Clear across Australia

 Telecom Australia
Perth, Western Australia
May 1986

To Alan Chynoweth

*In appreciation of your time
and knowledge shared with
the people of Telecom.*

Len Caudle
State Manager
Dec. 1985

Clear across Australia

A history of telecommunications

Ann Moyal

NELSON

Thomas Nelson Australia
480 La Trobe Street Melbourne Victoria 3000
First published 1984
Reprinted 1985
Copyright © Telecom Australia 1984

National Library of Australia
Cataloguing–in–Publication data:

Moyal, Ann.
  Clear across Australia.

  Bibliography.
  Includes index.
  ISBN 0 17 006266 X.

  1. Telecommunication — Australia — History.
  I. Title.

384'.0994

Typeset in Baskerville 12/13 pt by Abb–Typesetting, Melbourne
Printed in Australia by Globe Press

To the Telecommunication Pioneers

Foreword

by Professor Geoffrey Blainey

This is the story of an Australian miracle: how people who were far away came closer and closer.

When the first British settlers arrived, a letter they sent home was unlikely to be answered in the space of two years. There was no post office in Sydney for the first twenty-one years, and when it did open its door its charges were so high that many residents must have forfeited letters and parcels addressed to them rather than pay the postage. Slowly a postal network was set up, and the mail was carried on foot and horseback, in carts and storm-tossed sailing vessels. The movement of the squatters far inland, the opening of ports thousands of miles around the coast, and the sudden gold rushes to remote gullies — all strained the postal service. The first telegraph lines were laid in the 1850s, and soon the processions of telegraph poles were not far behind the rush of gold diggers. In 1872 in Darwin the telegraph cable arrived from Europe and Asia, and the long overland wire with its forest of poles and sixty thousand insulators linked Darwin and the cities of the far south. This was one of the crucial events in Australia's history but it was perhaps less important than the remarkable quickening of communications in the last twenty years: the swift transmitting of television pictures by satellite across the world, the coaxial cable, the STD phone, telex and a variety of innovations within Australia.

Ann Moyal's book describes and explains how our isolation was whittled down. For years she has believed that technology is one of the great moulders of our history, and in this lucid, pioneering book she shows how and why. Many readers will find illumination in her pages: those who work in telecommunications, those who read Australian history and those who write it, and the politicians, businessmen and civil servants who have to make decisions on how to harness, effectively and economically, the next wave of innovations.

Contents

Preface

T he history of technology has, until recently, been a neglected subject particularly as it concerns its social, economic and political impact on human affairs. This is now no longer the case. There is, for example, a flourishing school in Europe centred around the work of the great French historian, Fernand Braudel, and there have been major breakthroughs in the USA, such as Elizabeth Eisenstein's monumental study of *The printing press as an agent of change* (1979). By contrast, in Australia, with the luminous exception of Geoffrey Blainey and his pioneering studies of mining and *The tyranny of distance*, most historians have tended to treat technological history with suspicion tinged with contempt.

One technology that has had a crucial influence on Australia, with its vast distances and isolation from the rest of the world, is telecommunications, a technology that remains a prime agent of change today. In 1979 the question of a history of Australian telecommunications was raised by two non-historians, political scientist Henry Mayer, and Queensland economist Don Lamberton, who recommended the idea to the management of Telecom Australia. The following year managing director Mr J.H. Curtis commissioned a history of his youthful and dynamic statutory authority set against its background of evolution from colonial times, through the 74-year institutional management of the Postmaster-General's Department (1901–75), and into the contemporary period.

History, as one practitioner observed, is often thought of as a study 'contentedly remote from the present, as a hobby of scholars who have elected to fly into the dead and gone past'. In this case nothing was further from the truth. The work had two prescribed purposes. It should provide a 'scholarly and popular' history that would trace important developments in telecommunications and shed light on the men and women who had pushed out the spreading network and services and brought them into popular use. At the same time it should offer an objective evaluation of past decision-making and 'interactive processes' with a view to using history to illuminate contemporary concerns.

Clearly, at the outset, neither Telecom nor I fully appreciated the size of the task in view. It was originally intended that the work should be complete and published by October 1982 to mark the managing director's retirement. Political and other events, however, intervened. I accepted the commission in February 1981 and completed an extended study in November 1983. The book now covers the span of Australian telecommunications from the first telegraph line erected between Melbourne and Williamstown in 1854, with an introduction on the early Australian post, and surveys events up to the end of the industrial and political upheavals involving Telecom in the 1980s until the election of the Hawke Government in 1983. Following the early retirement of Mr Curtis in July 1981, managing director Mr W.J.B. Pollock has given the historical venture his most active interest and support.

A commissioned work, centred upon an institution, must to some extent emerge as 'history from the top'. Major developments tend to be attributed to Directors-General or managing directors when they are, of course, the results of collective efforts. Similarly there is a tendency, in dealing with a Federal organisation, to give greater emphasis to the affairs and decision-making at Headquarters than in the States. Within certain limits, I have tried to keep this bent in mind. I have attempted to indicate the individual character and contributions of the States and, while marking the influence of men and ideas, I have sought to depict the leaders and planners yet to discern the part played by individual and team inventors and innovators, the influence of the engineers, the role of the trade unions, the key participation of women in telecommunications, the ongoing work of line construction and upkeep, and the wider economic, financial and social interaction of telecommunications with the developing community.

Faced with a huge task, my aim has been to open up a pioneering field of study to scholars in a variety of disciplines. There are large and fertile areas to be explored and each chapter invites the prospect of more detailed and specialist studies. At the same time, I hope to engage the interest of the many Australians who have participated in the rise of national telecommunications — in Telecom, the former PMG, OTC, industry and elsewhere — who have been the lifeblood of a great enterprise and to whom this book is dedicated.

There are some special features of this historic assignment that need recording. The scholarly independence and authority of the work was assured by the appointment of a distinguished editorial board whose members were Professor Geoffrey Blainey of Melbourne University, Mr Stuart Sayers, literary editor of the *Age*, Professor Henry Mayer of Sydney University, and Mr W.F. Cox of Telecom Australia. In assembling the material I have received remarkable assistance from members of Telecom Australia at Headquarters and in the States and from former members of the organisation and of the PMG. The generous commitment of their time and knowledge represents a vital component of the book. A significant part of the evidence for the work, particularly in more recent times, has come from oral history. Despite access given me by Telecom to its archives up to the end of 1976, it was soon apparent that these resources were not arranged for historical researches nor did they readily retain the evidence of the thrust and turn of technological and institutional decision making. The interviewing of participants hence became a fundamental part of the methodology of the book. Particularly for the later chapters I have had the benefit of discussion with former senior administrators of the PMG's Department and Telecom Australia, with members of the Australian Telecommunications Commission, Telecom's managing directors, State managers, head of divisions in Headquarters and the States, several Ministers of the portfolio, civil servants, trade union leaders and a range of other staff. These interviews have been conducted by me in travels about the country. But I have also had the back-up of the telephone. Historians, correctly, agree that this instrument has become the destroyer of documentary evidence, replacing letters and leaving the researcher with brief aide-memoires and bland reports. For my part, however, I have found the telephone an indispensable aid in setting up interviews, trapping oral recollections, eliciting clarifications and corrections, and drawing on the opinions of participants and experts that, without this facility, may have remained inaccessible or have been lost forever. I am grateful to Telecom for this special use of its network.

Oral history, however, has its hazards. It is time-consuming; it calls for extensive checking and cross-checking to establish its accuracy and care has to be taken with the more colourful 'remembrancers' in separating the wheat from the chaff. In respect of accurate facts, I have also found it necessary to verify and correct information and some illustrated material published by the PMG and Telecom on aspects of their history.

Acknowledgements

Many people have contributed to this book. My thanks are due, first and foremost, to Mr J.H. Curtis and Mr W.J.B. Pollock for their interest in commissioning and encouraging a major history of Australian technology. I also extend my appreciative thanks to the members of the editorial board who, in their individual ways, have made valuable and characteristic contributions. Mr E.R. Banks, in whose directorate the history has been assembled, has throughout given me his most constructive support and made many pertinent inputs. Mr Fred Cox and Mr Stephen Lindner of the corporate analysis unit, business development directorate, have been responsible for the administrative management of the work and I thank them for their protracted contribution. I also express my gratitude and admiration for the feats of typing performed by Mrs Lina Salutari and Miss Gwen Butler in preparing the draft chapters and the final manuscript.

Several people have helped me notably in various stages of the work. Michael Harold, who became my first research assistant on loan from Telecom, furnished me with important and perceptive early research. Grant McBurnie and Kerry Lee in Melbourne also contributed helpfully to aspects of the research, while in Canberra Adrian Stevens proved a resourceful part-time research assistant. In the illustration of the book, I have had valuable assistance from David Grigg, from the information and publicity offices of Headquarters and the States, from Alan Tulip, and in recent months from John Barth who has made a striking contribution to the final production. I thank them all for their participation.

My particular thanks are due to Mr J.F. Moynihan of Telecom WA who has given me constant assistance throughout the writing of this book. An engineer and 'unofficial historian' himself, he has generously lent his time and much of his own material to ensure the accuracy and comprehensiveness of the work.

In writing an institutional history, it has been stimulating and valuable to me to have been invited to spend two years as visiting fellow in the Department of Economic History of the Australian National University. I owe much to my colleagues, Professor Noel Butlin, Dr Alan Barnard, Dr Jonathan Pincus and Dr Ian MacLean, for their economic stiffening and interest in my work.

The following people assisted me greatly with interviews, discussion and material that added significantly to the history and I thank them: J.P. Ahern, T.J. Alford, J. Anglin, F. Arter, D.M. Baker, John Baker, the Hon. Lionel Bowen MP, P.R. Brett, George P. Brown (and for his father's press cuttings), D.F. Burnard, B.W. Byrnes, W.L. Caudle, D.M. Coleman, J.P. Coleman, J.H. Curtis, L.W. Edwards, R. Ellis, A.H. Freeman, B.J. Fuller, M.J. Gooley, A. Gough, the late F.J. Green, Peter Green, I.M. Gunn, Joan Hancock, L.M. Harris, W. Harris, Sir Alan Hulme, H.R. Hutchison, B.F. Jones, S. Kaneff, A. Kellock (and for his father's memoirs), J.J. Kennedy, Sir John Knott, E.F. Lane, R.B. Lansdown, G.W. Larsson, I.J. Lefevre, C. Leonard, G.L. Lindenmayer, C.J. Livingstone, R.N. Lowe, N.J. McCay, W. Mansfield, S.C. Moon, J.F. Moynihan, K. Newham, P.I. Nolan, the late F.P. O'Grady, B.J. O'Sullivan, E.E. Payne, J.K. Petrie, A.D. Pettersson, the late R. Pitcher, A.B. Poulsen, W.J.B. Pollock, M.J. Power, D.M. Rowell, J. Ross, E.F. Sandbach, L.D. Sebire, the Rt Hon. Ian Sinclair MP, H.G. Shaw, J.L. Skerrett, G. Slater, G.N. Smith, J.R. Smith, D.R. Snowden, R.D. Somervaille, A.A. Staley, R. Stradwick, F.L.C. Taylor, A. Traill, A.J. Truss, K.C. Turbet, R.W. Turnbull (and for his written material), Sir James Vernon, N.C. Watson, Sir Frederick White, Harold White, K.F. Work, H.S. Wragge.

In addition others helped me in a variety of ways in providing specific information and illustrations and in facilitating my efforts, and in responding patiently to my requests: John Bangsund, J. Bateman, P. Bethell, M.L. Brindley, D. Brooke, J. Brown, R. Buddrige, J.D. Catto, Cynthia Cockerton, C.T. Colliver, C. Coogan, M.P. Cousins, Tric Cramsie, Ailsa Cross, W. Dair, L.J. Derrick, S. Doull, Liz Ford, D. Gimm, F.S. Gubbins, Marjorie Hall, Sylvia Hall, the late Harold Hinckfuss, Mimi Hurley, D. Irons, Anthony James, V.J. Kenna, T. Klenk, J.E. Linton, J.L. Lightfoot, R. Lorimer, B.G. Luscombe, Stuart Macdonald, J. McKinnan, T. McNamara, L. Maher, D. Morrow, National Library of Australia, Australian Reference staff, P. O'Callaghan, P. O'Donoghue, Postal-Telecommunications Historical Society of Queensland, A.J. Rawady, W. Rhode, David Richards, Judy Ryan, R. Saunders, D. Shaw, Joy Shackcloth, Judith Smith, N. Stange, N. Stubbersfield, J.C. Sutcliffe, B.A. Taylor, Telecom Headquarters Library staff and Engineering Research Laboratory staff, G.W. Todd, S. Townley and S.R.E. Warner and S.A. Young. Fay Donlevy and Bettina Stevenson compiled the index.

Throughout my work, I have had many pleasant dealings and enlightening talks with Telecom drivers, technicians and telephonists met while visiting exchanges, and with engineers and linemen whose names I do not know. Rising early to reminder calls, constantly using Directory Assistance, I have formed the highest regard for the courtesy and good nature of the many telephonists I have encountered. Throughout my meetings with Telecom members and former members of the PMG, I have also learnt that no history of their enterprise can be complete without a generous tribute to the wives.

Finally, I should like to thank my husband J.E. Moyal, mathematician and engineer, whose knowledge, critical judgement and support has been the greatest encouragement to me throughout the making of this book. In the parlance of the cinema credits, he has been in every sense, my 'Chief Grip'.

ILLUSTRATION ACKNOWLEDGEMENTS

Most of the photographs and drawings in this book came from Telecom Australia files. The author and publisher are also grateful to the following for permission to reproduce illustrations: Advertiser Newspapers (p. 219); the *Age* (p. 382); Amalgamated Wireless (Australasia) Ltd (pp. 130, 131, 131, 133, 135, 141); Art Gallery of New South Wales (pp. 5, 9); Australia Post (p. 55); Australian Telecommunications Employees Association (pp. 322, 323, 324, 325, 382); Australian War Memorial (pp. 107, 163, 163, 164, 164, 165); Battye Library, Perth (pp. 12, 149); Brisbane *Courier-Mail* (p. 192); Hobart *Mercury* (p. 210); National Library of Australia (pp. 10, 47, 49, 51, 64, 107, 136, 137, 149, 243); Peter O'Donoghue (pp. 270, 298); Ray Pratley (p. 60); Royal Historical Society of Victoria (p. 7); D. Solomon (p. 209); and Mr S.A. Young (p. 215).

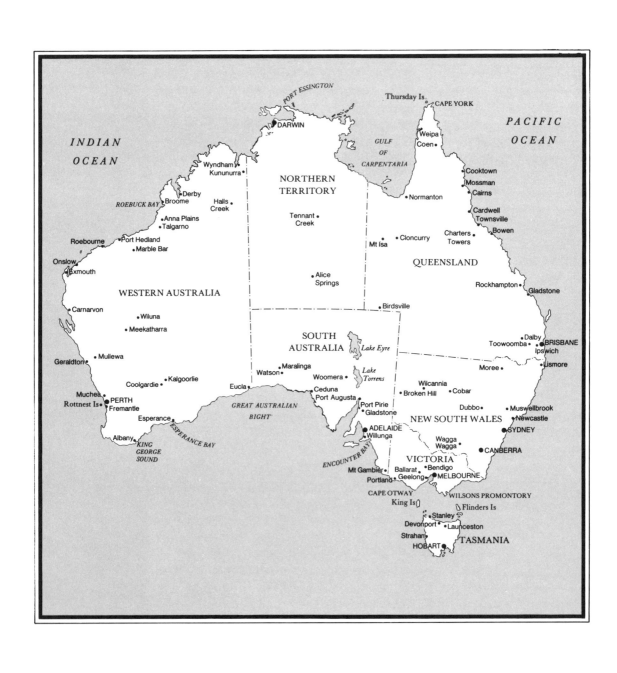

1 News from Home

Large fires were lighted this morn about 10 o'clock', wrote the young naturalist Joseph Banks in his Journal when, on the first sighting of Australia, HMS *Endeavour* began to tack her way up the southern coast of New South Wales. The date was 25 April 1770 and the fires, which were then seen repeatedly by Captain Cook and his men and were taken at first to be cooking fires, were in part the Aboriginals signalling the presence of strangers along their shores. The columns of rising smoke, with their alerting message of change, were the earliest telecommunications to be used in Australia and, for the British explorers, marked the first sign of human communication seen in the remote fifth continent which, within two decades, their country-men would settle as a penal colony and as a bastion for trade and Imperial expansion in the southern seas.[1]

In the course of its development, communication would become the lifeblood of the distant Colony. But the first consignment of immigrants — the ragtail population of 759 convicts and almost as many military gaolers who landed with the First Fleet in January 1788 — knew only the sense of exile and excommunication that the name 'Botany Bay' implied. So rare were ships sailing between Australia and England that Governor Arthur Phillip and his officers also shared this excommunication. Two years would pass before the Governor's first despatches to England received an answer back in New South Wales, while the shipwreck of the supply ship *Guardian* off the Cape of Good Hope in 1789 pushed the infant settlement to the edge of starvation. When the long awaited Second Fleet arrived in June 1790 preceded by the *Lady Juliana*, she was greeted by Sydney-siders with cries of 'Hurrah for a bellyful, and news from our friends'. They shouted for letters and trembled as they tore them open. 'News', wrote Watkin Tench, 'burst upon us like meridian splendour on a blind man.'[2]

The convict settlement had been sited far from England both for trade and to prevent convicts returning when their sentences had expired. Detachment, not contact, was envisaged for the malefactors at the antipodes of the globe. The illiterate convicts — a large company — accepted an enforced alienation. But to those who could read and

A general view of Sydney harbour. The first, and for many years the only, link with 'home' was by mail sent on sailing ships. Even at best, 'return of mail' could mean a wait of from six months to a year.

write, the determination to maintain connection with the homeland, to exchange news and the binding expressions of love and affection with those they had left behind, propelled them to seek every means of getting letters back to England.

It was the Scottish artist, Thomas Watling, sentenced for forging guinea notes on the Bank of Scotland and transported in 1791, who began a series of letters to his aunt in Scotland which, consigned by private hands and published in Scotland as *Letters from an exile in Botany Bay to his Aunt in Dumfries* (1794), shed critical light on the little known conditions in the penal colony. Margaret Catchpole, transported for life for the theft of a horse in 1801 and assigned to various families about Sydney, also wrote vivid letters to friends in Suffolk providing eye–witness accounts of events in the Colony, the Aboriginals, the countryside, the strange wildlife, and the savagery and immorality of the imported Colonial inhabitants. Her letters, reproduced later in literate form, excited lively interest in the Colonies.[3]

Letters were the sinews that bound the growing populace to the Mother Country conveying social, economic, political and scientific information to Britain and Europe. By 1800, with the Second Fleet, there were over 5,000 'European' residents in Australia. At first official despatches and personal letters were consigned to any ship's captain that would take them. Mail was a private affair and private arrangements and payments were made by communicators at both ends of the line. In more distant Van Diemen's Land where, from 1803, military outpost settlements stretched thinly from Risdon Cove near Hobart to Port Dalrymple and George Town, letters were entrusted to the captains of whaling and sailing ships operating in Bass Strait and southern waters who would ultimately get them to the mainland. Even for official correspondence the means for establishing contact was improvised, Governor King in New South Wales authorising his Deputy Lieutenant Collins in Tasmania to pay 'thirty empty salt meat caskets' for carriage of despatches to the island.[4]

For the first fifteen years of settlement arrangements for incoming and outgoing mail were ad hoc and disorderly. Only one ordinance offered any guidance for handling mail. A notice in the *Sydney Gazette* of 10 July 1803 authorised boatmen plying between Sydney and Parramatta to make a twopenny charge for each private letter carried. But for overseas mail conditions bordered on the chaotic. When ships from England docked in Sydney, residents simply stampeded on board to collect their correspondence eager to be brought in touch, even if months out of date, with England, 'beautiful and beloved', and the life they had left behind.

The abuses inherent in such a procedure in time prompted official action. On 25 April 1809 the *Sydney Gazette* notified that complaints had been made to the Lieutenant–Governor that 'numerous frauds' had been committed by individuals repairing on board ships 'personating others' and that, to prevent such abuses, the Lieutenant–Governor would establish an office to which all letters and parcels addressed to residents of Sydney would be deposited before distribution. Isaac Nichols, assistant to the naval (customs) officer, was placed in charge of the mails and his fine house at Circular Quay, Sydney, became the first post office in Australia. Nichols, as first postmaster (1809–19), assumed the duty of boarding all ships that docked in Sydney to collect mail while the names of the addressees were published in the *Sydney Gazette*. A year later the scheme was extended to the whole Colony. Nichols collected the not inconsiderable sum of 1s a letter, 2s 6d for parcels under twenty pounds, and 5s for heavier articles, partly from Customs and partly from his clients. Official sponsorship and private enterprise thus launched the first postal system in Australia.[5]

An artist's impression of Isaac Nichols, Australia's first Postmaster, boarding a ship to collect the mail. Nichols, a former convict, was also step son-in-law of Lieutenant George Johnston, reputed to be the first man ashore on the arrival of the First Fleet in 1788.

But if excommunication was a key feature of the Colony's birth, efforts developed across scattered fronts to link the tiny settlements and to re-establish vital lines of communication with the Mother Country. The remote settlement of Van Diemen's Land (renamed Tasmania in 1853) proved — perhaps because of its greater isolation — a postal innovator. Its first postmaster, John Beaumont, appointed in 1812, lasted an ineffectual twelve months; but his successor, James Mitchell, former quartermaster from the First Fleet frigate *Sirius*, prospered from both cattle and mail in Tasmania and negotiated the first direct post from the island to England on a South Seas whaler in 1816. Letter bags were kept open before the departure of ships 'for the reception of all letters from those who wish to write to their friends in Europe' and incoming mail was similarly advertised in the *Hobart Town Gazette*. Mitchell developed other services. Under him, W.T. Stocker pioneered the north–south service between Hobart Town and Launceston as official government messenger providing the first 'overland mail delivery service' in Australia. Convict messengers were also employed on the routes extending inland. Trusted not only with the mails but with a musket to defend themselves against attacks by bushrangers or Aboriginals, they covered the ground on foot and trumpeted their arrival by blowing a horn.

Mitchell's efforts in Tasmania (which became an independent Colony in 1825) outstripped those of his senior in New South Wales. By 1820 a weekly postal service ran between Hobart Town and the northerly point of settlement at Port Dalrymple. When he retired in 1822, Mitchell handed over a postal service that spanned the island from south to north and serviced a circle of hamlets around Hobart. The fees — a shilling a letter from Hobart to Launceston — made communication a costly business when a labourer earned little more than a shilling a day. But people paid for business and human contact, 'the cherished link that solaced the human heart'. Even convicts were not excluded from the postal service provided they could pay, though their frequent movement from gaols or between assignments to settlers meant that they often missed out on precious mail. By 1824 post offices flourished at Launceston, George Town, Sorell, New Norfolk, Macquarie Plains, Hamilton, Bothwell and the military station at Green Ponds.[6]

In New South Wales, where the population had passed 30,000 by 1821, the first Act 'to regulate the postage of letters' was introduced by the new Legislative Council in 1825. Under it, postmasters were appointed for the first time outside Sydney in an arc that reflected the spread of agricultural and pastoral settlement to Parramatta, Campbelltown, Liverpool, Penrith, Windsor, some 80 miles across the Great Dividing Range to Bathurst, and north to the coastal settlement at Newcastle. But private schemes continued to supplement official plans. So outrageous was the price demanded by the Sydney–Parramatta Monitor Coach Service for the carriage of newspapers and letters to the inland postal towns that the Government introduced its own twice weekly horse–drawn coach service to Newcastle and Port Macquarie in 1828. Prices were graded by distance carried, 4d for a letter to Parramatta, 8d to Campbelltown, with a special penny rate for all newspapers printed in the Colonies. By the same ordinance, sea postage fell to 4d for a single letter.[7] George Panton, Nichols's successor, became the master of this expanding official empire, having received the title of Postmaster–General on his accession to office in 1818.

Nonetheless Tasmania was the real pacesetter for postal reform. Following a committee of enquiry appointed by its Legislative Council in 1828, the Colony restructured its postal service four years later to become a government department. Fixed salaries were settled for the postmasters to replace payment on handled mail; Postmaster–General Collicott received a handsome £400 a year; 14 deputy postmasters were appointed (some doubling as district constables or police clerks); a code was drawn up for all postal employees, and all postage was paid into the general revenue fund. Importantly, the cost of inland postage dropped dramatically. Letters weighing up to two ounces cost a penny for delivery in Hobart or Launceston and within a radius of ten miles, and 3d more for a radius of ten miles further. But, though a weekly service ran between Hobart and Launceston linking with an intricate network of convict messengers along the route, the difficulty of the terrain, the illiteracy of the convict messengers, and the delays caused by bad weather, sparked criticism and led to the introduction of a horse–drawn mail cart, let by tender, to carry mails twice weekly between the points.

Other Colonies launched their mail services promptly. In Western Australia postal services began some five months after settlement, in December 1829, with the appointment of Lionel Samson as post-master at Fremantle, and shortly afterwards James Purkis became postmaster at Perth. Both Samson and Purkis were freelance, cash-basis postmasters who took their fees from postal levies. But Samson, a leading member of local society, soon found that the mails brought scant return. He used to 'dread the arrival of a ship'. The one privilege he stipulated was 'that he might read his own letters first' and then came the duty of distributing those letters to his friends who 'would borrow for them to pay the return postage, not return it, and drink

'From a distant land'. An 1889 oil painting, now in the Art Gallery of New South Wales, by David Davies.

about a gallon of brandy while waiting for, or reading them'. By 1835 Government had taken charge. Perth post office became the official GPO with branches at Fremantle and Albany, while Albany (originally known as King George's Sound post office) served as the key south coast port through which all overseas contract mails passed until the building of a navigable harbour at Fremantle at the century's end.[8]

Free enterprise also characterised early postal efforts in Victoria and South Australia. Port Phillip's post office, established in 1837 was run by the Clerk of Petty Sessions, E.J. Forster, and a succession of businessmen. Mails came and went by sailing ships between Melbourne and Sydney, Melbourne and Tasmania, and were soon received direct from England. A post office in the charge of a storekeeper — a traditional combination — opened in Geelong in 1840, and a third, for the collection of mail by coasting vessels, opened at Portland. Government intervened in 1841 and an official post office was erected in Melbourne. At Victoria's separation from NSW in 1851, there were some 36 post offices in the new fledged Colony.[9]

Thomas Gilbert, postmaster and general storekeeper in South Australia, discharged his duties from a hut beside the Torrens River soon after Adelaide's first colonists landed in 1836. Two years later a Post Office Act established post offices at the Colony's crucial entry ports of Port Adelaide, Port Lincoln, Willunga and Encounter Bay. Mail was an important ingredient of expansion. With a postal charge fixed at a uniform rate of 3d a letter or parcel, South Australians fared better than their neighbouring colonists and the enterprising took advantage of this seductive rate to post off chests of tea and other bulky commodities to inland points. Adelaide, entrepreneurial city of the south, also captured the role as a key mail port by shipping all sea mail at an attractive penny rate.[10]

By virtue of size and citizenry, New South Wales became the hub of a spreading postal empire. Following Tasmania's lead, the Colony's postal service became a government enterprise in 1834 with lines of delivery and collection extending west, south and north 600 miles away to the outpost penal settlement of Moreton Bay.[11] An overland mail service using coach and pack horses linked Melbourne and Sydney. Along scattered land lines, across Bass Strait, and across 1,000 miles of ocean to the penitentiary of Norfolk Island, written communication reached outward, and mail and inexpensive postal circulation of local newspapers quickened a growing sense of colonial identity.

From the outset, Australia's postal service was noticeably egalitarian. Convicts, Aboriginals and women contributed to its workings. Convicts and ex–convicts became leading participants. Australia's first postmaster, Isaac Nichols, reached Sydney as a convict. Transported for stealing in 1797, Nichols so impressed Governor Hunter with his competence that he was appointed chief overseer of the convict gangs labouring around Sydney. When his own seven–year sentence expired, Nichols launched a successful career on government granted land as a farmer, and later, as a shipbuilder, constructed the vessel *Governor Hunter* which he used on the Newcastle, Hawkesbury and Bass Strait trade. His appointment as postmaster in 1809 followed two public appointments earlier that year as superintendent of public works and assistant to the Naval Officer.[12]

John Collicott, postmaster in Tasmania, was the son of a convict transported 'for his failure to affix duty stamps to bottles of medicine'. Collicott emigrated to Australia to join his father and built up a number of profitable businesses in Hobart Town. As Postmaster–General he made extensive use of convict messengers.[13] Some 35 were appointed by the official post office between 1834–9. Paid a shilling a day, they slept in a separate ward in the penitentiary and were permitted to sleep out on the job. Their issue of two new suits a year — dashing blue jackets with 'M' on the collar, blue waistcoats, blue trousers, four pairs of shoes, two shirts, a blue forage cap and one black silk handkerchief — were the envy of many free settlers. They formed a postal elite that contained some rogues but generally recruited men determined to gain access to a new life by conditional or free pardon.

By 1830 the Australian population numbered 70,000. Twenty

Getting the mail through involved a lot of detailed planning by local inhabitants. Part of an application by two prominent squatters for a mail route between Yass and the then newly settled Port Phillip. From the collection of the Royal Historical Society of Victoria.

years later, from swelling tides of immigration, the figure stood at 400,000.[14] By the half century Australia was one of the most urbanised countries in the world. About four out of every ten of its population lived in the main ports of Sydney, Melbourne, Geelong, Adelaide, Hobart and Launceston, and more than half the population lived in towns and villages. Financially the Colonies rode on the sheep's back and on the profitable whaling and sealing of the South Seas. Nationally the Colonies were joined together and sustained in their commercial progress by the interconnecting mails. In the 19th as in the 20th century information lay at the base of social growth. Colonists depended for the export of their wool, wheat, flour, manufactured goods and, ultimately, their minerals on knowledge of the state of the market overseas. The wait for this news could be as long as eighteen months or two years while the sailing packets plied their way from Sydney to London via the Cape of Good Hope and back again. For nearly a century the high masted ships ran the gauntlet of the Indian Ocean, battling its strong winds and waves and its sudden airless calm. Across time and distance Australian merchants hung on news of the fluctuating market overseas. The time–lag affected the decision–making of traders, investors and entrepreneurs. Falling prices in England hit trading houses in Sydney and Melbourne months later, while a strong rise in price reverberated in the Colonies in delayed, but resounding, financial booms.

Until the 1850s all mail travelled by sailing ship, at the captain's discretion, and on payment of sums individually negotiated by the separate Colonies. In 1852 the first Australian mail contract for steamer carriage was made by the British Government with the Australian Royal Mail Steam Navigation Company to transport mail every alternate month between Southampton and Sydney via the Cape, calling at King George's Sound, Adelaide, and Melbourne. But the arrangement foundered on long delays. The following year a contract was signed with the Peninsular and Oriental Steam Navigation Company to carry Australian mails in company vessels either on the China and Japan run as far as Singapore, or from Southampton to Alexandria by steamship, overland to the Red Sea, and by steamship to Ceylon and Australia. Though the service was disrupted when the steamers were converted to troopships for the Crimean War, by 1858 a monthly P & O mail steamer brought comparatively quick and regular connection for correspondence and newspapers between Australia and England, via Galle in Ceylon.[15]

On land, horse–drawn carriages provided by contractors were used for mail transport on major routes in all Colonies from the 1830s and 1840s. The 'Sound' mail rattled by spring–cart the 250 miles to Perth from King George's Sound via Albany post office from 1841. In Tasmania, the 'Royal Mail Service' ran between Hobart and Launceston from the early 1830s, started by the contractor John Cox, and transformed into a flourishing business of seven coaches and 150 spanking horses by his wife Mary Ann. When Cox died, Mrs Cox (with her eight dependent children) was a spirited precursor of a cavalcade of enterprising women who, individually and collectively, played a sig-

Coaching was not
always quite so easy or
fast, as this photograph
taken near Marysville in
1900 shows.

nificant part in the growth of communication services in Australia.

Freeman Cobb, an American by origin, offered a service far
superior to any in the Colonies with his leather–springed light
American–styled coaches painted a brilliant red. Cobb first ferried
passengers and mail to the Victorian goldfields in 1854, and the
enterprise spread. By 1862 Cobb & Co. had become the major official
carriers of the Colonies' mail. They were harnessing 6,000 horses
across eastern Australia by 1870 and extended their activities to
Western Australia's goldfields of Kalgoorlie and Coolgardie during
the 1890s.[16]

The gold rushes of the 1850s placed enormous strains on the postal
services of Victoria and New South Wales. As shiploads of gold–
hungry immigrants docked in Melbourne, a flood of international
correspondence deluged the city mail centres and the makeshift post
offices set up in rooms or shanties near the burgeoning goldfields.
Total post office business quadrupled in Victoria between 1851 and
1853. 'The increase in business in the Post Office Department', the
Victorian *Annual Report* noted anxiously in 1853, 'was almost
unexampled . . . and the increase in correspondence with the United
Kingdom, with the adjoining Colonies, and indeed with the whole
civilised world, caused such an amount of business as could not be
satisfactorily disposed.' Bendigo Creek, a major gold–post centre,
struggled with one postmaster and four clerks, and letters handled in
the Colony rose from more than half a million in 1851 to over two
million in 1853. Revenue also leapt from £8,000–odd in 1851 to
£25,000 two years later.[17]

Within each Colony the creation of post offices followed the movement of population. Outlying colonists pressured their Postmaster-
General. It was customary for groups of townspeople to petition for the
establishment of a post office. The need and rationale varied from
place to place. Size of town, its economic connections, and its role on a

Welcome news; gold
diggers reading their
long-awaited post. From
an oil painting of ca
1860 by William Strutt,
now in the Art Gallery
of New South Wales.

route to other outposts were frequently pressed. In Bourke, New South Wales, in 1862 petitioners argued that in addition to a sizable citizenry 'a Court of Petty Sessions is held here weekly with a resident Police Magistrate and his staff, Police Force etc. which the establishment of a Post Office would greatly accommodate and benefit'. In the same Colony the residents of Yetman urged that they had 'over one hundred inhabitants with two hotels . . . the nearest post office is distant seventy

Canberra's first post office (1862 to 1913), at the foot of Mt Ainslie, which, like many other country post offices, also served as a shop and boarding house. From an oil painting by Joseph Wolinski, now in the National Library of Australia.

miles so that the inhabitants of this township and district are at a serious inconvenience regarding their correspondence'. Stockmen passing that way to Queensland also urgently needed a convenient place for registering letters with their remittances.[18] Post offices appeared beside goldfields, along transport arteries like the River Murray, in spreading suburbs and townships, and, as the railways moved out from coastal cities carrying mailbags and competing with inland coaches, at junctions and railway stations.

There were still isolated regions requiring bizarre arrangements for mail. Booby Island, a northwesterly speck off Cape York Peninsula, was used throughout most of the 19th century by seafaring men as a house of call and 'post office' where letters were deposited to be taken up and 'favoured' by the next passing ship.[19] But there was a growing regularisation of the postal system. Government had intervened, postal departments were the seats of authority in each Colony. Uniform postal rates were temporarily agreed upon throughout the Colonies by 1849; the practice of prepayment of postage by adhesive postal stamps was introduced in the Colonies between 1852–5; while postal matters became matters of important and often heated debate at the periodic Intercolonial Conferences. Across the broad span of the continent and outwards across the seas, there was a veritable hubbub of words and messages (unnoted except by the staff of the postal departments of state) that expressed the inner life, the business and the knowledge practical, political and scientific, of the Colonial community.

The 'postie' and the bush mailman were distinctive figures of the Australian scene. The latter was often 'a gentleman'; some had military backgrounds; all had to be competent hands with a horse. As one explained 'A mailman has to be highly respectable and trust-worthy'. Mailmen worked to a 'line'. As long as they kept up the time, they were fairly independent, 'got all the first news' and were 'always made welcome wherever we go'. Their bed and cutlery were kept for them at homesteads along the route. But the going in all weathers, on primitive tracks and across swollen rivers, was not without challenge. 'We aint supposed to swim rivers', one reflected, 'in fact, we're not allowed to cross a river or creek if it's over the saddle flaps. Not but that we do. A man isn't going to camp with nothing to eat and no matches or tobacco, perhaps, when there's a station to be made by just swimming a few yards. Of course if the mail's lost, we catch it.'[20]

But there was another hazard. Bushrangers preyed on mailmen. The Postmaster–General of New South Wales reported in 1862 that 'the number of mail robberies has increased to an alarming extent . . . the loss to the public and the inconvenience caused to the Department by the perpetration of the robberies can hardly be overestimated'. But it was more than an irritant to mailmen. Some were shot dead and there was, not surprisingly, 'a disinclination to tender for the con-veyance of mail'. Western Australia, with its vast reaches, adopted the practice of employing Aboriginal mail carriers on some routes. During early settlement, the leader of a tribe who camped on the flats of the Brunswick River, nicknamed 'Governor Peter', carried mail (the Europeans' 'yabba paper') over surprising distances on foot, as far north as the Pinjarra, and south to Busselton. Aboriginal labour was cheap. The men received a ration of flour, meat and tobacco, plus a clothing allowance, and 6d 'spending silver' a week. The remarkable 'Governor Peter', however, never adopted the white man's garb.[21]

In general the postal service was staffed on a shoestring. Though Colonial postal departments paid handsome sums to inland mail contractors, the railways and shipping companies for transport by sea, it knew how to economise, particularly in the sparsely populated country districts, in accommodation costs and staff. Almost anyone was eligible to become a postmaster — schoolmasters, farmers, car-penters, gaolers, storekeepers, resident magistrates, public servants, though inn–keepers were little favoured. The salaries offered were often tokens, as low as £5 a year and, in the case of a government servant, sometimes nothing at all. By the 1880s sums of £60 to £95 a year could be paid to postmasters at major country centres and as much as £485 at key city posts. But the practice of encouraging 'semi–official' agency post offices, where small commissions were meted out to those in charge, flourished in rural centres and ancillary suburban districts and in 'flash in the pan' gold mining towns.

Women flowed into the postal service as an economic expedient.

Despite the advent of motorised transport, the traditional mailman on horseback remained, until recently, a common sight to those living in the remoter country areas.

Sydney postmen of the 1890s. Until Federation in 1901, all the activities of the post office were under the local control of the various colonial governments.

From the 1860s and particularly from the 1870s postmistresses were widely appointed through the Colonies. The contrast in their salaries was instructive. Postmasters in Victoria earned between £150–£485 a year in the 1870s; postmistresses from £60 to £180. In Queensland, a Colony where 'manly' virtues were enshrined, the 'postmaster' at the Brisbane GPO was Mrs Elsie Barney who succeeded her husband Captain John Barney, the Colony's first full–time postmaster, on his death in 1855. Energetic and efficient, Mrs Barney presided for eight years over postal development of the Colony at a time of considerable

Trained as a telegraphist by Bishop Salvado (founder of the Benedictine Abbey of the Holy Trinity, New Norcia, WA) Ellen Kuper née Paugieran was the first postmistress at New Norcia, WA, in 1867. She is pictured here with, on her right, Waregian, and on her left, Isabel Tubian, together with Buyacan and Marrian Imbich.

expansion of sea and inland mail. In Western Australia Ellen Kuper (sometimes called Cuper) was appointed postmistress at the mission station of New Norcia in 1874 and became the first full–blooded Aboriginal to attain such a post in Australia's public service. In Victoria the number of postmistresses rose steeply in the mid–1870s and, by 1879, were in charge of more than half of Victoria's 127 post offices. One was Henry Handel Richardson's mother, Mary Richardson, who began her work at Koroit, Victoria, through the patronage of the Postmaster–General. While the novelist described her mother's position in a society where a working woman was generally considered 'outside the pale', postmistresses were respected by the community and were superior in education to many of their customers. Their sustained, if underpaid, service to their communities was recognised after Federation by the frequent appearance of country postmistresses in the Royal Honours Lists as Members of the British Empire.[22]

One of a hardy breed, Thomas Cambridge, a postman in NSW from 1835 to 1861.

Under government auspices, the postal service ran at a deficit in the Colonies. Yet no one questioned its importance. The concept of a 'people's service', of 'getting the mail through' became deeply embedded in the philosophy of the 19th century departments of post, though the costs of transporting the mail into every corner of the countryside made deep inroads into Colonial Exchequers.[23] It was a people's service staffed by men and women drawn from all sectors of the community. By foot, horse, camel, bicycle, spring cart, coach, ship and railway, the mails travelled daily, weekly, monthly or at longer intervals over a huge continent. Distance and isolation were alleviated. A thousand post offices had emerged to form the structure onto which

A country 'splendid in their post offices'. Sydney's General Post Office in 1887. The tower was to be dismantled in 1942 as a wartime precaution, but was re-erected in 1963.

Melbourne's Elizabeth
Street post office, in
1867 (and before the
addition of a third
storey).

speedier, more complex communication systems could be grafted.
The country's postal system was fragmented, moulded by the 'huck-
stering notion of statemanship', which left Australia with disjointed
railway gauges, unco-ordinated traffic systems, and persistent
intercolonial rivalry and disagreement over postal rates, overseas
connections and terminal points for mail steamers as the century wore
on. Still bickering, the Australian Colonies joined the Universal Postal
Union in 1891.[24]

Yet the staggering task of internal and external communication
had been achieved. Visiting Australia in 1871–2, Anthony Trollope,
British novelist and a long–time British postal official himself,
perceptively observed the importance of the post in a country so
gigantic and remote. 'I was gratified', he wrote, 'by finding that the
Colonies generally were disposed to be splendid in their post offices
rather than in any other building, for surely there is no other public
building so useful.'[25]

2 'The Most Perfect Invention'

By the mid–19th century the speediest form of communication over short distances in Australia was the semaphore system. Operated widely at capital ports and headlands to announce the sighting of shipping, the semaphore formed a visual telegraph that conveyed messages alphabetically by the positioning of its two arms. The town of Semaphore, nine miles from Adelaide, is a contemporary reminder of its use. But in Tasmania human as well as shipping movements were tracked by the device. Until 1846 a chain of semaphore stations dotted the Tasman Peninsula. Convicts attempting to escape from the fiercely guarded penitentiary at Port Arthur knew the system to their peril. From the strategic heights of Mount

The Hobson's Bay signal station in Victoria, replaced by the telegraph network, was then one of many semaphore stations around Australia.

The Morse code

A	• ▬
B	▬ • • •
C	▬ • ▬ •
D	▬ • •
E	•
F	• • ▬ •
G	▬ ▬ •
H	• • • •
I	• •
J	• ▬ ▬ ▬
K	▬ • ▬
L	• ▬ • •
M	▬ ▬
N	▬ •
O	▬ ▬ ▬
P	• ▬ ▬ •
Q	▬ ▬ • ▬
R	• ▬ •
S	• • •
T	▬
U	• • ▬
V	• • • ▬
W	• ▬ ▬
X	▬ • • ▬
Y	▬ • ▬ ▬
Z	▬ ▬ • •
1	• ▬ ▬ ▬ ▬
2	• • ▬ ▬ ▬
3	• • • ▬ ▬
4	• • • • ▬
5	• • • • •
6	▬ • • • •
7	▬ ▬ • • •
8	▬ ▬ ▬ • •
9	▬ ▬ ▬ ▬ •
0	▬ ▬ ▬ ▬ ▬

Cunningham, Eaglehawk Neck, Mount Raoul and Mount Nelson to Hobart Town, messages of their sighting could be transmitted from Hobart to Port Arthur and back in under fifteen minutes. There were, however, several drawbacks to this 'optical telegraph's' use despite its historical adoption in peace and war. Rain, fog, mist and snow dimmed its power; it was labour–intensive and totally ineffective at night.[1]

It was electric telegraphy that would transform the business of communication in Australia and bring a mercurial speed to the flow of news, information and human exchange that underpinned the structures of a rapidly advancing society.

Electric telegraphy, an area of wide experimentation in the early 19th century when Faraday's work on electromagnetism opened up the field, had produced more than one practical form of communication between distant points before the mid–century. In Britain a telegraph system patented by Charles Wheatstone and Edward Cooke using deflection by magnetic needles (where signals caused the needles to point to letters of the alphabet) was widely adopted for signalling on British railways. But the invention by Samuel Morse in the United States of an electric telegraphic system conveying a code of letters tapped out by a keyboard and recorded at a distance by a register and a moving stylus on a strip of paper gained rapid world acceptance and spread speedily in North America and Europe. It was nine years after Morse had tapped out his famous message 'What Hath God Wrought' across the 40 miles of newly installed electromagnetic telegraph line from Washington to Baltimore in May 1844 that Australians responded to the prospects of the new technology.

It was a young Canadian, Samuel McGowan (1829–87), who brought telegraph technology to the Colonies. At 24, McGowan was already an expert telegraphist and experienced entrepreneur in the flourishing North American telegraph development. He had studied briefly for the law but, in 1847, entered the field of telegraphic experimentation, studied under Samuel Morse, became associated with Morse's colleague, Ezra Cornell (inventor of the first telegraph insulators), managed for a time the New York–Buffalo line that took the telegraph towards Canada, and was one of a bevy of successful entrepreneurs who canvassed subscriptions for America's spreading private telegraph companies.[2]

When news of Victoria's gold discoveries reached the United States in 1852 McGowan saw his opportunity. He consulted his former instructor, Professor Morse and, fortified by his advice, embarked for Australia. McGowan reached Melbourne early in 1853 with a specific plan for electric telegraph development, equipped with several complete sets of Morse instruments, batteries and insulators, and accompanied by a 'first class electrician'. It was the first transfer of modern telecommunication technology to Australia.

McGowan's plan was to develop a private company to construct and work telegraph lines from Melbourne to the Ballarat and Bendigo goldfields and to link Victoria's golden capital with those of its neighbouring Colonies. He was soon in touch with interested backers and a demonstration of the working of his Morse apparatus in Melbourne in June 1853 stirred excited praise. 'To us, old Colonists who have left Britain long ago', the *Argus* editorialist reflected the next day, 'there is something very delightful in the actual contemplation of this, the most perfect of modern inventions. We call the electric telegraph the most perfect invention of modern times ... as anything more perfect than this is scarcely conceivable, and we really begin to wonder what will be left for the next generation upon which to expend the restless enterprise of the human mind ... Let us set about electric telegraphy at once.'[3]

Government intervention, however, was to forestall the growth of privately sponsored telegraphy in the Colony. At first, distanced from the remarkable advances of the technology in America and Europe, Colonial Governments evinced no interest in the electric telegraph.[4] McGowan's evidence and enterprise transformed their inertia. As plans for his company took shape, the Victorian Government in September 1853 called tenders for the construction of an experimental electric telegraph line from Melbourne to Williamstown and indicated to McGowan that any independent approach would meet 'the utmost resistance'. At the same time they offered him a leading place in the management of public telegraphy. Confronted by bureaucratic impasse and persuasively solicited by Governor La Trobe, McGowan conceded. The contract for the 11-mile Melbourne–Williamstown telegraph line was let to him.

The work of establishing Australia's first telegraph line was completed with home–made wooden poles cut from the tallest trees and imported British galvanised iron wire. McGowan had great

Samuel Walker McGowan, the Canadian of Irish extraction who founded Australian telegraphy, and who, from 1854 until 1887, served as superintendent of Victoria's electric telegraph department.

The Geelong (Victoria) Customs House, which later served as its first telegraph office. The first message, sent on 6 December 1854, advised of the goldfield riots at Ballarat.

trouble with the insulators. Melbourne had no glass house, Sydney's one manufacturer 'botched' the production, and McGowan himself had to devise and manufacture a quantity made from shellac and tar. But, on 3 March 1854, the first telegraph line in Australia began operation (just six months before the first Australian railway line was opened between Melbourne and Port Melbourne on 12 September) and McGowan himself was gazetted as general–superintendent of the new electric telegraph of Victoria.[5]

His vision of riches had been thwarted but McGowan quickly applied the qualities of a dynamic telegraph entrepreneur to those of an active superintendent. By December 1854 the first experimental line had been extended to Geelong, and to Queenscliff by January 1855. Keen to reach the goldfields alive with people, commerce and news, the department installed a line from Melbourne to Sandhurst (now Bendigo) in July that year and an extension linked Geelong and the Ballarat goldfields in 1854. Within three years of McGowan's appointment, Victoria was webbed by a network of overhead tele-graph lines stretching from Melbourne to Ballarat, some 200–odd miles to Portland near the South Australian border, and north and north–west via Wangaratta and Wodonga to the Murray River. The closed circuit system of Morse transmission was employed and the received signals were recorded on an embossing recorder. 'The line', reported the *Argus* on 11 March 1854, 'is one of the kind known as Professor Samuel F.B. Morse's American line of magnetic telegraphs . . . The galvanic batteries which are used are known as Groves's batteries.' With instruments, recorders and techniques derived from American experience, Victoria's first telegraph statute of 1854 was based on Canada's Telegraph Act legislated eight years earlier, a copy of which McGowan prudently brought with him to Australia.[6]

Victoria's initiative stirred other Colonies. Its example was encouraging. Nearly 4,000 telegrams were despatched in the first year

A Morse key for the sending of telegraph messages, and opposite, a Siemens Bros Clockwork-driven Morse register for their automatic recording on paper tape.

of operation in 1854. Two years later the figure had tripled bringing in some £5,500 to the Colony's electric telegraph department. Telegram rates were set at 1s 6d for the first ten words any distance under 10 miles, and rose steeply for distances over 20, 50 and 100 miles. Yet, despite the cost, the telegraph system immediately fed into the mixed strands of Victoria's burgeoning commerce, linking trade and transport, dispersing news from Melbourne to the Murray, connecting investors with markets, gold diggers with buyers, and adding its own dynamism to a vigorously progressing Colony.

The point was not lost on the neighbouring Colonies. By late 1854 the Government of South Australia was soliciting help from the Colonial Office, London, to find them a suitable superintendent of telegraphs. Their choice fell on Charles Todd (1826–1910), a grocer's son, who had begun his scientific career in 1848 as 'supernumerary computer' at Greenwich Royal Observatory. He later became assistant astronomer at Cambridge University where he participated in the determination of longitude by telegraphic means between the observatories at Cambridge and Greenwich and, back at Greenwich in 1854, was superintendent of the galvanic apparatus for the transmission of

time signals. Not surprisingly Todd, steeped in and fascinated by telecommunications, was a prime candidate and was supported by the Astronomer Royal, Sir George Airy, for the South Australian post. While he had never built a telegraph line, under Airy's guidance he had supervised the acquisition of equipment and stores, made important contacts in the British telegraph and submarine cable world, and had assimilated British telegraphic methods and skills.

While Airy wondered in private if his young protégé 'had the boldness and independence of character which may be required in an Australian establishment', Todd himself dreamed of great telegraphic ventures, writing to the Australian explorer, Captain Sturt, soon after accepting office in February 1855: 'I look forward to . . . the time when the telegraph system will be extended to join the several seats of commerce in Australia and also, it is no idle dream in the present age of wonders, when I shall be able to meet Dr O'Shaughnessey [telegraph experimenter in India] by connecting Asia by submarine cable thence via Calcutta to London.'[7]

Todd's post in Adelaide combined the superintendent of the electric telegraph with that of astronomical observer. He arrived in November 1855, bringing his young bride Alice, a technical assistant, E.C. Cracknell, and a good array of British telegraphic plant, the first British telegraph equipment to reach Australia. But Todd declined to follow instructions to bring out some operators, intending to raise his own core of telegraphers in the Colony. Plans for a telegraph line from Adelaide to its port and to Semaphore in St Vincent's Gulf had been partly inspired in 1854 by the Crimean War and the nervous, if irrational, fears of the Colonial Government that small, remote Adelaide was vulnerable to Russian attack. Todd began work at once. But, by an irksome irony, the real urgency had been snatched from the project by the opening, on the very day of Todd's arrival, of a private telegraph line from Adelaide to its port built by private entrepreneur, James McGeorge. McGeorge had brought his equipment, at his own expense from Europe the previous year, and, although the Government and the chamber of commerce adamantly refused assistance, had gone ahead and completed the job himself. His achievement was short-lived. In 1856 the South Australian Government bought the competing line at a purchase price of £80 and dismantled it.[8]

Meanwhile Todd, acting on British specifications, completed his telegraph line from Adelaide to Semaphore in two short months. The British technique he transferred to Australia was the undergrounding of telegraph cable, a method adopted disastrously in Morse's initial attempt on the Baltimore–Washington line. Todd, too, quickly regretted his uncritical dependence on the British undergrounding technique which, he wrote, 'added very greatly to the cost and was very soon an endless source of trouble as indeed were all underground wires laid in England . . . owing to the insulation becoming defective'. The British Henley magnetic double needles, which Todd also used on the line, were subsequently superseded by closed circuit Morse instruments as the telegraph system grew.[9]

Most vital to South Australia's progress was an intercolonial

Early days. The first telegraph station at Hergott Springs (Maree), South Australia.

telegraph connection with the prosperous port of Melbourne. The Government placed £20,000 on the estimates for the project in 1857 and Todd travelled to Melbourne to meet his colleague, Samuel McGowan. Both agreed that the line should be built as one uniform and successful system using Morse's technology, that the advancing Victorian line be extended to the South Australian border, and that Todd should build a line of over 300 miles from Adelaide to join it. The discussion with McGowan touched Todd's dream of a telecommunication link with India and Europe and the joint report to their respective governments bore this out. They saw their intercolonial telegraph connection as but 'a step in the direction of our ultimate telegraph communications, via India, with England, a scheme vast and difficult [which] . . . will, we doubt not, at no very distant date be carried out'. The Adelaide–Melbourne electric telegraph line, strung securely above the ground, was begun in April 1857 and opened in July the following year.

In contrast to its southern neighbours, the Colony of New South Wales was altogether slower, more cautious and hidebound in its response to the revolutionary new system of speeding the transfer of commercial and social information. In July 1855, with telegraphic activity booming in Victoria, New South Wales Governor Sir William Denison, an engineer by training himself, responded negatively to a question in the Legislative Council put by Henry Parkes and declared that, despite an exhibition of a telegraphic machine and estimates of £500 per mile given by the Magnetic Telegraph Company, there did not appear, in the present state of the Colony, to be 'such a demand for the adoption of these rapid means of conveying intelligence' to justify the outlay required. Some opposition stemmed from the NSW commissioners of railways, who, while rejecting the argument of telegraphic need, clearly wished to dominate any future development of the technology and link it with the railways.[10]

McGowan's plans, however, depended on a Sydney, Melbourne,

Now occupied by the Lands Department, the former telegraph repeater station at Beechworth (Victoria) dates from 1858, and was one of a number of such stations on the route north to Sydney.

Below: Beechworth, November 1983. To mark the 125th anniversary of the opening of the telegraph line between Victoria, New South Wales and South Australia, Morse messages passed once again between the state capitals. Here, Michael Duffy, Minister for Communications, receives the Adelaide message from ex-telegraphist Bill Edhouse.

Adelaide telegraph triangle and he pressed the neighbouring Colony that they should first build an electric telegraph within their own borders to understand the working of the telegraph system before plans for an intercolonial link were made. Parkes's interest proved crucial. In October 1856 he moved in the new Legislative Assembly for a select committee of Parliament to be appointed to investigate the question of telegraphic communication and particularly 'with reference to the rapid extension of that means of communication in the adjacent Colony of Victoria'. After long deliberation, the committee advised that immediate steps be taken to connect the cities of Sydney and Melbourne by electric telegraph and that a sum of £38,000 be placed on the estimates.[11]

Tenders for construction of the line from Liverpool to Albury were arranged in May 1857, while the New South Wales Government undertook the erection of the 20-mile line from Sydney to Liverpool itself. With some hitches in operating skills, the local line hiccoughed into operation on 30 December 1857. Under Governor Denison's watchful eye, the first message ran: 'Can you read my writing?' No answer was received for several minutes, the *Sydney Morning Herald* reported next day, but on the question being repeated 'an answer arrived that the pen of the instrument at Liverpool did not mark and was out of order'. Secondary messages like 'Have you got my writing plain' met silence and at last a terse reply from the Liverpool telegraphist that he 'did not get it plain enough'. 'Whether he was unable to rectify the defect in his instrument', the *Herald* mused, 'or believed from not being able to read the writing that all queries were at an end, we are unable to say.'

Despite human inexperience, New South Wales was soon ringed about its pastoral landscape by the humming electric telegraph wires. Todd's assistant, E.C. Cracknell, appointed assistant superintendent of telegraphs in New South Wales in January 1858 on Todd's strong recommendation and superintendent in 1861, strengthened the enterprise. He opened the Colony's third telegraph line on Australia Day 1858, registered the growth of 36 telegraph stations by 1862 and, despite contracting problems, completed the 200-mile line to Albury to join the Melbourne–Albury line in October 1858, a mere four months after Todd's successful completion of the Adelaide–Victoria stretch.[12]

Edward Charles Cracknell, superintendent of telegraphs in NSW from 1861 until 1893. He and his brother, William John Cracknell, the superintendent of telegraphs in Queensland, started a tradition of family service in telecommunications.

Queensland (separated from NSW as an independent Colony in 1859) would join the intercolonial telegraph nexus in 1861. Tenders for the construction of a line from Brisbane to the New South Wales border were called for in September 1860. Contractors Messrs Brown and Sherry undertook the project at £38 5s 6d a mile, and the line was ready for operation at Ipswich 24 miles down the route from Brisbane in April 1861. The line to the border was completed in November and linked with Sydney via Tenterfield in New South Wales where the separate Colonial staffs decoded the weakening message from each capital and transmitted it on.

Colonial Governors, in their congratulatory greetings, took the occasion to stress the increased prosperity and strengthened intercolonial activity the telegraph could provide. 'The wire', declared New South Wales' Sir John Young, speeding the first message from Sydney to Brisbane on 6 November, 'is an emblem of the congenial feelings which unite them to rejoice, each in the resources and advancement of the other'. An ominous silence followed his words. Had well–known Colonial rivalries muzzled the machine? Had Queensland's Governor Bowen nothing he wished to add? In the event, a storm had fused the lightning conductors at Tenterfield and it was three days before the Queensland Governor got his chance to reply. When he did so, his message was equally harmonious. He praised the telegraphic union of the two great Colonies and prayed telegraphically that the new bond might prove a symbol 'of mutual goodwill and of rapidly increasing prosperity'.[13] Gubernatorial hopes were justified. The spread of repeater stations with their staff and buildings contributed to the growth of country towns, while many a country postmistress found a congenial husband among the new company of telegraphists.

One cementing factor was the appointment of E.C. Cracknell's brother, W.J. Cracknell, as stationmaster at Ipswich in 1861 and as general superintendent of telegraphs at Brisbane in 1863.[14] It was the beginning of a significant tradition of family service in communications in Australia that blossomed in each Colony and State and has remained a distinctive feature of communications to the present day. W.J. Cracknell presided over the mobilisation of a vigorous telegraph growth, pushing lines out from Brisbane along the coast north to Bowen and Cardwell and inland to serve the spreading pastoral settlements that followed in the wake of Queensland's separation from New

London-born William John Cracknell (centre), superintendent of telegraphs, Queensland, 1863–80, surrounded by his staff in Brisbane, 1869.

South Wales. The Colony's population itself rose from some 23,000 to 34,000 in its first independent year and had almost doubled by 1865. That year, the Colony's Electric Telegraph Department handled over 50,000 telegrams and its messages were transmitted internally over more than 1,000 miles.

Eleven years after McGowan's initiative, several thousand miles of Morse's 'lightning lines' silhouetted the Australian countryside. Over long distances repeaters were installed, initially human operators who read the incoming Morse signals and re-transmitted them on to their destination. Much of the growing expertise was of American derivation, though Britain's Wheatstone automatic instrumentation for passing on messages in minor city and suburban offices, and its evolutionary improvements, were diffused throughout Australia from the early 1860s. The work of contracting and installing was experimental and difficult. Linemen and telegraphers had to be trained but, in city and suburb and in the remote country repeater stations, they impressed a new technology upon society.

Tasmania, dangling below the mainland, faced special problems. An internal electric telegraph joining Hobart and Launceston was completed during 1857 (the third Colony to get under way). Funded by Government and equipped from Government stores, the line was erected by a firm of Canadian contractors, Messrs Butcher, Estage and Carroll, who had carried out telegraph construction work for McGowan in Victoria. In true Australian tradition the senior partner and engineer, W.H. Butcher, was taken on by Government as their superintendent of telegraphs at Hobart, while his brother, G.B. Butcher, became the operator at Launceston. Ancillary lines stretched quickly through dense terrain 40 miles from Launceston to George Town in March 1858 and an easier installation joined Hobart to Mount Nelson in July, and Low Head in October that year.[15] While the public eagerly followed telegraphic progress, a peevish resistance greeted its replacement of the semaphore shipping signals on Mount Nelson. 'Since the line of electric telegraph has been extended to Mount Nelson', Hobart's *Mercury* fumed on 24 July 1858, 'the whole of the efficient and well-understood arrangements previously in existence have been thrown into disorder. We hate the meddling spirit that cannot let well alone!'

Despite spurts of local Luddism and the loss of favourite landmarks, the real challenge, both human and technological in Tasmania, was the provision of a submarine cable that would bind the isolated island to the trade, commerce and general progress of the mainland. The Governments of Victoria and Tasmania discussed the question as early as 1856; Butcher argued persuasively for the cable in a letter to Tasmania's Colonial Treasurer in August 1857, but the technology of submarine cabling, formidable and expensive, was in its infancy. Butcher might sincerely press that 'There can be no question that unless this Colony is . . . connected with the sister colonies, our commercial, agricultural, and general interests will be materially injured': the problems of a great undersea mechanical artery challenged the most enterprising enthusiasts.[16]

Overseas experience enjoined caution. Britain's first attempt to thread a cable across the Channel to Cape Gris Nez in France in 1850 had given one evening's spluttered and unintelligible communication before a French fisherman caught part of the cable in his trawl and, seeing the copper wire embedded in its gutta percha, rejoiced in the strange new seaweed with its core of gold. The same British company, the General Oceanic and Subterranean Electric Printing Telegraph Company, succeeded with another crossing the following year and submarine links were subsequently made with Ireland, between Britain and Belgium and Denmark, and, in 1857, between India and Ceylon. But frequent interruptions and erosion from rocks and shoals menaced the fragile lines.

Tasmania's plan for a submarine cable was highly pioneering in 1857. Soundings were taken in Bass Strait; Victoria and Tasmania agreed to share the costs; Samuel McGowan visited Tasmania to consult the Government in February 1858; tenders were sought; and Butcher, finding a ready successor in his brother, resigned his post as superintendent of telegraphs to join the successful contractors, Messrs McNaughtan & Co. of Launceston to proceed to London to oversee the construction of the cable. The contract, signed in February 1858, fixed the price at £45,000 and provided for 240 miles of cable with a single copper conductor armoured by iron wire. J.H. Henley, engineer, carried out manufacture in England. While the great cable grew, a flock of interested scientists and engineers gave advice and, after a trial submersion of several months, pronounced it 'extremely well manufactured'. 'Its insulation is so perfect', one expert vouchsafed, 'that it will retain a visible charge of electricity for several minutes.' Henley staked his reputation on the work. The cable, completed late in 1858 and coiled like a gleaming serpent, reached Melbourne aboard SS *Omeo* in 1859.[17]

The first route for the all important connection, surveyed by Tasmania's marine surveyor Captain Ross whom McGowan accompanied, had sought the longest utilisation of land lines. (See map.) The actual route chosen was more direct, used more submarine cable, came ashore at Three Hummock Island in place of Hunter Island, and joined Tasmania at Circular Head near Stanley.

SS *Omeo*, accompanied by the Colonial vessel SS *Victoria*, left Cape Otway, Victoria, in July 1859. Three-quarters of an inch in thickness, the cable was played out over a large drumwheel and dropped over a 'girding wheel' projecting from the stern of the ship. Watches of 12 men were stationed to release the cable and prevent it getting fouled and the playing out was halted at intervals to join the cable ends. The ubiquitous McGowan closely supervised the complex task. The difficulties were great. The telegraphic points established on the two islands worked imperfectly; fractures were found and repaired but, at last, on 18 August 1859, the cable and batteries were landed by whaleboat and a mainland telegraph circuit made the eagerly awaited connection with Launceston.

One hundred and seventeen miles in length, the Tasmanian cable was the longest yet laid. (Britain's submarine link with Holland ran a

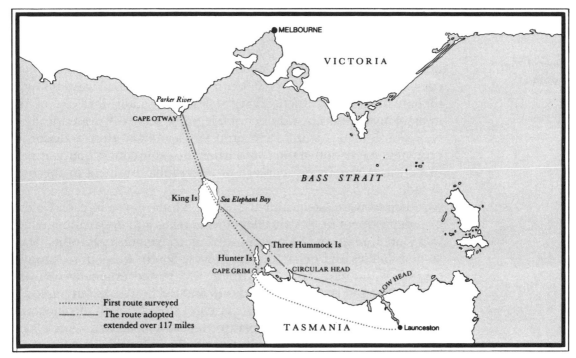

The Bass Strait cable, 1859

close second at 113 miles). But its life was erratic and short. The line, reported the superintendent of telegraphs, F.A. Parker, 'was never in regular working order . . . and business was seldom commenced until 11, 12 or 1 o'clock'.[18] The section between King Island and Three Hummock Island broke frequently, repairs were challenging, and the total cost — shared by Victoria and Tasmania — escalated to £53,000. Yet, when the shoals and sharp rock beds near King Island finally cut the connection in January 1861, the 'mechanical artery' had provided a telling foretaste of what telegraphic linkage between Tasmania and the mainland could achieve. Hasty, and certainly inadequately prepared as were the marine surveys of the dangerous passageways of the Straits, the men who pushed the cable had the future in their bones.

Advances in submarine technology, reaped from the struggle to lay the Atlantic cable, accomplished successfully after several attempts by the *Great Eastern* in 1866, contributed to the second Bass Strait undertaking in 1869. Then, Tasmania alone bore the financial cost of £70,000. The Victorian Government, twice shy, paid only for the line that joined the cable on their shore to the telegraph line to Melbourne. Yet, so valuable was the contribution of the Bass Strait cable to Tasmania's commercial life, that it was duplicated to cope with demand in 1885 and again in 1909.

By 1869 a distinctive pattern had emerged in Australia. The countryside was ringed around by telegraph lines, concentrated about the capital cities and market towns, the goldfields, and the denser agricultural and pastoral settlements. Smaller country towns were channelled into the arteries that bridged the capital cities. Use of the

This pole once marked, as a warning to shipping, the spot where a submarine telegraph cable linking Victoria and Tasmania came ashore at Apollo Bay, Victoria.

telegraph was extensive. Colonial statistics confirmed that the new technology had become a vital instrument of government and business. The prosperous and populous 'gold Colony' of Victoria led the field, despatching over 130,000 telegrams internally and intercolonially between 1854–70.[19] South Australia's record was also high, though their Government charged less and made less use of the intercolonial lines. The number of telegrams sent rose dramatically in New South Wales from 1858, and in Tasmania, after a period of economic stagnation in the 1860s when the cable connection snapped, there was a significant increase of telegraphic business in the next decade.[20]

All lines were Government–owned, administered in each Colony by a department of electric telegraph or telegraph department which was joined, in accordance with need or convenience, to other State responsibilities and departments. In New South Wales, for example, control of the telegraph department was vested originally with the Minister for Internal Communication and Public Works but passed to the control of the Postmaster–General in 1867, although the telegraph and post office remained separate departments, each with a permanent head. In South Australia Charles Todd combined the posts of superintendent of telegraphs and astronomical observer until the amalgamation of the departments of posts and telegraphs in 1869 elevated him to Postmaster–General and Government Astronomer. Similar amalgamations between posts and telegraphs occurred in Victoria that year and through the next decade in the other Colonies. But everywhere the well–established practice of grafting telegraph (and later telephone) staffs onto country and suburban post offices demonstrated the integral relationship of communication services.[21]

Only Western Australia, the great 'western third' with its small seaboard population, lagged behind in the developing telegraph's spread. When they participated, in 1869, it was private not public enterprise that spurred them on. In a Colony apathetic towards the telegraph, or of its relevance, Perth newspaper proprietor, Edmund Stirling, was one man who had become dissatisfied with the slowness of communication between Fremantle and Perth. Dependence on intercolonial mail and newspapers landing at Albany and proceeding overland to Perth, already placed Perth well behind the other capitals in its access to commercial information and news. Hence, in February 1868, Stirling presented a plan to Colonial Secretary Barlee offering to build a telegraph line from Perth to Fremantle if the Government would supply and erect the telegraph poles. Barlee initially declined to support the venture. Early in 1869 he agreed to provide convict labour for the erection of both poles and wires on an agreed concession for official messages carried on the line.

By a gentle irony, Western Australia, a Colony that had stoutly resisted convict transportation until a chronic labour shortage forced their acceptance from 1850–68, became the only Australian Colony to employ convicts in the construction of telegraph lines. Fortuitously, an ex-convict James Fleming, would furnish the expertise. Fleming had been deported from Scotland for defrauding fellow Glaswegian tea

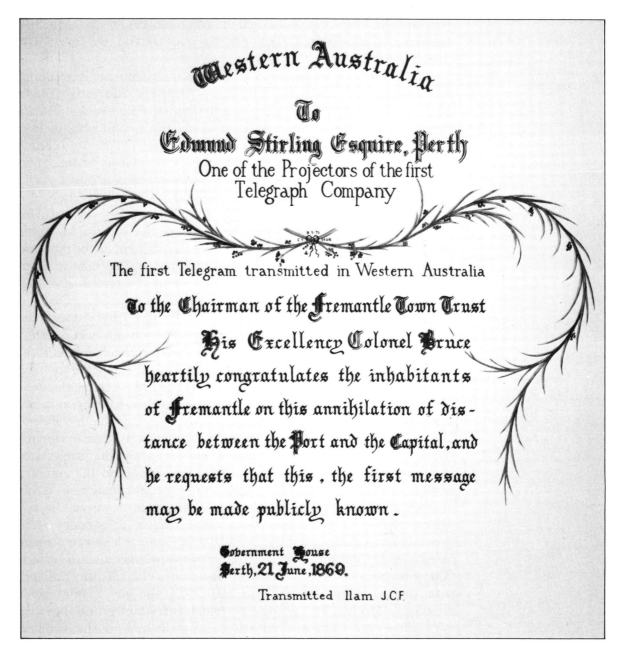

𝔚estern 𝔄ustralia

𝔗o

𝔈dmund 𝔖tirling 𝔈squire, 𝔓erth
One of the Projectors of the first
Telegraph Company

The first Telegram transmitted in Western Australia

𝔗o the ℭhairman of the 𝔉remantle 𝔗own 𝔗rust

ℌis 𝔈xcellency ℭolonel 𝔅ruce

heartily congratulates the inhabitants

of 𝔉remantle on this annihilation of dis-

tance between the 𝔓ort and the ℭapital, and

he requests that this , the first message

may be made publicly known .

𝔊overnment ℌouse
𝔓erth, 21 𝔍une, 1869.

Transmitted 11am J.C.F.

merchants in 1864. But a 'ticket of leave man' for good behaviour within a year, he quickly became headmaster of the William Street Boy's Academy and later reporter on the *Inquirer and Commercial News*. Most germane, he had acquired a considerable knowledge of the principles of telegraphy before his exit to the Colonies and was an able telegraphist. Stirling snapped him up to oversee the construction task. The first telegraph pole was planted in Perth on 9 February 1869 and, under Fleming's direction, convicts cut a wide swathe through riverside bush from Perth to Fremantle, dug in the jarrah poles, while linemen strung the overhead wires. Telegraphic equipment shipped from Melbourne was installed in a room in the Perth town hall and in a Fremantle shed; Fleming trained the first three telegraphist cadets, and the first cheerful message from the Governor, tapped out by

The first telegram transmitted in Western Australia, 1869, from Colonel John Bruce, the Administrator of WA, to Edmund Stirling, who, with Alexander Cumming, founded the Western Australia Telegraph Company in 1868.

Fleming on 21 June, congratulated the inhabitants of Fremantle on this 'annihilation of distance' between the capital and the port. The distance was 12 miles.

Further private initiative would push the lines outward from Perth. A second private enterprise, the Electro–Magnetic Company, bought Stirling out and in 1870 the Legislative Council, under pressure from residents of the towns, agreed that it would co–operate with the new company in getting telegraph connection from Perth to Albany, Bunbury, York and Toodyay. The Albany–Perth connection had great significance for the Colony's press. News reaching Australia by ship could now be quickly transmitted to Perth from Albany before it reached other Australian ports. On 1 January 1873 Western Australia's Government purchased the assets of the Electro–Magnetic Company and reconstituted its post office department as the post and telegraph department. With a background most Western Australians would prefer to forget, James Coats Fleming became the first superintendent of telegraphs in the Colony.[22]

Western Australia now joined the fervour for telegraphic information and exchange. Colonial enthusiasm for this 'most perfect invention' was not surprising. Well before the Australian continent was hooked up with telegraphic networks overseas, the impact of the new technology was dynamic and diverse. Telegrams became the new currency of quick communication. Australians took to telegrams like ducks to water. There was something about the laconic staccato style of the communication that suited their unloquacious temperaments. While costs varied from one Colony to the next, they rose proportionately everywhere with distance from the centres, and the remoter settlers early paid the price for long distance communication well over that required from their city cousins. High prices, however, did not inhibit the telegraph's use. By far the largest consumers were government, business and the press. But the telegram served a social need. Good Morse training was essential. But it was not always perfect. 'Come home at once', urged one message, 'father bad.' Father, indeed, was 'dead'. Another family was alerted by the gay if mysterious message, 'Mother sailing past',[23] while smart telegraph boys in Melbourne learnt to add to telegrams delivered to the Chinese business community the productive words 'Give Boy Ginger'!

Nowhere was the effect of the new technology more evident than in the business of communication itself. As lines spread, provincial and city newspapers began to publish a few inches each day, by–lined 'By Electric Telegraph', presenting intelligence from neighbouring Colonies, news of the movements of shipping, the price of goods, reports from parliament and, whenever possible, sporting events. Until the 1870s overseas news was telegraphed from Adelaide as the first point of shipping entry with telegraphic connections with the east. Its position gave that city a strategic and financial boost. At first, Charles Todd reflected, 'we had but one intercolonial wire and on the arrival of every English mail, there was an exciting amount of rivalry between the different newspapers in Melbourne and Sydney, great efforts being made to secure first possession of the line'.[24] Long chapters of the Bible were not infrequently despatched, at considerable expense, to ensure one newspaper's monopoly of the line while its correspondent compiled his news report. Messages of 8,000 to 10,000 words were not uncommon, boosting the returns — even at the more favourable rates for newspapers provided by South Australia's department of telegraphs. In 1859 Todd reported that the pressure on one single line was so great that a second intercolonial line had immediately to be planned from Adelaide to Melbourne via Wellington, New South Wales, and this was open for business in 1861. At the same time a duplicate line linked Melbourne and Sydney. Yet, despite Todd's endeavours, no direct line was installed from Adelaide to Sydney until 1867.

For the business community, the rapid dot–dash of the telegraph code tapped out prosperity and wealth. Business demand for telegraph services was pivotal. City and country town telegraph offices became the commissioning points for orders, the centres of market and banking intelligence, and the place where key decisions on buying, selling, importing and exporting were despatched. In the rich Western District of Victoria, where pastoral transactions often involved the large scale movement of flocks, 'squatters with interests in Queensland and New South Wales', wrote one historian, 'had frequent resort to [the telegraph].' Niel Black, a leading district pastoralist buying Queensland stock to be driven south to fatten, 'found the telegraph service indispensable when arrangements for the herd's management had to be altered'.[25]

Businessmen were impatient customers who forced governments to duplicate lines. In Tasmania the telegraph department pressed the

The hub of the nation — the operating room of Melbourne's chief telegraph office.

need for a second wire between Hobart and Launceston arguing pertinently 'that fully 50 per cent of the messages are presented for transmission during ordinary "business hours" between 9 and 4' and, unless they could go forward with ordinary promptness, 'a large proportion of them would become comparatively useless to sender and receiver'.[26]

Business was the stick that prodded the telegraph out and across increasingly difficult landscapes. In Tasmania, the gold discoveries at Mangana and Waterhouse in 1870 and 1871, and the tin finds at Mt Bischoff later that year, forced extensions while the opening of other fields in the island's mountainous west speeded telegraphic construction and maintenance that placed heavy burdens on the linemen. Plunging across snowfields, eating 'badger and bacon', drying the telegraph poles by a warm campfire each night, linemen on the Ouse–Strahan line experienced fierce environmental conditions that were very different from those endured across the continent as the lines marched out from Perth to Wyndham in the remote north easterly goldfields of the Kimberleys in 1893.

The telegram also served as an important instrument of central government in the large Colonies, issuing instructions and orders, announcing appointments, transferring public servants, conveying legal judgements and directives and, in police hands, tracking blackguards and criminals. The capture of Ned Kelly, bushranger extraordinary and national folk hero, became the subject of rapid telegraphic intelligence.

The relation between the telegraph and the railways, pivotal in England and Europe where telegraphs historically served the safe management of the railway lines, varied in Australia. In New South Wales the links were closer than in other Colonies and telegraph stations were not uncommonly attached to country and suburban railway stations where a stationmaster doubled as telegraphist. In the remoter Colonies telegraph lines often skirted the railways route and railway staff kept watch in distant areas on needed telegraph line repairs. At times the combination of the two services saved lives. In South Australia and the West, cases were reported where lost bushmen, parched and close to death, cut telegraph lines to announce their feeble presence, and were rescued either by telegraph linemen or railway staff. But administrative co–operation between the two services was sometimes difficult. Throughout the Colonies the telegraph generally preceded the railroad in forging extra–local and interregional links between merchants, the business community and entrepreneurs.

One important duty of the telegraph system was to keep the time of the nation. Time signals were transmitted to all telegraph stations throughout each Colony at one o'clock every day. Lines were kept clear for the transmission and clocks provided to all the city and the more important country post and telegraph offices.

Science, too, shared early the benefits of the new technology. Todd used his position as Superintendent and Government Astronomer to place weather stations in the hands of country post and telegraph officers with instructions to gather precise information on climate, winds, rain and storms. The advent of the overland telegraph would extend these reporting stations to the Northern Territory. But from the 1860s the intercolonial telegraph lines served to circulate information of storms and weather and to build up a telegraphic meteorological service with the co–operation of the Colonial Government astronomers that would serve into the next century.[27]

Todd also used his British experience of establishing longitude by telegraph when, in 1868, with the help of the Government astronomers in Victoria and New South Wales and free access to those Colonies' telegraph lines, he made an accurate determination of the 141st degree of east longitude to give more precise definition to the boundary line between South Australia and Victoria. For this under-taking, telegraph lines were linked up to Sydney observatory and to Melbourne's Williamstown; the two observatories were connected in direct circuit, and the transit of fifteen selected stars was observed and recorded on the Melbourne chronograph via information transmitted to Melbourne. 'The signals transmitted from Sydney', Todd explained, 'were received by a repeater at Melbourne, the armature of which automatically repeated them to the Chronograph.' The time lost in repeating was 0.027 seconds which was subtracted from the time of each Sydney transmit by the Melbourne clock. After further observations and recordings made near Wentworth on the boundary site 'Messrs Cracknell and McGowan', recorded Todd, 'having kindly arranged to give me direct circuit with the Melbourne Observatory, via Deniliquin and Echuca, all intermediate telegraph offices being cut out', a true boundary was established.[28]

Towards the close of the century Australia had become one of the largest national users of the telegraph. 'In no country in the world', wrote the statistician T.A. Coghlan in 1900, 'has the development of telegraphic communication been so rapid as in Australasia, and in none has it been taken advantage of by the public to anything like the same extent.'[29] It was true that the Colonial telegraph departments were more often in the red than in the black. Costs of line extension were constant; plant and buildings ate into returns and, although the gap between revenue and expenditure narrowed, there was an accept-ance by Colonial Governments, acknowledged at the Intercolonial Conference of 1873, that in a vast country telecommunication was and

The men who built the network. A South Australian line party camped in the bush.

Linemen camped at
Ducie River, below
Cape York, Queensland.

should, if necessary, be maintained in the Colonies 'at some pecuniary loss'. It was a question that would engage governments in debate and scrutiny in the decades ahead.

The colourful and energetic personality of the Australian progenitor of telegraphs summed it up. McGowan expressed his pride in the remarkable new system of communication that he had introduced by having a dinner service made in England elaborately decorated with cable and Morse motifs in brilliant red and white with a compass centred on each plate. It was a vivid gesture to a new age.

3 Wiring a Continent

T wo feats that became a legend and brought the greatest impetus to the telegraph in Australia were the striking enterprises by planners, contractors, back–up forces and linemen that stretched the Overland Telegraph line across Australia in 1870–2 and, five years later, built the East–West Telegraph around the Great Australian Bight to bring Australia's western half into electric telegraph contact with the east.

Even before Charles Todd reached Australia in 1855 dreaming his dreams of a telegraphic link that would unite the Antipodes with India and England, there was eager enthusiasm in England, the United States and Europe to girdle the earth with wires and cables that spanned continents and islands and passed along the ocean floor.

No technology held such glamour, or was so heroic and compelling, as the 'magic' submarine wire. By the mid–1850s cables reached out from England to the continent of Europe, crossed the Mediterranean, crept across the floor of the Black Sea to link Britain with its troops in the Crimean war, struggled to cross the Atlantic Ocean, and moved out towards India and Asia. Cable entrepreneurs in Britain and America drew investors like pied pipers, though the problems of the technology were such that thousands of pounds, and more dollars, often sank with the fragile cables to the sea bed.

To several entrepreneurs in Britain and America, the Australian Colonies beckoned as vital terminal points for their overseas cable schemes and in Australia 'cable fever' pervaded the Colonial Governments. As early as 1854, the year that Samuel McGowan swung the first telegraph line into the Australian sky, the British entrepreneurs, Brett and Carmichael, builders of the Channel cable, addressed the Colonial Governments with charts of cable lines originating in the Mediterranean and projecting expansion to Aden, across India to Madras, and on, via Ceylon, across the Indian Ocean to Perth. The plan, utopian in 1854, became a crucial starting point for cable schemes and speculation about the all–important integration of Australia into overseas networks that drifted in the heads of Governors and superintendents of telegraphs in the Colonies for nearly sixteen years.

'For the first time I realised the vastness of the undertaking.' Charles Todd, planner of the overland telegraph line.

One persistent and seasoned cable agent was Lionel Gisborne, an American promoter involved with the problematic Atlantic cable and founder of a family of cable and telegraph companies that changed names, amalgamated, divorced and collapsed without apparent damage to their chief. In 1858, as director of one of these, the Red Sea and India Telegraph Company, Gisborne approached the British Secretary of State for the Colonies with a proposition to connect the Australian Colonies with a contemplated Dutch cable from Batavia to Singapore. The plan, which hung on the Indian Government's readiness to extend its lines from Rangoon to Singapore, envisaged connecting Java by cable to Port Essington on Australia's north-west tip, and thence by a giant submarine loop around Cape York Peninsula and south to Moreton Bay.

The proposal caused a flurry in the Colonies. Rivalry and the keen desire of the Colonial Governments to maximise on the overseas connection by having the cable terminate on their territory, heightened the political interest. One man who grasped the political potential of the scheme was Sir Richard MacDonnell, Governor of South Australia. Despite obvious imponderables, MacDonnell saw four possible pathways between England and Australia emerging from the advancing cable routes: Brett's route from Ceylon to Western Australia stopping to join the cable midway across the Indian Ocean at Cocos (Keeling) Island; a submarine cable from Timor Island to the northern coast of Australia near Cambridge Gulf thence by overland route to Adelaide; a possible line from Banjoewangi in Java around the Western Australian coast to Perth; and Gisborne's Port Essington to Moreton Bay route.[1] (See map.)

Committed as he was to extending South Australia's pastoral interests into the unknown north MacDonnell favoured the overland route. He consulted his superintendent of telegraphs. Todd replied: 'I should prefer the fourth (Gisborne's) [route] which would require comparatively short lengths of cable in shallow seas, where the cable could be taken up and examined in case of injury.' Although, as Todd saw, the overland route to Adelaide would reduce the distance, be less costly and be more easily repaired, in 1858 the desert lay uncharted and empty and Todd considered that it should at least be shown to contain 'country available for settlement' before the concept of an overland telegraph should be taken up.[2]

McGowan, superintendent in Victoria, expressed other views. Technologically more experienced and better informed than Todd, he drew attention to the 'unsuitable nature of the bottoms' of any cable route involving Australia's coast to the north and north-east since it was, he understood, 'mostly composed of coral intersected by sharp angular ledges of the same material occurring suddenly and in unexpected positions'. But McGowan was not disposed to endorse the South Australian overland route. Even if it were possible to overcome the difficulties likely to be found in attempting to cross the interior's barren wastes, he reported to his Government in January 1859, the 'constant liability or molestation from the incursion of hostile native tribes, the nearly total absence of suitable timber for several hundred

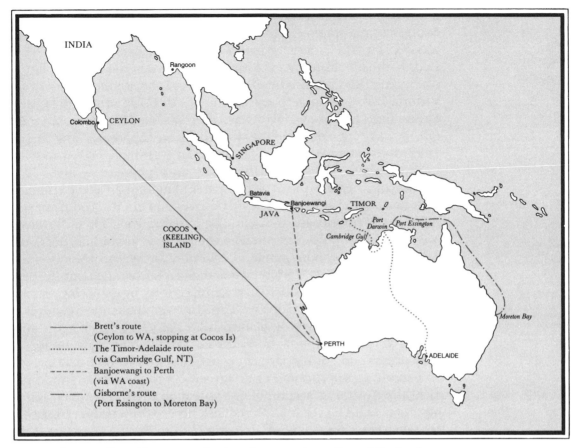

Proposed routes for cable communications between Australia and England, 1854–9

miles, want of natural fodder for beasts of burden, and the scarcity of water, would all tend to raise difficulties'. He cast his vote on 'a causal consideration' for Brett's Indian Ocean–Western Australia route.[3]

In New South Wales Governor Sir William Denison, who also administered Queensland until its formal separation in July 1859, favoured the Gisborne route and its link through Moreton Bay. A convert to telegraphy since the opening of the first Sydney line in 1857, he knew the trouble experienced in the Colonial links from lines that passed even briefly under water. Cables under the Murray River had been carried away 'more than once' and he had kept closely in touch with the progress of the Bass Strait cable plan. But nonetheless, writing to cable expert McNaughtan in Tasmania in March 1859, Denison affirmed that 'we (New South Wales) shall be disposed to assist any company which may be disposed to try and connect us with Batavia and India and so with England'. A few months later he had firmed his view. 'My idea of the route for the line to Batavia', he wrote then, 'is from Sydney to the Northward ... 1,000 miles would be done by N.S.W and Moreton Bay — from thence to Cape York into the bottom of the Gulf of Carpentaria and so on to Batavia [which] would be taken by the Company, making the sea lines as short as possible.'[4]

Yet, despite evaluations and the readiness of both the New South Wales and Victorian legislatures to commit themselves to subsidies for

37

the scheme, Gisborne's plan aborted. South Australia's reaction, expressed in a statement of the Legislative Council in January 1859, was explicit. The Governor had postulated the overland route. 'Until steps had been taken by exploration to ascertain the practicability of connecting this Province by Electric Telegraph with the mouth of the Victoria River, or some point on the North Coast of Australia, near Cambridge Gulf, or even westward thereof', the Executive statement ran, it was 'not advisable ... to decide on supporting any line of Telegraphs intended to connect Australia with India or Europe.'[5]

But what of Todd? Historians and popular writers have traditionally cast the quiet and competent Englishman as the visionary who first conceived Australia's epic overland route. Todd, indeed, claimed the priority for himself. The initial moving force, however, was not the able public servant who would carry out the line, but South Australia's exploration–minded Governor, Sir William MacDonnell. Already during 1858 MacDonnell had given encouragement to South Australian explorers to open up pastoral country by exploring country west and north of Lake Torrens. The same year he made overtures to the Lord Commissioners of the British Treasury for financial assistance for an overland telegraph, but received a resounding rejection for his risky plan. Todd, for his part, clung to Gisborne's scheme and in 1859 prepared a prospectus and draft agreement for a company to imple-ment the Australian section of the operation to Moreton Bay. But in July 1860, at his Government's request, he also drew up an estimate of probable costs for a line of telegraph from Port Augusta to King George's Sound, and there registered some anxiety at contemporary risks of 'long submarine lines'. 'I am more than ever disposed', he wrote then, 'to think we shall yet connect ourselves with India by an overland line to the northern coast, and thence, by a comparatively short submarine section to Java.' But he was not against a route to King George's Sound which he saw as linking with the central overland route.[6]

Todd has been charged — some 40 years after the event — with misrepresenting his initiating role. His accuser is Henry Strangways, lawyer and politician, who served in seven South Australian ministries from 1860–70 and who, first as Attorney–General (1860–1) and later as Premier and Attorney–General (1868–70), held a ringside seat at the critical cable negotiations. 'Sir Charles [Todd]', he wrote in a private letter of 1908, 'has no claim to speak of the Central Australian line as his pet project.' Todd, Strangways asserted, was essentially the diligent public servant and not the man who held responsibility for settling the important overland line. Todd's recollections had certainly consoli-dated and streamlined his own participation when he came to write up the story officially in 1884. But contemporary evidence suggests that it was Stuart's successful inland exploration of South Australia in 1860 that clinched Todd's positive overland view.[7]

Inland exploration of South Australia would change many per-spectives in 1862. John McDouall Stuart (1815–66) had responded to the South Australian Government's overture to open up pastoral country in 1858. A year later the Government's offer of £2,000 to the first person to cross the continent and reach the north or north–west coast (an offer made during Gisborne's visit to Australia in 1859) called him out again and, in April 1860, he reached and named the geographical centre of Australia near a mountain he called Central Mt Sturt (now Stuart). Pausing only to raise the flag and express the hope that it might be 'a sign to the natives that the dawn of liberty, civilisation, and Christianity, is about to break upon them', Stuart completed his journey in good pastoral land and, attacked by the natives McGowan so profoundly feared, turned homeward. Stuart made two more attempts before he finally reached the north–west coast at the Mary River on 24 July 1862 and, honouring a promise he had made to the Governor, 'washed his hands and face in the warm water'.[8]

Stuart had proved that the continent could be crossed; that the idea of an inland sea was a myth; and that enough water could be found to support men and beasts. In the preface to his *Explorations in Australia: The Journals of John McDouall Stuart*, published in London in 1864, he attested that a telegraph line could be routed through the interior. Stuart's successes had strengthened Todd's changing view. The explorer's arrival at the Mary River also influenced Gisborne who negotiated with the Indian Government to close the Rangoon–Singapore gap and resolicited the Australian Colonies in 1862 with a proposal, this time as director of the Australian India and China Electric Company, for a heavier and more effective cable and for a larger subsidy from the participants. Todd now wrote positively of an overland route. 'In a letter addressed to myself', he reported to his Government in October 1862, 'Mr Gisborne says the promoters would be prepared to meet Australian lines at whatever point that could be completed by the end of 1864.' Gisborne, it was true, had doubts about 'having a long land line traversing an unsettled country with a hostile or mischievious native population' and urged the difficulty of its maintenance. But Todd had grasped the nettle. 'The way for a land line', he now declared, 'seems clearer now than it did, even two years ago.' Indeed, he believed it offered 'so many collateral advantages beside its diminished cost, that I cannot forbear urging the desirableness before pledging ourselves to Mr Gisborne's scheme ... of immediate steps being taken to determine the feasibility of carrying the wire to the North Coast.'[9]

Todd's enthusiasm, however, had come too late and a hiatus occurred in the 1860s. The problems of longline submarine technology, the Bass Strait fiasco, and the failure to achieve an enduring trans–Atlantic cable (until 1866), quelled Colonial enthusiasm and the Intercolonial Conference of 1863 declared unanimously against discussion of Gisborne's latest scheme.

The politics of an overseas telegraph connection would reach its crescendo at the decade's end. Other actors had appeared. The young colony of Queensland was equipping itself for the task. There, W.J. Cracknell had pushed his Morse lines up the northern coast to pass Rockhampton and reach Port Denison in 1866. Cracknell clung tenaciously to the concept espoused by Gisborne of terminating the

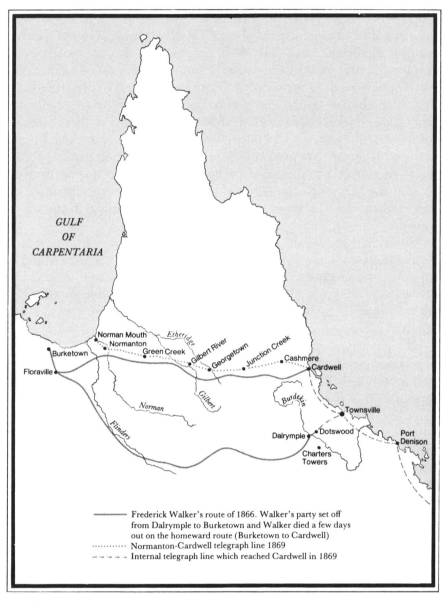

GULF
OF
CARPENTARIA

———— Frederick Walker's route of 1866. Walker's party set off
from Dalrymple to Burketown and Walker died a few days
out on the homeward route (Burketown to Cardwell)
·············· Normanton-Cardwell telegraph line 1869
– · – · – · Internal telegraph line which reached Cardwell in 1869

The first telegraph line erected in Australia, 1869, to meet the international
telegraph link

overseas cable connection within Queensland's domain. More pre-
sumptuous than the other superintendents of telegraphs, in 1866 he
arranged for an exploratory expedition to survey an overland route for
a telegraph line from Cardwell on the northern coast directly across
country to Normantown from where it could connect to the eastern
coast of the Gulf of Carpentaria at Burketown and make a suitable
cable join. The distance was some 450 miles. A party of 12 men, led by
the bushman and pastoralist, Frederick Walker, and including a
number of Cracknell's own telegraph department staff sent to
examine the quality of the trees for poles, set off in June 1866 from
Dalrymple near Charters Towers. Three months of hard slogging later
they reached Burketown.[10] While Walker paid for the endeavour with
his life and died from fever a few days out on the homeward route,
both Houses of the Queensland parliament approved the erection of a

line on the route surveyed when the internal telegraph line reached Cardwell in June 1869 and proclaimed the undertaking as 'a great step towards placing Australia and New Zealand in telegraphic communication with India and Europe'. Contracts were let in two sections from Cardwell to Etheridge River, and from the Etheridge to the Gulf, and work was set in train that marked the first construction undertaken by any Australian government to meet the international telegraph link.

W.J. Cracknell evidently thought the cable connection was in his bag. In January 1870 the Governments of Queensland and New South Wales entered a provisional agreement with the newly formed British Australian Telegraph Company (BAT) whose prospectus was not only to lay a cable from Singapore to Java and a further cable to link Java with Port Darwin, but to 'construct land lines from Port Darwin to Burketown to connect with the Queensland telegraph system'.[11] The construction contract to install both submarine and land lines went to the Telegraph Construction and Maintenance Company (of which BAT was a subsidiary) whose director, Captain Sherard Osborne, put himself into touch with the Colonies. Osborne particularly advised the South Australian Government that the cable would come ashore at Port Darwin and he sought their permission to build the overland connection across the Northern Territory now administered by the South Australian Government.[12]

The news fell like a blow upon the Government in Adelaide. While they agreed that they would give permission to the company to erect the line, their clear preference was for a line to be constructed from Port Darwin to their southern telegraph station at Port Augusta. They went further. The South Australian Government was prepared, the Colonial Secretary notified the company's co-director in Adelaide, Commander Noel Osborne (Sherard's brother), to put before parliament a Bill to authorise a direct line between Port Darwin and Port Augusta to be erected either by the company under guarantee or by the Government. Todd discussed the matter with Noel Osborne. 'I pointed out', he reported, 'the great advantages such a line would possess over one which kept for so great a distance in the tropics and flooded country of the Northern Territory and the lowlands around the Gulf of Carpentaria. I also showed that our line would be much shorter, and that Queensland could easily tap it by an extension from Normantown.'[13]

Hairbreadth competition now spurred fearless action. The Port Augusta to Port Darwin Telegraph Bill was introduced into the South Australian parliament on 8 June 1870 to raise the finance for the venture. For this proposal all subsidies were set aside. Todd, drawn into the hub of negotiations, estimated the cost of the overland line at £120,000. His commitment was unequivocal now. 'If we fail to accept these terms', he advised his Government, 'we must be prepared to leave to Queensland the exclusive honour of having, through her own unaided enterprise and energy, afforded to the Australian Colonies the immense advantages of telegraph communication with the whole civilised world. Our geographical position and our intelligence alike prohibit this.'[14]

Cracknell, within sight of success, was bitterly aggrieved. Outmanoeuvred, he would not forget. South Australia's offer relieved the British Australian Telegraph Company of the cost and construction of an overland line, while the South Australian Government pledged to have a telegraph line stretching across the continent from south to north, open and ready for traffic, by 1 January 1872. The Bill, passed by a large majority, received the Royal assent from the Governor on 16 June 1870 within eight brisk days. Public opinion thrilled to the ambitious enterprise. The fevers and vacillations of the past twelve years had been resolved within three nerve–wracking months. South Australia had borne off the prize. Todd was placed in charge. 'Then', he reflected sombrely, 'perhaps for the first time, I fully realised the vastness of the undertaking I had pledged myself to carry out.'[15]

In 1870 the technology available for the 1,800–mile Australian overland telegraph project was experimental and rudimentary. It rested on practical experience accumulated over fifteen years from telegraph construction in the settled parts of South Australia and from materials imported from overseas. Countries as geographically different as India and America had developed telegraph networks built across arid plains, over rivers and mountain ranges and through the great canyons of the United States. But each experience of trans-continental telegraphy was individual and unique. To span the length of the Australian continent from south to north, to string a telegraph line from settled districts through the unknown 'dead heart' of the continent, carry it north through unexplored country from the Roper River (where Stuart had diverged to the west) and join it to an overseas cable timed to come ashore on the Australian mainland exactly 18 months later, was an undertaking of epic and unpredictable proportions. Technologically, it was the 'greatest engineering feat' to be carried out in 19th century Australia. In human terms, as one official speaker declared on the line's completion, it was 'the greatest and by far the most wonderful event that has ever occurred in the history of this country'.

From its origins, the procedures of the overland telegraph line were unorthodox. Todd's instructions, issued by the South Australian Government, were stringent and precise. He was to build a telegraph line from Port Augusta to Port Darwin 'in the most substantial manner' and to have it ready for traffic by 1 January 1872. Action under the empowering Act, however, would only become official with the signature of the British Australian Telegraph Company on the formal contract sent by mail to London. The Act became operative on 12 October 1870. Meanwhile, in June 1870 Todd embarked on the project without delay. His only guide to the long overland route — Stuart's *Journals of Exploration* — was fragmentary. These revealed nothing of the area adjacent to the explorer's track and were eight years out of date. Nonetheless, Todd recalled, 'How eagerly I read Stuart's journals and with what feelings I tried to realise all I had to contend with, work out plans by which I could hope to overcome every obstacle and carry the undertaking to a successful issue.'[16] Dug into his office in King William Street Adelaide and working with enormous concentration and speed, Todd was both sanguine and determined. They were qualities on which the whole superstructure of the enterprise would depend.

Organisationally and logistically the overland telegraph plan was immense. While the technology of the undertaking was familiar to Todd, the forward planning of each interlocking segment of the scheme had to be precisely prepared, with prudent attention to detail and with a judgment of both geography and men that, at least initially, could only be crudely guessed. Essentially it was a *management* plan. With a bare 18 months at his disposal, Todd quickly determined to subdivide the project into three sections: the first, the southern section extending from Port Augusta 500 miles to the northwards; the third, the northern section stretching from Port Darwin to the Roper River near Stuart's Attack Creek; and the second or central section, 'the longest and most difficult', covering about 600 miles of country as yet devoid of human landmarks which could best be defined as a slice of territory 'falling between Latitude 27 degrees and 19 degrees 30 minutes on the map'. The first and third sections Todd put out to private contractors; Edward Bagot in the south, Joseph Darwent and William Dalwood for the northern section, while the Government took on the unknown, chartless central section. There were five working parties, designated A,B,C,D and E, each with an overseer, charged to cover a degree and a half of latitude, or about 100 miles. To meet the unrelenting deadline, construction was planned to take place concurrently across the entire length of the route.[17]

With the scantest knowledge of the interior north of Lake Torrens, except for the corridor described by Stuart, Todd immediately appointed John Ross, enterprising young manager of Thomas Elder's far northern cattle stations, to begin an expedition at Mount Margaret, with a surveyor and three assistants, to survey and plot a northerly route for the line. Ross needed to take account of such factors as the timber suitable for poling, available water, conditions for transporting material, and the nature of the ground for the poles. Appointed on 7 July 1870, Ross was due back with a pilot route no later than October.[18]

A month after Ross's departure, the northern contractors, Darwent and Dalwood, embarked for the north. The South Australian Government had appointed Captain Bloomfield Douglas as Government Resident, in the Northern Territory in April that year, believing that the cable would come ashore at Port Darwin and be linked by overland route to Burketown, Queensland. In July 1870 Port Darwin was little more than a camp, a remote outpost inhabited by the Resident family and a few surveyors and police. Their lives would be transformed by the new overland telegraph plan.

Darwent and Dalwood were splendidly equipped. Fitted out with wire and insulators, wagons, drays, bullocks, 28 horses, forage, supplies, food and with 80 men chosen from the 400 applicants who had hustled forward from city and country to join the adventure at 4s 6d a day, they left Port Augusta on 20 August 1870 on the SS *Omeo*.

With the contractors and their assistants — for supervision and reinforcement were the benchmarks of all Todd's plans — went two Government overseers, William McMinn and R.C. Burton, both with experience of the Northern Territory and both responsible for overviewing separate sectors of the contractor's work. In addition, there were two assistant inspectors, two telegraphists and four linemen to work on the extending telegraph line. Sunk almost to its bulwarks with its cargo, SS *Omeo* sailed out into Spencer's Gulf watched by a thousand spectators. The hymns and prayers of the service held a week before at St Paul's Church to commend the members of the northern telegraph expedition to Divine protection still echoed in the participants' ears. They would need this protection when, landing at Port Darwin, they ceremoniously sank their first pole on 15 September 1870, gave three cheers for the Queen, three more for the Governor and his seven daughters, three for themselves, and began their expedition south.[19]

Todd's most elaborate planning was thrown into the organisation of the central section of the line. 'The fitting out of the working parties for the interior', he reported later, 'was a matter of grave concern, as upon it, and the selection of good officers and men, their success mainly or entirely depended.' The 'good officers', five Government overseers chosen largely on the recommendation of the surveyor-general, were Richard Knuckey appointed to subsection A; G.R. McMinn to B; J. Beckwith to C; S.T. Woods to D; and W. Harvey, who accompanied Ross on his first exploring sortie, appointed to the distant section E. Each party also had a sub-overseer, an assistant and between 16 and 19 men. Later, to focus hierarchical responsibility, Woods was made chief officer of the whole central group. But their lines of operation soon rapidly dispersed. As Todd himself stressed, 'It will give some idea of the difficulties and the distance to be travelled over when I state that Mr Harvey's party did not reach the scene of their operation (Section E) until the 24th May in the following year.'[20]

The equipping of these huge parties, ready by the end of August, was reminiscent of the great overland wagon treks across the wild west of the United States. The range of the men recruited testified to the self-supporting nature of their task. There were carpenters, black-smiths, farriers, drovers, horsemen, labourers for cutting trees and building the stations and huts, storekeepers, cooks, linemen, tele-graphists, overseers, surveyors, a surgeon for each section, and cadets. Transport was crucial. Everything except the tree poles had to be carted to the site. Bullock and horse-drawn vehicles carried the men and materials. In the central section, two camel caravans, in the care of two Afghans, joined the 15 horse wagons, 17 bullock drays, a bullock wagon, five express wagons, some 200 bullocks and almost as many horses. Nothing was more important than that technological backstop, the horse, and the most elaborate instructions were spelt out to overseers for their care.

Not surprisingly, the provisioning of such an assemblage impinged deeply on the city of Adelaide. One saddler alone made 27 sets of

five–horse heavy harnesses, 45 pack saddles, some 300 horse collars, plus instrument cases and patent leather haversacks for the officers. He used over 600 hides and kept 40 men at work from dawn to late at night for six weeks at a bonus of ten per cent of their earnings to soften their exhaustion. The Sarina Timber–yard in Adelaide also turned out an astonishing 30,000 ironbark insulator pins, while other Adelaide suppliers built the light but strong transport wagons to Todd's special design. The imported equipment reached gargantuan size. Three thousand wrought–iron poles came from Britain to be used where suitable wood could not be found and, over a period, more than 1,800 miles of single–strand galvanised wire was brought from Britain, together with insulators, batteries and other equipment.[21]

Todd, tireless supremo, set down highly specific instructions for his overseers to observe. Every overseer was held responsible for the strict discipline, health and morale of his men. The tools, implements and stores were to be protected from injury; waste was the enemy; trustworthiness vital; and accountability was scored through every sentence of the text. Rest came on Sundays though it was recommended that an overseer 'read a short service to his officers and men on that day', even if, as some noted, attendance was, mercifully, 'voluntary'.

The midnight oil burned low in Todd's office as he set down his detailed instructional manuals. All the knowledge and portents of

Carriers of the inland — camels, like these from India being unloaded at Port Augusta, South Australia, were used as transport during the building of the overland telegraph line.

45

survival garnered by explorers were embedded in these documents. Here Todd received particular assistance from Benjamin Babbage (1815–78), one of the most remarkable men in the Colony. The son of the eminent Charles Babbage, Professor of Mathematics at Cambridge and inventor of the calculating machine, Benjamin had trained as an engineer with some of the most distinguished names in England. From 1842–8 he gained experience in planning and building railways under Isambard Brunel in Italy and England; he worked in engineering and in waterworks and had dabbled in creative experimental telegraphy before he left England. He came to South Australia on the recommendation of the head of the British Geological Survey in 1851 to make a geological and mineralogical survey of the Colony. Babbage became a noted explorer in Australia. Sent by Government to search for gold as far as the Flinders Ranges, he discovered the MacDonnell River and Mt Hopeful and dispelled the prevailing notion of the impassibility of the Lake Torrens 'horseshoe' by finding a gap through to the Cooper and Gulf country. In further excursions between Lake Torrens and Lake Gairdner and westward and north, Babbage delineated the western shores of Lake Eyre South, surveyed and mapped the country and, never hurrying, acquired an intensive understanding of its ways. His slowness indeed led to some public and parliamentary clamour, and he was superseded in 1856.[22]

Todd appointed him overseer to Bagot's section in the southern section, but he also used him in plotting the overland route and in drawing on his unique knowledge of the country. 'All bright green places should be visited as being spots in which drainage water has collected', the instructions to overseers ran. 'Mound springs may sometimes be discovered by a fringe of rushes or reeds upon an apparent sandy hill . . . Water is, as a general rule, more likely to be met with in the gullies amongst hills rather than upon the opposite side of the hills . . . If the main creek dies away on an arid sandy plain, water may very likely be found lower down the valley, either on the surface, if the nature of the soil changes and becomes retentive, or by digging.'[23] Babbage's scientific knowledge of geology, agronomy, drainage and botany bolstered the overseers' skills.

In late September 1870 Babbage and the second overseer W.H. Abbott, appointed to the southern section, left Adelaide with the contractor Bagot and made rapid headway. Bagot supplied his own men and timber (at £41 per mile) and wire and insulators came from Government. Babbage's role was to survey the northern end of the section but the absence of good timber caused problems and poling was permitted at ten poles to the mile instead of the prescribed twenty to meet the connection deadline. While the party awaited shipment of 1,500 iron poles for the line near Strangways Springs, Bagot, working in more settled areas, readily met his contract; his wire up and telegraphic contact made with Adelaide by the end of 1871. He was fortunate; the contracts were stringent, designed to stir up a lively speed, a penalty of £20 a day without appeal, while no man could be withdrawn from the workforce until the overseer had inspected and certified the work.

Under such pressure it was not surprising that anxiety and apprehension steamed off the pages of the overseers' diaries which Todd, strict taskmaster, had enjoined them to keep. J. Beckwith, overseer on section C of the central section, became ill from heatstroke on the outward journey. Though an experienced surveyor, he was already anxious, five days out of Adelaide, confiding in his diary, 'I must have all the horses fresh before leaving this station.' When heatstroke overtook him he was, he wrote, 'much afraid'. 'I feel bodily ill . . . my health seems quite broken up.' Struggling with fever, he worried and fussed about the horses. It soon became obvious that Beckwith was not fit enough to tackle the journey north and Todd, who was at the depot, replaced him with the sub–overseer W. Mills. 'The failure of my health', wrote Beckwith piteously, 'has caused him [the Superintendent] a great deal of trouble.'[24] Beckwith was the line's first casualty. Lonely, and denied much sympathy from the men of a returning transport team who brought him back, he maintained his diary until 31 December but died shortly before reaching Adelaide.

Christopher Giles, sub–overseer on the central section A, left a vivid picture of daily life on the line. 'The working hours at the main camp', he recorded, 'were — Begin work at 5.30 am, breakfast at 7.30 am to 8. Leave off work at 11, begin again at 2.30 and work till 6.' A large steel bell suspended on a rope served to strike the hours that showed on a sundial which Giles himself had made and placed in the centre of the camp. At night there was the great emptiness under the

Construction party on the line. From the *Illustrated Australian News*.

open sky. It was a melancholy land, silent except for the noise made by the horses and the men moving in the tents. The food was basic — monotonous tinned meat, preserved potatoes, tapioca and dried vegetables pressed into 'Hash me grande' stews or baked under the mysterious name of 'Lobscouse'. In such surroundings the presence of the Afghan 'Jemedars' lent an eccentric touch. Hadjee Meer Ban, a commanding figure in his pure white robes which he changed once or twice a day, 'was the most cheerful and jovial disposition', reported Giles, 'when not at his devotions (he had been to Mecca) or expanding in his broken English on the merits of his faith.' As the 'Jedemars' knelt at sunset to pray, Giles reflected 'Strange to think that in this *new* country, the echoes should be waked by the worship of the Eternal in the oldest living language in which He is known.' Yet the Afghans were 'a most valuable auxiliary contingent to the expedition.'[25]

In this human and technological enterprise, men's ingenuity and endurance were pressed to straining point. Instructions conveyed that wooden poles, tapered to specifications and not less than nine inches in diameter at the butt, were to be hoisted and fixed 'in a most substantial manner' and positioned at not fewer than 20 to the mile. In softened ground, each pole was strutted with a 16–foot pole to prevent the line wire pulling the pole over and, in a region of the highest lightning incidence in Australia, every second pole was fitted with a lightning rod. The bare wire rested on insulators fastened to the pins or spindles attached to pole or crossarm and overseers kept written check of the daily work of each man, the poles cut and erected, and the length of wire put up each week into the silent sky.

In this early telegraph line installation, contractors and overseers knew little of theory. In any event, conditions in central and north Australia were novel and unremitting. One constant enemy was leakage from the insulation along the line. Insulators (60,000 in all across the line) were challenged by conditions that began in temperate zones and experienced every variation in atmosphere from misty rain, dry aridity, dust, monsoonal downpours, and temperatures ranging from below freezing point to those as high as anywhere in the world, which resulted in frequent signal failure. 'In the 1870s, knowledge of the characteristics of insulators for open wire was naturally fairly elementary', wrote Frank O'Grady, a later Director–General of the Australian Post Office.[26] Insects also made unremitting invasion of the insulators' semi–enclosed undersides. White ants were to remain a permanent scourge of telecommunication in Australia. In 1871 they gnawed their way through wooden poles and were barely daunted by the steel poles imported from the firms of Siemens and Oppenheimer. Many poles, hanging like skeletons, had to be replaced entirely in 1883.

For these and other maintenance reasons 'repeater' stations were essential. These were established at every 150–180 miles, close to available water, in charge at first of one operator to receive and write down the signal and retransmit it on to the next section of the line. Eleven repeating stations were established at Beltana, Strangways Spring, the Peake, Charlotte Waters, Alice Springs (named for Todd's

The Powell's Creek telegraph station. From the *Illustrated Australian News* of 21 May 1887.

wife), Barrow Creek, Tennant Creek, Powell Creek, Daly Waters, the Katherine and Yam Creek. In time these stations would be staffed by a station master, as many as four operators and a lineman. But in 1871 demands on the inventiveness of the lonely linemen and telegraphists kept them alert. Strange false currents played havoc with the line. Slowly it was learned that these related to weather conditions and sunspot activity and construction proved instructive to contemporary research.[27]

In the event, an uncalculated and almost fatal threat to the exploit came from the tropical northern section. With the first pole 'well and truly fixed', the contractors, on overseer McMinn's directions, consolidated their men on the first part of the line immediately south of

Erecting the first pole of the overland telegraph line at Port Darwin on 15 September 1870. Harriet Douglas (to the left of the pole), one of the government Resident's seven daughters, performed the ceremony.

49

Darwin. The two working parties made good progress and over 200 miles of poles and some 100 miles of wire were erected when torrential rain, heavy clearing work, transport breakdown and short supplies interrupted progress in mid–March 1871. Conditions were calamitous. Up to 10 inches of rain fell in a day; tracks swelled to rivers, rivers to lakes, and the telegraph line holes cascaded with water as soon as they were dug. With supplies shrinking, weevils and grubs rampaged through the flour and rice; the men would not eat and, for the first time on the line, 56 men voted to strike. McMinn, rushing to the Roper, found little to cheer him there, panicked, cancelled the contract with the contractors and sailed for Adelaide. His excessive zeal and apprehension threw the whole line into jeopardy. With the benefit of hindsight, it is clear that with new supplies pending and good weather ahead (for there was a particularly good summer that year) the northern section could have been completed on time. Todd, however, stood by his overseer, though Darwent and Dalwood immediately announced legal action and claimed that their section could have been completed within a few weeks of the contract date.

Todd now wanted to transfer the northern section base at Port Darwin to the Roper River but in this he was overridden by Government. Instead, on 13 July 1871, as time closed in, the Government interceded, appointing Robert Charles Patterson, assistant engineer of the Department of Works and resident engineer of the South Australian Railways, to lead an expedition to Darwin with huge reinforcements of bullocks and horses, and a further contingent of 200 men, chosen once more from an army of twice that number who responded to the advertisement in the *Adelaide Advertiser* on 15 July. The inland, and the purpose and romance of the venture, attracted men as nothing short of war would do.

Patterson set out on SS *Omeo* and arrived in Port Darwin in August 1871. Todd's report of the culminating struggle and perturbation in the north, written over a long perspective in 1884, is judiciously clear. 'It was hoped', he wrote,

> that the large force and transport power placed at the disposal of Mr Patterson would have been ample to enable him to join, by wire, on to Mr Harvey's work [section E. central section] — not by the end of 1871, that was impossible, perhaps, but certainly by March or April 1872 . . . but, unfortunately, further disasters occurred to prevent this. Mr Patterson's expedition arrived at Port Darwin during the dry and hot months immediately preceding the setting-in of the north–west monsoon. The country was bare of feed, and long stages had to be performed without water. Before wells could be sunk, and all materials carted up from Southport, a wet season of remarkable intensity was upon them, and all work stopped: 20.986 inches of rain fell in December, and 18.261 inches in January, up to the 24th. Very severe losses of stock were sustained . . . and Mr Patterson, after despatching the *Bengal* with stores and material to the Roper, where he subsequently met her, having proceeded overland, had to send Mr Little from the Roper, in a boat to Normanton, and thence to the nearest telegraph station (Gilbert River) in Queensland, to telegraph for further help.[28]

The situation could hardly have been more desperate. For one thing, on 7 November, as Patterson prepared for his journey to the

Roper, the fleet of the Telegraph Construction and Maintenance Company started to bring the cable ashore. Lying at anchor like three ghosts in Port Darwin Bay, the company's ships, *Edinburgh*, *Investigator* and *Hibernia*, were a pertinent reminder that time was running out. By 9 a.m. the cable fleet's men had the cable on shore and, placing it in a trench to the cable house, had linked it up to the instruments. Without delay, *Hibernia* set off playing out the copper cable that would link Port Darwin to Java. *Hibernia* carried the shore and intermediate cables and, when these had been laid, the *Edinburgh* spliced on the deep–sea section and carried the task forward. On 16 November, in the Bali Straits, the deep–sea length ended. With the cables cut and buoyed, the ships steamed on to the local shore terminal at Banjoewangi. The shore cable was landed on 18 November and, the following day, 19 November 1871, Australia was linked up by international connection to the world overseas.

Hence it was not the bustling cities of Melbourne, Sydney, Adelaide nor Brisbane which heard the first remarkable message; but Port Darwin, the tiny, raw settlement named for the *Beagle*'s scientist who had elucidated a theory of the evolution of species and left his surname in this remote domain. 'Advance Australia' exhorted the message sent to the Government Resident of the Northern Territory by Captain Halpin of the cable fleet. 'I have the honour', he telegraphed, 'to announce to you, in the name of the Telegraphic Construction and Maintenance Company, that we yesterday completed perfect submarine cable communication with your colonies, and with Java, the mother–country and the Western World. May it long speak words of peace.'[29] Yet penalties of £70 per day would begin on 1 January 1872. It was five weeks away.

Although the southern and central section lines were substantially erected and messages travelled across internal sections of the line, chaos and anxiety prevailed in the north. At Katherine, on 21 Nov-

The telegraph station at Port Darwin during the line's construction. From the *Illustrated Australian News* of 16 July 1872.

ember, Patterson consigned himself to gloom: 'I am utterly weary of the whole thing' he wrote in his diary. 'Can see nothing but blackness and suffering ahead. Fear expedition must collapse.'[30] Worse: W.J. Cracknell, nursing his grievance, had struck out publicly against the overland telegraph plan. In his annual report to his Government of December 1870 the Queensland superintendent of telegraphs had sharply contrasted the merits of the overland and the Carpentaria lines and poured scorn on the 'impractical' route that lay in desert country 'devoid of permanent surface water' and cattle feed. 'The Queensland lines', he countered conversely, 'traversed settled country throughout. They have been severely tested in all seasons, and prove to work both regularly and well; they are better cleared and more substantially built than those in course of construction by the Government of South Australia, and therefore less liable to interruption.' Despite the overland line's progress in full swing when he wrote, Cracknell argued that it should be abandoned until the country was more thoroughly opened up. Todd answered the charge with customary thoroughness, regretting that Cracknell should have 'spoken so positively and disparagingly without first ascertaining his facts', but Little's necessary journey to Normanton and the telegraphic appeal for help across Queensland's wires was a harsh hair–shirt for Todd's back.[31]

Todd himself was quickly back in the field at the Roper River by 27 January 1872, reinforcing his enterprise with animal power, more horses, more bullocks and bringing his own brand of confidence and

52
*Clear Across
Australia*

Charles Todd and his overseers at the Roper River depot. From left: J.A. Little, R.C. Patterson, Todd, and A.J. Mitchell.

perseverence to the completion of the line. (As Napoleon had found, 'the morale is to the material as three is to one.') The Roper River now became the headquarters for the last assault. Todd, arranging for the *Omeo* and a paddle steamer, *Young Australian*, to carry the animals and supplies four or five miles up the river above the mouth, saw himself confidently 'opening up to the commerce of the world a new and very fine river, destined I should think to become of considerable import-ance to this portion of northern Australia.'[32] The tone differed strikingly from Patterson's.

But it was April before the weather permitted work on the line to resume and a northerly gap of some 300 miles to be poled and wired. On 22 May, Todd sent the first (if truncated) trans–Australian telegram. The wire had reached the Elsey River under Patterson, and Todd despatched his message from Port Darwin to a temporary station on the Elsey whence Knuckey carried it over the long gap to Tennant Creek. From there it was telegraphed to Adelaide. Todd arrived at Daly Waters on 22 June 1872. The remaining gap now lay between Daly Waters and Tennant Creek. For some weeks a pony express (or 'estafette' as Todd preferred to call it) travelled weekly carrying messages between the two arching ends of line. On 24 June, as excitement mounted and progress was assured, the cable between Port Darwin and Java failed. There was no more talk of compensation then.

Ironically it fell to the melancholy Patterson to join the final point of the telegraph lines near Frews Ironstone Ponds on 22 August 1872. Eight months behind schedule, the overland telegraph line had been completed in two unforgettable years. Although the cable line was not restored until October 1872, communication with Java, India, Europe and on to England had been wrested out of and built into the central ranges, forbidding desert and swollen rivers of Australia. Todd, camped at Central Mt Stuart that night and linked up to the telegraph with a portable relay instrument connected at a joining point, was deluged with messages of congratulations from all over Australia. Stunned, perhaps, but jubilant, he remained working the instrument until he was frozen and fatigued.[33]

'Little more than two years have elapsed since the actual work of constructing the Overland Telegraph was entered upon', the *Adelaide Register* spread news of the achievement on 23 August 1872, 'and we have now the gratification of announcing the completion of the line. At one o'clock on August 22nd the Government received a message direct from Port Darwin, intimating that the last length of wire had been stretched and that uninterrupted communication across the continent had been established.'

The overland telegraph line became a legend. The men who built it, flocking from all parts of Australia to participate, knew both the reality and the dream. Some of them paid for the experience with their life. Thirst killed C.W. Kraegen, a telegraph operator due to take charge at Alice Springs, as he rode from Charlotte Waters to Alice Springs to meet Todd. His two offsiders, travelling behind, survived by killing a horse and drinking its blood. One lineman was lost in the bush;

Charles Todd's portable Morse key set used when the overland telegraph line was finally joined at Frew's Ponds on 22 August 1872.

another drowned. A teamster died of consumption. Daniel Kavanagh, 23, from Maitland in New South Wales, working on the northern section, died from fever at the Roper River. Delirious, talking about his friends, the line was engraved on his mind as he died. There were eight deaths, including the luckless Beckwith. The cost in strain, exhaustion and death among the transport animals could never be assessed.

In this large-scale penetration of a continent, what of the indigenous inhabitants? Little enough was known of their myths or realities in 1870-2. Fear of their hostility and imagined depredations was built deeply into the reactions of many who contemplated, and rejected, an overland route. There was no attempt by the planners to secure an Aboriginal as an adviser on possible directions of the route. Todd's instructions to his overseers urged them to deal moderately with the native inhabitants, treating them 'kindly but firmly' and firing only 'in the last extremity.' It was clearly hoped that they would prove helpful as the stringent instructions to avoid all contact with native women were mitigated in the case of 'any woman engaged by [an overseer], in the absence of a man, as a guide to point out the situation of water.' Native camps or burial grounds were to be left untouched. But there knowledge or understanding ended as the technical and human caval-cade plunged unwittingly through tribal lands and near vital water holes.

The Aboriginals, in turn, found their rewards in aiming their spears at the white porcelain insulators 'of the best approved pattern' made by the Berlin Imperial Pottery to claim new cutting shards, in making fishhooks from the wire, while the iron foot-plates used to increase soil resistance and keep poles upright were, Todd reported later, 'dug up, broken, and made with much ingenuity, into tomahawks, of which I possess some very creditable specimens.'[34] Silently they watched proceedings, venturing sometimes, as Giles reported, with friendly interest to the camps. Their own messages signalled along the route can only be guessed. In Africa, where telegraphs were being constructed, the Ashantee tribemen were reported as regarding the telegraph as 'the white man's fetish', holding it in wholesome respect. They looked upon it as 'a powerful charm' and parties of British engineers engaged on the construction of line in the Ashantee War discovered a white cotton thread suspended from the trees for a distance of many miles in obvious imitation of the wire. In Queensland, if not in the Central and Northern Territory, strings of stolen wires were set up by Aboriginals on the Cardwell–Normanton Line, post by post, in a mimic attempt at the technology.[35]

There were more serious encounters. In the immediate post-construction period an attack was made, in February 1874, on the station at Barrow Creek which was very close to an Aboriginal water-hole. The staff, including station master Stapleton, an assistant and six station hands, were suddenly showered with spears one Sunday evening while sitting smoking outside the station. Stapleton was mortally wounded. The assistant tapped out the details of the attack to Alice Springs which passed the news quickly to Adelaide. At the GPO,

Gun turrets, such as
these on the corners of
the Cape York outpost,
were common on many
northern Queensland
telegraph stations as
protection against
attack.

Todd sent his carriage to bring in Stapleton's wife. Todd himself took
down the pathetically brief message from the dying Stapleton whom
his men had lifted to the keys. 'God bless you and the children', it
read.[36] A punitive expedition was despatched against the Aboriginals
and troopers and telegraph men scoured the district for months
reputedly killing every Aboriginal seen. But Todd made no allusion to
this development in his official report. A similar attack occurred at
Daly Waters the following year when the station master was fatally
speared while bathing with his staff in the river.

It would be some years — towards the end of the century — before
Aboriginals were employed as station staff, decked out amazingly at
Alice Springs in scarlet coats with gold buttons, the discarded uniforms
of the South Australian postal services, which an inspired and practical
official had sent to the overland telegraph.

Todd had reasons for satisfaction. His dream had been achieved.
The cost, somewhat larger than his 'guess estimate' of £120,000 of
June 1870, was set at £479,174 in 1884.[37] But the work was sound.
When the explorer, John Forrest, came upon the overland telegraph at
a point between the Peake and Charlotte Waters in September 1874,
he found it impressively solid. 'The telegraph line', he minuted in his
diary, 'is most substantially put up and well wired and is very
creditable at this spot; large poles of bush timber, often rather crooked

The Charlotte Waters,
Northern Territory,
telegraph station, 1879.
Aboriginals soon
became associated with
station staff and were
eventually to find
employment on the
line.

Finis coronat opus — the end crowns the work. The memorial to Todd and his men at Frew Ponds, NT.

and iron ones here and there . . .' Moreover, Alice Todd, as her husband had urged her, had practised economies during his sojourns on the line and he found 'a good balance in the bank' when he returned. Since he remained Postmaster–General until the age of 76, he had long opportunity to see the returns on his work. But he did not receive the hero's welcome. No statue was erected in Todd's honour (though, figures of the failed heroes, the explorers Burke and Wills, contrastingly dominate a prominent Melbourne square) and he received a knighthood 21 years after his remarkable achievement. But a memorial plinth, erected by the South Australian Line Training School of the PMG's department to Todd and his overseers, now stands in the quiet landscape at Frews Ponds.

The triumph of the overland telegraph line was widely recognised by the Colonists. 'The earth', said the Governor of New South Wales, Sir Hercules Robinson, inaugurating the overseas connection with Sydney in November 1872, 'has been girdled . . . with a magic chain.' The once isolated inhabitants of the antipodes could 'speak' with friends in England and were brought in touch with every important post in Europe, Asia and America. The daily press now contained information of political and commercial events that took place within 48 hours throughout the civilised world. It was not surprising, as historian Geoffrey Blainey remarks, that the international telegraph link of 1872 which carried news so fast was more 'miraculous' for Australians than the first half century of aircraft.[38]

All the Colonies except Western Australia were joined to the Adelaide–Darwin line that November, yet, despite the early and, as it proved, fanciful schemes to bring the first overseas cable ashore on Western Australian shores and link the Colonies by telegraph from Albany to Adelaide, Australia's great 'western third' remained detached, cut off from telegraphic contact with Europe and England, and isolated from electrical communication with the other Colonies by the barren tracts of the Nullarbor Plain. Slow to adopt telegraphy in their own Colony, Western Australians were at first reluctant participants in telegraphic development of which they would become prime users by the century's end.

By December 1873, over a year after the overland telegraph began transmitting regular messages to England and Europe, one enthusiast, Western Australia's Governor Weld, was in contact with Todd and other South Australian officials. Though Weld expected 'violent opposition' in his own Colony, he sought 'to insert the thin edge of the wedge in the matter of the telegraph line' by getting his Legislative Council to bring down a definite proposal in the first session of 1874. Weld's plan to link his Colony with the continental network depended on this Legislative Council's willingness to finance the 750–mile 'western sector' of a line from Albany to Eucla beside the Western Australian border with South Australia, and reciprocal support from South Australia for an equidistant extension of their telegraph line from Port Augusta to Eucla. Despite havering — for South Australia had less to gain — Todd saw the scheme as essential to complete the

Australian network and as an obligation which 'our geographical position compels us to fulfil.'[39]

Both Colonial legislatures voted the necessary sums in 1874. But the empty 1,500 miles of inhospitable country stretched dauntingly between Albany and Adelaide. What route should the telegraph take? John Forrest's successful crossing of the continent from east to west in 1870, retracing in reverse the steps of the explorer, Eyre, some 30 years before, proved that a well–equipped expedition *could* cross the Nullarbor. This cast the decision for the coastal route. In his last act as Governor of Western Australia, Weld planted the first ceremonial pole of the route at Albany on the first day of January 1875.

Undoubtedly the construction of the 'east–west' telegraph line was another enterprise of epic human and technological proportions. Begun effectively in both Colonies in April 1875, three years after the overland telegraph line was complete, it derived much from the knowledge and experience acquired on that feat. Yet many of its problems were local and distinct. From their distant ends, two Colonies (one with meagre experience of long–line telegraphy) sought to bridge an expanse of desert known principally for its desolation and con-ditions treacherous to man. Not surprisingly, the job attracted no contractors when tenders were advertised in the Colonies in January 1875.

On the second bid, J.G. Flindell, a wiring contractor, and J.J. Elsegood, a carpenter in the building trade, tendered for the Western Australian contract, while Walter Thomson, a settler experienced in the building of South Australia's telegraph lines, tendered for the eastern sections from Port Augusta to Port Lincoln and on to Fowlers Bay. But there were no contractors for that remote and hostile sector of the country from Eucla to Fowlers Bay. Here, Richard Knuckey, one of Todd's most experienced overland telegraph overseers, was put in charge by the Government with 38 men and 89 horses to assist him to construct the most rugged and challenging sector of the work.[40]

For the Western Australians the solutions for transport, equipment and materials lay with the sea. Ships chartered in Bunbury and Fremantle carried the wire, stores and the 14–foot long jarrah wood poles (tapered, and squared to prevent their rolling in the vessels) to coastal depots along the route. There were no ports. The bays and protected bights ended at Israelite Bay and the small sailing ships, anchored off a sandy beach, were buffeted by fierce winds and the 'long, high, incessant swells' of that little known stretch of coastline. Poles tied in bundles were cast off and rafted ashore to a waiting team of linemen. Building material and stores followed in small boats. On shore the poles, the stores, and the building material for the stations and huts were winched up the perpendicular cliffs by derricks or hauled by straining horse or camel teams. One ship, anchored at Point Culver with the object of landing poles, succeeded, reported Western Australia's superintendent of telegraphs, 'in landing one hundred and seventeen poles, after waiting ready at all times to slip the cable and put off to sea no less than six days for opportunities.' The contractor's cutter, *Tribune*, was dashed on rocks and wrecked near Bellinger Island in July 1876 though for twelve months, Superintendent Fleming noted regretfully, this vessel had carried on the service remarkably well in face of many dangers discovered and avoided over an almost unknown coast.[41]

Contractors and men threw enormous effort into their task. James Fleming himself reconnoitred and pegged the first and worst 40 miles of the western route and moved by ship and horseback to supervise the extending line. In South Australia, from Eucla to Streaky Bay, the total lack of timber for poling again forced Todd to use imported galvanised wrought–iron poles from Britain along this sector of the route. Ferried overland, or landed with the iron water tanks at Fowlers Bay, Knuckey's 1,000 iron poles were laid at intervals of five chains in temperatures that rose feverishly that September 1876. 'I would not willingly undertake such another work', Knuckey wrote later, 'and

The Overland Telegraph and the East–West lines

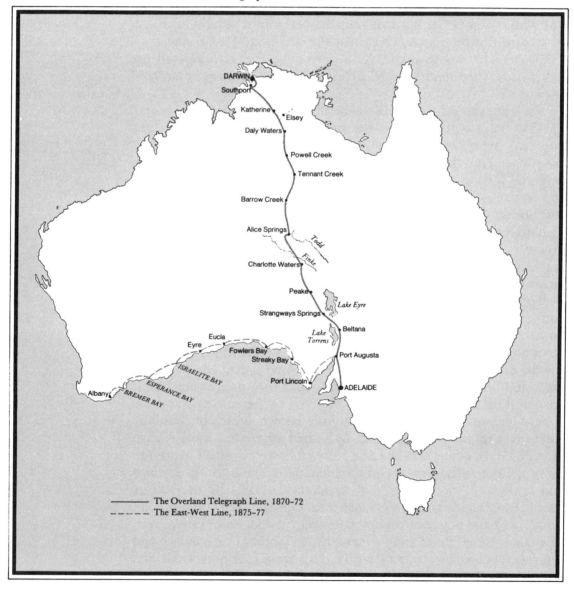

───────── The Overland Telegraph Line, 1870–72
– – – – – The East-West Line, 1875–77

have to start it at the same time of the year.'[42] Yet his courage and his men's persistence conquered the terrain.

In the inner South Australian sectors some timber was on hand. Contractor Walter Thomson took it as it came. 'Crooked was how God had made the poles', he stated, 'and the Government inspector would have to put up with poles that way.' But there were other problems. The matter of sinking pole holes into the tough limestone (a persistent challenge to telecommunication construction in South Australia) led to a new technique of using a 'gad' made of a thick steel bar sharpened at one end to drive a hole some 8 to 10 centimetres in diameter into the rock. The operation requiring two men, one steadying and rotating the gad while the second struck blows on a sledge hammer, was typical of the *ad hoc* approaches devised to speed construction.[43]

Eight repeater stations were erected to boost transmission along the line; in Western Australia at Bremer Bay, Esperance Bay, Israelite Bay, Eyre's Sandpatch (later Eyre) and Eucla, and in South Australia at Port Augusta, Port Lincoln and Fowlers Bay. At Bremer Bay, a woman joined the enterprise. Mary Wellstead, one of six daughters of an isolated settler of the region, was assigned as telegraphist at the station in March 1876 and maintained the post until a station master was appointed at the end of 1877. From the first connection at Bremer Bay, linemen patrolled constantly to indicate to the Aboriginals that the advancing wire was under surveillance. The precaution was unnecessary. The indigenous inhabitants were timid and apprehensive. 'The natives, completely wild', Fleming reported, 'haunt [*sic*] by themselves, and run to the thickets at the approach of a white man.'[44]

By late 1877, two and a half years after poling began, the eastern and western wires were joined at Eucla. Sunburn, heat, the sandy rock–strewn desert, toil, strain and the sea mists that drifted in at night to destroy insulation and block transmission on the lines had been battled and overcome. 'Saturday 7 pm [8 December 1877]', ran the first triumphant message to Perth. 'Eucla Line Opened. Hurrah.'

The telegraph station at Eucla would constitute a vital, if bizarre, border station for almost a half a century. Built within sight of the sea in Western Australia, close to the South Australian border, it operated as

The Eucla telegraph station's operating room, 1898. The Western Australian staff sat on the left of the partition, the South Australian on the right.

Eucla today.
Abandoned to the
drifting sands, it has,
however, taken on a
new role as a popular
tourist sight.

two Colonial terminal stations, 'an example of the confusion and solemn make–believe common in pre–Federation days.' Here Western and South Australian telegraphists, seated on their respective sides of the operating table, took down the Morse signals tapped out from their capitals (in differing telegraph alphabets) decoded them and passed the written message through 'hand–holes' in the head–high partition to their opposite number. Clocks monitored the different time, 90 minutes apart, in the two Colonies and the transcribed messages were transmitted onwards. At Federation in 1901, the dividing partition was ceremoniously taken down, electromagnetic repeaters decimated the staff from 50 to five men in 1909, and in 1927 Eucla (called 'Yirkla' by the Aboriginals after the planet Venus) was abandoned to its ghosts and drifting sand.

But its first year of operation proved its need. Nearly 11,000 telegrams passed back and forth across the circuit, a total that mounted steeply with every year. Western Australia was now in touch with the rest of the world. Distance, if not annihilated, had been subdued and the desert barrier conquered. Morse code, in its various Colonial inflexions, could pass 'clear across Australia'. To the inhabitants of its cities, country towns, goldfields, farms and pastoral stations, the miraculous feat of electrical communication united a continent.

4 From Telegraphy to Telephony

T he impact of the overseas cable on the Australian Colonies was immense. Offering fast communication with the money of London, the telegraph became a generator of economic development in the Colonies and a pervasive agent of social change. In a country rich with minerals, where goldfields speckled the spurs and gullies of the Great Dividing Range and outcropped from Queensland's northern Palmer River, through New South Wales, through the rich deposits of Victoria to the western mountains of Tasmania, the telegraph, with its international and intercolonial axes, served as the communication link for an upsurge of mining from the late 1870s that finally surpassed the resource development of the glittering 1850s.

Even before the overland telegraph was completed, the line emerged as a generator of speculation and mining growth. In early 1871 three linemen working 100 miles south of Darwin washed gold near Pine Creek and the following August G.F. MacLachlan, overseer of the northern sector, found five ounces of the metal close to the poling route. News sped to Adelaide and within a year a group of speculators, including the contractor E.M. Bagot, had mustered the capital, formed the Northern Territory Gold Prospecting Association, and despatched John Westcott and a party via Darwin to camp and dig at the site. In August 1872 the telegraph operator at Pine Creek relayed news of a proven goldfield. At repeater stations installed at the gold fields on Shackle Creek and Pine Creek, news of yields and new companies flashed back and forth along the desert line. By May 1874 60 companies had been floated in Adelaide and £67,000 reputedly paid to organisers and promoters. 'The overland telegraph', comments Blainey, 'had opened the goldfields, and now was the magic instrument that raised the capital.' As prospectors spilled across the arid Northern Territory landscape and Chinese miners flowed in from Darwin, one Victorian mining expert noted with some astonishment 'In the whole history of mining never before were claims floated by telegraph, without even a plan'.[1]

In Tasmania tin and tin prices dominated the singing of the wires. In December 1871 James Smith plunged his pick at Mt Bischoff into

61

'the greatest lode of tin then known to man'. Two years later he sold it to the Mt Bischoff Tin Mining Company and tin prospectors fanned out across the rugged north–west Tasmanian mountains. The tele-graph lines followed the settlements outwards. As business boomed, inland telegrams for 1873–4 at least doubled those of the previous year; by December 1875 they had jumped significantly again while intercolonial messages added to the volume on the lines.[2]

The overseas cable connection would spur foreign investment as the decade of the 1880s advanced. Initially, distance favoured local ownership of mining in the Colonies. By the mid–1880s Australians owned almost all the mines in their own continent. At first slowly, hampered by the breakdowns that plagued the overland telegraph line and the sudden interruptions of the sea cable, the overseas telegraph evolved as the medium of speculative foreign investment in the Colonies. Successful speculation depended on the quick exchange of information of price fluctuations. Before the cable era, many South Australian copper mines, acting on postal reports from London, vigorously produced copper only to find from later intelligence that the metal's price was so unfavourable their mine was working at a loss.[3] With instant cable connection, Australian gold and base metals became increasingly attractive to British speculators. While Victoria, the richest gold Colony in the British Empire, could raise its capital readily on the local stock exchanges, Colonies such as Queensland began to turn to British speculators to pour money into their gold mines situated at a distance of over 1,000 miles from the capital at Brisbane. By 1886 British money buttressed Queensland's golden city of Charters Towers while along the 8,000 miles of the Colony's telegraph wires over a million messages, both business and social, flowed between Brisbane and its country and city stations. By the early 1890s so great was British investment interest in Australian minerals, stimulated by the quick exchange of information, that London replaced Melbourne as the great investing centre for the Colonies.

Colonial Governments as well as mining promoters also sought British investment by cable. From 1872–3, writes the economic historian Noel Butlin, capital outlays began to rise quickly reaching peaks for Australia as a whole in the mid–1880s. Rapid communi-cation underwrote stable and confident investment. Funding from British merchant bankers flowed into 'go–ahead' Colonial programmes that pushed roads, railways and the telegraph lines themselves outward; built harbours and bridges, and nourished the spread of ancillary activities in the Colonies.[4]

For the business community, telegraph and cable services were pivotal to growth. Merchants, wholesalers, importers, mining investors, exporters, land dealers, manufacturers, bankers, farmers and ship–owners were quick to grasp the opportunities afforded by the miraculous new communication with England and Europe. The flow of goods and orders between Mother Country and Colonies grew. With knowledge of the market transferable within 24 to 48 hours instead of slow weeks by sea mail, goods could be supplied in realistic quantities and gluts and scarcities diminished. The impact of the overseas cable, often ignored by economists, bolstered the prosperity of a country which depended heavily in its remoteness on accurate information for the successful transaction of its overseas trade. Major pastoral companies used the cable service extensively to convey information on prices of wool and meat, on rainfall, and the sale and purchase of sheep and bulls.

The Australian Agricultural Company, founded under Royal Charter with headquarters in London in 1824, had large pastoral and coal mining interests in New South Wales. It cabled frequently from London and used the cable as a tool of business intelligence and control. The tighter direction and supervision of colliery and pastoral business that the cable allowed threatened the relative autonomy built up by the AAC's Australian superintendents as an outcome of distance and as one of its rewards. Edward Merewether, general super-intendent at the Newcastle colliery, clung doggedly to mail com-munication and shied away from the expensive but expedient com-munication that the cable afforded. When he did send a message, it was annoyingly concise. 'You really must make up your mind to use the wires more liberally', a letter from head office chided him in September 1873, 'if you have recourse to it for the transmission of important matter.' The rest of the letter bore testimony to the cable's new force. 'If in your judgment it was essential to get permission to commence the work at once (and we agree with you in thinking that it was) you should not have starved your message, or shrunk from the cost of repeating it. If your calculations are correct the profit derivable from this new Pit ought to be £16,000 a year from the month of completion, that is, you will recoup the cost within the 12 months, and for such an object it could not signify much whether you spent an extra £100 in sending a full message and repeating it.'[5]

In any event, most companies quickly adopted general cablegram codes in which a word represented a whole sentence, together with their own private cyphers for special matters in the interests of security and costs. Such messages as 'Thomson augury abdominous rhomboid' (meaning 'Thomson £1,500. Pay this sum as he requires, and debit our account') sometimes ran into tangles on the Java section of the cable in its transmission forward by Dutch telegraphists. There were frequent complaints in company correspondence about botched messages. Nonetheless the security aspect justified the cypher's use.

In a company such as the Australian Agricultural Company, with investments in collieries and a large employer of miners, it was not without significance that two out of five of their Sigma code words related to strike matters. Both the telegram and the cable became important communication instruments for breaking strikes. Strikers also used the telegram to make plans and needed to ensure that they steered clear of the electric telegraph regulation, common in all Colonies by the 1890s, that 'telegrams which appeared to contain seditious language' must be submitted to the chief telegraph office before being submitted.[6] Despite the exorbitant price of cables to England — £10 for 20 words (and 50 per cent more for all words over the first 20) — and some inevitable muddle on the line, the convenience and effectiveness of cable communication cancelled out its early deficiencies. Inter–firm messages often ran to fifteen typescript pages including codes. One such, despatched on 27 July 1893 from Goldsborough Mort and Co. in London via the overland telegraph line to the company's Melbourne office, was interrupted by a post office and telegraph department memorandum notifying that 'the manager at Adelaide . . . has had to stop transmission of your cable to work off some of the accumulated traffic [and] will resume shortly'. Partly transmitted at 11.35 a.m., it was completed by mid–afternoon.[7]

Occasionally for business, the overseas telegraph link proved to be something of a two–edged sword. While the cable enabled Australian firms, including importers, to call up supplies more rapidly, it also allowed British manufacturers, directly or through their offices in London, to respond more quickly to notices for tender that had formerly favoured local companies. As a result swift competition from British firms pierced the isolation that in one sense had succoured local manufacturers and meant that Australian business lost the lead time of several weeks gained by sea communication for preparing plant and training workers for effective tendering.[8]

The question of wider, more reliable, and cheaper cable contact occupied the Colonies when they gathered at their intercolonial conferences. In February 1876 cable connection was established with the 'seventh Australasian Colony', New Zealand, one which was recognised as highly important to the mercantile community of the eastern

Bringing the New Zealand cable ashore at Botany Bay, February 1876.

Colonies.[9] By the 1880s moves were afoot to strengthen existing cable routes to India and England and to forge submarine connections with other countries. Todd's South Australian evidence made the point: 'Immediately following the construction of the overland telegraph', he reported in 1884, 'the commercial progress of this colony was remarkably rapid: trade increased, agriculture extended over the northern area, and railways and telegraphs were pushed on in all directions.'[10]

In 1880, moved by frequent breakdowns and interruptions and prodded by Cracknell in NSW, the Eastern Extension Telegraph Line duplicated its cable from Madras to Darwin. Queensland and New Zealand negotiated with the French telegraph company in New Caledonia in 1893 for a cable which terminated at Burnett Heads, near Bundaberg, Queensland. And in April 1889 a submarine cable linking Australia and England was laid between Roebuck Bay (Broome) WA, and Java as an alternative route for Western Australian traffic to Europe and as a back-up for the overland Darwin–Java link. So rich was the flow of intelligence and news, so important the widening links with information sources overseas, that, when for 18 days in July 1888 no cable messages arrived, the deprivation felt in the Colonies by the citizens and merchants was so great that it was, said the *Sydney Morning Herald*, 'like a sudden onset of blindness or deafness'.[11]

Pivotal to the business community, cables also became major arteries of the Australian press. At first the Melbourne *Argus* was the only Colonial newspaper to receive cabled public news. It represented the Associated Press and its overseas material was distributed to all newspapers in Victoria, New South Wales, South Australia, Queensland, Tasmania and New Zealand. With press rates at 10s a word in 1877, even a shared service offered highly abbreviated items of news, but these were proclaimed under bold headlines to achieve the maximum effect.

Direct Telegram from Europe
(By Submarine Cable)
Berlin, June 16
The Emperor William is Improving in Health.

Another, of more burning interest published two years later, informed Colonists of progress in the bloody 'Kaffir War'.

TELEGRAM
(Via Adelaide and Eucla)
Adelaide, February 24. London February 20.
All the attacks made at the Cape by the Zulus have been repulsed. The situation is serious, but the British are confident of being about to maintain their position until the arrival of reinforcements.[12]

In a service that informed both country and cities, sport found some place and London prices for wheat, metals and wool completed the ration of international events. Certainly, the eyes of European news had been picked by the time the fortnightly mail steamer from Europe reached Colonial ports. Cable rates fell as the century advanced. J.H. Heaton, a Tasmanian representative at the International Cable Conference in Berlin in 1885, claimed the responsibility for an agreed reduction of press charges to 2s 6d a word. Heaton spoke French which most of his Australian colleagues did not. In 1891 press rates fell again to 1s 10d a word, and to 1s 0d in 1902. In contrast to the early scraps of overseas news cabled in 1873, metropolitan daily papers were handling an average of 700 words a day by the century's end.

It was not all plain sailing. There were delays in the transmission of news. Shoals and an occasional submarine volcano between Java and Darwin broke the line. The press had no priority and the 'infamous' Dutch telegraphists often so mutilated the messages that there was much huffing and torment late at night at the *Argus* office when cables transmitted via Java came in.

> Depetris declared Italy cannot abandon Treaty Paris (read one). All essays approval all refrentum Gatnffs despoleres approving their decision. Kabinck deferred resolution occupation Bulgaria pending reference Queen. Propose 6,000 Belgians occupancy. Disrealig Fortress Begrade fired Australian monitor.

The torment lent variety. 'Thus it often happens', an *Argus* representative told the Colonial Cable Conference of 1877, 'that we find different interpretations of the same message given in all the Colonies, owing, in great measure, to so much being left to guess work'.

Despite frequent complaints by press and merchants of the imperfections of the telegraph service and its delays, it was the industrious and lonely telegraph operator, often at obscure repeater stations in the centre of the continent or on its southern–most border, who got the cables through. Telegraphists, both urban and outback, made up a new and distinctive group in Colonial society. Drawn usually from well–educated or aspiring backgrounds, they grew out of the dynamic new technology, developed technical skills, and often possessed scientific knowledge and some scholarly attainments. 'The telegraph operator's is brain work, requiring close and unremitting application', one professor summed up the new calling. 'The mental effort involved in receiving from a sounder [Morse code] was exactly similar to that in which a shorthand writer was engaged when report-ing a speaker verbatim, and it took as long to train a good telegraph operator as a good reporter.' But there was more. In order to do his work intelligently, the telegraphist 'must be well in touch with the politician, the sportsman, and the man of commerce; and after becom-ing an expert manipulator of the key, he must acquaint himself with technical duties. It should also be remembered that the most delicate and momentous secrets are entrusted to his discretion, and his work is of a highly confidential character.'[13]

Telegraphists were an elite. In city and suburban post and telegraph offices they occupied a position between the manipulative classes of telegraph messenger, letter carrier and postal sorter, and the managerial classes of supervisor, postmaster and superintendent. Their training and skills, and the sense of commitment that their duties inspired, turned them into a cohesive group, with conventions and 'in–house' codes and jokes and a deep sense of camaraderie. Better educated than most other members of the public service, urban tele-graphists showed their middle class alliance by dressing fashionably. Dapper in gloves and brightly coloured waistcoats, they completed their ensemble with a cane. Even in the inland's torrid heat, there were few concessions to comfortable dress. The telegraphists at Eucla confronted each other across the border partition sartorially correct in flannel trousers, white shirts, ties and the ornate Victorian waistcoat.[14]

But men who took these jobs and wended their way overland on horseback to the east–west and overland telegraph stations, driven by ambition or the strong sense of wanderlust that empty lands stir in men of vigour, were workers of extraordinary commitment. Individualists were moulded by country and calling into assiduous and solitary habits. Yet mateship flourished along the lines. Frederick Simmons, a 16-year-old boy from Geelong, Victoria, joined the Eucla station in 1897 to find a 'tough and primitive service', a stern test of ambition and self-reliance, but a 'wonderful camaraderie and fellowship among the men working and living together in such places'. At Eucla, wives joined the growing settlement of telegraphists, two supervisors and linemen. They bred large families, carefully conserved their stores between visits of sailing ships and steamers with supplies, rejoiced in a monthly mail service by camel or horse buggy from Fowlers Bay and, in accident or illness, took down the vital instructions from the doctor at the end of the line.[15]

In November 1895 J.H. Lawrence, a member of Fremantle's telegraph staff hoping for an increase in pay, took ship for Israelite Bay, was rowed ashore and plodded on horseback the long miles to Eucla to serve as senior of the Western Australian telegraphists. In his nine years at the 'border' station, the staff grew from six to 16 telegraphists on both the Western and South Australian sides, providing two cricket teams and some backstops. (Western Australia staffed the station entirely from 1909.) Lawrence saw the second iron east–west line built from Eucla to Coolgardie in 1896, turning somewhat inland from the original exposed sea route with its 'ancient and salt-encrusted aerial'. 'Had Aspros been available in those days', he later wrote, 'they would have been in great demand by the operators of those soul deadening avenues.'[16]

From the 1890s Eucla became the busiest telegraph station outside the capital cities, the conduit for cables coming to and from Western Australia and the eastern Colonies. Gold discoveries in the northern part of Western Australia in the late 1880s gave a great thrust to its internal telegraph lines and, after gold was discovered at Kalgoorlie in 1893, the lines streamed out eastwards from Perth and its adjoining network until the Colony could boast some 9,000 miles of telegraph line by the century's end. Throughout the 1890s the wires ran hot from Adelaide investors eager to spark the mining bonanza and to despatch an army of prospectors to Western Australia's eastern goldfields. A post–cum–telegraph office, established at the goldtown Coolgardie in September 1893, struggled with a staggering flow of traffic and collapsed frequently under the strain. The telegraphic department, observed the *Coolgardie Review* in 1895, was 'unable to cope'.[17]

A large flow of Western Australia's international cable traffic left the Colony via Broome — its cable connected and working in 1889. But Eucla became the re-transmitting centre for a deluge of inter-colonial messages with their burden of mineral demand and specu-

The eventual introduction to Eucla of automatic telegraph repeaters in 1909 was to bring about a ten-fold reduction in staff.

lation that poured in from the gold investment stock exchanges scattered as far afield as Charters Towers, Queensland, through Broken Hill and Silverton, Ballarat and Bendigo to Zeehan in Tasmania and from all Colonial capitals of which Adelaide was the busiest investment centre of them all. It was Morse's insistent 'dot–dash' that transferred the words of mining and investment intelligence that rekindled Australian mining prosperity in the 1890s and, in 1895 alone, brought huge sums of revenue into Western Australia's once insignificant telegraph department.[18]

At Eucla the men were mustered into shifts. Staffing was organised on a 24–hour basis. When the duplex system (a two–way system of simultaneous incoming and outgoing line transmission) was introduced on this line, three pairs of telegraphists (representing each Colony) were scheduled for shifts of eight hours. The least popular shift — between 11 p.m. and 7 a.m. — brought no lessening of the work. By 1898 each Colony had a duplex and a quadruplex system in use. Staffs were also doubled up at major repeater stations along the east–west and overland telegraph line. The pressure generated placed enormous strain on the telegraphists. It also stimulated sensational transmitting speeds. There was no pausing between messages, Lawrence recalls. The task became both a 'gospel' and a 'craft'. 'To average 70 messages per hour for the entire staff was', he wrote, 'our objective'. Discretion and integrity were paramount in their work. The remote telegraphists working through the night on inland stations were the first to receive official tidings of important events whose cyphers were not always obscure. On one occasion they handled a secret cable from London designated for all Colonial Governments which warned: 'We have reason to believe war Russia not probable but possible advise preparation but quietly as possible.'[19]

Despite their real pride in achievement and the contribution they made to their Colony's wealth, Western Australia's telegraphists were poorly rewarded. Working long hours they confronted physical lone-liness, low pay, no allowance for isolation, the disturbing vigilance of natives and constant pressure to get the traffic through. R.A. Sholl, the tough–minded Postmaster–General of the Colony, described them as 'excellent but underpaid officers' yet he practised a niggardly parsimony himself. Despite a number of requests for a billiard table to relieve the monotony for Eucla's staff, Sholl refused to add the item to his department's expenditures. The table arrived five years after Federation when the bulk of the telegraphists were beginning to be transferred elsewhere.[20]

The Colonies varied in staff remuneration, telegraphic charges and in the running of their telegraphic affairs. In Tasmania the telegraphist pay was pitifully meagre. As early as 1877 the Colony's superintendent of telegraphs, F.A. Packer, pointed to the 'never–varying attendance of 12 to 13 hours a day for the small salary provided' (then less than £30 a year) and stressed the danger of losing these 'most valuable, trust-worthy and competent officers' to better paid, but less skilled, areas of Government service.[21] Victoria and New South Wales offered their telegraphists higher rates.

The first attempt to form a telegraphists union was made in New South Wales. In 1881 Sydney telegraphists elected their first open–job 'Committee of Seven'. The committee received notices of grievance and made formal representations to the telegraph department. But there are no records or reports of its activities and it appears to amalgamate in 1885 with the NSW Operators Society, renamed the Electric Telegraph Society in 1891. The Queensland Electric Tele-graph Society and the South Australian Telegraph Officers Association were both formed in 1890. Sydney's Electric Telegraph Society produced one of the earliest and liveliest of union journals, *The Transmitter*, in 1891 edited by the society's secretary, E.C. Kraegen (son of C.W.I. Kraegen, casualty of the overland telegraph line).[22] The journal focussed problems of salaries and classification and increas-ingly raised questions of the job–induced illness among telegraphists which began to show up in muscular pains in the fingers, hands, arms and shoulders of the operators' 'sending side', which a British House of Commons Inquiry of 1895 designated 'telegraphists' cramp'. Eye strain and nervous trauma were also common complaints among the overworked band of Morse transmitters.[23]

It was in the Eastern Goldfields Association of Western Australia (an offshoot from Perth) that telegraphists first took militant action. Late in 1895 they called a strike that involved telegraphists up and down the Eucla–Albany line, in the eastern goldfields, and on the networks reaching out north–west to Broome. Lawrence at Eucla was a reluctant union recruit. He chose to be 'suspended' rather than join the strike, though he was quickly reinstated. The strike, he records, 'proved fatal to the principal advocates, ending in dismissals, suspensions and transfers to remoter localities'. Yet despite the negative outcome of this strike, the telegraphists — a conservative white collar group, whose loyalty to their employers and whose patriotism and commitment was high — became the torchbearers of a Commonwealth–wide union, the Australian Commonwealth Post and Telegraph Officers' Association formed in 1901. Significantly, as unionist John Baker points out, it was the new technology of communications, with its international links and sympathies, that created a special brand of unionism in Australia under the eyes of a paternalistic bureaucracy.

By the end of the century there was much to indicate the wide impact of the telegraph in Australia. Economically, through boom and bust, the Colonies had been dovetailed even more closely than in pre–telegraph days with the Mother Country, while their trade connections with Asia were significantly enlarged. Colonial Governments now had speedy access to the Imperial Government and their own agents–general abroad, while the perpetually fragile relationships between the Colonies found common cause, and some collaboration, around the issues of improved communication, cable extension and cheaper telegrams for all.

The overland telegraph, strung out like a life–line across the continent, had, as the explorer Ernest Giles saw it, split the country in halves and brought much impetus in the latter years of the century to the exploration of the little known western half. To this end, the telegraph and cable were crucial in establishing longitudes. In 1882 all the Colonies (except Western Australia and Tasmania) contributed to the cost of determining the different longitudes between Darwin and Singapore. Pietro Barrachi, a recent recruit to the Melbourne Observatory, received the cable signals at Darwin and co–ordinated the longitudes from January to March 1883. He went on to determine Australian longitudes by telegraph signals for Darwin to Adelaide, Adelaide to Melbourne, and Melbourne to Sydney. At Todd's request in 1890 the Western Australian Government exchanged telegraph signals to establish longitudes from HMS *Penguin* at Roebuck Bay (Broome) to Adelaide Observatory.[24]

One of the most remarkable cables despatched illuminated Australian science. Since their first arrival in the Colonies, naturalists had been trying to solve the puzzle of platypus birth. But these unique Australian monotremes ('one–holers' as they were colloquially called) kept their secret. Did they produce young like a reptile by an egg? Or did they give birth to live offspring in their burrows? For almost a century the problem lay in observing the creatures in the process of birth. In 1884 a visiting British zoologist, William Caldwell, settled the matter. He shot a platypus on the banks of the Burnett River, Queensland, which had laid one egg and held a second containing an embryo ready for laying inside. Caldwell sent off immediate word to Professor Liversidge at Sydney University. Liversidge's splendidly terse cable to the British Association for the Advancement of Science meeting in Montreal, Canada, that year, conveyed the long–awaited news to the scientific world: 'Monotremes oviparous ovum meroblastic' [monotremes produce young by means of eggs expelled from body before being hatched, egg softshelled].[25] Telegrams, indeed, would become the fast shorthand language of major discoveries and priority in science.

Despite cost, the colonists increasingly used the cable and telegram for personal news. Marriage, birth, death, sickness, success, were elemental facts needing to be communicated in a country founded by migrants, and not all communications from the medley of prospectors dispersed across the country related to Mammon. The cable links conquered alienating distances for colonists. Importantly they also became a key factor in 'moulding and unifying the consciousness of Australians about being one homogenous people' in spite of the barriers of distance and transport.[26]

If the telegraph was the tool of business and commerce, the foundation of a new information society in Australia, that remarkable instrument, the telephone, invited repercussions of a different kind. The transmission of voices, human communication between two people at considerable distances from each other, the exchange of opinion and gossip, let loose a force that would alter and liberate the habits of society. 'I think', W.C. Kernot, Melbourne's Professor of Engineering, summed it up in 1897, 'if a prediction of coming achievement had been made to any intelligent person in 1837 . . . of all modern inventions, the telephone would have aroused the greatest scepticism.'[27]

Scepticism and disbelief certainly greeted early attempts to establish voice communication. But Professor Alexander Graham Bell's brisk message, 'Mr Watson, come here, I want to see you', communicated by a telephone instrument and a connecting wire between two rooms in a Boston boarding house on 10 March 1876, and the demonstration of his talking model at Philadelphia's Centennial Exhibition that year, took the scientific world by storm. Britain's distinguished physicist, Sir William Thomson, pronounced the telephone 'the greatest by far of all the marvels of the electric telegraph', while Bell's patent stimulated a rush of experimentation around the world.

Australian inventors, both amateur and official, were quickly caught up in the epidemic of 'telephone fever'. In contrast to the introduction of the telegraph in Australia, where the cutting and trimming of wooden poles and some hastily devised insulators represented the range of early local innovation, Bell's invention

The model for many early Australian telephones — Bell's telephone of 1877.

The first telephone made in Victoria, 1878, now in private hands in Geelong. The mouthpiece also served as an earpiece.

71

provoked a burst of creative experiments in the Colonies. Detailed information of the 'wonderful instrument', with illustrations of its workings, reached the Colonies by steamer from July–December 1877 through two 'carriers', the *English Mechanic and World of Science* of 6 April 1877 and the *Scientific American* of 6 October 1877. It is not clear who deserves priority for creating the first successful telephone in Australia. Inventive ardour stirred a cluster of experimenters from Tasmania to Queensland. In Victoria W.J. Thomas, a customs inspector at the Geelong Customs House, using a home–made instrument and connecting wire, managed to link houses in his district with music and song late in 1877 and later, more ambitiously, to transmit 'Yankee Doodle' over the telegraph wires between Geelong and Queenscliff.[28]

In Tasmania, Alfred Biggs, school teacher at Campbelltown Public School, an amateur astronomer and scientist whose work on stellar observations and earth tremors won him a rare Fellowship of the Royal Society of London, constructed three hand–type telephones from Tasmania's beautiful Huon Pine and, after telephoning over short distances, made the first long distance call in Tasmania from Campbelltown to Launceston, a distance of 50 miles, in 1878.[29] In Brisbane, a medical practitioner, Dr Severn, alert to the potential benefits to his own calling from a telephonic link, also experimented from home–made instruments over a mile of telegraph wire on 28 January 1878.

One of the most fertile of the early telephone researchers was Henry Sutton of Ballarat, Victoria. Sutton (1856–1912), the son of a goldminer who had established a music warehouse at Ballarat, showed a youthful interest in science and engineering, absorbed the engineering journals of the well–stocked Ballarat Mechanics Institute and, between the age of 14 and 21, designed an ingenious assortment of machines and models, including electric motors, vacuum pumps, an 'ornithopter' and other heavier–than–air flight machines. By late 1877 Sutton had devised and constructed some 20 telephone instruments all working on slightly different principles. But he resisted the practice of patenting his designs on the grounds that 'discovery' should benefit fellow workers in science. It did. Sixteen of his telephones were subsequently patented by others overseas. Bell himself recognised the importance of Sutton's work and, during his visit to Australia in 1910, journeyed to Ballarat to inspect the telephone system which Sutton had installed in the family warehouse.[30]

No one, however, was more successful in telephone development than the British migrant, J.E. Edwards. Born in London and reared in an environment of mechanical and electrical work, Edwards had actually conceived the idea of transmitting musical and other sounds in 1858 when, at the age of 17, he was employed in a large firm of London electroplaters. Later, on the staff of the leading telegraph workshop of Messrs Siemens and Halske, he found he could make most kinds of electrical contrivances. He emigrated to Victoria in 1866 and at once joined the workshops of McGowan's telegraph department. There his ranging imagination had full play. In August that year

Edwards conceived the idea of calling members of Parliament to a division by electric bells fitted in all the rooms and operated by a combination switch on the Clerk of the Assembly's table. Possibly the first of its kind in the world, it sent politicians hurrying, and John Edwards himself to fit up other systems of electric bells in Government buildings and lunatic asylums. When he left the telegraph department in 1877, he set up his own company of 'electrical engineers' and contracted to make relays and other telegraph equipment for the Victorian Railways.[31] It was hardly surprising, then, that telephones proved John Edwards's special 'meat' and he implemented his youthful plan for transmitting music and speech by wire. Unlike Sutton, he patented his technique in August 1878 and in his flourishing Melbourne business made and sold telephones of his own design until 1885.

Compared with this entrepreneurial expertise, other Colonial experiments depended heavily on Bell. Todd used 'Bell-type' instruments made in his department workshops to achieve telephone voice communication between Semaphore, Adelaide and Kapunda in January 1878 and to carry out the first major 'trunk' telephone connection in Australia over the telegraph line between Semaphore and Port Augusta. Conversations were also heard on the remote overland telegraph line from Beltana 200 miles north to Strangways Springs. In Tasmania the pioneering interests of the telegraph department and the Extension Cable Company combined to trial the new technology in a telephonic link between the chief operator of telegraphs at Low Head and the Tasmanian manager of the Cable Co. stationed at George Town.

Other telegraph departments joined in the experiment and research. E.C. and W.J. Cracknell achieved something of a family duet. In January 1878, 'E.C.' conducted experiments by telephones made on the Bell principle to converse over a short distance between Sydney and La Perouse and, on a visit to Maitland, NSW the following week, transmitted songs and a bugle blast to Sydney on the same instrument over 140 miles of telegraph wire. In Queensland 'W.J.' carried out the first telephonic experiments in that Colony on 26 January 1878, beating Dr Severn to the post by a short two days. But W.J. Cracknell was clearly dissatisfied with his crude instruments and, securing a promise of improved models direct from Professor Bell, informed the Queensland Parliament that further experiments of 'this scientific wonder' would be made.[32] Across the continent successful experiments with telephone working were carried out over the Perth–Fremantle line in March 1878.

At first Bell's device, carrying bugle and songs (at times to concert audiences), threatened to become a means of social entertainment. Melbourne's businessmen, however, seized on the larger potential of the instrument. In July 1879 Robison Bros, the Melbourne firm of engineers and brassfounders, installed the first commercial telephone to link their Flinders Street office with their foundry in South Melbourne. Far–seeing developers of the telephone's use, the firm retained the 'No.1' telephone number in Melbourne until the 1920s

With names still
familiar to Melburnians
today, Australia's first
telephone directory of
September 1880.

The men behind the
idea. William Henry
Masters, electrician and
importer, was a
shareholder in, and
chairman of, the
Melbourne Telephone
Exchange Co. Ltd,
which was registered in
July 1880 with a capital
of £5,000.

Melbourne Telephone Exchange Company
LIMITED.

H. BYRON MOORE, Manager.

LIST OF SUBSCRIBERS.

1. ROBISON BROS. AND CO.
2. EXHIBITION.
3. JAMES HENTY AND CO.
4. E. C. WADDINGTON AND CO.
5. FANNING, NANKIVELL AND CO.
6. W. F. DIXON AND CO.
7. BLAKE AND RIGGALL.
8. W. W. COUCHE AND CO.
9. CONNELL, HOGARTH AND CO.
10. BEATH, SHIESS AND CO.
11. WM. M'CULLOCH AND CO.
12. H. WERTHEIM.
13. DR. JAMES.
14. JAMES SERVICE AND CO.
15. E. ANDREWS.
16. HENRY FRANCIS,
17. APOLLO CANDLE COMPANY.
18. JAS. M'EWAN AND CO.
19. W. H. ROCKE AND CO.
20. M'LEAN BROS. AND RIGG.
21. SWALLOW AND ARIELL.
22. W. B. JONES.
23. ALLIANCE INSURANCE CO.
24. NEWELL AND CO.
25. LIVERPOOL AND LONDON AND GLOBE INSURANCE CO.
26. HENRY MOSS.
27. LYELL AND GOWAN.
28. W. F. WALKER.
29. COMMERCIAL UNION INS. CO.
30. THOS. WALKER.
31. COMMERCIAL BANK.
32. BANK OF AUSTRALASIA.
33. JOHN ZEVENBOOM.
34. NEW ZEALAND LOAN AND MERCANTILE AGENCY CO.
35. BRISCOE AND CO.
36. KITCHEN AND SONS.
37. WM. SLOANE AND CO.
38. F. W. NEEDHAM.
39. W. H. MASTERS AND CO.
40. MACK AND ELLIS.
41. SUPERINTENDENT'S OFFICE (TELEPHONE CO.) 60 Little Collins-street East.
42. H. BYRON MOORE (Office).
43. H. BYRON MOORE, private residence, Ascot Vale.
44. EXCHANGE.
45.
46.
47.
48.
49.
50.

51.
52.
53.
54.
55.
56.
57.
58.
59.
60.
61.
62.
63.
64.
65.
66.
67.
68.
69.
70.
71.
72.
73.
74.
75.
76.
77.
78.
79.
80.

when it was transferred to the city's Roman Catholic Cathedral, St Patrick's. Other point–to–point connections quickly linked Melbourne's three daily newspapers with Parliament House and a dozen or more commercial companies connected their offices, factories and warehouses on the Edison–Bell instrument and closed circuit wires.[33]

But 'point–to–point' was a restricted service allowing communication from one fixed point only to another. The first commercial telephone exchange, which enabled a 'subscriber' to replace the individual connecting wire with a single set of connections between the instrument and a central switching exchange — a major advance in the telephony system — had been opened in Connecticut, USA, in 1878. Two years later, in September 1880, Australia's first telephone exchange opened for business in Melbourne.

In contrast to the Government–controlled telegraph system introduced some 24 years before, the Melbourne Telephone Exchange Company was a private concern owned by W.H. Masters and T.T. Draper who patented their own system (Bell's application for a patent on his invention was refused in Victoria) and succeeded in the face of competition from an exchange designed and patented by J.E. Edwards. Masters and Draper leased part of the city's stock exchange building in Collins Street, installed a 100–line switchboard, connected up the existing point–to–point lines and, under the go-getting management of H. Byron Moore, developed an expanding business. Within a year, the initial subscribers list had grown to 127.

London-born Thomas Draper was a builder, contractor and electrician. He was responsible for the first electric lighting of a Melbourne building (the Public Library), and introduced the process of nickel plating.

The telephone, the list advertised, 'secures economy of time, money and energy'. One journalist appreciated the remarkable advantages the telephone conferred. An invention, he wrote, 'that enabled a man sitting in his office to ask his bank manager for an overdraft, order a coat from a tailor, and send his wife any reasonable excuse for his non–appearance at home at the usual hour', deserved a first–class certificate.[34]

Melbourne's leadership in telephony influenced other Colonies. The secretary of Sydney's Stock Exchange visited Melbourne and, impressed by what he saw, sought to develop a trial telephone between Sydney's 'Royal Exchange' and the General Post Office. He encountered the sharp resistance of Edward Cracknell who, in spite or because of his own experiments, believed that all the shouting and singing through a telephone instrument across telegraph wires did not offer a sufficiently clear system of vocal communication and declared that the 'Yankee Toy' needed considerable improvement before its introduction in New South Wales. But Cracknell was overruled. The intervention of the director of the Exchange, Alexander Campbell, Member of the Legislative Council (and later Postmaster–General in New South Wales) led to the installation late in 1880 of Sydney's first private telephone line at the Royal Exchange linking the city's businessmen with the wool sheds at Darling Harbour. Essentially the device was a telephone bureau to which lines gradually became attached between wharves, wool stores and commercial offices. Users

The manager of the Melbourne exchange, Henry Byron Moore, a land agent, surveyor and later stockbroker. The broker who handled the formation of BHP in 1885, he was, from 1881 until 1925, Secretary of the Victoria Racing Club.

erected their own lines at their own expense and paid an annual maintenance fee to the postal department.[35]

Tasmania's superintendent of telegraphs, Robert Henry, also crossed Bass Strait to see the Melbourne Telephone Exchange Company in operation. He found 'several forms of telephones in use': at the Telephone Exchange, the Edison–Bell solely, and, on private lines between Government departments and other offices, forms such as the British or American 'Crossley, Gower–Bell, Theiler and others'. Opinions differed as to the best system. But there was no doubt about the importance of the technology and Henry pressed for Government-owned telephone exchanges in both Hobart and Launceston.[36]

The Melbourne telephone exchange in 1880.

Henry's evidence was revealing. What happened to indigenous invention in Australia? Clearly, with the exception of Edwards's locally manufactured telephones and his telephone exchange, overseas designs prevailed. Masters and Draper was an American firm and the telephone equipment for Sydney's, Brisbane's, Adelaide's and Hobart's exchanges — instruments, receivers, transmitters and switchboards — were imported from British or American companies which employed local agents in the Colonies. The best of the early instruments used in telephony in Australia were built by the Consolidated Telephone Company of England (known as Blake or Blake Bell), a Bell Telephone subsidiary. Transmitters also came from

Two of the earliest Ericsson table telephones imported into Australia before the turn of the century were, left, the rare and ornate 'Biscuit Barrel', and right, the more common, but equally attractive, 'Coffee Grinder'.

When traffic on the poles exceeded that on the roads: telephone 'trees' in George Street, Sydney, in the mid-1880s.

Bell though instruments from Siemens Bros, London, Swedish Ericsson, and a steady flow of switchboards from Western Electric Company of Chicago penetrated the system. The failure to generate and manufacture local telephone equipment in the Colonies would appear to have its roots in a contemporary tendency to ignore indigenous inventiveness and, in a country of small population and small markets, to turn to technology sources overseas. Henry Sutton's indifference to patenting his many inventions (an attitude shared in aviation by Lawrence Hargrave) and his creative versatility — for he moved on to photography, motor cars and a 'walkie-talkie' radio by the century's end — probably also contributed to this negative trend.

By 1883 all the Colonies, except Western Australia, had telephone exchanges in their capitals. The telegraph department, Brisbane, launched a Government-run switchboard in 1880. Hobart mustered ten subscribers for its exchange in 1883, with 35 in Launceston. Adelaide began with 48 subscribers the same year though Sydney's and Melbourne's exchanges, Todd admitted, 'put ours to the blush'.[37] By Federation all were Government owned. E.C. Cracknell was converted. In March 1882 a Government exchange was brought into service in Sydney's General Post Office. With ten lines and a junction with the switchboard at the Royal Exchange, the Government and the free enterprise telephones functioned side by side until a fire conveniently knocked out the Royal Exchange switchboard late that same year. Reconditioned, it was transferred to the General Post Office. By the end of 1883 the NSW's annual report noted with satisfaction that over 400 persons 'had taken advantage of' Sydney's telephone service. In Western Australia, a cost benefit evaluation of the telephone initiated by the Legislative Council in 1882 led to the opening of the Perth exchange in December 1887 and an exchange at Fremantle two months later. Following the established Australian pattern, the Victorian Government bought out Masters and Draper and J.E. Edwards's private exchanges in 1887.

Like the telegraph, telephone services were expensive. As with all new technology, telephony favoured the 'haves'. Lines were connected at the expense of the subscriber who also paid a maintenance fee per mile for the line and for the telephone instrument 'recommended by the Department'. Costs rose steeply the greater the distance from the exchange. Nonetheless, for those who could afford the technology, the telephone offered a personal service very different from the telegraph. City business operations, long dependent on cables and telegrams, were speeded by telephone service. There were other clients. Fire brigades, police stations, hospitals, were among the earliest connections. Leading doctors took out subscriptions (the respected Dr Crowther commandeered No.1 of the Hobart telephone exchange for many years). Banks, solicitors, insurance companies, auctioneers, printers, importers, brokers, merchants and the press made early use of the striking new facility. One of the world's first 'call-girl' networks was established in Melbourne in 1891 when telephones were connected to city brothels. One biologically-minded Melbourne publisher saw the city's telephone exchange as the '*cerebellum* of the social and commercial system of the busy city ... incessantly receiving and transmitting from and to every portion of the vital organism'. In Melbourne the number of calls made each day reached 8,000 in 1887, the greater part in business hours. Public call boxes or exchange bureaux offered calls at 6d and, it was noted, that on hot, cold or wet days, telephones were more frequently used than in clear fine weather.[38]

At the nerve centre of the system were the ladies of the telephone exchange. For a technology that would come to play such a prominent and enhancing role in the lives of women, it was significant that women immediately entered the workforce of telephony. The trend, begun with the economic move of employing postmistresses in country towns and extended gradually to telegraphy, found an unrepressed outlet in the employment of women in the telephone exchanges. The pattern, set in the USA, was transferred with some display of cultural resistance to Australia. Mechanisation of factories had already opened avenues of employment to Colonial women but these were concentrated traditionally in lower status work areas of clothing manufacturing, jam and pickle factories, where skilled tasks were jealously reserved for males. Women of higher education and social standing were found in nursing, sales and teaching. The progress made by women in telegraphy and telephony — skilled mechanical operations requiring training and examinations and endowed with status traditionally beyond the reach of women — marked a striking departure in Colonial industrial practice and a notable (and as it proved enduring) union between women and the new communication technologies.[39]

The New South Wales Postmaster-General, John Burns, was the first to employ women as telegraphists in his department. Western Australia's superintendent of telegraph used the local girl, Mary Wellstead, for the east-west repeater station at Bremer Bay; Bishop Salvado trained Aboriginal Ellen Kuper as a proficient telegraphist at New Norcia mission station; while 'ladies of good education' were employed later in the 1870s as country telegraph operators in Tasmania on a shoestring at 1s 5d a day. In Victoria the Postmaster-General, T.L. Jackson, employed a regiment of women in his country stations where the amount of business was insufficient to 'justify the appointment of a male telegraphist'. The women doubled as postmistresses, penetrated the larger suburban and country stations as assistants and, by 1880, Jackson found that he had 66 women in charge of country stations and another 62 female assistant telegraphists in other stations. They were clearly an economy measure — though the assistants could earn £52 a year, a fortune compared with their exploited sisters across Bass Strait. But while, on Jackson's own admission, they performed their duties with 'intelligence and zeal', he judged them inferior to men telegraphists and even the best 'unable to bear the strain of continuous exertion to anything like the same extent young men are capable of enduring'. There seemed no

Australia's first telephonist, Isabella Cliff began work in the Melbourne exchange in 1880. She continued there after the service was taken over by the Victorian government in 1887.

basis for Jackson's assertion. The young women themselves were not, as their male colleagues fondly fancied, all waiting for married bliss, that 'more congenial and benefitting station' where Morse code played no part. They trained; they exhibited initiative and dedication. They were, also, in the straitjacket of the period, expendable and vulnerable, though one or two gamely put in applications for promotion.[40]

By contrast, the telephone became a woman's preserve. They were gentler and more biddable than men. In Melbourne, Byron Moore, profiting from American experience, launched the Melbourne telephone exchange with eight women telephonists. By 1887, when the Victorian Government took over the Melbourne exchange, there were 24 'fair and nimble–fingered operators'. Essential attributes were good health, good eyesight and hearing, clear speech, a good arm reach (for they stood at the controls until 1890 when they were allowed to sit down), speed, a neat appearance, 'politeness on all occasions', self–reliance, and tact in dealing with distress. Recruited between the ages

A job for middle-class girls. Connie Letch, Western Australia's first telephonist, 1887, and her letter of appointment.

of 16 and 18, their salaries were relatively good for women at £45 to £63 per year (1898). At first they worked with ordinary receivers and transmitters, receiving and routing the calls at the exchange. Headphones came in during the 1890s. These cradled the head and were supported on a breastplate which weighed two pounds. The harnesses were not welcomed by the girls, the pressure 'provoked headaches and excited hysteria'. The telephonists were overviewed by a supervisor, at first a man, dapper and self–important, but matronly figures soon dominated the role and kept down excitement and strain. 'There is no shouting . . . no apoplectic straining into the machine's mouth', one journal described the Melbourne Wills Street exchange in September 1887. 'There is a soft sighing murmur in the room; and one could easily imagine the spare forms to be automatic figures; and yet the little pouting delicate mouth is wrestling with the pangs, groans and tempers of 100 subscribers, that number being attended by any one lady operator.'

The ladies of the Brisbane exchange, 1899. Front row — Mary Armstrong, Ada Warburton, Frances Wall, Mrs Dick (supervisor), Eleanor Ferguson, Annette Bowler, Lil McDonnell. Back row — Kate Sheldon, Annie Murray, Edith Aulsebrook, Amy Abraham, Edith Hawker, Sarah Gallagher and Alice Hibbert.

'A soft sighing murmur in the room' — the main switchroom of Melbourne's Wills Street exchange. Empty of switchboards, the building is now a Salvation Army hostel.

In Sydney, for some years, the route to the telephone switchboard was barred by the crusty figure of Edward Cracknell. 'The experiment' (of employing women), he wrote, early and inaccurately in December 1878, 'has been tried . . . in other parts of the world and has proved an utter failure'. Women, he sensed, were incompetent at fixing mechanical problems. Instead young boys were employed at the Sydney exchange. One well qualified young woman, Jane M'Ilwain, trained in Melbourne, slipped through in 1882 and was despatched to be an operator at Gladstone, NSW. It was not until the mid–1890s that a phenomenal growth of telephone subscriptions, brought on as a result of reduced costs (together with Cracknell's disappearance in 1893), turned the Public Service Board's gaze to the fairer sex. Six girls were appointed in 1896, selected from pupil teachers in the Education Department. It was no longer a matter of competing with men: the job was seen as a dead end for male employees. The salary could not exceed £100 a year and women were expected to resign before marriage. Taken on as 'cheap and docile labour' they, nonetheless, filled exacting jobs and enjoyed considerable autonomy and position.[41]

The 'cheap and docile labour' was at first supervised by men. Here, the postmaster oversees telephonists in the original Port Adelaide exchange.

Yet the appointment of the girls stirred the male chauvinists of Sydney's press. 'The telephone girl has arrived and the telephone man is ordered to move on', declared the *Telegraph*. 'Her voice is said to be better adapted to the instrument, just as it is to a knot–hole in the back fence through which the female conversation is known to excel.' At the *Star* another journalist fumed at the thought of 'the frizzy haired houris

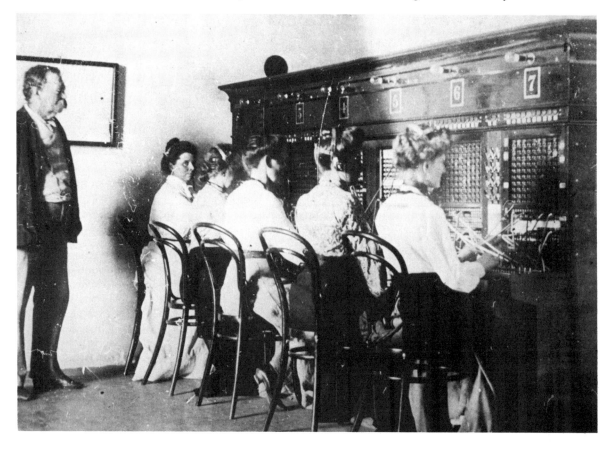

of other Colonies who attend upon your telephone and answer your ring when they do not happen to be reading the latest novelette or conversing with their best boy'. The female operator, he found, had a fatal habit of saying 'beg pardon' and switching you off without further notice if your voice was elderly.[42] It was in vain: female telephonists were here to stay, though they stood on the shifting ground of social change.

By 1901 telephone bells rang in 33,000 offices and houses in Australia. The instruments, now often mounted on walls, fine objects in their sturdy polished cases of wood, gave rather unpredictable service; hearing was not very good, interference a common complaint, and there was much irritable waiting on the line for the operator's connection. Urban use dominated the lines. The 1,000–odd miles of wires recorded by Colonial departments at the century's end coiled largely around the city and suburban telephone exchanges. High–cost long–line telephony moved slowly. South Australia and Tasmania (eager innovators) claimed the first trunk services from Adelaide to Semaphore and New Norfolk to Hobart respectively (both about 23 miles) in 1888. The 1880s and 1890s saw trunk services established between Melbourne and the well–heeled burghers of Ballarat, Bendigo and Geelong. In New South Wales trunk lines linked Sydney with Newcastle and the popular Blue Mountain resort towns of Katoomba, Blackheath and Mt Victoria; and similar short distance trunks developed in the other Colonies.

A later Ericsson wall telephone of a type that served Australians for well over fifty years from its introduction in the 1890s.

The Ericsson wall telephones undergoing modifications in the PMG's Melbourne workshop, 1910, for Australian use.

Typical of smaller
exchanges with their
100-line switchboards is
this early example at
Port Pirie, South
Australia, 1899.

While the first
underground telephone
cable was laid in
Melbourne's Queen
Street in 1884, it was
not until this occasion
in 1898 that the
experiment was
repeated.

Early telephone lines were single-wire earth return circuits strung up aerially on poles. As city and suburban demand mounted, the poles with their bunched crossbars and unsightly wires created visual pollution and obstruction to the thoroughfares. In New South Wales Cracknell tackled the problem by designing a frieze which he had erected along the length of George Street from the GPO to Railway Square. Ornamental yet substantial, the frieze formed a uniform verandah for all the houses along the street. Specially built cables carrying 50 wires were laid by hooks in the frieze and passed in iron pipes laid below each street crossing. This ingenious system obliterated a maze of wires and won commendation at the Adelaide Exhibition of 1887. But undergrounding cable was troublesome and, despite praise, Cracknell's scheme did not prevent the cavalcade of cross-arm telephone poles from dominating city landscapes.

By the decade of the 1890s the idea was dawning that the telephone might supersede the telegraph or at least cut into its phenomenal use. Telegraph boys, those buttresses of the telegraph system, the 'look sharp' lads who kept the office hardware polished, delivered the telegrams on foot or bicycle, and kept a weather eye on the prospect of training and promotion, felt a whiff of distant events in the depression years of the early 1890s when some lost employment in city offices. The telephone, too, rapidly invaded the railway communication system which had been built up (often around the combined country telegraph and railway station) by the departments of telegraph and railways. Tasmania, for example, recorded nearly 500 paid railway messages in 1877 and some 18,000 'service messages'.[43] But the telephone with its greater speed began to edge the railway telegraph system out.

Comparisons of telephone and telegraph traffic proved difficult. Colonies recorded different statistics in their annual reports. (See Appendix I.) But, in both services, rates dropped across the Colonies from 1895, business and domestic demand escalated and, even in fine weather, Australia's people were making noticeable use of public telephone bureaux. Australia's telephone services numbered 24,700 in 1901.

A telegraph messenger boy, 1900. For many it was the first stepping stone to a glittering career.

The 19th century, however, was the telegraph's golden age. By Federation 43,000 miles of telegraph lines girded the country while nearly six million telegrams (sent and received) were handled nationally and internationally that year. An evolving science, telegraphy updated constantly and its changing instruments, available in the Colonies, were works of art. Exhibited at the Adelaide Exhibition of 1887, they ranged across a miscellany of British inventions, the new Wheatstone galvanic instruments, Henley's magnetic electric instruments, the five Needle Cooke, Wheatstone's alphabetical magnetic telegraph instruments, Siemen's alphabetic instruments.[44] The Colonial telegraph departments were keen up-daters, replacing and interlarding the old with the new. The rapid evolution and adoption of new telegraph instruments in the decade 1877–87 increased speeds of transmission from 40 up to 400 words a minute.

Given the pace of technological change and the desire of the

The 'golden age' of the telegraph. One of a series of Christmas greetings sent by Melbourne telegraphists to their suburban and country colleagues.

Colonies to exploit it, local attempts at innovation conducted in departmental workshops could not keep up with instruments from well–established and research–oriented laboratories abroad. Innovation aimed modestly at local needs. Todd designed a new insulator for use on his iron poles, the porcelain umbrella (the butt of outback Aboriginals and city larrikins) protected by an iron shield screwed to an iron pin which served as a lightning conductor. Charles Kopsch, a member of Todd's staff, designed and improved Blake galvano telephones with vibrating bells, and there were many other such modifications that went unrecorded. Essentially Australian telegraphy and telephony were adaptive. Their developers kept abreast of overseas technology through the choice and modification of competitive systems and equipment. Each Colony thus early shaped a forward–looking and confident communication policy based on the knowledgeable purchase of imported materials and testing for its efficiency and range.

Administratively, Colonial communication systems were hotch-potch, as disjointed and unco-ordinated in their intercolonial relationships as the railway networks that left their differing and disconnected gauges at each Colonial border. They differed in their rates of progress, in the instruments and equipment they adopted, in their codes and training facilities, and in the very titles and responsibilities of their senior officials. But by 1890 all but one Colonial telegraph departments and their telephone branches were joined administratively to the Colonial Postmasters–General. The exception was New South Wales. There E.C. Cracknell's entrenched resistance to any connection with the post office kept his telegraph and telephone department distinct. But after an overtaxing day at a parade on 14 January 1893, Cracknell died. The breath was scarcely out of his body when amalgamation was ordered by the Postmaster-General and completed in February 1893. Government–owned and administered, the telegraph and telephone had achieved a deceptive uniformity in the Colonies.

5 Brothers in One Service

The Federation of the Australian Colonies, planned for over a decade before its official inauguration on 1 January 1901, brought marked changes to the organisation of communications. The Constitution Act of 1900 empowered the Commonwealth Government to 'take over, control and administer' the posts and telegraph departments of each State of the new Commonwealth and, on 1 March 1901, the former separate and distinctive Colonial departments were brought together to form the Postmaster–General's Department of the Commonwealth. A new era of institutional development had begun.

Even at its birth the new body was a giant. Its assets were valued at £6 million; it employed almost 16,000 and accounted for 90 per cent of Commonwealth Government's manpower. Its 7,400 offices were speckled across the landscape of the continent. During its 74 years of growth (until its partition as two separate Statutory Commissions for post and telecommunications in 1975), the Postmaster–General's Department (PMG), or the Australian Post Office (APO) as it came sometimes to be called, handled more money, employed more men and women, carried forward the tradition of family employment that had no counterpart in other Government departments, and developed as the country's major technological instrumentality.

Its birth pangs, however, were severe. Colonial Postmasters–General, accustomed to power and position in their own bailiwicks, entered the Commonwealth with reluctance. 'It is with much regret', R.A. Sholl, Western Australia's Postmaster–General conveyed his unhappiness in his last report to his Colonial Secretary, 'that I am compelled to sever my official relations with the State Government'. The mood was no more cheerful in South Australia where as one new Federal MP testified 'almost to a man and woman, South Australia opposed the proposal to federate the postal service'. In New South Wales, the Colonial Postmaster–General Joseph Cook (who would lead the nation as Prime Minister in 1913), declared on the eve of Federation that, though it had always been assumed that the post office should be taken over at the Commonwealth's formation, he

'Brothers in one service'
— an undergrounding
line party at Mount
Gambier, South
Australia, 1916.

himself 'had not heard a single effective argument in favour of doing so'.[1]

Nonetheless despite the behind–the–scenes disenchantment and a lurking State-ism that would bedevil PMG affairs for two decades, telegraphists across the States from Darwin and Perth to Eucla, from Wagga Wagga to Hobart and Brisbane joined at noon Adelaide time on 1 March 1901 to sing 'God Save the King', to clasp a metaphorical hand across the wires and to express their feelings of 'brothers in one service'.[2]

The problem of integrating the disunited State administrations would prove a politician's nightmare. No fewer than eleven ministers held the PMG portfolio in the Commonwealth's first 13 years. That reluctant Federalist, the Western Australian Sir John Forrest, was appointed first Federal Postmaster–General on 1 January 1901 and held the post for 16 days until the sudden death of the Federal Minister for Defence, Sir James Dickson, raised him to the higher and less frustrating post. Prime Minister Barton wanted Robert Philp, Premier of Queensland to take the vacant post, for Queensland's resistance to Federation had been high. The telegraph wires ran hot between Brisbane and the seat of Commonwealth Government in Melbourne. But Philp declined and the Colony of Queensland's former ministerial Postmaster–General, now Senator James Drake, was appointed Federal Postmaster–General on 5 February 1901.[3]

It now fell to Drake to harness the disparate arms of the postal, telegraph and telephone services, to harmonise the six Colonial Acts with their differing practices and regulations, and to build a central administration. After some delay, while he sped about his new domain, Drake introduced the Post and Telegraph Bill in the Senate on 5 June 1901. The debate was an important curtain raiser. It examined central issues about the management and policy of the new communications colossus, and touched off those fundamental philosophical and interpretative questions that would re–echo in parliamentary debate on postal and telecommunications matters across the century.

Essentially the new Government saw the Federal post and

telecommunications system as a Government monopoly inherited from the Colonies. As several historians have noted, Colonial socialism or Colonial 'governmentalism' had long been a conspicuous feature of the Australian colonies, encouraged by both entrepreneurs and wage–earners in their own different interests.[4] Moreover, as Postmaster–General Drake pointed out, the notion of a communications monopoly was reinforced by British and European practice. In Australia, he argued, the Government would ensure that a centralised administration would be worked in such a way as 'to be of the very best service to the people of the Commonwealth'. On the question of a telegraph monopoly (and telephones were included as 'other communications by telegraph' within the Bill), Drake advocated that 'a telegraph monopoly . . . enables us to look ahead; take advantage of every innovation, and adapt it to the benefit of the public.' If the telegraph service had been in the hands of a private proprietor, he noted, 'I am inclined to think that it would have fought against the introduction of the telephone service . . . Instead . . . the Postal Department, having the monopoly, welcomed the telephone system, and assisted, to a great extent, in making the invention of practical value to the community.'[5] It was a concept of a steadily expanding and upgrading service that would in general, though not invariably, underlie telecommunications practice and development in Australia.

In 1901 these ideas had wide acceptance. 'A little State Socialism', as one MP put it, could do no harm. Its advantages in the postal and telegraph service, Drake insisted, were 'fully appreciated by the people'. Senator Major Gould (NSW) might argue briefly for the convenience, in cases of urgency, of allowing some persons to make a profit by carrying letters for hire in thickly populated areas: the Postmaster–General defended the monopoly position. 'By allowing private companies to transact business in the particular districts where it is most profitable to carry letters for a lower rate than the departmental charge', Drake countered, 'it would become impossible for the Postal Department to carry out the service in the remote portions of the State.'[6]

On the larger question of PMG management and responsibility, some ideological differences did arise. Should the department accept a policy of 'running at a loss' to assist the development of the country, offering services in distant and uneconomic places and making up the drain on departmental revenue through taxation? Or should the department run its business as a 'commercial concern', balancing revenue and expenditure, and carrying out its programme through loans on which interest must be paid? The Postmaster–General favoured a policy of management as far as possible 'on business lines'. He found timely support from senatorial colleagues in Tasmania, Western Australia and Queensland. But Victorian Senator Best made the case for a 'more service–oriented department' and claimed that there could be too great an emphasis on the commercial aspect of the measure. 'We have here', he put the proposition, 'a vast undeveloped continent . . . and a duty to render to those who do not crowd themselves into cities. We ought to offer them every possible facility with a view to making their lives as agreeable as possible.' It was, Best articulated, the concept of service to the bush, 'a general principle we should all bear in mind'.[7]

In the House of Representatives there was a kindred refrain. But many members considered that the transfer of the postal and telegraph function was premature. Anti–Federalism cast its long shadow across the debates. Amid the confusion and mismatch of the different Colonial services, some members believed that an imposed centralism was a 'pig in a poke'.[8] The pre–Federation cry of 'one destiny, one people' might sometime be achieved: it was demonstrably harder to realise 'one people, one postage stamp, one penny'.

The Post and Telegraph Bill was assented to on 16 November 1901. Yet, in terms of Federal policy, little real progress was made. The Commonwealth Government was given responsibility for all postal and telegraph (telephone) transactions, except in such cases where State Government Railways should have authority to erect and maintain telegraphs within the railway boundaries; and no attempt was made to unify rates. Indeed, with rate structures that bore on the economy of individual States, State regulations were to be maintained under the Commonwealth Act at the discretion of the Governor-General. A year later, the *Post and Telegraph Rates Act* of 1902 fixed uniform rates for telegrams and newspaper postage; but eight years elapsed before the *Postal Rates Act* of 1910 repealed all State rates and regulations and provided for uniform and reduced rates for letter-cards, printed papers, books and magazines, and the long hoped–for universal penny postage.

The problem of forging a 'national' telephone and telegraph policy thrust a thorn into the Postmaster–General's flesh. Drake grappled with the matter early in his regime. In May 1901 he called together a Departmental Electrical Committee chaired by Todd, and made up of departmental chief electricians, J.Y. Nelson, NSW, H.W. Jenvey, Victoria, and J. Hesketh, Queensland, to conduct a thorough inquiry into the existing systems of telephony and telegraphy. Adhering to their elaborate terms to provide an efficient and uniform national system covering maintenance, working, management and rates, the committee inspected the telephone and telegraph systems in most States, took evidence from electrical and telegraph engineers, poked about electrical workshops, made special tests of telephone–speaking over State lines, investigated the telegraph messenger service, drafted revised instructions for telegraph and telephone use, evaluated their management and construction in the States, and submitted a detailed report for reform of the systems plus a practical estimate of costs.[9]

While few of the committee's more ambitious proposals saw the light of day (the complete replacement of Melbourne's obsolete telephone exchange and the addition of new exchange boards for Sydney and Adelaide exchanges were among them), their widely researched report with its expert guidelines on telephone trunk line development between capitals, telephone equipment, the choice of exchange switchboards and branching equipment, high speed telegraph systems between capital cities, and even the replacement of wooden by iron poles, laid down a long-term blueprint for communications development that would shape evolving practice.

In 1901, however, a wide disparity existed between the political process and expert advice. Funds for development were in short supply. Importantly, the famous 'Braddon clause' of the Constitution prescribed that, for at least five years after the imposition of uniform custom duties, the Commonwealth Government should return to each State the difference between all revenues collected in the State and the outlays made in a particular field, together with a per capita share of Commonwealth expenditures.[10] And a special parsimony developed in Treasury thinking for developmental expenditure on posts and telegraphs. Long after Drake's departure from the portfolio, the permanent head of the PMG complained that the Department 'was not allowed to act upon the recommendations of the committee of Experts of 1901' and had been compelled to 'live from hand to mouth extending out-of-date equipment'.

Yet, despite administrative handicaps, some technological developments followed an imperative of their own. On 13 March 1902 a wooden barrel was pushed ashore from HMS *Anglia* into the surf at Southport, Queensland. It carried a rope at the end of which, coiled on board, was the Pacific cable that, starting from Southport, would join Australia with Vancouver and forge an Imperial communication link between Australia, Canada and Great Britain. Watched by an eager crowd, the cable end was ferried ashore and, amid cheers mingled with the pounding of the surf, was entrenched and sited in the waiting cable house. Eight months later the long join of the cable had been made via Norfolk Island and Fiji to Canada. In a flurry of Imperial fervour, the first message was relayed to King Edward VII. 'As the

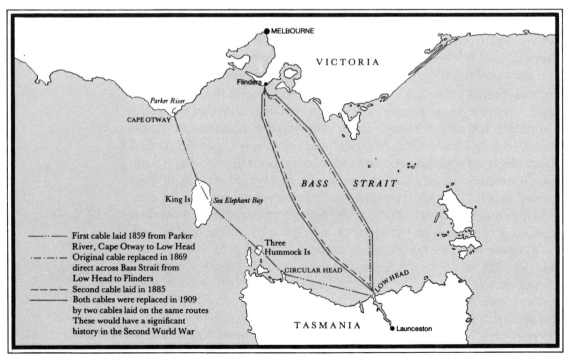

The 1909 Bass Strait cables. These cables would have a significant history in the Second World War.

cables are entirely British', the greetings read, 'this first message to pass the sunrise by one route, and the sunset by another, is appropriately addressed to the Sovereign of the British Empire on which the sun never rises or sets'.[11] With the 'Africa cable' from Durban landed at Cottesloe, near Perth, via Mauritius and Cocos Island a few months earlier and extended by sea to Adelaide in March 1902, Australians could send cable messages to London through either the eastern or the western hemispheres, while the 'all red' Imperial line heightened both their sense of Empire solidarity and national security. Two cables (replacing the 1885 cable) were laid between Victoria and Tasmania in 1909.

In the early years of the century demands for both telephone and telegraph gathered pace. By 1907 two recommendations of the 1901 Committee had been acted on. All telephone traffic was placed in charge of a new engineering branch established in the PMG and, in July 1907, the first intercapital trunk service, (the 'nerves of the whole system' as Bell described long distance telephony), was opened between Melbourne and Sydney as a major pilot scheme. Its success led to the second trunk line, between Melbourne and Adelaide in 1914, and trunk connections between other State capitals following the First World War.

Behind the thrust of technological advancement was the leadership of John Hesketh, Queensland's electrical engineer. Hesketh was the first British post office engineer to join the Australian postal service. Recruited to Queensland in 1896 at the age of 26 to organise its telegraph and telephone services, he was so successful that the committee of departmental experts omitted Queensland from its major recommendations for network reform in 1901. In 1904 Hesketh

Erecting a pole on the Perth–Adelaide line, 1876.

The technology improves. While the above was a common method of erecting poles for many years, even at the turn of the century new ideas were being introduced, as with this mobile unit seen in action below.

visited America and Europe for the Commonwealth Government to investigate developments in telegraphy and telephony and to report on the incipient field of wireless telegraphy. Travelling at a time when substantial advances in telecommunications technology were being made, he was able to make some important evaluations of forward developments and to press them upon the Commonwealth Government.

Serious and perspicacious, Hesketh sought to pluck from overseas experience a 'mean' of adopted practice where 'the highest efficiency and soundest development go together'. With this in view, he advocated the adoption of a series of new technical innovations and

The Evolution of the Strowger Automatic Telephone

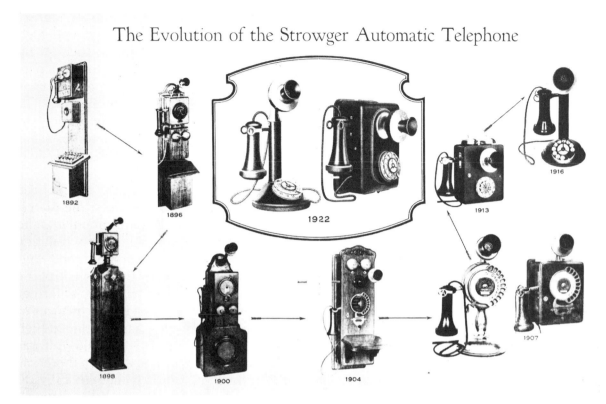

1892   1896   1922   1916   1913   1898   1900   1904   1907

brought reinforcing evidence from overseas to bear on practices that were already penetrating the Australian network. Importantly, he urged the introduction of American–style country 'party lines' in remote areas, the adoption of the 'measured' or 'toll' system of telephone tariff (where the payment varied with the extent to which the service was used) and the introduction of the British Wheatstone automatic high speed system for long distance telegraphy between State capitals. At the same time he advised against any early introduction of the 'step–by–step' automatic telephone exchange system, patented in 1889 by the Kansas City undertaker, Almon B. Strowger, (to prevent, it was said, his grave business passing via the telephone girls to competitive firms), then in growing use in the USA. Hesketh, instead, favoured upgrading Australia's 'magneto' system by the adoption of the 'Common Battery System', a manually operated system introduced into America about 1896 by which telephone instruments were fed current from one central, common battery situated at the exchange and which was capable of serving both large and small exchanges. This system, Hesketh considered, was more suited to Australia's stage of telephone development. His advice rested on technical and economic grounds, and he was quick to note that, while the automatic exchange saved on operators' salaries, it added considerable costs for maintenance paid to fitters and mechanics.[12]

In March 1906 Hesketh was appointed the PMG's first chief electrical engineer. With tight funds and Treasury imbued with a spirit of narrow conservation, he inherited a communications system he found largely 'obsolete' and in which, he told a later committee of inquiry, State engineers could not bring their systems 'to a proper

By the First World War, Australia had two varieties of these Strowger telephones in service, the 'Candlestick' and the metal wall telephone.

John Hesketh, the PMG's first chief electrical engineer. His overseas visits played an important part in updating the telephone and telegraph system.

pitch'. Yet under his influence and direction the first Common Battery System was installed in Hobart in 1908; the Wheatstone system of high speed telegraphy between capitals was accepted and introduced by 1910, and encouragement given to country dwellers to erect tele- phones for 'party' lines, Hesketh himself drafting the simple guidelines that told farmers how to put up a telephone line in the same way as they built a wire fence.[13] In 1910 a universal toll system of metered telephone charges replaced the flat rate system. Despite obstacles, Australia's telephones reached the 100,000 mark in 1911, a three–fold increase on the Federation figure.

As a department of State, however, the PMG had reached the doldrums by 1907. Lack of planning, tension between the States' deputy Postmasters–General and the central administration, and the inexperience of politicians in dealing with the running of a complex but unco–ordinated technical instrumentality, exposed conditions close to chaos.[14] The situation was exacerbated by the presence of the 'parsimonious Treasurer', Sir George Turner, who, as a former Premier of Victoria charged with managing the flagging finances of that Colony during the depression of the 1890s, had developed both his reputation and his advanced cheeseparing skills. In 1906–7, it was impossible to get funds voted for postal reform. In addition there was mounting dissatisfaction among the PMG Department's clerical staff, mechanics and linemen at their heavy workload and at what they saw as the oppressive role of the Commonwealth Public Service Board Commissioner in fixing wages and conditions to ensure that 'decisions did not press unduly upon the resources of the Treasury'.[15] There was also an overt hostility among Department officials against the infant but growing trade union movement in communications.

At the centre of the system was the secretary of the Department, Robert Scott. Born in England, but a Queenslander by upbringing and education, Scott had joined the Brisbane post office as a clerk in 1862, rose to superintendent of mails, and reached the Colony's top position as undersecretary and superintendent of telegraph in November 1899. He was chosen in July 1901 as first head of the new PMG Department with the title of 'Secretary'. His appointment under Senator Drake's political leadership, and the rapid addition of fellow Queenslander Justinian Oxenham as chief clerk (and assistant secretary in 1907), established some tradition of Queensland leadership which moved the Melbourne *Argus* to remark that 'Queenslanders will do well in the Federal postal service.'[16] The newspaper was prescient. Not only did the first two heads of the PMG's Department, Scott and Oxenham, T.A. Housley (1965–7) and the last Director–General, Eber Lane (1972–5), come from that State, but the appointment of Queenslander J.H. Curtis as first managing director of Telecom Australia 1975–81, proved that geographical distance was no obstacle to the 'glittering prizes'.

Scott, effective in Queensland, plainly lacked the administra- tive calibre needed to direct and integrate the new Commonwealth communications giant. He faced intemperate obstructions from State deputies. A court case and much publicity marked 'Deputy'

F.L. Outtrim's attempt to secure something like his old Colonial authority in Victoria when Federation arrived. Senator Drake also cultivated the habit of inviting the public to bring their troubles to him. There was clear want of management planning. No Annual Reports were issued for the Department until 1910–11. Accounting practices were non–existent or incomplete; the vital office of Commonwealth chief electrical engineer was not provided for until 1906; professional electrical engineers found themselves used for clerical work; and, despite criticism of a high centralism, there was, on the evidence, no attempt to fashion a clear system of Commonwealth adminis-tration.

So chaotic, indeed, were PMG affairs that in July 1907 Alfred Deakin's minority Government (in office since 1905) was defeated on a motion to adjourn a debate demanding a Royal Commission into the post office. The instigator was William Webster, Labor MHR for Gwydir, NSW, a quarryman turned trade union official who, having become acquainted with post office affairs the previous year, was appalled by the rudderless progress of that ship of state. Contrary to normal parliamentary practice on defeat, Deakin did not resign but, after consultation with the opposition, he yielded the point and in March 1908 arranged for a cabinet committee to look into the matter.[17]

The cabinet committee's findings led to a Royal Commission into the post office appointed by the Governor–General in June 1908. The commission, made up of seven politicians drawn from all parties, was assigned specifically to investigate the management, finance and organisation of the PMG's Department; the extension of the service into country districts and particularly in remote and sparsely populated parts of the Commonwealth, and complaints about the service. In practice, its task was a top–to–toe examination of the Department and of its technological development. Not surprisingly, politicians of all parties were unwilling to serve. Senior members from both Houses invited to become commissioners were found to be heavily committed in their electorates. The Hon. Joseph Cook became the committee's reluctant chairman but resigned at the end of the year. The Hon. William Wilks, a committee member, replaced him in the chair. Of the seven appointees (Senators Hugh de Largie and Edward Mulcahy, and MHRs Cook, Wilks, Charles Salmon, David Storrer and William Webster), only Wilks, Webster, Storrer and de Largie remained on from December 1908 to conduct the committee's business and to sign its lengthy report.

As Webster recalled, the task was 'arduous and unsatisfactory'. PMG staff saw the commission as a 'battleground', and hundreds of pages of evidence underlined their tense rivalries and discontents. In a marathon venture that took two years to complete, the commissioners circled the capitals of each State, held hearings, examined witnesses, took detailed evidence from the States' electrical engineers, heard a defence of his arbitration processes from the hard hitting public service commissioner, Duncan McLachlan, interrogated staff administrators and union representatives within the PMG, and manfully sought to unravel the finances of the Department. As a result of its protracted business, the commission bore a singular stamp. Some of the reforms it recommended were carried out before its formal report was complete.[18]

Before finalising its proceedings, the commission took evidence in August 1910 from the father of telephony himself, Dr Alexander Graham Bell who, on a world tour was fortuitously visiting relatives in Australia. Bell's testimony given in Parliament House, Melbourne, was a refreshing medley of opinion on technological developments abroad,

Dr Alexander Graham Bell, telephone inventor (above), addressed a meeting of the Postal Electrical Society in 1910 (right).

the dilemma of Australian experience, the pros and cons of automatic telephony (he, like Hesketh, favoured the common battery switchboards — 'the most perfect system at present existing'); the need for metallic circuits, and the undergrounding of wires to obtain a satisfactory telephone service in the Commonwealth.

Bell stood in no doubt as to the deficiencies of the telephone system in Australia. He had gone to some trouble in Sydney to ferret out facts, and he considered that, on the rates charged, the present system must run at a loss. Unlike America, he had remarked earlier, 'the telephones here are not yet part of the people's life'. He believed, however, that the public should be educated to underwrite the costs of a complex technology like the telephone and should 'pay a fair price for a fair service'. To the lasting joy of telephonists, he defended the much maligned women operators and declared that his own private testing had revealed the curious and significant fact — an early example of a time and motion study — that the telephone operator took one quarter the time to make the connection as it took the subscriber to answer his call. 'Let the public generally treat the telephone girl with courtesy and consideration', said Bell, 'and let the Department appoint someone to hear complaints.' Bell was a feminist. Writing from Lennon's Hotel to Queensland's Deputy Postmaster–General after a visit to the Brisbane exchange, he confided, 'I am glad that I had something to do with the opening up of a new occupation for women. I do not think that any industry offers more opportunity for the advancement of women than the Telephone Industry.'[19]

It was not surprising that Bell's interrogation by the commissioners was lengthy and intense. His fertile mind turned a searchlight on the differences between Australia's struggling Government telephone

'Let the public treat the telephone girl with courtesy.' Melbourne telephonists on their outing to Port Campbell, Victoria, 1906.

system and America's free enterprise development. He saw the patent system, founded on British lines, as inhibitory to the inventive process. Australia, like America, he urged, should stimulate invention and protect inventors in the ownership of their creations. 'One of the great dangers in a country like Australia', he stressed 'is that Government ownership is going to interfere with the improvements of inventors by stopping the financial rewards that are before them.' It was very important, Bell added, 'that the Postal Department should have a laboratory to test all new ideas . . . and if good, adopt them'. Since the Australian Government tended to be a buyer of new inventions, Bell envisaged a 'testing laboratory' and a staff of experts to try out the medley of new inventions burgeoning overseas, and give sound opinions on them. His realistic idea was adopted in the 1920s. From American experience, Bell also argued for rapid updating of obsolete equipment. The process of transition, he emphasised, should be short. Australia, with its mix of old and new equipment, was unduly 'prolonging the period of change'.

His final word was on professional expertise. 'Do you think', he was asked about the office of Commonwealth chief engineer, 'that a high class man would save his salary over and over again?' 'Yes', replied the forthright 63–year–old bracingly, 'You cannot economise on brains.'

The Royal Commission presented its report to Parliament on 5 October 1910. Its recommendations on administrative, postal and technological matters, agreed by the commissioners, totalled 175. Conceptually the commission was committed to large–scale reform. It

Some of the staff of the PMG engineering branch, South Australia, 1918. The PMG was actively encouraging officers to undergo engineering study, and even by 1911 was willing to pay the fees attached to approved study courses.

made no secret of its verdict that the amalgamation of the country's postal and telecommunications service had been made too soon. It found defects 'due to lack of efficient management' and defects inherent in the system of control. 'When however', it concluded sharply, 'an inferior system is associated with a weak and limited management, the results are disastrous.'[20]

In its overall findings, the report gave even–handed justice. It censored the State Deputy Postmasters–General for 'an incomplete conception of the Federal spirit' but found, equally, that the Secretary had tended to identify himself with day–to–day matters instead of shaping a policy of uniform administration, sound finance, and ongoing technological development. It found the Treasury culpable of want of foresight and of 'a total lack of consideration' for the new Department. But the Department itself had also failed to alert the Postmaster–General of the effects of a 'starvation policy'. In the light of much evidence heard, the report recommended that staff matters should be removed from the control of the Government's public service commissioner. While the recommendation was strenuously opposed, it marked an opening salvo against the Public Service Board's influence on staff matters in the PMG that, fuelled over many years by the union movement, found specific outcome in the recommendations of the second Royal Commission into the Australian Post Office in 1974.

The report's most sweeping reform centred on its proposal for the establishment of a board of management, made up of three directors; a general manager as chairman, a postal director and a director of telegraphs and telephones. Such structural rearrangement, it was argued, would ensure that the Minister kept control of matters of policy but that the board, through its chairman, would act as a 'connecting link' between Parliament and the Department, supplying reliable advice on the financial conditions of the service, issuing annual reports, and bringing business–like management and accounting procedures to the running of the Department.[21]

Radical as it seemed, the proposal was not without precedent in the former Colonies. The railway commissions of the last 15 years of the 19th century had provided some successful experiments in corporation management that blended the proven methods of private enterprise with the public ownership and funding of huge and, initially, loss–prone national enterprises. In such models of statutory authorities, Australia led the world.[22] In 1910 the commissioners saw board control of the unwieldy PMG Department as a means of achieving a more streamlined and publicly accountable administration. Behind their proposal lay the evidence of a severe malfunction of a Government department that had notched up a deficit of nearly £3 million in eight and a half years. While no proper accounting existed, the imbalance arose, in the commissioners' view, from a series of reductions in rates — telephone trunk rates in 1901, telegraphs in 1902, general telephone rates in 1907 — which aimed at granting concessions to the public without due consideration of the ultimate cost and its collective financial effect. Bell's advice on 'a fair price for a fair service' had found its mark.

At the same time the commissioners believed that the monopoly position of the PMG's Department had led to 'monopolistic unconcern' that raised vital issues of accountability. A board of management would, they argued, counter such unconcern and ensure that a 'correct relationship' (absent in the past) would exist between revenue and expenditure. Essentially the rump of commissioners who remained to hear the long evidence taken in every State were moved by the view that the PMG's Department came in contact with the life of people more than any other institution in the nation. Its facilities, they found, 'tended to develop the country'.[23] They also recognised that the country's communication system should be treated as 'a complete financial proposition' in which those parts of the service that made a profit should sustain and cross–fertilise those that did not. City people would produce profits that the PMG should spread, using them to provide services to the countryside. States with large populations and large volumes of business should make up losses on services in less populous States. It was an extension of the concept of cross–subsidisation of areas and services (already apparent in Colonial post and telegraph days) to the federated States.

Ten years into the new century it was the postal services that paid. Telegraph and telephone services — operating with largely out–of–date technology — did not recoup departmental outlay. Yet, while these proportions would shift and change widely in later years, the Royal Commission's report focussed a theme that became an important touchstone for recurring debates on the financing, growth and purpose of the massive PMG's Department.

In city, town and country, the lines spread. An example of aerial 'pollution' in Barrack Street, Perth, 1915.

High spirits, linemen at Maryborough, Victoria, 1910.

102

The aerial trunk route
from Melbourne to
Sydney crosses the
Murray River near
Albury.

From their long recommendations it was evident that the Royal
Commission wanted a telecommunications system that was strat-
egically planned, technically up–to–date, watchful for new developments, ready to scrap obsolete systems and instruments on forward-
looking, economic grounds, and capable of developing its own
inventions and some manufacture. The commission had imbibed
much from their technical witnesses, Bell, Hesketh and the State
engineers. They wanted provision for training, greater use of
engineering expertise, 'modern materials', and a system that would
march equitably across the country in close kilter with telecommunication development overseas.

By 1913, 130 of the report's recommendations had been adopted.
Pushed by the energetic Hesketh, technological improvements moved.
By May 1911 a 100–line private automatic exchange was commissioned for internal use in the Sydney GPO and on 6 July 1912 the first
public automatic telephone exchange, the Strowger type, was installed
in the busy market town of Geelong, Victoria, with 800 lines. In the
British Empire, Australia followed Canada and Britain with the
introduction of automatic exchanges. Canada led off with the first
successful installation of Strowger at Whitehouse Yukon in 1901 and a
number of other automatic exchanges (not all of the Strowger type)
followed at regular intervals.[24] Britain opened its first automatic
telephone system at Epsom a mere two months before Australia, in
May 1912. With a second overseas tour behind him in 1912, Hesketh
had been converted to the virtues of the automatic exchange and the
Strowger 'step–by–step' was imported and installed in three inner
Sydney suburban exchanges (Newtown, Balmain and Glebe), in
Brighton, Victoria, and in Perth all in 1914. Attached subscribers could
now ring up another person in their locality at their exchange without
having to give the number to the operator. A calling dial was attached
to the subscriber's telephone. The user put his finger in a slot

The automatic exchange arrives. The installation supervisory staff for the Geelong automatic exchange, 1912. The system they installed was invented by Kansas City undertaker, Almon B. Strowger, who died in 1902.

The installation staff in Geelong's Ryrie Street, under some of their handiwork.

corresponding to the digit required and turned the dial until his finger reached a stop. The dial rotated back to its original position on release and, in the process, sent a series of pulse signals corresponding to the number required along the line to the automatic switch. At the exchange each pulse moved a shaft one step further towards completing the call. The Strowger switching system depended on moving wiper blades connected to the shaft to complete a connection by means of the electro–mechanical step–by–step process. An intermittent buzz signalled if the number was engaged or a series of clicks were heard if the called line was free. (The familiar dial, ring and busy tones in use today were not introduced for many years.) Metering was automatic when the called party answered. The first generation of automative switching machinery had arrived. It would spread in the postwar period to the capitals of other states.

Left: Cable hauling between Perth and Fremantle, Western Australia, 1916.

Good progress had also been made in the recommended use of metallic circuits: 40 per cent of lines in metropolitan areas were of this kind and, as the annual report confirmed, 57 per cent of Australia's total telephone conductors were embedded in cables underground. The trend came none too soon. The visual pollution of aerial telephone lines and crossarms was a feature of capital city streets. Telephone use was largely concentrated in city and major towns; only 2¼ per cent of the population had a telephone by 1911, but the PMG's Department actively encouraged country residents to erect their own lines, when not far distant from an established route, and accepted and paid for the labour involved.[25] Most importantly, an auditing system of 'commercial accounts' was introduced into the Department in 1913. An essential groundplan was hence laid. By August 1915 Robert Anderson, appointed to report on the business management of the

Top: Part of the original Geelong exchange equipment, a 'step-by-step' selector switch. The central arm moved both up and across to select a required number.

Above: The first appearance of the dial in Australia. One of the Automatic Electric Company of Chicago's automatic 'Candlestick' telephones, of a type used at Geelong.

Department, could affirm that 'good work is being done in forecasting requirements for telegraphs and telephones' — a process very different from the *ad hoc*, 'spasmodic financing' arrangements of the previous decade — and that an 'effective scheme' based on the view that the Department, if not its separate branches, should pay its way, was in use.[26]

Personnel had also changed. Sir Robert Scott, a target of some criticism from the Royal Commission, retired in 1911. He had been knighted for his services in 1903 and persuaded to stay on for several years past his retiring age in 1906. Ironically, Scott received high praise for his contribution to the management of the Department in the PMG's first annual report of 1910–11, a record of development and accountability that he had persistently disdained to use. His post went to Oxenham, then assistant secretary, who, as the terrier-like watchdog William Webster complained in Parliament, was a clerical officer who had not served at the instruments used by the operators, nor worked in an engineer's room, nor knew anything about the practical task of inspecting or managing post offices.[27] The problem of enlisting top men for top jobs at a salary of under £1,000 a year, as Bell noted, was a severe handicap in the Department's management.

Yet, aided by the remarkable Hesketh, the 1910 report had large effects. Only one of its major recommendations was ignored: the proposal for a board of management. Despite Webster's clear influence as a member of the commission, his own Labor Party, which took office under Andrew Fisher as the Royal Commission drew to a close, declined to accept this central administrative reform. The board of management proposal was ahead of its time. Though it would resurface in Parliament several times under Joseph Cook's and Fisher's successive Governments from 1913–15,[28] and Webster as Postmaster-General made a bid for its adoption in 1919, the concept of a board of management was set aside. Sixty-two years later the second Royal Commission into the Australian Post Office, appointed by the Whitlam Labor Government, would find an interesting historical blueprint in the recommendations of its precursor, six decades before.

The war of 1914–18 interrupted telecommunications growth. Although Webster himself became Postmaster-General in the Labor Party upheaval that brought W.M. Hughes to the Prime Ministership in October 1915, war quashed hope of major departmental reform. Staff left for the battlefields. Nearly 4,000, including a large number of technical personnel, enlisted from the PMG, many to serve at Gallipoli and in France. At home, untrained temporary staff filled the vacant posts. Construction work ground to a halt, expenditure on both telegraph and telephone fell dramatically in the wartime years, while the depleted staff coped with the challenge of AIF mails. The introduction of duplex and quadruplex apparatus allowed more traffic to be packed on telegraph and telephone channels already set up. It was just as well. In 1914, Australians were sending more telegrams per head of population than almost any other people.[29]

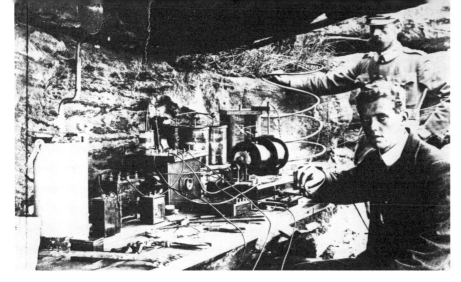

Communications in the
Great War. The first
radio message being
sent from Gallipoli,
1915.

Australian Signallers laying communication lines during the Passchendale
offensive in Belgium, September 1917. The middle man in the trench, Harold
Hinckfuss, would return to spend his career with the PMG In Queensland.

War, however, stimulated technological advance. Within the
Department innovation, normally discouraged by easy access to
equipment imported from abroad, received a timely thrust and work
began in the PMG workshops on the construction of steel and copper
appliances. In every case, one politician reflected, 'they are not only as
good, but in many cases superior, to imported articles'. Australia's
wartime isolation from supplies of imported copper telephone wire
also spurred local manufacturing. By 1918 copper wires were being
fabricated by a consortium of non-ferrous mining interests, Metal
Manufacturers of Port Kembla, New South Wales, for the PMG. From
small beginnings, the company moved on to the production of paper-
insulated lead-covered cable and made its first deliveries to the Department in 1923. The thrust to PMG workshop innovation, however,
was not cemented in the postwar. Despite evidence of PMG capability
to make 'valuable improvements in certain appliances', the postal
department was sending its orders abroad 'as soon as peace was
declared'.[30]

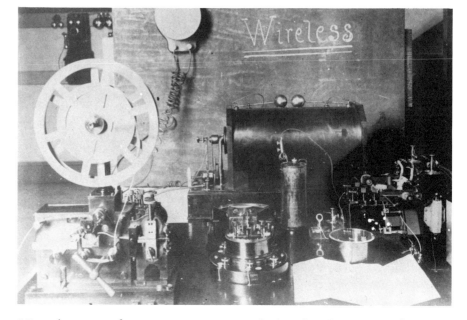

An early Australian experimental wireless set-up.

Most importantly, war was to speed the development of a new technology that would open up a vivid chapter in telecommunications history: wireless telegraphy.

Experiments in the electromagnetic field of wireless telegraphy had been publicly conducted in Australia as early as 1897. Nine years earlier the German physicist, Heinrich Hertz, had shown experimentally that low frequency electromagnetic radiation could be produced in the laboratory and detected at a distance. In 1896 the Italian experimenter, Guglielmo Marconi, gave the first practical demonstration of communication by wireless telegraphy — telegraphing without wires — near Bologna, Italy, and a year later followed this feat of virtuosity by a demonstration of 'ship to shore' wireless. A triumphant Marconi formed the Wireless Telegraph and Signal Company Ltd (later the Marconi Wireless Telegraph Company with its various subsidiaries) in 1897.

Hertz's findings filtered to Australia. There, William Bragg, the youthful Professor of Physics at Adelaide University (who would win the Nobel Laureate for his work on X–ray analysis in 1914), became deeply interested in the energy of electromagnetic waves. Though Bragg's interest was initially theoretical, in September 1897 he gave the first public demonstration of the working of wireless telegraphy in Australia, at Adelaide University, using 'Marconi apparatus' constructed by the university's talented technician and instrument maker, A.L. Rogers. Bragg met Marconi on a visit to England the following year and by May 1899 he and his indefatigable father–in–law, Charles Todd, managed to establish wireless communication on one of Rogers's two–way installations between Adelaide Observatory and Henley Beach. The distance was miniscule (less than five miles) but public enthusiasm was immense. Bragg capitalised on it with three public lectures on the new medium at Adelaide University in September that year in which he explained to a packed audience in the university library that, while light waves were short and could move forward only in a straight line, long waves of wireless telegraph could swing easily round obstacles and signal around or over hills.[31]

Much interest, both public and official, sprang from the prospect offered by the new technology of linking the lighthouse on Althorpe Island (at that time joined by a temperamental cable) to the South Australian mainland. Similar hopes ran high in Western Australia where G.P. Stevens, manager and electrician of the telegraph branch, concluded, after making some rough tests with a six-inch coil as a transmitter and an unexhausted coherer as a receiver made in the departmental workshops, that wireless telegraph could be used to connect Rottnest Island (and the Governor's summer residence) with Perth. Tasmanians, long plagued by unreliable cables, also urged their Government and the Commonwealth to embrace the new technique.[32] These sponsors were precipitate. Wireless telegraphy was in its infancy at the end of the 19th century and had many experimental years ahead.

Even so, Australia's constitutional founders had already grasped the broad implications of the embryonic new technology. *The Commonwealth of Australia Constitution Act* of 1901 was oddly worded. It gave Parliament specific control of postal, telegraphic, telephonic 'and other like services'. The notion of extending Government authority beyond the control of the established 'posts, telegraphs and telephone system' had emerged at the Constitutional Committee's important drafting session of March 1891. Several committee members were interested in science. It was commoner in the 19th century to find lawyers and politicians conversant with advancing scientific theory than it is in the age of scientific specialism today. Committee members Sir Samuel Griffith, John Forrest and Bernhard Wise were all members of the newly formed Australasian Association for the Advancement of Science at whose Melbourne meeting in 1890 the Professor of Physics from Sydney University, Richard Threlfall, gave a gripping address on 'The Present State of Electrical Knowledge'. Threlfall had privately repeated Hertz's exact experiments at Sydney University in 1888. He now outlined the nature and importance of the German scientist's experiments and speculated on a system of electric signalling through space, without wires. His ideas found constitutional form. At a later meeting of the Constitutional Committee in 1897, Threlfall's brother-in-law, Wise, moved that the sub-clause defining Commonwealth authority over 'posts, telegraphs and telephones' be extended to read 'and other like services within and beyond the Commonwealth'. For various reasons, the extra territorial phrase was dropped but the vital 'other like services' remained.[33]

Australian communicators quickly took up the revolutionary new medium. Even before Marconi had flashed the letter 'S' across the Atlantic from Cornwall to Newfoundland in December 1901, experimenters using Marconi-type apparatus — a spark coil, a plain aerial transmitter, a coherer detector and a Morse receiver — were trying their hand at the new wonder. Walter Jenvey, Victoria's chief electrical engineer, set up an experimental wireless station at Bluff Head, near Elwood, and gallantly attempted to welcome the then Duke and

Duchess of York (later King George V and Queen Mary) arriving to open the first Federal Parliament in Melbourne on HMS *Ophir* on 1 May 1901. From his hilly encampment, Jenvey maintained contact with the escort warship HMS *Juno* some two miles out to sea (messages between the escort and the *Ophir* went by semaphore) and thus accomplished the first recorded wireless telegraph communication between ship and shore in Australia.[34]

There were scoffers and critics. 'Marconi', reported the *Sydney Telegraph* on 14 March 1902, 'is still looked upon askance' and even if he did succeed in signalling all round the equator, the newspaper argued, telegraph wires and cables would continue to provide the most efficient communication service. 'Wireless telegraphy', it observed darkly, 'will gossip to the wider world.'

At variance with their early pronouncement that they would take advantage of 'every innovation' for the benefit of the public, neither the Department nor Government were ready to take a plunge on wireless telegraphy or enter into liaison with the eager Marconi. The Commonwealth Government deliberately delayed the introduction of wireless telegraphy in Australia. But Marconi was a persistent suitor. From 1902 his company deluged the Government in Melbourne with offers to establish wireless telegraph connections, the first a service between Australia and New Zealand at a price that lopped about £150,000 off the cost of a proposed new submarine cable. But the Government, pressured by a British post office hostile to Marconi, continued to refuse. It declined again in 1903 when the Marconi Company offered to found a service between Victoria and Tasmania despite the verdict of that experienced Departmental trio, the State electrical engineers, that 'there is no doubt that telegraphical communications can be established by the Marconi system between Victoria and Tasmania'. Nor was the Government susceptible to offers of other wireless telegraphy systems from a cluster of budding companies including Telefunken, Lodge Muirhead, T.E. Clark, Heincke, and De Forest and Shoemaker, that poured into Australia between 1902–5.[35]

One point was clear. The Department wanted absolute control over the new communications system. In October 1905 a short *Wireless Telegraphy Act* ensuring Government monopoly passed through Parliament. The Act reserved the system of 'transmitting and receiving telegraphic or telephonic messages by means of electricity without a continuous metallic connection between transmitter and receiver' to the Commonwealth Government. It also required that all experimental stations engaged in such transmission must be licensed by the PMG's Department.

In 1906 the Marconi Company moved again. Hopeful of convincing the Australian Government of the benefit of wireless telegraphy over long distances, the company erected two transmitting and receiving stations at Queenscliff (Point Lonsdale), Victoria, and at Devonport, Tasmania. From these points on 12 July 1906, the first professional wireless communication by land station in Australia was conducted over a distance of 200 miles. Prime Minister Alfred Deakin

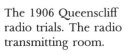

The 1906 Queenscliff
radio trials. The radio
transmitting room.

The condenser room.

presided. 'Wireless telegraphy', he told the assembled dignitaries with some foresight, 'seems likely to transform economic, political and warlike proceedings all over the world.' It was the first time an Australian Prime Minister had launched a major communications technology. The event also signalled some public association between the Government and Marconi though the link was shadowy. While a cairn to mark the spot where the transmission took place, in the reported presence of the Australian Prime Minister and Marconi, was erected at Point Lonsdale, Marconi himself, detained in America, never graced the historic proceedings. The plaque is misleading. In addition, the Government flatly declined to purchase the stations from the company, although £10,000 was placed on the estimates for wireless telegraphy development in September that year.[36]

The Government procrastinated for another three years. It was not until September 1909 that W.H. Kelly moved in the House of Representatives that a chain of wireless telegraphic stations be immediately erected around the Australian coastline for the three-fold purpose of the use of merchant shipping, the gathering of information on the advent of 'hostile forces', and the saving of life and property at sea. The Royal Australian Navy added support. A report by Rear-Admiral Henderson loosened Government thinking. Henderson argued that the establishment and operation of wireless stations for commercial and other purposes, including those on ships, should be retained by the Commonwealth as a monopoly, and should be sufficiently revenue-earning to permit their maintenance in a state of high efficiency.[37] While the Admiral pressed the larger purpose, his real object was an effective naval and military wireless organisation.

Now Government response was positive. £10,000 for wireless telegraphy reappeared on the estimates and tenders were invited in October 1910 for the construction of two high-power wireless land stations, one at Sydney, the other near Fremantle, to command the seaward approaches on both sides of the continent. The contract went to a newly formed syndicate of Sydney businessmen, trading as Australasian Wireless Ltd, with equipment and engineering supplied by Marconi's rival, Germany's Telefunken. Not surprisingly, Marconi brought action for patent invasion and the problem was resolved by the merger of Australasian Wireless, the Marconi Company and Telefunken to form Amalgamated Wireless (Australasia) Ltd (AWA) in 1911. The Marconi Company held half the shares while the other partners split the remainder until Telefunken lost its shares at the outbreak of war in 1914.

As war loomed, wireless stations rose rapidly around Australia's coastline. Their development quickened with the appointment to the PMG's Department of John Balsillie, distinguished engineer in radio-telegraphy. A Queenslander, Balsillie had gone to England to study electrical engineering in 1903. He devised a magnetic detector, joined a company erecting wireless telegraph stations in England and later in Russia, and, with inventive skills and qualifications in great demand, he worked in Germany, Siberia and China before returning to England to form the British Radiotelegraph Company where he marketed his own 'Balsillie system' of wireless telegraphy. Australia's Prime

Minister, Andrew Fisher, met Balsillie in London in 1911 and promptly snapped him up for the communications Department at home.[38] By May 1914, 19 wireless stations dotted the Australian and New Guinea coast using some Telefunken but largely Balsillie's own system of wireless communication. Erected by contract but operated by the PMG, stations were situated at or near Port Moresby, Thursday Island, Cooktown, Townsville, Rockhampton, Brisbane, Sydney, Gabo Island, Melbourne, Hobart, Mt Gambier (SA), Adelaide, Esperance, Perth, Geraldton, Broome, Roebourne, Wyndham and Darwin. In 1916 the Department also acquired the experimental working wireless station at King Island, Bass Strait, from an unusual vendor, the Roman Catholic priest, telegraphist and wireless equipment manufacturer, Father Shaw.

The wireless stations provided a unique and vital link between shore and shipping, carrying overseas telegraph traffic on to warships, convoys and merchant vessels and providing important communication between Australia and its islands off–shore. They also contributed to the chain of radio telegraph stations that linked Australia via Ceylon and South Africa to the European theatres of war. Their value in protecting Australia and its troop ships was demonstrated in the early months of war. On 9 November 1914 a lone German raider, the *Emden*, was sighted off Cocos Island, the small coral atoll south of the equator where a cable and a Marconi Company wireless telegraph station joined Australia with Ceylon. Since the outbreak of war in August, the *Emden* had already sunk 15 ships, bombarded Madras and Penang, and was preparing for a surprise attack on the communication centre at Cocos Island. The same day a convoy of 38 ships was steaming in the area from Albany to Colombo carrying troops and supplies under escort of four warships. Alerted by a wireless message from Cocos that a 'strange ship' was in sight, the Australian cruiser *Sydney* detached herself to investigate and sank the lethal *Emden* before noon.[39]

It was a triumph for the Navy and the new communications service of wireless telegraphy. Yet it highlighted a growing rivalry between the department of the Navy and the PMG. When a PMG wireless operator innocently transmitted an uncoded message on the movement of Australian troops, the Navy department sought the transfer of wireless telegraphy to its control. Prime Minister Hughes consented; Balsillie left the service, and the PMG's wireless branch (then numbering 120 members) was handed over to the Navy in 1915. Postmaster–General Webster neither grieved for its departure nor welcomed later proposals for its return. The service was costly. It lost £16,000 in 1916 and Webster informed Parliament that 'he would be loath to resume control of such an unprofitable service'.[40]

Yet technological developments would outpace political prejudice. By the war's end, dramatic new prospects for wireless telegraphy and telephony were emerging overseas. The thermionic or vacuum valve but especially the amplifying applications of de Forest's vacuum tube triode were transforming the transmitting range and receiving capacity of the medium. A new era of science–based telecommunications had arrived.

A lineman at work in Tasmania. There the rugged terrain demanded unusual solutions.

On the Eucla route, a different type of terrain produced a choice of transport for this Western Australian lineman.

Across the first two decades of the 20th century the wide–flung workers of the PMG developed their own sense of commitment and fraternity. The spirit of brothers in one service grew. Styles and needs varied in different States. Innovation and ingenuity took many forms. Despite some mismanagement, the Department was a huge public service where people of talent could find a place. Qualifications could be acquired by learning along the way. The Postal Institute, established during the war, was conceived to provide 'in–house' courses, libraries, and infuse a sense of corporate purpose and identity. As it grew and spread, it also became a focus for much social enjoyment in the PMG. Away from the centres, the frontier activities of linemen and telegraphists went on in every State. The men who chose the outback stations belonged to a breed of robust pioneering stock. Their lives were often spare and lonely: their accommodation makeshift. They lived 'on the job'. Upkeep and long trips for maintenance filled their days. Many of the lines strung took small account of landscape, marching up hills, across swamps and lakes in search of good timber and the shortest route. Maintenance was often difficult. Some of the remoter staff lived on Aboriginal land and their attitudes often reflected the harsh outlook of the times. East-west line telegraph operators on the Nullarbor won the doubtful distinction of becoming the first men to find (and scratch their names and initials on the walls

of) decorated Aboriginal caves. Wives who ventured into the lonely outposts were brave and stoical women. One story is told of a wife in Queensland's Gulf country who gave room on her verandah for a period to a large box containing the disinterred bones of a former telegraph officer. He had died from malaria, was buried, and after a suitable interval, disinterred for transport and reburial in Brisbane. The consignment was shipped as 'a case of returned Telegraph material'.[41]

At headquarters and in the States, engineering and technical knowledge formed an increasingly important part of the Department's affairs. British engineer J.M. Crawford ('JMC' as he was widely known), successively superintending engineer in Victoria and New South Wales, particularly encouraged the recruitment and training of mechanics and engineers and promoted the work of their Postal Institutes. The brilliant Hesketh died in July 1917 at the age of 49 and his place as chief engineer was taken by Frederick Golding who had been transferred from Sydney to act during Hesketh's final illness, in December 1916. Golding had worked his way up since joining New South Wales' Colonial telegraph service in 1880. As chief electrical engineer, he was watchful of innovative development overseas and, in 1921, conducted an official visit to Britain and Europe to inspect the new apparatus of high frequency telecommunication. But Golding fell foul of the secretary of the Department, Justinian Oxenham. A tiff between Golding and the British Customs over some dutiable items he brought in from France, gave Oxenham his chance and the chief engineer was brought before a board of inquiry in Melbourne on a series of allegations of 'misconduct' laid by Oxenham in October 1922.[42]

While the Melbourne press battled with technical questions of terminals, electron tubes, rotary line switches, duplex and multiplex technology for more than a week, the real thrust of the public hearing turned on a personal vendetta on the part of Oxenham against his key engineering chief. Golding's technical ability was not in doubt. His preference for multiplex over duplex high frequency apparatus to clear congestion on the busy Melbourne to Sydney trunk route proved the point, as did his active preference for rotary subscribers line switches over earlier imported 'plunger' forms. The inquiry itself conceded as much. Golding's arrangement to procure these, it pronounced with fine administrative logic, 'turned out to be a good one, but it was against the principle of the department'.[43] Clearly to Oxenham and his lieutenant, the chief inspector of the Department E. Woodrow, a member of the inquiry team, Golding was a thorn in their flesh. The inquiry's verdict of misconduct stuck. It was a case, said Golding's defending QC, where secretary Oxenham was in the remarkable position of being 'the accuser, the selector of the tribunal to hear the charge, and the adviser of himself as permanent head as to the nature and extent of the punishment'. Golding, said his counsel, had been 'treated like a dog'. He was demoted to 'B' class engineer after the trial and retired on his 60th birthday in June 1923. Neither the inquiry, Golding's name, nor his departure is mentioned in the annual reports of 1922 or 1923. He became a 'non–person' in Departmental affairs. His story, however, is untangled from the spacious cover given the inquiry by the Melbourne press.[44]

The case, critical for Golding, was also crucial for the PMG. It focussed a deep malaise in the administrative management of the Department that prompted Prime Ministerial intervention. During 1918 the Hughes Government's terrier–like Postmaster–General, William Webster, had frankly admitted that he had only 'with great difficulty been able to keep the Service off the rocks — it is still in the breakers'. Four years later it was Hughes who would find a passage through the shoals. Late in 1922, faced with demands across the country for telegraph and telephone services in the wake of war, and with the resolution of the 1921 Royal Commission into Public Expenditure of the Commonwealth of Australia that 'some hundreds of thousands of pounds could be saved annually in the Post Office' resounding in their ears, his Government grasped at that age–old panacea of administrative ailment, a general review, and turned for help to Britain.

6 The Long Reign of 'Pooh-Bah' Brown

In January 1923 Harry Percy Brown, a small rotund Englishman, stepped ashore from a liner at Port Melbourne with his wife and four children. Assistant staff engineer of the British post office, a prominent member of the British Institution of Electrical Engineers, highly experienced in telephone and telegraph traffic in the British service, H.P. Brown had accepted the role of expert adviser to the Australian Government on loan from the British post office to investigate and assist in the reform of the Postmaster–General's Department. The son of a former superintendent of the London telegraph office, Brown had held responsibility for the technical planning and management of all telegraph and telephone plant in England. In 1913, he was adviser in India to the East India Railway Company on telegraph, telephone and railway traffic control and, three years later, headed the emergency communications of Britain's wartime home defence. From wide experience and his natural powers, Brown was held by his colleagues to be 'the most capable man' in Britain.[1]

Sir Harry Percy Brown, outstanding leader of the PMG from 1923 to 1939.

Prime Minister Hughes had met H.P. Brown at the Imperial Conference of 1921 and in October the following year, as the PMG's administrative troubles flapped blatantly in public view, himself negotiated Brown's appointment as adviser to the Australian Government. Yet, when Brown arrived in Australia three months later, Government had changed hands. Hughes was out; the first Nationalist–Country Party (Bruce–Page) coalition was in, and Australia's first Country Party Postmaster–General, W.G. Gibson, became chairman of the three–man postal advisory committee inherited from the Hughes Government to draw up a programme for the extension and reform of postal and telecommunication services. Brown, second member of the committee, was 44. He came on temporary loan for a year, accepted the offer of permanent head of the Department in December 1923, and remained for the rest of his life.[2]

It was Gibson, a Victorian farmer who had the distinction of being the first Country Party member elected to the Federal Parliament, who was so impressed by Brown's abilities that he manoeuvred the early retirement of Justinian Oxenham and secured his adviser's appointment to the secretaryship of the PMG at a salary that soared far above that of any other public servant.[3] Public outcry was loud. Was there no Australian equal to the task? Were none invited to apply? The answer was No. From a debut of press and parliamentary outrage, Brown 'the human whirlwind' was here to stay. Dynamic, rosy, with a bald pate usually kept from public view by a jaunty trilby hat, Brown would become one of Australia's public service 'giants'. For the first time, there was an engineer at the top. The idea charmed one professional engineering journal which suggested that Mr Brown was appointed less because he was an acknowledged telephone and telegraph expert than 'because he was an engineer'. He was thus a 'trained thinker preferable to anyone who had not been taught to think'.

During 16 years as permanent head (he was named Director-General of Posts and Telegraphs after persistent struggle in 1927), 'Horse-Power Brown', as the press quickly dubbed him, was to make a significant impact on the PMG's Department in areas that ranged across telephony and telegraphy, wireless and broadcasting, training and research, and in the hitherto non-existent field of public relations.

Brown's first task was to reshape the central administration and to build it — as the British post office stood — on a base of sound engineering management. Hitherto, as one senior administrator re-called, 'the engineer and other men with direct technical responsibilities were looked upon as "necessary evils" subservient to the reign of clerks.' Brown changed this 'clerkly' system. With determined speed, he restructured the Department's organisation so that eight senior men reported directly to him covering the whole gamut of operations: engineering, telephone traffic, telegraphs, postal services, accounts, personnel, wireless and stores. 'For the first time in its history', wrote S.F. Kellock, former Deputy Postmaster-General in New South Wales, 'the Department had a logical working organisation'.[4]

Brown's capacity for streamlining and delegating delighted the technical staff. Before his arrival every directive or memorandum bore the Secretary's name. Brown required branch heads to sign their own directives and to take responsibility for policy action within their sphere. Morale rose. Quiet, consistently courteous to his subordinates, averse to profanities (he was heard to say 'Damn' the day he died), the new Secretary acted with a directness and persistence that had not been seen in the Department before. In the broader field of policy making there was also change. It was now the permanent head who (in some contrast to his predecessors) gave strong policy guidance to his politicians. Brown and Gibson worked in close accord.

Technically Brown was to leave a singular impress on his Department. With the wartime development of the thermionic valve and the use of voice frequency repeaters, a new era of scientific telecommunications and voice transmission had arrived. Brown, with his own special knowledge and experience, saw the telephone — that

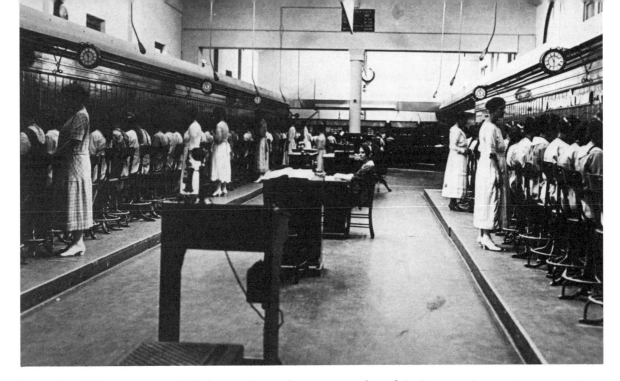

branch of the service which 'came in such a personal and intimate contact with the community' — as the paramount field of postwar attention. He gave it his driving attack. In 1924–5, faced with formidable demands for new telephone connections hanging from the aftermath of war, he set in train a major reorganisation of the telephone branch, dividing its activities into 'traffic' and 'commercial', and further breaking down these two areas of social and business service into sections with clearly defined responsibilities. A similar decentralisation was extended to the States. Country telephone 'districts' were formed and management responsibilities more widely diffused. With improved man management behind him, Brown pushed for that hitherto elusive requirement, the standardisation of telephone and exchange equipment throughout the Commonwealth. He also required that telephone lines and other materials be purchased on a bulk basis to meet standard demands across the country. Having federalised the system, Brown introduced the procedure of letting contracts outside the Department for the erection of telephone lines to meet widely existing demand. In 1924–5 alone, six million miles of telephone wires were erected by contractors.[5]

His policy paid dividends. For the seven years to 1926, Brown later reported, the mileage of wire used on local telephone exchange systems (a measure of urban, suburban and rural development) had jumped by 103 per cent and, for trunk line communication, by 137 per cent. In addition, automatic telephony, delayed by war and postwar financial strains, received a significant forward shift. 'Step-by-step' automatic exchanges, eliminating the manual operator and making it possible for the telephone system to deal automatically with large numbers of subscribers, were installed in suburban areas, and a major automatic city exchange opened in South Brisbane in 1925. By June that year, there were 22 automatic exchanges in Australia. The first rural automatic exchange was opened in 1927. For the first time, with

'Personal contact with the community' — a major city exchange, Adelaide, South Australia, in the 1920s.

119

An example of some
step-by-step switching
equipment.

An early variety of
Rural Automatic
Exchange (RAX), at
Thornton, Victoria, and
its modern equivalent,
with microwave
connection, at Wye
River, Victoria.

the backlog behind it, and encouraging new trunk telephone rates charged on 'crow fly' distance between caller and correspondent introduced in 1924, the Department could begin to canvass for telephone orders. 'Today', Brown noted with justifiable pride in August 1927, 'it is believed that the rate of growth of the Commonwealth telephone service is almost the highest of all telephone administrations.'[6]

Australia, with 6.9 telephones to every hundred of its population, ranked seventh in telephone density per population in the world. Technologically and financially, telephone construction and upgrading had lifted the Department to a new status. In the four years ending 30 June 1926 Brown announced, 'the expenditure on the creation of new assets had exceeded that incurred during the previous twenty–one years'.

Brown was the instigator of a number of strategic planning decisions which would modernise Australia's telecommunications system. The systematic extension of automatic telephone exchanges was such a one. Automatic technology would form the growing, and financially profitable, basis of the network. The development of long–line, inter–State trunk services was another strategic plan designed both to stimulate and service national business and social needs. Brown's personal experience and knowledge would transform the rudimentary trunk services that had been launched between Melbourne and Sydney in 1907. In a new era of telephony, as Golding had foreshadowed, it was now practicable to carry several channels of high quality voice communication on one pair of wires by employing differing electrical frequencies, a system known as 'carrier wave'. When Brown learnt soon after taking office that Golding's plans for technological development were not being pursued and that two copper wires were to be put up between Melbourne and Sydney and between Melbourne and Adelaide, he quickly intervened. In January 1924, with J.M. Crawford, whom Brown himself appointed chief electrical engineer, he marched across sections of both routes and counselled his team of central office engineers to return all materials and start planning afresh. Over a year later, in September 1925, carrier systems were launched when three channels of greatly improved trunk line telephone communication were opened between Melbourne and Sydney. Similar carrier services rapidly extended from Sydney to Brisbane, Melbourne to Adelaide, and directly from Sydney to Adelaide in 1926.[7]

Telegraph technology also benefited from the introduction of 'carrier wave'. The first telegraph carrier system was opened between Sydney and Melbourne in 1927 and the system spread. Telephone plant was also used to its fullest capacity to carry telegraph traffic by dictating telegrams across the lines. The telegraph service needed all the help it could get. Overtaken by competition from its sister service, the telephone, the telegraph began to show substantial losses from 1925. Brown tackled the problem across several fronts. During 1925 a teletype system of printing telegrams was successfully tested on the Melbourne to Bendigo line and sets of new apparatus ordered for other circuits. He also assaulted the matter on the human side. 'Office drag', he told members of the Victorian Postal Institute in 1927, 'is a term which does not appear to be very well known here . . . I want every telegraphist to talk of "office drag" first thing in the morning, and get rid of it. "Office drag" is the delay which is occasioned in the collecting, circulating, and despatching section of telegraph administration, and the most expert telegraphic treatment of messages may have its value nullified completely if this is permitted to assume an undue magnitude.'[8]

Engineering solutions of telegraphic problems were also joined to carrier wave. By 1927 the Murray Multiplex system of telegraphy was introduced on long distances to replace the outmoded Wheatstone–Creed system of Morse telegraphy. The new system permitted the use

The Melbourne-Sydney telephone carrier system, 1925. More than doubling capacity, it allowed for five telephone channels instead of the previous two between both capitals. The carrier system's terminal being installed in central exchange, Lonsdale Street, Melbourne.

The marvel of the age. Officials listening to four conversations being carried on between Melbourne and Sydney. Speakers were attached to each channel, and stenographers took notes of the conversation. From left to right — W.G. Gibson (Postmaster-General), H.P. Brown (Secretary), J.M. Crawford (chief electrical engineer), R.N. Partington (state engineer, Victoria), S.H. Witt (engineer, research), J.S. Jammer (Western Electric Company) and C.E. Bright (deputy Postmaster-General, Victoria).

The telephone carrier system's Wangaratta (Victoria) repeater, which amplified the signals on their way north and south.

of up to eight channels or circuits over the one line by a system of electro–mechanical multiplexing. The Murray Multiplex not only radically reduced the length of tape used for message transmission, it concentrated the task of sending and receiving messages in the hands of one instead of two operators and thus signalled the beginnings of a decline in numbers for the once elite profession of telegraphists.[9] A further service, the picturegram, or wire photo, was introduced between Melbourne and Sydney in September 1929, a facility made available to other capitals in later years.

Much of the importance of Brown's administration lay in the organisational reforms and technological developments he implemented in his first seven years. In new specialist divisions and sections,

A forerunner of the picturegram. AWA's experimental apparatus of 1929 for the reception of pictures by wireless has the face of Ernest Fisk emerging from the machine.

This was the first 'commercial' picture received by the Beam Wireless Picturegram Service from England. It was published in Australian morning papers on 17 October 1934, and depicts C.J. Melrose beside his plane at Mildenhall aerodrome, England, preparing for the start of the Centenary Air Race.

Brown laid foundations upon which others in the service, several future Directors–General among them (McVey, Chippindall, O'Grady), could later build. Essentially he encouraged an engineering culture and secured the growth of a technological institution that would find explicit expression in Telecom Australia in 1975. Brown's was the ground plan.

Early in his advisory role to Government, Brown had urged the wisdom of founding a PMG research laboratory to keep Australia abreast of telecommunications developments abroad. The idea took root. A one man research section was established in the headquarters building at Treasury Place, Melbourne, in June 1923 and grew to a five–man unit with the status of 'Research Laboratories' in 1925. Its charter was to 'keep in touch with the latest discoveries, inventions and developments in electrical communication', to undertake experimental work, formulate standards for telephone transmission, and to gear research discoveries to the work of departmental engineers. The 'one man' founder was S.H. Witt. A slim, spry man, Witt had a creative and ranging grasp of telecommunications science. He had propelled himself upward in the service from junior instrument fitter in 1910 to assistant engineer using the Department's internal training courses. Witt accompanied chief engineer Golding on his overseas study tour in 1921 which led to Witt's participation in the planning for an Australian trunk network and his selection for the research post. From 1924 he worked to Brown in the important introduction of voice frequency repeaters in spreading trunk telephone links and in integrating the trunk carrier wave system. By 1926, when Australia's first major body for government scientific research, the CSIR (Council of Scientific and Industrial Research), was launched, Sid Witt's small Research Laboratories (which he led for 22 years) was shaping to become the nucleus of advanced telecommunication studies in Australia.[10]

Little has been written in Australia about the 'style' of the country's foremost public servants or the ingredients of leadership and purpose that shaped their work. As one political scientist has noted, our lack of knowledge cramps our understanding of public administration and of the character of our policy making.[11] Brown's style was that of a first–class engineer who brought skills of planning, resource management, research and public relations to the task in hand. Analytical, inventive, attentive to detail, and warmly aware of the diverse army of employees working under his command, Brown combined the capacity of the forward–planning technologist with a strong and simply–expressed sense of institutional goals. 'He never made a complicated statement', one staff member recalled. The mixture inspired the enthusiasm of subordinates and created a new image of the PMG.

Brown's mind resembled a grinding sieve, drawing in points of view, assimilating local conditions, and churning out a flow of initiatives and developments. The breeze stirred not only at Melbourne headquarters but in the labyrinthine offices of the States. Brown himself went quickly about his kingdom, listening to State problems, encouraging direct links between parallel State and central office branches, and finding time when travelling to dart into country post offices, emerging an hour or so later with long lists of needs which a surprised postmaster had brought to mind. Mrs Brown on country holidays became a familiar, if resigned, figure, sitting in a waiting car while her husband established personal contact with the country managers of his domain. Not only had a new era of engineering leadership arrived, an era of concerned personnel management had begun.

From the moment he set foot in Melbourne, Brown exercised a powerful attraction for the press. Modest and conservative in speech and dress, but with a faultless eye for the human dimensions of his Department's work, he caught their cynical imagination. He was always accessible. Reporters called on him 'morning and afternoon'. He stored their writings in voluminous press cutting books. 'These visits and articles', Brown recalled later, 'were of the greatest possible value to me for I was kept informed of weaknesses in the Department's services and could immediately take steps to put things right.'[12] PMG branches throughout the country were instructed to send cuttings to Brown with suggestions on how to improve the services. Journalists nicknamed him alternatively 'Pooh-Bah' (after the Lord High Everything Else in *The Mikado*) or 'Horse-Power' Brown (after his initials) as his reforms poured in, and praised him as 'almost indecently efficient'. Mr Brown, wrote *Punch* in December 1925, 'has managed to have his name bandied about on the tongues of thousands of postal officials ... What has produced this miracle of devotion in a department that has never developed Mahomet's knee in the practice of salaams?' The answer came rousingly back. It was not entirely the personality of the man, 'but rather his way of getting things done, of producing striking results with a minimum of friction and delay. To look at him [said *Punch*], mild-eyed and gentle, wrapped in courtesy ... one could never suspect his playing the part of strychnine to the drowsy heart of the feeble service. But the lion is lying down in the lamb which careless people think is H.P. Brown.'[13]

From a reproduction of a cartoon in *Punch*: H.P. Brown, 'almost indecently efficient'.

For all his lamb-like qualities, Brown had a very shrewd eye for public relations. He was a pioneering propagandist and publicist for the PMG. During 1927 he authorised the production of leaflets and posters for display in post offices and public places which urged the populace to 'Say it by Telephone' and, with a modernity that has hardly been surpassed in 50 years, cajoled the public, 'When travelling keep in touch with your home and business: use telephone trunk line services'. Not all the coverage he personally attracted was unleavened praise. Sydney's *Smith's Weekly* deplored the well-paid Brown. His salary (£4,000 in 1928) excited their rage. They found his energy across the broad field of telecommunications a 'fearful interference' and when Brown, dissatisfied with the antiquated methods of human mail-sorting at the Sydney mail exchange, turned to home-grown talent, the PMG engineer A.B. Corbett, to build a mechanised letter-sorter — the first of its kind in the postal world — they lambasted him and his 'monstrous' creation in headlines that informed, 'Pooh-Bah Brown starts confetti industry at Sydney GPO'.[14] Yet in praise or prejudice,

With the spread of automatic telephony and the trunk network, press advertisements like these became common in the late 1920s and early 1930s publicising automatic telephony. Publicity shots extol the convenience of the portable bedside telephone.

Brown was the media's man. Lunching with leaders of commerce and industry, giving public addresses, or merely publicly exhorting the telephone girls to 'smile in their larynx' so that the caller could hear it, his public charisma glowed.

One of the most pressing problems of Brown's growing technological enterprise was the need for a highly trained staff. New developments in long line telephony, the very extension of the complex system of automatic telephony across the continent, and the growing sophistication of telegraphy depended on the skill and training of mechanics and engineers. Wireless communication and broadcasting would add significantly to this demand.

Colonial progress in stretching communication networks outwards had rested predominantly in Australia on the precept of 'rule of thumb'. Ingenuity and the backslogging determination of linemen and fitters had wired the great continent while telegraphists and telephonists mastered operational skills. But while there were 'schools of telegraphy' in all the Colonial Departments of Posts and Telegraphs for 'respectable lads of good education' to become telegraphists, and rather more summary classes for the 'golden-voiced' girls who would connect telephone conversations across the land, there was limited opportunity for the training of mechanics or engineers. Sutton, the versatile inventor at Ballarat, ran classes in the early 1880s in electricity and magnetism at his local School of Mines. Mechanics Institutes across the country also provided access for the working classes to emerging scientific knowledge and expertise. In Colonial capitals and major industry townships, the Institutes offered occasional lectures and growing libraries in technical subjects to those who cared to pursue learning on their own. But the few 'mechanicians', as they were called, employed by telegraph departments in the 19th century were seldom more than self-trained.

The problem of training in engineering was just as acute. The Australian universities were dismally slow in providing academic training for electrical engineers. Tuition in general engineering existed from the mid-1860s at Melbourne University where W.C. Kernot, MA, gained the first certificate in engineering in 1866. Kernot, in turn, taught civil engineering, became first Professor of Engineering at Melbourne in 1883, and later took part in a Victorian inquiry on the undergrounding of telephone wires. But he offered no instruction in electrical engineering fields. His counterpart at Sydney University, Professor W.H. Warren, appointed in 1884, founded an engineering school where he built courses on American rather than British lines and established three major teaching streams which included electrical engineering by 1910. But professional training with telecommunication components was not available either at Melbourne and Sydney, or at the engineering schools that rose on the campuses in the early years of the new century at the universities of Adelaide, Queensland and Western Australia.[15]

The Royal Commission into the Post Office of 1910 exposed an urgent need for training in all the Department's technical fields. Hesketh was obviously eager to build up a competent engineering branch. As one outcome of his efforts, PMG engineers were upgraded managerially in each State after 1906. But trained engineers remained scarce on the ground. The chief engineers of Victoria and New South Wales, Walter Jenvey and J.Y. Nelson, were local men without university training though their competence supplemented Hesketh's in his sustained attempts to upgrade the Commonwealth network. The first trainee engineers, three in number, joined the service in 1906. One was R.V. McKay who, qualifying seven years later, was rapidly appointed divisional engineer at the age of 21. But Departmental attempts to encourage in-house training among technical members of their engineering branch met poor response. A plan with added financial inducements to staff to undertake approved correspondence courses in telegraph and telephone engineering 'at any recognised institution', announced in 1911, foundered within three years. Hesketh, reporting in 1912, stressed that the supply of engineering staff had been 'insufficient' for the past six years, 'and there appears to be no sign of relief'. It proved, in fact, impossible to recruit qualified engineering candidates for the telecommunications enterprise in Australia. Local advertisements for the post of assistant electrical engineer in 1912 drew no response and Crawford was brought from England to fill the post. Over the next three years, four more British post office engineers were enlisted, R.L. Lawson and R.N. Partington in 1914 and S. Gleed and J. Kilpatrick in 1915, all of whom rose to high positions in the service.[16] It was one of several tugs on the Imperial apron–string, a recurring if intermittent appeal for engineering reinforcement, that continued into the early 1970s.[17]

The development of training for mechanics also proved uphill work. In 1912 classes were started in each State, and the rapid intake of over 400 mechanics and some 700 junior mechanics from outside the Department, with several hundred from within, testified to a gaping need. Nevertheless the thrust towards co-ordinated training for the mechanics came most usefully through the Postal Institute introduced within the Department in 1915–16. It was the Institute, with branches emerging in each State, that organised wartime classes in electrical telephone and telegraph technology and engineering drawing and opened a route whereby technical staff could proceed by in–house training and experience through the grades of fitter mechanic and, if sufficiently motivated, up the training ladder to engineer. The technology itself provided an attractive lure. 'Little groups formed to help each other,' recalled one participant, 'people got deeply interested in the technology and this prompted individuals to learn more.' Self–help became a distinctive training concept within the PMG.[18]

Brown's advent and Crawford's initiatives added to the motivation of PMG engineers. Both men put their stamp on a scheme for cadet training which encouraged talented young officers to acquire a science degree by part-time study or assisted leave and to gain the necessary 'topping off' in telecommunications on the job. Several engineers with a Director's baton in their pocket and many key engineers who guided the Department's growth in headquarters and the States got their training by such a route. Cadet training, indeed, formed the basis of professional engineering in the PMG service. At the outset it was less than formal. It depended, said G.N. Smith who rose to head the Victorian PMG, 'almost entirely on the inquisitiveness of the cadet and the willingness of certain of the engineering staff to assist'. Nonetheless the daily routine was full of contrast. 'A cadet would leave the manhole, trench, workshop, wash himself, travel to the university for lectures then return to the workplace', wrote Smith, 'for further diverse chores.'[19] It was not until the mid–1950s that Australian universities generally offered degrees in electrical engineering that suited the PMG's professional need. This failure on the part of the universities illustrated what became a marked compass error in university education in Australia. While the prestigious engineering schools of Europe and America were turning out electrical engineers in considerable numbers by the last quarter of the 19th century in order to provide the manpower of an electrical age, Australian tertiary education set its course against practical technological training in favour of an emphasis on pure and non–applied fields. The rapid conversion of the technically oriented University of Technology, founded in 1946, into a more 'establishment' University of New South Wales was an evident symptom of this.

From the outset of Brown's directorship, wireless communication was moving to the centre of the stage. Several years before his arrival some significant commitments had been made. Stretched across the far mid–southern sector of the world's atlas, the continent of Australia received its first direct wireless transmission from England in September 1918. Given the experimental state of the art, it was something of a miracle that a series of Morse letters could be despatched from the Marconi Company's station at Caernarvon, Wales, and be distinctly heard and recorded in Sydney using an 80–foot aerial erected at Wahroonga by AWA's enterprising young managing director, E.F. Fisk. From that moment, the long, angular figure of Fisk became the impresario of wireless advance.

In August 1919 Fisk conducted the first public demonstration of

A facsimile of the first direct wireless messages sent from England to Australia, 1918, bearing news from Australia's Prime Minister, W.M. Hughes, and his Minister for the Navy, Joseph Cook. The messages sent from the Marconi station at Caernarvon, Wales, and received by AWA at Wahroonga, New South Wales.

wireless telephony on AWA equipment at the Royal Society of New South Wales and, having established an intimate friendship with the Prime Minister, Billy Hughes, secured the 'Little Digger's' backing for his long–distance wireless communication plans. Hughes, in Britain for the Peace Conference in 1918, was actually present at Caernarvon with the Minister for the Navy (and one–time Postmaster–General) Joseph Cook, when the first coherent wireless telegraphy message was sent. Fascinated and fired by the magical potential that wireless communication held, he urged the British Government that a direct commercial wireless service should be established between the two countries without delay. At the Imperial Conference of 1921, Hughes went further and resolutely resisted the scheme (presented by Sir Henry Norman's Wireless Committee) that Australia should form the end–link in a chain of low power wireless relay stations scattered at intervals through India, Singapore to Darwin which would leave Australia as the butt end of message interruptions and delays.[20]

Hughes's stand had far-reaching consequences for Australia and

The AWA central radio office, Melbourne, in the early 1920s. The service, known as 'the world's trusted messenger' employed operators, using Morse transmitting and receiving equipment, who decoded and typed up messages from perforated tapes. 'Beam boys' then delivered them around the city.

The beam traffic was to become extremely popular and grew rapidly. The central radio office, Melbourne, a few years later with improved equipment, new destination boards and female operators.

the pace–setting company AWA. Against a backdrop of protracted parliamentary debate, the recommendations of a Parliamentary Committee appointed to examine the matter in 1921-2, and the dissenting opinion of one of the committee members, Labor MP, F. Brennan, on both the feasibility of long-range wireless communication and the morality of a joint Government–commercial undertaking in this field, Prime Minister Hughes pushed through an Act authorising a partnership between the Commonwealth Government and Amalgamated Wireless Australasia Ltd. While the venture had some precedent in Australia in other fields, it was as Fisk rightly pointed out, 'unique in its details in the world of wireless'.[21]

The agreement was signed in March 1922. Under it, the Commonwealth Government acquired control of 500,001 of AWA's one million £1 shares (giving the company's capital a healthy boost), while AWA undertook to establish high–power and feeder stations in Australia for direct wireless telegraph communication to Britain and Canada providing a 24–hour wireless service to England at a charge a third less than that of existing cable rates. AWA also took over from the PMG's Department (returned to them from the Navy in October 1920) its 29 coastal wireless stations including those in Papua and New Guinea. They were to remain under AWA control until 1946. To aid the marriage and alleviate the strains of 'settling–in', Hughes shifted the remaining control of wireless communication from the PMG's Department to his own Prime Minister's Department for a period from June 1922 to March 1923. The agreement also called for a representative board. Seven directors were to be appointed, three by the Government, three by the company, with an independent seventh director chosen to hold the balance. When press and political uproar exploded at the choice of AWA's former chairman of directors, Sir Thomas Hughes, as the seventh balancing wheel, Billy Hughes, with comic logic, took the vacant place himself. He remained a director of the Commonwealth–AWA board for the rest of his life.[22]

The very existence of the agreement posed large questions of mixed Government and commercial undertakings that were hardly ventilated in 1921–2. Brennan's dissenting opinion in committee came closest to the point. 'The requirement for safety of lives at sea, the defence of the Commonwealth, and the convenience of persons in remote parts of the country', he summed up, 'should not be subordinated to the speculations of capitalists.' He saw the agreement as 'subsidising a gamble' on long–distance radio telegraphy and, worse, as likely to turn the Government into 'a cog in the wheel of a very large trust indeed'.[23]

But Fisk, whose mind teemed with a succession of far–reaching scientific ideas (all his children bore the names of famous scientists), saw the arrangement in rather different terms. AWA, which held the patent rights to the principal wireless systems of the world and had a well developed organisation for the manufacture of apparatus and the development of commercial wireless services, 'had joined hands with Government and has now become a national undertaking'. The arrangement, he stated in 1923, had 'effectively solved' the two main problems confronting other countries in wireless advance: the need for a form of effective Government control and the capacity of commercial enterprise to offer a service that could keenly compete with the older cable and telegraph services.[24]

Fisk was himself already imaginatively involved in extending experimental wireless connections. From his first demonstration of wireless telephony in Sydney in 1919, he sought (like many of his wireless peers abroad) to develop wireless, or radio as the Americans were calling it, as 'a pleasure instrument'. In October 1920, with the backing again of Prime Minister Hughes, he transmitted a concert by wireless telephony from a Melbourne suburb to the Queens Hall, Parliament House, rousing the drowsing Federal politicians with 'Rule

Britannia' and 'Advance Australia Fair'. He built on this feat with the claim that the time was rapidly approaching when country people would be able to receive news, music and even political speeches by means of their own small-scale wireless apparatus. Hughes, appropriately, became the first Australian Prime Minister to make a political broadcast when a speech he made at Bendigo in 1922 was transmitted to an outside audience. With the novelty of opening up Australia to a wireless programme service using AWA's own manufactured wireless sets (the British Broadcasting Corporation had begun broadcasting in 1922), Fisk in November that year sought the PMG's Department's permission to expand AWA's embryonic broadcasting to every State.

Ernest Fisk, AWA's managing director, testing early wireless receivers at his Wahroonga, Sydney, home.

A series of intricate steps now marked Australia's evolving wireless and broadcasting policy. With Hughes's Government out of office, in May 1923 the Coalition Government's Postmaster-General called a conference in Melbourne of Government and industrial interests to discuss the future of broadcasting. Brown, then advising Government, was an influential figure in the wings. Sir Earle Page's account of the meeting sums up unfolding events. 'Despite some misgivings ex-

The Victorian Police were the first in the world to use mobile wireless communications, in May 1923, Morse messages being relayed to the patrol car from the Domain wireless station, Melbourne. At first fitted with receivers only, two-way communication was later developed by F.G. Canning. Here, the first police wireless operator, W.R. Hutchinson, sits on the running board of the police Lancia beside his AWA Marconi receiver. Canning is seated in the back, and F.W. Downie, 'father' of the wireless patrol, is standing to the right.

pressed by Brown, [he wrote in his autobiography] the Conference adopted a scheme for the "single wave system" submitted by Ernest Fisk. Under this, broadcasting stations would be permitted to forward programs on definite wave lengths to persons holding "sealed sets". Sets were to be sealed (or locked on one wave length) to ensure reception from one station only. It was considered that this system would give full opportunities to the broadcasting industry and, at the same time, avert the danger of detrimental monopolistic interests being established.'[25] Page omitted to say that the PMG's Department would collect a 10s licence fee in addition to the subscriber's contribution to the station of his choice. The 'sealed set' regulations were issued by Government in July 1923 and broadcasting began officially in Australia on 23 November 1923, when the first licensed station, Sydney Broadcasters (2SB, later changed to 2BL), broadcast a concert on equipment designed and manufactured by AWA. Twelve days later, a second Sydney station, 2FC, came on the air. Stations 3AR Melbourne and 6WF Perth began regular broadcast services the following January and June.

But the system was not a success. Audiences wanted wider than one station fare. In a nation of tinkerers, simple crystal and valve sets with their trailing leads, honeycomb coils, condensers, headphones and mysterious switches rapidly appeared in stores and graced the mantelpieces of many adventurous households. Listeners found they could boycott the 'sealed set' scheme. In some cases, the return on the licence fee (an amount that ranged widely in the different States and stations between 10s and £4 4s a year) sowed doubts. Wool prices, readings from Dickens, poetry, stock exchange reports, weather and music formed the substance of the daily programme. But there were

An Australian family
tunes into the news and
entertainment bought
to their home by
AWA's Radiola wireless
set, 1926.

also unnerving pauses between segments. 'To fill in loose time', wrote
one observer, 'listeners were regaled with the solemn ticking of the
metronome.' The countdown proved symbolic. 'The public have
shown us in no mistaken manner', declared one interested set of
broadcast investors, that 'they should be allowed to "listen–in" to any
service.'[26]

The outcome was a revised set of regulations issued under the
Wireless Telegraphy Act in July 1924. These jettisoned the unpopular
'sealed sets' and replaced them with the 'dual system' of 'A' (national)
and 'B' (licensed commercial) class stations. The genesis of this idea
came from Brown, and has remained the basis for Australian wireless
and television broadcasting. 'One of the first of the Department's
tasks', Brown himself summed up the innovation, 'was to devise a
comprehensive plan for the allocation and utilisation of channels so
that as many stations as practicable, both National and Licensed ("B
class"), could operate satisfactorily within the International medium–
wave band. This band lies between the limits ... in approximate
terminology of wavelengths [of] 200 metres to 545 metres. This plan is
based on fundamental studies of radio propagation phenomena, the
topographical features of the Commonwealth, its distribution of

population and social and commercial communities of interest.' Brown saw the basic plan as a 'scaffolding within the meshes of which some flexibility exists to allow for the adjustment of specific allocations to meet special or local circumstances'.[27]

Under the new scheme it now became legal for any person holding a receiving licence to operate any type of receiving equipment for an annual fee of 35s. The revenue collected from the Post Office from licence fees was apportioned among the companies permitted to operate in each State. The regulation limited the number of revenue-earning stations on a population basis to two each in New South Wales and Victoria, and one in each of the other States, with the provision that stations could be called on to establish relay stations to serve country areas. In addition, licences were to be granted to other companies desiring to operate 'B' class broadcasting stations, which would not receive revenue from listeners' fees, but would be permitted to broadcast advertisements without restriction.

The Mulgaphone, an early radio receiver manufactured in 1924 by Westralian Farmers, and used to receive the first broadcasts in the Augusta (Port Leeuwin) area, WA.

While the former sealed set stations such as 2FC, 2BL, 3AR, 3LO, 5CL, 4QG, 6WF and 7ZL became the 'A' class stations in the respective States, the first 'B' class licence was issued by the PMG to G.V. Stephenson whose station 2EU (later changed to 2UE for greater euphony) began transmission from his Sydney home late in 1924. Other commercial stations soon filled the air. Flappers danced to the broadcast syncopated jazz rhythms of the 1920s, and 'I heard it on the wireless' became a common by-word of daily city and suburban exchange. Country people would wait longer for the entertaining electronic toy. It was the urban housewife, of whom the Australian poet, Judith Wright, could write:

> And as the evening meal is served
> we hear the turned-down radio
> begin to tell the evening news . . .
> Of murder, famine, pious wars . . . [28]

The PMG's Department's part in the spread of broadcasting and in the diffusion of an instantly companionable, entertaining and informal medium was both administrative and technical. From 1925 the

Research Laboratories staff were involved in the transmission of radio broadcast programmes over the trunk network and in field strength measurements associated with short-wave transmission for radio frequencies. During 1925 they engineered the first simultaneous inter-state broadcast — a network hook-up of six stations across which the Commonwealth Treasurer promoted a Commonwealth wartime Conversion Loan. Between 1925-7 the Laboratories equipped themselves to conduct radio frequency measurements on the medium frequency broadcast transmitters. On 9 May 1927 PMG staff would help to carry out the grandest yet national radio transmission when Parliament House was opened in Canberra.

The transfer of the Commonwealth Government from Melbourne to Canberra, after 26 years of Federal Government, already involved the PMG's Department in a massive expansion of capital equipment. Staff members themselves heaved a sigh of relief that their own headquarters did not share in the great upheaval and remained in

Melbourne. But additional trunk lines from Canberra to Sydney and Melbourne had to be installed and subscriber equipment introduced for the new Departmental buildings and houses mushrooming around the centre of the bush capital. In addition, telegraphic facilities were required for the 'gentlemen of the press' to despatch their stories from the press gallery and, for the big event, a public address system, primed to cater for his halting speech, was needed to transmit the Duke of York's (later King George VI) ceremonial opening speech to the public outside Parliament House. Since no national broadcasting then existed, Postmaster-General Gibson offered to provide stations in the eastern States with a land-line transmission of the Canberra proceedings without charge. While wireless and amplification systems played their part, 14 telegraphists were on hand to send 170,000 words over the wires to tell Australians and the world that a new democratic forum existed in Canberra.[29]

The long row of telegraphists busy transmitting the news of the opening of Parliament House, Canberra, 1927, and the cascade of telegraph tape they engendered in just a few hectic hours.

Engineering management fell to Crawford, chief engineer. But the last word went to Brown. It was, he told an exhausted but happy staff at the ceremony's end, 'by far the heaviest day's work in the whole of Australia'.

Australia's swift participation in domestic wireless technology marked it as a country ready to exploit advancing communication techniques and to use them to enhance life in that land of 'magnificent distances'. But H.P. Brown, in his first year as secretary in 1924, already had severe misgivings about the Government's 'share' agreement with AWA. Wireless communication under the 1922 Agreement had run at a net loss of £62,736 between 1922-4. Writing to the secretary of the Prime Minister's Department in July 1924, Brown, firm but tactful, asked in effect, 'Should Government be responsible for such a loss?' If it continued at its present rate, he estimated that, even without interest and depreciation, the loss could escalate to over £300,000. In such circumstances, Brown questioned, was Government responsible for keeping AWA afloat?[30]

Brown's concern at AWA's financial performance found echoes of a different, but disturbing, kind among a bevy of would-be broadcasters in Australia. AWA's monopoly in royalty payments over all wireless broadcasting functions in the country was a source of friction and dissatisfaction both to broadcasting stations and manufacturers alike. From 'A' class stations alone, AWA took some 20 per cent of their total revenue in licence fees. When in December 1926, therefore, the Bruce–Page Government announced the appointment of a Royal Commission into Wireless under the chairmanship of J.H. Hammond KC, a flood of critical evidence poured in.

The commission's findings proved a stepping stone towards a policy of closer national control of broadcasting. Shored up by evidence, the committee condemned the royalty charges levelled by AWA on broadcasting companies and radio dealers as 'detrimental to the development of wireless services within the Commonwealth' and required that these be significantly reduced. It also recommended the appointment of an Australian Wireless Committee to advise the Minister and that the relationship between the Postmaster–General's Department and Amalgamated Wireless Australasia Ltd be 'more specifically defined'.[31]

By mid-1928 the concept of a national broadcasting service had taken root. The problem of country services alone touched sensitive nerves in the Nationalist–Country Party coalition. As the Country Party's leader, Earle Page, noted 'there were no "A" class stations located in the areas where people had most need of a service to help remove the feeling of isolation'. While the Royal Commission itself saw no pressing need for a national broadcasting service, the Government perceived its role as owning and operating the 'A' class broadcasting stations while contracting out the programming. In July 1928 Prime Minister Stanley Bruce appointed an advisory committee on broadcasting to give expert advice to the Government. Its chairman was H.P. Brown and its membership included the radio researcher Professor Madsen and former Royal Commissioner Hammond.

Brown, absent overseas for part of that year, nonetheless infused the committee with his views. Essentially, the advisory committee's recommendations would culminate in the foundation of the Australian Broadcasting Commission in 1932. In a period of transition, the committee recommended that control of all broadcasting activities should be vested in the Postmaster-General and that the PMG's Department should be technically responsible for the installation, operation and maintenance of the complete service of a national system. 'A' class stations were to be purchased on the expiry of their licences between July 1929 and December 1930 and serviced by the Department. To preserve the 'dual system', 'B' class stations would continue to be operated by private enterprise. By December 1930 all 'A' class wireless licences had expired for purchase. A three-year contract for programmes went by tender to the Sydney entrepreneurs, Australian Broadcasting Company, in May 1929. Most importantly, the Australian Broadcasting Commission (ABC) was founded by Act of Parliament as a national broadcasting commission responsible to a Minister on 1 July 1932.[32]

From its pragmatic, political and technical beginnings, the national broadcasting system in Australia took form. Broadcasting was already flourishing when the Australian Broadcasting Commission assumed its functions in July 1932. The national network then consisted of eight main and four regional stations (4RK Rockhampton, 2NC Newcastle, 2CO Corowa and 5CK Crystal Brook, SA); the financial crisis of 1929 delayed funds for a fifth station in Western Australia, and there were also 48 commercial stations. By February 1932 the 350,000 licensed listeners in Australia represented a national broadcasting audience of possibly three-quarters of a million. The efficiency of the national network derived from the PMG Research Laboratories planning and engineering skills. Telephone trunk circuits were adopted for inter-connecting broadcast stations to provide simultaneous transmissions: the regional stations were linked by land lines with capital city programme centres and, as Brown characterised it in 1932, 'provision has been made for the simultaneous grouping of any of the stations covering a partial or comprehensive broadcasting chain throughout the Commonwealth stretching between the extremes of Rockhampton in Queensland, and Perth in Western Australia, a distance of 3,805 miles'.[33]

Brown's own part in the shaping of the national broadcasting structure had been pivotal. Working closely with Gibson and later with the successive Postmasters-General of Scullin's Labor Government, J.A. Lyons and A.E. Green, he had steered decisions on a Government-backed broadcasting system and integrated the technical functions of his Department with the evolution of the ABC. It was Brown's drafting that defined the relationship between the statutory body and his Department in the enabling Act by which the PMG remained responsible for the technical side of national broadcasting, a link he prized. Brown also cared keenly that the high technical efficiency of national broadcasting be steadfastly maintained. 'It is vital', he wrote to Departmental personnel working for the national broadcasting service on the eve of the new ABC programme service, 'that nothing should be left undone to make it an outstanding success under the new conditions'. Despite financial tightening, the PMG's technical achievements in simultaneous broadcasts had been, Brown affirmed, of 'outstanding merit'. Yet the vital question was 'what we propose to do in the future. There is only one reply', the dynamic Secretary answered himself. 'Whatever the job may be, it will be done even better than before, and it will be done in a manner to be unexcelled. Put all your enthusiasm into the job', he exhorted radio staff, 'enhance the prestige of the Department, and maintain the best traditions of our great public service.' It was impossible not to respond![34]

Beyond the Department, however, Brown met some antagonism. Though he served as an active intermediary between his Minister and industry interests in the arrangements for 'B' class stations, he was generally held to be a 'thorn in the flesh of laissez–faire'. With Fisk, he was increasingly at odds. Yet his certainty of purpose for the social future of broadcasting was never in doubt. 'The influence which this scientific achievement will have on the world', he summed up in 1932 in one of those statements which, while profoundly true were often quickly overtaken by other technological advance, 'will probably do more to alter the relationships, the outlook of knowledge, the culture and the tastes of the world than any other inventions which history has to record.'[35]

On the overseas front, a 'beam wireless' telegraph service had finally been established between England and Australia in 1927. From a technical breakthrough pioneered by Marconi's leading engineer C.S. Franklin in 1923, short–wave wireless communication replaced the projected long–wave connection and established an important new communication infrastructure. Fisk received the first experimental signals in the 90–metre band in February 1924 but it was not until 8 April 1927 that the direct Australia–England wireless telegraph service began the use of the 'HF beamed transmission' technique which Franklin developed.

Although then in the midst of world–wide poverty and struggle, technological progress pushed on and, in 1930, Australia's overseas telephone system with England came into action using beam wireless. This, the PMG annual report explained, was 'a complete trunk line . . . made available by development of an ingenious assembly of apparatus known as the radio link telephone terminal equipment'. Politicians and the people were more impressed by the end rather than the means. Speaking to his counterpart James Scullin in Canberra at the inauguration of the UK–Australia service on 30 April 1930, Britain's Labour Prime Minister, J.R. Macdonald exclaimed: 'What an age, my dear Mr Scullin, we are living in. What would our grandfathers have thought of it!' AWA's part and particularly that of Fisk was notable here, conducted within the Government–Company Agreement of 1922. Fisk had engineered three world radio broadcasts from Australia in 1927 and from 1928 had conducted demonstrations of radio telephony from Sydney with New York and London. Bruce as Prime Minister had talked for ten minutes to the Secretary of State for Dominion Affairs, Lord Passfield, from AWA's Sydney boardroom in a stunningly clear run–in of the service in August 1926. With the official ceremonies completed in Canberra eight months later, AWA made a

The AWA radio centre, Pennant Hills, NSW, in the 1920s. Used for broadcasting and trans-oceanic telephony, it was via this station that the first Australian overseas telephone call, between Canberra and London, was made in 1930.

The novel overseas link brought its own peculiar problems. A cartoon from the Melbourne *Herald* of 16 May 1930.

radio telephone connection between Australia and New Zealand within a few days. Connections with Europe, relayed via the Australian–UK circuit and British post office facilities, followed in a matter of months.[36]

Such overseas telephone calls were confined to high politics, or high drama. £6 for up to 3 minutes was beyond the means of the man in the street. Anglo–American journalist, Alistair Cooke, recalls the tension and prestige conveyed to the man in London in the mid–1930s by the words, 'There is a telephone call from New York'. 'Long before the transatlantic cable, when the radio circuits had to go to exotic places like Tangier', he writes, 'telephone calls between London and the United States were placed only by the Rockefellers, Presidents of the United States, and export–import millionaires.'[37] When the habit of telephony overseas became more common, the imagined sound of the great distances and the shock of the spoken word, reduced many communicators to tears.

In the midst of these technical advances, the 'Depression without parallel', as Scullin described it, halted all aspects of Australia's growth. After years of expansion, the PMG's Department services and man-power froze. In the first year of Depression in 1929 postal services showed a profit, but telegraph and telephones ran at a loss.[38] For the first time telephone cancellations now exceeded telephone connections. Indeed, so widespread was the people's plight that local telephone calls fell by nearly 23 million and trunk calls by five million between 1931 and the end of 1932. Staff suffered great internal change. The number of permanent PMG staff declined — over a thousand were not replaced between 1929–31. Others were regressed though Brown publicly assured his workers that no dismissals would

141

take place unless rendered 'absolutely necessary', a promise he managed to keep. Internal accommodations, however, went on. Engineers in training interrupted their professional tuition and moved to clerical work. All technical training ceased until 1937 and junior mechanics, grateful to have a job, were transferred about the country to postal delivery and other clerical jobs. In all States, some were sent out onto the road as salesmen pushing the sale of telephones. The procedure proved surprisingly successful. From 1932–4, orders for over 30,000 new telephones were obtained in this way, while new clients were further wooed with postcards to advise friends and clients of their new connection.

Throughout the Depression Brown worked persistently to keep departmental and national morale high. Telegram drives, wide press cover, the introduction of cheerful Christmas and New Year greeting telegrams, plus a spate of slogans for telegram and telephone use, were useful springboards in 1929. In the critical year of 1931 Brown rose to the Government's pledge to employ members of the unemployed for special Government undertakings for a period of a month and absorbed large numbers of workers on buildings and the construction of telegraph and telephone lines. At Prime Minister Scullin's bidding, Brown also became the leader of a national campaign to ginger up public morale. His response was to cancel stamps at post offices throughout the country with slogans which read bracingly, 'More Work', 'Give Employment — Assist National Recovery', 'Australian Products Are Excellent', 'Use More Wool', and started a tradition of national postal mottos in Australia.

In spite of the Depression, the establishment of the first telephone connection between Adelaide and Perth brought remote Western Australians into voice contact with the other States. That giant of a

---

142
Clear Across Australia

WA's Premier, Sir James Mitchell, making the first telephone call across the Nullarbor, from Perth to Melbourne, 18 December 1930. From the *West Australian* of 19 December 1930

Advertising the new service, 1931. It was not a cheap service. A transcontinental call then cost the equivlent of about $36 today for a three-minute call at day rates.

Western Australian Transcontinental TELEPHONE SERVICE

Now Available between FREMANTLE and the EASTERN STATES

TARIFF	Day Rate 9 a.m. to 6 p.m. 3 Minutes		Intermediate Rate 7 a.m. to 9 a.m. and 6 p.m. to 9 p.m. 3 Minutes		Night Rate 9 p.m. to 7 a.m. 3 Minutes	
	S.	D.	S.	D.	S.	D.
ADELAIDE - -	12	0	9	0	6	0
MELBOURNE -	14	0	10	6	7	0
SYDNEY - - -	17	0	12	9	8	6
BRISBANE - -	18	0	13	6	9	0

Full information obtainable G.P.O. Perth, P.O. Fremantle, or by Telephone to B 071 or B 072

G.P.O. PERTH, W.A. 2nd January, 1931.

S. R. ROBERTS, Deputy Director Posts & Telegraphs

territory, Western Australia, again lagged behind the rest of Australia in intercontinental telecommunications through the sheer cost and circumstance of geographical distance. In 1930 Western Australians were reportedly the largest users (except for New Zealand) of telegrams in the world. By the late 1920s these messages still flashed along the old Eucla–Adelaide line. A copper telegraph line had been erected on the Transcontinental Railway between Port Augusta and Kalgoorlie in 1917 but was used exclusively for internal railway needs. From 1927, the PMG moved to upgrade telegraph facilities by joining the railway route. The Eucla repeater station and the coastal route for interstate telegraph traffic was accordingly closed that year. In 1929, as the Depression grew, a Parliamentary Standing Committee examined the proposal to install a telephone link along the railway route. While they reported that there was no great demand among the Adelaide commercial community for a telephone link with Perth and that 'no large amount of business connection could be expected in that quarter', Perth businessmen, with parent companies in the eastern States, pressed vigorously for the join.[39] With approval to go ahead, a voice frequency telephone channel and a carrier telegraph system were installed on one pair of wires by the PMG between Perth and Adelaide in 1930. A carrier channel for radio broadcasting was added to the same two wires in 1933. The first telephone conversation between Perth and Adelaide, over one of the longest land–line telephone circuits in the world, took place between the Premier of Western Australia, Sir James Mitchell, and Postmaster–General Lyons in Melbourne on 18 December 1930.

The telephone voice of Australia could now be heard across the broad girth of the continent. Its boost to business was immense. Five years later, pressed by a deprived community, Tasmania joined this

The cable laying ship *Faraday*. Launched in 1923, it was lost to enemy action in March 1941.

Part of the original submarine cable carrier equipment at Apollo Bay, Victoria, 1935. Updated and extended many times, but finally replaced by a microwave link, the equipment and submarine cable were to remain in service until 20 March 1980.

important national telecommunication axis. In November 1935, SS *Faraday* spooled out the submarine cable from Apollo Bay, Victoria, across Bass Strait via King Island to Stanley, Tasmania. The cable traversed 160 nautical miles with capacity to carry six telephone, 12 telegraph and one broadcasting channel. Made and contracted for by Siemens Bros of Woolwich, London, it was the longest and the most modern cable of its kind in the world. Business opened in March 1936 and the following month the old 'heliograph capital' of Australia, tiny Rottnest Island off Fremantle, WA, was similarly joined by the *Faraday*'s effort, by a 12-mile cable bringing telephonic contact with the mainland and the rest of the world. PMG engineers had put a girdle round their earth.[40]

Brown would preside over the strong recovery of his Department from the Depression. From 1933-8 the net profit of the PMG's Department was a striking £18 million. Many developments contributed to this dynamic lift. The first overseas airmail service, begun officially between England and Australia in 1934, was such a one. Brown put

himself strongly behind the development of aviation in Australia. He sent personal letters on the first flights arranged by Australian National Airways to London in 1931, keeping the BBC's governing director, John Reith, informed of the decidedly different developments planned for the ABC, and pressing Government that 'all first class mail should travel by airmail wherever possible in Australia' to assist the struggling field of aviation. Brown saw the facilities that his own Department and civil aviation might provide as two of the most important develop-ments in a country beleaguered by scattered population and distances. His progress was slow, but he personally supported Charles Kingsford–Smith whose epic flight from America to Brisbane in 1928 depended substantially on the carriage of mail. When flying the first airmail from New Zealand to Australia, Kingsford–Smith ran into problems with a propeller. He got a message through direct to Brown asking permission to dump the mail. Brown's reply was characteristic. 'Dump the mail, but get back.' The broken propeller, which Kingsford–Smith presented to Brown on his return, hung as a memento in Brown's office for many years.[41]

Telephone connections and calls also picked up dramatically from 1934. By that year one in every 13 people in Australia had a telephone, an average much higher than Great Britain where the idea of personal telephones for all classes of the populace was slow to take root. By 1934–5 the ground lost as a result of the Depression was wholly made up in the telephone field. In 1933 the handset phone was introduced giving particular encouragement to local manufacturing industry through a contract to AWA to supply the instruments. Hitherto, sub-

Another of H.P. Brown's developments, the inaugural airmail to London leaving Melbourne, 24 April 1931.

145

Australia's standard bakelite table telephone of 1933. The bellset beneath the telephone could be removed and placed elsewhere to give it an even slimmer appearance.

scriber handsets were imported traditionally from Britain and the parts assembled by AWA. But AWA had entered the local manufacturing field in the 1920s with the steady production of broadcasting receivers and transmitters for the national and commercial networks. In 1933 it set up a subsidiary company to manufacture electron receiving and transmitting tubes. By late 1934 it began producing the bakelite parts for telephone bodies and handsets. The entry in the 1930s of Australian subsidiaries of the British electronic companies, Standard Telephone Company (STC) and Philips, contributed, with AWA, to the growth of a self–sufficient radio industry that proved important at the outbreak of war.

By the mid–1930s, Director–General Brown had achieved a striking metamorphosis in his Department that had no counterpart in other Government fields. The annual turnover of the Department exceeded £147 million: its capital investment in fixed assets and plant was £54.5 million per year: it was one of the largest business undertakings in Australia and continued to be one of the greatest employers of labour. Moreover, as Brown understood, there were few in the country who did not depend in some way on its multifarious services. Their very range and size demanded flexibility that called for modification and adaption of methods and the updating of systems and machinery to replace old equipment with new.

There was movement across the whole field of Australian tele-communications in the 1930s. Rural automatic exchanges (RAXs), the small unit–type exchanges that handled a minimum of 50 subscribers already in the two major eastern States by 1927, were introduced in Western Australia, South Australia, Tasmania and Queensland in 1935.[42] The number of private branch exchanges, manual and automatic (PBXs and PABXs), acquired by business and Government departments also spread, providing alternate and attractive employment for telephonists who would find themselves increasingly displaced as automatic exchanges took over their manual work. Through strategic planning, trunk line inter–city services expanded rapidly as the 1930s closed building a capacity that stimulated the growth of a national telephone market. Meanwhile, country services grew on the back of the 'party-line', those natural carriers of shared experience and gossip and on lines self–installed by remote individual subscribers. The presence of the telephone, particularly in the bush, transcended the senses of isolation, fear and loneliness. Human contacts grew. Love and affection could speed along the lines. Countless proposals were made by telephone. The prolonged, repetitious 'goodbye' became a feature of women's telephone conversations from the start. While some British and American writers of the 1930s repined the 'blissful quietude' of pre-telephone days, such themes found no expression in Australian literature. Rather, a little known poem of Henry Lawson's, while clearly no literary treat, offered a paean of praise to the party line of bush telephony on the isolated coastal border of Victoria and New South Wales.

> O the folk are never lonely that the telephone can reach!
> There are three undreamed of places with a telephone at each . . .
> She was lonely, she was frightened, she'd been very ill indeed,
> And the haunting fear was on her that the bush at night can breed,
> She was nearing her confinement and had thought that she would die,
> And the terror grew upon her when she could get no reply,
> There's a telephone to Kiah, Green Cape, and the Gabo Light,
> But down here in Mallacoota, one hears rings at dead of night;
> 'Tis an angel responding to the kindest deeds and best,
> Ringing Eden, ringing Gabo — ringing Mallacoota West.[43]

There were still remote areas that the telephone did not reach. Here the telegraph remained the life–line, the distance–stretching sentinel that conferred both material and psychological benefits upon bush families. Many outback people owed their lives to the telegraph. In the days before the inland wireless system, it was not uncommon for a city doctor to give instructions for an operation or medical treatment over the telegraph wires. A famous operation took place at a remote northerly–westerly repeater station in Western Australia in 1917 when a stockman sustained serious internal injuries after falling from his horse, 300 miles from the nearest doctor or nurse. Friends took him to Fred Tuckett, postmaster and telegraphist at Halls Creek. Tuckett, with St John's Ambulance training behind him, made contact with a Perth doctor and gave him a description of the condition of the injured man. The doctor diagnosed a rupture of the urethra, blocking the bladder passage. Only an operation could save the man. But there were neither instruments nor anaesthetics at Halls Creek. With morphia, permanganate of potash, a razor, a pocket knife and considerable strength of mind, Tuckett followed the meticulous instructions telegraphed down the line by Morse code. The stockman survived for thirteen days but died of pneumonia.

This epic event and the continuing hazards of accident and birth stimulated the launching of the Flying Doctor Service at Cloncurry in north-west Queensland in 1929. Founded by the Rev. J. Flynn and the Australian Inland Mission to serve Australia's most isolated residents and, in Flynn's words, 'to make the dumb inland speak', the service was designed to throw a mantle of safety over the outback. Outpost stations spread quickly in Northern Queensland, South Australia and Western Australia on call sign 8AC allocated by the PMG. The pedal wireless, devised at Flynn's request by Adelaide engineer and wireless experimenter A. Traeger, and using bicycle parts and footpower to drive a generator, was its linchpin. Initially the pedal wireless sent telegrams by Morse transmitter. In 1932 Traeger introduced a keyboard which, adapted from a standard typewriter and using a spring-operated drum and perforated strip to produce the Morse characters automatically as the corresponding letter pressed on the keyboard, obviated the need for remote settlers to learn Morse code. By 1935 the system had changed to the simpler use of wireless telephony in many outback and mission stations. Using such devices, isolated settlers could communicate their needs and receive information and help from base and outpost stations. Diagnosis was made instantly over the network, treatment prescribed, and the Flying Doctor rapidly airborne in cases of serious care. The first School of the Air was also based at Alice Springs in June 1951. Neither the Flying Doctor Service nor the kindred Bush Church Air Society Flying Medical Service were PMG services but they were subject to PMG supervision through the issue of licences for base and outpost stations and for approval of transmitter power and equipment.[44]

The PMG's own mantle of communication, however, fell widely across the continent as the 1930s advanced. Multi-channel systems were imposed on many lines and, through technical improvement, 'howling, frying, and excessive side tone', as one advertisement advised, was eliminated in transmission on telephone lines. The connections, the slogging installation of circuits and cables, the extension and improvement of radio and telephone communication, and the ingenuity required in linking different communications networks sparked a special ingenuity among the planners and operators of the PMG. In a country of sportsmen, where cricket was a passion as well as national spectator sport, it was significant that, as early as 1932,

Alfred Traeger using an early Morse example of his 'bicycle wireless' transmitter.

Traeger's pedal wireless was to transform the lives of women in the outback. Here, Mrs Irene Fuller of Newry Station, NT, uses it to contact the Flying Doctor Service base at Wyndham, WA, 1938.

The Revd Skipper Partridge, on patrol for the Flying Doctor Service, operates a pedal wireless in outback South Australia, ca 1930.

listeners across the country could follow live on radio the 'ball to ball' battle for the Ashes. Sometimes the achievement was an inventive mix of telegraph and early broadcasting skills. When the English cricket team toured Australia in 1932, broadcasters were able to reproduce, with accompanying sound effects, the movements of play by reading 'hit by hit' descriptions of the game which were transmitted by skilled telegraphists stationed at the cricket ground and linked up by land lines to the national broadcasting stations in all capitals. When the Australian cricket team in turn toured England in 1934, this feat of virtuosity was enlarged by messages received at frequent intervals by cable, transmitted by Morse around the Australian capitals, and telephoned to broadcasting station announcers. The exercise involved an astonishing two minutes time lag between the action in England and its detailed broadcast by the ABC.[45]

Throughout the decade, Brown lent a drive to the spread of services that, as he predicted, would shape the behaviour, commercial enterprise and habits of the nation. No other Director–General would equal his 16 years tenure of service or his influence on the Department under his charge. The ingredients of his leadership were themselves distinct. Organised, enthusiastic, a tactician who saw the distant end–point of the decision in hand, he pursued a functional mode of thought that consistently linked Australia with telecommunication progress abroad. His critics saw him as a 'centralist'. Much of his achievement, however, lay in a rare combination of humanist and engineer. His concept of his Department drew instant recruits. 'There is not one soul in this great Department', he said, 'who need feel that he or she is denied the opportunity of labouring in the best cause which is known to humanity . . . service to our fellows. The Post Office is a great civilising agency . . . We need only to realise what our service means to the life of the nation, and the rest will follow.'[46]

One further component of his long–term achievement was Brown's rapport with politicians of all parties. He served nine Ministers during his regime, from W.G. Gibson (who transcended the quip that he had inherited a 'political grave') through J.A. Lyons, A.E. Green, J.A. Fenton, R.A. Parkhill, Senator A.J. McLachlan, the ebullient A.G. Cameron, and E. Harrison in 1939. Brown reputedly left the fruits of his experience in a cluster of notes on 'How to behave in the political arena' to his successors. One Minister who long predated Brown, A. Chapman, Postmaster–General from 1905–7, also had good reason to recall him. During Brown's first year in office in 1924, Chapman, who had a reputation for the use of colourful language, telephoned Brown at his home one night to complain with some vividness that he had had a most unsatisfactory conversation with a Sydney subscriber over No. 399–400 (telephone lines were, and still are given a number). Brown interrupted the caller's explosive flow. 'Unless you are prepared to speak civilly, Mr Chapman', he advised, 'I will stop this conversation now. Secondly, I can tell you that you will not be able to have a good conversation with Sydney for at least two years.'[47]

Ironically, it was E. Harrison, Postmaster–General in Robert Menzies first Government of April 1939, who would bring Sir Harry Brown's distinguished regime to an end. Awarded a CMG in 1934, Brown had been knighted for his services to Government under Lyons's administration in 1938. During 1938–9, he had sat on the defence communications committee completing arrangements for the wartime control of Australian communications. With his First World War experience in Britain and a Department in solid working order, Brown, at 59, might reasonably have expected to remain at its head for the challenging years of the Second World War. He was, instead, ousted from his role. On 20 September 1939, with war announced, Brown visited the Minister in Sydney to discuss aspects of the control of commercial broadcasting. An intimation from Harrison revealed plans to divest the PMG's Department of some technical broadcasting powers and to transfer some authority to Sir Ernest Fisk. When Brown made clear his strong opposition, the atmosphere, as one PMG official reported, 'became electric'. The Minister threatened to sack his Department head. Back in Melbourne next day, Brown wrote out his letter of resignation. With leave due, he indicated that he would terminate his duties in a matter of two weeks. His official retirement is dated 31 December 1939.[48]

Harrison and Menzies had dislodged their premier public servant. Though Sir Harry Brown would go on to hold important posts in wartime organisation and later commerce, this act at a time of national crisis remains a stain on Menzies's early administrative record. Brown himself agonised over the problem. 'I found it very hard to make up my mind on the step which I have now taken', he wrote to an old colleague, 'principally because of the consciousness that I would sever a connection with so many colleagues in the Post Office and in the Commonwealth Service as a whole. I doubt whether any man has been more fortunate and blessed with the goodwill of his colleagues to the extent I have, and it is due to these personal relationships that I have had so happy a life and have been credited with so much others have done.'[49]

His farewell was characteristically modest. Yet in 16 years Brown had lifted the Postmaster–General's Department and established it as a major technological authority. Inevitably he bears the title of the 'father' of the Department. 'I think I can say with justification', his letter of resignation summed up, 'that the affairs of the Department are in a satisfactory condition and that there are no outstanding matters of importance or unsolved problems.'

Main telephone and telegraph routes, 1939–45

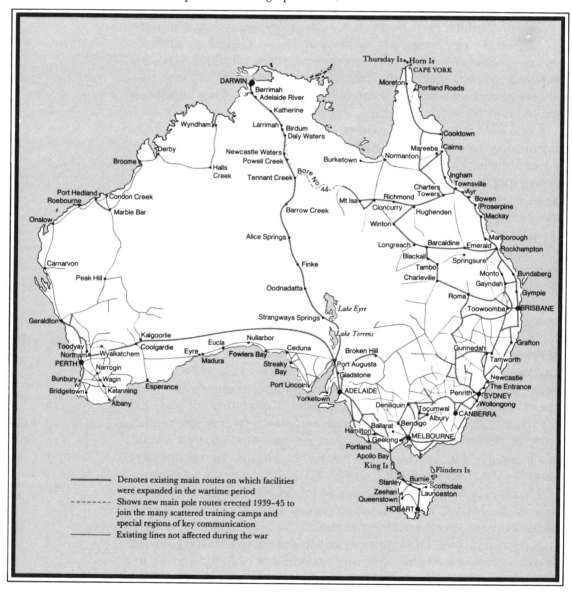

7 The Telecommunications War

From Troy to Vietnam, communications lay at the heart of warfare. The First World War of 1914–8, that agony of trench warfare which held men down for years in mud, barbed wire, and scarred miles of battlefields in Europe and on treacherous Gallipoli Peninsula, has sometimes been called the 'Telephone War'. Both sides laid vast networks of cable for their own communication and to tap the enemy's messages. Field telephone cable carried commanders' orders to their embattled troops. The Second World War has alternatively been labelled the 'Radio War'.[1] But the description is inadequate. Radar and telephony in all its forms and the wide use of that most covert of mediums, the telegraph, made it essentially the 'Tele-communications War'.

Isolated from the northern theatres of battle, yet sending off her fighting men, and threatened by assault from Japanese troops who occupied the northern coast of New Guinea from 1942, Australia's wartime participation and defence hung on the lines of its communication both internal and overseas. From the end of the Depression until September 1939 trunk telephone and telegraphs had extended steadily in Australia. Local lines and exchange plant increased. The Australian network, with its basic trunk line axes from Hobart to Melbourne, Melbourne to Adelaide and Perth, and north to Canberra, Sydney and Brisbane, catered for the growing but sub-stantially coast–clinging population. The PMG's telecommunications programme, with its internal cross–subsidisation from telephone to telegraph services and from profitable urban and inter–city telephone trunk–lines to costly rural growth, was set on a forward plan.

War changed this situation. From its outbreak on 3 September 1939 the Department's immediate priorities took clear shape. They were to strengthen weak links in domestic communications; to begin the connection of telephone and telegraph to the network of Army training camps springing up around the country; to organise the distribution of overseas and internal Service mail, and to co–operate with the Defence Department and the three Services in conducting research, design and development at their Research Laboratories for varied Service telecommunications needs. PMG mechanics were at once declared a 'Reserved Occupation', though a considerable number of departmental engineers left to join the Second AIF Signal Corps. By war's end some 7,500 of the PMG's workforce had enlisted in the fighting forces, more than a third of the total permanent workforce.[2]

The most pressing need was to strengthen the continental telephone and telegraph networks that, moderately used in peacetime, would be converted in wartime into round–the–clock communication lifelines. At Japan's entry into the war, with the bombing of Pearl Harbor in December 1941 and the fall of Singapore on 15 February 1942, Australia became the central communications centre in the South Pacific and the military base and boarding point for the US troops' northerly assault into the Pacific islands. The need for a large extension of trunk telephone and telegraph facilities assumed formidable urgency.

From the outbreak of war, Darwin's role as a garrison town was immediately identified. This sleepy tropic outpost had a small population and few facilities. From November 1939 two hospitals and a hotel were erected. RAAF aerodromes and buildings rose like mushrooms. Navy headquarters were established and PMG engineers, mechanics and linemen despatched from Adelaide to install the considerable network of telegraph and telephone lines and the exchanges required to give the garrison town an instant voice. Engineers H. Hawke and C. Leonard, both from Adelaide, led this communication thrust. Darwin's post office was also upgraded with additions of staff. H.C. Bald volunteered to return as postmaster with his wife and daughter in August 1940, having served there in younger and quieter days from 1928–34. Darwin itself had declined as a cable and telegraph centre after Bald's recall. The Pacific and Indian Ocean cables had cut severely into the outward flow of cable traffic through Darwin via Java and this route was closed down in 1935. Now the post office, the telephone exchange and telegraph communication centre acquired crucial importance for defence. Two senior women telephone operators who had volunteered also arrived from Adelaide to run the exchange assisted by Mrs Bald. Army camps ringed the township requiring their own telecommunication connections. In mid–1941 a radio link to Sydney was established from the bustling port and lines supplied by the PMG for transmitting and receiving stations.[3] Its days were short–lived. After December 1941 the Japanese found the wave length used by Sydney and jammed it with a stronger signal.

The historical overland telegraph line remained the sole connection with the south. Todd's iron wire had been augmented in 1898–9 with a copper wire which was added to the original line with a minimum of ceremony and fuss. This gave a two–way simultaneous transmitting and receiving capacity and a useful back–up when the intense climatic conditions of both wet and dry seasons in that harsh territory blotted out part of a line. Telephone connections had been set up locally in Darwin and from some of the OT repeater stations where 'phonophore' telephone facilities gave connection of a kind over a radius of 200 miles. But there was no trunk telephone connection with the south. If Darwin were to serve as the northern sentinel of communication, the situation demanded nothing short of the reconstruction of a greatly upgraded overland telegraph/telephone line. In April 1941 the war cabinet authorised the provision of a copper bearer circuit suitable for 3–channel telephone carrier operation from Gladstone, SA (136 miles north of Adelaide), to Darwin. This required the purchase and installation of two 3–channel telephone carrier systems, one to operate between Adelaide and Alice Springs, the other from Alice Springs to Darwin, plus the purchase and installation of two 9–channel voice frequency (VF) telegraph carrier systems to operate over one telephone channel in each of the 3–channel telephone carrier systems. 'To string the whole of the 1800 miles', a dispassionate official note recorded, 'a total of 320 tons of copper will be used.' Work began in June 1941.

On this second major overland communication enterprise, there were no horse or bullock drawn drays to transport the line and stores. The camels and their Afghan drivers would play no part. The tents were there for the 270 or so men who would work in more than 30 parties scattered through South, Central Australia and the Northern Territory. The enterprise was a joint PMG and Army Signals Corps operation, the Southern Command Signals Corps supplying the initial 66 volunteer army signal personnel (trained by the PMG to handle and splice the stay wires) and the Department providing senior experienced linemen. As the work progressed it drew Signal Corps

Vital wartime upgrading being carried out on the old overland telegraph line route, NT.

volunteers from across Australia to man the three–monthly working shifts. This time there was no track to be cut. The copper wire was strung to the old overland telegraph poles, though some were strengthened by the linemen and new cross arms placed on alternative poles. But four holes a mile had to be made for the new transpositions and wind stays, and steel tower structures replaced the steel poles across the wide beds of the torrential Finke and other northern rivers. Over the 70 years since the first OT line was erected, some new devices had evolved. One was the 'snow shoe', developed by the Adelaide engineering branch and used for walking over the soft drifts of sand and sandhills of some sections of the line. Time was of the essence. Planning envisaged that the new telecommunications would terminate at Adelaide and Darwin, with two 'back to back' terminals at Alice Springs. By this means, Adelaide–Darwin channels could be split at the dead centre point at Alice Springs to give flexibility in the adjustment for traffic flows.[4]

So it was that on the morning of 19 February 1942, J.L. Skerrett, PMG engineer from central office transmission section, was engaged at the Alice Springs repeater station linking the telephone carrier line through to Adelaide. The high speed telegraph channel with its teleprinter connection had been working across the length of the line for a mere five days. Six more joins in the telephone circuit, with amplifying repeaters at Barrow Creek, Tennant Creek, and four northerly repeater stations had yet to be made before the telephone between Darwin and Adelaide would speak. Late on that hot February morning Norman Lee, the telegraph supervisor at Alice Springs, came into the equipment room to report 'we've lost contact with Darwin'. Skerrett, taking up the measuring equipment, diagnosed a suspected fault very close to Darwin. He expected it would be quickly restored. But time went on. Neither he nor Lee suspected how fateful the fault would prove. Skerrett went into the telegraph office where Lee had a galvanometer plugged into the Darwin line. This instrument flickered when lines were being mended. As the two men talked, the needle on the galvanometer moved. 'My God, that's Morse', said Lee. With the new technology high speed transmitter and teleprinter installed, it was the last kind of message they expected to receive. Lee plugged a sounder into the line and answered the signal with his Morse key. As he translated from the old, now displaced Morse medium, Skerrett wrote down the words: 'Darwin bombed at 10 a.m. and no known details of damage and loss of life'.[5]

The day had begun ominously in Darwin. Since December 1941 most of the civilian population had been removed. It was a military town with staff for essential services. The remaining townspeople were growing used to practice air raid alerts. Coincidentally, that same day, the Sydney operations manager of Qantas Empire Airways wrote to the Director-General of Civil Aviation warning that, from Qantas's own information from their operations in Sumatra and Malaya, 'the most likely period for bomb raids on Darwin would be between the hours of 10 a.m. to 2 p.m.'[6] He was prescient. That morning, A.T. Halls, one of two supervisors of telegraphs, who had arrived in Darwin a few days before, was testing the telegraph circuit to Adelaide at the Darwin post office building.

'There's another air raid alarm', Halls tapped, 'I'll see you shortly.' But he then went on: 'The Japs have found us and their bombs are falling like hailstones . . . I'm getting out of here, see you later' — followed by the laugh signal (three dashes and a dot).[7] It was the last message from the Darwin post office. The bombing of the first Japanese raid on Darwin was expertly planned. The first bombs fell on the wharf where the Timor convoy had anchored the night before. The second drop hit the communications arteries. A 1,000–pound bomb fell on the post office killing outright the nine people sheltering in the near–by trench, Hurtle Bald, his wife and daughter, four telephonists, including the two senior girls from Adelaide, Freda Stasinowsky and Eileen Mullen, Jean Mullen who had joined her sister in Darwin a few months before, and a temporary telephonist Mrs Emily Young, Archibald Halls, and postal clerk, A.W. Wellington. The overland terminal and Darwin's new telegraph connection with Adelaide was totally knocked out by the second raid at midday.[8]

Certain conflict surrounds the messages transmitted of the fateful news. No written evidence of the first messages has been preserved. The Prime Minister's voluminous papers hold no key and the records of involved PMG senior officials, if set down, have not survived.[9] But oral and other evidence suggests that several messages reached PMG headquarters independently that day. Austin Jones, superintendent of telegraphs, South Australia, received the telegraph call from Halls at 10 a.m. In his own testimony in 1971 he noted that, having personally received the information in the operating room, 'I immediately contacted Mr E.H. Bourne, Chief Inspector (Telegraphs) Central Office Melbourne who immediately contacted the military authorities'.[10] Meanwhile, Harry Hawke, supervising engineer, had extracted a Morse key sounder from the rubble of Darwin's postal hall and, accompanied by W.T. Duke, the second and surviving telegraph supervisor, had moved eight miles down the line from Darwin, hooked up the line, and dictated the message that Duke tapped out of destruction and death. It was this message that Skerrett intercepted at Alice Springs. There, using the telephone connection completed the previous day, Skerrett immediately contacted PMG headquarters in Melbourne and spoke to L.B. Fanning, the Acting Director–General of the PMG, who, keeping Skerrett on 'hold', telephoned the Prime Minister, J.J. Curtin. Fanning came back with instructions to Skerrett to burn the original message and remain silent on information that would be censored out of the newspaper reports.

Duke, meanwhile, also established direct communication with Adelaide and maintained it later that day from a point 21 miles south of Darwin. Other communication points conveyed the news.[11] Two telegrams only, located among the records of the Department of Civil Aviation, provide written evidence of events. One timed 2.07 p.m. 19 February, sent from outside Darwin from radio inspector E.W. Betts, was received at Cloncurry, north–west Queensland, and transmitted in code to the Department of Civil Aviation, Melbourne. Decoded it read:

'Darwin bombed machine gunned 20 Japs 30 minutes 1000. Nineteen civil buildings and radio room minor damage. Fire tender hangar some RAAF buildings burnt. Drome OK think Eleven Mile [an RAAF station] OK. All staff [radio] OK. Stop. Later. Second attack started 1210 still in progress.' Betts's message to Civil Aviation concentrated not unnaturally on the state of RAAF buildings and communication and was conveyed to Fanning. A second short telegram was also later received by the Department of Civil Aviation from Perth: 'At 1414 Darwin reports all clear normal working resumed'.[12]

But nothing was normal, and devastation was immense. While the capital city newspapers disclosed next day that 72 enemy bombers accompanied by fighters had carried out the first raid on Darwin, and 21 bombers the second raid at midday, information was closely censored. 'The Government', Prime Minister Curtin announced, 'regards the attack as most grave and makes it clear that a severe blow has been struck on Australian soil. Information does not disclose details of casualties.'[13] On 22 February the metropolitan press published the news of the death of nine members of the postal staff and the injury of eleven others. In all, the major newspapers variously reported casualties as between 15 and 19 people killed and 21 injured on 19 February. But the total number of dead was in fact 243. 'It was a blitz', said the *Sydney Morning Herald* truthfully, 'of the most ferocious kind.'[14]

Darwin itself was effectively destroyed as a communication and flying base centre by the raid. With engineering help sent from Adelaide, telecommunication headquarters were transferred, along with RAAF headquarters, to Larrimah, 116 miles south of Darwin, and the links of the telephone carrier wave system were completed there in April 1942. A year later this overland telegraph terminal was shifted to the Adelaide River and finally removed to Berrimah, eight miles south

Darwin, 19 February 1942. The surprise Japanese air raid destroyed the post office, killing most of the staff. Shown here (from left to right) are the ruins of the postmaster's residence, telegraph office and cable company building.

of Darwin, when operational needs changed in the middle of 1944.[15] But it was not until post–war days that a new Darwin post office was opened for service in an act of remembrance on 19 February 1946.

The threat from Japan and the concentrated build–up of both Australian and American troops, who reached Australia early in 1942, placed extraordinary demands on the PMG's Department to meet urgent yet often shifting needs. For operational purposes each branch of the Services required one or more communication channels for its own individual and immediate use. Moreover, the telegraph channels required by the Forces were those capable of operating teleprinter or teletype over long distances between headquarters located in the capital cities and forward stations which were at times as far away from headquarters as 2,000 miles. In practice this meant that, instead of traffic being brought to one centre and passed to other States over a few channels using machine systems, a procedure the PMG's Department normally employed, the demand grew for numbers of separate multi–channel carrier telegraph systems for long distance trunk links.

At the outset, the demand placed precarious overloads on the existing main trunk–line circuits, Melbourne–Sydney, Melbourne–Adelaide, Melbourne–Canberra–Sydney, and particularly on the carrier service from Sydney to Brisbane where the US Army were headquartered. The situation had clear elements of 'Catch–22'. For, just as demands for communication lifelines reached their peak, Australia was virtually cut off by war from sources of overseas manufactured telecommunications systems and equipment on which the growth of their network depended. All carrier telegraph equipment installed in Australia before 1942 was entirely obtained from abroad. 'With the single exception of one 18–channel system of B.G.E. (British General Electric)', one PMG official confirmed, 'no carrier telegraph equipment could be secured from any source outside Australia . . . from 1939–44.' The UK subsidiary, Standard Telephones and Cables Pty Ltd, in Sydney planned to begin local manufacture in 1942, but no supply could be expected for a year. In a situation where necessity urgently fathered invention, PMG central office, the Research Laboratories and the Melbourne workshops began the planning, manufacture and assembly of a prototype 4–channel VF carrier telegraph (Type 'R'), which was in design early in 1942. Two of these systems were pressed into service on the Adelaide to Alice Springs, Alice Springs to Darwin route at the beginning of the year; but many more were needed.

Need, indeed, wonderfully concentrated the PMG's approach. A major difficulty in manufacturing these sophisticated systems with their greater number of channels turned on supplies of high permeability core material for making filters and for sensitive telegraph receiving relays. A limited amount of suitable core material was located in a Melbourne firm. The innovative PMG engineer, S.T. Webster, developed a suitable relay (PR 10) and manufacture of the relays began in the Melbourne workshops. To step up production, contracts were let for components and the manufacture of several units was contracted out to transmission engineers, while Sydney, Adelaide and the Melbourne workshops supplied the filters and relays. So adept, indeed, did the 'in–house' manufacturing system become that 15 systems providing four, six or nine channels each were produced and installed during 1942–3. STC Sydney completed four 9-channel systems in the same period, while the Department's Melbourne workshops turned out fourteen 4–channel terminals for use on mobile communication units by the Army Signals Corps in forward areas and for combat use outside Australia.[16]

Most critically for Australia in the years of Japanese menace from the north, the new carrier communications systems were thrust into service across 234,040 miles of country by December 1942 and nearly 360,000 miles by December 1943, doubling in a single year the distance of carrier telegraph mileage built up in Australia over the past 15 years, and almost trebling it in 1943. War, that great prime mover, gave indigenous telecommunication technology a powerful spurt.

Moreover, as the war demands quickened and US communication requirements from General MacArthur placed insistent pressure on the Brisbane to Melbourne line, PMG engineers and linemen, aided by US troops, carried out extraordinary feats of improvisation, juggling existing networks, pulling out and replacing working services to transform the network and strengthen it where the greatest need lay. In mid–1942, in one swift manoeuvre, circuits were taken out of the Melbourne–Canberra–Sydney carrier telegraph system and replaced in a complex permutation by several Type 'R' systems. While the Melbourne–Canberra–Sydney service was, in fact, reinforced, the juggle freed an 18-channel telegraph carrier system for use as a direct service from Brisbane to Melbourne. Arrangements with the US Air Force assured the transport of the terminal with all its accessories from Canberra to Brisbane. On a winter morning the strange airfreight, weighing 18 hundredweight, was stacked into the bomb bay of a Liberator aircraft and shifted from Canberra to Brisbane airport. Within a matter of days, the service was operating direct from Brisbane to Melbourne along selected telephone channels without any intermediate telegraph equipment at Sydney. 'The whole operation', R.E. Page summed up, 'was completed . . . without the loss or closing down at any stage of any of the existing telegraph channels which comprised some of the most important circuits in the Common-wealth.'[17] It was a triumph of planning and improvisation. Moreover, it was accomplished in 21 days.

In wartime such exploits could not be publicly hailed. They found muted, and largely technical, description in issues of the *Tele-communication Journal of Australia* when the heat was off. Their planning, however, was shaped by the Defence Communications Committee made up of representatives of the Australian Army, Navy and Air Force, the US Army and Navy, the PMG's Department and the Departments of Munitions and Defence. The PMG's representatives on the Communications Committee were initially Sid Witt and, from 1941, Norman Hayes, superintending engineer, Victoria, and R.E.

Lt-Col. Norman James McCay, Army Signals Corps, was a key planner of the extended wartime eastern trunk network. A pre-war PMG engineer, he returned to the Department in 1946 as supervising engineer of the then new transmission and long line equipment section and became head of the PMG research laboratories from 1953 to 1960.

Page, supervising engineer, transmission headquarters. The Australian Army representative, Lieutenant–Colonel N.J. McCay of the Army Signals Corps, was also a former long–service PMG engineer who had installed the first major 3–channel carrier telephone systems between Melbourne and Sydney, and had been concerned throughout the 1930s with transmission and carrier equipment. McCay became the key architect in planning the strengthening and extension of major trunk line systems up the eastern coast of Australia and in detailing the phases of extension of lines from Brisbane north to Cape York, inland to Charleville, Hughenden and Cloncurry, westward to link the overland telegraph to the major coastal routes, and on to extend communications across Torres Strait into New Guinea.[18]

All planning decisions required War Council approval. In the actual execution of the work, the PMG's Department acted in close collaboration with their Australian and US Army colleagues. Several of the Signal Corps officers engaged in the extensions were ex–PMG engineers, in line for high office in the postwar years. With a background of expertise, they undertook the organisational work. As the threat to national security deepened and fears of Japanese invasion centred on Queensland, PMG linemen, overseers and mechanics were shifted north from headquarters and from other States to get the services through. PMG engineers and line inspectors directed the Army signalmen in an unusual reversal of wartime roles. The Americans brought in major long line carrier telephone equipment which was assembled by PMG staff while US Army personnel played a significant part in erecting the line from Brisbane to Rockhampton and west to Mt Isa and Tennant Creek. G.N. Smith, PMG divisional engineer in Brisbane, superintended the work. A former (and later) PMG engineer, Major J.W. Read of the Army Signals Corps, supervised the construction of the trunk route from Cairns to Cape York. PMG engineers, H.V. Pilgrim, H.G. Fraser and R.J. Kanaley, overviewed for the PMG. Construction was performed by Signals

Corps troops from both Australian and US Armies with PMG line inspectors in a technical assistance role. On some routes modern trunk carrier services appeared for the first time. On others, old lines were replaced or reinforced with the new copper wire carrier technology. Repeater stations were built hurriedly along the extensions. Part of the large scale equipment, the terminals and teleprinters and some telexes associated with the technology, were built in the PMG's Melbourne workshops and flown north in roomy DC3s, while human grit and ingenuity pushed the new extensions out. The telecommunication line to Cape York was completed on 9 December 1943.[19]

The *coup de main* in this furiously–paced national communication exercise was the linking of Australia's northern–most tip, Cape York, with the New Guinea Peninsula where Australian forces were pushing back the Japanese. Dexterity and bold improvisation paved the way. In Melbourne, McCay conceived the plan of hauling up one of the old Bass Strait submarine cables of 1909 and placing it across the Torres Strait. Both cables laid that year were still in use between Tasmania and the mainland though the modern telephone carrier cable laid by the *Faraday* in 1935 had superseded much of their use. In pursuit of the plan, Captain I.M. Gunn, one of McCay's Signal Officers, an ex–PMG engineer (who would also become a future Director of Posts and Telegraphs, Victoria), surveyed Torres Strait from Horn Island off Cape York along the shortest route to the New Guinea coastline at Sabai. But the Sabai launching site, straddling a stretch of swamp south of the Fly River, proved unsuitable for the cable plan. When this news reached McCay in Melbourne, he determined to pull up both cables and lay them across a longer sector of Torres Strait, end to end.

With the New Guinea side of the operation in charge of Read and Gunn, exploit 'Heath Robinson' began. In Bass Strait the coastal collier turned marine–cable–laying ship, SS *Mernoo*, fitted out with bow sheaves and a turning–over winch, wound up the two iron–clad cables that had lain peacefully on the sea bed for over 30 years and carried them, coiled aboard, under escort to New Guinea. Now that distance was less constraining, the site picked for the second launching was Boera Point, 30 miles to the west of Port Moresby. The project, however, met obstacles from the start. On its first venture on 1 October 1943, the *Mernoo* turned too far south and, with inadequate charts, lost 60 nautical miles of cable when it broke in deep water. Another starting point was chosen at Delena, a native village, some 90 miles west of Moresby. On the second run out, Read was in charge of paying out the cable. In the dark tropic night calamity struck again. A day and a half out from Delena, while the cable payed out over the ship's bow, the naval escort vessel detected the presence of a submarine and it became essential to 'black out' the cable hold. But it was not possible to stop the cable laying. Read pulled the cable crew out of the hold where they faced possible decapitation in the darkness. But without manual control, the cable churned itself out in elaborate loops and over 150 miles of cable were laid in 50 dark miles of sea. Daunted, yet not dismayed, Read landed the cable end safely at Cape York.

Despite mishaps, the vital connection had been made. It was now

SS *Mernoo* off Boera
Point, New Guinea,
1 October 1943. A
barge tows the cable
from ship to shore.

Under the supervision
of Major J.W. Read,
troops of the Signals
Section, New Guinea
Force, splice the shore
end of the antique
cable.

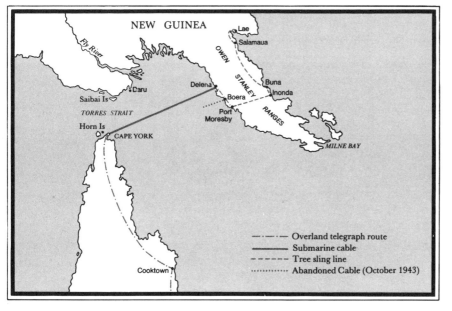

Routes of the
submarine cable laid
late in 1943 to link
Australia with wartime
operations in New
Guinea. The cable
launched from Boera
was abandoned when the
cable broke in deep
water.

arranged that General Blamey, Commander-in-Chief, Australian Military Forces, then in Melbourne, should be the first to use the cable line to send a message to his General Officer Commanding New Guinea Force. But already some cause for additional anxiety had appeared. Captain Gunn, in charge of installing the land-line link between Delena and Port Moresby, was grappling with copper wire in a newly introduced insulation material, polyvinyl chloride. Resistant to heat and sun, it had, however, in its early experimental stage, rapidly hardened and become brittle at joints, which made it both difficult to detect and mend breaks and faults in the interior communication wire. Faults were known to exist between Delena and Galley Reach — a large expanse of mangrove swamp. Blamey's message hence travelled by Morse telegraph up the eastern coast of Australia to Cape York, across by (looped) submarine cable to Delena where the message was decoded and transported physically across the break and telephoned on to Moresby. There it was encoded back to Morse. Sir Leslie Morshead, GOC New Guinea was, as it happened, at Milne Bay and received the message from Port Moresby by encyphered radio. Waiting at the 'fault line', Gunn and his men expected a telegraph message for return communication to Blamey within a couple of hours. They stood by for three weary days. Unaware of the drama and, it seems, of the achievement, General Morshead had replied direct to Melbourne by the slow and tightly encyphered radio route. The submarine cable, however, completed in December 1943, worked for over three months before its unusual loops broke in the high tides of Torres Strait in April 1944. But it had gallantly served its time. Out of place and time, the historic cables of Bass Strait had provided a remarkable holding operation in the northward drive for communication until they were replaced by a new cable that year. Early in 1944 a newly made submarine cable was also laid to replace the fault-prone aerial line between Delena and Port Moresby.

Gunn would carry the New Guinea communications network onward. Acting on plans devised by McCay in Melbourne, Gunn, in 1944, designed a 'tree sling' line capable of taking a 3-channel carrier system from Port Moresby across the precipitous Owen Stanley

Above: Mounting insulators for a signal line, Sogeri Valley, New Guinea, 1943. The use of living trees, instead of specially erected poles, saved time and materials, while the foliage provided camouflage.

Right: Army Signallers working with communications cable in dense jungle terrain near Lae, New Guinea.

Ranges and the damp forests of the Kokoda Trail to Inonda near Buna. In that environment, 'tree sling' took on new meaning. In PMG parlance a tree sling line was normally a galvanised iron wire strung tautly from tree to tree. But in the rain forests of New Guinea, creepers grew up the trees stretching their deep tendrils along the copper lines in 'a matter of hours'. Technology, however, would triumph in the lush forests of New Guinea. Here the tree sling line was designed with lots of sag and free ties of light wire forming a 'fuse' that broke when a tree fell across the line and allowed the insulated line wire to continue to function. In sylvan undulations, the line wound its way on from Inonda west to Salamaua and on to Lae. British Army representatives, in some wonderment, came to look and later adopted the technology for their communications lines in Burma.[20]

War opened up a rich vein of creativity in PMG telecommunications. From a position of dependence on carrier technology from abroad, a stream of ideas and designs welled up within the PMG Research Laboratories and in different technical sections of the Department for bolstering the national network and thrusting it, via field engineers and linemen, into little known and often unpronounceable places. In this 'crafting' of a wartime network, the Australian Type 'R' system formed the key. In its initial design, carried out in the Research Laboratories, many played a part. Webster, a scientist from the telegraph section of the chief engineers branch, Melbourne, conducted vital work on permissible telegraph distortions and carrier receive relays; E.H. Palfreyman of the Research Laboratories prepared the important filter design, while W.N. Boswell, also of the Laboratories, designed the oscillators, static modulators and amplifier detectors. In Adelaide Frank O'Grady, supervising engineer (and later Director–General of the PMG), made improvements to the Type 'R' system and modified the imported 'B' type carrier system to fit in with Australian equipment.[21]

In terms of locally manufactured carrier systems, the record was impressive. Thirty–two telegraph carrier systems had been manufactured by the Department by October 1944 providing 4, 6 and 9 channels for use over the Department's lines throughout Australia.

The New Guinea campaign depended on good lines of communication. Part of the trunk telephone and telegraph carrier terminal station, Lae, 1944.

One separate 9–channel uni–directional carrier system (designed by the engineers A.J. McDevitt and K. Boyle of the PMG transmission section in Sydney) had been made for the use of the RAAF, and other diverse channel systems were manufactured for use in New Guinea, with ten complete mobile terminals of communication equipment. Most of the work was done in the Department's Melbourne work-shops. An immediate impetus to one important local upgrading was the loss by enemy action of a convoy carrying underground cable equipment for the Sydney–Newcastle–Maitland circuit, a route covering approximately 150 miles. The cable and carrier equipment was subsequently made under the Department's direction. In all, the Melbourne workshops produced 25 carrier telegraph systems and ten complete mobile communications systems as well as reconditioning and adapting some 60 teletype (teleprinter) units brought in from the USA. When, towards the end of the war, Skerrett and Webster revealed details of this large–scale and dexterous crafting and production of Australia's wartime communications, it became, in Skerrett's words, 'an international exposé of carrier telegraph technology'.[22]

Throughout the war the Research Laboratories, under Sid Witt, at 59 Little Collins Street, Melbourne, fulfilled a versatile national role. Independently, and variously in conjunction with the Munitions Laboratories, the CSIR's Radiophysics Laboratory at Sydney University built early in the war for radar research, and AWA's laboratories, the PMG Research Laboratories were used for an extraordinary range of telecommunications research, design and development required by the three armed services and for highly secret radar research.

With CSIR, the Department had shared a close research interest in radio since the CSIR's establishment of the Radio Research Board in 1926. H.P. Brown had been a central and active figure of the Board which met under the chairmanship of Sydney University's J.P. Madsen, the first Professor of Electrical Engineering in Australia and acknowledged 'father' of the Board. The Board had a membership of four and its aim was the support of 'pure' radio research to ensure, as Madsen put it, against 'a slavish application of experience' from radio research overseas. In this it had succeeded, sponsoring individual researchers at Sydney and Melbourne universities and producing both a core of research men who joined AWA's laboratories before the war and the handful of gifted workers who laid the foundation of Australia's independent radar research. Under Brown, the PMG's Department had contributed £8,000 to the Radio Research Board in 1928 for a period of three years, while his strong protection of the sum from Treasury bureaucrats as Depression struck made him a pivot of the Board's success. The Board's independence was its strength. 'It would certainly have completely altered the whole nature of the scientific radio research effort', a leading radio researcher summed up, 'if the Public Service Board and Department influence had taken over the Radio Research Board' as was proposed.[23]

The dynamic Sidney Herbert Witt, first Head of the PMG Research Laboratories, from 1923 to 1945. Joining the Department in 1910 as a junior instrument fitter, he was to play a vital role in telecommunications over many years, particularly in wartime.

Now in wartime, the CSIR Radiophysics Division and the PMG Research Laboratories undertook to collaborate in the development of some 20 highly secret radar projects, information for which was brought to Australia by CSIR radiophysicist, Dr David Martyn, after an official visit to Britain in 1939. Due to the highly secret nature of the projects, great responsibility devolved on Witt's cramped and decidedly dingy little Research Laboratories at Collins Street, Melbourne. While the CSIR's radiophysics research team prepared the 'prototype' for Australia's radar equipment, all the development and production of radar had to be carried out by the PMG. The challenge was immense. Sir John Eccles, the Australian–based New Zealand neurologist (and later Nobel Laureate), who offered his services to the Government to assist in war, visited the PMG Research Laboratories and privately declared that it 'was impossible to carry out intellectual work in such surroundings'.

More serious was the acrimony that developed between the pressured PMG research staff and the 'boffins' of the CSIR. L.M. Harris, a participant in the programme, who rose to head the Laboratories in 1960, recalled that while the CSIR radiophysics scientists 'built the breadboards and handed them over to the PMG research staff', it was the PMG Research Laboratories who 'proposed specifications, production design and drawings, costed the development, advised the Department of Munitions on having radar apparatus manufactured in quantity, and kept account of the whole operative costs'. In effect, said Harris, they 'carried out development of the concept from scratch'.[24] In this way, the ASV (air–to–surface vessel) equipment, as one example, was developed on the British model for the RAAF's extensive use. It was a clear example of the sundering of research from development and of the arrogance and detachment of the 'pure' scientists from the all–important applications of their work, a tendency which some critics have noted as a disturbing hallmark of some CSIR and CSIRO scientific work.[25]

Collaboration would improve from 1941. With the unexpected departure of Professor Madsen, chairman of the Radiophysics Advisory Board, the Government seconded Professor F. White from the Physics Department of Canterbury University College, New Zealand, to take charge. White, who became both chief of the CSIR Division of Radiophysics and chairman of the Radiophysics Advisory Board, acted as 'pacifier' between the clashing laboratory heads Martyn and Witt and, importantly, served as the intermediary between the PMG Research Laboratories and the Services to relax secrecy and to approve certain manufacturers to assist the production of radar equipment. In time, responsibility for radar supplies was transferred to the Department of Supply.[26] The contribution of the PMG Research Laboratories, however, has never been given full due. CSIR was quick to claim public credit for Australian radar work although the major part of the undertaking that brought radar into operation was the engineering task performed by the small, creative and persistently determined PMG Research Laboratories team.[27]

The Research Laboratories' other wartime projects ranged widely.

This wartime radar (AA No2 Mark VI) control system for directing searchlights was designed and developed by the PMG Research Laboratories. With the participation of the Laboratories, radar was quickly lifted from the prototype to the operational stage.

Equipment design and testing for the Services included work for the Army on wireless sets operated through field telephones, the manufacture of model microphones for aircrews, and the development of high frequency direction finding equipment. Research staff also designed and tested intercommunication equipment for RAAF low pressure training chambers to permit pilot training at simulated altitudes. Special amplifiers and switching facilities were required to allow communication between a large group of people using oxygen masks under low pressure conditions which, one report clarified, 'also affect efficiency of the voice and electro–acoustic instruments'. Various forms of telephone equipment were further perfected and encased in divers' helmets to assist salvage operations on vessels sunk by enemy action (a device already used by the PMG's Department for divers engaged in repairing the Bass Strait telephone cable in 1937). Other special telephones were developed for use in observation chambers at depths of 450 feet. Research was also widely linked with acoustics (work which drew John Eccles to the Laboratories) including the measurement of acoustic noises in tanks; and work was done on the design of equipment for the detection of practice torpedoes, the development for bomb release controls and, always, the design of radio systems and transmission lines for defence stations. In all, said one report, 'investigations of telecommunications problems connected with the design and construction of special equipment for the Defence forces was carried out continuously. There were over 400 separate defence investigations' in the Research Laboratories.[28] Begun with 'one man' and his assistant in 1923, the Research Laboratories under Witt had reached a position of national importance by 1945.

On the industrial front, war consolidated Australia's already well developed radio and electronic industry which was largely concentrated in the hands of Amalgamated Wireless (Australasia) Ltd. In 1939 AWA was joined by the respective American and Dutch subsidiaries, Standard Telephones and Cables Pty Ltd and Philips. AWA also collaborated with the CSIR Radiophysics Laboratory on the manufacture of the 'early warning' radar sets which General MacArthur used throughout his Pacific campaign. And in all laboratories tropic proofing investigations and the tropicalisation of materials and electronic equipment went on. 'It was no exaggeration to say', the chairman of STC, Sir Samuel Jones, later summed up, 'that the Australian radio industry led the . . . allied world . . . in the techniques of building equipment capable of withstanding the rigours imposed by the ecological conditions encountered in the tropical regions of the Pacific and other such areas.'[29]

Little had been said of the administrative and political leadership of the wartime PMG's Department. In the period from September 1939 until Japan entered the war, Menzies, as Prime Minister, evidently held the PMG portfolio in low esteem. Brown himself privately believed that he had been snubbed by Menzies, and no less than four Postmasters-General held the portfolio in the war years from September 1939 until October 1941 when the appointment of Senator W.P. Ashley, under Labor Prime Minister Curtin, brought a continuing presence to the important wartime portfolio.

Brown's successor as Director-General was Daniel (later Sir Daniel) McVey. A former PMG engineer and superintendent of the Sydney mail exchange, McVey had left the service in 1937 to become Assistant Commissioner of the Public Service Board and in 1939 Menzies appointed him as permanent head of the new Commonwealth Department of Munitions (later Supply and Development). Big, impressive, charming, and with renowned managerial skills, McVey was already known in press and Government circles as 'Australia's Public Servant No. 1' when he accepted the vacant Director-Generalship of the PMG late in 1939. But despite brilliance, he was largely an 'absentee landlord' in the role. While he remained nominally Director-General until industry called him in June 1946, he distributed his managerial manna across a maze of homefront war activities, establishing the Department of War Organisation of Industry and serving at times concurrently as chief executive officer of the production executive of cabinet, secretary of the Department of Aircraft Production, and as Director-General of Civil Aviation. He was a model of the high powered technocrat.[30]

Against this background it fell to two men, Assistant (later Deputy) Director-General L.B. Fanning and chief engineer, R.V. McKay, to contend with the day-to-day administration of the complex decision-making and planning of the wartime PMG. Fanning, a Tasmanian, had come up on the telephone side. He had headed the central office telephone branch since 1918, building it managerially and commercially under Brown's restructuring of that area into an efficient and prominent field. An articulate communicator, Fanning, as wartime Acting Deputy Director–General, developed strong links with politicians and, despite a natural caution, sought the limelight.[31] Yet the real power in war planning and its implementation lay with the brilliant engineer and tactician, Roy McKay. McKay's career epitomised the rise of an internally trained PMG engineer. He had joined the Department in 1908 as one of its first cadet engineers; was appointed the youngest divisional engineer in the service in 1914, and seven years later became supervising engineer, telephone equipment, Sydney. In 1931 he moved as superintending engineer, equipment, to central office where his drive and influence extended over the telephone equipment of the whole country. In 1940 he succeeded Robert Lawson to the chief engineer's chair. With his wide technological knowledge, McKay worked in close harmony with the itinerant McVey. But it was McKay who dealt directly with the US forces in determining the PMG's overall communications back–up, responded to the communications committee's programmes, and made his own imaginative and at times unorthodox input into the Department's overall wartime schemes.[32]

In addition to the eastern thrust towards New Guinea, developments were nation–wide. In Western Australia Broome and Wyndham were raided by Japanese bombers shortly after Darwin in 1942 and fears formed that there might be an attempt at invasion at deserted Jurien Bay, midway between Geraldton and Perth. General Blamey despatched the 3 Australia Signals Corps group there under the command of Lieutenant–General Gordon Bennett (who had escaped from Singapore) in 1942, and aerial channels were erected on the coast and inland in a broad arc around Jurien Bay and manned by the Signal Corps. In May 1943 the enemy threat moved north with Japanese bombing of the US submarine base at Exmouth Gulf. There telecommunications had been strengthened by PMG staff during 1942–3 with construction north from Geraldton (where the pre–war line ended) to the submarine base. Heavy construction of land and sea cables was also carried out in the Cockburn Sound area south of Perth to serve the large Royal Australian Navy base. Simultaneously, work was implemented by both Western and South Australian PMG staff in the critical years of 1942–3, when Australia's vulnerability grew, to upgrade the vital east–west telegraph and telephone communication lines.[33]

Within the whole arena of planning, one central responsibility, common to all combatant countries, was the preparation of emergency fall–back communication systems in the event of an enemy attack on the main exchanges or of invasion of the country. 'Shadow' exchanges were set up, furnished by main cable terminals, some distance behind the main exchanges so that in an emergency the main exchange could be bypassed. Alternative centres of communication contact were established in all capitals; in Perth in a popular restaurant, in Sydney (the most vulnerable of the cities) in the great retail building of Grace Brothers, where the PMG also constructed a special com-

Hidden behind the screens (rear of picture) in Paterson's Dining Rooms, in the heart of Perth, WA, was one of the many wartime emergency shadow exchanges.

munications headquarters for General MacArthur, and in the unused underground tunnel of St James Railway Station, a position especially pressed by the American High Command who urged the wisdom of undergrounding. In Brisbane, the persistent demands of General Douglas MacArthur, as Supreme Commander of the Allied Forces in the South–West Pacific, led to a veritable warren of fall–back emergency communication centres.[34]

Plans were also made for a 'scorched earth' policy of demolition of the capital city communication centres and for a retreat to alternative centres established in major country towns. The back–up behind Townsville was a notable case in point. Despite high preparedness, fortunately the 'shadow' equipment was never called into service. Three major new communication links overseas were also established. In recognition of its essential defence ties with the United States, the Australian Government sidestepped Empire wireless agreements and established two direct radiotelegraph circuits between Sydney and San Francisco in December 1941 and April 1943, and a link with China in 1942.[35]

Civilian demands for PMG's Department services did not lessen with war: they ballooned. With military personnel, the militia and even landgirls flung across the continent, the internal use of telephone and telegraph boomed. On the outbreak of war the private use of radio and telephone was embargoed between Australia and countries overseas. Concessional telegram rates for members of the forces, introduced in May 1940, and trunk line calls offered at half rate 'from any telephone office in Australia' to members of the forces in uniform, caused the wires to sing. Inevitably war made the PMG's Department a healthy profiteer. In mid–1939 all the Department's services were favourably in the black. Revenue exceeded expenditure by nearly £2 million. By June 1941 profits had soared. Three months later the Government increased telegraph charges as part of a budget package to finance the war effort and creamed off £1.5 million from this. The number of telegrams were up by 10 per cent in 1941 on the previous year — 'a record number', said the annual report. They rose 17.7 per cent more the following year, and a further 25 per cent in 1943. It was not until 1945 that telegraph usage began to fall. Telephone and wireless profits also climbed.[36] While the PMG and the Army Signals Corps worked strenuously to get the vital wartime telecommunication links through, people at home depended as never before on broadcasts, newspaper news despatched by coded telegraph from theatres of war, on tele-phone calls, and on mail from service men everywhere.

Increasingly, women were pressed into PMG occupations as male staff joined up. Some PMG women enlisted as telegraphists with the WRAAF and, as the Navy slowly admitted women into its shore stations, with the WRAN. But a total of 6,000 women had been recruited for 'men's work' in the Department by 1944. In a major social breakthrough, they were permitted to wear slacks to work 'at least in the winter months' to make up for the shortage of silk stockings. They were, however, 'temporary'. Postal and telegraph unions negotiated firm arrangements with the Department to ensure that enlistment (the 'reserved' mechanics excepted) covered the staff member's re-employment, superannuation, promotion, increments, and examinations. At the same time, unionists and other staff formed themselves into a post office volunteer guard to protect post office establishments in Australia. Importantly, from 1942, groups of engineers and technical staff formed themselves in each State into special PMG 'reserve units', known as 2 Australian Line of Communications (L of C), whose members trained to form a highly skilled group capable of maintaining PMG telecommunications as military personnel should war conditions require. Finally, telegraphists lent their skills to the extensive training of servicemen and women in Morse code in some 450 depots throughout the country.

Essentially, the human face of war, its loss, sacrifice, grief and joy surged across the PMG's communication lines. One of the most demanding wartime duties fell to the telegraph messenger. Telegrams became the official communication of all the armed forces to notify death, wounding, capture or 'missing in action' of service personnel. Sealed in special white regulation envelopes, the telegrams were delivered by hand. Officially, regulations required that such messages be delivered by PMG messengers accompanied by a parson or priest. The duo was rare. Most often it fell to the youthful messenger, often a boy of 15 years, to handle this harrowing traffic of war. It was a duty they remembered all their lives.

8 'The Ringing Grooves of Change'

The atomic bombs that blasted the Second World War to its end in August 1945 changed the fortunes of every country. In Australia the war's end ushered in a period of buoyant prosperity. From war itself a new age of science and technology had been born. In the struggle for survival, old technological practices had been overturned while a revolution in electronics had lifted the experimental gadgetry of the 1930s into working components of a large-scale telecommunications system. In every sense, Australia entered a new age. In the field of social and economic development, the PMG's Department would play a crucial part. Aviation, and all forms of transport, would shrink distance as never before: but telecommunications would heighten a sense of national cohesion and of the mastering of geographical distance that had singular social and psychological effects. From the postwar years, and notably the 1950s, telecommunication services would offer a veritable cornucopia of new developments in automatic telephony and telegraphy, television, electronic computers, microwave radio, rocketry, transistors and other solid state devices that would alter the style of our lives. 'Forward, forward let us range,' wrote Tennyson of another age, 'Let the great world spin forever down the ringing grooves of change.'[1]

The story of these developments could crowd any volume. The interest here is in the way the technology was incorporated into the Australian experience. Basic decisions about the direction of telecommunications development were made immediately after the Second World War. The origins of these decisions and their implications for Australia's future were rooted in two concepts which, while appreciated prewar, drew special force from the experience of 1939–45. One was an understanding of the geographical distance of Australia, both internally and in terms of its contacts with the outside world: the other was recognition of the need for a strong and expanding engineering organisation that could implement and project the technologies that would tame these distances.

One wartime lesson had emerged with special sharpness. Never again could Australia allow itself the 'technological nakedness' that

One of the many new technologies introduced after the war was that of very high frequency (VHF) radio. This experimental FM station was established by the PMG at Jolimont, Melbourne, in 1946 and operated until 1961 when its frequency band was taken over by a country television channel.

McVey and McKay —
Scots-born Daniel (later
Sir Daniel) McVey, who,
after a short period on
the land, began his
career as a cadet
engineer with the PMG
in Queensland,
becoming Director-
General of Posts and
Telegraphs, before
moving to private
industry after the war.

Roy V. McKay joined
the Department as
cadet engineer in New
South Wales in 1908
and rose to become
chief engineer under
McVey in 1940. He
retired in 1956 to
return to London as the
Australian member on
the Commonwealth
telecommunications
board.

had rendered it so dependent on overseas equipment and had demanded such effort to marshal the massive communication back-up required for its role as a base headquarters of the Pacific War. The lesson struck home. Those who had been most closely involved in the PMG's wartime leadership now made judgments that would ensure that Australia would step up the local manufacture of telecommunications equipment. One of the PMG's Department's first postwar acts was to give assistance to its native industry and to encourage the major Australian-based firms in the production of automatic switching equipment, private manual branch exchange switchboards and the universal type telephone attachments whose manufacture they had begun in wartime. The second and related plan was to design strategies that would gear the Department for the long-term technological consolidation and integration of an advancing national network.

One strategy was a commitment to progressive automation. This policy was hardly new. An early Postmaster-General, Josiah Thomas had enunciated it in 1911. H.P. Brown had pushed the policy forward. Australia became the first country in the world to introduce rural automatic exchanges and, spurred by Country Party pressures ('rural automatic telephones' ex-Postmaster-General Gibson told Parliament 'are my pets'), these small imported exchanges spread about the countryside bringing round-the-clock services to isolated country settlements and saving on the cost of all-night operation in areas of small populations. Their local production won high priority.

Key figures behind the manufacturing planning were Director-General McVey and his chief engineer. 'McVey and McKay', one close observer recounted, 'were up to their eyes in the political and commercial pressures to sponsor the development of local automatic switching equipment in Australia.' In 1945 Australia, as a long-time importer of systems and equipment, stood at the crossroads of telecommunications progress, one foot on a hotch-potch of British and American exchange systems and their switching equipment, the other poised to move towards a more rationalised system where disparate local and trunk systems (and their signalling equipment) could be fused into a co-ordinated Australian system. Two firms won government support: Standard Telephone and Cables Pty Ltd (STC), the Sydney branch of the British subsidiary of IT&T which had already been involved in Australia's wartime communications effort and Telephone and Electrical Industries (TEI), a consortium owned by five British companies — the precursor of Plessey Telecommunications Ltd. Accordingly in 1948 special pricing arrangements were offered to both firms for ten years with the requirement that they should manufacture one standard Australian system of automatic switching equipment on a guarantee of a minimum annual order from the Government.[2]

McVey also threw his formidable management skills into obtaining access for STC to the British patent (the British post office 2000 type step-by-step automatic telephone exchange) which McKay had selected for the Australian model. At the same time, similar arrangements were worked out for the manufacture of Australian

The Melbourne-Sydney coaxial cable marked a major new artery in Australian
telecommunications. Begun in 1960, it was to take two years to complete.
Here, an excavator prepares the route for the cable to be laid while, following
on behind, a cable jointer connects two lengths of the route together.

telephone and telegraph cables, an industry of recognised local achievement. Agreements were signed between Government and Austral Standard Cables Pty Ltd for a ten year period and later with Olympic Cables Pty Ltd and Conqueror Cables Pty Ltd for the production and supply of standardised underground cables.[3] (These contracts were later extended. The first interstate coaxial cable between Melbourne and Sydney was, for example, contracted in 1959 to the West German firm Siemens on the basis of 50 per cent manufacture in Australia by Olympic Cables. All subsequent coaxial cables were also manufactured in this way.)

With McVey's departure to head the STC Sydney subsidiary himself in June 1946, the new Director–General L.B. Fanning, inherited this ground plan. He also inherited the PMG's bustling postwar growth. In the four years of the Chifley postwar Government, telephone progress surged ahead. Wartime priorities had greatly lengthened the lists of waiting customers for both business and private telephones. Some subscribers had actually been disconnected because of wartime communication needs. But as ex–servicemen returned home newly aware of the benefits of telecommunication, peace released a clamorous demand for telephone services that escalated as economic conditions boomed.

A second spur to PMG activity was population growth. Together with the need for technological self–sufficiency, the need for more people to populate a large and exposed Australian continent became one of the major policy planks of the Labor Government. 'The days of our isolation', said Immigration Minister Arthur Calwell, launching his

The need for skilled staff was to show itself in local notices, such as this from Warragul, Victoria, of the early 1950s.

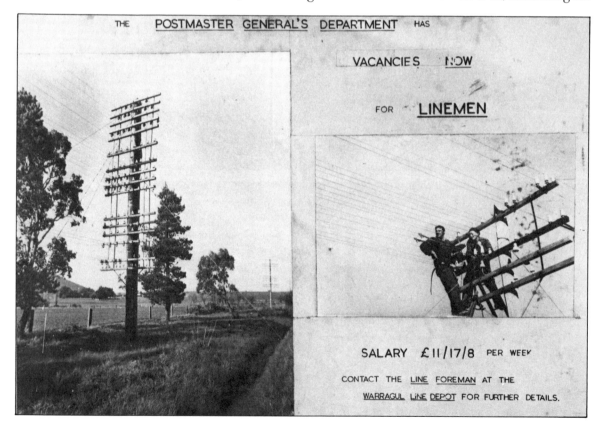

THE POSTMASTER GENERAL'S DEPARTMENT HAS

VACANCIES NOW

FOR LINEMEN

SALARY £11/17/8 PER WEEK

CONTACT THE LINE FOREMAN AT THE
WARRAGUL LINE DEPOT FOR FURTHER DETAILS.

scheme of assisted immigration in November 1946, 'are over'.[4] Now, not only did the historically favoured British migrant make speedy use of cheap passages to the land of sunshine and prosperity, but labourers, technicians and professional men and their families from an arc of European countries landed at Australian ports to help build the basis of a new age. By June 1950 the PMG's Department had absorbed 1,250 'New Australians', many with technical skills. All but 50 were pressed into the large engineering projects to build up trunk and subscriber telephone lines. While some of the new arrivals were the first to suffer when Prime Minister Menzies demanded cuts in the Public Service 'to restore economic balance' in the recession of 1951, migrants in the long term added vital manpower and a new segment of service demand to communications expansion in Australia.

By the decade of the 1950s telecommunications had advanced on every front. Five hundred rural automatic exchanges were in operation, some 60 more on order from Britain, while the Department was now designing its own. Some 150 carrier telephone systems and 1,000 new trunk circuits had also been added to the network including extra trunk–line channels on all the major interstate routes excepting Adelaide–Perth. Capital city exchanges too were increasingly converted to automatic, a development that led AWA into manufacturing local switchboards; while city and provincial telephone subscribers multiplied. The telephone echoed the throbbing commercial and social pulse of the nation. In keeping, the Department introduced a mobile radio telephone service in 1950, extended this to taxi services, ambulances and the police, adding a new dimension of speed to

Not only was there a shortage of staff, but also of equipment in the immediate post-war years. Here, a Geelong (Victoria) technician makes good use of an ex-army jeep, 1948.

telephone services. In broadcasting, there was kindred progress. Ninety–five per cent of Australian homes had radio receivers by 1949. 'Broadcasting', Postmaster–General Donald Cameron told Parliament that year 'has become a part of every citizen's daily life'; broadcasting of Parliament itself was started by the ABC in June 1946, while the PMG's Department was 'a vital factor in the business and domestic life of the whole country.' The progress made in the telephone and telegraph development since the war, said Cameron, was 'staggering'.[5]

The war's end brought one major change to the organisation of Australia's overseas telecommunication and its internal interrelations in the termination of the Government's long and at times controversial agreement with AWA. The resolution, which also bore McVey's stamp, of this complex business would prove as sinuous and labyrinthine as the underlying submarine cables themselves.

From the earliest extension of its overseas communications, Australia had joined an Imperial communications club. With the special exception of the radiotelephony circuits opened between Australia and the USA and China during the war, Australia had, from the 1870s, operated within an Empire telecommunications system based firmly on the major British cable companies. By the First World War the Australian continent was served by submarine telegraph cables that linked its western, northern and eastern coasts to Empire posts in India, South Africa, Canada and Great Britain. There were good reasons for an 'all red' Imperial route. The security and privacy of an Empire communications network were important in peace and war. In addition in true colonial fashion Australia extended her telecommunications contacts through Britain to countries elsewhere. But the introduction of the short wave beam wireless telegraphy service from Britain to Canada in 1926, and to Australia, India and South Africa in 1927, disturbed this harmony. Beam wireless services operated in Australia by AWA now competed advantageously with the more capital intensive and costly submarine cable routes. Indeed they quickly threatened the economic viability of the cable companies. With potential international competition for the British submarine cables and a recognised need for an Empire cable system — for interruptions and 'fading' on the beam wireless service at the very least made a reliable back–up system a necessity — an Imperial Conference was called in London in 1928.

The solution accepted by members was to fuse Empire cable and wireless interests to ensure unity of operation and direction and a 'common purse'. The Eastern and Associated Cable Companies thus merged with the Marconi Wireless Telegraph Company to form Cable and Wireless Ltd in 1929. This new concern was empowered by charter to operate the whole of the overseas cable and radio–telegraph services in Britain. It quickly acquired the entire cable service system interconnecting the Empire and leased the four beam wireless telegraph stations in Britain communicating with Australia, Canada, India and South Africa.

Despite the private monopoly character of the venture, British and Dominion Governments' interests were safeguarded by the Imperial Communications Advisory Committee (later the Commonwealth Communications Council) which supervised company activities and rates. But Cable and Wireless Ltd retained the right to control all beam radio extensions. Not surprisingly, the arrangement was soon found to limit the activities of the Dominion companies. In 1930 a frustrated AWA sought to negotiate a merger with Cable and Wireless Ltd, a move the Scullin Labor Government opposed. Prime Minister Menzies later proved more responsive. During 1941 his Government endorsed a proposal from AWA to amalgamate Australia's cable and wireless services in a new telecommunications company operating a tripartite agreement between AWA, Cable and Wireless Ltd and the Australian Government, but the proposal found scant favour with Cable and Wireless Ltd.

In wartime Cable and Wireless Ltd's monopoly met storms. On the outbreak of war with Japan, America demanded direct wireless circuits with its Empire Allies. Nor was the Australian Government ready to terminate the radio connection with San Francisco at the war's end. By 1944 it was already apparent that structural changes to the organisation of Commonwealth telecommunications must be made. At two meetings of the Commonwealth Communications Council held in 1944 and July–August 1945, McVey and his fellow PMG representative Sid Witt, played a pivotal role in opening the way to change. It was the Australian and New Zealand 'ANZAAS plan' that proposed the replacement of Cable and Wireless Ltd dominance by a group of 'autonomous but interlocked government–owned telecommunications entities', to be set up in the UK and in each of the Dominions of Canada, Australia, New Zealand, South Africa and India. In future, government, not private enterprise, would control the country's overseas, as well as its internal telecommunications.[6]

In the light of the intense political haggles over the role of the Overseas Telecommunications Commission (Australia) in 1975, it seems generally to have escaped notice that the Commission owes its inception to a Labor Government. The Overseas Telecommunications Bill was introduced in the Senate by Chifley's Postmaster-General, Donald Cameron, on 18 July 1946. It provided for a new statutory authority, the Overseas Telecommunications Commission (Australia) (OTC), that would acquire the ownership and operate the overseas telecommunications services of AWA and function under the aegis of a Commonwealth Communications Board established as a corporate body in Britain. Similar commissions were set up in the other Dominions. Ironically only one parliamentarian, Alan MacDonald, Liberal Senator from Western Australia took exception to a separate overseas telecommunication body, 'when officers of the Postmaster-General's Department are capable of undertaking the work'. Their part in the negotiations, MacDonald added, was already a 'monument to their capacity and patience'. But Director-General McVey and collective Dominion opinion shaped the plan. The legislation, moreover, carried the stamp of no less than three former Postmasters-

General — W.G. Gibson (CP), Senator Ashley (Labor), and the leader of
the Liberal Opposition in the Senate (and Postmaster–General in the
Menzies Government 1940–1) Senator George McLeay.

There was inevitably a close overlap between the function of
PMG's Department and the new instrumentality. The Postmaster–
General remained responsible for administering the Wireless
Telegraphy Act. The Department retained responsibility for land lines
and their connection with overseas facilities, providing both
switchboards and the operators who handled international telephone

Telephonists handling
calls at the international
manual assistance
centre, Sydney, 1952.

traffic plus the operators who switched the calls through the OTC
'gateway' exchange to the international circuits. With the Overseas
Telecommunications Act's passage in August 1946, the embryonic
Overseas Telecommunications Commission was born. Into their bag
(by Government purchase) went Australia's coastal radio stations and
AWA's international high frequency transmission stations in Victoria
and New South Wales.

OTC assumed full control of the radio beam services, absorbing
many of AWA's former radio staff, in February 1947. The long alliance
between private enterprise and Government had ended. Instead, a
strategic marriage had been arranged between the PMG's Department
and OTC. As in many marriages there would be tensions and conflict.
Rivalries would flare for the positioning of exchange 'gateways', the
sites of satellite earth stations and submarine cable landfalls. The large
family of PMG engineers would tilt at the small band of OTC brothers
as a 'cushy and exclusive club'. But the fundamental relationship
between the partners jogged along unquestioned for 25 years. With

the Royal Commission into the Post Office appointed by another Labor Government in 1972, the question of OTC's future assumed all the infighting and bitterness of divorce (see chapter 11).

On the vital question of engineering, Australia entered the postwar period critically short of technical manpower. While her total population rose towards 7 million, there was, said the PMG annual report of 1949–50, 'a dearth of qualified men'. As in previous years, the solution lay in a timely appeal to Britain. During 1950–1 over 70 British engineers were recruited and the following year 100 technicians, including cable joiners, were lured from the UK under Australia's immigration scheme and added to the Department's permanent staff. Plans for new engineering training also shaped. By agreement with the Public Service Board, a cadet engineers scheme was initiated in 1949 by which second year engineering undergraduates were recruited from the universities and earmarked for a PMG career. Twenty were chosen in 1949. By 1952 there were 212 cadet engineers and over 1,600 technicians–in–training. The Department recruited by advertisement, its sense of image heightened by the public relations sections formed in 1947 at headquarters and every State.[7] But there was also that ongoing, distinguishing stream of recruitment of sons and brothers of PMG men reared in the tradition of the service, many of whom as brothers rose jointly to high places, outstripped or equalled the careers of fathers, and followed in the footsteps of a grandfather or greatgrandfather to form generations of PMG men.

In general the Department offered attractive opportunities for personal advancement. In Brown's time a 'typical chart' outlining such opportunities urged the entire gamut of junior assistants, clerks, messengers, linemen, mechanics, telegraphists, telephonists, engineers, district inspectors, supervisors, carpenters, and even sign-writers and French polishers to scramble up their respective ladders to propitious heights. A telegraph messenger, said the chart, rightly, could rise 'by his own efforts' to the highest position. Another message assured that clerks too could travel 'to the top' by a series of routes if they 'want to work'. Courtesy, civility, attention and diligence were the qualities stressed. 'Learn your job and become efficient' was the cry. Brown's hand could be clearly seen. But it was a dictum carried forward from year to year reinforced by a broad commitment to in-house training for the engineering cadet, and Postal Institute and other technical courses. Job mobility was indeed more marked in the PMG's Department than in any other Australian Department of State. It was both the largest employer of labour and the most motivated. Changing technology contributed its part. 'All sorts of people' recalls a former New South Wales State director 'were studying for exams.' Small groups helped each other and, when a new technique or system appeared, 'the technical staff clambered everywhere, eager to understand the new developments'.[8]

Brown's directorship had highlighted the rise of a major engineering enterprise in Australia. The Second World War confirmed the trend. Indeed, until about 1948, the only PMG staff members who generally boasted a tertiary education were engineers. With the strong policy commitment to automation and technological consolidation pushed by McVey and McKay, the Department's engineering character was affirmed. Yet surprisingly, with McVey's departure in 1946, professional technological competence was not reflected in PMG's directorship for some 13 years. Engineering leadership remained in the hands of chief engineer, R.V. McKay. With his technical abilities and wartime contribution, it was generally expected that he would follow Fanning to the Director–General's post. But with Fanning's departure to head the newly formed Australian Broadcasting Control Board in March 1949, the PMG top job went to the long–time Departmental and wartime administrator, Giles Chippindall.[9]

Chippindall belonged to that elite corps of PMG messenger boys who carried a director's baton in his knapsack. 'Chip', as he was widely known, had joined the Department in Victoria in 1908 and rose on the clerical side of the engineering and telephone branches to become the first inspector of personnel in 1936. In 1941 he was one of a large number of officers who transferred from the Department to serve in wartime administrative roles, first as Deputy Director–General and later Director of the War Organisation of Industry, as chief executive officer of the production executive of cabinet and later as Secretary of the Department of Supply and Shipping. He returned as Assistant Director–General to the Department in 1946.[10]

To some extent, Chippindall's career was a non–technical mirror–image of McKay's. But Chippindall had political supporters. A tough minded wartime administrator, he won reputation as 'a man who gets things done'. Bluff, ambitious, and a powerful lobbyist, he was quickly selected by the Labor cabinet for the Director–General's post. In the competitive world of men and power, no one was surprised when McKay was despatched abroad to become the PMG's first liaison officer in London. If unwittingly, Chippindall showed foresight. He created a London post of first importance for tapping and assimilating forward developments in telecommunications overseas and founded a centre for the transfer of British and European technology that functioned effectively until it was abruptly terminated by Prime Minister Fraser one summer morning in 1976. McKay's engineering influence was thus preserved, for as he was wont to remind his Director–General in times of dispute, he retained his title of engineer–in–chief. As such he was a key force and exerted crucial influence on the direction of telecommunications planning in the PMG.[11]

Under Chippindall's directorship from 1949–57 the PMG enjoyed a period of progress interwoven with financial loss across all services in the inflationary years of 1949–54. With more trained staff, quicker delivery of material from local manufacturers, and additional line staff to clear connection backlogs, telephone traffic soared. Telephone subscribers reached the million mark in 1949. Automatic exchanges steadily replaced the manual system. Perth became the first capital city with an all automatic telephone network in 1953, and by 1957, 98 per cent of telephones in capital cities were automatic. At the same time

Melbourne-born Sir Giles Chippindall, 'adroit in the corridors of power'. He rose from telegraph messenger at South Yarra, Victoria, in 1908, to head the PMG as Director-General, Post and Telegraphs, from 1949 to 1957.

the number of small rural automatic exchanges reached over 900. Local and trunk telephone calls doubled in their millions in the decade to 1957, buttressing the country's economic progress and serving in suburbs and countryside as a cohesive agent of social exchange.[12]

Over the period of its penetration, the telephone had enlarged the scope of human and commercial contact more than any other invention. One American writer confidently asserted that 'the telephone had changed the behaviour of Western man more than any other technology in history'.[13] In Australia certainly the stock exchanges and the economic pattern of business pivoted on the telephone operation as it had on the telegraph some decades before. But it spun faster and more densely as a result of telephone use. In the high turnover market where millions changed hands each day, information and the competitive business of dealing hung on the telephone. Pressure from the business community in 1957 and a shortage of technical staff led the PMG (in the teeth of opposition from the Postal and Telecommunications Technicians' Union) to authorise manufacturing companies to sell, rent and install PABXs (private automatic branch exchanges) of approved specification to business firms to connect them to the national system.[14] Overseas telephone calls were also increasingly used by the business community.

The Queen's visit to Australia in 1954 focussed a need to strengthen and upgrade telephone links abroad, but the holding of the Olympic Games in Melbourne in 1956 gave striking impetus to all forms of telecommunications in Australia including the installation of a telephone network for the 15 scattered Games venues, new channels for use by an army of international press reporters using telephone and telegrams, a permanent telephone communications facility and extensive developments in radio broadcasting. The radio telephone exchange from Sydney to London was supplemented immediately before the Games by a new radio telephone exchange at Perth linking London with two new channels through a joint undertaking by the PMG and OTC, and the original two radio telephony channels from Australia to London increased to eight.[15] Victorian supervising engineer, Ivan Gunn, was honoured with an MBE for his planning of the Olympiad telecommunication that year.

For country people, the telephone wrought immense and deepening changes to a lifestyle that, in the remote areas, still bore the outward semblances of a century before. Even with a concerted push towards automating country exchanges, the vast majority, 75 per cent, were still manually operated in 1957. Such exchanges offered contact and a real sense of companionable assistance from the operator — almost always a local girl or woman — through daytime working hours, but it also meant silence and isolation at night. If Postmasters–General were inclined to harp on the spread of RAXs in the national Parliament, it was because, as they knew well, automation put country people in round–the–clock communication with their doctors, their emergency services, their relatives and friends.

Psychologically, the telephone was coming to have a pervasively transforming effect both in business and in the home. Business

A typical small country exchange at Yaapeet, Victoria. The switchboard was manned by the postmistress, Mrs Isabel Dillon, for over 31 years until its automation in 1981.

Less typically perhaps, Mrs Dillon's dedicated service to the local community was, like others, to be formally acknowledged when she received the Order of Australia Medal from the Governor of Victoria, Sir Henry Winneke, 1981.

Despite the increase in exchange automation, there was still a great need for telephonists to handle subscriber inquiries and operator connected trunk calls, such as here at the manual assistance centre in Melbourne's City West exchange.

telephone communication established both expediency and directness in commercial dealings. It lubricated business and official exchange. It also protected the individual. A man, argued one marketing analyst, 'felt safer talking through an instrument he can cut off at will than conversing face–to–face'. Direct dialling detached the user further from personal involvement with an operator. Few had yet come to view it as a hydra–headed monster threatening the individual's privacy. The American humourist, Robert Benchley, discerned in the telephone a means of feeling more important than one was. 'There is something about saying "OK" and hanging up the receiver with a bang', he observed, 'that kids a man into feeling that he has pulled off a big deal, even if he had only called up Central to find out the correct time.'[16] For women, the telephone became an instrument of social freedom and, for some, control. Sometimes it was a tyranny as Dorothy Parker's impassioned essay, 'A Telephone Call', showed. 'Why can't that telephone ring? Why can't it, why can't it? Couldn't you ring? . . . You damned, ugly, shiny thing . . . Damn you, I'll pull your filthy roots out of the wall, I'll smash your smug black face in little bits. Damn you to hell!' The Australian novelist, Shirley Hazzard, carried the image forward in more feminist terms. She has one of her women characters of the 1950s say: 'Women have got to fight their way out of the dumb waiting at the end of the never ringing telephone . . . the *receiver*, as our portion of it is called'.[17]

Organisationally in business, the telephone produced hierarchical effects. It was worth noting at what level an executive no longer answered his own telephone calls. There was also a broader social distinction that the telephone made. White collar workers, but not most blue collar workers, could use the telephone at work. Un-doubtedly the large and diverse effects of the telephone on the

186

A PMG advertisement of 1937 publicising the advantages to business of the still novel teleprinter service.

organisation of economic and social developments and its possible national differences, offers a fertile and little explored field for research.

As the telephone extended its hegemony, that old–timer, the telegraph, experienced a fundamental alteration in its commercial use. Telex entered the Australian telecommunications network as an important component in 1954. The teleprinter, an electrical typewriter whose message was transmitted by relatively high speed telegraphy was first introduced in Australia in the mid–1920s following its introduction by Siemens Ltd as a public telegraph service in Germany. Initially Australian teleprinters were 'point–to–point' in operation, linking post offices in different towns. In wartime, when supplies of the overseas teleprinter expired, spare parts were manufactured in the PMG Melbourne workshops to keep existing machines in service for vital war telecommunication use. Several private teleprinter services were in operation in the early 1940s as the PMG's Department leased units to a handful of businesses — (Qantas's precursor, Queensland and Northern Territory Aerial Services, was a case in point), while a few industrial companies used them for transmitting messages between head office and their branches.

The value of the teleprinter was self–evident from the start. As simple to use as a standard typewriter, they provided speedy communication of printed messages that could be directly received on paper on a corresponding, and unattended, teleprinter machine. Swifter in transmission than the telegram (because the delivery time was removed) and cheaper than a trunk telephone call, teleprinters became a powerful challenger to the business telegram. In 1954 a breakthrough occurred. A manually operated telex exchange was set up by the PMG to link teleprinter terminals and receivers in Sydney and Melbourne and subsequently in other capitals. Four years later Australia's first overseas telex service was opened by OTC. Now business houses and other operators of PMG–leased telex services could conduct direct exchange of printed correspondence with similarly equipped offices both at home and overseas. By June 1959 the Australian telex service was available in 27 countries, a figure that leapt to over 100 in 1968 and to double that by 1975.[18]

New South Wales and Victoria dominated the telex scene. In the first year of the exchange's operation there were 48 telex services in

Telex became a linchpin of business and international affairs from the 1960s: the telex manual assistance centre, Sydney, in the 1970s.

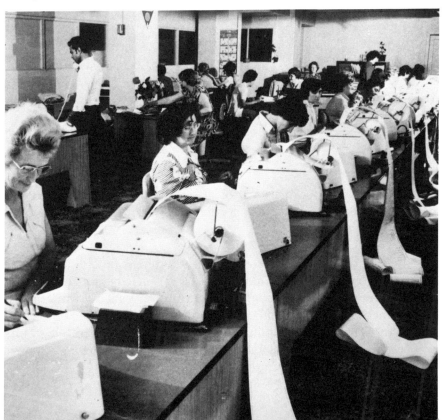

New South Wales, 47 in Victoria and, with high business concentrations, the two States remained pre-eminent users. At first telex tended to take on in the wholesale trade, transport and the machinery and equipment manufacturing industries: but by the end of the 1950s traffic was dispersed. International traffic also soared. The department of Foreign Affairs made early use of telex services in a large number of its embassies and consulates abroad, while Government departments, newspapers, airline offices, stock exchanges, business enterprises, and later hotels and motels, universities and other organisations turned to the new and easy telecommunications system. When, during 1966, the PMG's manual telex exchange system was converted to fully automatic switching, subscribers could 'call direct' to a multiplicity of government, business and organisational subscribers in Australia.[19]

Inevitably telex held far-reaching consequences for the traditional telegraph traffic and its corps of skilled practitioners. Ticking in an office corner, hammering out multiple messages in a stock exchange or newspaper room, telex was the bell-wether of the post-industrial age, the precursor of a new, automatically-linked information society whose metallic clicking sounded the knell of Morse code working in Australia.

In this mini-technological revolution, where did the Australian telegraphist stand? In the immediate postwar years most telecommunications workers, technicians along with management, greeted with optimism the promise of a flourishing technological age. Automation, the *Tele-technician* enthusiastically editorialised in October 1950, 'is an advance in the field of human endeavour to build a higher standard of life with less labour'. More realistically the Telegraphists' and Postal Clerks Union linked the vision of a technological utopia with 'adequate planning and training to place workers in more highly

Teleprinters in use in the telegraph operating room, Sydney, 1957.

technical jobs'. With the proposed introduction of the telex exchange, telegraphists sensed their impending decline. The introduction of an interstate teleprinter network in the Commonwealth Meteorological Office in 1953 was one telling case in point. It brought to an end the PMG's Department's historic responsibility for receiving and transmitting daily weather and climatic reports from telegraph and repeater stations around the country and signalled an important inroad into telegram traffic. Departmental losses on telegrams already touched £1 million in 1953. Three years later the telegraphists' predicament was plain. The reduction of telegraphists amounted to over 400 between 1954–7 and fewer recruits were accepted annually. By 1954 the last of the old Murray Multiplex tape systems was replaced by teleprinter equipment (except on the Sydney–Brisbane line), and by 1957, 60 per cent of all telegraph operations was done on teleprinters. In the same year Morse was eliminated as a subject in the training courses of telegraphists and postal workers.

Yet even more directly threatening to the telegraphists than the magic telex was the plan for the large scale mechanisation of the telegraph system through the introduction of a new switching system, the teleprinter reperforator switching system known beguilingly as TRESS.

In the postwar years a number of powerful automatic, teleprinter transmission systems had been developed for telegraph transmission by telecommunications companies overseas. In Europe where distances were short, these systems were 'point–to–point'. Only in America did Western Union operate a 'reperforating' model which stored the messages to be transmitted for handling and redirection using tape. A cluster of headquarter's engineers including R. Kerr, P. Bethell, D. Richardson and J. Coghill devised the TRESS system based on the use of automatic switching equipment and a reperforator/transmitter machine made by Siemens to Australian specifications. TRESS relied on the presence of automatic switching centres in each capital plus teleprinters in all large post offices. Telegrams were transmitted by teleprinter from the outstation post offices to the capital centre where they were automatically stored temporarily on perforated paper tape. When the line to the destination became free, stored messages were then switched automatically to that line and retransmitted from an automatic tape transmitter. Some messages

TRESS, the Teleprinter Reperforator Switching System, offering fully automated message (telegram) switching, was an Australian innovation which hastened the end of Morse telegraphy.

and particularly those from interstate, passed to semi–automatic positions where a switching operator inserted routing information by push button. In time, the system evolved to switch messages auto-matically in both the State of origin and destination, making the semi-automatic positions redundant. The telegram received by teleprinter was finally delivered by telephone or messenger.[20]

Designed on a shoestring, TRESS was a major and highly successful innovation which grew from scratch in Australia in response to local conditions and distances. In manpower terms, its implications were clear. 'Considerable staff savings' the *Australian Telegraphist* observed darkly, 'will be made in Chief Telegraph Offices where hitherto messages had been received and transmitted manually.'[21] Before TRESS a telegram despatched from a country town in, say, South Australia to Newcastle, NSW, would pass through the hands of six operators. After the introduction of full automatic switching in TRESS, only two operators, one each at the sending and receiving ends were required, while the actual transmission time for a TRESS telegram was reduced from 40 to seven minutes. Projected initially in 1953, TRESS was due for installation late in 1958. In the polished jargon of Director–General Chippindall's 'Ten Years Report', the new telegraph auto-mation was seen in compelling, cost–saving terms. 'The problem facing the Department in dealing with telegraph business [said the Report] has been tackled with vigour and realism, and staffing and techniques are being overhauled continuously and adjusted appro-priately to changing conditions.'[22]

But to the involved telegraphists and postal clerks, the problem was not so smoothly solved. Between 1954 and the system's installation in 1959 their union protested vehemently against the projected scheme. TRESS, with its caressing name, would indeed become the focal point for the early public examination of automation and its impact on the skills, working hours, health and job satisfaction of employees whose work would be transformed by capital intensive mechanisation. It loomed over telegraphists as a programme designed to effect economies at 'giant cost' cut from their collective salaries through redundancies. In such circumstances Chippindall's words were far from reassuring. In August 1957 senior representatives of the Telegraphists and Postal Clerks' Union, J.E. Hickey and John Baker, met with PMG management to seek transfers of redundant staff to positions of equal status and retraining. 'From the outset', the *Australian Telegraphist* summed up, 'we opposed TRESS. It is the Union's job now to adjust its policies to the new situation and fight on the question of safeguards.'[23]

But the writing was on the wall. TRESS was cut into service in Adelaide in August 1959 and extended to all mainland States by 30 June 1960. The cutover to TRESS was completed in Hobart and Launceston later that year. TRESS rapidly fulfilled its automative promise. In operation throughout the country by 1964, TRESS, said the PMG *Annual Report*, 'has mechanised the public telegraph service'. The last Morse message on the eastern network was sent between Bombala, NSW, and Sydney's central telegraph office early in 1963,

The last Queensland Morse telegraph message is sent from Brisbane to Thursday Island, 24 June 1964. Watching veteran telegraphist Hector McDonald are (from left to right) E.C. Lather, Queensland's Director of Posts and Telegraphs, Sir Alan Hulme, Postmaster-General and J.W. Robertson, assistant director (telecommunications).

while the last Morse sent exclusively by land line in mainland Australia was to the far northern outposts of Wyndham and Halls Creek, WA, in mid–1963. In Queensland the last Morse message was sent by combination of land line and radio to Thursday Island in 1964. Morse continued to be sent by radio circuits in WA, the last messages being from Roebourne to Onslow and Wittenoom Gorge in November 1968.

The number of telegraphists employed by the PMG fell dramatically from more than 16,000 in 1954 to some 500 in 1980. Wastage took its toll. Over the years telegraphists found their way into clerical and other positions in the telephone and engineering branches, while similar accommodations were effected for postal clerks. A small number of telegraphists joined the swelling ranks of technicians who, 9,000 strong in 1954, would double in number by 1980 to form the key workforce of a modern telecommunications organisation. But the 'elite' professional telegraphist disappeared. No longer was there the 'Knighthood of the Keys' where telegraphists had their own signature intonations, where each 'heard' not 'read' the message and quickly wrote it down; and where on major race days — those 'holydays' for Australians — the keys and sounders rang hot between race course and the nearest telegraph office with a cryptic language only the telegraphist could understand. The 'Australian Telegraphists Ode' written by 'Spru', the Western Australian telegraphist, Frank Spruhan, which first appeared in the 1920s, said it all.

I well remember Charlie Teede
Who used to work the races;
No need, indeed, to ask for speed,
He'd pace it with the pacers.
Lord help the man who 'broke' him once
Or questioned his 'creations';
On him a flood of scorn was turned,
The atmosphere with brimstone burned,
And Pitman, green with envy, squirmed
At his abbreviations.

The field got wl awa to ti
and as ty settld dwn
Te Shicer frst to brk te li
Ws flwd bi Jo Brown
In close proxim ws Tired Tim,
Tn cme Arbtratn,
Behind te bunch ws Cntr Lunch,
Gd Luk and Hi Taxn
they whizzed along (and so did Charles)
Without te least cessatn.

C R T B te topwt jumped
And got on trms wi Shicr,
Who tn and tre his bundl dumped
Wh labld him a twicer
I scrambled after Charlie
Like a trailer round a bend,
Then gave OK — but queried
'C R T B' u send.
Now wot is it in aid of?
Enlarge a bit my friend.

W'l I mst sa its te bst displa
Of ignrce Ive hrd,
Of all te sqrts in W.A.
Ur certnly te bird
And ani harsh rmks Ive mist
Tey all cn b inferd.
'C R T B' — its known bi rote,
Wt wld u ha me send?
Its cmg rnd te bnd, u goat —
COMING ROUND THE BEND![24]

As one technology departed, another waited in the wings. As plans for TRESS shaped in 1953, the Australian community was far more concerned with the question of whether, and if so, how soon, the country might invest in the new technology of television.

Long forgotten, but of striking foresight, one Australian had probed the mystery of visually transmitted communication in the late 19th century. The creative inventor, Henry Sutton, of Ballarat, designed an apparatus he called 'telephany' in 1887 which is now generally conceded as being the first theoretically feasible television. Sutton was activated by his determination to let the citizens of Ballarat (some 70 miles distant from Melbourne) view the famous Melbourne Cup. His 'telephany' design combined such recently achieved devices as the Kerr effect, the Nipkow disc (which John Logie Baird would adopt in the 1920s), and the selenium photocell. But its fatal flaw as a

Dispersed into many leading positions in the community, former telegraphists gather for a 'Morsecodian' dinner, October 1951. The distinguished group included (far left back) S.F. Kellock, Director of Posts and Telegraphs, NSW, (fifth from left) H.L. Anthony, Postmaster-General, (third from right) Sir Alan Potter, (far right) A.S.V. Smith, and (fourth from left) Rupert Henderson. Their invited guest, Giles Chippindall, Director-General, Posts and Telegraphs, (centre) stands between (to his left) E.R. Knox, Chairman of CSR, and Lt-Gen. Sir Leslie Morshead.

working means of transmitting images lay in the fact that the signal had to be transferred via telegraph lines which were far too slow to relay the flashing hooves of the horses of the Melbourne Cup. Sutton wisely did not bother to construct his ingenious device; but evidence suggests that Baird's first television system of the 1920s owed something to the early Australian experiment.[25]

Baird projected his first image onto a 'television screen' in 1925. Two years later he demonstrated 'a distant electrical vision' over 400 miles of telephone line between London and Glasgow and, in 1928, engineered the first experimental transmission between London and New York. But the BBC's flirtation with the new medium of television was cautious. Though they inaugurated an experimental television service using the Baird system in 1929, six years later two systems went on trial — Baird's telecasting with a 240-line screen and EMI–Marconi with 405 lines. In February 1937 the BBC's adoption of the EMI–Marconi system for British television led the world.

In Australia, in April 1934, a small group of amateurs in Brisbane were transmitting television radio signals that carried 25 miles to a receiving set in Ipswich. For three years the group, led by Tom Elliot, assembled equipment and followed experiments abroad. Using the electronic scanning method after broadcasting stations had closed at night, they sent out messages from the top of the Brisbane Observatory on Wickham Terrace for any enthusiasts who cared to pick them up. In 1935 the Brisbane broadcasting station 4CM was granted a licence to conduct experimental television broadcasts. 'Tom Elliot and his associates', the Brisbane *Courier–Mail* reported later were 'effectively transmitting pictures of 9 inches by 4 inches with almost 100 per cent clarity'.[26]

In October 1935, while television trials were under way in Britain, Elliot and his team made a public transmission from the Brisbane Observatory to the *Courier–Mail*'s building a few miles away, when a copy of the *Courier–Mail* itself was 'clearly legible on the screen'. Initially transmission began with objects taken from rolls of sound films, and later close–up 'stills' of movie stars. But the amateurs quickly moved on to animated television using rather cumbersome methods. War ended their experiments. Yet in 1935 Elliot optimistically claimed

194

that Australia 'can have television here and now if the authorities are willing to co-operate. There is no reason to delay. An efficient system of low-definition television could be put on the air almost immediately and then Australia would be practically abreast of the world in the new science.'[27]

If Tom Elliot sought PMG help, his appeal left no record. At the Research Laboratories, Witt and J.H.T. Fisher were conducting television research. In March 1939 Fisher published a laboratory report 'Studies of overseas developments in television in relation to possible future services in Australia', which surveyed requirements for a national television service based in Melbourne. But, as in England, war clipped television experimentation in Australia, Fisher moved to the Army Design Directorate to work on radar, while Witt's energies were widely dispersed. However, a year after the BBC launched television with a 405-line system in June 1946 and the first coaxial cable transmitted TV from New York to Washington, the PMG Research Laboratories were engaged in the examination and planning of an Australian television service.

Yet television broadcasting did not begin for ten more years in Australia. Why, despite achievements, did Australia have to wait so long? And why did Government relinquish its monopoly control of a new mass medium in a way it had never dreamt of doing with telephony or telegraphy?

Technically, Australia with its long distance and dispersed population posed formidable problems for national television development. Research concentrated on methods and techniques of waveform testing for the best frequency use in Australia and on video transmission circuits and relay links. During 1948 an unexpected input came from Europe. Four German scientists whom the Australian Government had acquired rather late in the Allies' scramble for advanced scientific talent among former enemy scientists, were transferred to Australia and to the PMG's Research Laboratories. The quartet, Albert Seyler, Ernest Rumpelt, Frederick Ruf and Wilhelm Otto, all held PhDs and had been staff members of German universities or scientific institutes. Transferred to Australia, initially for two year contracts, all but Ruf opted to remain when their contracts expired. Seyler, an engineering graduate from the Technical University, Munich, and a wartime radar researcher for the German Air Radio Research Institute, would make an important contribution to television research. He immediately joined Fisher's television team and his fundamental investigations with Z.L. Budrikis on coding and processing of visual information ultimately established the Research Laboratories as one of the major contributors to television signal coding research. In the early 1950s Seyler and J. Potter would develop an innovative 'pulse and bar' waveform test concept which was embodied in the 'Video Transmission Test Set'. As a later outcome, the first solid state operational pulse and bar waveform test signal generator was developed by the Laboratories with Seyler and manufactured by Australian industry for the national network and for export.[28]

J.H.T. Fisher, the first Australian television engineer, and former PMG employee, who was to be honoured in 1974 with the Television Society of Australia's Penguin Award for his pioneering work in, and research on, television.

Dr Albrecht Seyler, a wartime radar researcher, was one of the four German scientists brought to Australia under contract in 1948 by the Government to work at the PMG Laboratories on television research. Awarded the degree of Doctor of Applied Science by Melbourne University in 1966, he headed the Research Laboratories' advanced techniques branch from 1964 until his death in 1977.

With technical investigation well under way, Prime Minister Chifley gave national television a green light.[29] But the process was careful. After consideration by a cabinet sub–committee on broadcasting and recommendations from the Australian Broadcasting Control Board in mid–1948, the Government authorised the PMG's Department to invite tenders for television transmitters (two for Sydney and Melbourne, and one for each other State), leaving it to the manufacturers to come up with specifications. Eleven tenders were received from UK, the USA, Holland, France and Australia by 1949, and in June that year cabinet approved the principle of the introduction of television services in Australia to be provided initially in six capital cities with relays at other points. Following the British precedent, and arguing that commercial interests could not afford the cost of setting up a new infrastructure, the Chifley Government contended that every capital city was 'equally entitled to the benefits of this great discovery' and that Government should meet the approximate operating costs of £1,400,000 a year. Arthur Calwell, Labor's spokesman in the House of Representatives, announced that television programmes should be provided 'only on a national television service in Australia'. 'We decided to make television a national monopoly' he explained, because 'we believed that the harm that had been done in the field of commercial [radio] broadcasting by those who had been lucky enough to get licences and who had exploited the public should not be repeated in the field of television'. The PMG would proceed with arrangements for further technical investigation and training technical and production staff, and the Government would pioneer an improved transmission system using 625 lines on screen (compared with Britain's 405 line and America's 525) as the most scientifically advanced and suitable system for Australia.[30]

The groundplan laid by the Chifley Government was, however, abandoned by the Menzies Liberal–Country Party Coalition Government elected in December 1949. High caution and deep ideological attitudes now played a part. One Liberal MP, C.W. Falkinder, had put one imputation plainly in the Parliament a few months before. Commercial broadcasters, he alleged, would not be permitted to use frequency modulation under Labor's national television plan. 'Unless the commercial radio stations give the most modern service, such as frequency modulation', he summed up, 'they will not obtain advertising upon which they depend, . . . and they will be gradually but completely forced out of the business.' Other Liberal members supported this view. Howard Beale saw national TV as the death knell for all forms of radio broadcasting. Some members of the coalition fraternity continued to condemn television as a 'luxury'. R.G. Casey, Menzies's Minister for National Development, somewhat paradoxically opposed the proposal for telecommunication growth on the grounds that in a period of planned national development and resource marketing needs 'we should not add to our already overcrowded market for public entertainment in Australia'. However there were others among the new Government who believed that television should be entirely handed over to private enterprise.

Menzies's Country Party Postmaster–General, H.L. Anthony, surprisingly, fixed his position on another point. He challenged the 'unfitness' of a policy of introducing television stations before much needed housing construction was carried out. In his view 'television was a non–essential product' in Australia. His was a stance of 'wait and see' while he announced his Government's intention of introducing one television transmitting station to Sydney as a pilot scheme.[31]

Deep hesitations about this 'strange new electronic instrument in the home' were also reflected in the wider community. Socially there was anxiety that the unregulated introduction of the spectacular new medium, might have baleful effects upon the community. 'Prometheus or Frankenstein?' asked one journal anxiously. Economically there was the strong objection in the recession of the early 1950s that the provision of television to the Commonwealth would be of enormous cost. Australians were deeply divided on the scheme. To a wide range of educationalists, churchmen, businessmen, economists and even the newspaper fraternity, television was 'one more frippery' in a country which urgently needed hospitals, schools, better roads and telephone connections and, for some, better defence.

Unusual pro and anti–TV groups formed. A former Country Party Postmaster–General Archie Cameron, contended (on behalf of the committee of the Liberal and Country League of South Australia) that Australia could not afford to devote manpower and money to television, while the National Farmers' Union of Australia (speaking for such rural leviathans as the Graziers' Federal Council, the Wheat Growers' Federation, the Wool and Wheat Producers, and the Primary Producers Council) pressed eagerly for the new service which, they believed with foresight, would by means of scientific rural extension work, lead to greatly increased production in primary industry.[32]

Menzies's role in the proceedings proved important. Though he himself was not, as one of his biographers, Cameron Hazlehurst, points out, greatly interested in TV and was a man easily bored by detail, he took a nationalist position on a matter of policy.[33] By 1950 his Government had adopted the principle of a dual national and commercial television service similar to radio. But they hastened slowly. Indeed as the redoubtable Labor MP, Clyde Cameron, accused 'the Government has decided that the Australian people are to be denied television services until private vested interests are ready to provide them.'[34]

During 1951 a television advisory committee, made up of Jim Fisher, Charles Moses of the Australian Broadcasting Commission, and J.M. Donovan of the Australian Broadcasting Control Board were sent abroad to investigate television developments in Europe and America and report their findings to the Television Advisory Council. With a mass of technical and other evidence already before them, the Commonwealth Government on 11 February 1953 appointed a Royal Commission on Television to take submissions and hear evidence. Two months later they pushed through the Television Act of 1953 to provide legislative authority for the establishment of both national and commercial television stations. Postmaster–General Anthony had changed his mind. 'No matter how we may differ in detail as to how it should be done', he now proclaimed with some simplicity in introducing the Television Bill to the House, 'we are all agreed that television services with their great potential benefits for education, culture and entertainment should be made available to the Australian people.'[35] Australia was scarcely in the van. The metropolitan inhabitants, at least of Britain, USA, Canada, Sweden, Denmark, Switzerland, Italy, Holland, Spain, Japan, the Philippines, Argentina, Brazil and even Mexico and Cuba were already enjoying the spectacle of the flickering black and white television screen.

Australia's first television broadcast was made from a commercial station TCN 9 Sydney on 16 September 1956. The first two national stations, ABN 2 Sydney and ABV 2 Melbourne, opened on 5 and 18 November. Much opinion had been ventilated. The Royal Commission had been expressly charged to recommend the number of both national and commercial stations that could be 'effectively' established and operated in the Commonwealth. They formed the conclusion, as 'inescapable as it is socially unfortunate', that the high costs of television must for some time limit the medium's use to large concentrations of population in the cities. But the rural lobby had large influence. In a country dependent for so much of its exports on primary produce, rural television assumed prominence. So great, indeed, was its potential lure seen to be that the commissioners considered that its early extension to country areas would serve to retain vital rural settlers on the land. In consequence, they declined to establish a priority for national stations and urged particularly that licences should be issued for commercial television stations in country centres 'as soon as possible'.[36]

The ABV-2 transmitter tower on Mt Dandenong, high above Melbourne, Victoria, from which both radio and television signals are broadcast.

The commission, however, rejected the proposal that television should be operated on a basis for joint participation by a national authority and private enterprise. Licences would be issued to commercial stations by the Australian Broadcasting Control Board: the board would have responsibility for allocating channels and formulating a complete frequency allocation plan, while the object of all licences was, in the greenhorn days of the mid–1950s, to provide programmes that would have the effect of raising standards of public taste. The 'democracy of the turning knob' was seen as a guarantee of good quality. One feature of the Royal Commission's evidence, and of the subsequent Inquiry of the Control Board into licensing, stood out. Apart from the pressure for rural interests, there was no real lobby for Australian television except those who wanted to sell. As one observer wrote later of the control board's inquiry: 'The bulk of the proceedings revolved round the problem of whether this or that applicant was able to run a TV station, whether it would fail, or whether it would make money eventually . . . The effect of the medium upon the community at large, and the need to erect some safeguards, either did not occur to the Board or did not concern them.'[37]

On the PMG's advice, Australian television services were developed and expanded using very high frequency (VHF) channels: ultra high frequency (UHF) became available later. Here the Director–

General's advice was positive and influential. He believed that, even at a proposed budget of £1 million, the launching of national television would not interfere with telephone trunk line erection or other essential telecommunication services. Rather, he saw the establishment of a number of television stations throughout Australia as giving an impetus to the provision of coaxial cable or microwave links that would facilitate the installation of additional telephone facilities.[38] Chip's prediction proved correct.

By 1955 the Government had acted on the broad advice of its Royal Commissioners. A 'dual' policy was established. By amendment to the Television Act of 1953, the PMG's Department was given responsibility for organising buildings for television transmitters, procuring under contract the necessary towers, aerials and associated transmitting equipment and radio links between transmitters and studios, operating, installing, commissioning and maintaining the transmitting equipment and organising the training of operating staff for the national television service as it had done for national sound broadcasting since 1932. The Department also held responsibility for providing programme relay facilities for commercial stations operation.[39] The Australian Broadcasting Commission was appointed the 'national' television authority; while overall control of planning, technical and programme standards of all Australian television stations, and the issue of licences to commercial stations, was vested in the Australian Broadcasting Control Board.

With its official launch both commercially and nationally in September and November 1956, Australia established a world tech-

Melbourne's television operating centre boosts and switches television programmes between studio and transmitter for stations throughout Australia. Shown here is the control console and the video testing and patching array.

The Melbourne Olympic Games of 1956 was one of the factors in the early
popularity of Australian television, despite the (then) high cost of sets.
Organising the full array of communications necessary for the world's press at
the Games was to be another PMG success story. Here, a radio broadcast is in
progress.

nological lead in the adoption of a 625 line service, a lead Britain would
catch up with when it introduced colour television in the 1960s. As the
Australian plan unfolded, Phase 1, with one national and two
commercial stations each in the major cities of Sydney and Melbourne,
was ready to cover the Olympic Games in Melbourne in November
1956. The occasion spurred both the establishment of the service and
the hire and purchase of TV receivers. Phase 2 extended the services of
one national and two commercial stations to Perth, Brisbane and
Adelaide in 1959 and to Hobart in 1960. Phase 3, completed in 1962,
created 13 new television stations, national and commercial, in
provincial centres in all States. In the same year the completion of the
Sydney–Melbourne coaxial cable made possible the first regular interstate television relays.

Sir Giles Chippindall — he had been knighted in 1955 — had presided
over a series of major technological evolutions during his term in office
and had led the Department in a period of striking innovation and
change. When he laid down his director's baton in May 1958, he had
the satisfaction of knowing that the country's telephone service had
literally doubled in the decade to 1957, while the assets of the
Department had multiplied by a factor of four touching £403 million in
1957. Indeed, as Chippindall himself pointed out, the value of the
Department's engineering and telecommunications divisions alone,
was 'somewhat greater than the fixed assets of the Broken Hill Pty Ltd,
the Snowy Mountains Hydro–Electric Authority, General Motors
Holden's, and Imperial Chemical Industries combined'. The PMG, or

the Australian Post Office as Chip started to call it, was not only an organisation with large interactions with the community, but a significant instrument in the capital market.

Little has been said in this volume about the 'pricing' or 'tariff' policy of the PMG. But, by the 1950s, the effects of such a 'policy' could be clearly seen at least for the telephone in the amount of cross-subsidisation that flowed from the profitable trunk line services to the 'bush', as well as in the evolutionary adoption of such items as connection, shared facilities and installation fees. Pricing had much that was arbitrary about it; much that was 'rule of thumb'. Its complexities offer a study in themselves. To date only one scholar has tackled the question, economic historian, Dr Ian McLean, and he admits to considerable difficulty. But McLean poses three questions that are relevant here:

1 What were the objectives of the PMG's pricing behaviour?
2 How far did political influence determine the level or structure of subscriber prices of the telephone?
3 Was the PMG an instrument of government development and redistributive policies?[40]

Historically, the PMG took over telephone rates in all their unevenness from the Colonies at Federation, and the colonial 'flat rate' (by which subscribers paid the same annual rate regardless of telephone usage) was maintained throughout the Commonwealth until 1907. In 1908 the 'measured' or 'toll' rate was introduced for new subscribers (chief engineer John Hesketh, back from an American visit, was a strong influence here) and this involved both a rental charge and a charge that took account of the number of calls made over the first 1,000 free calls in any account of a six month billing period. There was no installation or connection fee. But, typical of that confused period, the old 'flat' rate and the new 'measured' rate ran side by side until the measured rate was universally introduced by Postmaster–General Thomas in 1910.

One interesting principle was established early in the business of levelling telephone charges: it was costlier to be linked to a large exchange than to a small one. The Report of the 1910 Royal Commission on the Post Office rounded out the point: 'It is obvious', it announced, 'that a telephone service with a large number of subscribers is of greater value to each subscriber than a service with a small number'. This established, and a measured charging rate affirmed, the basis of a comprehensive telephone charging policy got under way in 1911. Yet it was not straightforward. Changes in telephone call rates were comparatively rare. Fee reduction for volume disappeared in 1915 and a single fee of one penny per local call was adopted nationally. The charge rose to 1¼d in 1920 and, except for a temporary change, remained thus for a record period of 21 years until it moved to 1½d (to assist the war budget) in 1941. It reached 2d in 1949 and 4d in 1959. Local call charges were thus clearly not related to fluctuating costs. 'In the half century before 1960', McLean sums up, 'the local call and the Sydney–Melbourne trunk call charges were raised only six times, and the annual rental charge on only eight occasions.'[41]

But there were other variants in the pricing scheme. Frequent adjustments were made by regulation to the conditions of levying telephone charges. In 1924, for example, the radius of local calls was extended from five to ten miles for metropolitan subscribers and extended again to a radius of 15 miles for subscribers in Melbourne and Sydney in 1929. The year 1951 gave an illustration of how network size affected cost when a fee for subscribers on networks with 5,000 subscribers was raised to 3d a local call, while subscribers on smaller networks paid 2½d, or a halfpenny less per call. Party line subscribers paid a lower rental than subscribers with exclusive use; but from 1914 annual telephone rental carried a loading for those living beyond certain distances from the exchange. Country people paid heavily for installing lines beyond a prescribed, and usually short, distance from an existing exchange; but no general telephone connection fee was introduced in Australia until 1956. Significantly in terms of cross–subsidising, or favouring one set of customers above another, from January 1934 business subscribers paid a higher tariff than residential customers (£1 a year) for a period of nine months, a practice that was then abandoned, resumed again in 1941 and sustained until it was dropped in 1964. A decade later the differential was reintroduced in the larger rental charged to business customers from 1974.[42]

Trunk tariffs added another element to the pricing roulette. Peak and off–peak rates were introduced as early as 1915 and remained a constant concession of 50 per cent for 14 years. An intermediate off-peak concession was introduced from 1929 to 1949 then abandoned until 1978. Distance was a factor in every reckoning. Distance loadings were large in relation to telephone rent. When it came to trunk charges, three distance segments appeared, one up to 100 miles, the second from 100–400 miles, and the third from 400–800 miles (to be enlarged as lines marched outwards), with different charges operating within each 'step'.

With such complexities, who determined telephone pricing policy for the PMG? Telephone charges, unlike telegraph and postal charges, were settled by regulation and were influenced by Departmental officers, the Postmaster–General, politicians and such interest groups as businessmen and farmers. The procedure was for the PMG to make recommendations and, while they were often examined in detail by the Minister and cabinet and sometimes discussed in Parliament, they lay strictly outside parliamentary control (except for the unusual step of disallowance of a regulation). Archie Cameron, a former Postmaster–General, alerted to the anomaly in 1941, vainly attempted to make a change. The Minister and the Department retained control over telephone pricing although it was a game Minister who got too far out of step with his Party.[43]

There was no doubt however, that, through the labyrinth, and through successive and different Party Ministers and the administrators within the PMG, both the 'equity theme' of a fair service for one country and the theme of a PMG 'public service' versus a 'business enterprise' loomed large. Dr J. Forbes, Federal member for the rural electorate of Barker, South Australia (a political scientist by training and later a Liberal Minister), took telecommunications as his special field. Speaking in the House of Representatives in September 1959, he expressed a clarifying view

> Since its inception, the Postmaster–General's Department has always recognised its special obligation to provide services to remote areas. In many, perhaps in most cases, these services have been provided at a rate below the actual cost of installing and providing them. Since the war, the Department's acceptance of this principle has been exemplified by the priority it has given to the telecommunications side of its activities, at the expense of all others. On the telecommunications side, the greater proportion of the money available per subscriber is spent in the country. It is because of this that such a policy has played a great part in improving communications in rural areas . . .
>
> But despite the emphasis inherent in these priorities for rural dwellers, rural electorates know that there is still much to be done before the situation can be described as satisfactory. There is still the 'submerged tenth' of the telephone users who operate within very restricted hours. There are still too many overloaded party lines. There are still too few trunk lines, and this causes long delays in making long–distance calls.[44]

The costs of expanding telecommunications were recognisably high. Forbes said he himself could testify from his own electorate to the very high cost of automative working. In the town of Mt Gambier, an automatic exchange to serve 2,500 subscribers recently opened cost the best part of £400,000. There were 70 rural automatic exchanges in his electorate alone, the average costing £16,500.

Forbes was one of many politicians who put the argument strongly that the PMG should raise its charges to a level where 'in the overall operations of the undertaking, revenue will cover all costs'. This, he judged, still justified calling it a 'public utility', for through elaborate systems of pricing and cross–subsidising it made no profit 'in any conventional sense of the word'.

Chippindall's regime focussed much of this thinking. His approach to running the PMG was as 'a great business undertaking' using budgeting as an aid to management through the use of 'needs' budget and a 'realistic' budget, and centred on resources and priority planning.[45] The method occasioned frequent reviews and won him some reputation as a martinet. But in this, he himself was under pressure from 1954 onwards. After six years of financial losses, the Department fell beneath the incisive gaze of the Joint Committee on Public Accounts. Since the chaos of its first decade, several accounting procedures had been adopted. Profit and loss results, cash expenditure and receipts, and the value of fixed assets became available from 1913; yearly details of engineering activities were published from 1927, and plant construction and maintenance totals were made public from 1932. But by the 1950s it was apparent that the Department's basis of commercial accounting was seriously out of date. Departmental efficiency, said the joint committee, had been 'primarily concerned with technical efficiency', while business management and a full appreciation of accounts and costs of the undertaking had been 'relegated to a less important position'. In the committee's view, the provision of telephones and other services in country areas below cost, the adoption of tariff schedules that did not in many instances relate to costs of giving service, and costs outside the Department's administrative control such as bushfires and floods required more careful reckoning.[46]

The criticism struck home although it was not until Chippindall had left the Department in 1959 that the appointment by Postmaster–General Charles Davidson of an ad hoc committee of inquiry into the commercial accounts of the post office cleared the financial air.

While dissenting groups within the committee grappled with the old question of the extent to which the Department should be regarded as a business enterprise, and minority and majority reports were produced, the upshot was that from 1960 the PMG was required to regard the Treasury as its business financier. The change marked a watershed. To bring the Department and parliamentarians back to a realisation of what true and fair cost meant in a period of considerable inflation and disappearing profits was, wrote economic historian Alan Barnard, 'a feat of considerable political consequence'.[47]

Chippindall's other contribution during his years in office was to set his hand to major institutional reform. In 1952 he introduced three streamlined divisions, telecommunications (containing telephone, telegraph and wireless), engineering, and postal and transport services. His influence on the Department was directly felt in his administrative strategies. Much given to committees, he set up the post office headquarters advisory committee under his own chairmanship early in 1953 to act as a consultative body of the heads (Assistant Directors–General) of the three new divisions, the Assistant Directors (centurions of the 'branches'), and 'a selected' State Director. In Chippindall's view, the committee gave all divisions and branches a part in the overall management of the Department. If the States felt somewhat left out, their regional councils were designed to model their discussion on the headquarters pattern along with supplementary items of local importance, while the 'selected' State Director rotated on the central committee.[48]

Basically Chip's plan was hierarchical, designed to keep lines of communication open from management downwards. The headquarters advisory committee, said his own report of progress, 'ensured that the ideas arising from the top level control will be pursued with proper enthusiasm and speed through the whole organisation'. It was a distinctly different and a less harmonious style of management than Sir Harry Brown's. Some members of the Department found an abrasiveness in the system, a sense of 'excessive inquiry and overview'. Engineers complained of an absence of participation in policy approaches from innovative staff members at lower points on the hierarchical scale.

In retrospect possibly Chippindall's most singular attainment as Director–General was his direct connection with political power. He enjoyed both the personal friendship and the high opinion of the Prime Minister, Robert Menzies. Tweed suited, his briefcase conspicuously stuffed with papers, his expression earnest but mild, he was an inveterate visitor to Canberra where he played golf with Menzies and a small group of Ministers, and was an informal, but powerful lobbyist, with a reputation for tough action and 'punch'. Chip's golf and his friendship undoubtedly lifted the Department in the Prime Minister's eyes. To some the alliance seemed unexpected. But while the PMG portfolio stood at 26th place in the Ministerial hierarchy, Chip's presence and influence was seen as 'pure gold'.

As the PMG flourished, what role did its political masters play? Their passage was often swift. (See Appendix II.) From Federation until 1963, 30 Postmasters–General were appointed in twice as many years, and a number used it as a stepping stone to higher office. The portfolio's position on the Ministerial totem pole was low: 27th in Senator Donald Cameron's time in the Labor Government of 1945–9 and 26th for the Country Party's H.L. Anthony under Menzies, 1949–56. Yet there were clearly rural votes in communications and in the spreading telephone and television lines, a point recognised in the appointment from the 1920s of Postmasters–General drawn from the Country Party and often from the Upper House.

Both Country Party and Labor Ministers were vigorous spokesmen for country needs. Chippindall served a mix of three. The Victorian Labor Senator Donald Cameron, whom Prime Minister Curtin appointed at the age of 67, had spent his early life as a swagman and gave keen attention to linemen's needs. In the severe floods in NSW and Queensland in 1949, he demanded and got mobile changing huts and eating rooms for the drenched restorers of communication, and succeeded in sheeting home PMG responsibility (which had been rejected at Federation as a legacy from Colonial times) for providing proper accommodation for country postmasters and rural staff. Cameron was an able Postmaster–General who steered through the formation of OTC and presided over the portfolio through the remarkable years of postwar telecommunications and postal, growth.[49]

His successor Larry Anthony, a countryman from the northern New South Wales seat of Richmond, enjoyed a distinction that made him unique. He started his career as a country telegraph messenger boy at Peak Hill, NSW, and died in harness as the nation's Postmaster–General in 1956. Anthony had held other portfolios since entering Parliament in 1937. Assistant Treasurer and Assistant Minister for Commerce in the Menzies Government of 1940 and Minister for Transport in 1941, he combined the portfolio for Civil Aviation with the Postmaster–Generalship from 1951–4. But, unlike Cameron who had his office at PMG headquarters and kept in close touch with Departmental staff, Anthony rarely visited Melbourne but shuttled by train between Canberra and his banana–growing seat. The seat went on his death to his son, Douglas, who would lead the Country Party and its retitled National Party of Australia, and become a long–time Coalition Deputy Prime Minister. Supportive of his Department, Larry Anthony was no pace setter and ran into considerable flak during the long hiatus over television. Overall he seemed to have imbibed the advice given by Curtin to his wartime Postmaster–General, Senator

Ashley, 'Don't interfere too much with them, Bill. They're doing all right.'

Chip's last Minister was C.W. (later Sir Charles) Davidson, Country Party member for Dawson, a sugar growing belt of Queensland situated between Mackay and Bundaberg. A popular Lieutenant-Colonel in New Guinea in the Second World War, where 'Charlie Hill' and 'Davidson Ridge' commemorated his success, Davidson made rather a spectacular entry into Federal politics in 1946 when he beat Labor's Deputy Prime Minister and Minister for the Army, Frank Forde (one more telegraph boy original), in the Queensland seat of Capricornia. Tall and clipped, Davidson had a staccato military style and, when he travelled, his suitcase glittered. It was made from aluminium taken from the wreck of a Japanese war plane. A sugar grower himself, he was returned for the seat of Dawson in 1949, became Country Party whip, Deputy Leader of the Country Party in 1953, Minister for the Navy in 1956 and, concomitantly, Postmaster-General on Anthony's death later that year. He combined the portfolios of land and sea for two more years.[50]

As Postmaster-General until 1963, Davidson presided over some major telecommunications planning and growth. For some Victorian members of the PMG's Department, he proved a special hero. When the Report of the Royal Commission into Alleged Improper Practices by 'persons employed in the Postmaster-General's Department in Victoria in relation to illegal gambling' (a matter that cropped up with some regularity in the PMG) with its criticism of the State administration's failure to co-operate with the police, was ready for tabling in Parliament, a fracas at question time diverted the Speaker's attention from Davidson's formal request to table the Report. Sweeping up his papers, Davidson left the House. The Report, resultingly, was never tabled in the House of Representatives and took a proverbial 'armchair ride' through the Senate.[51]

Not everyone saw the Postmaster-Generalship as a glittering prize in a career of talent. Clement Semmler, a former senior official of the ABC which, had 'tumbled willy-nilly into the [PMG] portfolio', wrote acidly that 'some of the honorable gentlemen I knew in those posts were barely literate, and very few of them showed the slightest interest in or knowledge of broadcasting. The ABC was an unwelcome fungus on the Post Office tree.'[52] Essentially the increasingly technological character of the office posed problems. Anthony (who as a sapper worked in the wireless section at Gallipoli in the First World War), when questioned about the adoption of very high frequencies for Australian television, candidly declared he was no 'expert'. 'I simply accept', he said, 'the advice of men who have devoted their lives to the study of these problems.'[53] It was a stance that would undergo perceptible change in the regime of the later portfolios of 'Posts and Telecommunications' and 'Communications' from 1975.

9 Distance and Diversity

W hile policy direction for the PMG (or the APO as it was called from the 1960s on) was set at Melbourne headquarters, the great part of PMG action took place in the States. Administratively the States were largely a mirror image of the headquarter scene. Headquarter divisions of engineering, postal and transport services, telecommunications, finance and general services, branches of accounts, personnel, buildings, stores and contracts, and organisation and methods were replicated in each State and, on matters of current operations and broad planning, headquarters usually worked in close communication with senior management in the States.

From a birds–eye view, one might consider that headquarters was the cyclops eye and mind of the great Commonwealth body and the States its functioning limbs. Certainly in an organisation that depended on new technology for its forward growth, overall strategic decision-making rested with headquarters while State directors of posts and telegraphs were brought to Melbourne several times a year (some thought too infrequently) to discuss their current problems and be provided with information of national plans. But there were significant anomalies and differences between the States. Population, and telecommunication subscribers, were distributed most unevenly among the States. Ten per cent were in South Australia, another 10 per cent in the West; fewer in Tasmania and some 40 per cent in New South Wales. Hence, despite the national framework of telecommunications, some States wielded more authority than others; there were some long fostered interstate rivalry, strong State loyalties, and a feeling at least among the remoter States staff of the 'they' of headquarters and 'we' in the field.

The very breadth of the continent and the varieties of its climatic conditions created singular differences in the rate and character of its communications growth. If the concept of a national telecommunications network was consciously fostered at the Melbourne headquarters, those who lived at Wilpena, South Australia, at Wyndham in Western Australia, at Birdsville in south-western Queensland, or at

207

Strahan on the inhospitable mid–west coast of Tasmania, saw the matter in a different light. Moreover the geography of a continent with a land surface of almost three million square miles bore little resemblance to a country such as Great Britain from which so large a part of Australian knowledge and equipment came. A telephone circuit between Melbourne and Perth, Adelaide and Darwin, or Hobart and Brisbane was equivalent in length to an international circuit connecting London to Moscow with many countries in between.

There were also large and striking differences between communications in the bare and rugged outposts of the continent and in concentrations of urban populations in cities and country towns. Although a telecommunications overview of Australia revealed that there were some ten million miles of telephone circuits and over 20 telephones per 100 of population in 1959, there were still many country–dwellers out on a 'telegraph–only' limb.[1] Radio broadcasting had yet to be provided to the remoter corners of the countryside, and television would not reach large sectors of the rural community until the mid–1960s and, for some inaccessible regions, not for another two decades. At the same time the old manual forms of telephony in common battery and magneto exchanges continued to function interwoven with fully automatic and continually advancing forms. The country's telecommunications network resembled an evolutionary biological form. The species of the genera were undergoing change; yet what was as extinct as the dodo in Melbourne or Sydney could still be functioning very effectively in a small Western Australian town. By the same token, dramatic and unexpected events could stimulate change in parts of the organisation remote from the centres of major advance.

The smallest State, Tasmania, hanging like a pendant below the mainland, illustrated one set of circumstances that underlined its besetting problems of distance and geography. The island's dependence on a submarine cable connection with the mainland was

Bottoms Up! Linemen inspecting a submarine telephone cable the hard way, by pulling it up over a raft, between Cygnet and Shipwrights Point, Southern Tasmania, 1962.

its Achilles' heel. The record–setting submarine coaxial cable of 1936 (the longest and most intensively used submarine telephone cable of its time) connecting Tasmania to the mainland by voice, was silenced by faults on four occasions: in 1938, during the vulnerable years of war in 1940 and 1943, and again in 1957. During 1939 a unique underwater cable inspection was made using a diver 'riding the cable' on an underwater sheave towed by a ketch. This 'eyeball' inspection not only provided valuable data on the state of the line, but vital information on the hitherto unknown conditions of the ocean bed.

Yet the cable, like its historic forebears, suffered severely from abrasions to its southern sector from the Sea Elephant Shoal rocks off King Island where the Naracoopa repeater station stood. Other abrasions also occurred at places where the cable rubbed against loops formed from excess slack. Repairs carried out in 1957 marked the culmination of a long deterioration in insulation resistance that began to show itself eleven years before. The delicate, costly and technically demanding location of the fault points by pulse echo techniques led to a substantial replacement of cable sections that year. The cable's burden of voices and business increased dramatically in the postwar years. During 1953 seven more telephone channels were added to its facilities, while a team led by L.M. Harris of the Research Laboratories managed to achieve an Australian 'first' in their assault on troublesome electrical noise by 'bridging the greatest attenuation' in Harris's words 'that had ever been bridged in terrestrial communications up to that time'. During 1955 Tasmania's links with the 'northern island' were improved when a radio telephone system with six high grade channels was cut into service between Lilydale, near Launceston and Wilsons Promontory in Victoria.[2]

Tasmania's problems also hung, not only on its vital telephone connections with the mainland and the deep sense of psychological isolation that even the briefest break inspired, but on its rugged terrain, the snow and ice–topped mountains, and the critical business of hauling equipment up the inaccessible surfaces of its outer islands and

Tasman Island, on the sea approach to Port Arthur, south-east Tasmania, may look picturesque but landing men and telecommunications equipment by means of flying fox and haulway for the island's radio installation would prove to be a particularly hazardous job.

its distant peninsular points. The River Derwent, emptying into Hobart's estuary, was deeper at its mouth and more difficult to cross with telecommunications cables than Sydney Harbour. The Furneaux Islands of Bass Strait offered the challenge of getting communications to an isolated sea–girt site; while men pitted their strength against Tasman Island, the guardian of Storm Bay, to pull telecommunications equipment and material up the perpendicular cliff to the radio station with its antennae perched on top. Inspection visits to the station were hair–raising for staff. 'We crossed to the Tasman Island light', recalled radio inspector, Eric Bowden, 'where you are hauled about 1000 feet up the cliff after being lifted in a basket from the ship's life–boat to a ledge about 80 feet above the sea.' On one inspection, 'the whole basket contraption [including several people, he wrote] broke loose and fell into the sea at the base of the cliffs among the kelp'.[3] There were no casualties, but the Government was quick to despatch a wireless officer on the lighthouse steamer to ask those involved to sign and absolve the Department from all blame! Nonetheless staff continued to risk life and limb on the old flying fox and haulage way of Tasman Island until the Department of Transport condemned the system and introduced helicopters in 1975.

K. Newham, recruited among the contingent of British post office engineers in 1951 and appointed group engineer in charge of southern Tasmania found it a 'colossal area to an Englishman'. The rugged challenges of this landscape — the dolorite rock that made cable-laying a nightmare and occupied linemen for days digging a few holes for poles for an aerial route impressed the new arrival who recognised that a small and geographically difficult State like Tasmania demanded a special versatility from an engineer who needed to attend to a mixture of technologies in one place. Newham soon found that it was important to be 'master of all trades and jack of none'![4]

One major environmental hazard, critical for television broad-casting in Tasmania and a continuing challenge when the installation of the microwave radio system transformed the island's telecommuni-cations network, was the icing–up of aerials on the high mountains where transmitting and repeater stations were built. The tower on Mt Wellington, erected in 1960 to serve Hobart's population, was the

Man and snowplough battling the severe winter conditions at the Mt Wellington microwave tower, near Hobart, Tasmania.

The protective steel plate cladding the Mt Barrow television transmitter tower, near Launceston, Tasmania, was yet another engineering adaptation to peculiarly Australian conditions.

highest television transmitting station in Australia and attracted the freezing Antarctic air. Although tests and consultations with the European manufacturer of the equipment had indicated otherwise, ice air formed on the windward side, building up long glittering streamers. Every year large chunks of ice fell off damaging the antennae and tower to such an extent that, in the great freeze–up of 1960, the pipes on the back of the aerial iced up and, when tempera- tures fell, 30 tonnes of ice descended, engulfing the aerial and crushing the protection on the cable.

Australian icing experiences differed from those overseas. The Antarctic blew up super–cold moist air. European ice–ups were not wet. In Tasmania one such experience was enough. When the Depart- ment erected their second transmitting tower on Mt Barrow near Launceston, the second highest station in Australia, they clad the tower entirely with steel plate and the antennae in fibre glass. By trial and error, environmental planning and experience superseded data and 'know–how' imported with systems from abroad. Nonetheless snow– climbing machines vital to telecommunications teams in Tasmania were directly copied by Ivan LeFevre (State manager of Telecom Tasmania 1979–83) from snow–climbing equipment imported from Switzerland during 1958 for work on the Snowy River Hydro–Electric Scheme.[5]

In sharp contrast, bush fires were summer time enemies. On 7 February 1967 a bush fire of holocaust proportions ravaged parts of Hobart and southern Tasmania. Fanned by winds of 60 miles an hour, it consumed houses, people, farms, greenland and forest, and destroyed and interrupted communications. More than 60 people died in the blaze, among them fire fighters who, as *Time Magazine* graphically reported, were stuck like gum to the eucalyptus trees. Such a fire had a profound effect on communications. Not only were two country telephone exchanges completely destroyed, trunk and most channels out of Hobart and many country trunk line circuits were interrupted while another eight exchanges were isolated by damage in the fire. Five hundred subscriber services were destroyed and 3,000 more interrupted by damage to the lines.

Black Tuesday bush fires of 7 February 1967 were to cause severe loss of life and property in a large area of southern Tasmania. Yet the vital communication links, such as this severely damaged aerial trunk route between Hobart and Launceston, were quickly restored to normal working.

The news of the disaster swept the world. Hobart's telegraph office battled for several days with daily telegram traffic more than 450 per cent larger than normal. Yet, within a day, 33 men, comprising a complete aerial party, a mole plough team and ten jointers, plus plant and material worth over $340,000, were sent from Victoria to restore the island's telecommunications. Natural violence could exact heavy and sudden penalties, but the impact on future telecommunications was profound. Before the fire, Tasmania had more aerial lines than any other State. After the holocaust, cables went underground, and underground multi–channel carrier cables plus tightened emergency planning were the phoenix–like products of the fire.[6]

South Australia (which administratively included the Northern Territory) was a 'small' telecommunications State despite its spectacular early leadership on the telegraph scene. Beyond Adelaide and its surrounding circles of ports and towns, the population was scattered in thin fringe settlements across semi–arid pastoral and arid land. Compared with other States, South Australia's progress to rural automation was fairly slow: it boasted 12 rural automatic exchanges in 1940, but the State established leadership in other ways. Before the war the ingenious Adelaide engineer, F.P. O'Grady, developed a system of single frequency dialling giving South Australia a network of trunk lines over which operators had direct dialling to subscribers years ahead of other States. By February 1942 a three–channel carrier added voice connection over the length of the circuit from Adelaide to Darwin, while new telecommunications train control systems, developed in Adelaide, were placed on the Port Augusta to Kalgoorlie and the Adelaide to Alice Springs railway lines.

Soldier settlement pushed the rural population outwards in the postwar years. Trunk routes were built through the Murray Valley to furnish direct circuits from Adelaide to Sydney, and lines went increasingly underground. By 1950 some 13 PMG–made RAXs were put into service in country towns powered usually by wind–driven

The single wire telegraph line being built across Western Australia's Great Sandy Desert between Marble Bar and Lagrange, 1925. Replacing a sea-spray damaged coastal line, and upgraded in the early 1960s for telephone working, it was to remain in service until the opening of the Kimberley solar-powered microwave network in November 1982.

generators mounted on steel towers. South Australia's telecommunication founding father, Charles Todd, had said in the previous century, 'telephone flashes our thoughts over hundreds and thousands of miles'. South Australian field staff knew this spacious sense of distance well. Engineers, mechanics, linemen were forever 'travelling between jobs'. One divisional engineer at Murray Bridge, SA, reflected that it seemed 'as if he were seldom engaged in the work itself but in the spaces in between'. With constant absence, much fell upon the divisional engineer's wife. One reputedly developed practical but tactful skills. 'I have heard him say', she was apt to remark when appealed to on a point during her husband's frequent absences elsewhere, 'that, in the circumstances, he would do such and such.' She would then go on to give a detailed description of procedures for restoring a damaged line.[7]

Western Australia had certain similarities. In terms of size it could swallow the State of South Australia thrice and fit Tasmania some 14 times within its expansive spaces. Here in the great 'western third' voice contact was not available beyond the central towns of Meekatharra, Wiluna or Carnarvon one third of the way up the long indented coastline, until 1959. Carnarvon had been connected to Perth by telephone circuit via Northampton and a repeater station in 1938. But voice connection was poor. In the immediate postwar years the coastal town was provided with a standard copper trunk line, a three-channel telephone carrier, and a superimposed 9–channel telegraph system connecting it via Mullewa to Perth. At the same time the installation of a reliable radio telegraph channel between Perth and Broome diverted some of the traffic from the old 19th century telegraph line that stretched from Carnarvon to Port Hedland, Broome and Derby and on to Wyndham via Halls Creek. Apart from the telegraph, only the pedal radio and the Royal Flying Doctor Service kept pastoralists, farmers and a scattering of miners and fishermen in touch with the wider world. During the 1950s radio broadcasting spread. But despite a demand for telephone connection, the sparse population of these westerly regions remained cut off by the expense and expanse of distance, joined to their fellow countrymen by an umbilical telegraph line.

Western Australia's telecommunications, however, like South Australia's, were to grow during the late 1950s and 1960s as a result of an external pressure — Australia's participation in Britain's long range missile project and atomic bomb trials. In 1948 Frank O'Grady left the South Australian PMG for a period to become chief engineer of the Australian Government's newly established Weapons Research Establishment, South Australia, which formed part of the Australian joint role in Britain's 'Blue Streak' missile research. He was joined by other PMG staff including Bill Boswell from the Research Laboratories who subsequently rose to head the Woomera Weapons Research Establishment and later the Australian Atomic Energy Commission. At the same time the PMG in South Australia maintained a special Woomera Project Division to cope with the large volume of work.

The Woomera enterprise and the missile facilities, controversial in their later outcome, brought marked benefits to telecommunications in the outer States. While the Department of Supply assumed major responsibility for the establishment of the Long Range Weapons Establishment at Salisbury, near Adelaide, and for the construction of the missile firing centre at Woomera in South Australia's central desert, the PMG's Department provided the sophisticated communication facilities for both Salisbury and Woomera and for the initial telecommunications lines designed to span westward to the distant impact point of Talgarno near Anna Plains, a barely discernible speck on the atlas between Port Hedland and Broome.

Planning for Woomera began in 1948 with close co-operation between the Department of Supply, the PMG, and the Department of the Army, who acted as contractors to the PMG. From Woomera the first stage of a main telephone, telegraph and aerial route was pushed out by the Army under PMG technical supervision to Mt Eber station, south of Miricata in the Stuart Range. There, for a period, it languished, serving some delighted pastoralists, until it was abandoned as the trajectory line for missile testing, although it was later extended as part of South Australia's telecommunications development to the Coober Pedy mining fields.

While short range missile and other weapons testing continued at Woomera, communications for the Maralinga site for the British atomic tests set a few hundred miles within South Australia's western border, fell to the PMG. Here the Defence Department's requirement was for an advanced telecommunications circuit from Port Augusta to Woomera and on some 350 miles along the East–West Transcontinental Railway to Watson situated a short distance south of the Maralinga site. The connection of two open–wire telephone and telegraph lines, plus a radio circuit to monitor and report the test proceedings, begun in August 1955, was completed in a brisk eleven months. Atoms served a pacific purpose. Not only did the new communication link effectively service the Maralinga tests, transmitting a mass of data back to base, it became a catalyst for the upgrading of the entire east–west telecommunications line from Port Augusta to Kalgoorlie which, completed in September 1958, proved a bonus to the West.

Three years later Western Australia gained again. It was now proposed to take the sophisticated telecommunications circuitry required at the Blue Streak missile impact site of Talgarno, west from Woomera, straight over desert country, and north from Perth via the communication system that in 1959 extended from Perth as far as Carnarvon and inland Meekatharra. It was easier, explained Len Caudle, engineer in charge of the north–west project team, 'to develop the spikes of the wheel than put in a new rim'. The decision turned on an inland thrust upgrading the route from Mullewa to Meekatharra and erecting a trunk line from Meekatharra to Marble Bar and on to Port Hedland and Talgarno — an enterprise that involved building 500 miles of new trunk lines, and stringing wire over 1,000 miles across the northern reaches of the State.[8]

Men and 'tower truck' working on the north-west project, near Port Hedland, WA, 1960. The metal poles, welded on site, were made of track from the old Port Hedland to Marble Bar railway.

On WA's Nullarbor Plain, it wasn't just linemen that found novel solutions to the barrenness of the landscape. Their ingenuity was to be matched by the magpie whose efforts are portrayed in this reconstruction: it built its nest on a PMG 'tree' from wire discarded on the east-west route.

The struggle, the surveying, the shifting and restructuring of old lines, the location of new river crossings, the building of repeater stations, the assessment of the fierce windloadings that tore at the copper wiring, the transport of foodstuffs, the quest for drinking water, the assault of sandflies and the sudden bogging of vehicles in country that turned from desert to instant quagmires after a rain, were reminiscent of the building of the overland telegraph line, though the technology and the transport would have dazzled the line teams of those distant days. The common factor was improvisation and endurance, and in 1958 the need to find novel solutions to problems of a telecommunications connection that required the highest reliability to transmit information on missile testing to Woomera and Perth.[9]

In the event, Talgarno never heard the thud of rockets. Britain terminated the Blue Streak Project in 1959. It was 'something of a mirage', reflected Caudle, yet it was a mirage that drew the remote settlements of Western Australia into first class telephone and radio communication with the rest of the continent. The Perth–Derby radio telephone system opened in 1959, and was later diverted to link the US radio base at Exmouth to Perth. By the mid to late 1960s telephone lines were pushing out from Talgarno beyond Broome and Derby into the old 'top north' pastoral settlements of the Kimberleys. They would also reach the red–brown orefields of the Pilbara just as mining companies began exploding like a new form of rocket at the end of that adventurous decade.

Giles Chippindall, as Director–General, once wrote with unaccustomed eloquence of the difficulties and hazards of his vast domain. The duties of his technical staff and linemen (as well as his postal carriers), he said, took the PMG's service to remote settlements, to lonely lighthouses at Cape Capricorn, to the perilous Tasman Island station, across the flood waters of Queensland's rivers and even past crocodiles that menaced certain routes. In Queensland experienced linemen were wont to warn young recruits against the dangers of sheltering snakes and the unlovable cane–toads that nestled in country manholes. Beehives also formed menacingly in cable jointing pits.

Of all the States, Queensland was 'different'. Its difference was a challenge and a strength. It early acquired a reputation for leadership. In 1901 its telecommunications system was pronounced the best in Australia. Queensland had also produced the first permanent head of the PMG Department, the forgettable and forgotten, Robert Scott, and John Hesketh, the well–remembered first Commonwealth chief electrical engineer. The first 'established' Postmaster–General was a Queenslander, Senator Drake. Over 16 years of lusty telecommunications growth, 1956–72, the Postmaster–General's portfolio was also in a Queenslander's hands. First Sir Charles Davidson and later Sir Alan Hulme had their ministerial headquarters in Brisbane.

From early times Queensland had demonstrated its individualism. While all the other States had adopted the American model Strowger step–by–step exchanges for the growing automation of their telephone systems, the Queensland PMG chose a step–by–step model made by Siemens Bros, England — the Siemens 16 — for its first automatic exchange at South Brisbane. By 1930 its three major city exchanges were all Siemens 16–type, and suburban and small town exchanges took up the theme. The decision, based as it proved on dubious economic grounds (for the Siemens' tender omitted the conversion of subscriber equipment in its costs), set Queensland on a different track, although country exchanges and major towns such as Cairns and Townsville opted for the Strowger exchange. The State's eccentricity caused problems. The Second World War cut Siemens' supplies, but major city exchanges extended their Siemens equipment in the postwar years. While the nationally adopted British '2000 type' exchange was introduced in Brisbane's Fortitude Valley exchange in

1947 and earlier at Rockhampton, the last Siemens' models did not disappear from Queensland's telephone network for nearly 30 years. At the same time the small model Siemens 16 proved the training aid for all PMG technicians employed in automatic telephony in Queensland until the 1960s when a model crossbar exchange was installed for training.[10]

Of all the States Queensland found itself at the end of the Second World War with greatly upgraded carrier wave telephone and telegraph services which stretched along its seaboard from Brisbane to Cape York. Wartime wires also ran to the State's western boundary beyond Cloncurry and Mt Isa, and out from Brisbane to Charleville, Longreach and Hughenden. New pole routes, following army encampments, criss–crossed erratically across the State. But there were also large areas of silence. The Brigalow country north of Rockhampton was such a one. The Diamantina shire with Birdsville in its southern

Jointing in shallow estuary water on the Sandgate to Redcliffe cable, Queensland, in the early 1970s.

corner was another. The river system of the flat channel country draining and flooding into Lake Eyre, prevented telephone connection going out westward from Charleville. When the telephone came to Birdsville to connect ten subscribers in 1975, it was radio telephony brought in from the north and later connected to Brisbane. The Gulf country was also a telecommunication doldrum. Normanton, the lively 19th century copper and gold port, continued to be linked to Burketown by one galvanised iron wire. Even Davidson's muscle as Postmaster–General could not lift his one–time electorate of Carpentaria out of its depressed communication state. Costs and low population density held back the voice of the outside world. It was the opening up of mineral deposits — that aphrodisiac of telecommunication progress — that brought telephone connection to the country round the mission town of Weipa, where drilling in 1964 revealed that the area held roughly one quarter of the world's known bauxite resources. In the mid–1960s Comalco's presence at Weipa brought radio telephony to miners, the mission, Aboriginals and capitalists alike.[11]

Queensland exhibited two differences from other States. More than half of its telephone population lay outside the capital which, for historical reasons, perched at the far bottom end of the State. Secondly, its country population was widely dispersed. Homesteads dotted the landscape from the Darling Downs to Cape York. By contrast, Western Australia's rural dwellers clustered about the edges of the empty desert. Accordingly, many of Queensland's outback subscribers erected their own telephone lines as private or party connections that ran out from small PMG exchanges to their homes. There were, thus, more small rural exchanges and more telephonists in Queensland than in any other State.

Yet Queensland and Western Australia faced some similar challenges. Cyclones swung in along the Queensland coast from Thursday Island south as far as Brisbane, shattering telephone communication and isolating inhabitants along the route. Cyclonic winds that whipped up the coastal desert sands of north Western

Despite the havoc caused, in 1960, by cyclonic winds near Geraldton, WA, the circuits on these badly twisted poles were still working, and the calls got through.

Australia also blew down aerial lines, uprooted and twisted telegraph poles, and damaged the radio masts that edged the vital communication links slowly northwards. In both States heavy rain driven by harsh winds was a familiar and uncomfortable enemy of country staff. In Western Australia the cost of telecommunications structures escalated to meet the remarkable velocities of the winds. Western Australia, too, knew the constant threat of lightning that crashed across the flat landscape, struck wires, cables and poles at random, and occasionally blazed and crackled into the ears of customers using the telephone. The problem led to research on a 'lightning tracker' in the Pilbara and to public warning about the use of telephones during electric storms in telephone directories.

Queensland also shared other recurring weather challenges with its neighbour New South Wales. Heavy floods periodically deluged many parts of Queensland and northern New South Wales. The restoration of broken lines called for considerable courage and skill.

After one such disaster in the spring of 1949 Postmaster–General Donald Cameron paid special tribute to 'the very fine work' accomplished by the employees of the Postal Department in Queensland and New South Wales when hundreds of miles of telegraph and telephone lines were washed away. 'When the disaster occurred', Cameron observed, 'it was not necessary to make a special appeal to them to do their utmost to assist the unfortunate people in the affected areas of restoring the Department's services'.[12] Employees voluntarily worked extremely long hours, in some instances under the worst possible conditions. Telephonists stayed on duty at their switchboards for periods up to fifteen hours. Linemen and others worked chest–deep in flood water for hours, restoring vital telecommunication lines. It was a story reported around the country in each decade. Later in Charles Davidson's time a special award, the Certificate of Merit, was introduced for 'exceptionally meritorious service' for PMG staff in times of State and national disasters.[13]

In the aftermath of flood, access to damaged lines is always a problem. Here linemen use boats to aid repairs to the Adelaide trunk route during the 1956 flooding of the River Murray at Renmark, SA. In Western Australia, less formality prevails. A liney sheds all to swim the Gascoyne River to repair damage in the 1943 flood.

Lineman Chris Byrnes, shown here during the flood of June 1952 at Leeton, NSW, was awarded the British Empire Medal for his work in repairing the lines.

Despite some problem sharing with their neighbours, New South Wales and Victoria were the premier communications States. There, with their large urban populations and a dominance of telecommunications business, the newest technologies were given trial. The largest underground cable was ploughed directly into the ground by mole plough between Melbourne and Geelong in 1938, the first major use of the technology. That great distance shrinker, the microwave radio system, was also first introduced in Australia between Melbourne and Bendigo at the end of 1959, launching the revolutionary new broadband trunk system across the very region where Samuel McGowan

The Prime Minister, the Rt Hon. R.G. Menzies, officially opening the
Melbourne to Sydney coaxial cable route in the presence of Charles Davidson,
Postmaster-General, 9 April 1962.

had pushed Australia's first outer–city telegraph a century before.
Microwave radio and coaxial cables, both carriers of broadband
frequencies, would transform telephone trunk facilities before the
1960s ended. The construction of Australia's first interstate coaxial
cable from Melbourne to Sydney via Canberra, begun in 1960 and
carrying some hundreds of telephone and telegraph channels, was
ceremoniously opened for business by R.G. Menzies as Prime Minister
in April 1962. Harry Kaye was the headquarter 'anchorman' for this
important scheme.

But there were subtle differences and strong rivalries between the
major States. The Victorian PMG enjoyed the advantage, and suffered
the disadvantage, of being only a block or so away from headquarters.
Inevitably there were more Victorians at headquarters and a greater
staff mobility and interpenetration of staff between administrations in
Victoria than in other States. With a heavy wartime backlog, Victoria
also made dramatic headway in the postwar years. Victorian superintending engineer C.J. Prosser was the author of the major 20–year
plan to convert the whole Melbourne metropolitan area to fully automatic working by 1963. New buildings for exchanges were acquired
and built, while 'portable exchanges' made from army galvanised huts
were pressed into temporary 'branch exchange' use. Management
threw itself keenly behind the plan. W. Sandbach, later Victoria's chief
engineer, put his skill for co–ordination and forward thinking into the
task of extending a huge network of cables and conduits, and PMG
staff in Victoria was augmented to enlarge and upgrade the network
with materials and equipment now manufactured substantially in
Australia.[14]

Bush fires ravaged the Victorian countryside across four terrible days in January 1962, and destruction of telephone and telegraph lines was immense. The event would coincidentally focus a national need. Prime Minister Menzies had a month before taken an initiative to restore the civil defence committees of the Second World War. His invitation to all State Premiers led to a meeting at the end of January 1962 at which the PMG's Department, along with other Commonwealth departments, was represented. With the memory of the bushfires still searingly fresh, delegates gave special attention to the problem of peacetime disasters rather than civil defence. The Victorian State Disaster Plan, DISPLAN, was the valuable fruit of this conference. The Victorian PMG headed the vital communications division of DISPLAN with responsibility for controlling and co-ordinating 'counter disaster action'. It was a model that would spread quickly to other States as a crucial linchpin in a national scheme that overviewed emergencies of bush fires, floods, and search and rescue operations on land and sea.

Fire was a national enemy. On 21 September 1961, ignited from within, it totally destroyed a 2000 type exchange at Civic, Canberra, with over 5,500 working lines. Miraculously, with a portable exchange and hard work, service was restored to every telephone subscriber within a fortnight and a new enlarged exchange of 8,400 lines built in 51 days.[15]

If Victoria influenced the larger national planning of the PMG, New South Wales was the country's 'premier' communications State operating some 40 per cent of telecommunications business and managing telecommunications activities larger than those of Queensland, South Australia, Tasmania and Western Australia put together. Unlike Victoria, which was comparatively well settled across its girth, New South Wales combined high density urban and suburban population with an often thinly populated countryside. It saw itself as the 'median State', but it undoubtedly faced the biggest problems and

The destruction of communication links by fire, although lessened by the removal of aerial lines, is still a recurring problem in Australia. Here, cable damage is repaired after fires in the Adelaide Hills, February 1980.

usually faced them first. Accordingly from its role and size, it achieved an autonomy in its planning and performance that Victoria did not have. Perhaps for the same reason it was noteworthy that New South Wales had significantly younger managers than those in other States. Promotional opportunities were recognisably less elsewhere. 'People who hold senior posts in Queensland and Western Australia' one staff member pointed out, 'are usually ten years older than those who hold them in New South Wales.'[16]

New South Wales PMG also cultivated a distinct, and distancing 'style'. At interstate conferences its representatives were known for a nice disregard of others' activities. 'We always do this in New South Wales [they would say]; we don't know if it applies elsewhere.' New South Wales management, it was suggested, 'took its own line and went its own way when it chose'. It was also known to carry things off 'in deliberate defiance of headquarters'. Significantly identification tags handed out to engineers in all States to give them ease of access when travelling and co-ordinating in other States were perceived not to work well in New South Wales. 'Tell the bastards nothing', was the cry remembered by one young Victorian radio engineer despatched to Sydney to initiate an interstate broadcasting task. The feeling was two-way. The Victorian 'bastards', said one New South Welshman, told New South Wales 'nothing when they chose'.

Problems of forward planning, however, particularly plagued a State like New South Wales. The spread of population to new suburbs was a challenge that recurred constantly and called for careful forecasting and a reliable data base. New South Wales management would experience its most acute challenge with the rapid development of the central and northern coastal regions and of Sydney's western suburb of Penrith in later years where the inadequacies of tele-communication facilities and a misjudgment of sudden population density and subscriber needs sparked strong and continuing public criticism. But planning could go awry in other ways. Telecommunications preparations for the expected growth of the Federal capital Canberra, which fell within the jurisdiction of New South Wales, led to the building of the long idle Deakin exchange, based on the report of the National Enquiry into Population — the Borrie report of 1975. 'We never believed in the Borrie Report', said M.J. Power, the then chief engineer and now deputy State manager of New South Wales. But in the case of Canberra, the Department could claim that the NCDC (the National Capital Development Commission) was 'the planner' in this case, while the PMG's Department, despite some original questioning, supplied the facilities. But New South Wales took care that the same mistake of oversupply should not be repeated in schemes for Orange or the Albury–Wodonga plan.[17]

Overall the engineering ethos of the PMG continued to predominate. Most State Directors of Posts and Telegraphs were drawn from engineers, though there were notable exceptions in W.J.B. Pollock who was promoted to head the Victorian administration in July 1974 and the former Sydney language school master, H.G. Shaw, who entered the PMG service in New South Wales as an inspector of postal legislation and research in 1954 and became Director of Posts and Telegraphs in Western Australia from 1973–8 (and later WA's first State Manager). Shaw was one State Director who believed that the image of the PMG (and Telecom) 'as an engineering fraternity' should be broken down in the light of its diverse activities and the contribution of its staff.[18] In some areas it was. Despite a strong tendency towards centralism and some *'faits accomplis'* landed on the States, State initiatives could develop in response to the influence of individual Directors of Posts and Telegraphs and the flair and ingenuity of State engineers.

By the late 1950s one strategic policy of high importance would weld headquarters and State management in a massive overall national plan. In Melbourne, during Chippindall's time in 1957, a master plan took shape under the Director–General and his Assistant and Deputy Directors to form a small committee of carefully chosen headquarters staff — the Automatic Network and Switching Objectives committee (known familiarly as ANSO) — to project a national telephone plan that would eventually bring about a totally integrated automatic (STD) dialling system in Australia.

The plan's rationale stemmed from the very diversity that had grown up around the various systems and approaches to telecommunications in the States. As R.W. Turnbull, superintending engineer, who was placed in charge of ANSO observed, 'The States were all developing projects for annual estimates, but no one was watching the end results'. Australia's telephone situation called for overview. There were two distinctive features of the Australian scene. More than 75 per cent of the nation's calls were connected automatically by the late 1950s (somewhat less than many countries overseas) but operators still handled over 200 million calls a year. Secondly, the cost of the geographically 'long haul' Australian system was reckoned to be proportionately higher in capital than in most other countries of the world.[19]

Customers themselves had scant idea of what it cost to install a suburban or city telephone. It cost the PMG a substantial £270 in 1959 but consumers were quick to complain. Remote rural subscribers required to pay for their own extensions beyond a certain mileage from the country exchange were persistent and articulate critics. Yet the labyrinthine rural networks and the small exchanges were pushed out by the PMG at huge capital cost. Popular ignorance was not surprising. Costs and charges were seldom debated in Parliament. The Department's pricing policy was intricate, as we have seen; judgments about rates and the timing of increases rested on both political and economic grounds. Certainly the internal cross–subsidies of the Department were not publicly disclosed. As one Labor MP put it critically in 1959, new proposals were presented 'with a fair amount of deceit'.[20]

By 1959 overseas advances in switching and transmission systems offered attractive reductions in overall costs. In addition, the promise of world–wide automative telephony when the Commonwealth

COMPAC cable, launched in 1956, would link Australian subscribers to New Zealand and Canada (and thence by microwave across Canada and by cable onto Europe), pointed to the need for strategic planning that would mesh new and existing technologies into a comprehensive national plan.

The two central figures of the ANSO Committee were its chairman, Ron Turnbull, a senior engineer, and Bill Pollock who would become Telecom Australia's second Managing Director in 1981. Turnbull (appointed superintending engineer, planning, at headquarters in 1955 after a career that combined the planning and installation of local and trunk networks, telephone transmission and traffic engineering) was widely experienced for the chairman's role. A conceptual thinker, he brought a strong sense of systems planning, 'of fusing the branches of technology as a whole' to the task. Pollock focussed on the commercial and customer aspects of the plan. One of the new breed of administrators who added a Bachelor of Commerce to his PMG work, he had been assistant controller, planning and development branch, telecommunications division, at headquarters since 1955. Others, notably the engineers, B.F. Marrows and G. Hams, and the 'young Turks', E.R. Banks and I.A. Newstead, contributed to the national planning at different times. ANSO enjoyed the full resources of headquarters; its strength, however, was its size: 'smallness was the trick'. State committees were established in New South Wales and Victoria, reflecting the importance of the Sydney and Melbourne networks in a national scheme; other countries' administrations were examined, and careful and co-ordinated forethought became the hallmark of the committee's approach. It was also democratic. Members of the team and other staffers visited and consulted regularly with all the States ventilating and testing the schemes' principles as they emerged. Administrative, financial, technological and logistic plans were stirred into the ANSO melting pot.[21]

By 1958 the plan's broad outline was complete. It aimed at conversion to automatic telephony in local areas, the updating of country telephone lines, and the eventual spread of subscriber trunk dialling throughout Australia. ANSO's long-term aim was, in short, to take the operator out of the telephone call. Central to it, and most immediate, was the decision to adopt a national telephone numbering scheme. Like most countries, Australia's telephone system was based on a combination of letters and numbers (XY 3562). But by 1958, so great had Sydney's telephone density become that the city was, 'reaching the end of the 6th digit dialling stage towards a 7 digit public telephone system'. The question for the planners was whether to add a third letter to increase the dial range or to opt for a system with an exclusively numeral dial. To choose for Sydney was to cast the die for the nation. Turnbull saw it as an 'immense decision'.[22] It was certainly ahead of Britain and the USA.

The decision made, all figure telephone numbers were introduced progressively in Australia from mid-1958. Under the evolving 'community telephone plan' area codes, beginning with zero plus a local number were allocated to groups of exchanges based on a 'community of interest'. These zones, named ELSA (extended local service areas), appeared from mid–1960. The zoning also offered pricing advantages. Calls within each zone and between adjacent zones were to be treated as untimed local calls. All subscribers shared the benefits. A typical country subscriber could now obtain a 'local' call over 25–35 miles, a distance much longer than that available before the 'community' plan. Further restructuring reduced the country-wide number of tariff charges, while multi–metering to monitor and charge the new subscriber dialled trunk calls (STD) was added to the package.

Dialling STD blithely across Australia today, it is difficult to comprehend the complexities of restructuring the old automatic telephone system that had, with some standardisation and upgrading, done sterling service since 1912. The all numeral system had to cater for Australia's telephone needs for the next half century. Demographic studies of population served as a predictive base. But forward judgments of financial, accounting and administrative policies, plus technical standards and new developments, had also to be absorbed. The community telephone plan served up by the planners and announced to Parliament by Postmaster–General Davidson on 1 September 1959 made history. Despite some opposition, the plan — implemented progressively through the 1960s — formed the foundation of the integrated automative telephone service of today, while the 'all figure' dial system became the model for telephone numbering plans in Britain and in other countries. For the PMG it was a rare piece of technology transfer in reverse.[23] At home, Turnbull, 'father of ELSA', won the Professional Officers Association Award of Merit for his work.

The national plan's evolution now hinged on the introduction of important new switching equipment, then in competitive develop-ment around the world. Two Directors–General who followed Chippindall in swift succession had carriage of the plan. Both P.E. Vanthoff and M.R.C. Stradwick belonged to the prototype of telegraph messenger who made his way triumphantly to the top. Vanthoff, a long–time and influential Deputy Director–General held the Director-ship for the last year of his career. Stradwick, a former Assistant Director–General of Telephones at central office and head of its telecommunications division since 1954, succeeded him in January 1960. But he too would leave within less than two years to take up two key positions in the telecommunications industry.[24]

Under Stradwick, detailed evaluations began of the international switching equipment suitable for a nation–wide automatic telephone system. One new system, the 'crossbar system', had strong appeal. Technically, crossbar was a major step from the bi–motional Strowger automatic system where each single digit dialled caused a switching step to be made to complete the connection. Crossbar treated the telephone number as an entity, and its control devices — the key to its functioning — routed the call along the best available transmission path. One leading manufacturer was the Swedish firm, L.M. Ericsson Pty Ltd, which, starting with the production of telegraph equipment in

1876, had expanded into a world–wide telecommunications enter-prise manufacturing telephone instruments and systems. Ericsson had early become a key supplier of magneto telephone equipment to Australia from Colonial times. Their stylish 'coffee grinder' and 'biscuit barrel' magneto handsets appeared in Australian homes and offices in the 1890s, while their Magneto Wallset became the Commonwealth standard after Federation.

Ericsson's pre–war Sydney agent, James Paton, had pushed the company's magneto telephones in country areas where their operational reliability was much praised. But the Swedish firm's market had declined in Australia in the face of British influence and closed during the Second World War. The advent, however, of Ericsson's new agent L.G. Rowe in Sydney in 1949 and the establish-ment of an Australian subsidiary company, L.M. Ericsson Telephone Company Pty Ltd, in Melbourne in 1951 brought the firm forward as an important competitor to the Sydney-based British subsidiaries of STC and TEI.[25]

Within the PMG the Department's long dependence on British technology was also undergoing change. It was part of Australia's historic conditioning that 'British was best'. Such technological imperialism had been exported strenuously throughout the 20th century, and before, and was much strengthened by the contractual arrangements made for joint Australian and British manufacturing of telecommunications equipment with TEI and STC in 1948–9. Chippindall was strongly pro–British; but the rising planner at headquarters, Frank O'Grady who had returned to the PMG from Woomera in 1957, became deputy engineer–in–chief at headquarters and subsequently Deputy-Director General in charge of planning, was not. In 1959 O'Grady led a team to investigate the new switching systems in Europe and Britain. Competition between crossbar and other switching systems offered alternatively by Siemens Ltd, ITT's French subsidiary, ITT's Belgian subsidiary, Bell Antwerp, and various enhancements of the basic Strowger concept offered by British firms including one from Ericsson's British subsidiary, provided a complex sorting task. But after laboratory studies, on–the–spot comparisons of European telephone systems, and close consultations with the Swedish Telecommunications Administration, the decision came down for Ericsson's crossbar. This decision was both technical and economic. Swedish crossbar switches designed for large, medium and small exchanges, particularly suited Australian needs. The system also had strikingly low maintenance (as Swedish experience proved) and made low demand for spare parts. Importantly, Deputy–Director General O'Grady was completely won over to the scheme.

The PMG's choice would strongly affect the telecommunications industry in Australia and abroad. It caused much heartburning overseas. 'We were inundated with experts from all over the world', O'Grady reflected. The British were especially put out. They had taken the firm view (disastrous as it proved) that the Strowger system should be substantially retained until fully electronic switches could be introduced throughout the network. One visiting British post office team spoke to the PMG, said one official, as if to a Colony: 'We know what's good for England and what's good for you'! In the event, though the first fully electronic exchange was installed at London's Highgate Wood in 1958, the British were forced to adopt crossbar for their big city exchanges before the 1960s were out.[26]

For Ericsson, the PMG's choice marked a breakthrough. 'We have now reached the almost unbelievable position', Rowe wrote to S.T. Aberg, a senior company official, as negotiations firmed, 'where our crossbar system has virtually been sold to APO, as the one and only standard switching system for the future.' Australia was not only a key market in itself. It was the influential proving ground for tele-communications technology imported from abroad. Aberg's response to the final decision in July 1959 confirmed the point. 'It opens certainly wide vistas for the crossbar system — in as much as APO is internationally well-known for being independent and sincere in all their dealings.'[27]

Crucially for Ericsson, and local developments, the final agreement required that crossbar equipment and exchanges be manufactured in Australia at an early stage. Without adequate facilities of their own, Ericsson in November 1959 contracted with both TEI (to which Chippindall on retirement had migrated as chairman of the board) and STC. Through this alliance, Ericsson supplied the technological know-how for the production of crossbar exchanges for ten years in return for a licence fee. Even so, a large number of deliveries were made by L.M. Ericsson, Sweden, to get the system off the ground.

The PMG established its first main crossbar exchange with 6,300 lines at Toowoomba, Queensland, in 1960. Other installations followed across the country, stretching the capacity of the TEI and STC factories to their limit. Encouraged by the scope of the market, Ericsson's Australian subsidiary LME early in 1961 concluded a merger with Trimax Transformers Pty Ltd, a Victorian company already supplying the PMG with long-distance telephone equipment. In November 1962 the united Ericsson–Trimax company began construction of a production plant at Broadmeadows outside Melbourne. By a series of adroit strokes, aided by the financial clout of Trimax's major owners (Australian United Development Pty Ltd), L.M. Ericsson both penetrated the telephone industry in Australia and would shortly dominate a significant section of the market.

Two factors spurred Ericsson's run during the early 1960s. The PMG approved the adoption of Ericsson's private automatic branch exchanges, the PABXs, which would gain increasing significance in telephone business in ensuing years. More compellingly, the PMG's postwar agreement with STC and TEI to stimulate indigenous production and delivery of local and rural exchanges, was due to expire in mid-1963. Ericsson saw its chance. Their enlarged Australian subsidiary now sought to ensure that PMG purchase of crossbar systems should be made on a tender basis. The move was sharply resisted by STC. LME, however, enjoyed the advocacy and influence of Sir Ian Potter, doyen of the Melbourne Stock Exchange and a director of the Trimax empire. Thus as cement poured into the foundations of the new Broadmeadows plant, Postmaster–General Davidson, with his Department's assent, agreed that the PMG's contracts with the British subsidiaries should not be extended. Instead, orders were to be distributed among the three suppliers for a transition period of two years on the basis of each factory's capacity to deliver. Competitive tendering would be then introduced.[28]

The new arrangement was healthy for developing realistic competitive tendering in the Australian industry, and for Ericsson the result was striking. Within two years of the completion of its factory, LME had acquired a third of the Australian telephone market and a quarter of the market for PABXs. Major crossbar exchanges at Sydney and Melbourne, and a Sydney intercontinental telex exchange were further supplied by Ericsson's Stockholm headquarters, while in 1967, L.M. Ericsson Australia acquired a sizeable share of Conquerer Cable Co. Sydney. The prizes had gone to technical excellence and some adroit and purposeful marketing.[29]

For the PMG crossbar marked a milestone in its telecommunications policy. Across the country, engineers, technicians and draughtsmen plunged into the demanding task of translating the

Using a mobile test unit, a technician tests the crossbar switching equipment in a modern telephone exchange.

Ericsson prototype into a system that suited Australia's conditions, producing, in effect, an 'Australian crossbar'. Technical experts from third world countries such as Nigeria, India and Singapore came to inspect and emulate the system. Contrastingly the British post office declined to move significantly into the new switching field. By the late 1970s 80 per cent of Britain's telephone network was still dependent on the old Strowger step–by–step and Britain had lost its leadership role in the international telecommunications industry.

10 The Technologists

In 1961 the PMG's Department was on the crest of a fast-moving technological wave. Fortuitously, the man who would steer it, tighten its organisational and research framework, and bring a personal technical mastery to its direction was the Adelaide engineer and innovator, F.P. O'Grady.

The choice of the head of Australia's largest and most technically-oriented Department of State was a matter of some importance. Sir Harry Brown had set a standard of farsighted engineering leadership. Yet there were considerations other than technology and engineering in the running of the nation's 'post office'. Hence, with the exception of the wartime Director–General, Daniel McVey, none of Brown's successors in office from the mid-1940s were engineers. How important was this? The answer was 'increasingly so'. For, despite a hierarchy of engineers dispersed through headquarters and the States, and the planning advice and input of the Department's chief engineer, the permanent head's knowledge of telecommunications technology, his grasp of the technical choices available for policy–making and of their economic and social implications for Australia were essential to his sound advice to his responsible Minister.

One of Australia's great public servants, Sir John Crawford, defined the function of the permanent head as 'the general manager and controller under the Minister, with the ultimate responsibility to the Minister for all the activities of the Department'. He must, said Crawford, be able to put before the Minister the possible alternatives, to select the weaker points in the specialist's case, and give his own opinion of rival theses.[1] He must also, as Sir John Crawford omitted to point out, be able to translate the complexities, and flag the dangers, of large–scale technological developments and their consequences for the country. Postmasters–General were particularly reliant on their Directors–General for judgments on the now financially pre–eminent and expanding telecommunications front. Ministers from every party brought a political awareness of the postal side of the Department's activities and to the importance of 'getting the mail through'. They also responded to public pressure to make sure that telephones and other

230

facilities were more equitably distributed. But they turned to their permanent head to educate and steer them on the new technologies of communications. More than in any other portfolio (although the Department of National Development, with its responsibility for nuclear energy, became a similar case in point), the Postmaster–General relied on his permanent head to explain and justify the 'thinking and planning function' of his Department, although the policy itself remained the ultimate responsibility of the Minister.

The appointment of O'Grady in the decade of 'white hot technological revolution' was a breakthrough. His selection by Menzies's Postmaster–General, Charles Davidson, was indicative of Davidson's strengthened handling of his post. O'Grady was a first class technologist. Gentle mannered, modest, with a puckish sense of humour and interrogative deep blue eyes, he towered above his predecessors in office (since Brown) in his creative interest in telecommunications technology. Born of an Irish–Catholic family with strong loyalties to his kin (which, some said, led to some show of favouritism in his career), he became a boyhood addict of the telephone. He had an uncle who was a bookmaker who asked him what he was going to do when he left school. 'I told him that I was keen on telephones', O'Grady recalled. 'He said I know Lew Griffiths who has something to do with telephones: he bets with me every Saturday.' (L.F. Griffiths, then in charge of operating and commercial branches of the Adelaide telephone, subsequently became superintendent of telephones in South Australia and later Director of Posts and Telegraphs in the State.) The advice Griffiths 'the telephone wizard gave me on what happened inside a telephone exchange', O'Grady wrote later, 'set me on the right course. So is history made.'[2]

Frank P. O'Grady, 'maker and shaker': deputy Director-General from 1959 to 1960, and Director-General from 1961 to 1969.

Frank O'Grady entered the PMG as a temporary messenger in Adelaide in January 1915. He fell out of the system when permanent staff returned from the war and joined the Adelaide's electrical engineering firm of Uhnehaun and Johnstone, where he extended his interest in electrical technology. Five years later he rejoined the Department as a mechanic through an open examination and almost immediately noticed a vacancy for an engineer. He swotted for the examination and got the job. His engineering career was diverse. Telephone equipment design, instructing mechanics in techniques for the new carrier equipment (a course that flowed into the 'little' *Red Book of Carrier* which APEU published), design work for the national broadcasting system in South Australia, long distance signalling, and the development and installation of a train control system were all grist to his mill. He planned and designed the 3–channel carrier system installed in emergency wartime conditions between Adelaide and Alice Springs, Larrimah and Darwin, while his leadership in radio transmission fields would equip him as Deputy–Director General (1959–60) to select the equipment for the broadband radio system planned from Brisbane to Cairns.

An optimistic communicator, O'Grady probably lectured more often and, wrote and published more papers (often in the *Telecommunication Journal of Australia*) than any other member of staff. He was never without a notepad, jotting down concepts and plans. When he died long in years in 1981, colleagues remembered him as 'a bushranger of a fellow who grabbed ideas, used them, encouraged his staff to do the same, and got things done'. To others he was a philosopher, a kindly but positive leader, a 'tinkerer' who, even as Director–General, would take anything new to pieces and reassemble it on his polished executive desk. To the historian of L.M. Ericsson, the company's crossbar victory hung substantially on the prominent technical influence of the man.[3]

During the four years of his Director–Generalship (September 1961–December 1965), O'Grady put his stamp upon a progression of major telecommunications plans. In Australia revolutionary engineering changes were taking place. Coaxial cables with their multiple and high quality communications circuits were reaching from Melbourne

Above: The microwave tower at Surrey Hills Radio Relay Terminal, Melbourne, 1963.

Right: Coaxial cable laying in Queensland in the 1960s.

and Sydney on a telecommunications backbone of broadband cable and radio systems that stretched to Cairns and carried television relays and high telephony transmission for the national STD (subscriber trunk dialling) plan. At the same time crossbar equipment and exchanges, designed in co–operation between Ericsson and the PMG were being installed, the first in all mainland capitals in 1963, and 100 more in other city and provincial exchanges by mid–1964. Two years later there were over 250 crossbar exchanges working across the country, while STD served more than 100,000 customers.[4]

From his first days in office O'Grady seized on the importance of the Research Laboratories in preparing the Australian Post Office for the telecommunications revolution ahead. Since Witt's departure from their leadership in 1945, the Research Laboratories, vital in wartime, had sunk into a doldrum. Neither Fanning, Chippindall nor Vanthoff — the non–engineering Directors–General — grasped the real potential of their Department's research arm. Their attitude was reflected in the fact that no permanent appointment was made to Witt's post of supervising engineer, research, for eight years. E.P. Wright, one of the original two–man research team, 'acted' in the position until 1953. 'To a large extent', one research head reflected, 'the Laboratories ran itself.' The appointment in 1953 of N.J. McCay, the wartime communications Lieutenant–Colonel and a postwar PMG transmission and long line engineer, brought a hardline 'military' administrator to the research post. While important experimental work on crossbar, coaxial cables, broadband and microwave developments went on, there was frustration and unhappiness among the Laboratories' engineering, scientific and experimental officer staff. Chippindall as Director–General scrutinised and queried every minor item of funding for the Research Laboratories' work. In his period, total allocation of funding for research moved slowly. There was also an inhibiting influence from the Public Service Board who feared that the PMG's Research Laboratories might overlap some of CSIRO's functions or, worse, 'do things more properly done by private industry'. When McCay retired in 1960, there was a prevailing sense of loss of mission and confusion in the deployment of the different grades of the research staff.

Compared with the major government research bodies of the day, the CSIRO (Commonwealth Scientific and Industrial Research Organisation) with its programmes of basic and applied research and the more mission–oriented Australian Atomic Energy Commission set up in the early 1950s to keep Australia abreast of nuclear science and development overseas, or the laboratories of the post–war Defence Scientific Service, the PMG's Research Laboratories were a poor relation, uncertain of their direction, and with inadequate resources of men and equipment to face a period of rapid telecommunications change. An internal investigation, convened hastily during Stradwick's last months in office, which looked also at other establishments, advised a thorough review.[5] Towards the end of 1960 a three–man committee made up of McCay's successor, L.M. Harris, G.F. Brown of the organisation and management division of the PMG, and E.W. Dwyer of the Public Service Board, was appointed to carry out an examination of the Laboratories and their staffing, and its findings were submitted to O'Grady in April 1962.

The 'Harris–Brown–Dwyer Report' saw the Laboratories' functions in specific terms. Principally it recommended that the Laboratories should conduct research and development aimed to develop telecommunication theory and practice 'in respect of the Australian region'. It should investigate technical development in telecommunications systems and, with the help of other PMG divisions, branches and sections, adapt and bring them into service, and conduct field trials. The Laboratories should also, it emphasised, provide specialised testing facilities, scientific and engineering consultative services, and collaborate with the planning branch of the engineering division in appraising world developments in telecommunications techniques to determine their technical suitability for Australia. To achieve these objectives, the committee suggested restructuring the Laboratories into a number of sections concerned with special discipline concentrations and the allocation of appropriate categories of engineering, scientific, and experimental officer staff.[6]

O'Grady endorsed the report. He went further. During 1962, he upgraded the Laboratories as a separate research branch of the engineering division and reorganised their structure into 22 sections that ranged from theoretical and mathematical concepts, through engineering design and development, transmission physics and materials, to the smallest details of practical design. Two years later he established a new planning and research division as part of an internal reorganisation of the PMG. As a result, O'Grady was often called the 'father of the Research Laboratories'. But the title belongs to Brown. Rather, O'Grady, was 'the godfather' who grasped the importance of strong Research Laboratories, enlarged their role and funding, and equipped them for flexible contemporary advance. Under him, two creative research heads, L.M. Harris and P.R. Brett, would lift this important Departmental asset into forward areas of telecommunications research.

Len Harris had spent the greater part of his career as a research engineer in the Laboratories from 1930–54. An intellectual who kept a cool eye on the tensions that flared at times between the research group and practical engineers, he rose quickly from research head to become first assistant director–general in charge of the planning and research division in 1964 where he continued to guide the Laboratories' programmes and growth. As the first non–university chairman of the Radio Research Board (which the APO helped finance), he fostered research links between the Department and the universities, served as a member of Melbourne University's engineering faculty, and encouraged PhDs to join the Research Laboratories. After a shaky start with academia (Professor Laby, Melbourne's Professor of Physics, had expressed profound contempt for the Laboratories when he visited them in the early 1930s), the Laboratories achieved scientific respectability. Melbourne University's first post–doctoral degree in applied science awarded for work done outside the University went, in the mid–1960s, to the Research Laboratories' Albert Seyler.[7]

In a telecommunications age, these important research links grew. Rollo Brett, Harris's successor as the Laboratories' head in 1964, would

The scientist turned administrator, Rollo Brett, being congratulated by His Excellency the Governor of Victoria, Sir Brian Stewart Murray, after his presentation of an OBE, 1983. P.R. Brett, who served as head of the Research Laboratories from 1964, was appointed Telecom's Victorian state manager in March 1980.

also widen them as member of the engineering faculty and the Radio Research Board, enlarging the latter's field from radio and ionospheric research to include the whole spectrum of telecommunications research. Links between the Department and universities were also cultivated in the States, where senior research–oriented engineers were invited to join the State universities' engineering faculty boards. The liaison was useful to the APO. Board membership influenced courses to take account of the Department's engineering needs, while the APO presence could speak for national manpower telecommunications needs.

Brett would lead the Laboratories for eleven years. A physicist with special training in radio physics who entered the Laboratories in 1944, he joined the small team of physical scientists — physicists, metallurgists and chemists — growing up under the leadership of D. O'Donnell. As Director, Brett expanded research on materials, their components and environmental performance, diversified the Laboratories' operation, and introduced three year rolling programmes of research. The Laboratories' funding rose from $1.5 million in 1964 to $9.3 million in 1975–6. Publicly, Brett also presented a cogent philosophy for the importance of research. Active Research Laboratories, he said, provided an important entry point for men of professional talent in telecommunications research and a 'reservoir of skill and knowledge' for use whenever required. They were a power-house of relevant expertise.[8]

Essentially the Laboratories' work focussed on applied rather than pure research. But, with an enhanced presence within the PMG, their staff was well respected overseas. When O'Donnell himself, 'a born researcher who could do more with a Bunsen burner than any other man', visited the Bell Laboratories in the USA, the comment was made that he was 'the best informed visitor Bell ever had in the Labs'.

O'Grady, with his passion for technological advances on the far horizon, stirred his forward–thinking into the Laboratories' plans. Investigation into satellite methods and systems had begun at the Laboratories in 1960 when news of the early 'passive' communication satellite, ECHO, arrived. Australia with its inaccessible, 'dead' tele-communication areas had much to gain from a 'radio repeater in the sky'. As space rocketry and the US Apollo project took off and President Kennedy pledged himself and his country 'to put a man on the moon by the end of the decade', the Research Laboratories assigned a small team to keep abreast on the satellite front. The launching of the US 'Telstar' by NASA in July 1962 — the first active artificial satellite for commercial communication — sparked sanguine, if speculative views. 'We can put into almost any desired position in the sky above us', O'Grady told the Professional Officers Association members in 1963, 'equipment which could carry the necessary radio receiving and retransmitting equipment to pick up any kind of communication (telephone, telegraph, data transmission or television), and rebroadcast.' While astronauts orbited the globe, Telstar was already relaying telecasts of their launching to the entire European network. To produce 'artificial mountain tops', said O'Grady, was 'a very exciting stage of development'.[9]

The ABGV-3 television transmitter site on Mt Major, near Shepparton, Victoria, showing the microwave signal pick-up mast and the larger transmitter mast.

There were some immediate problems. The question of carving up the radio spectrum to take account of international needs for frequencies created by the new forms of telecommunications relay was such a one. The Research Laboratories provided the leadership of a significant Australian delegation to the first international conference held on the topic at Geneva in 1963. Through OTC, Australia also became one of eleven foundation members of the International Tele-communications Satellite Consortium (INTELSAT) the following year.

On the ground and on Australia's terrestrial mountain tops, substantial progress was being made. Television, slow to start, reached all Australian capital cities by 1960, and spread outward to the countryside. Thirteen independent licences were granted by the Postmaster-General as the 1960s dawned, drawing a ground-plan for a web of stations from Ballarat, Bendigo and the La Trobe Valley, Victoria; the Canberra region; the Goulburn Valley, Illawarra, the Central Tablelands, and the Richmond-Tweed areas of New South Wales; the Darling Downs, Rockhampton and the Townsville areas of Queensland, to the north-eastern areas of Tasmania. The planning of dual national and commercial stations, and the installation of their equipment and towers called on the skills and ingenuity of PMG radio engineers and technicians in every State. To get television to the outback was almost as challenging to the Australian Post Office as it was for NASA to get American manned satellites into the sky. It was a matter of priorities, politics and costs.

Radio broadcasting had forged ahead. Ever since Harry Brown had urged his staff to put their best foot forward to get national radio to the people in 1932, prodigious, if sometimes little recognised, efforts had been made. There were 17 licensed radio sets for every 100 members of the population in 1939, a ratio that put Australia seventh in the world of radio ranking, after countries like Sweden (22 per 100), the USA, Denmark and New Zealand (21 per 100), and the UK (19). Canada (with only 11 per 100) ranked a comparatively low 14th. Throughout the Second World War and after, these statistics grew. By the late 1940s to possess a radio was no longer a mark of affluence. There were nearly two million licensed radios in 1949, while the PMG's Department provided the transmission for ABC radio programmes, music, drama, sport and entertainment that bound the listening countryside in a sense of common culture. When the ABC introduced its own news service in 1947 you could, wrote one remembrancer in 1983, 'walk any street from Hobart to Atherton at 7 p.m. and be certain to hear the theme music and the words "Here is the news from the ABC"'.

The songs, the chat and the very advertisements of the commercial stations also arrived by courtesy of the technical input of the PMG. Yet workers in this field were often unsung heroes. Radio broadcasting was pushed from the front page of technical achievement, just as, in another technological age, news of moon orbits and landings would soon move from stunning headlines to the third pages of the daily press. But radio engineering and research remained a major arm of the PMG's work. Throughout the 1960s technical upgrading went on. Radio engineers and technicians continued to plan and install the separate national and commercial radio towers in the cities (shared towers with two antennae were common features of the country towns); to set up relay stations and the 'unattended' automatic national transmitting stations of the remoter areas and, until 1964, to provide technical control for all ABC sound studios.[10] There was little choice of programme in some country regions. Severe fading plagued certain geographical locations, and in the far outback, listeners were forced to depend on shortwave broadcasting bands on which the national broad-casting service transmitted national programmes to the inland.[11] More widely, Radio Australia relayed by booster station from Darwin conveyed special programmes to countries overseas.

Radio was the companionable medium. But there was more glamour in the high–towered television transmitters that straddled the country's mountain tops and carried the black and white image (colour TV would come to Australia in 1975) of a wider and more dangerous world. It was one thing to hear of the assassination of President Kennedy on radio. It was another to see the brutal event televised a few hours later with all the shock and horror of sight. Death entered the suburban living room along with the faces of people one knew, or did not want to know. Television was the 'intrusive' medium. Australian periodicals fattened on the analysis of its impact — on children, on criminals and delinquents, on education, on the isolated elderly, and on the viewing community at large.[12] Whatever the predictions of social change, the PMG faced unremitting pressure to get the medium further and further out. With government support it did, supplying both the country's expanding national service, and a highly subsidised technical service for commercial television's profitable enterprises too.

Fortunately the TV transmission links, whether by coaxial cable or microwave radio relay, were high capacity telecommunications facilities that provided multiple telephone channels to remoter regions as well. Yet television enjoyed a spectacular growth. While Sydney and Melbourne commandeered most of the country's entire ownership of about 738,000 sets in 1959, the figure leapt nationally to nearly 2,500,000 in 1965. Four years later, the 2,650,000 TV sets licensed across the land exceeded the number of licensed radios by some 20,000 sets.

During O'Grady's regime, plans went ahead for the extension of these microwave systems that would fling the great transmitting towers against city and country skylines. Coaxial cables, with their packed components of telephone and television transmission circuits, found their way underground, weaving out like primaeval snakes in the rocky substructure of the earth. The communications lines that now began to web the continent were very different from the aerial open wires of 50 years before. The men who installed them were also more highly trained. Approaches to the landscape, if at times transforming, were also made with greater forethought and environ-

New technology was changing the landscape. A typical microwave tower, part of Australia's broadband communications network, at Townsville, Queensland, formed a link in a chain that stretches from the east across to Darwin, NT.

Coaxial cable laying in Western Australia, 1968, and in the rocky terrain traversed on the Ceduna, SA, to Cobar, NSW, coaxial cable project, 1978.

mental care than in earlier years. The country, of course, offered its quiet, or hostile resistance. For terrain north of the 26th parallel in north-west Western Australia, the concept of a 'hostile environment' passed into the language. There the country was known to react tempestuously when disturbed. 'Plough a coaxial cable in', said one experienced engineer, 'and the lightning goes "zapp", striking instantly through to the cable along a line of stones, or via small trenches formed by roots.' When it came to coaxial cables and all equipment containing solid state physics devices, nature could be very powerful in the North. One woman in Perth had occasion to remember it. She had her panties burnt off while talking on the telephone while she leaned against her refrigerator. While the Research Laboratories developed direction finders and monitors to locate lightning faults that plagued the Port Hedland–Carnarvon and Mt Newman coaxial routes, staff were given strict instructions not to work on external plant when electrical storms were about.[13] Across the whole continent, however, powerful machines lumbered into action, explosives shattered unyielding rock, moleploughs rolled out the cables and buried them beyond the reach of other destructive assaults. Coaxial cables and microwave relay systems would girdle the continent before the decade of the 1960s was out.

Automation in the post office advanced on every front. The telex network was fully automated by 1966. Computers, outriders of another communications revolution, were introduced in the Research Laboratories during 1963 and in the data processing service in Sydney in 1965. Of special interest to the customer was the new Australian lightweight 'colorfone' introduced in the early 1960s in five different hues. The 'colorfone' offered a more modern shape than the standard black telephone and featured a self-cradling, 'non-fatiguing' handset and coiled cords. Though the telephones were manufactured in Australia by STC and AWA, the choice of colours (with a strong Australian preference for the quiet light ivory) was based on 'an exhaustive study ... into the colour preferences of subscribers overseas'. As one economic historian noted, Australians were 'copycats'.

One feat, started in Chippindall's time and carried on under successive Directors-General until its completion by O'Grady's successor, T.A. Housley, in 1967, was to link Australia's land lines with the telecommunications networks of other continents via the massive new submarine coaxial cables winding around the world. In 1956 the first powerful transatlantic and transoceanic coaxial cable 'TAT 1' was laid between Britain, Canada and the USA. So great was its success that it led to the first all-Commonwealth coaxial cable link, CANTAT I, completed between Britain and Canada in 1961, and to CANTAT II a year later.

Australia had contributed to many international conferences which had as their object the compatibility of national networks with an ultimate single world network. Now evolving TAT cable plans led to Australian plans to participate in two Commonwealth coaxial cable

Developed from the 'Assistant' telephone designed by the Bell Telephone Manufacturing Co of Antwerp, Belgium, but modified considerably for Australian use, the new standard table telephone, the 'colorfone', was introduced in January 1963.

The Touchfone 10 was introduced in the 1970s as an optional alternative to the colorfone.

schemes — COMPAC, an 80–voice channel submarine cable that
would link Vancouver via Hawaii, Fiji and New Zealand to Australia;
and a northerly twin–SEACOM — that would take the 'all red'
connection from Australia via New Guinea, Guam, Hong Kong, North
Borneo, to Singapore and on by microwave to Malaysia, Europe and
Britain. COMPAC, planned by a group of Commonwealth Overseas
Telecommunications authorities, reached Sydney and began operation in December 1963. SEACOM, planned in 1961, pushed south-
wards from Singapore to come ashore in Australia in 1967.[14]

The site of SEACOM's Australian landfall stirred dissent. OTC,
Australia wanted the cable to land at Sydney to connect directly with
COMPAC's 'gateway' exchange. But the PMG, alive to the vast
impetus to land communication that a more northerly landfall could
provide, pressed for a landing at Cairns. Economically and politically,
their reasoning scored. The decision, argued by O'Grady and the
Queensland–based Postmaster–General, Alan Hulme, to make Cairns
the linchpin in a vast Commonwealth submarine cable chain foreshadowed massive telecommunications development in Queensland
and west to Darwin.

The coaxial cable routes

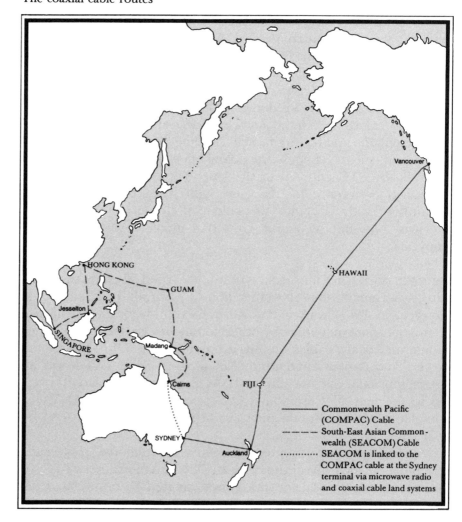

An important plan shaped in the early 1960s for a duplicated microwave system to carry the international traffic south from the OTC gateway at Cairns to Brisbane, from where already developed cable and microwave routes would convey the traffic to Sydney. To chart the best route for the 960 miles from Cairns to Brisbane, teams of engineers, surveyors, technicians, chainmen and linemen measured nearly 3,000 miles of some of the toughest country in that State. Slashing their way up the densely covered mountains of Queensland's mid–northern coast, they mapped access routes and fixed the positions for 29 repeater stations that would carry the television and telephone traffic between Brisbane's terminal station and the distant settled north. A useful aid were the US Army designed 'Kytoons'. These balloons enabled accurate height readings to be made and, attached to flares at night, floated like plump glow–worms above the mountain tops.

The Brisbane to Cairns microwave service was brought into service in April 1966 and by May 1967 Brisbane and near–by Ipswich subscribers had 'gained access to STD to Cairns, the Gold Coast, Lismore (NSW), Rockhampton, Sydney and Townsville'. When the SEACOM cable came ashore amid pomp and ceremony at Cairns later the same year, Queensland's telecommunications 'super highway' linked the world.[15]

Trevor Housley, general manager of OTC Australia from 1956, had substantially masterminded the COMPAC and SEACOM

In the Glasshouse Mountains, 1963. Surveying the route, for the Brisbane to Cairns 'super highway' microwave radio link. Project engineer, V.J. Griffin, examines maps on the vehicle.

schemes. On O'Grady's retirement in December 1965, Housley returned as Director-General to his 'first love', the PMG, after an absence of 20 years. Many remembered the large, prematurely grey-haired, young man who joined the Department as a junior mechanic-in-training in Queensland in 1926. Housley, with many of his confrères, had been pushed onto the roads to drum up telephone customers during the Depression years, and proved so good at it ('a bit too good' said one old crony remembering the subscribers whose payments later fell away) that he was held up each week as 'the model salesman'. Later, as a qualified engineer with a University of Queensland BSc, Housley joined the Queensland PMG radio section and worked in Pacific defence communications in the war. He left for the Department of Civil Aviation in 1946 and, five years later, became assistant general manager of OTC. Housley enjoyed the corridors of power; but he liked and was greatly liked by his colleagues and unionists. He brought high administrative skills plus phenomenal energy to the Director-General's task. Forever pulling on a pipe, he worked, in the knowledgeable words of his driver, 'the greater part of 24 hours a day, the greater part of seven days a week'.[16]

Dramatic spin-offs from the fast advancing international telecommunications systems marked Australian progress in 'the Housley years'. Housley himself had been a key participant in the international discussions of 1963 that led to Australia's part in agreements governing global commercial satellite systems. In April 1965, the United States launched 'Early Bird', its first synchronous satellite (one that, while geostationary, kept time with the rotation of the earth), positioning it above the Atlantic. Managed by INTELSAT (the International Telecommunications Satellite Consortium), INTELSAT I, as the 'bird' became known, provided all forms of communication services between North America, Britain and Europe. When, in October 1966, a trio of larger satellites, INTELSAT II, were launched to hang like bright stars above the Pacific and Atlantic Oceans, Australia was drawn into one of the great adventures of the age.

A large land mass in the southern hemisphere and a foundation member of INTELSAT, Australia offered attractive sites for land 'hook-ups' with the Pacific satellites. Such land-to-satellite links were vital in a data-gathering chain designed among other purposes, to serve NASA's rapidly advancing Apollo space programme. OTC's first earth station was built at Carnarvon, WA, and opened late in 1966 with seven circuits on open wire lines across the Nullarbor connecting Australia via satellite to the USA. Again old technology was married to the new, at least until the open wire circuits were replaced by the east-west microwave system in 1970. When, in 1968, OTC opened a considerably more sophisticated earth station at Moree in north-west New South Wales, Australia's telecommunication network was linked with the national system of Canada, USA and Japan.

The link integrated data, telephone, telegram, telex and TV circuits. Most popularly for the community, most Australians could now for the first time watch overseas events on their television sets as they occurred. The heading 'By telegraph from London', so remark-

The dish antenna at the OTC satellite earth station, Ceduna, SA.

able in Victorian times, found its amazing counterpart in the reign of Queen Elizabeth II in the words 'By satellite' on the news service of TV. Flynn of the Inland's poetic phrase used of radio broadcasting 40 years earlier, 'to make the dumb inland speak and its deaf distances hear', now stretched to sight. Carnarvon in Western Australia stood as a sentinel of the most modern communication system in that once 'backward' State. Although its earth station belonged to OTC, the service spilled over into local use. By arrangement, 24 satellite circuits were introduced for telephone traffic between Perth and the eastern States late in 1969 to relieve pressure pending the completion of the east–west microwave. 'It was the first time in the free world', wrote John Moynihan, Telecom WA's unofficial historian, 'that satellite circuits were used for intracontinental telephone circuits'. When, during that year, a second earth station was opened at Carnarvon with a large dish–antenna, TV relays made connections across the State. Australia's fourth earth station at Ceduna, South Australia, opened in 1970, linked Australia through a new generation of INTELSAT satellites hoisted above the Indian Ocean to the telephone and television networks of Asia, Africa, Britain and Europe.[17]

The moon landing of 20 July 1969, the fulfilment of President Kennedy's promise, brought Australians numbering millions into awed community with people from all round the world. The PMG had been involved in the various US space programmes since the first Australian tracking station was set up near Woomera in 1957. Since then a complex network had been constructed to provide communication for the Mercury, Gemini and Apollo ventures. There were gratifying rewards. NASA data circuits in Australia, the engineers' and technicians' house journal *Telegen* noted, averaged a reliability of 99.8 per cent which 'compared favourably with other national sections'. John Glenn, the first astronaut to orbit the earth on 20 February 1962, streaked across the coast of Western Australia near midnight, and exclaimed, 'I can see the lights of Perth! Thank everyone for turning on the lights.' It was more than the lights. PMG technicians and engineers had laid a skein of lines to bring Glenn's message from Muchea to Perth.[18]

With the Apollo 11 mission to land a man on the moon, additional facilities were required. Circuits to carry the video signals with special data information were provided from the radio telescope at Parkes to Canberra, and on to the satellite earth station at Moree. At Sydney a 'split' off the television relay was transmitted to the ABC studios at Gore Hill where it was converted to Australian television standards. From there it was relayed to Australia's 39 national and 43 commercial television stations. Science and technology outstripped all television ratings on 20 July 1969. 'One small step for man', said astronaut Neil Armstrong as his foot found firm lunar ground. Yet it was also a giant step for the booming business of communication, data transfer, scientific and technological information, and ever expanding commercial and human exchange. The PMG's Department noted the achievement in more parochial terms. 'In Australia', the Annual Report announced in 1969, the telephone network 'contains enough wire and cable to stretch to the moon and back 50 times', and more than 6,000 telephone exchanges were serving from 20 to 20,000 inhabitants each.

In these persistent technological advances, what of the men? What of the engineers, the technicians and linemen who mastered the technologies, contrived their integration, laid and jointed the long coaxial cables, and installed the microwave towers and relay stations that carried the television transmission and STD facilities further and deeper into the countryside?

The engineers were at the heart of the telecommunications system. Under differing titles — for their roles and responsibilities changed as the technology moved on — they were the 'makers and shakers', the planners, innovators and overseers who, in key positions in headquarters and widely dispersed in the States, chose the systems for present and future needs (microwave versus coaxial cable, telex for remote mining business where telephone links were poor), and who introduced and modified the equipment and carried out the continuing task of upkeep and extension.

The Australian network, it was widely acknowledged, evolved differently from telecommunication networks in other parts of the world. This difference sprang essentially from the function of the engineers. At first, as we have seen, staff worked their way forward from junior engineers to engineer by in–house study and open examination within the PMG. From the 1920s cadet engineers were introduced with a BSc gained by part–time study during office hours added to engineering and technical work in the branches in every State. But it was not until after the Second World War that graduates trained specifically in communications engineering started to emerge. The University of Queensland led the way with the first graduates in this field in 1949, a group who included ex–serviceman, J.H. Curtis, destined to become the first managing director of Telecom. By the mid–1950s Australian degree courses in electrical engineering had been upgraded and tailored to meet sophisticated electrical and communication engineering needs and in–house courses on the new technologies were also offered to PMG engineers.[19]

Their knowledge was more than a watching brief. Departmental engineers were the professional manpower who applied both their theoretical knowledge and practical experience to make overseas technologies fit local conditions and conceived original answers to problems at the Antipodes. Their innovative qualities were widely recognised abroad. In the vital evaluation of systems overseas, their work was careful and informed. The Report of the Royal Commission of Inquiry into the APO of 1974 gave them public praise. Staff, they noted, 'spared no effort to ensure the best possible deal for the APO and . . . are to be commended for the expertise and competence they have displayed'.[20] In the larger field of State deployed superintending, supervising, divisional and other engineers, they proved a versatile breed of problem–solvers who exercised a high degree of independence in overcoming difficulties and responding to customer needs.

Necessity mothered invention across the States. As a result it often proved difficult to identify individual inventors. War spotlighted a few. Particular innovators were known to colleagues in their State. Some, who crossed State boundaries in different posts, influenced several local scenes. But there was a style of corporate anonymity. Teamwork was the key. Major projects were collaborative drawing on the efforts of numerous draughtsmen and engineers. The Australianisation of crossbar was a case in point. At least two men were known as 'Mr Crossbar' for very different contributions to the art: Ron Turnbull for his part in the planning of the national switching scheme, and Allan Pettersson, chief engineer of Telecom WA (1975–83), who as district engineer responsible for the maintenance of the first crossbar exchange installed at Toowoomba, burnt the midnight oil to probe the new equipment and developed the automatic disturbance recorder (the ADR) which was adopted nationally as a standard installation for supervising the working of the crossbar exchange.

There was, inevitably, duplicate invention. State innovations did not always flow into national designs. Engineers across the country, for example, hatched their own multiple versions of the moleplough for digging in and laying cables in different types of terrain. Many thought their own processes were unique. This phantom rivalry, or 'reinventing the wheel', eventually led headquarters to devise a register of research, development and innovation to record all national research and innovation work in progress.[21] Yet happily it failed to curb the inventive gusto of the scattered individual telecommunications engineer.

Not all engineers were creative. There were many industrious plodders. There were also some, high on practice and at times in influential places, who undervalued the importance of ongoing PMG research. Contributions varied. Engineering roles embraced maintenance, the ordering of equipment and material, slogging installation, the checking on performance of all systems, planning and management, as well as the exhilarating assault on puzzles that demanded ingenuity on the spot.

Engineers' attitudes to their roles varied. C.P. Snow, that sharp observer of two cultures, once asserted that engineers tended 'to be technologically bold and advanced but . . . to accept any society into which they happened to be born'.[22] His comment proved both false and true. There was certainly boldness in the stringing of the longest telephone lines, in Australia's forward international place in radio and telephone density, in its adoption of progressive transmission and switching techniques, and in its ambitious stretching from the 1960s of the wholly new and advanced broadband networks across an immense continent. Telecommunications engineers altered the nature and improved the standard of living of their society. As such they served as key agents of social change.

Yet, as Snow suggests, some were far more perceptive of this social role. Witt and his research engineers and a successive contingent of engineering planners had an articulated philosophy of the social implications of their work. For them, national long–term needs, economics, technological and community progress were closely intermixed. But there were also the 'linear' technologists who performed their jobs as pragmatic practitioners, inflexible in their attitude and with certainty that all they did carried a grinding justification of its own. The early invasion of Aboriginal territory, with its disregard for tribal sites and ownership, arose from this. It reflected the values of the time. Environmental impact was a substantially foreign concept to engineers. From telephone line to microwave transmitters, telecommunications proved a visual polluter until public pressure demanded that reasonable accommodations must be made. Yet there is no doubt that the generality of PMG engineers were gripped by the potential of their craft and shared a strong sense of providing the 'best' community service at a minimum cost. Engineering, as one early practitioner put it, 'is the art of doing well with one dollar what any bungler can do with ten after a fashion'.[23] Most often they saw themselves as reacting to and stimulating social demand rather than as conscious ambassadors of change.

Yet despite the engineering presence at the centre of the system, there was a paradox. Brown had stressed the importance and accelerated the training of qualified engineers. During the 1930s their stature grew. But while the engineers themselves had a keen sense of their own importance — 'over esteem' was a term heard along office corridors — they were not professionally well recognised in Australia.

The PMG's Department employed the largest group of engineers in the Commonwealth. But, slow to organise themselves industrially, they (and their colleagues in State and other Commonwealth Departments, statutory bodies and private industry) were linked industrially alongside much larger associations of employees, and their industrial awards and agreements were partly determined by the industrial interests of these. It was not until September 1946 that the Federal Association of Professional Engineers Australia (APEA) was formed to bring together a number of existing State groups and to stimulate newly formed branches in the laggard States of Tasmania and Western Australia. Thereafter the APEA became the spearhead for improving the status and salaries and focussing the common vocational interests of Australia's professional engineers.[24]

Progress was tortuous. It took 15 years to secure the Association's recognition as the profession's industrial organisation. Resistance welled from State Governments averse to the 'intrusion' of a Federal organisation in the salaries and conditions of State engineers, and from self-determining Commonwealth Statutory Authorities. Hearings, tribunals, transcripts studded the course. A State Instrumentalities Case of 1951–2 and a Private Industry Case the following year began a procession of arbitration actions aimed to register the APEA under the Commonwealth Conciliation and Arbitration Act. When after two years of hearings from 1959–61, also involving the participation of the Professional Officers Association, the Conciliation and Arbitration Commission handed down its decision on the Professional Engineers or the 'Main Case' (as the Association called it), the struggle, as one writer put it, 'had assumed the proportions of an Odyssey'.[25]

In pronouncing judgment, Justice Richard Kirby, President of the Commission, recognised the costly and 'dispiriting' nature of the skirmish and the depressed status of a major profession in Australia. Much had been said at the hearings, and much would be said again, about the engineer's service to civilisation. Roads, transport, bridges, communications hung upon his skills. The Commission's verdict underlined the point. It defined a uniform national minimum salary rate for qualified and experienced engineers that lifted the annual base rate by an instant £800. Overnight engineering became one of the best-paid callings in the land. Equally, the Commission's verdict recognised the once unacclaimed 'servant of society' as a true-blue professional group.[26] Professionally, economically and psychologically, the APEA had scored a triumph.

But on the economic front, the case's repercussions were widely felt. The quantum jump in salary, as one engineer recalled, 'left the Commonwealth Public Service Board gasping'. The board's response would introduce significant changes in the work organisation of the PMG. The board's initial resistance to salary increases for higher than base grade engineers led the following year to the Professional Engineers Case No.2 of 1962 which established new salary standards for more senior Commonwealth public service engineers. But within the PMG, the Public Service Board turned its pruning eye on areas where cuts and adjustments might be made. It fell, in a period of shortage of qualified professional engineers, on engineers-in-training acting in positions and earning the salaries of qualified engineers. Subsequently it identified qualified engineers doing 'unprofessional work'. While the in-training group were merely scrubbed out of the new salary range, the board's second reform led importantly to the creation of a new sub-professional 'technical grade' that threatened job areas of engineers.

Within the Department, battle lines were sharply joined. O'Grady as Director-General resisted the board's pressure for a 30 per cent reduction of engineering ranks. A compromise, agreed after a long review, led to a reduction of 20 per cent of classified engineering positions in favour of office-based 'technical officer' positions open to technical and engineering staff alike. By the late 1960s the twin concerns of salary increases and the engineers' professional position versus technical officer grades surfaced in a major case brought before the Commonwealth Public Service Board by the Professional Officers Association (the POA) who represented the majority of PMG engineers. But, despite a further large salary increase that flowed from the judgment in December 1969, engineers again faced significant organisational changes of role. For the engineers, financial victory had, ironically, proved to be a two–edged sword.

The judgment of 1969 would provide the stepping stone for the more fundamental decision (taken by Telecom Australia in 1977) to place 'principal technical officers' in managerial positions in charge of technical staff. It marked a shift from the engineer's traditional and to them pivotal control of technical line staff which held long–range implications for the institutional role of Australia's telecommunications engineers.

It was the technicians and their unions who would challenge the hegemony of an 'engineering culture' in the PMG. The technicians formed an upwardly mobile group. Like the engineers, their education and industrial progress advanced significantly through the 1950s. Again like the engineers, their title and classifications also changed with the technology. 'Technicians' belonged to the 20th century. In Colonial times the telegraph and telephone systems were maintained by 'instrument fitters' and a rare supervisory 'mechanician'. By the end of the first ten years of the new century, the PMG's Department's need for technical workers, and the workers' need for higher wages, ushered in the Federal Australian Postal Electricians' Union (the APEU) in 1911. Later the same year the instrument fitters became 'mechanics'. In the mid–1920s, with the appearance of the new carrier systems, classifications into mechanics grade 1 and grade 2 (for the more experienced workers), and junior mechanics–in–training came in response to union action.[27]

From the first decade of the century the PMG's mechanical workforce was aware of the close relationship between new technology and its changing role. In its First Report of 1911 the Department plainly indicated its intention to utilise technology to reduce labour in order to provide an advancing network at minimum cost. Presenting the Report, Postmaster–General Josiah Thomas proudly claimed that 'the Department is thoroughly alive to the desirability of employing mechanical devices, with the view to economising labour and expediting work as far as practicable'. From the advent of the automatic Strowger 'step–by–step' exchanges, the mechanics recognised the need to press for training and, in its absence, to make provisions for their own Departmental training 'on–the–job'. The wartime Postal Institute and its State branches attempted an educative role, while the Union journal, the *Australian Postal Electrician* and its successor, became major channels for the dissemination of technical information. With departmental training either non–existent or inadequate, union membership became a virtual necessity for technical employees wishing to 'get on' in the service and keep abreast of change.

During 1931 the APEU, motivated by its executive's decision to 'make special efforts to have described in plain language the general features and principles of the systems installed', published a book of collected technical articles. It sold for 1s 6d. Members were strongly advised to acquire a copy 'due to the difficulty of obtaining text books or information on these matters by the general body of mechanics'. Clearly the union had a low expectation of the PMG, for a decade later it lavished praise on the Department for providing members with a technical instruction manual at nominal cost.[28]

Through self–help, rudimentary training, the postal institutes, and some new courses elicited from the Department in the hectic years of innovation in 1941, the mechanics (as a reserved occupation) became the pillars of the vital wartime telegraph, telephone and radio systems. This gave them fighting power to obtain industrial rewards for their expertise. Their success precipitated change. In 1942 the union's journal was reborn as the newly titled, hard–hitting *TeleTechnician* while (after some Departmental and Public Service Board resistance) the union itself changed its name in March 1943 to the Postal Tele-communications Technicians Association (Australia) (PTTA). A year later, Senator Ashley, Labor's Postmaster–General, acceded to strong union pressure for a change in designation from mechanic to technician.

Industrially the technicians were on the move. The union produced a crop of able and aggressive negotiators to state their cause and carry their case before both the Conciliation and Arbitration Commission and the High Court. At the core of their struggle was an attempt to obtain training to improve their knowledge of telecommunications systems and to win status and financial recognition for their work. Training schemes were a barometer of technological change. Under pressure from this increasingly educated group, Departmental courses changed from the manipulative to more analytic and diagnostic skills. As expertise and specialisms grew, senior technicians were added to the technical assistant and technician classifications while two streams — technician (telecommunications) and technician (trade) emerged in 1950. The demarcation was plain. Telecommunication technicians saw themselves as white–collar employees who understood the concepts of changing telecommunications technologies, who were often the only technically able people in isolated country districts, and who depended increasingly on theoretical training and retraining in their jobs. By contrast trade technicians were 'blue collar' workers, practically trained through four or five-year apprenticeships and working under supervision.

During the 1950s the thrust of automation spurred the technicians' moves. TRESS and its impact on telegraphists sounded the alarm. 'Planning and training', proclaimed the *TeleTechnician*, 'must be introduced and applied prior to the extensive introduction and extension of automation to ensure that unemployment is not caused and that the worker in industry reaps in full the benefits that should accrue from its introduction.' On the issue of redundancy, the technicians had little to fear. Five hundred technicians had been imported from Britain in 1951 but the shortage remained acute.

Nonetheless they intended to link the accelerating process of automation with greater training, more highly technical jobs and a share in the returns from the technological revolution that their skills sustained. During 1957 several 'Raise Our Sights' forums initiated 'to lift morale and provide excellent means of bringing the technicians into collaboration with management' won union and PMG support. Yet, as Departmental engineers and leaders projected the national telephone plan, the *TeleTechnician* sharply prodded Director–General Stradwick 'from his somewhat ethereal castle at Central Office' to make available to all technicians a book published by the Department on the community telephone plan. 'Here is a chance for our D.G.', it exhorted, 'to get in a real blow for improved efficiency, better staff relations and increased technological knowledge. How about it D.G.?'[29]

Numerically and industrially, the technicians had made important ground. The 8,000 or so employed by the Department in 1951 had grown to over 11,500 by 1965. Their classifications had been upgraded; telecommunications technical officers and senior technical officers appeared in 1960. Classifications, like clothes, made the man. Changes in technology and related training had increased their responsibilities and skills. When, early in 1962, the engineers' 'main case' broke, PTTA members rightly predicted that some engineering functions would be 'priced out' and in future performed by their own sub–professional group.[30] Technicians had become the centurions of a new technological age.

It was inevitable that deep rifts would form between technicians and engineers. 'Without the co–operation of the technician and craftsman', said the PTTA journal stoutly in 1961 'the engineer is bereft of the means of execution; in short, nothing can be achieved because there is nothing to transfer the idea into an accomplishment.'[31] The notion flowed into the industrial blood stream of the PMG. There were certain key injectors. One was George Slater, the fresh–faced general secretary of the Amalgamated Postal Workers Union of Australia (APWU). Automation hit postal areas forcibly in the 1960s with the introduction of the TEI manufactured electronic coding, letter–sorting machine at Sydney's Redfern mail exchange. The machine, and its threatened impact on experienced male postal workers, excited intense union reaction. For the three years of preparation before the installation, there was no management discussion with the APWU and the PMG had, clearly, failed to apply the lesson of their co–operative experience with TRESS's introduction when it came to the automotive mail machines. Slater himself fought a spirited fight against 'the flood of female labour' that, he believed, would deluge the male Redfern mail exchange and protested against the 'take it or leave it attitude' of PMG management. Active on the tumultuous Redfern front, he later assisted technicians and higher grade postal clerks against engineering job dominance in certain fields.[32]

In a Commonwealth Department that employed over 77,000 people by 1970, harboured its own network of unions and supported a maze of hierarchies that occasionally overlapped, tension and job jostling occurred. Technical staff, for example, chafed at the supervision of postmasters in country towns. Engineers resisted any loss of supervisory role. Clerks were not invariably sympathetic to technicians or engineers. Yet while differences simmered, within the huge telecommunications enterprise of the PMG, manpower segments functioned as a service team.

If the technicians were the 'centurions', it was the linemen who, historically and contemporaneously, were the footsoldiers of telecommunications advance. Without them, nothing went in. They strung the aerial wires, dug in the cables, built the steel structures for the radio and television transmission towers, and installed the evolving equipment and systems that influenced the customs of a nation.

From early in this century, they formed strong unions. Registered as the 'Australian Telegraph, Telephone Construction and Mainten-ance Union' by the Commonwealth Arbitration Court in 1912, they became the Postal Linemen's Union in 1919, and amalgamated six years later with the APWU.[33] For years their training and know–how was obtained on the job. By the 1950s it became the formal responsi-bility of the engineering division. The linemen's journal *On the Line*, founded by V. White, was launched from the division in 1957. White's influence also lay behind improved lines staff training and an emphasis on aspects of safety in tool kits, clothing — attitudes which have reached rigorous standards in recent years. *On the Line* was an educational forum in itself mixing the message of safety practice and precaution with humour, human stories, and instruction in new devices and skills.

As lines went underground and coaxial cables had to be laid and jointed, the 'liney's' work was industrially upgraded although it retained much of the essential 'craft tradition' of its earliest days. Lines work bred independence and ingenuity, and a versatility that was passed on across the country from father to son. Over the years both the lineman's range of work and his appearance changed. Hard white protective helmets with leather head bands replaced the traditional digger's hat. Yet, while the helmets were designed to withstand pressure and long exposure to rain and sun, the heads inside needed to be as steady as those of their more casual forebears to the hazard of climate, environment and heights.

Linemen of the future. Protective linemen hats being tested for weakness over long exposure to the elements at the Research Laboratories, Victoria.

In Australia there would be no communications service without the participation of women. Women were vital. Initially as postmistresses and some telegraphists (often combining the two roles), they carved a career path in telecommunications in the 19th century and, from the inception of telephony and throughout the 20th century, dominated the working of the manual telephone exchange. Both the nation and the fairer sex had much to gain. Colonial post and telegraph departments, and subsequently the PMG, found access to an 'economic' workforce at modest pay, while educated women found entry to a congenial and respectable occupation that gave them social status, a sense of community service, and responsible authority.

In city exchanges the work was demanding. Bertha Cleminson, a country girl from Rockhampton appointed to the Brisbane central exchange in 1903 later recalled the role. 'On the Magneto switchboard at that time there were approximately 1,520 subscribers' shutters connected at the central exchange ... Normally each telephonist attended to a hundred line section of the switchboard, but teamwork was expected from all telephonists at rush time.' The telephonists were allowed lunch–time and a morning and afternoon 'break', but their work was constantly monitored by the supervisor, Mrs Dick. Mrs Dick showed her martinet qualities when the electrical engineer (then John Hesketh) did his rounds. 'Then the girls would hear the stentorian tones of the Supervisor "take that call" if a second elapsed before a calling subscriber's shutter dropped.' This was not surprising. John Hesketh sternly overviewed his workforce, noting holes in their stockings with distress and parading up and down the length of the switchboard 'like a caged lion'. The discerning Bertha (who was awarded a medal for her speed and efficiency in connecting emergency calls by journalists of the Brisbane *Telegraph*, and rose to serve in a top clerical position in the PMG) 'had a feeling one would see a lashing tail had one dared to look around'.[34]

The work also carried certain strain. There was the irritant of jumping up and down to move plug cords (once the girls no longer stood all day), the burden of headphone and chest equipment, and the pressures of busy periods of traffic during the working day. Certain 19th century preconceptions also pervaded male attitudes to this innovative sphere of 'women's work'. The Royal Commission of Inquiry on Postal Services of 1908–10 illustrated this. Despite

Progress in headset design. For many decades Melbourne telephonists wore headsets almost as awkward as those of the 1880s (right). Telephonists at the old Newcastle (NSW) exchange in the 1970s (opposite page) are wearing sets of a less cumbersome design.

Alexander Graham Bell's rousing defence of the 'hello girls' in his evidence before the commission in 1910, a more common view was offered by Dr Leschen, whose testament presented telephone operators as frail, nervous, hysterical creatures whose real purpose was motherhood and whom the clatter of telephone technology might derange.

'My experience of female telephone attendants', Leschen observed, 'is that many of them are kept far too long at their work. The complaint a majority of them suffer from is neurasthenia, or practically breakdown of the nervous system. This, in my opinion, renders them entirely unfit for the duties of motherhood. I have strongly recommended many of them to resign, and they have done so.' Questioned earnestly by the commission, Leschen reasoned that men did not suffer to anything like the same extent. A woman, he said, was 'much sharper in her wits, much quicker, and much more expeditious'. A man would last longer, but would not be so quick at the work. To the query, were the women, then, being 'sacrificed for speed?', Dr Leschen answered 'it was a woman's nature to act quickly' but that such quickness was clearly detrimental to their 'usefulness as women and citizens of the State [presumably as mothers]. It is altogether too nerve straining.'[35]

Despite nerve straining, women continued to preside at city, suburban and country exchanges. In rural exchanges, responsibility and job satisfaction was large. In a small community, the telephone operator was its focal point, providing connections (and comfort) and speeding help in times of emergency and distress. 'When people are in a panic', one operator recalled, 'they don't look up phone books. They ring the exchange and ask for help.' 'You are a cross between a Dorothy Dix and a know-all', another long-term operator serving 26 subscribers summed up, 'I was always a shoulder for the callers to cry on. It's more than just a telephone service.' Some elderly people rang the exchange, 'just to hear a voice'; men would call for cooking advice, and schoolchildren coming home to an empty house would ring the operator to find out their mother's whereabouts. Hours could be long (44 hours a week and 40 for night service); and night duty dragged. 'It was sometimes very lonely', one Tasmanian operator recalled, and 'we occasionally spoke with other exchanges'. Knitting and reading helped to pass the quiet hours.

While the Department took pride in this petticoat service, the low rates paid to their female operators kept the overall price of telecommunications services down. Ironically, the introduction of the step–by–step automatic exchange at Geelong in 1912 — the 'girl-less, cussless phone' as inventor Strowger proudly called it, presaged the gradual phasing out of the operator's job. Yet legions of Australian women made careers at the telephone exchange. There were over 9,000 telephonists in the PMG in 1951; 10,000 when STD was introduced in 1956; a decline into the 9,000s from 1959–64, and from 10,000 to 10,600 in the decade 1965–75. Until a significant break-through in Commonwealth public service regulations in 1966, only single women could apply, and there was an inevitably large turnover in female telephonists through marriage. As one American writer observed shrewdly, 'the very quality that made them good operators made them good wives'.[36]

In 1914 telephonists formed their first union, the combined male-female Commonwealth Telephone and Phonogram Officers Association and elected Miss J.S. Roddy as first Federal president, a position she held for thirty years. Miss K. Hester succeeded Jean Roddy from 1944–66. Health and pay were central issues — equal pay was actually achieved between 1914 and 1920 when the Commonwealth Public Service Board again fixed 'single female' rates. Across the years, sick leave, rates of pay, overtime payments, higher duty allowance, Saturday and Sunday penalty payment and meal allowances were negotiated and won. A single triumph was the attainment in the late 1920s of a 34–hour week for staff at the busy main exchanges at Sydney, Melbourne, Adelaide and Brisbane. Country telephonists worked longer hours, varying between a 36 to a 40–hour week (until Telecom introduced a 36¾–hour week across the board). Women could ascend the career ladder from telephonist to monitor, supervisor and travelling supervisor (overviewing the work standards of rural exchange operators) and could move into clerical grades. But the way was tough. There was evident sexual discrimination in the PMG. After persistent union struggle, women were allowed to enter the 3rd division of the Commonwealth public service in 1949.[37] Soon after, Kate Coffey, who began her career as a telephonist, became the highest paid woman in the Department as administrative assistant to Director-General, Giles Chippindall.

Over the century the social background of telephonists widened and changed. The 'quickness', friendliness and sense of community remained. Telephonists, both men and women, worked far beyond their normal duty when flood, fire, or other havoc struck country or city lines. Women at first substantially serviced the 'wake up and reminder calls' first introduced in 1946. Regular users of this service formed cosy relations with the telephone girls. Edged out in metropolitan centres by the late 1970s by an impersonalised computer delivery of the time, 'wake up' telephonists recalled how they rang subscribers to remind them to feed the cat, catch a plane, take medication, remember birthdays, arouse students to complete an essay, and to serve a medley of individual needs. Monday and Anzac Day always registered the highest national service demand.

But automation was spreading. All metropolitan exchanges were fully automated by 1962, and while telephone instruments increased almost seven–fold in Australia in the three decades from 1950–80, telephone operators varied between 9,000 and 8,500 in that time. The movement towards redundancy was gathering pace. In cities telephone operators moved into directory assistance and a range of new work linked with computerised machines. But rural exchange operators were hardest hit. For them geographical location and, for some, a husband's occupation, ruled out alternative employment remote from home. As a result, only about 360 of the 2,500 telephonists made redundant by automation between 1974–80 accepted alternative positions offered by the PMG and Telecom. In many country towns the friendly local community contact was receding before the technological efficiency of the machine. Some manually operated exchanges would, of course, remain, but total automation of the telephone system is expected in Australia by 1990.

One factor, however, has undergone change. Under full–time general secretary, Sylvia Hall, the power of the renamed Australian Telephone and Phonogram Officers' Association has grown. Redundancy, working conditions in the new automated exchanges, window-less air–conditioned offices to suit computer machines, and the eye strain of prolonged video work, have combined to form a pressing platform for reform. 'What price progress?', a Sydney Telephonists Action Group asks. The role of women in telecommunications' technological progress has swung full circle to conditions often reminiscent of the original telephonists' fatigue and nervous strain.[38]

Across the field of employment, engineers, technicians, linemen and telephonists faced alteration and attrition in their work. The happy family atmosphere of the PMG was undergoing change. A new deal was needed to face the realities of modern industrial conditions that had, across 70 years of the century, overtaken the huge Department of State. The time was ripe for change.

11 The End of an Era

After six decades of operation, the Australian Post Office was a goliath. Its workforce touched 115,000; its assets were almost double the size of Australia's biggest private company, BHP; and its postal and telecommunications system constituted the largest capital enterprise in the country. To add to its complexities, it was also a Department of State administering two inherently different operations — the labour–intensive postal system and the capital–intensive telecommunications services with its technically trained workforce and a technology whose changes bore importantly on its future planning and manpower needs. The Janus faces stared outward on divergent resources, management and means.

The Department's postal activities in the 20th century lie outside the scope of this history. But, in a dual enterprise whose economies were institutionally joined, it is noteworthy that, since their important contribution and upgrading in the Second World War, Australia's postal services had operated at an almost perennial loss. After a spectacular profit of nearly £3 million in 1946–7, postal returns fell into the red in 1948–9 and dropped to a £2.5 million deficit in the national economic crisis of 1953. Indeed, with steadily rising manpower and materials costs, the postal services suffered a sizeable financial deficit until a brisk gust of profit blew across the ledger for 1960 and 1961, and again more mildly in 1963 and 1964. Otherwise, in the years 1948–75, the Department's postal returns, either for political reasons or from costs, were balanced substantially by revenue from its tele-communications side. See Appendix V.[1]

There had been several major postal developments since 1901. Large improvements in postal delivery came from the spread of airmail in the early 1920s. The pioneering flights of Western Australian Airways begun from Geraldton via coastal ports to Broome in 1922, later from Perth to Derby, and from the inauguration of Queensland and Northern Territory Aerial Services (Qantas) in remote Queensland and, successively, from Sydney to Brisbane and Melbourne, from Adelaide to Perth, were all operating by 1930. In addition, the decision taken by the mid–1930s to carry all inter–capital mail by fast night flights free of airmail surcharge, quickened the delivery of mail across the land. The first overseas Qantas services for regular airmail flights from Darwin to Singapore (and thence by other flights to England) and their extension to other countries in 1938, which Brown as Director–General negotiated and spurred, offered remarkably cheap rates and in the single year of 1938–9 lifted incoming airmail to Australia by 600 per cent!

There was still the challenge of 'getting the mail through' to the remote outposts, often as real in the 1960s and 1970s as in 1901. A great part of mail service was long haul. The volume of internal mail had waxed as population grew and the effects of large–scale immigration, the annual report noted in 1958, 'were graphically illustrated by the increase in the volume of mail overseas'.[2] Curiously, there was always more overseas mail entering Australia (to be handled) than that going out (on which charges could be made). So great, in fact, was this rising inward tide, that the Department for this and other reasons introduced high speed mail sorting machines into Melbourne, Sydney and Brisbane during 1955. Even so, as one economic historian observes, 'the postal services found it difficult to maintain quality, let alone improve it, without incurring large increases in cost'. Despite such assistance as faster delivery by trucks and better roads, the carriage of most internal letter mail by air from 1959, the introduction of the postcode in 1967, courier services from 1970, and motor bikes for postmen, postal productivity so heavily dependent on physical handling, crept forward only minimally assisted by technological change. Contrastingly, from the post–war, telephone productivity jumped annually at double and later at six times the postal rate, while the battery of telecommunications advances in transmission and switching and the new broadband systems of coaxial cable and micro-wave, propelled telecommunications output forward (with only occasional annual deficits) at a dramatically accelerating rate.[3]

With mounting disequilibrium in its activities, the financial management and accounting of the PMG showed singular features of its own. Several studies of these processes have recently emerged from the Research School of Social Sciences' Department of Economic History, Australian National University. Their titles — 'Service at any cost'; 'Cui bono? The Post Office at work', and 'Telephone pricing and cross–subsidisation under the PMG, 1901 to 1975' — suggest their thrust. 'No private business of its size', Jonathon Pincus writes in 'Service at any cost', 'would have survived as long as did the Post Office in the first stage when it drew upon taxpayers.' The Department's historical exemption from tax — a privilege conferred in Australia essentially on public service organisations, charities and pension funds — gave the public enterprise a clear edge in competition for resources. For almost 60 years, moreover, the Department's capital works were financed largely through interest-free loans from the consolidated revenue fund. The year 1959 brought signal change. In the policy which Charles Davidson announced as Postmaster–General, based on the (Fitzgerald) Ad Hoc Committee of Inquiry of that year, the concept of financial budgets was introduced and the Department required to pay the Treasury interest on its outstanding balance of capital each year at the ruling bond interest rate. More crucially, the principle was applied retroactively to Federation so that in 1959 the Department was debited to the amount of £340 million. The rise in interest charges on all capital accordingly moved from 0.8 per cent of revenue in 1958–9 to 12 per cent in 1959–60, a leap that was mirrored in the sudden drop in telecommunications profit from nearly £6 million in 1959–60 to about £0.4 million in the following year. Charges for services rose. New costs of telephone calls and connections and for letter and newspaper postage expressed keener acknowledgement of the concept that the 'user pays'.[4]

An amendment to the Postal and Telegraph Act of 1968 marked a further though different change. By it, Departmental appropriations were altered from the standard itemised departmental form to a single–line trust account. While Parliament still gave its approval to the PMG's annual accounts, it forfeited control over the detailed itemisation of the expenditure. The PMG hence acquired greater flexibility, with Ministerial and Treasury concurrence, to determine its charges, its surpluses and major financial goals.

Historically the character of the PMG's financial and accounting methods concealed much of the real economics of the game. Cross–subsidisation, first from the more profitable postal services to the growing telephone network and, after the Second World War, from the now burgeoning telephone service to the declining postal and telegraph services, underlay the fiscal display. 'In a multi–enterprise commodity like the Post Office', Pincus notes, 'the costs of supplying a particular set of customers is a disputed concept and we are forced to accept the methods used, but rarely spelt out . . . to distribute overhead or common charges between services.'[5]

There was also the politicised nature of cross–subsidy and PMG pricing which found its roots in a strong governmental commitment to 'assistance to the bush'. Cross–subsidisation from busy intercity trunk lines to country services kept rural telephone charges down, just as a distinction between business and residential telephone services established in 1941–64 brought a subsidy from the business community to the domestic or private telephone. A basic theme for politicians, with Country Party members articulately in the lead, was that the cheapening of country telephone services (and later, television) would encourage stable rural settlement and halt a critical urban drift. With the telephone, however, one point was clear. Call charges grew effectively cheaper across the century and, with the advent of new technologies, the service improved. Only the annual cost of telephone rentals kept ahead. £5 in 1920 and £6 in 1941, it reached £13 in 1956, £17 in 1959 and £20 in 1964. By 1973 it had climbed to $60. Additionally, the initially less visible connection fee initiated at £10 in 1956, was a revenue producer that rose steeply to £15 in 1964, $50 by 1971, and reached $120 in September 1975.[6]

Hence, despite some reforms in accounting and fiscal procedures effected by the late 1960s in the PMG, large questions remained about the Department's economic viewpoint, financing and costs. Was the efficiency of the country's communications colossus comparable with that of other large concerns? Was it, in truth, a 'business undertaking' endeavouring to use every modern method of business management over its equipment, purchases and staff? Or, with its clear commitment to new technology and engineering excellence, was the PMG delivering services that were 'too large, too quickly supplied, and too cheap'? Were these services technically efficient and soundly planned? And, given the widening gulf between costly postal service and the increasingly profitable telecommunication activities of the PMG, how could institutional efficiency be balanced and improved?[7]

Other problems were also gathering within the PMG. The decade of the 1960s exposed deep-rooted industrial strains. Tension rippled across several fronts. During 1965 the cumulative effects of TRESS and telex on the telegraphists' role, the unpopular mechanisation and centralisation of mail handling at Sydney's Redfern mail exchange, and a protracted fight by third division postal and telegraph staff against 'automation declassification', climaxed in a national strike of postal and telegraph workers, 'the first major group of white collar workers', as the *Australian Financial Review* noted, to be affected by technological change that centred on the threat of automation. Among other issues, the strike also turned on the ideological point that there should be an equitable sharing of the fruits of the PMG's rising productivity from technological advance by employees across the institution. The strike, said the *Australian* newspaper prophetically, 'opened a new chapter in one of the most important debates in Australian history. It brought to a head a deep dissatisfaction . . . felt in the Post Office.' It raised serious questions involving automation and the relationship between Government, the Public Service Board and the PMG.[8]

The PMG's long legislative relationship to the Public Service Board lay at the base of many Departmental problems. Despite some evolutionary delegation from the board, the Department was hampered by board jurisdiction in significant areas of its structure, management and recruitment. The great majority of PMG employees were white and blue collar professional and technical workers organised into associations or unions. Under existing arrangements, the PMG could not negotiate directly with its employees. In cases of arbitration, the board, not the Department, represented the official case. At the same time the Department had to solve what it saw as 'unique problems' in terms acceptable to the board, while it suffered lengthy delays awaiting board approval. The Public Service Board also presided over managerial classifications within the PMG maintaining a standard structure over the whole public service despite major differences between individual departments. From the standpoint of a business organisation like the PMG, the board's control in such matters as managerial classification, promotions, and hours of duty and pay hindered management action, created extra work for staff and lowered institutional morale.[9]

From its earliest history, there was, in fact, severe criticism of the

Public Service Board's dominance over the PMG. Three early investigations, the Royal Commission on Postal Services, 1908–10, the Inquiry into Business Management of the Australian Post Office, 1915, and the Royal Commission on Public Expenditure 1919–21, emphasised the point, and pressed for the formation of a governing board of commissioners to administer post office affairs free from Public Service Board control. The major postal unions took up the theme. The key Amalgamated Postal Workers Union regularly raised the question of the board's handling of union and staff affairs at its annual conferences. In 1957 the APWU's Queensland's branch went so far as to seek the commitment of the Federal Australian Labor Party in its constitution, platform and rules to free the Australian Post Office from Public Service Board control. In two submissions to the Federal conference that year, the union urged that a Labor Government repeal Section 66 of the Commonwealth Public Service Act which denied Commonwealth employees the right to strike 'under threat of penalty of dismissal', and endorse the principle that control of the Department should be vested in a commission and removed from the control of the Public Service Board. While the first submission was incorporated in the Party's platform, the second would wait another ten years before it was jointly pressed by the Queensland and South Australian branches of the ALP and added to the Federal platform of 1967. The new paragraph 6 of 'Economic Planning' pledged 'the severance of the Post-master-General's Department from the Public Service Board control and the Department to be controlled by a Corporation'.[10]

By the late 1960s additional organisational difficulties and the problem of delegating some real authority from headquarters to the States were also evident in the giant Australian Post Office. The institution was creaking at its joints.

Most seriously, the management and executive responsibility for this huge department of state had become too complex and onerous for one chief executive. Despite the existence of two Deputy Directors-General, nine senior headquarters personnel (the Assistant Directors-General), and six Directors of Posts and Telegraphs reporting from the States, the Director-General lacked appropriate powers to delegate much of his authority. The responsibilities of the deputies were ill-defined. They undertook projects and programmes for the Director-General on an assignment basis, stood in for him as need required, but were essentially 'deputies without portfolio'. As Frank O'Grady put it of his period in office, 'When I'm here, the Deputy Director-General does what I don't want to do. When I'm elsewhere, he does what I ought to do.' With the expanding scope of the PMG, the enlargement of industrial disputes and the pace of technological change, the administrative weakness and burden deepened. The point was grimly driven home in October 1968 with the sudden death of Trevor Housley during stiff union negotiations in Canberra.[11]

During Housley's own administration, the situation prompted moves for internal change. In December 1967 Brian Jones, Deputy Director-General to O'Grady and Housley submitted an internal paper recommending a separation of operative functions within the organisation along postal and telecommunications lines. The proposal, however, forwarded by Housley, met silence from Postmaster-General Hulme. Housley himself espoused a two–way system which contemplated dividing departmental operations into those distinctive to the PMG (postal and telecommunications operations) and those (clerical and professional) industrially related to the Public Service Board. The operative staffs could, he thought, be separated from the public service as 'a minimum step'. But the scheme, never widely viewed as 'a goer', foundered upon strong discouragement from the head of the Public Service Board, Sir Frederick Wheeler.[12] Frederick Wheeler.

With Housley's death, Jones floated the plan with the new Director–General, J.L. Knott. An academic–style administrator whom his peers saw as 'an intellectual in the works', Jones was primarily concerned to confront the different management problems in the postal and telecommunications services, provide a more effective administrative plan, and to boost morale. During 1969 he chaired a senior level consultative committee which looked beyond a possible two–way partition to a three–part separation of the administration into postal, telecommunications and construction responsibilities both in headquarters and in the States. The proposal, attractive to the majority of senior management at central office and the new Director-General, was strongly resisted by the State Directors of Posts and Telegraphs with the sole exception of Tasmania.[13]

John Knott had entered the PMG from outside. From a distinguished career as a company director, head of various wartime commissions and committees, and secretary of the Department of Defence Production and later of Supply, he was serving as Deputy Australian High Commissioner in London when Hulme called him home to fill the vacant PMG post. His advent caused a flurry at headquarters and among trade unionists who believed the appointee should come from within the Department. Experienced and urbane, Knott quickly established good relations. He was determined not to die in office. He delegated, used his resources well, and turned to younger men to bring in new ideas. Conscious of the need to lift morale, he quickly visited every State. 'I was amazed', he said later, 'at the retention of Colonial attitudes in the Post Office I had inherited'. From this came a spate of reforms. Knott reconstituted the old post office headquarters advisory committee established in Chippindall's day as the new 'central board of management' to review policies, corporate objectives, and long–term plans, and added to it younger executives as associate members along with senior staff. More than his predecessors, Knott's emphasis was on 'consensus at the top'. The board was replicated in every State where the director and heads of divisions and branches met regularly to address major issues affecting their affairs. Knott also set his stamp, after much industrial pressure and with the co-operation of the chairman of the Public Service Board, on an inquiry into engineering structures that led to plans for a basic reorganisation into a number of relatively self-contained area

Sir John Knott,
Director-General from
1968 to 1971. 'Tea and
sympathy' was his
innovative internal
approach.

Sir Alan Shallcross
Hulme, MHR for Petrie,
Queensland, became
Australia's longest
serving
Postmaster-General,
from 1963 to 1972.

headquarters in each State. Experienced in research management in defence and supply, the new Director–General appreciated the importance of the Research Laboratories then spread across some 18 sites. The Research Laboratories, he maintained, were 'quite as good as the CSIRO, only less publicly recognised'. His interest and discussions with the head of planning and research and others would lay the foundations for consolidating the Laboratories as the Telecom Research Organisation in a new research compound at Clayton, Melbourne, in 1976.[14]

Knott's influence spread widely. As an outsider himself, he tended to look outward, emphasising customer service and bringing a greater business orientation to the PMG. He also looked inward, sought dialogue at various levels and lifted morale. Women posties and messenger girls were put into Prue Acton–designed uniforms, while his institution of the famous Friday afternoon 'tea and sympathy' sessions for senior staff members generated a new sense of institutional morale. These 'get togethers', said Knott, were mechanisms for communication and transferring technical and administrative ideas. The one condition was to talk about work. However, despite Sir John Knott's private support for the concept of partition (he was knighted in 1971), in practice he deferred to the judgment of his Minister. 'The Post Office', he went on record as saying on his retirement in January 1972, 'is not committed at this stage to the concept of two managers. We must continue as at present or adopt an alternative on the lines proposed by the [Jones] Committee.'[15]

By 1971 Alan Hulme had presided over nine years of buoyant telecommunications growth. An accountant by training and twice president of the Queensland division of the Liberal Party when Prime Minister Menzies appointed him to the 'tough' PMG post in 1963, Hulme rose quickly to cabinet rank. The first Liberal to hold the PMG portfolio for over 20 years, he became vice–president of the executive council and an influential political figure who lifted the lowly Postmaster-Generalship to seventh position on the Ministerial scale. A sober man whose smiles were rare, he frequently attended headquarter conferences, consulted closely with his Department when policy and planning was in the making, and worked hard at understanding the telecommunications technologies advancing in every field.

But as MHR for the rural seat of Petrie, Queensland, Hulme favoured the interests of the States. As organisational problems sharpened in the 1960s, he saw the solution, not in the sundering of the PMG but in an increasing decentralisation towards the States. It was the State directors, he insisted, who, as the enterprise grew, knew best where needs arose, who received representations from parliamentarians, and who understood the important 'people factor'. In the remoter States, moreover, postal and telecommunications services were intimately linked. Any division of these services might, Hulme believed, produce a loss of influence in the States and a harmful economic impact as a whole. As Minister, he was hence a sturdy opponent of the partition idea.[16]

With such precepts, it was not surprising that Hulme (also knighted in 1971) should choose as Knott's successor after two years in office a man with unique experience of the States, his close associate and fellow Queenslander, E.F. Lane. If Hulme was grave and sober, Lane's career bounced forward like a Walter Mitty dream. From a youthful start as a telegraph messenger in his home town of Dalby, he was, like a telegram, 'quick off the mark'. His smile stretched broadly across his face. His career touched the organisation at many points. Laterally and upwardly mobile, he moved from telegraphist at Cairns and later Mt Isa, where he married the telephonist, to join the Queensland telephone branch where he became senior traffic officer. In 1956, he moved to Tasmania as superintendent of the telephone branch, quickly became assistant director of telecommunications and, in 1957 at the age of 46, was appointed Director of Posts and Telegraphs of the State. Four years later he joined headquarters as controller of the telephone branch and, within six months in 1962, accepted Director–General O'Grady's offer to make him Director of Telecommunications in New South Wales. Lane returned to his home State of Queensland as Director of Posts and Telegraphs in 1966. Humorous and chivalrous, a forthright 'man's man' who had the common touch, Eber (meaning 'father' from the *Book of Genesis*) lived by the rule 'Do unto others as you would have them do unto you'. It was not always easy. Asked on one occasion about his formal degrees of which he was happily free, he was given to reply that he had trained in the 'HSOFE', the Hard School of Flaming Experience.[17]

Eber F. Lane, last Director-General of the PMG, from 1971 to 1975. He had 'the common touch'.

With adjoining offices in Brisbane, Hulme and Lane found much in common. Both men resisted the pressures for major administrative change; both cared strongly for 'people's needs'. During 1971, adding another leadership role to his expanding list, Lane moved to New South Wales as Director of Posts and Telegraphs of this major State, and six months later, reached the Director–General's chair. He would carry his opposition to partition to the chief executive's post. Like Hulme, Lane's opposition rested on economic grounds. Any division of functions would add to costs. He also personally found that, despite the prevailing concern, the role of Director–General was well served by the existing organisation of staff. His appointment sparked one administrative change: the departure of deputy Director–General Jones to a post as senior lecturer in administration at Monash University. Jones's going defused the internal pressures for change and ensured, at least for the remaining period of the Liberal Country Party Coalition Government until December 1972, the perpetuation of the administrative status quo.

In the event, change in the PMG was politically inspired.

In 1967, after 19 years in opposition, the Federal ALP emerged with a policy platform of specific social and institutional change. With an emphasis on 'national' thinking and greater accountability in government, the Party saw a special need for 'remodelling and reinvigorating' government departments and for giving some public enterprises autonomy to pursue their objectives more effectively. A prime target was the cumbersome and unsettled PMG. In his policy speech for the Federal election of 1972, Labor's leader Gough Whitlam, reaffirmed the Party's plank that 'Australia's largest employer — the Post Office — will be severed from the control of the Public Service Board', and with Labor's election to office in December 1972, one of the first acts of the new Government was to set up an ad hoc committee of cabinet Ministers to consider the matter of a formal investigation.

A Royal Commission, 'The Commission of Inquiry into the Australian Post Office', was announced by the Prime Minister on 30 January 1973. Detailed plans for the commission, handed down in letters patent from the Governor-General, were devised in consultation between Labor's new Postmaster-General, L.F. Bowen, and senior staff members of the PMG. Its terms were far reaching. The commission was required to 'inquire into and report upon what changes, if any, should be made in the organisation, administration and operations of Australian postal and telecommunications services including:

(1) the range of services to the public and their adequacy to meet present and future needs;
(2) the financing of recurrent and capital costs;
(3) management/staff relations including the jurisdiction of the Public Service Board;
(4) responsibilities of the Overseas Telecommunications Commission and the division of functions between that Commission and the PMG's Department;
(5) urban and regional development;
(6) procurement of supplies with the aim of developing Australian industries;
(7) the performance of work by contract; and
(8) other matters arising during the course of the inquiry.'[18]

There was, however, no specific reference to the establishment of a Corporation.

The three commissioners appointed were Sir James Vernon, director and former chief chemist of Colonial Sugar Refining Ltd, Sydney, chairman; B.J. Callinan, CBE, managing director of the Melbourne firm of consulting engineers, Gutteridge, Haskins and Davey, and the Queensland company director, J.J. Kennedy. Sir James Vernon, Lane's nominee for the chairmanship, already had a notable record of public service for his work on the 1963 Commonwealth Committee of Economic Inquiry that bore his name. Its recommendations had been shelved and a rumour persisted that, in accepting the chairmanship of the APO commission, Vernon had pressed Whitlam that he wanted this commission's recommendations approved. The story was apocryphal. It was Bowen, not the Prime Minister, who appointed and interviewed Vernon, while Vernon in these discussions himself made it plain that it was not his intention 'to prejudge the issue'. He accepted the open-ended task, he said later, of investigating 'a gigantic worn-out organisation with spiritually related but worn out wings'.[19]

Callinan and Kennedy lent distinctive but complementary skills. The former, a man of wide engineering experience, a member of

The Commission of Inquiry paid many visits to departmental establishments. Here, Sir James Vernon, chairman (left), Bernard (later Sir Bernard) Callinan, commissioner (right), and J.J. Kennedy, commissioner (far right) relax with Muriel Gallagher, supervisor of the interstate exchange and President of the ATPOA, in the Perth GPO, WA, 1973.

Melbourne University's faculty of engineering and a commissioner of the Victorian State Electricity Commission, was professionally suited to examine an organisation substantially raised on the professional work of engineers. Kennedy had attested commercial skills. A one-time unsuccessful ALP candidate for the Queensland Federal seat of Mt Gravatt, he was something of a political maverick with connections with both powerful unionists and politicians of the right. He had made his name as a chartered accountant, built up a succession of electrical retail businesses and was known as one of Brisbane's millionaires. He had also the additional, if irrelevant, distinction of having been mistakenly billed for the Queen's telephone account during her official visit to Brisbane in 1971 when the Royal Yacht berthed at Newstead Wharf. He would, he said jovially, have gladly paid the $89 if this would make him baron of Breakfast Creek.[20]

The commission itself would provide an important vehicle for change. As A.F. Spratt, deputy Director–General of the PMG and an influential participant in the Department's preparation wrote later, 'It is salutary for any organisation particularly a large one to have its role, performance and organisation exposed to public inquiry'. Because of the multiplicity of vested interests, 'an outside independent inquiry may be the only way of effecting change within a reasonable time'. To a public concerned with rising charges and increasingly critical of postal and telephone services, the inquiry marked a watershed. The commission, observed the Melbourne *Age*, offered 'a complete overhaul of Australian postal services . . . from the delivery of letters to international communication by satellite'.[21]

The two deputy Directors–General, Spratt and J.H. Curtis, carried the charge of preparing the Department's submission to the inquiry assisted by senior staffers, W.J.B. Pollock, D.G. McQuitty, R.B. Cullen and J.L. Brady.[22] The cost to the PMG alone (in work effort foregone) was $2.5 million. The commissioners were assisted by three consultants, the Sydney firm of chartered accountants, Price Waterhouse and Co. who completed an independent report on the evaluation of financial management in the PMG, the Melbourne–based international management consultants, Cresap, McCormick and Paget Inc. who investigated and reported on the organisational structure of the Department, and consultant G. Paterson who reported on private contract work performed by the PMG. The consultants' reports, published as volume 2 of the commission's findings, and based on interviews with senior PMG staff, provide a wealth of detailed material on the Department.

In all, 482 submissions reached the commission, ranging from the PMG's own massive offering, submissions from PMG employees (54), Government departments and instrumentalities (10), local government bodies (56), organisations using post office facilities (25), chambers of commerce, PMG contractors and suppliers (12), Australian Post Office staff associations (25), political parties and party branches (6), industrial and professional associations (5) and from 212 members of the general public. In addition to its 659–page submission, the Department doggedly provided supplementary comments on incoming submissions. It would also provide supplementary material and statements on the submissions of other papers in response to a spate of queries which the commission raised.

Significantly, the submission of the APO (as the commission consistently called it) contained no recommendations for change. Differences on many matters within the Department ran deep. Rather, it advised on the history of the Department, the development of posts and telecommunications in Australia, and the alternatives available for future organisation plus possible outcomes of different paths. Phrases 'on the one hand' and 'on the other' peppered its reports. It was a strategy of 'wait and see' tailored to leave fundamental decisions on the future of the organisation to the Royal Commission.

After visits to Britain, Sweden, Canada and the United States the commissioners embarked in June 1973. on the lengthy hearing of major submissions and on the interrogation of senior APO personnel. Eber Lane as Director–General bore the major brunt of the questioning, assisted in areas of special knowledge by senior staff. Vernon himself noted the PMG's detailed submission as a 'very high class piece of work' and privately praised the objectivity of Lane's responses. 'He fell over backwards to be fair.'[23]

Submissions pressed differing themes. The Country Party, whose concern with communications had involved it closely with the Department's performance, commended the progress made in extending STD telephone service to many parts of Australia, but pressed its own extensive shopping list. It emphasised the need for more automatic exchanges in country areas, recommended the development of overseas links 'including satellites', and urged that concessional rates be offered to country dwellers 'as a general incentive to decentralisation'. But on one point, the Party, represented before the commission by Ian Sinclair MP, was dogmatic. It was opposed to any organisational division of the APO. It held, indeed, 'that the Australian Post Office should be regarded as an essential service and as an instrument of national development, and not as a statutory trading corporation, and that its capital expenditure and recurrent losses should be assisted by direct subvention from the Treasury and not only by recourse to loan funds'. It was a submission that Country Party leaders would later prefer to forget.[24]

Within the key unions, attitudes to change were mixed. Both white and blue collar unions were critical of the Department's heavy centralisation, the fragmentation of functions, and the reduced job satisfaction arising from automation, increasing technological change and inadequate consultation with management. The Administrative and Clerical Officers Association frankly regretted the breakdown between the engineers, telephone technicians, telegraphists, clerical administrators, telephonists and messengers, the 'old Post Office *esprit de corps*'.[25]

The case for the important Postal Clerks and Telegraphists Union was put by its former general secretary, John Baker. A theatrical figure whom his colleagues called 'the Count', Baker was the only testator to raise the chairman's ire and be ordered to 'sit down'. A fiery critic of management on the grounds of over–capitalisation of the APO for 'the benefit of multi–national corporations', Baker challenged the 'automation exercises' at the Redfern mail exchange and roundly condemned the conversion of the post office 'from a considerable profit earner to a consistent debit–maker in order to justify vast programmes of capital investment in high technology'.[26]

Baker's testimony revived the question (taken up originally in the late 1950s) of PMG productivity figures and their projection. During 1972 he and his union had commissioned Dr D. Bhattacharya, economist of Sydney University, to undertake a productivity study of the Australian Post Office covering the comparative period 1961–2 to 1971–2. Bhattacharya's conclusion, despite some acknowledged imperfection in the analytical model, suggested that the total productivity of labour in the Department had increased over 30 per cent in the period 1961–71; that the share of salaries and wages in total cash expenditure had concurrently declined from 55 to 48 per cent, 'while the more capital–intensive and labour–saving technology had been deliberately and continuously introduced'. In short, his argument ran, the APO had 'allowed over capital–intensive technology beyond the point warranted by existing conditions and economic considerations' and that there was 'a poor correlation between real wage rates and productivity'.[27]

Bhattacharya appeared as an expert witness for the union. He met a stiff challenge from APO's Dr R.B. Cullen, a former member of the school of business administration of Melbourne University (and later Telecom's first director of finance) for the false conclusion he drew from his analysis that the productivity function bore no relationship to technological change. In print and oral testimony, Cullen contended that the labour–intensive postal business 'showed only slight labour productivity and the technical change index remained close to unity'. Contrastingly, the telecommunications business was capital intensive and showed a high index for technical change.[28]

The submission of the key Amalgamated Postal Workers Union

stressed three interlocking themes. They sought to cut the link between the Department and the Public Service Board, closer consultation between management and workers on matters of technological change, and the immediate reduction of work contracted outside the Department by the PMG. Here the union believed that the Public Service Board's recruitment policies (when PMG plant installations, construction and traffic were rapidly expanding) were calculated to undermine APWU membership of the PMG. The PSB's 'totally unrealistic and selfish handling of recruitment levels', their submission noted, ensured that demands for work in the installation of automatic telephone exchanges, microwave systems and PABXs, could not be met by available Departmental staff. 'The bias that is shown in sorting the large, easy and profitable jobs from the difficult ones and the obvious bias in demanding and getting a high standard of construction from Departmental staff and at the same time allowing contractors to cut every corner and cheat the Government with sub–standard construction [they observed tersely], explains why the APWU has called a halt to all forms of contract work.'[29]

Pressure for 'day labour' as distinct from 'contract labour' for internal and external work would remain a controversial issue for the APWU. In 1973 the first step was clearly the elimination of Public Service Board control. 'If the APO were free to negotiate directly with the unions', their argument ran, forcefully presented before the hearings by union president Frank Waters and George Slater, 'there would be a much greater chance of involving employees in the need to provide the most efficient and reliable services to the public' and, at the same time, a much greater probability of industrial relations questions being solved successively by immediate negotiations.

Despite wide criticisms, many of the major unions and associations firmly resisted the concept of organisational change. Support for separation in the PMG came from the Professional Officers Association, the Telecommunication Technical Officers Association, the Postal Telecommunications Technicians Association and the Administrative and Clerical Officers Association. The APWU opposed a split on the grounds that 'significant management diseconomies could result from the creation of separate organisations'. The Union of Postal Clerks and Telegraphists also opposed it, arguing that 'the direction of technological change implied a greater unification of all forms of communication', while the Australian Postmasters Association, the Postal Overseers Union, and the senior group of Postmaster–General's Department heads of divisions and branches association (an elite group of 105) objected to partition in the belief that it would lead to costly duplication of activities and a lesser quality of service.[30]

Contrastingly, the Association of Professional Engineers' Australia and the Association of Architects, Engineers, Surveyors and Draughtsmen of Australia sat on the fence. The professional engineers, already battling to retain their professional strongholds against incursions from technical officers in the APO, were more concerned with this power struggle than the broader implications of organisational change. Their submission bore all the hallmarks of a codicil to the 1959 'Professional Engineers' Case'. 'Telecommunications services', they urged, should 'be under the effective management of professional engineers at all levels of decision making' both in operations and in respect of innovation and standards, and they pressed for the Area Management Organisation foreshadowed by Knott.[31] It was a submission strongly countered by the technical officers associations.

The commissioners also heard representatives from the manufacturing suppliers and contractors for the telecommunications industry in Australia, from the Treasury, Public Service Board, various Commonwealth departments and the OTC and from the Government's newly appointed adviser on women's affairs, Elizabeth Reid. 'Are there', asked Ms Reid, bracingly, plunging to the heart of the matter, 'any unarticulated assumptions about women which should be examined, such as that women should not be employed in jobs requiring team work or field work, that women are not capable of supervising men, that men resent having a woman as a supervisor, that it is unwise to employ an attractive woman, that late night collections of mail should not be made by women, that women inhibit protracted drinking sessions in hotel bars, that women are physically weak?' While the commissioners fell back before this 'appallingly wide though "valid" question', and hoped that Ms Reid was not suggesting that 'the Commission would have any expectation of arriving at the right answers here', the Department's comment was cautiously accurate. 'Departmental policy', it replied 'is that women are promoted on merit and there are many instances where women are promoted over men . . . [but] equal opportunity at senior levels may take time . . .'[32]

During the hearings, Commissioner Kennedy made the enlightening remark that, while everyone was saying that the APO should be 'streamlined', 'no one was telling the Commission how it should be done'. In practice, the commissioners' report stemmed from the importance of the historical evidence, their own cogent eliciting and evaluation of testimony, telling advice from the British post office (transformed into a corporation in 1970 with one board governing the two arms of the telecommunications and postal functions), and detailed inputs from the consultants. Throughout the inquiry Vernon's influence could be discerned. A quiet but probing chairman, he encouraged the commissioners to take a 'total view' of the Department and 'to stop short on decision before major recommendations were made'. With his familiar reminder, 'All systems work, some work better than others', he sought consensus based on a wide interpretation of the terms of reference and was disturbed by the commission's inability to find accord on one question, the future of the OTC.[34]

Fourteen months after its appointment and after the ingestion of thousands of pages of argument and evidence, the Royal Commission presented its report to Government on 19 April 1974. Its recommendations would lead to a fundamental restructuring of the nation's telecommunications and postal systems.

First and foremost, the commission, said the Report, 'came to the conclusion that separation of postal services from telecommunications would be desirable and in the general interest.' Each was a large and

'Splitting heirs.' The partition of the Australian Post Office, as seen by WA cartoonist POD (Peter O'Donoghue). On the left is H.G. Shaw, state manager, Telecom WA, and on the right, D.W. Buchanan, state manager, Australia Post WA, wrestling for possession of the Perth GPO.

important enterprise in its own right; both were essential community services but with basic characteristics of commercial enterprises, and it was apparent that the two services represented 'wholly different management environments'. The Department had also become so large that questions of possible diseconomies arose from its size and spread. The separation of postal and telecommunications functions, the commissioners summed up in their key recommendations, provides 'a unique opportunity for the reconsideration of all aspects of their future organisation and financing and, hopefully will put them in better shape to cope with future community needs'.[34]

In a detailed dissection of the Department's performance, the commissioners found much that was successful, but much that, in 74 years of development, was in pressing need of reform. On the 'pro' side of the telecommunications ledger, their Report judged that the present range of telecommunications services available in Australia was 'reasonably adequate for the needs of the present and the immediate future, taking into account the resources available to the APO'. Standards of performance for technical faults and plant congestion for local calls was generally satisfactory and the policy in clearing telephone service faults appeared comparable with that of most overseas telecommunications authorities. It also concluded, on

the basis of a report from its consultant, G. Paterson, that policy on purchases of cables was administered 'in a realistic and practical way' and that the existing competitive tendering system for major switching equipment adopted by the APO had been successful. It commended the Department 'for the way in which the purchasing policy for switching equipment had been developed and administered'. Similarly the Report affirmed that the policy of the APO in encouraging and assisting the development of local manufacturing capability 'has made an important contribution to the telecommunication industry in this country'.[35]

But, on the 'con' side the commission found that the APO was grossly oversized, too great in compass for the oversight of one chief executive, encumbered with organisational and management structures that were no longer in keeping with modern functions and needs, heavily over-centralised with adverse consequences for central planning of the States and, despite a fairly good industrial record in terms of man hours lost in Australia as a whole, in need of new measures to face what the commission saw as the 'biggest challenge' of industrial relations that lay ahead. In addition, on the key historical question of cross-subsidies, the commissioners believed that there was 'a tolerance beyond which cross-subsidisation of a minority of customers at the expense of the majority of users should not be extended . . . the tariff structures should not reflect a gross distortion in

As the Royal Commission investigated, the network continued to grow. Here, Mrs I.V. Alexander is presented with a plaque commemorating her as the one millionth telephone subscriber in Victoria, 19 April 1974.

271

favour of some categories or classes of users of a service at the expense of the majority of customers of the APO.'

In opting for two corporate bodies to replace the old APO, the commissioners were influenced by two formulations; one from the Public Service Board, the other from a report of the Joint Committee on Public Accounts. 'The essential criterion for the establishment of a statutory authority instead of a department', said the PSB, 'is the nature and degree of Ministerial and Parliamentary control to be exercised over the functions involved'. Statutory authorities were established to remove some matters from the direct control and responsibility of Ministers and there was generally a clear intention to limit the day–to–day responsibilities and powers of Ministers and to vest them in a separate legal entity.[36] The second statement, from the 1955 Report of the Joint Committee of Public Accounts on the Aus-tralian Aluminium Production Commission, further affirmed that the statutory corporation was 'the most suitable device for ensuring the public management of economic enterprises where there is need for flexibility in administration and for independence from close political control. These attributes, essential for successful business operation, are seldom present in ordinary Government Departments.'[37] Thus, more than half a century after the concept of a statutory corporation with a board of management was first suggested by legislators and review committees for the APO, the plan for corporate governance under 'board' management was finally sheeted home.

From the report's labyrinthine but well–informed discussions, the following major recommendations emerged:

Two statutory corporations, one for the postal and one for the telecommunications services should be established to achieve a new approach to the organisation, management and financial policy–making of the country's communication services. Each corporation should be administered by a board of seven commissioners. Each new corporation should be granted, under legislation, powers to determine the conditions of service, classifications, career structures and pay of its own staff.

Given the large and often unrelated spectrum of employees within the communications services, industrial disputes should no longer be dealt with by the Public Service Arbitrator but by 'separate arbitral authorities' established to hear and determine claims and matters arising from the service of each corporation. The Public Service Board, however, should work with the Department before the formation of the statutory corporations 'to structure the industrial relations divisions of the corporations' and to recruit suitable staff.[38] The commissioners were at some pains to stress 'the sound management practices for which the Public Service Board must be given proper credit' and, by such a caveat, dodged the intention (attributed to some unions) that the Royal Commission should become a Public Service Board 'heresy hunt'.

The Minister should be relieved of day–to–day administration of the corporations' affairs, should give management reasonable freedom to make necessary commercial and business decisions, place with management the authority and responsibility for organisational and staffing matters, and enable persons in outside government employment to contribute their skills and experience to the overall direction of the enterprise.

The setting of tariffs for individual categories of services (basic or standard services) within the proposed corporations should be largely a matter of corporation management 'subject to the approval of the Minister'. It should also be the corporation's responsibility to submit to the Minister, from time to time, proposals for changes in tariffs required for the achievement of their financial goals. In effect, the corporations should be given power to vary tariffs at any time, subject always, in the light of the acknowledged 'political sensitivity' of increased charges, to Ministerial approval. At the same time, the Minister, in exercising his powers in respect of tariffs, should be required to have due regard to the financial objectives of the Commission. In the setting of tariffs 'the aim should be to minimise, as far as possible, major distortions in financial performance; tariffs for an individual service should be set to recover at least its direct cost even though revenue may not always be sufficient to match fully allocated costs'.[39]

On the financial side both corporations should be given the financial objectives of obtaining, by way of charges for services, amounts necessary to meet all costs of wages, salaries, materials and services, depreciation, superannuation and long service leave provisions, and interest on borrowings. In the light of the nature of their services, they should be exempt from income tax, local government rates, payroll tax, sales tax, customs and excise, and motor vehicle registration. But both corporations would be required to pursue financial objectives of not only matching expenses with earnings, but of providing 'together with other funds generated internally such as depreciation and provisions' amounts equal to 50 per cent of capital expenditure in each year'.[40]

The present arrangement for financing by advances from the Treasury, (which carried interest at the rate current for long dated Australian Government securities), to meet the shortfall between estimated expenditure and estimated revenue, was 'appropriate and should be continued'. There was, the report said, little merit raising finance on the market. Indeed, both corporations in conducting their businesses should accept a certain amount of 'rough with the smooth'. It would hence be unwise, to introduce procedures involving calculation of losses suffered on particular services as a result of Government policy and matching such losses with a series of subsidies.[41]

In respect of borrowing, the boards of the corporations should be authorised to borrow from approved banking institutions by short–term overdrafts (a limit of $20 million to be set for telecommunications), in order to give flexibility in situations requiring a quick response.

On matters of organisation and management, the report laid the basis for a streamlined telecommunications corporation. The commissioners' advice drew heavily on the international consultant Cresap, McCormick and Paget for administrative reform. Both the commission and the consultant had found deficiencies in the top level organisational structure of the APO; strategic planning activities for telecommunications had become 'fragmented' and important areas of management were 'without specialist staff'. The report proposed a new scheme of telecommunications corporation management to be headed by a 'managing director' responsible for long range and external matters, and a 'chief general manager' responsible for practical and day–to–day management, but with clear lines of communication to twelve 'directors' responsible for specific areas. Three directors (external relations, finance, planning and internal audit) should be responsible to the managing director, while directors of research, customer services, personnel and industrial relations, automatic data processing, accounting and supply, and the 'chief engineer' would serve directly within the responsibilities of the chief general manager.[42]

In the central field of engineering, the report located a number of dysfunctions and lack of co–ordination in the engineering spectrum of the APO which were both 'inappropriate' and led at times to inadequate management of major technological change. The newly defined position of 'chief engineer' should co–ordinate the planning, programming and works functions of engineering hitherto performed in separate divisions of the Department and weld together the inputs of research, planning and plant engineers. For the better formulation of the planning of research, the Research Laboratories would be placed under a separate director of research.[43]

The report also determined that marketing activities were 'not effectively integrated into the Telecommunications business' and that the telecommunications marketing programme was 'more heavily influenced by technical hardware capacity than by customer marketing considerations'. A special unit under a 'director, customer services' should be formed to take responsibility for marketing and consumer–oriented programmes to improve the co–ordination of marketing and engineering and bring 'a marketing viewpoint into technical decisions'.[44]

In a reform of State and headquarter management, the report recommended a 'new organisation for the regional administration of telecommunications'. The commission perceived that the division of administrative regions based on State boundaries, as in the PMG, resulted in parts of the network being divided for administrative purposes when they could more sensibly be placed under a single management area. The report accordingly recommended 'that the boundaries of the regional administrations be determined on the basis of the business characteristics of the network and not on State boundaries', and that technical and commercial activities related to standardised services be brought together under 'district telecommunications managers' in each region. Despite the keenly argued testimony of the professional engineers to retain line responsibility for all engineering works, both commissioners and its consultant concluded that there was a need for opening up the career opportunities for technical and clerical officers engaged in telecommunications administration. They saw the position of district telecommunications manager 'as a true management position and not a position where professional engineering qualifications should be regarded as essential'.[45]

Finally, in their summary of major conclusions, the commissioners considered two subjects that had emerged forcibly in written submissions and at the hearings: contract work and the question of urban and rural development. On the matter of contracting out work from the APO to private firms, the report gave even-handed judgment. It found that despite the APWU's criticisms, Departmental specifications and procedures for contract supervision were 'adequate to ensure that required standards of work and working conditions are met, provided the supervisory staff exercise the powers given them'. It also found that the laying of conduits by contract in New South Wales was the cheapest way of doing work, but that installation of switching equipment by contract 'is only marginally cheaper than installation by APO staff'. Here special skills were required and 'the greater part of such installation work should be carried out by APO staff'.[46]

On one issue only did the Royal Commission forfeit its remarkable unanimity: the question of merging the proposed new telecommunications corporation with the Overseas Telecommunications Commission. Pressure for OTC's inclusion in the commission's terms of inquiry had come originally from senior APO planning staff in discussions with Postmaster-General Bowen. There were sound reasons for its consideration. There was a close link between the operational functions of the Overseas Telecommunications Commission with its earth stations and gateway exchanges for international connections for telephone and data services and the APO's national telecommunications services. OTC's international gateway exchange at Sydney, for example, comprised crossbar switching equipment together with interface equipment interposed to make the differing technical characteristics of the national and international circuits compatible.[47] The exchange was manned by OTC technical staff. When, however, an international caller obtained access to a subscriber in Australia via the gateway exchange, the call was switched automatically for STD or manual operation at the PMG exchange. Billing of all customers was done by PMG; due proceeds were credited to OTC, while the PMG's Department received payment for its services through 'a terminal fee per paid minute' for outgoing and incoming calls. In the case of rented or leased circuits, e.g. between the Cairns SEACOM terminal and the Sydney gateway exchange, negotiated rental charges were paid to the PMG.

Overseas telegrams travelled either from OTC offices or directly from Australian post offices via TRESS to the OTC Sydney operations room and were there converted to international format and switched into the international stream. Incoming telegrams followed a similar path. Telex messages could pass directly to automatically operated destinations overseas or for countries where direct automation was not available, they passed through an international telex operator at the Sydney gateway exchange. Rental charges for telex equipment and charges for telex calls within Australia were billed by PMG. Billing for international calls was carried out by OTC and the PMG received payment based on its assessed costs plus 10 per cent.[48]

Throughout its 28 years of development, OTC had proceeded profitably. 'The Overseas Telecommunications Commission', said the report 'has developed a substantial and profitable business which has required only a modest initiating investment of Government funds.' Its rather gilded role, indeed, gave rise to criticism and some rivalry at the PMG where, it was considered in the words of the Departmental sub-mission to the inquiry that 'taking telecommunications as a whole, the OTC clearly had the profitable segment of the business international services, while the APO had the relatively unrewarding task of providing the internal telecommunications network throughout Australia through which OTC obtained access to the senders or receivers of international communications'.

There were instructive international comparisons. The British post office was responsible for both domestic and international tele-communications services. In Canada the Canadian Overseas Tele-communications Corporation (COTC), a wholly government–owned statutory body established in 1946, operated the country's inter-national services (except those that linked Canada with the United States), while private enterprise companies were responsible for the internal network. The profitability of these two groups, with their more equitable division of service 'spoils', was found to be rather similar.[49]

In evidence before the commission, the APO pressed several points. It would be more economic to carry out international switching through its internally sited new generation of trunk exchanges than to concentrate them in a single specialised gateway exchange. The costs debited against the international network did not take adequate account of the large investment of the national network — the necessary prequisite to all international as well as national services. Existing billing arrangements caused confusion, while OTC was in a position to negotiate reductions in Australia's international tariffs that could lead to undesirable imbalances with the PMG.

The Director–General, Eber Lane, put himself behind this argument. Predictably, OTC presented a counter–view. They rejected the concept of a merger. The OTC, they told the commission, 'has moved from the 1946 pioneer phase to its 1973 position of a recognised leader in a highly sophisticated global industry'. The absorption of the international switching function into the domestic system would diminish their flexibility, slow their response to international innovations, and submerge their influence in the international telecommunications field. With the recognisable arrogance of an elite, they claimed that the charges paid to the national organisation, far from being low, were 'not only fair but generous'.[50]

Critically divided on the issue, the commissioners exposed their differences. Kennedy, with Callinan, saw no justification in divided control and believed that amalgamation of the two organisations would give coherence and improved service. Indeed they believed that OTC's role and its financial returns could confer economies of scale on a national network limited to trunk and local circuits. They strongly recommended the repeal of the Overseas Telecommunication Act, 1946–71.[51] But Vernon dissented. With personal links with the OTC board of management, he saw the OTC as 'a well developed and compact organisation, strongly market oriented ... and with established relationships in the international field'. Moreover, on the trusted maxim that when you are on a good thing, stick to it, Vernon saw no logic in destroying a going concern unless overwhelming advantages could be shown for the merger. Nor did he believe that telecommunications planning would be optimised by a single tele-communications planning authority.[52] The conflict of opinion would explode politically when the report's recommendations reached Parliament.

The Royal Commission's report offered a strikingly altered ground plan for communication services in Australia. It offered new bodies for new times. In a period of changing engineering and technical education, it recognised two streams of training and experience. It sought new and upgraded professional management experience to complement the once professionally dominant engineering 'culture' of the APO. With its adoption, the historic Postmaster–General's Department, dating from Federation, would be metamorphosed into two corporations formed as statutory authorities in which the Australian Government was sole shareholder, but which were con-stitutionally and structurally freer to determine better service and stronger economic and marketing development. No longer would it be possible for young men to aspire to climb the ladder from messenger boy to Director–General. That office, along with many other job classifications and career routes, would be swept away.

The commission's report was a singular public achievement. Its concepts marked the passing of an era. On the telecommunications front, a great new technological enterprise had been conceived. For the new postal corporation, the commission foreshadowed a clean financial slate and a fresh start. 'We thought the boards of these two new organisations', Sir James Vernon summed up later, 'should be charged with running an efficient show and making an acceptable profit.' The boards would determine the charges, the charges would be approved by Government and, should the Minister disagree, he would be required to show good reason.[53]

On one issue only did the commission fail to probe: the question of technological change. Despite its importance to the unions' sub-missions, this problem elicited remarkably little comment from the Royal Commission. The commissioners judged, on the evidence before them, that the APO's attitude to consultation with staff organisations had been 'a reasonable one'. They found that management had gone to considerable lengths to consult with staff organisations 'in advance of changes in procedures or equipment so that the implications of the proposed changes could be fully understood'. But their conclusion was not well based. Formal consultative processes had not been introduced into the APO until 1969. Moreover, on the beleaguered and tumultuous Redfern mail exchange, the report had 'no ready solutions to propose'. The commission, however, recommended that every effort should be made 'jointly by management and by staff organisations to codify and agree on consultation procedures' to ensure 'that necessary changes could be introduced in an orderly fashion with minimum disruption'.[54]

Within the APO itself, the report found large endorsement. Lane privately pronounced it 'a good thing with much to recommend it' and was delighted at the commission's lack of criticism of the management. There was some uneasiness among engineers. Some internal critics deplored the 'blatantly business–oriented approach' the consultant, Price Waterhouse, had imparted to the commission's findings, and there was some fear in the postal sector that despite the 'clean–slate' waiving of losses and accumulated interest on postal sector loans, the postal corporation 'might be down–graded or regressed'. For the Public Service Board, the report presaged severe demolition and decline. In a grim echo of concern, the Department of Labour and Immigration condemned the new corporations' proposed staffing arrangements as 'naive' and predicted serious leapfrogging and industrial chaos from their managements' freedom to negotiate with the unions and fix pay on independent lines.[55]

The report of the commission into the Australian Post Office, submitted to the Governor-General on 19 April 1974, was accepted in its broad recommendations by Prime Minister Whitlam five days later and the proposed creation of separate statutory corporations for the postal and telecommunications services announced. It was an exceptional outcome for a commission of inquiry in Australia. 'A package deal familiar to generations of Australians since Federation', exclaimed the Melbourne *Herald*, 'is to be broken up. The PMG's Department that has trendily called itself the Australian Post Office for the past few years has been no bargain for a long time. So with few political regrets, it becomes two new parcels.' More cautiously, the Melbourne *Age* noted that the commission's report offered 'the hope — but not necessarily the certainty — that two, more independent, specialist authorities can provide a more efficient, economic and attractive community service than the present monolithic, bureaucratic department had been able to maintain'.[56]

12 'Double, Double, Toil and Trouble'[1]

During the long passage of the inquiry, business proceeded at the PMG. Yet so comprehensive an investigation made disruptive demands on headquarter's senior staff. Moreover, as the Royal Commission proceeded with its inquiry, major trouble spots loomed into view. Eber Lane, Director of Posts and Telegraphs in Queensland, was famous for his retort when asked why, unlike other States, he raised no major problems for headquarter's discussion, 'We kill our snakes north of the border', he replied.[2] Two now lay coiled at the very centre of his organisation: one the common user data network, the ill–fated CUDN: the other a lively, but less dangerous species, the controversial environmental stirrer, Canberra's Black Mountain telecommunications tower.

In the data field the PMG had entered the transmission business in 1964 using telephone lines to transmit computerised information between stock exchanges and some business houses. Five years later the first on–line time sharing computer system was introduced by which the telephone network linked subscribers' computerised data equipment to a centralised computer. Australia had plunged later than many into the expanding, future–oriented, data transmission age. People would now not only deploy the telephone lines for their social, working, business, information–seeking, life–saving and life–enhancing use: telephone traffic would increasingly serve either a person sending data to a remote computer or two computers communicating with each other. With the PMG's 'datel service' of 1969, two forms of data transmission were supplied. Transmission could be made over the ordinary switched telephone network or along privately leased lines. Datel services of both kinds required a data modem supplied by the PMG at either end of the line. The modem converted the digital data from the computer into an analogue form suitable for transmission along telephone connections and reconverted it back into the digital form at the receiving end. Data transmission was commonly used in airline bookings between capital cities, in the transfer of information within firms from one centre to another and, in a country where the totalisator had been invented some 40 years before, in the co–ordination of totalisator betting systems.[3]

With the technique of centralised message switching in growing vogue abroad, PMG planners saw the advantage of developing a common user data network initially for itself and other Government departments, but expanding to serve business customers wanting to transmit data between their own computers and remote terminals on sub–networks derived from PMG common switching and transmission plant. The concept was pioneering and innovative in 1967. It was also ahead of wide customer needs. A conference with the Public Service Board (responsible for rationalising Government computer requirements) suggested this.[4] However, the Department of Civil Aviation, the Bureau of Meteorology and TAA (with the possible interest of Australian National Airways — Ansett's predecessor ANA) had defined switching needs. Accordingly, the planning and research division pressed Housley as Director–General to sanction large–scale studies and plans for a common user message switching scheme. The PMG, the argument conveyed, would not only be failing in its responsibilities if it did not offer up–to–date message switching facilities as part of its overall telecommunications service; but the lack of positive steps would, in the words of one senior planner, 'invite pressures from private consortia pooling traffic to gain benefits of scale'.[5] Such pressures, indeed, already threatened the role of the common carrier in Britain and the USA.

Yet despite the APO's well–attested reputation for locating and applying the most advanced telecommunications technology from overseas, not all her geese were swans. CUDN, the common user data network the Department now precipitated, was to prove a very troublesome and 'ugly gosling' indeed.

With a favourable response from three customers and considerable interest in the scheme abroad, it was agreed with the concurrence of an interdepartmental committee in 1967, that the PMG should establish a common user data network as soon as possible cutting its first two users, the Bureau of Meteorology and the Commonwealth Department of Health, into service in 1971. The small volume of traffic meant high starting costs, but there was a sanguine expectation that the combination of on–line computers with the message handling needs of large decentralised business would speed a mounting traffic flow. Planners recognised that attractive rates must be offered to customers to counter the lure of private switching systems on leased lines (the Department of Civil Aviation and Ansett in fact opted for these), and they also sensed the need to dispel any picture of George Orwell's *1984* type predictions of national data banks subject to unauthorised access or bureaucratic abuse.[6]

Tenders were called for service in mid–1969 and, at a time when large computing projects were in the experimental stage, Sperry Rand (Australia), a subsidiary of UNIVAC, USA, was chosen. The company's experience with the world–wide SITA network and the provision of airline reservation systems and its expertise with the majority of features required in CUDN secured Sperry Rand the contract in September 1970. It was agreed that CUDN would be established using United States UNIVAC equipment and that computer based message

The Common User
Data Network (CUDN)
central processor
equipment in
Melbourne's Lonsdale
exchange, 1974, and
the system in use at the
Commonwealth
Department of Health.

switching centres should be installed initially for the Commonwealth
Department of Health in Brisbane by late 1971, successively in
Melbourne, Sydney and Perth during 1972, and in Adelaide in January
1973. Installations would embrace central processors — UNIVAC
418–111 computer units, UNIVAC mass storage sub–systems,
UNIVAC peripheral processors, communication terminal module
controllers and magnetic tape sub–systems. The Melbourne, Sydney
and Brisbane systems would be 'mesh–connected' with Adelaide and
later Perth. In addition to transmitting and switching data traffic,
CUDN would provide message switching facilities for telegraph type
traffic, interfacing with telex and TRESS. UNIVAC had a 'turnkey'
responsibility to deliver a working system in accordance with
specifications at a fixed price.[7] The agreement marked a massive
transfer of computer technology from the United States to Australia
and was seen internationally as an adventurous but responsible
task.

But from the beginning CUDN collected problems. Even before its
inception, sharp criticism from the key customer, the Department of
Health, of 'grossly uneconomic' charges prompted tariff revision and
reduction.[8] Financial appraisals within the Department during 1970

also suggested that the estimated internal rate of return, crucial to the viability of the scheme, had dropped from a figure of 16–17 per cent per year before interest over a ten–year equipment life (the figures given to the Postmaster–General), to a low 8 per cent. With only seven customers in view for service by 1976, it was also clear that unforeseen additional capital costs 'would change the economics of the project'. Extra maintenance aids would also be required. Early planning capsized. Not only would customer charges need to be lower than originally planned: the anticipated rate of increase in customer use of the system was 'less than expected'.[9]

Bad news gathered like storm clouds on every front. By the time the contract was finalised and the relevant PMG unions informed of agreements to implement stage one, the date for starting the Brisbane installation had been advanced by ten months with subsequent post-ponements in other States. Customers such as the Departments of Commerce and of Customs, handicapped by lack of information on CUDN charges in planning their computer systems, tartly pressed the PMG for firm figures 'or, at least the principles on which they will be based'.[10]

In June 1971 Postmaster–General Hulme, with a sharp accoun-tant's eye on the oscillating tariff schedules, warned Director–General Knott that the Department should only participate in the provision of common user data network facilities provided the price schedules were kept under close review and if the prices quoted 'enable the customer some twelve months in which to instal his own equipment'.[11] As work began at Sperry Rand with the involvement of PMG technicians and staff, difficulties affecting both hardware and software computer planning programmes reared alarmingly.

CUDN clearly did not transfer easily. What went wrong? Planners later implied 'just about everything'. Internal minutes and letters document the trail. In a situation of transfer of a major computer project and of some Australian technological lag, the case study is instructive. There was a fundamental lag in agreed schedules. 'The Post Office noted', a letter from the PMG's Department to Sperry Rand charged in September 1971, 'that severe slippage of the project has occurred, more severe than your Company has at any time indicated.' Further, 'it was established by questioning UNIVAC personnel that interconnected sequences had been changed in what appeared to be a totally unplanned way and that the UNIVAC project management group was unable to objectively assess progress'. Sperry Rand's technical staff, it was inferred, were inadequately trained, system software development encountered particular snags, and there was want of precision in the managerial conduct and testing of the project. Technical reinforcements were in fact subsequently sent to Australia from UNIVAC, USA.[12]

On the contractor's part there was also recrimination. Sperry Rand complained that the personnel at the PMG were without sufficient understanding of computers and specialised computer techniques for such an advanced undertaking. There were problems, they suggested, 'because of the new techniques being used' and underlined that 'whilst

Department personnel will gain knowledge as the project advances, it is unrealistic to expect this knowledge, which is not reinforced by past experience of such systems, to equal that of UNIVAC Personnel'.[13] Lack of knowledge, they suggested, bred anxiety and suspicion. Whatever the faults, testing of the pilot Brisbane centre in March 1972 uncovered such a hornet's nest of problems that one PMG official wrote in alarm, 'it must be clear to the Department of Health as well as ourselves that the system's software was incapable at this stage of supporting traffic without failure for longer than a few minutes'.[14]

Brisbane's CUDN was eventually commissioned in November 1972 on a partial basis to carry traffic for the Commonwealth Department of Health Brisbane, and TAA. In April 1973 an interim system was commissioned in Sydney to handle Department of Health traffic from Melbourne, and leased line services were provided for both TAA and the Department of Health at CUDN rates. By July 1974 a 'further interim CUDN service' was installed to carry Department of Health traffic in Sydney. But poor performance, contingency plans, and customer dissatisfaction reached critical pitch by 1975. The time lag between CUDN's commissioning and the prospect of full operation stretched over more than five tense and expensive years.

Lane inherited the trouble-ridden enterprise from his pre-decessors, Housley and Knott. CUDN, in fact, would ruffle the composure and challenge the decision-making of several executive heads. With hindsight, Lane considered that he should have destroyed the snake when he took over as Director-General in 1972, or at least when he had time to assess the difficulties the following year. 'Had I done the right thing', he admitted candidly nine years later, 'I would have cancelled the whole project there and then and cut the losses.' Not to do so, he said was 'an error in judgment'.[15]

Not surprisingly, the commission of inquiry into the APO was explicitly critical of CUDN. There were, it concluded, errors of evaluation, scheduling, a shortage of expertise and an important failure in the considered planning of 'such a major innovative project'. It was also apparent from the evidence that poured in that, even on the PMG's revised financial assessment of the system and substitution of a 16-year equipment life for the original ten, CUDN would not reach break-even point after the payment of interest on all capital investment until about 1981-2. Yet realistically, the commission recognised that technical problems were always a part of the intro-duction of major new systems. It considered a cost-hike from $14.3 million for a larger than originally planned system to $18.4 million, 'a high but not altogether unreasonable overrun in view of the nature of the project and cost escalation'. Nevertheless they concluded that a time lag of about three years was not reasonable and reflected on all aspects of the problem. In short, they summed up, 'In retrospect . . . the CUDN system should have been studied in considerably more detail by both the APO and the successful tenderer and its operational requirements more clearly defined before a contract was let . . . Entering into firm five year tariff agreements at an early stage of such a system was a hazardous procedure.'[16]

In the industry there was some lip-smacking. 'The Vernon Commission', wrote Linton Simpkins, the *Australian*'s computer expert, 'confirms what the industry has always suspected that the CUDN project has been a series of mistakes and apparent mismanagement both by the APO and the suppliers, Sperry UNIVAC.' But in the long run, 'the local industry will benefit from the horrible example of this project'.

There were certainly lessons to be drawn. The venture had been bold and enterprising in 1969. The PMG was the first department of state to adopt computer technology in Australia. Moreover, as E.R. Banks told the Australian Computer Users' Association later, 'even the sincerely held expectations of suppliers and users could cause a service to be started for which there was insufficient demand'. The PMG's track record for importing and integrating systems was well renowned. But there was one ingredient that was new and specific here: the lack of experience in a large computer programme. It was not, then, simply a matter of a decision being overtaken by new technology. The major CUDN error lay elsewhere. 'Overtime, over-budgeted, and extremely overrated', as one industrial critic put it, it exhibited all the features of hasty planning, overconfidence and false estimates of risk factors that were not in general characteristic of PMG's planning approach.[17]

On the tried Departmental axiom that 'Australia was a country looking to apply the most advanced technologies as soon as we felt they were safe', CUDN was a faulty piece of decision making. The Royal Commission saw its management as the fatal flaw. 'The project', they observed, 'should have been made the responsibility of a special management group reporting regularly to top management.' But to reflective senior staff, the flaw lay deeper. 'We built something', said one, 'before we had the customers.' To others, the engineering planners had grasped hold of a potential technology but questions of its use and impact did not receive due attention. In a quest to conquer the Australian data network market, there was — as the 1974 Commission Report would indicate of the whole of the PMG — a serious failure of market research; while technical planning was allowed to blot out simple user requirement.[18]

The experience proved costly in time, money and men. The faults were not all on one side. Sperry Rand (Australia) contributed substantially to the muddle and miscalculations of the scheme. But the Department and its successor had much to learn and serious cautions to observe in the transfer of future computer and semi-conductor technology. Here CUDN proved an instructive process. It was Telecom Australia who would ultimately cut the painter. But while CUDN was officially established in all mainland capitals by October 1975 servicing its three customers, the Department of Health, the Bureau of Meteorology, and TAA, Director-General Lane and his planners had already decided that CUDN's message switching services should be withdrawn and the Department of Health transferred to leased private lines. By January 1977 Brisbane and Adelaide's CUDN centres were closed and the Department of Health's traffic moved to private lines.

By the early 1980s the 'ugly gosling' had been cannibalised for State and internal headquarter use.[19]

In October 1973 Sir Keith Hancock, doyen of Australian historians, sat down to write a book. He called it *The Battle of Black Mountain*. Its villain was the PMG. 'Black Mountain', he began, 'is "everybody's mountain", the incomparable scenic backdrop to Australia's national capital. Wherever you go in Canberra its benign profile, adorned but never concealed by trees, will remain within your field of vision'. Scientists and bushwalkers prized it: it was a 'valuable laboratory' for the scientific study of Australian insects; a flora reserve had been designated on its south–east side some 30 years earlier, and a decision gazetted as late as July 1970 to establish the Black Mountain reserve. If a telecommunications tower planned by the PMG were built, Hancock posed the question as earth movers stirred across the mountain top and Mr Justice Smithers listened to defence and advocacy on the matter in the ACT's Supreme Court, 'what will happen to the insects? In Australia as elsewhere, towers built on hills are invariably floodlit at night . . . Citizens and tourists down below will gape at the floodlit tower, but many species of insects on the mountain will be disturbed in their natural habitats and lured to their destruction.'[20]

The heated controversy that flared over the planned construction of Black Mountain Tower in the early 1970s would also prove costly to the PMG in time, material and men. But its outcome — a soaring pinnacle against Canberra's rolling skyline, was very different from the ill–starred CUDN. Nonetheless, the tower's planning and early preparation had all the ingredients of high drama. It also scored several firsts. It marked the first time in the PMG's history and in the history of the early Colonial administrations of posts and telegraphs, when a hostile citizenry confronted the authorities over the installation of telecommunications technology. And, in the protracted civic, bureaucratic, political and legal hubbub that ensued, it prompted Australia's first environmental impact statement.

The idea of a national telecommunications tower, structured and sited in the national capital, was initially the brainchild of Sir John Knott. As Australia's Deputy High Commissioner in London, Knott had dined at the top of London's post office tower and brought the vision of a glimmering city back to Melbourne. He floated the idea with Postmaster–General Hulme and despatched his telecommunications lieutenant, Deputy Director–General Evan Sawkins to inspect major telecommunications towers in Europe. Under two directors, Knott and Lane, Sawkins, assisted by W.F. Brigden of the PMG's building branch, and engineer F.L.C. Taylor, would become the prime mover and tenacious architect of the 'big bad Black Mountain Tower'.[21]

Other eyes than the PMG's had focussed on the telecommunications potential of Black Mountain. OTC had wanted this solid hump in the rim of hills for its second satellite earth station but had been fought off by the PMG after some critical clashes to Moree. The PMG itself had been under pressure for several years from Canberra's guardian, the National Capital Development Commission (NCDC), to clear its major radio relay station (the terminal and repeater station for high capacity broadband microwave systems on the Sydney–Canberra–Melbourne route) from one of Canberra's smaller ridges, Red Hill. The station, positioned since the early 1960s with its 39-metre lattice steel pylon supporting the radio antennae, would, it was said, spoil the view from the new Houses of Parliament planned for the vicinity of Capital Hill. Technically, moreover, the station could not be extended vertically to meet demands of growth.

Black Mountain itself already sheltered two slender television transmitting masts serving Canberra's national and commercial stations and the studio needs of Canberra Television Ltd's Channel 7. Their existence, and its position, recommended the mountain for the tower scheme. By early 1972 cabinet approval steered by Hulme was given for a 641–foot (195.2–metre) multi–purpose tower with rotating restaurant and viewing platform that would, technically, fulfil the telecommunications needs of the capital for the next 50 years. After lengthy hearings on the subject in August 1972, the Parliamentary Standing Committee on Public Works put its stamp upon the plan and fixed tenders for September 1973. In October 1972 one of the outgoing acts of the coalition Government under Prime Minister McMahon, was to give the go–ahead to the construction of Black Mountain Tower.[22]

But the scheme met stiff resistance from a group of ANU academics and the Society for Social Responsibility in Science (ACT). Their argument turned, as Hancock's rolling phrases indicated, first on ecological and aesthetic grounds and later on economic and tech-nological reasoning. They saw the projected tower with its rounded drums and spire, as an 'excrescence' on the pristine Canberra land-scape, 'a distortion of spatial and symbolic values' and as a threat to the peaceful, though often unseen, ecology of the mountain park. They also believed the structure could cost twice as much as comparable Australian facilities for radio, TV and radio–telephone equipment. Their technological case rested on the concept of qualified need. With such revolutionary new developments as underground optical fibre, cable television and a possible domestic satellite on the near horizon, the academics put the case for waiting until the exploitation of these new techniques could render so prominent a structure unnecessary.[23] To present their technical case, the committee of Citizens to Save Black Mountain enlisted Stephen Kaneff, Professor of Engineering Physics of the Research School of Physical Sciences, ANU, self–avowedly no specialist in telecommunications technology. Nonetheless Kaneff argued that the tower was not only 'technologically unnecessary' but likely to prove an impediment to necessary technological change in the not too distant future. He alternatively projected a less permanent single steel lattice–work radio and TV mast on the Black Mountain site and a radio telephony installation on Red Hill.[24]

The PMG's case also rested on need: the need to provide an evolving telecommunications system for the relay of telephony, television, radio, FM and data transmission for Canberra's expanding, Government–centred and nationally–oriented population. It is clear that many PMG planners also saw the tower as a symbol of technological achievement and prestige. On these points, with the exception of plans for the round and revolving restaurant, the PMG had the support of the NCDC.[25]

Politics kindled the confrontation. Labor had entered Government in December 1972 with stated commitments to environmental planning and conservation. Pressure from the Minister for the Environment and Conservation, Dr M. Cass, led in February 1973 to a cabinet decision that environmental impact statements should be mandatory for all developmental projects in which the Commonwealth was involved. One was clearly mandatory now. On the instruction of Bowen as Postmaster-General, Australia's maiden environmental impact statement on the tower project was hastily improvised by Sawkins and Taylor 'across a weekend' in mid-February 1973. 'It attracted strong criticism from opponents of the project', Taylor wrote later, 'much of which, in retrospect, was probably justified.' Hancock's criticism was pungent. The impact evaluation, he wrote 'was not conceived as a reasoned statement open to reasoned criticism by the Department for the Environment and by responsible citizens at public hearings. It reiterated the well-rehearsed arguments in favour of the tower and brushed aside every counter-argument.' Cass himself acknowledged that the impact statement was hardly 'an ideal first example' and hoped 'that in future environmental impact statements will be incorporated at the very earliest stages of planning for projects and not, as the Black Mountain statement had been, made at the end of what was virtually a predecided project'.[26]

But Postmaster-General Bowen was in the driver's seat. In August 1973 he and over half the Labor caucus and finally Prime Minister Whitlam accepted their Department's technical arguments for the contentious telecommunications structure on a vote of 41 to 35.[27] Labor politicians, like their coalition forbears, were clearly moved by the tourist and revenue-producing potential of the tower.

Not so the academics and their supporters. The committee of Citizens to Save Black Mountain determined to join battle and take their case to the ACT Supreme Court. Their claim rested on 'public nuisance'. Persisting through an initial 'interlocutory action', a verdict in favour of the tower's construction, a halt advised by Mr Justice Smithers in the same court on the grounds that Canberra's planning body, the NCDC, opposed the tower, a resultant suspension of construction in November 1973 (ordered by the Minister for Works), a cabinet decision a month later to authorise the construction of the tower, a cross-appeal by the plaintiffs, and a final High Court judgment that work on the tower could lawfully proceed, it dragged on relentlessly until June 1975.[28]

How important was the battle, and what could be learnt? As a case study of concerned citizens, bureaucratic and political manoeuvres, it offered a tangled skein. Certainly the role of the NCDC, first as critic and later as defender of the project, commended the National Capital Development Commission to neither side.[29] The protesters were highly motivated but less than adequately equipped technically to deal with a large technological department of state. The ANU has no Faculty of Engineering and their chosen adviser, Professor Kaneff, found himself in a difficult position as the technical lead. The academics, moreover, unversed in technological history, also proved ahistorical in their approach. PMG plans for upgrading telecommunications systems had an inbuilt ingredient of 'wait and see'. But lead–times were not indefinite and suggestions to await the largely experimental and commercially unproven optical fibre underground cable solution were economically and technically unsound.

The bureaucrats also behaved with more than bureaucratic zeal. They pressured politicians, won over their Postmaster–General, rejected geographical alternatives to Black Mountain on the grounds of greater expense, and fought tenaciously for the location of their choice. Key spokesmen for its construction made little attempt to liaise as accountable public servants with an active citizen group. The tactics of confrontation engendered deep antagonisms in the dispute. Predictably the politicians behaved politically. Despite a supportive environmental faction led by the Minister for Regional Development, Tom Uren, departmental, economic and technological arguments for a soaring telecommunications edifice overcame initial resistance from caucus. Prime Minister Whitlam added his assent. Bureaucratically and politically the episode bore all the hallmarks of closed government.

Begun early in 1973, suspended, and recommenced in December 1973, construction on the tower was substantially completed by 1977

The Black Mountain Tower, an expression of optimism about technology. Black Mountain Tower would give the national capital a mass audience.

and opened by another Prime Minister, Malcolm Fraser, on 15 May 1980. The shadow of censure, said the Prime Minister, had passed. The telecommunications tower on Black Mountain now stood as an integral and important part of Canberra, for many a national symbol and, technologically, 'a significant extension in the overall telecommunications facilities that we need as Australia gears up for the 1980s. I congratulate Telecom and all who have been responsible for the project.'[30]

Popular reaction tended to endorse this view. The tower has emerged as Canberra's logo. Visitors pour through its doors: well-heeled diners revolve in its restaurant, while tourists from all over Australia and abroad applaud the views from its circular lookouts that stretch spectacularly past the blue green city to the encircling hills. By night its beacon welcomes the traveller home. The novelist, Christina Stead, residing at University House two years before her death, found the tower framed in her window a source of daytime pleasure and a comforting presence at night. For others it remains a 'grotesque edifice'; a 'towering mistake'. Yet such criticism is reminiscent. When, after the excitement of the great Paris Exhibition of 1889 to commemorate the centenary of the fall of the Bastille it was decided that the Eiffel Tower (erected as a temporary structure to demonstrate French engineering skills) should remain, the literary luminary, Guy de Maupassant, furiously dubbed it 'monstrous'. Put to telecommunications' use soon after Marconi's advent, it stands today as the symbol of Paris.

In Canberra vindication for Black Mountain Tower came early and from sources close to home. In 1979 Black Mountain Tower was awarded a Certificate of Merit by the Concrete Institute of Australia for 'outstanding quality of achievement in design and construction of the concrete work' and, a year later, gathered another plaudit, the Royal Australian Institute of Architects (ACT chapter) 1980 civic design award, on criteria that commended the project's success in terms of functionalism, impact on the people, the environment, aesthetic appeal (at a distance and close up), and upon Canberra as a whole.

Although a smaller telecommunications facility would have undoubtedly fulfilled the technological purpose, the PMG, like many of its counterparts overseas, chose otherwise, arranging to finance the more imposing structure by leasing the tower's commercial facilities of restaurant and visitors' lift. The final cost of the project soared from the original tender of $6 million to more than $16 million.[31]

Yet while questions about environmental intrusion raised much heat and dust in Canberra, the PMG was undertaking another vertical conquest of space, the bizarre but beautiful Bellenden–Ker tower perched in the high rain forests of Queensland's Great Dividing Range, that would rank as a world environmental first.

Bellenden–Ker stood in the centre of rugged, impassable mountain country girded by rain forests some 1,500 metres above sea level, but with a direct 'line of sight' 50 kilometres north to Cairns. As such it suggested itself as a key site for a tower to provide both TV coverage

Below right: An
exercise in
environmental
planning. A helicopter
flies in mast sections
during the construction
of the Bellenden-Ker
television transmitting
towers, near Cairns,
North Queensland,
1971.

Below: A cable car
gives access to and
from the completed
towers for repair and
maintenance, a method
which prevents
disturbance of the rain
forest below.

for the growing tourist centre of Cairns and its neighbouring coastal
and mountain towns and to serve as a repeating station for a Cairns–
Atherton radio system. Not surprisingly, a protective Queensland
Forestry Department preferred the high but accessible Mt Bartle-
Frere which could give only obstructed television transmission, with
some ghosting, into some parts of Cairns. A solution between the need
for community telecommunications and TV services and an
untrammelled national park prompted compromise.

Feasibility studies by two Commonwealth Departments (Housing
and Construction and Services and Property) conducted largely by
helicopter revealed that a cableway could be constructed with long
spans across the national park involving a small number of trestles
nestled into the park's forest that required minimum clearing through
the undergrowth. Surveys were made by the Department of the
Interior to determine the route and twin structures designed by the
Queensland office of the Commonwealth Department of Works. A.B.
Poulsen, Queensland's divisional engineer, television, led the project
team of PMG engineers. Helicopters proved invaluable and Verey
pistols were used to fix line of sight. By April 1970 a contract was let to
McNamee Industries, Sydney in association with the experienced
Austrian cableway firm, Waagner–Biro, for construction of the
cableway and the buildings and tower on Bellenden–Ker.

The work of clearing the pathway, begun with the terminal station
near the Bruce Highway at the mountain base, was supervised by
Forestry controllers. Swift rain forest regrowth covered the scarring
tracks. Helicopters flew in materials and men. Clouds clung to the

soaring peak for days on end fending off the gnat-like airborne machines. But work proceeded persistently. Cement for the mountain top buildings was mixed at the base station and ferried in by air. Ten spans carried the steel track that, winched in, supported the cableway and ran in one continuous length over more than three miles. As such it formed the longest cableway of its kind in the world.[32]

Bellenden-Ker, a star in the crown of microwave and TV stations that girdled the continent, was opened by Sir Alan Hulme as one of his last acts as Postmaster-General in October 1972. Such environmental planning was well ahead of the Labor Government's legislation on environmental impact statements in February 1973. In its imaginative and collaborative approach, it marked a long step from the 'ad hocery' and 'get the connection through' attitude displayed by PMG engineers and planners in earlier years. An old era was waning: new attitudes, to be honed and strengthened in the Telecom era, were already spreading through the system.

Lane, elected at the close of a remarkable career to captain the PMG on what would prove to be the last lap of its 74-year journey, would go out with a bang. He had, recalled one senior colleague, 'steered the ship of state through a very difficult period'. At Christmas 1974 he faced national crisis. On Christmas morning radio stations around the country relayed the news of 'Cyclone Tracy' that, swinging in on winds of 200 kilometres an hour, had devastated the city of Darwin shortly after midnight on Christmas Eve.

Sixty-five people were dead, hundreds were injured, and thousands made homeless by what was soon identified as Australia's 'greatest natural disaster'. Communication with the shattered city hung on one link, the modern new microwave system that carried trunk connections from Darwin via Katherine, Tennant Creek, Mt Isa and Townsville to Brisbane, built to withstand cyclones and cut over into service in mid-1974. With channelling equipment damaged by water, only one circuit of this system, an order wire used normally for administrative and control purposes, remained operative to alert the nation. Cyclonic wind had destroyed the open wire pole route 25 kilometres south of Darwin and had severely damaged the Radio Australia transmission centre at Cox Peninsula. Outpost radio, TV, broadcast and local telephone services ceased to function. News of the disaster reached southern cities from 8 a.m. and the news was broadcast on the ABC at 11.50 a.m. Almost 33 years after bombing had exposed the northern city's vulnerability in February 1942, Darwin was 'off the air' again.

It was in this scene of almost total devastation that PMG staff began the job of urgent restoration of services. Major-General Arthur Stretton, placed in charge of the overall disaster organisation, later passed critical comment on the communications' collapse. 'The most unsatisfactory part of the Darwin disaster', he wrote, 'was the breakdown of communications on Christmas Day. Communications from Canberra to Darwin were disrupted for a vital period of some hours, there was a complete breakdown of communications within Darwin

The Radio Australia
transmitting site, Cox
Peninsula, near Darwin,
devastated by Cyclone
Tracy on Christmas
Eve, 1974. The scene
within Darwin, and the
Darwin post office, full
of Christmas mail.

itself and there was radio silence for thirty five hours.' Despite the existence of the one 'order wire', said Stretton, 'the PMG was not able to offer this facility to anyone in authority in either Canberra or Darwin on Christmas morning'.[33]

Yet Darwin exchange was operational by 11 a.m. and emergency services provided for connection to the trunk outlet. By 26 December trunk circuits and full STD facilities were restored to all States, public telephone facilities made available at the Darwin post office, outpost

Darwin residents take advantage of the free telephone calls made available by the PMG in the immediate post-cyclone days.

radio was given temporary service, and radio broadcasting resumed. By 28 December, one hundred emergency services were connected in response to requests and priorities set by the disaster organisation. Hundreds of other lines were serviceable but very few premises were habitable. As trunk telephone services were heavily in use by emergency services, the telegraph system was used for thousands of telegrams to and from all parts of Australia. Free telephone calls were allowed for three days. Postmaster–General Bowen then announced that reduced rates would apply to telecommunications charges in and from Darwin.[34]

Never had the PMG faced such urgent challenges as on Christmas Day. Engineers and telecommunications staff worked round–the–clock to restore contacts with all States although almost all experienced loss of property and possessions and most would see their families evacuated among the 35,000 people removed from the stricken city. Writing to the Director of Posts and Telegraphs of South Australia and the Northern Territory in the first lull, Eber Lane was to convey an expression of his lifetime feeling for the members of his huge, responsive, community–oriented team.

> They gave unstintingly of their time to help the local community, and their efforts, I am sure will not be forgotten . . . The manner in which damaged plant was restored quickly, and the manner which operating staff then effectively used it, was quite outstanding . . . It makes one feel proud to know one is surrounded by people who are prepared to go the extra mile in an emergency, or in fact in any condition in meeting the Department's obligation to provide the means for the people of Australia to communicate, be it by post, telegraph or telephone.[35]

Lane, highly pressured by the responsibility of restoring communications to the rebuilt city of Darwin, would lead the PMG's Department to its final day. There was much to be done.

With the Government's acceptance of the Royal Commission's broad recommendations on 24 April 1974, the stage for partition was set. Fourteen months and much hard labour later, Telecom Australia would arise.

'A Royal Commission', one British pundit noted, 'is like a broody hen sitting on china eggs: the administration that sets it up never intends any recommendation to hatch.'[36] The observation was singularly wide of the mark for the Commission of Inquiry into the APO. All but one of its major recommendations would pass into legislation. Moreover on its central recommendation for the PMG's partition, the Government had the instant backing of the Liberal Party. While the Liberal Party had made no submission to the commission of inquiry, opposition leader, B.M. Snedden announced his party's endorsement without delay. With the exception of the proposal to submerge the OTC, he stated on 25 April, the Liberal Party 'basically agreed with' the commission's recommendations. The coalition parties were due to issue their policy platform on communications, and, said Snedden 'it had been the Liberal Party's view that the postal and telecommunications services of the present department should be separated'. But there was no such endorsement from the Country Party. The coalition platform, *The way ahead*, issued in May that year, carefully avoided the partition question, placed its stress on improvements in efficiency and productivity of the PMG, but concealed, in effect, a hard–won measure of agreement for partition.[37]

Within the Department, the task of drafting the legislative blueprint fell to the two deputy Directors–General, Spratt and Curtis, working in close collaboration with the Office of the Crown Solicitor. Through weeks of drafting, they stuck firmly to the commission brief. It was by no means easy to split a long–lived and entrenched department of state. Change and amalgamations of Ministries and portfolios might come and go: but the PMG's Department was the most massive organisation of men and materials in the country. Its operations, as defenders of the status quo were wont to stress, reached from its core at Melbourne headquarters through the nerve centres of headquarters in the States, down to every small post office in the country. To divide the great body into two viable and effectively functioning parts, required clever and painstaking surgery.

Several mechanisms speeded the operation. Interim commissions (one telecommunications, one postal) were appointed to oversee the job, more than 40 APO task forces geared into action, and continuous consultation proceeded with a less than jubilant Public Service Board.

Political currents also shaped the timing of the legislation. After 18 months in office, Whitlam, hindered by a lack of majority in the Senate and a threat to Supply, called a general election of both Houses of Parliament in May 1974. His Labor Government's return, strong in the House of Representatives but without its hoped–for majority in the Upper House would cost it one important provision of the planned legislation — the amalgamation of the new telecommunications corporation and the OTC.

The double dissolution election also brought ministerial change. In June 1974 Bowen, who had held the Postmaster–Generalship since December 1972, was elevated to the new portfolio of Special Minister of State, and Reginald Bishop, a leading South Australian union official before election to the Senate in 1962, was brought into the Postmaster–General's chair.[38]

The two men were rather different. Lionel Bowen, a solicitor by training and a member of the New South Wales parliament before his election to the Federal House as MHR for Kingsford Smith, had steered planning for the APO commission of inquiry. Independent and un-inhibited, he had brought an individual flavour to the long–held Liberal–Country Party post. Reared by his mother in the egalitarian Sydney suburb of Randwick, he firmly identified with the workers. He accepted invitations to pay visits to the Redfern mail exchange (an informality much frowned upon by his Department) and publicly con-demned the Redfern 'chamber of horrors'. He also held open house for unionists at his Sydney office, and in October 1973, when go–slow bans and mail interruptions dominated the news, he joined postal workers in the Eight–Hour Day March in Sydney, and generally disconcerted the State Director of Posts and Telegraphs and the Director–General.[39]

Senator Bishop, a down–to–earth and affable politician, was more conventional. But, keen to learn, he had startled South Australia's Director of Posts and Telegraphs D.M. Coleman on appointment by immediately asking to 'see the plans'. With inputs from Sir James Vernon, it was Bishop who selected the Commissioners who, first as administrative caretakers and later for fixed terms, would guide the new Australian Telecommunications Commission into a new and more independent age.[40]

Appointments to Australian statutory bodies normally bore a political stamp. Bishop broke with this tradition. A.G. Gibbs, appointed chairman of the interim telecommunications commission was a doyen of the Liberal Party in Victoria, a former chairman of General Motors Holden, and prestigious chairman of the Victorian Railways. Although Gibbs would hand in his badge a few months after the formal con-stitution of Telecom Australia, he brought great verve and expedition to the corporation's initial tasks. Other commission members reflected a spread of community concerns. R.D. Somervaille, partner of the Sydney firm of Dawson Waldron, solicitors, and T.E. May, public director and consultant, mirrored Vernon's concern for financial and industrial expertise. The full complement of seven was made up by trade unionist, K.C. Turbet, Federal secretary of the PTTA (later ATEA), Mrs Joan Hancock, a consumers' representative on the South Australian Credit Tribunal, P. Lawler, secretary of the Department of the Special Minister of State, and J.H. Curtis, deputy Director–General.[41] The interim Australian postal commission showed a similar spread. Under the chairmanship of J.J. Kennedy, it included George Slater, general secretary of the Australian Postal Workers Union, and A.F. Spratt, deputy Director–General who, like Curtis for tele-communications, was in line to become managing director of the new postal organisation. The appointment of the two union officials was itself distinctive. While one or two top union officials served on statutory authority boards, Turbet and Slater were the only top union officials in Australia appointed to the boards of organisations which employed the bulk of their own union; the beginnings of industrial democracy in Australia.

It was Postmaster–General Bishop who introduced the three enabling bills — Postal Services, Telecommunications, and Postal and Telecommunications Commissions (Transitional Provisions) Bills — into the Senate on 23 April 1975. The Government, Bishop paid tribute, recognised the splendid service which the PMG's Department 'had rendered the people of Australia from Federation to the present day'. But overseas trends in postal and telecommunications management and Australia's own history now demonstrated the need for change.[42]

Two aspects of the bills sparked opposition amendments that could be met at once: a more specific definition of the two Commissions' roles, and a larger measure of direction for the Minister. But on one central point the battle lines were drawn — the marriage of the country's internal and international telecommunications services. The Liberal Party had signified its resistance to the merger; Vernon's dissenting opinion lent support, while the active lobbying of the Professional Radio and Electronic Institute of Australia (PREI), representing the largest number of OTC employees, and by OTC's own general manager, Harold White, had already stirred ferment before Parliament rose in November 1974. Energetic and mercurial, White pressed two insistent themes. He saw OTC as 'unique' and he was sharply critical of what he termed the 'divine right' of the APO as operator, regulator and adviser to Government. Under threat of submergence, White wasted no time in mustering the support of two powerful allies, the Overseas Telecommunications Users Association and the Sydney Chamber of Commerce, and in drafting a fighting speech for the Shadow Postmaster–General, Senator Durack.[43]

His politicking brought rewards. Four turns of the parliamentary wheel were required to complete the circle. Provision for the amalgamation of OTC and the Telecommunications Commission was contained in the original Bill introduced on 23 April. The Government firmly addressed the point. On 21 May the Senate, with its Coalition majority, carried an amendment excising the contentious clause, and the amended Bill was passed without further amendment in the House of Representatives on 27 May. Two days later the Government adopted the 'novel, if not unique tactic' (as Country Party member Peter Nixon put it), of introducing a Telecommunications Bill No. 2 into the House of Representatives through the Special Minister of State, with the original amalgamation clause restored. The Bill was carried in the Lower House. But in the Senate on 11 June its fate was sealed. Though Senator McAuliffe (Labor, Queensland) might infer that, if the measure were defeated, 'the Government will wheel the legislation back to the Senate in the Budget session and it will be established as a double dissolution measure', the threat was a paper tiger. The Telecommunications Bill No. 2 was defeated by a mere two votes, 27 votes to 25. The original Telecommunications Bill, with its Senate amendment, remained the valid legislation. The legislation trio, the Postal Act, the Telecommunications Act and the Postal and Telecommunications (Transitional Provisions) Act, received the Royal Assent on 12 June 1975.[44]

13 Telecom Rising

A sign of the times, as the PMG's Mercury logo gives way to those of Telecom Australia and Australia Post. From a cartoon by WA's Peter O'Donoghue.

The birth of 'Telecom Australia' inaugurated a new era of telecommunications in Australia. On 1 July 1975 the Australian Telecommunications Commission — trading as Telecom Australia — took over almost all of those responsibilities for Australia's public telecommunications network that had previously been the domain of the Postmaster–General's Department since 1901. The Act that created the country's new telecommunications organisation was carefully honed. The Australian Telecommunications Commission was constituted to plan, establish, maintain and operate telecommunications within Australia; perform its functions in such a manner 'as will best meet the social, industrial and commercial need . . . of the Australian people'; have regard to the desirability of improving and extending telecommunications services in the light of developments overseas; operate 'as efficiently and economically as possible' and make its services available for all people who 'reasonably' require them. At the special insistence of the Country Party, a clause was added that the Commission should have regard for 'the special needs for telecommunications services of Australian people who reside or carry on business outside the cities'.[1] The clause embraced the oldest inhabitants: Aboriginals had been classified as Australian citizens as a result of a Federal Referendum in 1967.

Under the Act, the Commission's powers were flexible and broad. It had the right to purchase, lease and sell lands, construct or demolish plant, machinery and equipment, make surveys, dig pits, sink bores, make cuttings and excavations (keeping a careful eye on roads and bridges) and, in all assaults on the landscape, 'cause as little detriment and . . . do as little damage as possible'.[2]

As the Royal Commission had foreshadowed, the Telecommunications Commission also acquired substantial powers to set charges for services (with Ministerial approval in the case of standard telephone and telegram charges and telephone rental), and to determine its own financial goals. The Minister's powers were precisely defined. He could, after consulting the Commission, give direction to it in writing about the performance and exercise of its powers 'as appeared necessary in the public interest'; but a copy of the direction had to be laid before each House of Parliament within 15 sitting days.[3]

In the fiscal field, as the commission of inquiry had intended, the Telecommunications Commission became responsible for securing sufficient revenue to meet annual expenditures and provisions for depreciation, superannuation and long service leave, and to provide for not less than one–half of the capital expenditure requirements for the financial year. It was exempt from tax, could borrow money with Treasury approval from Commonwealth sources, invest in approved banks and securities, but it could not enter the private money market.[4] The 'surplus' in any financial year (for the term 'profit' was at once taboo) was to be applied under Ministerial guidance.

Three key provisions of the Act embodied the concern for a tauter, more business–like direction of the Commission's affairs. The first was the appointment by the Governor–General of a managing director as chief executive and Commissioner, responsible for the long–term policy and management of the Commission and freed from ongoing matters to concentrate on fundamental questions and corporate goals. The incumbent would have the time, it was argued, to conceive long–term strategies from which to exert strong leadership over the direction of the enterprise. The second was the appointment of a chief general manager responsible for day–to–day operating problems and available to subordinate managers for decisions on a regular basis. By such an arrangement, in sharp contrast to the leadership of the PMG, external policy and strategic considerations were removed from the everyday demands of technological and operational problem solving.[5]

The third major step involved severance from the Public Service Board. Functions once reserved to the PSB were transferred by legislation to the Commission, while industrial disputes and appeals were to be submitted to and heard by the Conciliation and Arbitration Commission and not the Public Service Arbitrator. The commission of inquiry's more specific recommendation for separate 'arbitral bodies' for the two Commissions was, in the event, rejected by Labor ministers and the unions, though a consultative council of representatives of both the Commission and staff organisations was provided for in the Act.

For both Telecommunications and Postal Commissions their Acts marked singular departures from the long governance of the Postal and Telegraph Act. 'Vesting Day', 1 July 1975, the date of investiture, or 'V' day as it became known, signalled the end of a long trail. The two Commissions were formally constituted. J.H. Curtis and A.F. Spratt became respectively managing directors of the Australian Telecommunications Commission (Telecom Australia) and the Australian Postal Commission (Australia Post) and Eber Lane, last Director–General of the PMG, retired from office on 30 June 1975. 'The Australian Post Office', declaimed the Melbourne *Sun* in a burst of biological metaphors, 'gave birth to twins at midnight then quietly slipped into retirement.' Sir James Vernon, an official midwife, was also in two minds. It was, he compromised at the celebratory dinner held in Melbourne that evening, 'either a funeral or the birth of twins!' But the responsible Minister turned his gaze ahead. The main thing now, Senator Bishop told the historic gathering, 'was to sell the product at the price the public wanted'.[6]

Under the Transitional Provisions Act, individual members of the defunct Department were allocated to the two Commissions. For most the choice was clear. Within a matter of weeks, some 85,000 members of staff had joined the Telecommunications Commission and 35,000 joined the Postal Commission, although a period of five years was allowed for the disgruntled or uncertain to change sides. For the Public Service Board, the balloon had gone up. At one stroke, it lost well over half its membership.[7] A long, influential and, at times, stormy relationship had ended. For the newly–launched telecommunications flagship, 'Telecom Australia', with its crisp trading name and its modern Telecom gold 'T' symbol flying at its masthead, it was 'full steam ahead'.[8]

In the matter of governance, the interim Commission set the form. 'The Commissioners', the first decision paper ran, 'will administer the organisation in accordance with accepted principles of business management so that the efficiency and vitality of the Commission are constantly under review.' Matters of policy and consequence within the organisation were presented to the Commission by the managing director either as 'submissions for decision' or as 'information papers'. The latter required discussion only if a Commissioner so desired. But submissions for decision demanded the active involvement of the Commission, exploring alternatives, making specific propositions, indicating the pros and cons of a certain course of action, and offering firm policy and programme recommendations. Decisions of the Commission (or of a Commission committee) were promptly coveyed by the Commission Secretary to the responsible management area of Telecom and other interested branches. Despatch was a golden rule.

For questions involving Ministerial approval, the first Commission meeting laid down that, 'Papers of this kind should contain a clear indication of the need for Ministerial approval and the section of the Act under which the Ministers agreement is sought'. At the same time the Commission was responsible for keeping the Minister informed of important developments falling within its care. In short, in the expeditious approach of A.G. Gibbs, it was agreed that 'as soon as possible after the completion of each Commission meeting, a letter summarising the important aspects considered and decided upon by the Commission should be prepared by the Secretary for the Chairman's signature'.

Gibbs's expert guidance left a clear stamp on Commission affairs which Robert Somervaille would follow on his succession in November 1975. A major figure in the Commission's performance, however, was managing director Curtis. Relieved of the day–to–day administration of Telecom, Curtis played a formative role. He brought policy papers before the Commission, presented detailed statements of cases and, a quiet but determined leader, set directions and goals. He early achieved a close working relationship with Gibbs, a collaboration he transferred to Somervaille.

To enter Jack Curtis's office was much like visiting the bridge of a luxurious ship. There was a quiet disciplined air. The managing director's desk was whistle clean. The grandfather clock, once used by Sir Harry Brown, provided a historical link. Time was an instrument of control. A tall Queenslander with the head of a Roman Caesar, Curtis was not, according to associates, the 'obvious first choice' for the leader's post. But from action, his image grew. His biography was full of firsts. An ex-serviceman who had served as a flight lieutenant in New Guinea in the RAAF in the Second World War, Curtis joined the PMG's Department Brisbane in 1949 as one of the original graduates of Queensland University's post-war Bachelor of Engineering (Communications) degree. Employed successively as a construction, field, and later planning engineer, Curtis introduced the 'Queensland plan' in 1961, the first-ever telecommunications plan. After service as superintending engineer, planning, and later assistant director, telecommunications, of his State, he followed Lane as Director of Posts and Telegraphs, Queensland, in August 1971. Two years later Lane appointed Curtis Deputy-Director at headquarters where he helped lay the legislative ground-plan of the new regime. A rare bird among telecommunications engineers, the new managing director read widely in history and philosophy and, with BA and BSc. degrees acquired along the way, was something of a 'two-culture' man. But despite the contours of a Roman Caesar, he lacked an emperor's imperious way. He was, however, a consummate influence behind the scenes.

The Telecom ship was scarcely out of the harbour when the first squall hit. In the period of transition, the Public Service Board had, on the commission of inquiry's recommendations, been called upon to assist the new Commission in their classification, conditions and remuneration of former PMG employees. The board's role was purely advisory — the new Act empowered each Commission to decide how many officers it should employ and the terms of their employment. But, for reasons of convenience and history, it was agreed by Telecom and the PSB that the 'most realistic approach' in the short term was to continue using the PSB's examination system and similar selection processes. The task force on the matter held that in the long term 'the style and content of selection tests will be changed to relate more closely to the policies of the Commission'.[9]

Against this background of mutual assent, the Commission's announcement of its top management appointment brought Telecom its first baptism of fire. 'One of the first acts of the new Commission', wrote the *Australian Financial Review*, in some annoyance, 'has been to subvert the Government's wage indexation policies in a spectacular example of self-indulgence.' Both Commissions heard the shots. Not only had steep salary rises been made: five permanent heads within the two Commissions replaced the original single one, and of these, two were 'super permanent head' rate. 'Post Office "fat cats"', growled the *Review*'s headlines, 'cream it in.'[10]

The Public Service Board joined the fray. Telecom's handling of its management posts, chairman A.S. Cooley informed the Commissioners, had placed the public service in an 'untenable position'. His direct complaint to the Prime Minister that Telecom's management was 'over–salaried and over–classified' prompted Senator McClelland, Minister assisting the Prime Minister on matters relating to the public service, to intervene. To no avail; Senator Bishop declined to budge.

Bishop's position was powerful and secure. It was also anomalous, one of those puzzling loose ends that confuse researchers and arise from either political reluctance or inexperience on the part of Government to carry through an overarching administrative scheme. The commission of inquiry, aware of problems with the British post office and its new ministerial authority, had carefully sidestepped the nomination of a particular Ministry to manage the new Commissions. At first it was considered that the Special Minister of State might carry on the responsibility he and his Department had assumed for the interim Commissions. But there was the matter of a 'dangling' Postmaster–General. There was also the question of the Wireless Telegraphy Act and other unplaced sections of the PMG. Thus despite the dismemberment of the old Department on Vesting Day, Senator Bishop retained the portfolio of Postmaster–General. His Ministerial responsibilities encompassed the brand new Commissions, the OTC, and administration of the Wireless Telegraph Act 1905–73 (which, in its control of the radio frequency spectrum would now license Telecom Australia in the provision of its radio communication systems). The administration of the ABC and the Australian Broadcasting Control Board once within the portfolio had already passed in June 1974 to the Minister of the Media.

Bishop's new Postmaster–General's Department was the rump of its progenitor made up of members of the Australian Stores Supply and Tender Board group, staff in the process of transition between Commissions, and a small administrative staff for the three communications Commissions.[11] F.J. Green, a former secretary of the Department of Air and himself a PMG staffer from 1935–46, was appointed secretary. From 1 July 1975 he became the Department's representative on the Telecommunications and Postal Commissions and OTC. In a move to seal gaps and build bridges, R.W. Turnbull was appointed Telecom's representative on the board of OTC. Bishop would hold his position until the Labor Government was swept from office on 11 November 1975. He was, said one Commission chairman, 'a most impressive Minister, correct in his attitudes'. Undoubtedly Bishop's staunch support for his Commissions, in what was viewed as a Public Service Board bid to thwart the legislative intention and bring the two Commissions back under PSB control, was a crucial stand although a brusque attempt made by Senator McClelland to put pressure on chairmen Gibbs and Kennedy would cost the Telecommunications Commission the chairmanship of A.G. Gibbs.

With the fall of the Whitlam Government and the election of the Liberal–Country Party Coalition under Fraser in December 1975, the Postmaster–General's Department disappeared. In its place rose the new Postal and Telecommunications Department responsible for the country's three communication Commissions. In addition it took on responsibility for ABC radio and television broadcasting policy and for the policy, planning and regulatory function of the administration of radio frequency acquired from the short–lived Ministry of the Media. In a world of kaleidoscopic departmental changes, it would retain this title for the next five years.

Despite criticism, Telecom's advent marked a 'flashpoint transformation'. There was clear purpose in the upgrading of the public servants turned business managers, the executive inner–cabinet which would steer the streamlined telecommunications ship of state. The new top management structure offered a conspicuously different profile from the management organisation of the PMG. In Telecom headquarters there were nine functional areas. Two major directorates, finance and planning, and also the secretariat (headed by Dr R.B. Cullen, P.R. Brett, and S.C. Moon respectively) reported directly to the managing director. The chief general manager, W.J.B. Pollock, with deputy chief general manager, J.R. Smith, took direct responsibility for seven other key departments, engineering, customer services, research, industrial relations, information systems, accounting and supply, and personnel which were led respectively by F.L.C. Taylor, E.R. Banks, E.F. Sandbach, R.C. Stradwick, A. Kellock, S.H. Hansen and J.P. Ahern. This top management team remained stable for the first three years.

E.R. Banks, since 1980 Telecom's director of business development.

At the top of the decision–making tree was the Commission of seven which met and continues to meet on a regular basis once a month. Matters for decision by the Commission are submitted through the managing director in papers which canvass a particular issue and make a recommendation. The Commission may endorse these, refer them back to management for further study, or vary the recommendation. Commission decisions include recommending contracts involving over $0.5 million, determining tariff variations or seeking Ministerial approval for tariff variation of basic services, major organisational changes, borrowing levels, and loans. Additionally, the Commission directs top management on central matters concerning the objectives, operations and forward planning of Telecom.

To link decision–making and to co–ordinate planning, a Headquarters co–ordination committee of top management meets once a month, and quarterly with State managers in attendance, to review progress and act as an advisory and reporting body to the managing director and chief general manager.

Streamlining also occurred in the States. State heads, once Directors of Posts and Telegraphs now Telecom State managers,

Members of the first Australian Telecommunication Commission meet in 1976, to discuss plans for Melbourne's new Exhibition exchange. From left to right: K.C. Turbet, of Melbourne, federal secretary of the Postal Telecommunications Technicians Association; Joan Hancock, of Adelaide, of the South Australian Consumer Credit Tribunal; T.E. May (deputy chairman), of Sydney, marketing manager, Australian Portland Cement; R.D. Somervaille (chairman), of Sydney, solicitor; J.H. Curtis, managing director, Telecom Australia, and F.J. Green, secretary of the Postal and Telecommunications Department.

report directly to the chief general manager. Far–reaching plans were also developed on the advice of management consultants Cresap, McCormick and Paget during 1975 to restructure the very basis of State operational administration. The resulting introduction of 83 geographically organised 'Telecommunication District Managements' (30 in New South Wales, 21 in Victoria, 13 in Queensland, nine in South Australia, seven in Western Australia and three in Tasmania) marked 'the largest organisational change in scope and magnitude attempted for fifty years'.

Implemented gradually from 1977 and in full operation by the end of 1978, the scheme evoked expected opposition from many pro-fessional engineers long resistant to the intrusion of technical and administrative staff in field operations control. Their reservations were deep–seated, for they faced a basic change of role. The formation of district organisations would transform the cultural environment of their institution from one of 'the dominant reign of engineers' to a much wider ethos of communications industry management. While the Australian Professional Engineers Association (APEA) did not, on this occasion, take up the cause, it was vigorously pursued by the Professional Officers Association (POA) whose members contained the bulk of Telecom engineers.[12] It was only after several hearings of the case before the Conciliation and Arbitration Commission and a High Court decision against the engineers, that the scheme went ahead. In the outcome, engineering line management changed and Telecom's largest professional workforce, the engineers, were pressed into more consultative roles in the management, planning and product evalu-ation of the nation's telecommunications giant.

Fundamental changes also underlay the introduction of Telecom

Australia's corporate plan. Planning of all kinds, as this history shows, had become an essential part of the introduction, adaptation, and extension of the national network. Australian telecommunications, as Senator Bishop was to learn, rested on a veritable mountain of plans. Importantly, within months of Vesting Day, Telecom inherited a major ground-plan on which to build. *Telecom 2000*, a study carried out by a national telecommunications planning team of the PMG's Department and Telecom, published in December 1975, provided a speculative and ranging analysis of the social, economic and technological options for telecommunications in Australia to the year 2000. An innovative venture in 'open planning', which drew on three years of study and discussion with industry, government and academia, the report was acclaimed by one Department as 'the first attempt at technology assessment in Australia'. It also found critics in business and government.

Basically, *Telecom 2000* spotlighted the intense interaction between social structures and telecommunications, emphasised the 'turbulent' social conditions that lay ahead, and stressed the importance of decentralisation and flexibility in decision-making to avoid locking society into fixed telecommunications patterns. 'The dangers of increasing social dependency on a single mode of communications', said the report, 'are very real.' Planning for the future should look at real life social differences as they exist in this country, avoid generalised goals like 'The Wired City' or 'The Information Society', and develop 'adaptive' responses. Against this framework, the report projected a range of alternatives of growth and development of different types of telecommunications technology and services that could arise in response to Australian social and economic needs.[13]

While *Telecom 2000* generated less public discussion of these important issues than its authors hoped (*Outcomes from the Telecom 2000 report* summarised the response), it had a marked impact on Telecom managers and planners in orienting their traditional, engineering-based thinking to the concept that telecommunications development should be governed by broad forward and flexible plans.[14]

The commission of inquiry had also recognised the need for the new Telecommunications Commission to strengthen its strategic planning. The Corporate Plan, initiated in 1975 and launched in 1977, became the centre-piece of this edifice, 'superimposed', in the managing director's words, 'as a capstone plan, on top of, and to give guidance to, the already existing but incomplete set of plans and programmes that had been built over a number of years in the Australian Post Office'.

The description was a simplification. Tactical planning on technological, administrative, manpower, operational and financial fronts was central to an organisation like Telecom or the PMG. Corporate planning was strategic and institutional and directed at wide and fundamental long-term goals. In 1975 corporate planning was substantially a new discipline in Australia; a new tool for new times. Essentially it offered planning to identify and handle corporate issues, explore financial possibilities and timing, and formulate options and tactical as well as other approaches within an environment that was subject to considerable social, political, technological and economic change.

The adapters of the new technique were a small planning directorate team who shaped the plan with ongoing consultation with the managing director, headquarters departments, and operational inputs from the States. Telecom unions were given the opportunity to comment, but the major unions PTTA and APTU, considered the scope of the proffered participation to be inadequate.

The plan, encompassing Telecom's charter under the Act, had four corporate thrusts: service and its improvement to meet customer needs; efficiency in the organisational structure and work environment; staff relations and development, and technological improvement. Such aims were broad. For the ten years from 1977 to 1987, the plan projected a specific series of targets which included a continuing decline in the real cost of telecommunications; a continuing investment programme to provide the availability and diversity of services; particular attention to the needs of small businesses and rural subscribers; STD penetration of 90 per cent of the country by 1980, and 95 per cent by 1987; greater efficiency from the 'timely introduction of new technology'; and a telephone in nine out of ten Australian homes by 1987.[15]

The plan generated a spate of documents. Background papers and reports on 'corporate policies', 'planning and programming processes', flowed off the production line. Workshops generated more proceedings and more papers. As a recognised leader in corporate planning, Telecom representatives were invited to demonstrate and discuss corporate planning methodology with interested Australian organisations. Evolving, reshaping, and couched at times in daunting bureaucratic prose, the corporate plan cast its influence across the spectrum of Telecom activities. An overseas visit by the directorate's chief planning officer in 1979 resulted in recommendations to update it and introduce a regular cycle of re-evaluation every two or three years. Overseas 'telcos' had found it prudent to lean towards generalisation in their corporate plans and a similar course was urged on Telecom.[16]

Within the organisation, the plan's presence was symbolic. Vernon had personally emphasised the need for clear direction and new management skills. A 'target and achievement oriented management' became Telecom's pre-eminent institutional aim. While top management of the new enterprise was drawn entirely from PMG men, new staff were recruited at senior middle management level, management training was strengthened with the customer in view, and special importance attached to encouraging key engineering staff to adapt themselves via postgraduate training in business, commerce or management, to become 'management planners'. Of the leading management troika, only Jack Curtis was an engineer. Chief General Manager Pollock, a junior mechanic when he entered the Victorian PMG's Department, added a degree in commerce before he returned to the Department after wartime service. His deputy, Jim Smith, was an accountant with wide experience in administration.

Smith was essentially a 'no nonsense' management man. 'More management and less manpower' was his insistent theme. 'Opportunity' was another precept of his creed. 'It concentrated people's minds', he said. Appropriately Smith was assigned the task of overseeing the internal organisation of Telecom and of implementing the controversial telecommunications district management plan. It was largely his persistence and argument that overcame the engineers' entrenched opposition to the plan. The first eight districts were established at Canberra, Wagga Wagga (NSW), Camberwell, Ivanhoe and Frankston (Victoria), and Metropolitan Central, North and South, South Australia, in March 1977; others followed in the remaining States in July that year, and the scheme was fully operational by 1978. 'Telecom', Smith encouraged his engineers as results rolled in, 'exists to provide service. Parliament has given us a service charter. But Telecom has been told not to produce service at any cost; Parliament has also charged us with the responsibility to operate as efficiently and economically as practicable keeping tariffs as low as practicable.' The Government should have no cause for 'dissatisfaction with our performance'.[17]

J.R. Smith, Telecom's former deputy chief general manager, who, in 1983, was appointed chief manager of the Victorian State Electricty Commission.

After its first year, it was clear that bustling, business–oriented Telecom was off to a flying start. An overall surplus of $152.4 million spun off the pages of its first annual report. There had been careful financial target–setting. When the Australian Telecommunications Commission took over in July 1975, Telecom had net assets of approximately $4,000 million, 3½ million telephone subscribers, and a projected budget for its first year of operation of approximately $1,900 million. It needed, however (in addition to funds to meet inflation and expansion), an extra $32 million for interest on past profits which had been converted to Commonwealth advances and some $118 million for the policy set by the Act of financing at least 50 per cent of its capital expenditure from internal sources. Contrastingly, the PMG's Department had furnished only 38 per cent of its capital expenditure from internal funds. In short, Telecom required an additional $150 million in earnings to meet the financial gap in its first financial year. It was not surprising, then, that Gibbs's introductory act as chairman of the permanent Commission in July 1975 was to announce significant tariff increases to a total of 28 per cent across the telecommunications services board.[18]

Local telephone calls, an area of overall loss in country regions only minimally offset by metropolitan returns, rose across the nation from six to nine cents. Telegrams, a shrinking field of activity dogged by loss and rising operational costs, rose by three cents a word. Short distance trunk calls were increased (long distance trunks had risen the year before), and the cost of operator–connected calls — a labour–intensive requirement — rose in regions where STD could be used. The practice of charging higher rentals for business telephones had been reintroduced by the PMG in 1974. The new Commission endorsed the reasoning that 'the telephone was of greater value to the business sector' (its contribution to the 'equity' theme), and increased business rentals by 42 per cent against 31 per cent for non–business telephones. The charge for new connections, an area where buoyant growth was anticipated at least for another five years, rose by 50 per cent. Even so, as the Commission chairman made plain (for the consumer needed constant reminders of the point) the connection charge took care of only a fraction of the real cost of adding a new telephone to the network. The cost in 1975, which covered use of junctions, now averaged about $2,000. Telex and data modem charges also rose.[19]

Outside the established concessions to rural residents, there was only a faint nod to the concept that the 'haves' must support the 'have nots'. The 33⅓ per cent concession on calls and telegrams for Darwin residents introduced after Cyclone Tracy was maintained from January until September 1975. Similar 33⅓ per cent concessions on rental charges for certain pensioners were continued although Gibbs omitted to note that Telecom recouped the concessional difference from the Department of Social Security; and there were noticeable cuts in the list of charities once offered concessional rents. The new Commission set a 'hardnosed' business style. There was also a clear emphasis on customer 'needs' and plans were announced for the introduction in Australia of the internationally popular push–button telephone during Telecom's first financial year.

Such firm financial planning brought returns. Despite tariff jumps and stagflation (a combination of stagnation and inflation in the national economy), there were substantial rises in network growth at the year's end in June 1976. Telex services grew by 16 per cent, the small but fast moving data service rose by 50 per cent, telephone connections by 4.6 per cent, local calls by 5 per cent and trunk line calls by 7 per cent. The year's operation, Telecom's first annual report summed up, 'represented a quite formidable task of management'. Over and above the change from Department to Commission status, 'there were new financial and staffing responsibilities, the drive to improve service, . . . the general economic conditions, the continuing attention to industrial relations, and the requirement to establish in the public mind the existence of Telecom Australia'.[20]

In retrospect, Curtis attributed Telecom's instant 'lift–off' to the 'successful setting of financial targets'. But there was also one important political factor that got up a lively wind. The advent of the Fraser Government in December 1975 was to have profound consequences for the new Telecommunications Commission. In the first instance, it led, in the economic uncertainties of early 1976, to a Government call for restraint in public sector borrowing and expenditure. The decision impinged on Telecom's attitudes. Management views of improving efficiency found reinforcement in Government policy of cutting the public sector. 'It influenced top management', one executive summed up, 'and tended to reinforce our existing viewpoint.' The Commission's immediate agreement to reduce its borrowings by $11 million increased its internally generated funds from 50 per cent to 53 per cent. It was a commitment that would expand to 56 per cent in 1977 and to a dramatic 68 per cent in 1978.[21]

In Australia's telecommunications context, two very different

Governments tailored change. Whitlam's reforming Labor Government pioneered and created the new statutory authority with business effectiveness and greater independence in mind. The Liberal–Country Party Coalition Government's impetus to 'cutting public sector ceilings' added its influence to the Commission's early run.

Telecom Australia would strengthen its financial performance in the next two years. With pressure clamped on budget deficits, the Government in May 1976, pushed the Commission from budget funding to public borrowing. The first Telecom's managing director knew of this important decision was when, to his considerable surprise, he read of it in the newspapers. The move required an amendment to the founding Act.[22] Under Eric Robinson, appointed to the newly named portfolio of Post and Telecommunications in February 1976, Telecom was pushed into the loan market.[23] Other Commonwealth and State instrumentalities had obtained funds from this area for many years, and in the present tight economic circumstances, pressure on the market was large. Telecom's need to raise $200 million was a substantial entry into a highly competitive field.

What strategy should the Commission employ? Essentially Telecom needed to 'position' its loans away from the semi–Government loans. Information gathered from underwriting brokers and some merchant banks suggested that a new and forward–looking authority could differentiate its stock in the market by offering Telecom securities that were more marketable than other such loans. The plan meant attracting small investors by making it easier to sell stock should they need and to be able to obtain higher prices for this stock.

Yet Telecom's situation was unusual. A research survey commissioned to explore Telecom's prospects in the loan market in August 1976 yielded a grim scenario. Very early in the survey it became clear that a Telecom loan might be hard to sell. Basically, the public still viewed Telecom as part of the Government itself. There was little interest in Government loans and 'outright hostility' from those who believed that Telecom 'profits' were too high. 'Among a section of the investing public', said the consultant's research report, 'Telecom itself has a distinctly unfavourable image compounded of extravagance, inefficiency and high cost to the consumer coupled with large profits for itself.' To this sector, 'the idea of investing in such an enterprise for a comparatively scanty "government type" return is anathema'.[24] The Treasury added its warning that the best Telecom might hope to raise was a loan of $60 million.

The Commission, however, pressed ahead. Its notable innovation under amendment of its Act was to set up a market in its own stock and to trade on its own securities. As no other semi–Government body enjoyed this right by legislation, Telecom gained a marketing advantage which became a major plank in its loan promotional campaign. Directed to the small investor as well as to the major institutional market, Telecom's 'keeping you in touch with tomorrow' loan, was launched in September 1976 and fully subscribed to the required $200 million by 5 October that year.

Its success was instructive to both Telecom and other marketeers. It was the largest semi–government loan ever floated, four times larger than any previous Australian loan, and its underwriting agreement devised with Telecom's financial consultants, Hill Samuel Australia, offering small investors a 'readily marketable security' with Commonwealth Government backing, was a distinguishing step. It was also the first national loan campaign run by a statutory authority to take advantage of the post office network to receive applications throughout the Commonwealth. Telecom also enjoyed a further advantage over its competitors in the use of the telephone network at no cost to provide a free telephone loan inquiry service in each State. The loan's marketability was also rigorously tested by large institutional investors who moved large parcels of stock immediately after the loan closed. In the event, Telecom's loan promise had proven to be a fact.

The breakthrough into the open market would have fundamental consequences for Telecom. Henceforth its capital expenditure on its expanding network would be underwritten by successive annual loans varied in 1978–9 to use a syndicated approach.

But the matter of Telecom's annual 'surpluses' needed to be clarified. They reached $164.4 million and $185 million in the second and third financial years. Charges had been kept static, reduced Sunday rates were provided on STD, but the troublesome word 'profit' continued to bedazzle Telecom's affairs. 'The public and sections of the media', lamented the annual report of 1978, 'have difficulty in comprehending the need for a public utility to make a profit of this size.' The question of cutting prices and operating at a lower profit had been raised during the year. But the report argued, if prices were cut, alternative capital sources would have to be found to counter blockages in applications for Telecom service.[25] Would the public never learn! Had they access to the new statutory body's glossy annual reports (which had won an award from the Australian Institute of Management for 'distinguished achievement' in reporting in 1976–7), they would no doubt have imbibed the point that profits were available 'interest free and thus an important factor in keeping prices down'. The interest was paid, in effect, by subscribers who paid for services.

One man who publicly hammered this point was Robert Somervaille, Gibbs's successor as chairman of the Commission in September 1975. Somervaille, a lucid, fast talker from whom ideas and enthusiasm tumbled forth like spring rain, wanted strong growth, higher efficiency and upgraded service, and the ploughing back of profits for fresh capital expansion to keep customer prices down in the years ahead. Well connected with merchant banking, it was Somervaille who piloted and backed Commission strategy for Telecom's access to extensive loan funds and who proved an articulate advocate for an organisation and service that was taken for granted in almost every home.[26]

With top management, Somervaille also gave special attention to Telecom's business and marketing thrust. The internal direction of this operation lay with the general manager, customer services, Roger Banks. An engineer turned management planner, Banks had been a key participant in the national automatic numbering and switching objectives (ANSO) committee and community telephone plan of 1960, had assisted the introduction of the computer trunk switching technology (designated 10C) in 1969, and as a member of an APO Task Force had worked on the structuring of Telecom. Between 1972 and 1974, he had left the PMG's Department to become director of strategic planning for Plessey Telecommunications in Britain and brought an understanding of private industry to his experience. For Banks, 'efficient marketing' opened up a broad route for Telecom. 'The first challenge', he told a Telecom audience, 'is to ensure that we don't let our present monopoly responsibilities and our position as a Government Commission blind us to the need to perform in the market–place to satisfy customers.' Telecom, he stressed, needed to perform as 'a vital, respected, national telecommunications service utility with whom customers want to do business' and escape the danger of becoming 'a moribund bureaucratic monopoly only providing services which private entrepreneurs do not consider worth the effort: in short a gutter utility'.[27]

Banks's views were prescient. They were also well–informed. The concept of a monopoly common carrier, matured over the century in Australia, was deeply implanted in Telecom. But there were threatened incursions at home and abroad. In Britain early in 1978 Conservative leaders pledged that a returned Tory Government would move to 'liberalise' the British post office monopoly and allow competition by industry. Similar 'liberalising interconnections' had started in the USA a decade before at the expense of the monopolistic, though private, common carrier AT&T.[28] In Australia there was early movement. On Vesting Day 1975 the chairman of the recently formed Australian Telecommunications Development Association (ATDA), T.E. Hodgkinson, had published an article in the *Sydney Morning Herald*, declaring that the inception of the new Commission gave industry, the Commission itself, and the public an excellent opportunity to 'look afresh' at the whole business of providing telecommunications in Australia. There was, said Hodgkinson, 'no logical reason why the administration should do other than provide the network and act as the "common carrier" as long as the devices connected to the network meet the interface requirements'. The production of a competitive range of terminals, PABX switchboards, extensions and other services and add–on equipment, restrictively standardised under the control of the APO, he argued, should be opened to the competitive development of the Australian telecommunications industry.[29]

Such proposals were strong stimulants to Telecom. Clearly the Commission and management's brief and that of the State district organisation was to change the environment of service, widen its range and accessibility and offer a new spectrum of special business services. The approach marked an important passage. 'We in Telecom', Banks conceptualised, 'are moving from the first major period of telecommunications history when we built the networks, into the second major period where the challenge is to take and utilise these networks, relate the capability we have to our customers, and fulfil the first injunction in any book on business "to maximise returns on our invested assets".[30]

It was not mere rhetoric. By 1978 it was already apparent that Telecom Australia was a more efficient organisation in its financial and service performance than the one it had replaced. In providing telephone service, it had faced a near record backlog of waiting applications carried over from a decade during which the PMG failed to meet a steadily rising demand. By 1975 the high level of demand had been somewhat slowed by decline in the economy and by successive tariff increases in 1973 and 1974. The further tariff increase of September 1975 slowed demand again and placed Telecom in a good position, with its adequate plant reserves, to reduce the number of waiting applications and meet a high demand that was expected to continue for a number of years. When telephone charges remained constant after 1975, demand revived and increased beyond all expectations to record levels. After 1978 waiting lists grew again. It was then that the district organisations, with their strong emphasis on customer service, proved their worth. By 1978–9 the speed of new telephone connections had improved progressively towards the target of 90 per cent of new telephone service orders completed within three weeks.[31] 'After three years', Deputy Chief General Manager Smith summed up, 'target setting and target achievement have become embedded in our way of working. We are truly managing for results.'

Within the network, landmark developments were occurring. International subscriber dialling (ISD) was introduced in conjunction with OTC to 13 countries in 1976 and to some 70 by mid–1978. Not surprisingly in a country where postwar immigrants made up a quarter of the population, the impact of the service on national telephone usage was marked. Britain, the USA, New Zealand, Italy and Papua New Guinea headed the destination list. The image of a country in touch, linking its people intimately by a telephone dial to relatives around the world flashed its human and commercial message from television's advertising screens. It was a far cry from the total ex–communication of Australia's first emigrants and a significant jump from the manual bookings and often interrupted overseas calls of two decades before. The use of trunk services, spurred by advertising of lower charges in off peak hours, also soared. (See Appendix IV.)

On the domestic front the Commission celebrated a 'milestone in network development' when the four millionth telephone service was connected in November 1977. A year earlier the decision had been made to upgrade existing telephone switching equipment with computer controlled components. Telecom was positioning itself for a new age of computer controlled local telephone switching equipment for its urban exchanges, while digital switching was arriving to update links between telephone exchanges. (See Chapter 14.)

For the newly focussed business market, a procession of new services was in the pipeline. Telex advanced rapidly at home and overseas and new machines were added. Datel services also showed a notable rise. It was Pollock who had spurred these 'services of the future' in the last PMG years. Demand for datel services doubled between Telecom's first year of operation and 1978 as banks, business houses and industry moved into the transmission of computerised data by telephone for their geographically dispersed operations. It was expected, said Pollock as chief general manager in 1978, that while the bulk of Telecom's operations would continue to be centred around the flow of traffic generated by the telephone, data services would represent a growing proportion of the Commission's business as the growth of private networks and the development of facilities with greater compatibility and utility continues.[32]

In the field of broadcasting, Telecom, as contractor to the Department of Post and Telecommunications for the construction and maintenance of the national television transmitters, sped the spread of TV broadcasting. The PMG's Department had completed its long service to broadcasting with the introduction of colour television in March 1975. Telecom inherited the spread of this technology to cities and provincial regions. In terms of distance covered, the spread was fast. Penetration of black and white television in Australia had been surprisingly swift. From its first beginnings in 1956, television grew at a faster rate initially in Australia than in Britain or America where it had started 10 years earlier. Eighty–one per cent of Australian homes had television within the first 10 years (compared with 44 per cent in Britain and 79 per cent in the USA). As colour dawned, an estimated 94 per cent of Australian homes had television sets, a figure that Telecom helped push to 97 per cent in 1978.[33]

Like the population, however, distribution was centred around cities and country towns. In so large a country where transmitters were scattered across vast and often difficult terrain, reception was fluctuating and often poor. There were regions of total rural blackout. By the late 1970s television reached only a 44 per cent cover in the country of the Northern Territory. There were also pockets of radio silence. As the Australian Broadcasting Commission celebrated its 50th anniversary in 1982 (surprisingly free from any reference to the feats of technical transmission that carried it across the land), one irate resident of New South Wales complained that it remained 'a sick joke' that the ABC could claim that it would be 'inconceivable without the ABC' while thousands of Australians living in New South Wales coastal towns 100 miles from Canberra, 'have never ever had ABC radio!'[34]

Telecom would assist with a further major broadcasting development in 1976, the permanent introduction of FM radio broadcasting in Australia built upon the Whitlam cabinet's decision of September 1974. As Minister for the Media in 1975, Moss Cass had outlined plans for the largest single increase in the range of radio broadcasting services since the war and, after some resistance from Postmaster–General Bishop at the 'riskiness' of the scheme, formally announced the offer of new 'public interest' radio broadcasting licences in August that year. The project met snags. Peter Nixon as Postmaster–General in Fraser's caretaker Government of November

1975 wanted public interest broadcasting accommodated in off–peak periods by commercial stations in low rating times. However, the first four stations of the national FM broadcasting network began transmission on 24 January 1976. Just as new Australian settlers from Europe were able to telephone their relatives with greater ease, they would increasingly be able to use ethnic radio and television programmes to keep them in contact with their cultural roots.

The Telecommunications Commission had presided over phenomenal progress in its first four years. New concepts of service, organisation and planning had been introduced and a new mode of fiscal management begun. Telecom Australia registered an annual rise in productivity of 5–8 per cent in the period 1975–8, an increase of 2–4 per cent per annum above such rises in the telecommunications sector of the PMG's last decade. As managing director Curtis summed up progress, 'The Commission squeezed the network for the first few years'. In effect, productivity grew, while Telecom set itself to carry a reduced level of plant reserves. In a period of expensive capital and steep interest rates, one available 'squeeze' was to crop the amount of plant embedded in the system for use in future years by installing cables for shorter life–spans and reducing exchange increments from five to two years or less. It was a deliberate decision to build a network to finer margins so as to reduce capital investment and keep charges down. While the concept of 'fine tuning' made Telecom more vulnerable to forecasting inaccuracies and material delays, it made keen financial sense in the organisation's inaugural years.[35]

Yet Telecom Australia faced problems. Its important external borrowings depended on Government policy and Loan Council approval despite the favourable showing of its innovative loans. Indeed the very success of the loan achievements was to stir considerable hostility from the States. Its commitment to the introduction of new switching technology to update its network and increase efficiency raised turbulent questions on the industrial front. Finally the very strength of Telecom's performance posed a threat. A buoyant telecommunications authority testified plainly to the business community that telecommunications would be a profitable growth industry in the years ahead.

The Commission, however, had got up a lively speed. There was marked institutional confidence. As one journalist noted, there was an 'intense atmosphere that does not fit with the popular stereotype of the Public Service, be that fact or myth. It does seem after an hour's interview with these men, that mañana to them means the eager promise of tomorrow and what can be done with it.'[36]

14 The 'New Luddites'?

Despite its remarkable achievements, one aspect of Telecom that appeared conspicuously less than successful in its formative years was the management's relations with some unions. By 1978 Telecom Australia stood at the centre of an industrial dispute that shook the nation. In PMG days there had been a serious confrontation during 1966 over the introduction of an electronic mail sorter at Redfern mail exchange, Sydney, which culminated in a national strike. But there had also been much positive collaboration. The major unions and staff associations had contributed importantly to the commission of inquiry of 1972–3. The commission's report had praised the Department's general record of industrial harmony and, as preparations for the two new Commissions went ahead, a special PMG task force 12 was formed under Spratt to ensure close and continuing association between the 23 staff associations (see Appendix III), the Department, and the Minister. Three union task forces also emerged; the Telecommunications Union Group of 17 unions, cosily entitled TUG, PUG the Postal Union Group, and the combined Joint Union Group, JUG, which would work in consultation with PMG managers on problems common to both Commissions.

These groups dissolved on Vesting Day. In their place that day, the Telecommunications Consultative Council was established under the Telecommunications Act and its by–laws. Made up of seven senior representatives of Telecom and ten representatives of the staff organisations, its functions were plainly defined. It would look at conditions of employment, welfare, health and safety, staff amenities, training and personnel policies, and keep association members informed of Telecom's operations and progress. But it would not deal with pay and classifications and, significantly, the question of technological change and its consequences for staff was not included in its ambit.

This omission was a deliberate union choice. In the drafting of plans for the Consultative Council, the PMG had suggested that two further committees be established, one on 'notice of technological change', the other on dispute settlement.[1] But in April 1975 Alan

Kemp, spokesman for JUG, notified that neither matters came into the category of 'consultative processes' and should be handled in separate discussion between Telecom and each union, on an individual basis and case by case.[2] The decision bore two unions' stamp. The 26,000 strong Postal Telecommunications Technicians Association (PTTA) and the equally substantial Australian Postal Workers Union (APWU) declined to be hamstrung in their negotiations with management by a medley of small 'house' unions. A combined union consultative process on technological change and industrial disputes, would, as the PTTA's Federal Secretary pointed out, weaken his union's capacity to bargain and 'weave its way through the pack'.[3] The decision, emasculating to the Consultative Council, was to have fateful consequences both for Telecom and PTTA's successor, the Australian Telecommunications Employees Association (ATEA).

From its inception, Telecom's commitment to a steeply rising growth rate and improved customer services through a policy of manpower containment and organisational change unsettled the technical unions. Telecom Australia, as one staff bulletin put it, 'makes no apology for either seeking to sustain growth by improving productivity, or seeking to provide its customers with new and better facilities'.[4] Such imperative emphasis on high productivity and customer service was not singular to Australia. In the burgeoning environment of the mid–1970s, it was typical of 'telcos' around the world. But how could it be achieved? The answer was computerised automation.

Since the famous community telephone plan of 1959–60, to introduce a national telephone numbering system and STD, and the

Installation staff working on a new crossbar exchange of a type that was increasingly replacing the electro-mechanical step-by-step model around Australia.

related decision to adopt Ericsson's crossbar system for swifter connection of subscriber calls, electromagnetic exchanges had been upgraded across Australia. The original 'step–by–step' automatic exchanges still worked their way (reaching a peak of usage in 1964), but crossbar local and trunk switching systems — the ARF, ARK and ARM — with their evolving improvements, now formed the sturdy backbone of the great telephone switching network of the nation. Yet, with an increasing load of data and voice transmission in the telecommunications service, Australia, like other industrialised countries, needed to consider new computerised switching systems then penetrating telecommunications services in Europe, North America and Japan.

First the transistor, then the integrated circuit chip and later the microprocessor had revolutionised telephone switching abroad. The stored programme control systems — SPC as they were called — with their electronic components miniaturised down to fingertip–size silicon chips, and with modular packaging, offered striking advantages over the bulky and space–consuming crossbar equipment. SPC took the pressure off costly building space; it was cheaper to buy, simpler to install and more reliable to operate. It also provided computerised charging and billing systems, powerful diagnostic facilities for location and correction of network faults and improved network use. For tele-phone buffs it paraded a range of customer facilities. It could, for example, provide an absent subscriber service, install 'hot lines', offer automatic wake–up or 'do not disturb' facilities, trace malicious calls ('bad news for heavy breathers' noted the *National Times*), and furnish abbreviated dialling for frequently used numbers. Those concerned

The first SPC (stored programme control) electronic trunk exchange outside the capital cities was this Bendigo (Victoria) 10C exchange, opened, in October 1978, by the Hon. A.A. Staley, Minister for Post and Telecommunications, in the presence of (from left) Ken Medlin, district Telecom manager, Bendigo; Don Wake, supervising engineer, Bendigo; and Max Smith, Telecom state manager, Victoria.

with individual privacy did not fail to note that SPC offered substantial surveillance capacity.[5]

A first step towards adopting some part of this dynamic new generation of switching equipment had in fact already been taken by the PMG in 1969. In that year planners chose the 'Metaconta 10C system' developed by Bell Manufacturing Company, Belgium, and four years later accepted the successful tender of STC Australia for the system. 10C was brought into service in Sydney in 1974 as a large trunk switcher alternative to crossbar, and installations followed in major trunk exchanges in all mainland capitals.

During 1973 investigations had also been set in train to explore the viability of introducing computerised switching systems for *local* exchanges, an area of potentially large development in Australia. The one absolute requirement for their adoption, as for the adoption of the SPC trunk system, was compatibility with the existing network. The old must integrate with the new. It must also promise a long lifetime. Following an exploratory visit by a team of management and engineering planners to inspect the competing systems overseas, the PMG called for tenders for computerised local switching in December 1974 to evaluate its applicability for Australia.

Telecom Australia would inherit the decision-making for this stride forward into a new technological age. By mid–1976 the choice of local switching systems was narrowed down to two — to the 10C family system and L.M. Ericsson's 'AXE'. Further assessment and a

Below right: The first entirely electronic local exchange was this L.M. Ericsson equipped AXE exchange, which opened in 1981 in the Melbourne suburb of Endeavour Hills.

Below: Technician monitoring an AXE computer control terminal in Melbourne's Batman exchange, 1983.

visit to Sweden and Belgium to inspect the systems in operation led by managing director Curtis, Telecom's director of finance, Cullen, and the superintending engineer of telephone switching planning, K.W. Power, resulted in Telecom's recommendation for the Ericsson AXE. Despite a delaying review of Telecom's decision pressed upon the Government by STC Australia anxious to gain the marketing advantage in South–East Asia that the successful tenderer would reap, the Commonwealth Government announced its acceptance of the AXE system in September 1977. 'It was', commented Curtis, 'the biggest technical decision in the country's telecommunications history, and the most fundamental.' AXE — its name would gather dire connotations for the workers as time went on — was, in the managing director's words, 'the most suitable system for economic application in Australian urban networks'.[6]

In addition, before and behind this important decision, another link in the euphonious alphabet of switching systems was under way. Plans had been announced by the PMG's Department in October 1974 for the proposed modernisation of parts of the crossbar switching system by the addition of Ericsson's computerised 'ARE 11' equipment designed to upgrade local exchange capacity and provide an aligning bridge with the envisaged AXE local exchange. A model ARE 11 was installed at Telecom Headquarters in 1975 and staff were advised that experimental ARE 11 field trial equipment would be introduced in exchanges at Elsternwick, Victoria, and at Salisbury, South Australia, in 1975–6.

Hence from 1975–7, as a result of both PMG planning and decisions made by Telecom, Australia was launched into a wholly new phase of automated telecommunications technology. The technical decisions came traditionally from the engineers. There were supportive economic assessments. But the wider question of worker impact was not addressed. Technological advancement was taken for granted among the 'tribal culture' of PMG and Telecom engineers. The unions' Commissioner, Ken Turbet, was also involved in the decision–making of the special committee established on AXE. But in all cases, the determinations were virtual *faits accomplis* by the time they reached the ranks of the technical staff.

Deep concern about ARE 11 would surface as the field trials began. ARE 11 exchange equipment combining computer technology with electromechanical telephone exchanges was the first SPC (stored programme control) system to raise significant implications for technical workers. Essentially the computerised equipment augured massive changes in work style and organisation for many Telecom exchange technicians. Since their long haul to status and higher responsibility, the technicians had become the true inheritors of major telecommunications change. The progressive automation that, from the mid–1950s, had dislocated and diminished first the telegraphists and later the telephonists, swelled the technicians' ranks. Since crossbar's introduction, the technicians themselves had faced con-siderable and, for some, traumatic change. While crossbar, like 'step–by–step', was an electromechanical exchange it used control logic which some older technicians found difficult to grasp.

As one high–placed manager observed, 'technicians who imagined that a small bus was wheeling round the corner found themselves facing a high-speeding train instead!' ARE 11's stored programme control provided for highly centralised direction. Data covering subscriber, exchange and a network–dependent information were stored in one location. Supervision and correction of the network was carried out by remote control, while the old challenging, but satisfying, manual fault–rectification of the crossbar system was accomplished by a 'card changing technique'. Control management, once distributed across many exchanges, was lodged in national and regional support centres and in a small number (29 were proposed across the country) of 'exchange maintenance centres' (EMCs). The SPC exchange, as man-agement itself acknowledged, required 'a change in maintenance philosophy and practice'.[7]

To the 3,000 or so Telecom technical staff engaged in metropolitan exchange maintenance, however, the message had a deeper meaning. J. Kreger, a long time PMG employee and ATEA unionist, who worked in Telecom's training division before retirement, summed it up. The older technicians he said, were particularly alienated by Telecom's new 'gung-ho' style of management. Many of them 'had lived Telecom' (and the PMG). When Telecom dropped 'its paternalistic attitude' and began moving staff to meet new technological needs, the older men, said Kreger, 'started to hate Telecom and all the more so because they were trapped because of their age'. The organisation's change in maintenance philosophy and practice challenged the lifetime activity of these men and, in their view, 'just discountenanced and disregarded the contribution they had made to the system'. Inevitably the bond between these technicians and management broke. 'That sort of bond', said Kreger, 'doesn't come out of management training schools.'[8]

Certainly for all metropolitan exchange technicians, the ARE 11 meant lower manhour maintenance, the loss of satisfying fault-finding and correction tasks, and a decline in responsibility for important detection and maintenance work. It meant, in short, deskilling and, except for a small elite corps of trained specialist staff at the maintenance centres, loss of job satisfaction, lower classifications and reduced career paths.

Hence, while crossbar modernisation by ARE 11 was scheduled for completion in 1982, staff discontent rose sharply through 1977. 'They call us a bunch of Luddites', said ATEA Federal President, Colin Cooper, in a *National Times* interview, recalling the displaced textile workers who had smashed labour-threatening machinery as the first Industrial Revolution took off: but unionists believed (as the first Luddites had done) that there were vital social questions about the effects of automation and, in this case, computerisation that must be examined before a large-scale programme went ahead. The technicians did not object to new machines. The ATEA, in fact, had become one of the first unions in Australia to negotiate a working week of 36¾ hours in exchange for productivity increases. It was not the technology but the change in the social relations of production and in the freedom and dignity of work that threatened them.[9]

The Australian dilemma was far from unique. Repercussions of the computer switching revolution reverberated overseas. 'Electronic telephone exchanges', the general secretary of the Postal, Telegraph and Telephone International warned in 1977, 'will in a relatively short time, reduce levels of work, skills and qualifications of the staff in a manner for which there is no precedent in our sector.' Workers should insist, he advised, that the introduction of the new technology be determined 'not merely by commercial and technical considerations but equally by social needs and the necessity to protect the livelihood of workers'.[10]

Within Telecom Australia dissatisfaction turned on the lack of adequate consultation between management and staff. The general manager of industrial relations, Richard Stradwick, son of a former

PMG Director–General, had joined Telecom from the Public Service Board on Vesting Day. An effective, aggressive–style negotiator, it was Stradwick who issued the swelling flood of information bulletins on the planned operation of ARE 11 and who carried on discussions with the union as specific matters arose. Six years later from a directorship in industry, Stradwick considered that there was a failure in Telecom to plan on the human side. 'Planning for change did not', he said, 'find its way through the organisation as it should.'[11]

In perpetuating a polarised mode of consultation both sides were at fault. Without the existence of a top management consultative committee on technological change, a proposal the unions had flatly rejected in 1975, the technical staff found themselves on the receiving end of management explanations and messages on the new technology, some decidedly inane. 'The decision on modernisation', said one such, 'is a bit like moving up to a better and safer car. If you want to, you can fit safety glass, disc brakes, automatic transmission and radial tyres to your old model car; but frankly its cheaper to buy a new car fitted with these particularly when maintenance costs are taken into account.' Yet in a world of 'keeping up with the Joneses', there was no consideration that older technology, like old model cars, could serve satisfactorily for many more years. Union leaders also failed to address this point. Telecommunications technology carried its own persuasive imperative. Some union leaders indeed seemed more concerned with the threat to the size and authority of their organisation through shrinkage of memberships and subscription than with the larger themes. But the man in the middle, the involved technician, had reasonable grounds for fear, and management talk of 'natural wastage' plus assurances that staff 'could expect to be deployed to areas of higher priority but there were no retrenchments' did not alter the stark fact that, after years of training and rising status, technical career prospects appeared in jeopardy.[12]

The lack of a broad–based consultative process led to confrontations and, following management's definition of job roles in the ARE 11 exchange maintenance centres in May 1977, to a hearing before the Conciliation and Arbitration Commission in June that year. Commissioner Isaac's judgment that ATEA should submit its written proposals for the maintenance of the trial exchanges to Telecom management, while management considered the proposals in the light of the merits of the union case, formed the prelude for an unfolding industrial conflict that would disrupt the nation.

In the gathering clash two contrasting positions were clear. Telecom's approach to the computerised technology was governed by an engineering orientation tied to economic factors that, hitherto unchallenged, had shaped Australia's telecommunications development for the past 130 years. We need a new switching system, their argument ran, to provide a modern network of world standard and to furnish customers with facilities at least cost. Without the new technology, network costs would rise, demand for service fall, and overall staff requirement decline. Telecom offered altered responsibility and roles, substantial immediate improvement for top staff in metropolitan exchanges and an increase in these positions by 1985, a net reduction in middle order technical grades, but no reduction in the total technical workforce. Training would be provided to develop a pool of technical staff 'continually applying their skills'.

The ATEA's case, alternatively, rested on the fundamental human aspiration of job satisfaction for the full complement of its members, continuing apprenticeships and training, career opportunities, the retention of hard–won expertise, and the performance of functions that would meet the 'best interests of the Australian community'.

At the core of the difference was an important matter of degree. ATEA's proposal for management's consideration sought a wider spread of technical work groups (and hence technician responsibility) in all metropolitan exchanges where ARE 11 was introduced in place of the tighter concentration of specialist groups of technicians central to the new EMCs. This, Telecom countered, would add costs 'reaching at least $93 million by 1990'. It was, said Commission chairman Somervaille, 'a heavy price to be paid by our customers when the ATEA proposals offer no new service benefits'. As events unfolded, it was a stance on the introduction of technological, as distinct from social costs, that would cost Telecom Australia considerably more than $93 million by 1982.

The disagreement, stalemated internally in 1977, would erupt nationally in June 1978. Various discontents now coloured the technicians' case. One was the growing polarisation in Telecom's technical ranks. A new starting classification of 'tradesmen' had been established to replace the hierarchy of assistant technicians and their immediate tier of advancement in 1970–1. By 1978 numbers within the technical workforce had undergone significant change. 'Technicians' had dropped by approximately 1,000 since the establishment of Telecom, while the 'tradesman' classification had jumped in the

Key unionists at the heart of the rising dispute. On the left George Slater, APTU general secretary, who joined the PMG in 1950, and served as General Secretary of the APWU (later the APTU) from 1963 to 1983. A Commissioner of the Australian Postal Commission from 1975 to 1980, and a member of the ACTU executive from 1981 to 1983, Slater was to be appointed a Telecom commissioner in December 1983. On the right, Ken Turbet, ATEA federal secretary and a Telecom commissioner from 1975 to 1977 and, now a commissioner of the Conciliation and Arbitration Commission.

same period by over three times that amount. To a now belligerent ATEA, the reclassification denied the upward mobility of this latter group. Tradesmen were held back by written 'academic' exams that transcended experience in the field and a ceiling had been placed on their promotion prospects. A critical gap, said union officials, had developed between 'academic' and 'non–academic' technical staff.

The real issue, however, remained the broad impact on the technical workforce of accelerating technological change. When, therefore, Telecom management at last communicated its finalised policy on the adoption of the Ericsson ARE 11 local switching system to staff and unions in April 1978, the balloon went up. ATEA's response was to impose work bans on any type of communications service that would assist the implementation of the new equipment. The issue shaped as the litmus test on the introduction of major computerised technology in Australia.

'ARE eleven' would become a household word in Australia. Go–slow bans on telephone maintenance and installation, and specific bans on the computerised equipment impinged increasingly on network efficiency. Disruptions, begun in Queensland, spread to Victoria, South Australia and New South Wales. Four appearances of Telecom and union representatives before the Conciliation and Arbitration Commission through June 1978 brought no agreement and ATEA announced extensions of its bans in three States on 30 June. Faced with mounting failure in its network, Telecom stood down 150 technical staff on 31 July 1978.

Telecom's chief general manager, Bill Pollock, a former PMG senior assistant director general of industrial relations, put management's hard–line view. 'Telecom', he told journalist Ian Reinecke, 'is concerned that radical changes to the proposed work structure now being demanded by the ATEA will erode the quality and technical capacity of the workforce.' ATEA's new Federal secretary,

ATEA Federal officers confer at a special Council meeting during the 1978 technology dispute. From left: Peter Green, federal industrial officer; Mick Musumeci, assistant federal secretary; Colin Cooper, federal president, and Bill Mansfield, federal secretary.

The leaders debate: Bill
Pollock (left) and Bill
Mansfield (right).

Bill Mansfield's face
would become well
known to television
viewers during the 1978
dispute. Federal
secretary of the ATEA
in succession to Turbet,
Mansfield trained as a
lawyer and acted as
union member on the
Myer committee on
technological change.

Bill Mansfield, was no less frank, 'Telecom are spoiling for a fight with the unions ... they appear determined to bring about industrial warfare in the communications industry'.[13] Mansfield, who had succeeded Ken Turbet as ATEA's secretary in the heat of confrontation that July, was a long time trade union official who had earned a law degree by part-time study at Melbourne University. A listener by nature, Mansfield was a fair but firm negotiator when the gloves were down. A week on, after further ATEA bans on 'all revenue earning equipment' in four States and more Telecom stand-downs including middle management staff who had themselves declined to issue stand-downs to staff, he had hardened his line. 'We are looking for a total answer out of this', he announced then. 'The men are getting angrier and angrier ... We are not in a conciliatory mood now.'[14]

As the crisis sharpened, the press played an influential role. They selected from the complex strands of the technicians' case an evolving picture of a beleaguered group. The *Australian* was already featuring a series on 'The Computer Holocaust' when the rumpus broke. From the outset, the media and the public were sympathetic to the workers' cause.[15] The tide of computerisation was already lapping at the doors of other institutions challenging banking, clerical and insurance employees and the very newspaper industry itself. Influenced by events, the Australian Public Service Association (fourth division officers) announced their decision to ban word processors.[16] On the same day Commissioner Eric Clarkson of the Conciliation and Arbitration Commission conducted crucial hearings of the Telecom case.

A vigorous and experienced arbitrator clearly sympathetic to the wider social issues of the dispute, Clarkson was determined to effect a pause. Handing down his judgment on Friday 10 August, rather like a teacher holding a squabbling schoolboy by each hand, he urged a 21-day 'cooling off' period, the lifting of all work bans, the reinstatement of staff, and a three-week 'freeze' on the installation of ARE 11 exchanges while further negotiations went on.[17]

But, locked in conflict, both Telecom and ATEA declined to budge. Within minutes of the judgment, press sources reported, Telecom management had intimated its intention to apply to the Conciliation and Arbitration Commission for the insertion of a punishing penal bans clause in the union's awards. Weekend discussions within the union similarly damped down any inclination to bring the temperature down. Four days later, Telecom and ATEA both formally rejected Clarkson's plan.

In this conflict of interests, where did the Commission and the Minister stand? Since Telecom's inception there had been notable changes. Somervaille had succeeded Gibbs as chairman of the Telecommunications Commission in November 1975, and no less than three Ministers (Victor Garland, Eric Robinson and A.A. Staley) had occupied the portfolio of Post and Telecommunications. In August 1978 Somervaille was overseas and his powers in the industrial dispute went directly via Curtis to Stradwick's successor, general manager of industrial relations, Barry O'Sullivan. The power and authority of the Commission as such, was, hence, not publicly perceived and there was some sharp press criticism of its 'shadowy role'.

O'Sullivan, however, pushed a forthright line. Faced with disruptive bans over 18 months and losing revenue of some $700,000 a day, Telecom considered that it could neither concede the right to interfere in the new exchange establishments, nor accept the three weeks' moratorium proposed by the union on the installation and maintenance of ARE 11. It accordingly applied to the Conciliation and Arbitration Commission on 15 August for a hearing on the penal bans clause.[18]

The industrial storm now gathered across the nation. The business community, prime target of the union bans, suffered severe dislocation in vital telex operations. Telephone trunk delays and interruptions also

ATEA members packed halls around Australia to support their union's stand on new technology. Here, some 5,000 members gather in Melbourne's Festival Hall, 1978.

lengthened across the land. For some there were sunny moments. The collapse of STD metering systems meant that many subscribers could enjoy a bonanza of free–trunk line calls. One gratified customer, who rang Telecom to brag of her cheap long–distance calls from Adelaide to Perth, was promptly traced and sent a bill for $200. But business and community services felt the dispute's sharp bite. Most ominously, the deepening conflict threatened to explode into confrontation that would involve not only Australia's largest employer and the key union of the information age, but the Federal Government and the whole trade union movement itself.

It was A.A. Street as Minister for Employment and Industrial Relations who spearheaded official action. The interdepartmental industrial relations co–ordinating committee (first called into being by Chifley as Prime Minister in 1947) met throughout the dispute. Made up of representatives of the Public Service Board, the Minister for Employment and Industrial Relations and, on this occasion, Tony Staley as Minister for Post and Telecommunications, it advised Telecom and played an observing role. Street publicly defended Telecom. 'Telecom', he stated in a letter to the *Australian* at the height of the debate, 'has at all times acted responsibly and sought to have the dispute settled by negotiation . . .' The Government, he said, 'supports Telecom in the action it has taken'.[19]

Contrarily Telecom's own Minister maintained a Trappist silence. The fourth man in the portfolio in succession to Bishop, Staley was a Prime Minister's man, a youthful kingmaker who helped engineer Malcolm Fraser's rise to the leadership of the Liberal Party over Billy Snedden in 1974. A political scientist and one–time academic who had lectured on such subjects as democratic theory, Staley would loom large when the satellite question broke. But, on the burning issue of the industrial consequences of technological change, he kept out of sight. 'Mr Staley went into his umpteenth day of total silence', the *Australian*'s industrial reporter observed tartly during the dispute's third week. It was a strikingly different position from that adopted by Ian Sinclair as a strike–ridden Minister for Communications in 1980–1.

Commissioner Clarkson, however, joined the verbal fray remonstrating in private with both parties for their 'stiff–necked' attitudes and publicly criticising the Government's co–ordinating committee for throwing oil on the flames instead of 'cooling it'.[20]

It fell, however, not to Clarkson but to the deputy president of the Conciliation and Arbitration Commission, Justice Mary Gaudron, to preside at the hearing of Telecom's penal bans appeal. A Whitlam Government appointee to the Arbitration Commission, Mary Gaudron was both the only woman commissioner and, in her early thirties, one of the youngest arbitration judges in the country. A clever negotiator sensitive to the larger issues of the case, Gaudron's advice from the bench on 15 August was that action on penal bans could only widen the dispute and divert attention from real and immediate problems. Her tactic, to suspend action pending further discussions, gained a momentary breathing space.[21]

Prime Minister Fraser entered the arena on 21 August 1978. His

The technological 'gee-whiz' kid, Minister for Post and Telecommunications A.A. Staley pushed for the satellite.

message was categoric. The Australian people were not to be denied the benefits of improved technology. Both Telecom and the unions were there to provide service. Like Street, he applauded Telecom's 'extraordinary patience' and announced that the Government fully supported Telecom's policy of no work, no pay.[22] Commissioner Clarkson had the disputants back before him at the Arbitration Commission the following day. This time he offered a six-point 'peace plan' (to be determined before him at a compulsory hearing of the Commission on 24 August) that took comprehensive account of union goals. In essence, it proposed a restructuring of the classification of tradesmen and technicians, arbitration of tradesmen and technicians' salaries, arbitration of the question of promotion and standards for promotion, trials to be held and investigations made of exchange maintenance centres by two independent experts, one each from Telecom and ATEA, the participation of technicians in 'exchange maintenance centre' operations to assist in diagnostic functions and as liaison between centres and exchanges, and an ongoing plan for consultation on technological change.

But, in the rolling power struggle, ATEA's position had become entrenched. Even before the union's refusal was made final at the Conciliation and Arbitration Commission meeting of 24 August, public and press support for the unionists had ebbed. 'While Telecom and ATEA are huffing and puffing about the showdown', wrote a now critical *Australian*, 'Australia is heading for a close down!' National communications teetered towards the brink. The huge edifice of telecommunications connections, built up over more than a century, exposed an extraordinary vulnerability. For despite its increasing sophistication and automation, it depended, as the unionists had realised, on human co-operation. Those connected by the oldest telephone equipment fared the best and — compensation for Australia Post — telex-dependent business houses were forced back on priority mails. In a Telecom dispute, observed one newspaper sagely, 'it paid to be primitive'.[23]

ATEA's rejection of the 'peace-plan' now evoked wide criticism. 'By declining to budge an inch', the *Sydney Morning Herald* summed up a disenchanted public's view, 'the ATEA has aroused serious doubts about its *bona fides* and a strong suspicion that it cares nothing about hardship to the public.' The union's attitudes, indeed, had brought events to crisis point. As the city of Adelaide fell back on telegram-only communication across the land, Telecom made plans to have the ATEA deregistered, while a Federal Government team planned army assisted emergency telecommunications.[24]

Politically, there was also movement. On Friday 25 August, Robert Hawke, President of the Australian Council of Trade Unions (ACTU), was on a plane from Darwin summoned south to attend a meeting of the national labor consultative council (NLCC) convened by Tony Street for the following day. Hawke, the conciliator and negotiator, was in fine fettle that day: he had decided to enter Parliament. A tough debater, yet a soother and smoother, he knew that he had a national crisis to resolve. From his own sources, he was aware that the

Telecommunications Commission, in the chairman's absence, had delegated full responsibility for the negotiations to Barry O'Sullivan and that, in the previous week, Telecom had been brought closer under the Government's wing. He also knew of the deep divisions of opinion growing within the ATEA's State and Federal ranks.

Hawke went to the attack. He later recalled: 'The Government had got itself into a fine mess. It had not allowed Telecom management to negotiate with the unions which is the first ingredient for disaster.' At the Saturday meeting of the NLCC (which ATEA officers attended but from which Telecom was barred), he charged Street of asserting 'we must "talk"' but of preventing Telecom management from talking to the unions. With Street's somewhat startled consent, another meeting was consequently held later that afternoon at Telecom Headquarters attended by managing director Curtis, chief general manager Pollock, O'Sullivan, Peter Nolan (secretary of the ACTU and Turbet's recent successor as union Telecom Commissioner), Hawke, the ATEA's Federal secretary, Mansfield, the union president, Colin Cooper, John Ducker of the NSW Trades and Labor Council, and other unionists.

'The atmosphere was very taut', Hawke gave his version later, 'because Telecom believed that the introduction of new technology was a management prerogative and rejected the idea that the workers should have any say in how it was to be introduced. Telecom's management had welcomed the Government's support; they were feeling undermined by the change of Government position which I'd forced from Street. We had some pretty tough talking: I had to put it hard and clear to Telecom that it was facing a Luddite position, that if it went ahead and introduced the new equipment in disregard of the wishes of its employees the danger of sabotage was real.' As a second argument, Hawke suggested (as the media had been doing for weeks) that this was a fundamental social issue and, his own contribution, that 'the trade union movement was *not going to budge*'.[25]

Not surprisingly, Telecom participants saw the meeting in somewhat different terms. In a period of low national awareness of the human aspects of technological change, they continued to view the confrontation in 'network' terms. As Barry O'Sullivan described it, Telecom's representatives perceived the meeting 'as an attack on management's ability to make changes to the network which were designed to improve the standard of service to the customers while reducing that service's cost'. They also judged that, despite Hawke's assertion, the ATEA's position was becoming decidedly more conciliatory. Pollock's observation was particularly trenchant. He considered that until Hawke's arrival Telecom had been dealing with an internally divided and 'leaderless legion'.

Another round before the Conciliation and Arbitration Commission on Sunday 26 August was played out before formal agreement was reached. Again deputy president Mary Gaudron played a leading part. 'Bloody Sunday' would go down in the annals of both sides. Gaudron's handling was regarded as a *tour de force*. Across the long combative day, she sought resolution of the dispute. By 5 p.m. both parties urged a break. A stylish feminine figure at the centre of a fatigued, frayed group of men, Mary Gaudron broke temporarily, lit up her long cigar, and declined to allow either the disputants to go out or food to be brought in. Not unlike the college of cardinals refusing to release the brethren until an agreement on papal election had been reached, on this occasion, as one participant put it, 'it was only the language that was blue'. While Hawke won kudos for ending the strike, much of the acclaim belonged to Gaudron. 'Mary Gaudron', Barry O'Sullivan said later, 'is someone who profoundly understands the negotiating position and facilitates consideration of the logic of both arguments'.[26] Basically both sides wanted the delaying period that the final agreement sealed.

Essentially the 'Gaudron agreement' was open–ended. There were to be dual trials of ARE 11 exchange management. Nine 'exchange maintenance centres' (EMCs) worked according to Telecom's operational plan were to be installed (three in New South Wales, two in Victoria, and one each in Queensland, South Australia, Tasmania and Western Australia) while five 'exchange support centres' (ESCs) — the system of exchange maintenance favoured by ATEA — were to be established in all States but Tasmania. Trials were to be investigated by two assessors, one appointed by each side, who would consider the efficiency of operation, standards of service and technical efficiency, job satisfaction, career opportunities, and questions of retention of expertise, and the 'public interest' aspects of the two systems. The assessors' reports would be presented to the Arbitration and Conciliation Commission two years later for debate in open hearings. Yet, the trials could be suspended if network reliability was endangered and both parties were free to debate and reject the 'relevance of the results'. Additionally, the ATEA secured its demand for staff restructuring and classification, promotion opportunities through all technical ranks, and consideration of 'work value' and training.

While the unionists acclaimed the outcome as a victory of the ATEA, Telecom had secured one vital guarantee: there would be no industrial action on these matters during the two year trials.[27] Nearly three million Australians had been directly affected by the dispute.

What had the protracted conflict proved? With hindsight, Telecom management acknowledged that there was an inadequate grasp of the implications of this new phase of technological change in 1976–8. Management insistence at the time that 'changes are introduced with a full understanding of the human implications and in a way that causes the least possible concern to our existing staff' sounded less than convincing in 1983.[28] Yet such lack of understanding in management circles was Australia–wide in 1978. The Government was seriously at fault. Unemployment had been growing in absolute numbers since the early 1970s in Australia. But by 1978 structural change and unemployment had become widely evident in the tertiary (service) sector of the economy. The Telecom dispute highlighted an industrial problem that already ran deep. For an attentive press it focussed two central issues. In a period of high unemployment, should a statutory body like

Telecom have the right to steer its organisation into new technology that would reduce the community's store of jobs without proper evaluation of the issues? And why had the Government given no attention to the repercussions of technological change in the services sector?

One casualty of the industrial upheaval was Ken Turbet. As Federal secretary of ATEA and a member of the Telecommunications Commission, Turbet wore two hats. An active Commissioner associated with the many decisions guiding Telecom's forward thrust, Turbet saw himself as 'representing both the technicians and Telecom'. But his pioneering role, begun with hope, soon became uncomfortable and ultimately untenable. As industrial discontent grew, Turbet's union saw him as increasingly 'tainted by management' and unwilling to serve as a conduit of 'management information' back to them. Equally, Telecom's chief general manager acknowledged that he felt some reserve in reporting to the Commission on industrial strategy 'when there was a representative of the powerful opposition on the other side'. Hence in October 1977, with growing polarisation of Telecom and union views, the Federal Council of ATEA voted that Turbet should no longer hold the Commissioner's post. His resignation followed in a matter of days.[29]

The act was counter–productive. At one stroke ATEA lost a centrally–placed moderator of their views. The action also displeased the ACTU who had persistently pressed for union representation on Australian statutory bodies. In the event, however, ACTU's own secretary, Peter Nolan, filled the vacancy. A printer by training, articulate and well–educated, Nolan was a moderate who saw the struggle as 'neither a win or lose dispute'. Increasingly involved on the negotiations front, he believed that 'we can't wait and hold our breath' on new technology. But he was also aware of the wider problem of social costs and of the divergent attitudes that divided unionists' outlook in the States.[30]

Ultimately the long dispute of 1978 was a harbinger of the great industrial and social struggle of the late 20th century, in the words of one MP 'the first cab off the rank'.[31] On the question of best telephone exchange maintenance between the systems offered by Telecom and the ATEA, there would be tension and uncertainty before the review of the external assessors, Professor A.E. Karbowiak of the University of New South Wales for Telecom and Peter Robson of the New South Wales Trade Union Training Authority for the ATEA, reached the Conciliation and Arbitration Commission in February 1981.[32] In the meantime, Telecom management heaved a sigh of relief.

If 1978 proved memorable for the embattled debate over new technology, 1979 would become the calendar year when Telecom's fragile relations with its key union cracked like eggshells over a wages claim.

Both the APTU, which encompassed Telecom linemen, and ATEA's immediate ancestor, PTTA, had pressed for statutory corporation governance of telecommunications free from Public

Service Board control for solid reasons, to obtain greater leverage in wage negotiations with management and to secure a larger share in the returns on telecommunications productivity. Telecom's early years of 'profit' spurred them on, and the issue shaped publicly in March 1979 when ATEA lodged an 'ambit' claim for a 20 per cent pay rise across the board for its 26,000 members.

Their application stood on four grounds: the loss of wage purchasing power, the fact that technicians in State instrumentalities and private industry earned higher wages than those paid by Telecom, Telecom's demonstrated 'profitability' in its first years and, perhaps more curiously in the light of the acrimonious arguments over loss of responsibility and job initiatives of the previous year, the need for payment for 'increased job responsibility'. The claim hinged on comparative wage justice. A technician's wage, as union secretary Mansfield summed up, had declined from a rate of 14.8 per cent above the average weekly wage in 1975 to a modest 1.8 per cent above that wage in September 1978.

To Telecom, however, such a claim across the board lay significantly outside the wage–indexation guidelines set by Government. Two months after ATEA's application came before them, management accordingly in May 1979 formally rejected the application, refused to negotiate with the union, and advised that the claim be referred to the Conciliation and Arbitration Commission as a distinct 'work value' case. ATEA's response was to initiate a 'work to rule' campaign in support of the claim on 7 June 1979 and, four days later, a second Telecom dispute erupted in the Melbourne courtrooms of the Arbitration Commission.

To the public recovering from recent communications shock, the matter appeared menacing. That much misunderstood mechanism, the Australian arbitration system (which, writes d'Alpuget, is 'a social system, like marriage and . . . just as wayward in rational terms'), was again pressed to find solutions and again offered up its colourful cast of characters.[33] Its deputy president, Justice Staples, would become a controversial player in the dispute. A jurist who believed that the Arbitration Commission was a forum of final resolution and not of 'first resort', Staples called on both sides to enter direct negotiations on 11 June. Telecom's refusal to deny the unions right of direct negotiation over wages was, he said, not only a contravention of Telecom's own Act but, in the light of recent high salary rises granted to Telecom's chief general manager and to the Commission chairman himself, it threatened to create one rule for the rich and one for the poor. He also counselled the union to withdraw its limitations. On 2 July, having failed to make an impression on either side and with telecommunications breakdowns from work bans developing in every State, Staples recommended that the dispute be referred to a full bench of the Conciliation and Arbitration Commission on the grounds of Telecom's refusal to negotiate.[34]

Legally the recommendation was unprecedented, and it was not upheld. Like marriage, the president and deputy president disagreed. President Sir John Moore subsequently ruled that the dispute did not exist over Telecom's position on direct negotiations but on the 20 per cent salary claim.

In this new communications imbroglio, union members won less support. The dispute, complained the *Sydney Morning Herald*, 'is yet another instance of a union in control of a vital service trying to stand over its employer by making the public suffer'. The *Australian* took a softer line. Telecom, it reminded readers, had made considerable profits in the early years which laid it open to demands for more money from employees. At the very least, its management must meet the union more co–operatively 'and be more open about its plan'.[35] But Telecom was also a public service, ploughing back its profits in lower charges to the public. It was the point ATEA, press and public tended to overlook. The matter of a 'service' authority making annual surpluses to meet network extensions and community telecommunications needs remained the difficulty, the conundrum at the heart of the matter that continued to confront unionists as successive disputes with management flared.

In the light of its position as a national utility, Telecom's industrial problems rapidly became the nation's and the Commonwealth Government's too. Despite Justice Moore's further efforts, by 10 July the country's most sophisticated telecommunications systems were 'switchbound' by union bans. The Prime Minister's intervention to announce that day that, unless bans and limitations were discontinued within three days, he would proclaim and use the Government's anti–strike legislation, the Commonwealth Employees Employment Provision (CEEP) Act, increased the gravity of the dispute. CEEP would enable the Government to stand down or dismiss Government employees engaged in industrial action without recourse to the Conciliation and Arbitration Commission. There was no more formidable weapon in the Government's armoury, nor more dangerous. It could also backfire. The legislation, drawn up during a major postal strike in 1977, had already been condemned by the International Labor Organisation and by all union councils in Australia. In these circumstances, Fraser's warning drew an immediate threat from the Federal secretary of the Council of Australian Government Employees Organisation of a strike of all CAGEO affiliates if the legislation went ahead.

The Prime Minister was as good as his word. As private discussions with the union stalled, the Governor–General proclaimed the CEEP legislation on Friday 13 July 1979. Fraser defended his cabinet's stand. 'If we have to put ourselves way back behind scratch to get back to sanity in Australia, then so be it', he said.[36]

For Telecom the dispute, begun legalistically, had gathered ominous ramifications. With two major, if differently ignited strikes shadowing its public performance since 1978, its sunny future now seemed in doubt. One journalist framed the question. Given the particular vulnerability and the serious consequences to the private sector of industrial disputes of public sector monopolies such as Telecom Australia, was it not about time, he asked the Prime Minister, that 'a Liberal Country Party Government started to think about divesting itself of Telecom and other public utilities?' Fraser's reply was hedged. It was an 'interesting proposition', he said 'which had been promoted in some quarters'. But it ought to be understood that Telecom provided services in parts of Australia which were highly subsidised, 'because if they weren't you just wouldn't have the service in many remote areas, in many rural areas that could be afforded by the people'. It was, he said, not just a question of the overall profitability of Telecom. 'You need arrangements that will provide a service throughout Australia.' Significantly in July 1979 the Prime Minister considered that Telecom would be just as vulnerable to industrial action in the Australian environment 'if it were privately owned'.[37]

Throughout the crisis, Curtis and O'Sullivan kept in touch with their Minister Staley, 'the smiling Minister', had little to smile about that July. He listened to all the advice he got, said one Telecom participant, 'and agreed'. As a junior Minister, Tony Staley was not regarded as a strong cabinet member. His position on the Ministerial hierarchy was low. In times of industrial crisis, he also sought to distance himself publicly from his statutory commission. The political strategy that evolved flowed from other men, the Prime Minister and the coalition leaders, and the Liberal Minister for Employment and Industry, Tony Street.

Its flow gathered strong momentum on 13 July. On that day the Signal Corps of the Commonwealth Defence Forces were placed on emergency stand-by, Telecom stood down technical staff at Kalgoorlie under the CEEP legislation for refusing to clear faults in its arterial east–west microwave route, while unions threatened retaliatory action against CEEP. By afternoon the Conciliation and Arbitration Commission had intervened. Following talks with Hawke and the Federal secretary of CAGEO, a full bench of the Commission proposed a peace plan that would, if accepted, untie the now extensive and crippling telecommunications knot.[38]

But negotiations were not finalised until the full bench of the Conciliation and Arbitration Commission handed down the 'work value' wage claim settlement on 15 November which granted a 4.6 to 5.7 per cent pay rise across the range of technical staff. The tense industrial upheaval had given off much heat. 'A messy, confused dispute, born in bickering and continued in acrimony', concluded the *Australian* '. . . with angry overtones, threats and gaffes.' Certainly neither Telecom nor the ATEA emerged unscathed. In a minority addendum to the Conciliation and Arbitration Commission's decision, the independently minded deputy president Staples delivered a blunt broadside. Telecom, he suggested, was overcapitalised, its assets overvalued, its profits understated, and its charge for depreciation 'prodigious'. The Arbitration decision, he insisted, should not be used as a lever by Telecom to raise charges to meet the new wage costs. Whatever the truth of Staples's comments which Curtis publicly denied, it was evident that, despite union intransigence, Telecom Australia needed to get its industrial house in order.[39]

Fired by the technological change debate of 1978, some important moves were in train.

Early in 1979 Telecom's Telecommunications Consultative Council had prepared a document for joint management and staff associations' acceptance on 'Considerations of the Introduction of Technological Change'. Born of conflict, the paper signalled a significant shift in both management and union thinking from the adversary attitudes of the previous year. It frankly recognised the altered nature of technological change, both from the introduction of new systems and equipment and the upgrading of the old, and conceded that computerisation led to new work methods, the possible elimination of some jobs and occupations, and to 'substantial changes for individuals involved'. Importantly, it enunciated a principle, hammered out by a council sub–committee over several months that agreed that:

— Telecom and its unions recognise that technological change should only be accepted where there was demonstrable 'net benefit' to the community;
— proposed changes in technology with important impact on staff would be jointly considered before any decisions were made either to adopt change or purchase machinery;
— information given to unions would begin 'at the contemplative stage' when questions of the introduction of new technology were thought to be required, and union participation would continue up to, but not including, the tendering process;
— the timetable for the introduction of new systems or equipment would be jointly considered.

While no formal agreement was reached in 1979 or subsequently for inclusion on the problem of redeployment and retrenchment of staff from technological change, 'Considerations of the Introduction of Technological Change' established consensus in joint approaches to new technology that ranged from costs and financing of new technology, assessment of customer attitudes and requirements, retraining, the security and privacy of new systems, and job creation programmes, and it was endorsed by most Telecom unions by mid–1979.[40] Few saw it as a panacea for all problems. It placed no obligation on the unions to accept a particular technology after completion of consultation. But the agreement marked a national first. It led to the creation of a technology and change branch within Telecom's industrial relations department the following year and won praise from the national committee of inquiry into technological change (CITCA) which the Government set up at the close of 1978.

In the event Telecom's arrangement proved more effective than Government's. While the CITCA committee made up of chairman, Professor Rupert Myers, vice-chancellor of the University of New South Wales, Alan Coogan of Nabalco, and Bill Mansfield of ATEA as the representative of the trade union movement, was directly triggered by the Telecom dispute of 1978 and signalled Government recognition of the crucial issue of technological change, the committee's attempt to make recommendations and 'maximise economic, social and other benefits', 'minimise the adverse consequences of change' proved challenging in a country decidedly short of experts in the field of technological change.

Unfortunately the voluminous report issued in July 1980 was distinguished by its almost total failure to come to terms with the process of technological change. While the report represented the advantages of technological change, there was little consensus from committee members on the social justice, equitable distribution of costs and benefits, or public involvement in the decision–making process on the pace of such change. The report failed to satisfy the unions. Mansfield himself found it a scarifying experience, and its prime recommendation for a 'safety net' for those made redundant by technological change was rejected by Government.[41]

The argument had swung full circle. The spectre of change would not go away. There were tentative compacts but no real commitments as the 1980s dawned. One point, however, was clear. Telecom as a statutory body committed to high productivity and financial solvency was bound to go ahead with new technology as the decade advanced. A failure in its efficiency would open the doors wide to competitive private enterprise. It could, and had, conceded a measure of worker participation in major decision–making about technological change. But after consultation neither party was entirely bound. The question whether a Government enterprise could, or should, adopt a protectionist attitude in order to ensure more employment in place of greater productivity from new technology (a view advanced by unions) was moot, to say the least. In Australia's capitalist society, where Government ideology was geared increasingly to free enterprise and the market–place, such propositions rang hollowly in Telecom's ears. The challenge of computerisation was here to stay.

15 The Politics of Satellites

I f Telecom was to face industrial upheaval in its first formative years, it was also to find itself embroiled in a political and technological battle on one of the central issues of telecommunications in Australia — the 'servicing of the bush'. The changes imposed on Telecom Australia by the Liberal–Country Party coalition on its financing and loans, would extend in 1977 to its fundamental role as the common telecommunications carrier in Australia.

From 1960 the PMG's Department had, like authorities overseas, turned to the possibility of enlarging and diversifying its land–based telecommunications system through domestic satellite technology. In a country of Australia's size the concept of a radio communication station in the sky, capable of receiving, amplifying and rebroadcasting audio or visual signals to earth held alluring prospects for an organisation whose copper cable and terrestrial–based microwave technology was faced at times by insurmountable problems of terrain. The results of the Department's first satellite investigation were published in 1961.[1]

Australia was further drawn into satellite inquiry through its participation in the international INTELSAT projects and its active collaboration with NASA's 'ATS' projects (applications technology satellite), whose earth stations at Cooby Creek, near Toowoomba, and at Muchea, north of Perth, drew in a small corps of PMG Research Laboratories' staff. By the late 1960s pilot studies on the NASA equipment demonstrated the technical feasibility of linking a geo-stationary domestic satellite with Australia's network and offered the prospect of taking telephone connection to remote and inhospitable regions where land lines had not been built. OTC's earth stations at Moree (NSW) and Carnarvon (WA) already had their ground antennae transmitting to INTELSAT satellites, while OTC's earth station at Ceduna, SA, provided supplementary communication for transmitting to the Indian Ocean INTELSAT officially opened in February 1970.

There were basic problems. In considering a domestic satellite it was necessary to choose between a low–powered spacecraft and a large dish-shaped antenna, or a spacecraft operating at high power

The Telecom Research
Laboratories'
experimental earth
station, used to beam
signals to and from the
Intelsat IV satellite,
being installed in
Melbourne, 1981.

with small dishes on earth. Secondly, frequency bands used by
satellites could interfere with, or themselves be interfered with, by
microwave land systems. The PMG's approach was thorough. While
no claims were made that satellite technology was proven for Australia
on economic grounds, David Snowden's paper 'Small Station Satellite
Systems using Delta Modulation', proving the viability of small stations
to serve very small communities or individual households, delivered at
the IEE INTELSAT Conference in London in 1969, threw Australia's
hat into the investigative ring. During 1972, a special satellite task force
was formed in planning and programming at the Research Laboratories to extend technical studies and 'examine the need for, the
form, cost and timing of a satellite communication system for
Australia'.[2]

As in all APO evaluations, economic factors loomed large. There
would be no point, wrote laboratory director Rollo Brett, 'in establishing a satellite system if it would cost less to provide the service by
alternative means'.[3] But despite this engineering viewpoint, satellites
had glamour. They were an entirely new technology; they presented a
way of doing things that had not been tried before; they altered the
way TV was distributed, telephone calls transmitted, and business
information carried round the globe. They also worked from solar
energy, did not appear to threaten jobs or skills, and were a 'catalyst
for change'. Importantly also for a country like Australia, costs of

transmission by satellite were not governed by distance on land. It would cost, for example, as little (or as much) to relay television programmes to such outlying spots as Katherine, NT, or Burketown or Birdsville, Queensland, as to Sydney or Perth. In the early 1970s there were auspicious indications that a domestic satellite could be a logical new telecommunications systems choice.

Five years later such anticipations had been reduced. While *Telecom 2000* supported the case for an Australian domestic satellite by the early 1980s on the grounds that it could both introduce video–conferencing facilities between capital cities and on a point–to–point basis to provincial centres, and offer 'solutions to rural problems', Telecom's long–gestating *National Satellite Communication Systems Study*, released in November 1977, offered cautious judgment of domestic satellite communication on economic grounds.[4]

On technical feasibility, the Telecom study was 'go–ahead'. All the service facilities required for a national satellite system, it said, could be provided. The technical problems of the existing technology and its interface with terrestrial networks had been solved abroad. Canada had launched its first experimental domestic satellite in 1965 and the USA and other countries were now close behind. The technical difficulties could be solved in Australia though there would be some signals transmission delay between earth stations and satellites requiring echo suppressors and special signalling measures, and some 'careful management in an interwoven satellite terrestrial network'.[5]

International safeguard procedures would also need to be devised and suitable orbital positions determined. But if Australia were to proceed with such a system, the study advised that 'procedures to define suitable positions will have to be considered well in advance of the proposed operative date'.

On the economic assessment, however, conducted at home and on several visits abroad, the study joined engineering judgment with an analysis of national costs. And here the verdict was unequivocal. 'It has been concluded [ran the summary] that it is not possible at this time to establish a quantitative economic case to justify the provision of a national satellite system although the market for greatly improved TV programs distributed at rates which reflect costs is an important factor.'[6]

Such was Telecom's assessment in mid–1977 and its broad terms and conclusions were known in Ministerial circles before the final report reached Minister for Post and Telecommunications, Eric Robinson, in November that year. But there had been movement on the political front. Kerry Packer, chief executive of Television Corporation Ltd (now Publishing and Broadcasting Ltd), operator of TCN Channel 9, alerted to the prospect of using a satellite for distributing television programmes beyond the existing areas of metropolitan and regional cover, had commissioned a report from US satellite consultant, the Canadian David Bond. The Bond report or, more formally, *The Opportunity for Television Program Distribution in Australia Using Earth Satellites*, reached Government on 15 August 1977. Packer pushed a political barrow. His covering letter to the Minister of

Post and Telecommunications put the case that television services should be provided to areas not currently served and that the existing communications network was 'not satisfactory nor capable of providing such a service to the Australian people'.[7]

The Bond report had instant effect. It had important allies. In January 1977 IBM had received approval from the US Federal Communications Commission for a satellite project in which it was a partner. The prospect of replicating that achievement brought IBM into the Australian fray. Other lobbyists were also active. Accordingly, with cabinet approval, Robinson announced the appointment of a task force to investigate the desirability and implications of a national telecommunications satellite system on 22 September 1977. The Minister's position was already clear. 'Australia', he reminded Parliament, 'is a large country. The distances are vast. The cost of using current terrestrial systems to take these services throughout Australia is enormous and in some instances difficult to justify.' The Bond report, however, represented a plan for a satellite service that would distribute television programmes simultaneously throughout Australia. It proposed a 'national television distribution system', offered instructional TV, healthcare by 'telemedicine', closed circuit TV, long distance telephone trunk calls and digital data transmission, and the Minister added, could mean 'a reassessment of future telecommunications systems'.[8]

Although the Bond report itself was not formally released, the Government intended to move quickly on the matter. It was just three weeks before the delivery of its own statutory body, Telecom's detailed review. It was also the same day that Robinson, responding to a question in the House, replied that it 'has always been accepted in Australia . . . that it is economically advantageous and in the national interest to maintain one technologically compatible communications system'. The entry of a private operator into the telecommunication field, he said, would tend to lead to fragmentation and incompatibility between competing systems, particularly as telecommunications technology will continue to be subject to rapid change.[9]

Nonetheless the Commonwealth Government task force 'to enquire into all aspects related to a national communications satellite system for Australia' was appointed in mid–November 1977. Headed by Harold White, general manager of OTC, with a secretariat and executive secretary also supplied by OTC, and including OTC's assistant general manager, W.G. Gosewinckel, in its team, it had two representatives from each of the departments of Defence, Health, and Transport, J.P. Coleman from the Department of Finance, and one member only from Telecom, director of planning, Rollo Brett. Its goals were quickly set. The task force would propose the introduction of a domestic satellite with recommendations for its provision as soon as possible. White's championship and leadership set the tone. His capacities and connections had already been demonstrated over OTC's hard–won independence from Telecom Australia in 1975. He would prove a successful campaigner for satellite technology in 1978.

Remote area television via satellites was to be introduced in 1980 with
Telecom's remote area television service (RATS), which relays the ABC's
national television service from the Moree and Carnarvon earth stations, via
the Intelsat satellite, to re-transmissions stations in some 62 outback
communities. Standing next to the satellite receiving dish at Broome (WA) is
Paddy Sebastian.

Telecom's submission, based on its own conclusions, addressed
itself to the positive aspects of satellite use. Technically, it testified,
'remote area' TV and telephony would be an evident attribute of a
satellite scheme. If, too, there was firm demand for substantial
increase in TV programme distribution, this could be met by a
multiple purpose satellite system which presented remote subscriber
telephony and TV and other benefits. Other national advantages
included educational and medical TV, upgraded and specialised
facilities for Defence and Foreign Affairs, and future meteorological
use. But the question of funding the high capital and annual costs was a
crucial issue if the satellite was to be justified on national grounds. On
current estimates of $220 million capital required to service some
5,000 remote area subscribers by satellite, plus an ongoing annual
expenditure of $8,000 per subscriber, Telecom placed satellite priority
'low'. It would, it submitted, 'probably' be cheaper with the available
technology of VHF and UHF radio to service these remote area
locations by terrestrial means. But if a convincing 'national advantage'

or 'priority' for the satellite could be proven, the domestic satellite should form a part of the national network linked with existing systems but of necessity with subsidised funding to offset additional costs to the national subscribers, many of whom had only small gains to make.[10]

Powerful counter–advocates were, however, at work. IBM's managing director in Australia, Allan Moyes, gave testimony. Detailing his company's successful venture with the SBS (satellite business systems), he noted that, from his own experience, 'monopoly communications carriers with a vested interest in existing facilities and an obligation to provide nationwide telephone communications appear far less motivated than entrepreneurial entities to bring these applications into commercial operations'.[11] The US Hughes Aircraft Company, contractor for the SBS, also submitted its report which included discussion of a 'hybrid' satellite using both high and low powered transponders operating in the gigahertz frequency bands, a suggestion that would leave its influence on the White report. Six months and some 160 submissions from media, government, business and community interests later, the task force considerations were complete.

The report plainly reflected what Harold White had foreshadowed in a public reply to Kerry Packer in the course of the task force hearings. 'We'll get a satellite', he said then, 'the only issues are when, what design, who controls it, how much it's going to cost, who pays for it ...'[12] Telecom's argument for convincing national priorities was firmly set aside. The task force of 1977–8 marked the first time that the adoption of a major telecommunications technology was debated as a national issue outside the national telecommunications authority's central domain.

Its major recommendations were wide–ranging. Centrally the White report advised the formation of a new and separate 'national satellite commission' responsible for assembling user requirements, specifying planning, providing, developing, marketing and operating the space segment of the national satellite system and charged with prescribing the technical standards and operating procedures of the earth stations. The new commission should operate under the Minister for Post and Telecommunications in running the satellite and carrying telecommunications traffic in competition with the monopoly carrier. It should, in effect, be permitted considerable freedom in providing and marketing a full range of satellite communication services directly to the public with the exception of domestic and international telephone, telex, and telegram services.[13] Further recommendations included a direct broadcasting service for the provision of a national television and radio service to isolated communities and homesteads beyond the range of terrestrial broadcasting services, and possible tactical and strategic transponders for defence.

Despite these farreaching projections, the report was remarkably vague on the technical form the satellite should take and lacked agreement on user requirements and costs. The problems faced were immense. There was the important matter of frequency bands. Most microwave systems operated in the 4/6 gigahertz range, while the newer satellites used the 11/14 gigahertz higher frequency band. For the Australian domestic satellite (DOMSAT), the task force expressed a preference for a 'hybrid' spacecraft using 4/6 gigahertz for regional television broadcasting, 11/14 gigahertz for direct broadcast television and telecommunications, and 7/8 gigahertz proposed for use by the Department of Defence.[14] Even so, as informed observers noted, the recommendations posed formidable engineering problems for the systems designers.

It was hardly surprising that Brett, as Telecom's representative, and Coleman, the representative of the Department of Finance, dissented from the central recommendation of the report. In their joint verdict, no strong reason had emerged to depart from Telecom's responsibility as the national telecommunications carrier under the 1975 Act, while the assistance which Telecom prescribed for funding satellite services would need to be sought regardless of who might own and operate the system. 'We find it difficult to envisage a workable solution', their caveat stressed, 'in which two Government bodies, providing similar services and answering to the same Minister, can be in real competition.'[15]

It fell to Coleman, chief finance officer of the communication section of the Department of Finance, and the major economist on the task force, to put his overall dissent. 'In my view', he summed up 'the improvements to Australia's communications capacity which could evolve from the basic model system are marginal improvements to a communications infrastructure which provides already a sophis-ticated, high quality service by world standards. I am not satisfied that it has been established that these marginal benefits could be provided necessarily at less cost by means of a satellite system.' Coleman (a subsequent recruit to the Postal and Telecommunications Department) contended that it was premature to place weight on the attractions associated with satellite technology when the task force itself had indicated that each of the possible additions needed further consideration.[16]

Despite dissent and the task force's own recommendations for technical and applications trials, the report of the Commonwealth task force of July 1978 cleared the way for a *fait accompli*. It was, the enthusiastic new Minister Tony Staley (Robinson had moved to Finance in December 1977) told Parliament in presenting it in September 1978, a report 'of which the Task Force could be proud'. Not all members shared that view. Nonetheless Staley announced that the report 'will establish the pattern of development for Australian communications into the twenty–first century'.[17]

In this swift prejudgment where did Telecom Australia stand? It had been pushed from the centre of the stage. Despite unique experience and high performance, it was relegated to an understudy's part. Why? There were several reasons. Telecom had failed to communicate effectively with the politicians. There was very little understanding of satellite technology among politicians, the bureaucracy or community at that time. The coalition cabinet, increas-ingly committed to the private sector and responsive to lobbying, was a rapid convert to the nationalistic aspects of the satellite plan. It also bore Malcolm Fraser's seal. Packer, its committed instigator, later revealed his successful wooing of the Prime Minister. Before commissioning the Bond report, he 'saw the Prime Minister', he recalled, 'and I explained to him my understanding of what was happening in those areas . . . To his undying credit he grasped on it immediately and said, "Of course it's what we want. It's exactly the sort of thing we need to stop the drift of people into urban areas."'[18]

Telecom's political access was significantly less. The Commission's presence as a buffer between Government and Telecom, the growth in authority of the Postal and Telecommunications Department, and managing director Curtis's personal style all played a part. The Commission had backed the judgment of Telecom's *National Satellite Communication Systems Study* in 1977. Asking questions along technological and economic grounds, said Commissioner Joan Hancock, herself an economist by training, 'the Commissioners were bound to give a negative to the satellite. If the decision was to be taken as a "desirable social good", it had to be a Government decision'.[19]

This outlook was very different from that of the other involved statutory authority, OTC. It also differed significantly in style from the policy stance adopted by another statutory body concerned with major technology, the Australian Atomic Energy Commission, whose long-time chairman Sir Philip Baxter had exercised a determined influence over the nation's nuclear policy through advice to both successive Ministers and several Prime Ministers as well.[20]

'The engineer' – Jack Curtis, managing director of Telecom Australia from 1975 to 1981.

Curtis and Baxter came from different moulds. Yet, while Curtis's responsibility and that of his Commission chairman, was to inform and convince their political masters of the relevance and timing of technological projects whose importance for the community was long term, they encountered problems common in a technological portfolio of a lack of understanding and grasp. Moreover, despite his long and congenial relationship with Alan Hulme, Curtis failed to establish particular rapport with Robinson, while Staley found that Telecom's managing director was inclined to 'lecture him'. Curtis's relationship with his Ministers was hence courteous but scarcely close. They, in turn, admired him for his integrity, but he remained 'the engineer'.

In communicating on the satellite issue, both sides were at fault. As one close observer noted, 'there was a gross misunderstanding by Telecom officials of the political climate and a lack of understanding by the involved politicians of Telecom's basic goodwill'. Personality shaped events. 'Telecom', reported Reinecke, the watchful telecommunications expert of the *Australian Financial Review*, 'was behaving exactly like a good old-fashioned public servant and ignoring the political process.'[21] In one sense Curtis tended to regard himself as a Permanent Head of State. Central to his view was his concept of himself as the country's foremost telecommunications technologist whose prime responsibility was to provide a sound engineering assessment of the technology. He concentrated on that advice.

His influence on the Commission was profound. There, in a

triumvirate of chairman Bob Somervaille, the constitutional lawyer, deputy chairman, financier Tom May, and managing director, Curtis earned the reputation as the 'man who thought things through'. He appeared dominant. His administrative style was receptive and vigorous, but he objected to 'being told'. On the matter of the satellite, Somervaille played a retiring role. He himself did not feel as strongly as his managing director on the cost benefit analysis of the case. But he conceded to Curtis's view. Nonetheless, whatever their private convictions, there was a lack of political perspicacity on the part of the Telecommunications Commission and significantly less reason for their corporate low profile as evidence of the White task force's tactics became known. For undoubtedly its influential chairman and most of its members were concerned far less with solid economically–based engineering judgment than with the promise of the prestige and technical virtuosity of a domestic satellite in the sky.

One scholar spotlighted the problem. 'Telecom', wrote Dr Peter White, 'should either have created or had access to a government organisation or process which could have attempted to assess the "national advantages" that might be derived from a satellite–augmented telecommunications system.' This organisation, he suggested, could have been within Telecom, the Postal and Telecommunications Department, or elsewhere. Without it, Telecom had 'not been able to create a debate over the national advantages involved'.[22] Without this, and without the belief that it should express its readiness to come to the satellite party if the political decision overrode economic cost, Telecom and its Commission, showed poor political judgment. With its unrivalled record for telecommunications evaluation and its positive findings on the satellite's technical range, Telecom failed to communicate to good purpose with the politicians. Robinson accordingly believed that Telecom was 'moving too slowly', and there was a feeling in political circles that the Commission's 'economic negatives' were firmer and more categoric than a reading of Telecom's 1977 national satellite study showed. The minor role assigned to Telecom in the Commonwealth national satellite task force signalled both an erosion of Telecom's authority and a basic weakness in its lines of communication with Government.

With the task force findings before him, Minister Staley was prepared to move fast. A youthful cheerful Minister, who tended to begin and end his parliamentary speeches with a joke, Staley had been elected to the Federal Parliament for the Victorian seat of Chisholm in 1970 at the age of 31, and acquired his first portfolio as Minister for the Australian Capital Territory in 1975. Two years later he moved to the Post and Telecommunications post. An advocate of high technology, he commended the satellite as 'the solution to our problems in providing communications to remote areas and isolated communities' — a theme he would push persistently during visits to the bush — and quickly won the reputation among fellow parliamentarians as the 'Gee–whiz kid'. But he carried another ideology in his political bag, to diversify in the interests of efficiency, spur what he called 'electronic democracy' and 'encourage competition between structures'.[23]

Robert Somervaille, chairman of the commission from 1975 to 1980. With Jack Curtis, he later became a commissioner of OTC.

In September 1978 he therefore appointed a Commonwealth interdepartmental working group under the chairmanship of his acting head of department, Hugh Payne, to study the findings of the task force and invite submissions, and shortly after took off (with Payne) for Canada. Neither Telecom nor OTC were represented on the working group. It was exclusively bureaucratic and, made up finally of chairman A.P. Guster from the Postal and Telecommunications Department, three members of the Department of the Prime Minister and cabinet, two members each from the Departments of Defence, Finance, Science, and the Environment, and one each from the Departments of Health and Transport, it was not conspicuous for its technical expertise.

Relatively new to the complex field of telecommunications when he set out, Staley was, he told the author, 'seriously thinking of accepting Telecom's argument to delay the introduction of an Australian satellite into the 1990s'. But in Canada he was shown working models of the Hermes satellite, which operated in the 11/14 gigahertz frequency band, believed that Australia and Canada were 'environmentally alike', and developed what he characterised as 'a clear view of the nature of communications *now*'. Telecom, he consequently argued, was influenced by 'outmoded information'. Despite his public statements that he was backing satellite technology for those 'amazing people in the bush', Staley in reality saw it as a 'brilliant' means of diversifying power and information, putting computerised knowledge into the hands of the people, and offering electronic choice.[24]

Hence, while Telecom pundits were categorising their Minister as a 'technological romantic' and a convert to 'small boy technology wonderment', Staley was firmly convinced. Tabling the working group report in the House of Representatives on 18 October 1979, he announced the Government's decision–in–principle to establish an Australian communications satellite system.[25]

The working group's recommendations contributed to the decision. From their findings based on 150 new submissions, three major 'DOMSAT' conferences, and a buzz of community discussion over the investigative ten months, their report concluded that Australian telecommunications would be enhanced by the complementary use of satellite and terrestrial systems and that a domestic satellite would overcome some of the most significant limitations in existing telecommunications services. Benefits would extend to the provision of telephony, television and radio broadcasting, scientific data, and safety services into remote areas; the satellite would improve television and radio broadcasting for Australia generally, provide better services for bulk high speed data communications and give 'additional diversity and resilience to the terrestrial network'.[26]

Much had still to be determined. Despite a broad capital estimate over the period 1982–92 of $200–$260 million and annual costs to the public of approximately $24 million, it was not clear what the real expenditures would be, the extent to which the new system would generate additional revenue 'or merely shift revenue from Telecom', or the size of tariffs and customer demands. Yet despite the acknowledged cost uncertainties, the working group majority view was that a multi–purpose national communications satellite should be established 'as early as practicable', and that a national satellite commission should be formed to undertake responsibility for planning, organising and developing the scheme.

There was some dissent. One representative of the Prime Minister's Department counselled deferring an immediate decision to allow for an interim planning group to produce a costed planning proposal and a more business–like analysis of potential demand. The representative on the working group from Robinson's Department of Finance also plumped for delay. The use of a 'regional' satellite might, he argued, well be more cost–effective; Australia was a member of INTELSAT, and what might be lost of national autonomy could well be compensated by economic gains. On available evidence the Finance Department's dissenting opinion foresaw that 'the early establishment of a satellite system could add a substantial $17–27 million per annum to public sector costs from 1985–92'. It claimed also that it was by no means 'adequately' demonstrated that the associated improvements in communications were of sufficient priority to warrant these costs. The Finance Department's representative additionally took the view that the satellite would be better organised by a 'largely autonomous subsidiary of Telecom' than by a new and separate authority.[27]

Telecom's own substantial background evidence had also produced its effects. Much turned on the matter of the remote rural subscriber. The White task force had recognised the formidable technical and economic problems which Telecom faced in planning to provide services to isolated and thinly populated areas and its increasing thrust towards automatic exchanges. Might the satellite offer some solution? The working group thought so. It could provide route diversity, improve services to remote areas 'in advance of terrestrial means', restore links with disaster areas, introduce direct point–to–point private lines, and provide high–grade communications with newly developing communities'. Telecom itself, in its further submission to the working group, again acknowledged the long–haul capacity of satellite communications across the Nullarbor, northward along the Western Australian coast, and linking Darwin, Townsville and other places; but it continued to see this as 'back–up resilience' and as incremental additions to terrestrial routes already formulated into the 21st century.

Established planning and conflicting ideologies and motivations intersected in the findings of the working group's report. Industry played a persistent part. Its submissions were critical of Telecom. They included outback service complaints, a demand for long range data connections, and greater radio and TV broadcasting range and diversity. But there was a measure of divergence between pressures for greater 'national' television penetration and regionally originating groups. That great satellite primer, Packer's Publishing and Broadcasting Limited, expressed a gnawing unease. 'One of our concerns', it submitted with deceptive blandness, 'is that Telecom will come to have an undue influence on the life of all Australians'.[28]

Telecom had two staunch defenders: its powerful unions, the APTU and ATEA. In May 1979, as management and ATEA prepared to join battle on the embittering wage claim dispute, the unions' joint submission to the working group strongly condemned the concept of a second authority for the organisation and management of a tele-communications system that might 'skim the cream off Telecom Australia's higher profit operations . . . without commitment to serve the general public in an equitable manner'. The unions were also critical of what they saw as the lopsided nature of community dis-cussion of the satellite. 'The form of the Inquiry', they declared, 'at worst stifles, and at best fails to promote meaningful discussion in the community on the many significant issues which it ought to be raising.' Unemployment was such an issue where the working group clearly lacked expertise. 'We now appear', said the submission, 'to be going through a new phase in the substitution of capital–intensive technology for labour, one based upon computers, electronics and automation. Satellite technology has each of these characteristics.' In public ATEA's industrial officer, Peter Green, spelled out the widespread doubt. 'Telecom', he said 'would be penalised by having an unencumbered rival duplicating the small high profit part of the service using a valuable national resource for the private advantage of big national and multinational corporations.'[29]

On the basis of its working group report, however, Government action had firmed. DOMSAT was projected for launching in late 1984–5. Registrations of interest were to be invited in tendering for the system from selected organisations, a satellite project office was to be established within the Postal and Telecommunications Department, and private industry would be involved in the planning activities. The actual technology of a space segment of three satellites with two in orbit and one spare on the ground, plus two tracking and control stations, and an earth segment comprising major city earth stations was to be organised, controlled and funded by a national satellite authority. It was envisaged that there would be earth stations owned and controlled by users or consortia of users (including the ABC, the Department of Transport, OTC and Telecom), together with small earth stations for the reception of radio and television broadcasts at individual rural homesteads. Staley's figures for these small dish antennae, paid for by the householder, varied considerably on his outback tours. The estimated cost in 1979 was generally cited at $1,000. But figures as low as $400 were recorded in some rural newspapers after the Minister passed through.[30] He was, however, notably less forthcoming about the uses to which the satellite could be put by metropolitan business interests.

On the major issue of private industry consortia whose submissions had figured prominently in both Government inquiries, the Minister was noticeably vague. As the terrier–like Labor member Barry Jones pointed out, 'The most interesting thing about the Minister's speech [in Parliament] was what he did not say . . . There is not one sentence on the media context in which the satellite is to be introduced. There is not one sentence, not one phrase, on the pattern of media ownership in this country . . . What we do not have in the Minister's statement is the reality of who the big users are to be.'[31] The Labor opposition itself was not opposed to a domestic satellite; but it was defensive of Telecom. It was also critical of the 'looseness' of costs, and, in the imprecision and haste in timing, opposition members were frankly sceptical of the 'massive public subsidy' for a satellite that appeared to hold special benefits for large private and overseas industry groups.

As a study of a major policy issue, the Australian satellite presents a complex case. Its strands are diverse. A junior Minister holding 27th place in the portfolio hierarchy had served as the catalyst. (Ironically he would withdraw from political life before the election of October 1980.) The Prime Minister, in Staley's words, had 'seized the issue and become an ally'. Fraser, in fact, as later evidence revealed, had identified with the project from the start.[32] While Robinson as Minister for Finance from 1977 was one cabinet Minister who shifted from an affirmative to a 'hasten slowly' attitude as cost factors emerged, cabinet and Government seized on the romance of the outback to carry the expensive but prestigious policy through. Their triumph over the reasoned advice of their national statutory authority stands out in the long history of telecommunications in Australia. Never before had a Commonwealth Minister or a Prime Minister defied the advice of the bureaucratic 'head' on the matter of a major technology.

The role of the Postal and Telecommunications Department had reinforced the Government's stand. Closely involved in the movement for a satellite, they supplied the encouragement that Telecom denied. Acting secretary, E.E. Payne, headed the Commonwealth interdepartmental working group until he left to accompany Staley on his learning visit abroad. R.B. Lansdown took up the secretaryship of the Department in July 1978 at a time when the working group was already finalising its report and shortly before the important DOMSAT conference held at the Australian Academy of Science in September brought Canadian expertise and stimulus to the satellite debate.

Lansdown had moved to the Department from the Department of Environment, Housing and Community Development. When he entered the Department, he did not know, he admitted, what a transponder was. It was his job, he said, to appraise the matter 'on broad policy issues'. Speaking at a national science forum in Canberra in 1982, Lansdown acknowledged that 'he had given a lot of his time and something of his reputation to satellite technology'. The Department itself had scant resources for the planning involved, but OTC's and Telecom's resources could be marshalled. OTC's backing for the project was central to the scheme. Appraising the project on 'national' grounds, Lansdown believed that the satellite could provide special services for remote Australians. Despite Treasury and the Department of Finance's long negatives, he was assured that there would be adequate demand for the satellite's services, and he judged as 'an act of faith' that the substantial capital investment would lead to DOMSAT becoming self-supporting. Armed with these beliefs and with assurances on the technical front from Canadian experience, Lansdown led his Department in 'a unique piece of public policy-making'.[33] If neither Treasury nor Finance shared his view, he won support at bureaucratic level from, among others, the Departments of the Prime Minister and Cabinet and Industry and Commerce.

Lansdown, a cool bureaucrat, threw his support for the planning and policy of the satellite behind the OTC. He was critical of Telecom. Telecom had 'opted out'. Moreover, in the secretary's view, Telecom was too heavily involved in borrowing and loan problems to carry forward a satellite scheme. OTC alternatively saw the satellite in high national priority terms. The prize hence went to OTC. Lansdown chose W.G. Gosewinckel, OTC's assistant general manager of corporate services and a former task force member, to head the provisional planning body for Australia's satellite.

Telecom had suffered a self–imposed 'defeat'. In one sense it was a house divided. There were many members of the organisation who felt that Telecom should have backed the satellite cause. 'We have killed the satellite' said one senior State engineer. 'We are not used to working with entrepreneurs.' Despite the hopeful satellite forecasts of *Telecom 2000*, two years of further study caused management to change its view. In the final analysis, responsibility must be sheeted home to the managing director. Correct in his technological and economic judgment, Curtis 'dug in' and resisted the emotional and national appeal of the satellite. As other men of high integrity had done, he offered advice to his political masters that he believed to be true disregarding what he knew his Minister wanted to hear. Distanced from the event, it was, he admitted, a 'locking in' of an advisory attitude for which he felt some regret.[34]

Yet there were sound reasons for Telecom's adherence to their long–term terrestrial telecommunications plans. By a manifest irony, an idea conceived earlier in the Research Laboratories took shape in 1978 as the Commonwealth satellite working group formed. This would spur the development of a local innovation, the digital radio concentrator system (DRCS) which, in the special conditions of rural Australia, would use up–to–date digital radio transmission techniques to connect outlying subscribers to the terrestrial network. The integrated digital subscriber system (using very high and ultra high frequencies), used pulse code modulation and time division multiplexing (see Glossary) to produce the necessary 'non–overlapping transmission bursts' from the various subscribers.

The new system promised the remote rural homestead traditionally connected to a manual switch by private line, all the charms of modern telephony, privacy, automatic connection, round–the–clock availability and telex facilities. There were also the large advantages the network would reap, including reduced equipment costs from common channel signalling, reduced overall cost from the use of repeaters and the number of subscribers serviced from a single base station, and a capacity for incorporating supervisory and remote fault–locating facilities.[35]

If necessity was the mother of invention, competition proved an

The digital radio concentrator system (DRCS), the cheaper terrestrial method of bringing communications to remote areas developed by Telecom's laboratories, had a trial installation at Wallal Station, south-west of Charleville, Queensland in 1983.

active father here. Throughout 1979–80 collaboration between the Research Laboratories and headquarters engineering department related the new system to the operational requirements of the rural and outback telephone network, and the system was put out for contract in July 1980. In a further irony, at least to the historian concerned with the thrust given in Australia's remote communication outposts to fend off Japanese invasion in 1942–5 (see Chapter 7), the contract for the digital radio concentrator system was let in 1981 in accordance with Telecom's specifications to Nippon Electric Company, Japan. With luck, and Japanese punctuality, bulk supplies of DRCS would feed into Telecom's rural automation programme in mid–1984, a year at least before the scheduled launching of the domestic satellite.

By mid–1980, there was further back–up for the Curtis stance. The policy research branch of Telecom's headquarters planning directorate, aided by South Australia, Western Australia, Queensland and New South Wales — the four 'remote area' administration States, completed its in–depth Remote Area Telecommunications Study. This study, and a related socio–economic study in the Northern Territory commissioned by Telecom in 1979, marked the first attempt to identify and define the 'remote area' people who had been used so persistently as the political bargaining point of the Government's satellite argument.[36]

There were 44,000 inhabitants of 'remote' Australian areas, more than 22,000 living in the far Northern Territory, or who did not have access to modern telecommunications services. Of these, 66 per cent were Aboriginals. Modest numbers were hence involved in the project of lacing remote outback subscribers into Telecom's 'universal' network. Some 2,500 outback subscribers were forecast for automatic STD telephone services for 1985, an estimate that would expand to 5,000 by the year 2000. This number did not take account of any demand for telecommunications in mining areas for which expensive priority spur line arrangements with mining companies had long been made. Nonetheless, it was significant that, of the estimated demand, 38 per cent of the 1985 figure were for Aboriginals or Aboriginal-related settlements.

For these Australians, old and new, the greatest expressed need was for the telephone. Quantitative surveys of pastoralists and commercial interests revealed that they would be prepared to pay significantly more for the telephone than for other services such as broadcast radio and TV or mobile communications. As one journalist neatly wrapped it up: 'first of all at the top of the list they wanted a telephone, secondly, they wanted a telephone that worked, and thirdly they wanted a telephone that worked all the time'.[37]

Economically, Telecom's Remote Area Telecommunications Study favoured the use of the promising digital radio concentrator system in almost all locations, although the report agreed that there were a few locations which could cost less by using the satellite if space segment and other overhead costs were ignored. But as the Northern Territory study stressed, with either satellite technology or the DRCSs, the problem of planning appropriate telecommunications services for remote Aboriginals, designing a pay–as–you–use telephone to meet special Aboriginal requirements, and the need for participatory consultation with Aboriginals was essential before the technology was installed. It was a far cry from the gun–turreted Colonial telegraph station outposts of North Queensland of the nineteenth century!

A series of steps marked the evolution of Australia's satellite plan. During 1980 Telecom became an active participant in the technical planning stage. 'If there is evidence of a national will', Curtis had stated publicly at the final DOMSAT Conference the previous year, 'Telecom will want to be responsive.' Curtis and Telecom engineer K. Power became members of the Postal and Telecommunications Department's 'portfolio committee' chaired by Gosewinckel, along with secretary Lansdown, the head of the Department of Transport, and the managing director of the ABC. Thus despite allegations that Telecom was slow to move to planning and 'dragged its feet', it played a crucial planning role. There was, however, no question, in the political climate of the time, that any share in the satellite's governance would be given to Telecom.

One event suggested the predetermined nature of the planning's course. Well before the Minister's announcement of the Government's call for tenders for the Australian national satellite communications system in October 1980 (one of Staley's last acts on the political scene), Lansdown received a direct offer from the vice–president of satellite systems and services of the United States Western Union Corporation offering to provide a satellite system for Australia to launch in the second half of 1982. The offer had strong attractions. It suggested a 36–channel (or transponder) system spread over two satellites, 12 in one and 24 in the other, at a total cost of $112 million, a sum little more than half that contemplated by the satellite project office of the Postal and Telecommunications Department. The Western Union satellite operated in the 4/6 gigahertz frequency bands (C band), while the model favoured by the Department — a variation on the SBS and Canadian model — transmitted in the 11/14 gigahertz frequency. The technicalities were obscure to the layman, but the politics were not. An Australian satellite operating in the C band would, as its Western

 351
*The Politics
of Satellites*

Union sponsor alleged, 'require a simpler co-ordination procedure with the existing network and involve less administrative costs'.[38] It could, therefore, spur a Telecom claim to become the satellite controlling agency because of the need to co-ordinate with Telecom's microwave trunk network operating substantially in the C band. The politics of frequencies, which the Department controlled, determined their decision, and the offer was set aside. Rather, specifications for requests to tender were released for two operational spacecraft in a flexible configuration of high–powered and low–powered trans-ponders.[39] An additional tender invitation in October 1981 allowed an option for an additional spacecraft. Telecom prepared the tender requests and evaluated the contenders covering earth stations for telephony and relaying programmes of the National Broadcasting Service; OTC engaged three overseas consultants, COMSAT, US, the European Space Agency and TELESAT, Canada, to assist on the satellite front; while the Department of Transport covered air stations for air navigation and safety programmes. To complete the organisational arrangements, AUSSAT Pty Ltd was announced as the national satellite authority and incorporated as a company in the Australian Capital Territory on 6 November 1981. A month later the US company, the 'proven' Hughes Communications International, was named as successful tenderer.[40]

Australia's satellite would be operational in mid–1985. Made up of three identical satellites with associated tracking stations, two satellites would be launched by either the European Space Agency rocket ARIANE or NASA's space shuttle or Delta rockets at that time. Yet, on the ground, many problems were unresolved. Despite a decision announced by the Fraser Government that AUSSAT would (1) finance its capital expenditure on the satellite system and its operating costs by a mix of 49 per cent commercial loans and a 51 per cent equity contribution by the Commonwealth, (2) establish eight major city earth stations, and (3) private sector organisations would be free to set up their own earth stations to 'access' the satellite system on the same basis as AUSSAT, difficulties multiplied. Evidence was scant of the Minister's promise that every effort had been made 'to create oppor-tunities for Australian industry in terms of transferring technology to Australian firms, developing new techniques and processes and enhancing job opportunities'.[41] The major earth stations contract went to Mitsubishi. The involved unions, ATEA and APTU, protested the satellite's threat to the national carrier and to their jobs, while Telecom itself faced the prospect of critical competition to its profitable trunk telephone and data network from a subsidised AUSSAT (on whose board private and media interests loomed large). Even the media promoter, Kerry Packer, seemed far from satisfied. 'The stupidity with which the Government departments have handled the communication satellite', he declared roundly, 'is terrifying.'[42] Only one thing seemed certain during the Fraser Government's last months of office: the long reign of Australia's terrestrial telecommunications was coming to an end.

16 Time of Crisis

The decision to adopt a domestic satellite presided over by a new national authority represented the first real threat to what had been seen as Telecom's 'unshakable monopoly'. The Government's goal to join Australia to the growing ring of domestic satellites owners (some 35 by the time AUSSAT moved into orbit in 1985) brought Australia squarely into the circle of major industrial countries — the USA, UK, Canada, Sweden and Japan to name a few — where long–standing, if differing, institutional arrangements for the management of telecommunications was being challenged by both government and industry.

This challenge was not surprising. The landscape of telecommunications was changing. The decade of the 1970s had seen the transformation of the plain old telephone system — the 'POTS' as it was colloquially called, to a highly evolved electronic system of expanding variety and range. To 'POTS' had been added the 'PANS' — 'the peculiar and novel services'.

The 'PANS' were a medley of quickly evolving extensions, new voice and data systems, terminals, 'add–ons' and accessories directed chiefly to that highly responsive seeker after speed and novelty, the business customer. Many of the new developments were the products of rapid advances in microelectronics and digital technology and their farreaching impact on telecommunications. But there was another stimulus. By the mid–1970s many advanced industrial countries were nearing saturation point in telephone connections. In Australia telephone household penetration touched 73 per cent by 1977 and was expected to reached 93 per cent by 1985. A great majority of subscribers had automatic services and STD and, despite good old Australian teeth gnashing and a steady stream of complaints about faults or delayed services and connections that reached Telecom and the Commonwealth ombudsman (a flow that sparked Telecom's ironic self–title, 'the company you love to hate'), Telecom and its predecessors had, it was widely recognised, installed one of the longest and most reliable telecommunications services in the world.

But while Curtis's dream of a 'universal' standard of service

353

throughout Australia by the bicentenary year of 1988 had to be pushed through, there was clear evidence of need for a change of emphasis. The importance of greater business orientation and keener marketing, pressed by the Royal Commission of Inquiry, had been quickly grasped. Yet from the moment of its inception, Telecom had felt the hot breath of competition blowing domestically and from strong influences abroad. During the 1970s the regulatory pattern of the telecommunications sector altered dramatically overseas. The hard fought 'Carterphone' decision handed down by the Federal Communications Commission in the USA in 1968 had punched the first dint in AT&T's telephone carrier monopoly by permitting Carter Electronics Corporation to market a service that connected mobile radio telephone systems to 'Ma Bell's' massive network. The decision, which prevented AT&T from prohibiting connections but allowed it to establish required standards to be met by connecting devices, finally brought the anti–monopoly (anti-trust) principle to the American telephone industry and had rippling repercussions round the world. A decade later in 1978 litigation and increasing competition from a range of telecommunications and electronics companies involved AT&T in what one journal called 'the largest corporate reorganisation in its history'.[1]

There were further agents of change. The rise of the computer industries strengthened the movement towards monopoly deregulation. The insidious microchip, miniaturising, diversifying, altering technologies in a number of related fields, inevitably blurred the boundary line between 'old' telecommunications and the new computer industries. Importantly, computer technology shifted the original purpose of the telephone system from the provision of mainly voice communication routes towards the provision of enhanced voice plus data communication and brought the controversial, but irreversible, computerised switching and transmission into the telephony and telex systems. In the 'terminal' field, electronic automatic private branch exchanges (PABXs) for switching within a company's internal telephone system emerged as a highly competitive product while satellite technology fostered other advances including facsimile transmission of the written word (as well as pictures), videotex for homes and offices, and a host of new communications products and facilities appeared.

These new telecommunications patterns and their implications for the monopoly carrier, found strong reflection in Mrs Thatcher's free enterprise Government elected in Britain in April 1979. Amid major organisational changes within the British post office that carved out 'British Telecommunications' from the post office's rib, the influential new Conservative Secretary of State for Industry, Sir Keith Joseph, announced proposals for relaxing British Telecommunications monopoly and, in October 1980 appointed Professor M. Beesley to conduct an economic assessment of the implications of allowing complete liberalisation for add–ons to the network services. Beesley's findings (published in January 1981) promised new competitive opportunities for the telecommunications and electronics industries in the United Kingdom and confirmed the American message that, with the ubiquitous microchip pervading the telecommunications and electronic industries, it was no longer possible to define a 'national telecommunications monopoly'.[2]

Australia could hardly hope to escape these gusting winds of change. Nonetheless, with its elaborate corporate and forward planning, Telecom's own stance was firm. It had two prongs: a policy intention to provide new services including new types of 'value–added' or terminal equipment, and a consistent view that it should retain its historical centralised control (with some industry association and sharing) of the diversifying domestic telecommunications enter-prise.

The planning document, *Telecom 2000*, emphasised the point. The product of much navel–gazing and future musing, it sought to demarcate the new Commission's place in a number of rapidly expanding fields. In the competitive area of marketing Telecom would, it predicted late in 1975, 'introduce and actively market a public mobile radio–telephony service' at the earliest possible date. It would also 'consider marketing a facsimile service in competition with present suppliers, offering network interconnection with directory listing to Commission–supplied terminals' and in the upfront, but as yet undeveloped, word facsimile technology in Australia, Telecom should stimulate Australian manufacture of the system of transmitting a page in 30 seconds across the telephone network through a research and development contract to a local manufacturer.[3]

For cable television (debated in the USA since 1971 but a serious field for speculation in Australia only as the 1970s closed), the Commission envisaged owning the physical transmission plant and hence 'providing substantial economies of common provision' while leasing CTV capacity to CTV operators — the commercial entre-preneurs, institutions and community groups. For these develop-ments, *Telecom 2000* had in mind a Government–sponsored committee where representatives of Telecom, the Australian Broadcasting Control Board, the Postal and Telecommunications Department, and media and educational groups could investigate pertinent aspects of cable television resources.[4]

In the volatile field of computing and its complex relationship with the network, *Telecom 2000* also foresaw a leading role for Telecom in developing machinery to foster the development of the two sectors, again with a government body representing the Commission, telecom-munication and computer manufacturers, and public service and other users. It also concluded that, in the area of private data networks, Telecom should respond to user needs 'through further liberalisation' of policies relating to innovation and efficiency in private line utilisation along the lines of its existing policy of sharing leased lines and integrated modems, but that Telecom should 'maintain its present monopoly of public common carrier networks in the case of computer telecommunications'.[5]

At best *Telecom 2000* advocated, not the introduction of competition, a concept that ran against the grain of the dynamic new telecommunications authority in 1975, but the exploration of areas where, along clearly restricted fronts, future competition might be introduced. In short the Commission rejected services that, either by interconnection of subscribers, value–added services or by more direct competitive penetration of the network, would 'run counter to Telecom's role as the common carrier'.

To Telecom itself the publication of *Telecom 2000* was seen as a way of inviting open debate on the technological, social and economic future of telecommunications in Australia. But the business community's response was less ecstatic. *Outcomes from the Telecom 2000 Report* summed up the responses in 1978, 'registered objections to the view that it is in the national interest to retain a telecommunications monopoly'. One critic blamed Telecom's determination 'to reserve to itself profitable areas of development' for the slow rate at which new business and terminal services were becoming available in Australia compared with countries overseas, while another argued that private industry could find the necessary capital resources that presently limited Telecom's capacity to introduce new business services.[6]

Not surprisingly the computer industry was the most outspoken critic of Telecom's prospective scenario. Its spokesmen held that private enterprise should be free to lease transmission facilities wholesale, add user–oriented data services, and retail them direct to customers. It was a firm avowal of an anti–monopolistic creed from the rapidly developing 'market push' sector of the telecommunications industry that would gather considerable momentum in the next few years.[7]

By contrast, the telecommunications industry proper had developed a largely symbiotic relationship with Telecom which removed it substantially from the list of critics. By 1978 it had attained an important and a novel position in the Australian economy. Its progress since the path–breaking contracts made under the Chifley Government between the PMG's Department and the two Sydney-based overseas subsidiary firms, STC and TEI (later Plessey Telecommunications), for the local manufacture of step–by–step switching equipment in 1948, had laid the foundation for an industry that now met nearly 90 per cent of the Australian Government's needs.[8] The industry's progress followed its own step–by–step. The advent in 1963 of L.M. Ericsson's subsidiary company at Broadmeadows, Melbourne, to manufacture crossbar equipment for Australia had led in turn to licensing arrangements between Ericsson, Plessey and STC for sharing local crossbar equipment production. Similar contractual arrangements were also made between the PMG and the major cable–making companies Austral Standard Cables Ltd, Olympic Pty Ltd, and later Conquerer Cables Ltd.[9] A decade later, the dependence of the three telecommunications companies, Plessey, Ericsson and STC, on PMG contracts in terms of their total output stood at 92, 65, and 60 per cent respectively.

The Australian–owned Amalgamated Wireless (Australasia) Ltd, AWA, had also made headway, dominating the supply of PMG and Telecom telephone handsets since the first contract signed with the

PMG in 1933 and manufacturing some four and a half million of the coloured '800 Series' handsets from the early 1960s. AWA continued to develop its research association with the PMG and later Telecom Research Laboratories to produce new telephone models, dials, telephone testing instruments, small business multiple systems for outback locations and, from 1976, special optical fibre suitable for telecommunications. With growing connections with Hitachi (Japan), Western Union (USA) and Olex Cables (UK), AWA had diversified and was not exclusively or even highly dependent on the national tele-communications authority.

By 1973 a medley of both substantial and diverse small telecommunications companies jostled on the Australian scene. Their ownership and the distribution of their share capital was remarkably evenly divided between Australian and overseas. Of the 36 major company members of the Australian Telecommunications Develop-ment Association, an industry consortium formed in 1964, surveyed in connection with the Commission of Inquiry into the APO in 1973, 13 were companies owned wholly overseas (with a share capital of $37.5 million); 11 were Australian owned (with a share capital of $39 million); while ten companies were partly overseas, partly Australian owned and had a total share capital of $92.5 million, $42 million of which was centred in Australia.[10]

Their products and services read divertingly like a treatise on the development and servicing of all forms of telephone, telegraph, radio, television and satellite communications systems and — from miniscule to majestic — ran the gamut of cords, jacks, plugs, fuse clips, racks, levers, copper and aluminium rods, transmitters, amplifiers, radio and TV equipment and receivers, antennae, through the whole apparatus of telephone instruments, parts, cables, exchanges, switching and carrier transmission systems and equipment to teleprinters, modems, and on to microwave, integrated data, semiconductor, defence electronic, and information systems. In 1970–1, the industry had a turnover of $275 million a year, spent some $10 million annually on research and development, employed some 20,000 people and had a total annual export of $44 million. A decade later, this output had practically quadrupled.[11]

Yet there were features of the industry that were distinctive. The concentration of a large part of total production among six manufacturers (AWA, the Dutch Philips group of companies, L.M. Ericsson, Plessey Australia Pty Ltd, Siemens Industries Ltd and Standard Telephones and Cables Pty Ltd, and the four cable manu-facturers, Austral Standard, Conquerer, Olex and Pirelli Cables), reflected a world trend in telecommunications towards mergers and dominance by a cluster of multinational companies. The Australian telecommunications industry also based its development primarily on local marketing, and scored from the practice adopted by both the PMG and later Telecom of notionally adding tariffs to their tender price evaluations.[12]

But there were other distinctions. Unlike the stereotype Australian manufacturing industries with their problems of outdated and inappropriate technology, poor productivity and inadequate management, the telecommunications industry moved forward on a flood of innovations, new products and techniques. Yet among major systems manufacturing companies such as Ericsson, as its Australian director pointed out, there were high costs of developing telephone switching and transmission systems, while the 'support' for adapting and upgrading these systems over long lifetimes (ARF, ARK, ARM, ARE and AXE were cases in point) was higher still. There were also the problems in other parts of the industry of oversupply in a market that, while involved in vigorous growth, was heavily dependent on the national telecommunications 'common carrier' by competitive tender. Competition between suppliers across most fronts was, self-admittedly, 'very keen'. Nonetheless, the 1974 commission of inquiry into the APO had commended the technical capacity the industry had developed over many years, its ability to produce for local requirement, and its effective working relationships with industry.[13]

This local and competitive emphasis had persisted with Telecom. When the Ericsson AXE switching system was adopted in 1978 (Telecom's love-affair with Sweden, said the media), the equipment had to be manufactured in Australia and provision was made that at least one other Australian manufacturer be granted a licence to produce the equipment as a competitive supplier. By 1977 Telecom's industry policy ensured that most of its transmission plant including cables were of Australian origin, and all but 10 per cent of its total requirements of material and equipment were produced locally. If Telecom's tighter financial management meant some reduction in holdings of equipment stock and a restraint in its procurement investment for the network, the effects on the industry were not long term. By 1977 Telecom contracts let for the supply of telecommunications materials reached $222 million, a figure that rose to $400 million in 1978-9.

Not surprisingly, the telecommunications industry was dedicated to the concept that Telecom's control of the basic switched telecommunications network of Australia should remain undisturbed. 'A fragmented network controlled by competing interests' was, said the industry's national association, 'more likely to lead to a sub-optimal result with consequent adverse effects on economic efficiency and national development'.[14] Yet despite such interdependence, two points were clear. From Telecom's inception the industry had set its sights on a larger share in the terminal and 'add-on' market; and Telecom itself was formulating plans for important extensions into this 'interconnect' field.

Historically Telecom and its antecedents had held sole responsibility for approving, authorising and maintaining all telephone attachments. As new products developed, items such as telephone answering devices, loudspeaking telephones, automatic dialling telephones, alarm systems, radio pagers, and the important facsimile and data equipment were approved by Telecom but marketed and maintained by the supplier. There was also an increasing range of terminal equipment, for example, PMBXs and

PABXs (the private manual and private automatic branch exchanges), telex machines, small business systems, public automatic mobile radio telephone equipment, where Telecom–approved devices dominated certain areas of supply and installation, or shared the supply and leasing with industry manufacturers.

One area that was to assume critical prominence was the new generation of stored programme control electronic PABXs which lay at the heart of the 'interconnect' market. The reasons for their significance was plain. Not only did the electronic PABX act as a private branch telephone communication network (as its electro-mechanical forbear had done), it offered an entire management system for data networks and, hence, an information control system that would form the hub of the office of the future. Word processors, minicomputers, facsimile transmission units, store and forward message devices plugged into it and the integration was seen as a transformation in office technology. Indeed the electronic PABX was a vital cog in the increasingly sophisticated computerised equipment that could be connected to the telephone network to provide a prolifer-ating range of services over and above simple voice transmission. The French had a name for it, 'télématique', and it was, in the words of the Director–General of French Telecommunications (a Government 'telco' on the move), a 'phenomenon whose importance is comparable to the beginnings of railroads or aviation'.[15]

While Telecom clearly stood to gain from the greater use of the network opened up by the spread of interconnect equipment, they also saw their own growth prospects linked to a share of the action in this dynamic new business field. Plans for a radical new PABX policy were therefore shaped at Telecom during 1978. In the past, the PMG had been the exclusive supplier of the electromagnetic PABX which it leased to, installed and maintained in both the public and private sectors. From 1957 private suppliers were allowed to install PABXs with PMG approval, while the Department retained its former monopoly for Federal and State Government departments and instru-mentalities. By 1966, however, the PMG had become the minority supplier in a field which was then dominated by the big five manu-facturers and suppliers, Plessey, Ericsson, AWA, Siemens and STC.

Ten years later, as an outcome of the commission of inquiry's recommendation that there would be significant national advantages if the Telecommunications Commission assumed responsibility for supplying the PABX market in both public and private sectors, Telecom moved in this direction. But its approach was not approved by Government. Telecom's announcement at the beginning of 1979 that it would take a controlling initiative in the new electronic PABXs hence signalled a dramatic policy change. In January, Telecom authorised seven major suppliers to set up a number of trial electronic PABX installations for evaluation. It indicated its intention of allowing competition in its previously exclusive State and semi–Government areas, of entering into competition in the private sector market up to 50 extensions, and of 'revamping' its lease and rental options to Government departments and instrumentalities. The 'interconnect' battle had been launched. Competition in the industry, previously restrained, now became fierce and there were signs of deep perturbation. Telecom's further announcement later that year that the Commission would also enter the fast-growing telephone answering machines (TAMS) and facsimile unit supply markets by calls for tenders in these fields, added fuel to a gathering blaze and provoked open complaint from the industry that Telecom's entry into the private sector markets would result in a flow of work from the private to the public sector and create diseconomies and under-utilisation in the industry.[16]

The proposed strategies had explosive effects. By October 1979, as Telecom's tender choice for the PABXs narrowed to Siemens and Nippon Electric Company, the industry reacted sharply. The traditionally cohesive Australian Telecommunications Development Association split when representations from ATDA's chairman, A.T. Deegan, brought Minister Staley into the fray.

The Coalition's Government's attitude to Telecom's moves towards the interconnect and 'add-on' market, evolving during Robinson's Ministry, had hardened. Staley, an articulate free market advocate, ventilated the Government's reservations. 'We have left Telecom in no doubt', he told the *Australian Financial Review*, 'about our view about their ambition to expand into what has been hitherto the private sector of the market-place. We have done it formally and orally in all the usual ways. We have told Telecom that the private sector can operate perfectly well and for Telecom to go into that market is not only unnecessary but it would give them undue influence in the market-place.'[17]

The Minister's position on the PABXs was unequivocal: Telecom must restrict its private marketing sector of the advanced private telephone systems to key-systems providing no more than two to 20 exchange lines, while the PABXs in that sector were left to the industry. On the telephone answering machine (TAM) and facsimile question, Staley's stand went further. Lobbied by the Office Equipment Industry Association of Australia, the Minister quashed Telecom's tender offer. His refusal to approve contracts peremptorily removed Telecom from two lucrative equipment fields. It was a significant prohibition. The TAMs market was estimated to be worth $2.5 million a year while the facsimile market (cited at approximately $4-5 million annually) was exploding.

Government policy was now an overt obstacle to Telecom's business strategy. The widening gap between the Government's concern for the private sector and Commission plans to develop Telecom's commercial potential in a changing telecommunications environment was sharply, indeed roughly, signalled at the highest level in mid-1980. On 1 July, at the close of the Australian Telecommunications Commission's first five years, the Minister abruptly dropped chairman, Robert Somervaille. News of the unceremonious departure — the chairman's 'shock sacking' as the ATEA described it — underscored differences that had mounted between the Minister and his Commission chairman for some time.

Bob Somervaille had set his seal on strong growth for Telecom to boost its efficiency, upgrade subscriber services, and to take the Commission into the important 'terminal' market. He had also contributed significantly to Telecom's successful entry into the public loan market both at home and overseas, and was known to be critical of the Government's attempts to impose loan restrictions on the Commission's programmes. 'If you have a monopoly [so went his thesis], it's only justified if it's an efficient business service. It's essential that it be a red hot body without failure.' Clashes between Minister and chairman were tactical and philosophical. They went indeed to the

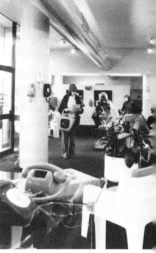

The first years after the formation of Telecom Australia were to see not only new buildings, such as this Telecom district office, at Murray Bridge, SA, and the opening of neighbourhood Telecom business offices, designed to provide better service to the customer but also numerous internal innovations designed to improve efficiency including the local engineering operations processing and recording of data (LEOPARD) system, a computerised telephone fault recording service, first tested in fault despatch centres like this in 1979.

very core of the purposes envisaged for the new Commission. Staley, with his orthodox free enterprise view and his satellite policy on the move, saw himself as anything but a 'rubber stamp' for Telecom. As the PABX matter flared, he told one journalist, 'I think Telecom thought "We only have to say jump and the Minister jumps". I do not accept this.' Somervaille, contrastingly, had joined the interim Commission, as the founding legislation to establish a statutory corporation with 'flexibility in administration and independence from close political control' was being prepared. Inevitably the different positions of the two men exposed a fundamental divergence in Commission and Government ideologies that was larger than personalities.[18]

Two events underscored the point. Six months earlier, in January 1980, the Government, with Telecom's agreement, announced its appointment of the international consultants McKinsey and Company Inc. to work in association with the Postal and Telecommunications Department, the Treasury, the Department of Finance and Telecom to advise on Telecom's assessment of the potential future demands of telecommunications, the appropriateness of Telecom's capital investment policies, and the impact — in a changing telecommunications market — of Telecom's investment policy.

The McKinsey report, 'Capital and Policy Requirements for the 1980s: Telecom Australia', presented to Government in June 1980 was essentially favourable to Telecom. Australia, it said, was receiving substantially greater value for its telecommunications investments than when Telecom was established five years before. Its network was efficient and nearing completion; its financial management was 'improved' and 'innovative', while the management of the capital programme since 1975 had achieved 'a one–third reduction in investment per service in real terms'. However the report advised that Telecom would need to increase its borrowings to fulfil its statutory obligations, it should be allowed a moderate increase in spendings of 8 per cent in real terms by 1990, that it would need to reconsider its cross–subsidisation of country networks and immediately enter the lucrative high technology market. At the same time, the report criticised Telecom for not adequately meeting demand from business, especially large business customers. 'Provisions', it said, 'lag behind their current needs for items such as leased lines and data links, and planning lags behind their need for services.' Telecom should undertake special market studies of the needs of these obligations. Prices of services, it recommended, should also be constructed to reflect costs and, in cases where Government required Telecom to provide a service judged to be essential — such as the rural telephone network — this should be funded by direct Government grant.[19]

The McKinsey report, so substantially supportive of Telecom's tactics, was retained by Government as a confidential document until it was leaked to the waiting press by the shadow minister for communications, Senator Button, a year after its completion in June 1981.[20] It was finally tabled in Parliament on 14 October 1981.

Meanwhile, as the McKinsey company compiled its evidence, the Commission itself, in an anticipatory stroke early in 1980, had appointed the US personnel consultancy firm, William M. Mercer, to advise them on changes in Telecom's organisational structure that would help provide more effective business service and a swifter introduction of new 'value–added' equipment. The resultant report, which appeared just as Staley's Commission changes took effect, hung fire. But its findings and the impetus of the McKinsey report led to a major restructuring within Telecom.[21] A new commercial organisation was introduced at Headquarters and in Victoria and New South Wales early in 1981, 70 key account managers were appointed to administer the needs of Telecom's biggest business clients, and Roger Banks was placed in charge of the new business development directorate which (absorbing the former planning directorate) would focus on planning and pricing policy for major new business ventures.

Five years out from its inception, Telecom was clearly under siege. To a lesser extent than America's AT&T and British Telecommunications but more so than in France and other European countries where the Government common carrier moved unimpeded into new fields, Telecom faced a fight with both Federal Government and the private sector. Staley's denying decisions, had, said deputy chief general manager Smith, created a 'climate of unease'. Banks was more direct. 'They seem to regard policy as their area', he said of Government, 'as though we are people in boiler suits who screw phones on walls ... They don't seem to realise that to run an enterprise like ours you must have something going for you ... [to make] decisions on the best possible basis.'[22]

As the Government's interventionist policy sharpened, private sector forces also gathered to challenge Telecom's entry into the competitive digital electronic and interconnect telecommunications fields. There were two prime movers: the multi–national computer suppliers spearheaded by IBM and a consortium of Australia's corporate giants. Under the banner of the Australian Computer Equipment Suppliers Association, IBM had gone public as early as November 1979 asserting that a public data network was needed in Australia, that such a project needed private enterprise involvement, and needed it soon.[23] Their corporate influence penetrated further afield. In September 1980 the company's Australian director, P. Holmes à Court, announced the formation of Business Telecommunications Services Pty Ltd (BTS), a consortium of 12 made up of such diverse and powerful enterprises as Australian Consolidated Industries, Broken Hill Pty Co. Ltd, Colonial Sugar Refining Ltd (CSR), Conzinc Riotinto Australia (CRA), AWA, Ampol Petroleum Ltd, the Australian Mutual Provident Society, James Hardie Ltd, Publishing and Broadcasting Ltd, Thomas Nationwide Transport Ltd, the Myer Emporium and IBM. The group's brief was to act as a 'research company' to define the long–term communications needs of Australian businesses; but its real intention was, in Holmes à Court's words, 'to develop economically feasible alternatives for the provision of advanced telecommunications services for Australian business'.[24] The end objective of both prime movers was undoubtedly the extensive privatisation of the national telecommunications system.

The new Commission that assembled in July 1980 was a Commission for altered times. Headed by acting chairman May (reappointed as deputy for two more years), it now contained, in addition to Departmental and union representatives Lansdown and Nolan respectively, a North Queensland cattleman C.B. Quartermaine appointed in 1979, and Mrs Elizabeth Manley, chairwoman of an Adelaide–based advertising agency who succeeded Joan Hancock. But there was no chairman of the Commission. By the year's end, with the Federal election of October 1980, the Commission would also inherit a new and senior Minister for the renamed portfolio of 'Communications', the powerful deputy leader of the Country Party, I.M. Sinclair.

While the new competitors mobilised on several fronts, Telecom Australia pressed ahead with a series of innovative approaches and products. At the centre of this activity were the Research Laboratories and the co-ordinated research programme planning developed within the organisation. Without the fanfare that has attended such Government research laboratories as the Australian Atomic Energy Commission, Australia's research leader, the CSIRO, and the Defence Science and Technology Laboratories, the PMG and later Telecom Australia Research Laboratories have tended to be downplayed in

Since their establishment in 1923, the PMG (later Telecom) Research Laboratories have occupied various addresses throughout Melbourne. In 1975 work was begun on these specially designed buildings on a new central site at Clayton, Victoria, next to Monash University.

Australia. Yet, since their foundation as one of H.P. Brown's initiatives in 1923, they performed consistently expanding tasks in the evaluation and adaptation of overseas telecommunications systems and products. By keeping themselves up-to-date on the swiftly evolving telecommunications technology, they served as a 'knowledge base' for informed decision-making. Their independent innovation, with input from some State engineers, covered switching and transmission systems and the more recent digital radio concentrator system (DRCS) due for operation in rural and remote areas in 1984. (See Chapters 9 and 15.)

Within Telecom (and the PMG), there were two distinct views of the Laboratories. Critics maintained that there was 'a large underbrush' of development applications and design work in the organisation but that 'cultural cringe' inhibited real innovation. Telecom and its predecessor, according to this viewpoint, had used contractors for innovative extensions to the network and remained derivative in its adoption of telephone and other equipment models from Britain, and more recently the United States. Another view, however, was that the Research Laboratories fathered many key inventions which, for want of local markets and 'development' funding, were either taken up by multinational companies for overseas

One of many research projects in the Research Labortories was the background work to the introduction of optical fibres. Capable of carrying far more telephone conversations than the conventional cable, optical fibre cable, seen here in comparison with its bulkier predecessor, was first installed in 1981 between the Laboratories and near-by telephone exchange.

Optical fibre cable being installed during 1982–3 into the public network under trial conditions in Brisbane and Melbourne, Victoria. A preliminary plough trial consisting of one kilometre lengths of four separate optical fibre cable designs is here being undertaken in the hilly terrain near Bacchus Marsh, Victoria, using the combined power of three tractors.

exploitation or jettisoned for economic reasons in Australia. In this context, two related inventions stood out. Research performed by the Laboratories in 1972–3 on stored programme control (SPC) electronic exchanges, with digital switching (installed in tandem with existing switch equipment in the Melbourne suburb of Windsor) was in the vanguard of such work overseas. Rollo Brett, then senior assistant director–general of research, put the matter publicly: 'In the switching area', he wrote in 1973, 'it has been our experience that, although in the past we have adopted overseas controlled exchange systems [Strowger, L.M. Ericsson Crossbar and ITT 10C processor], a great deal of special work has been necessary to adapt these systems to the Australian network. Clearly our network is becoming increasingly unique and in the Research Laboratories we consider it a possibility that the next generation of switching equipment will be developed and manufactured in Australia.'[25] The possibility of an indigenous SPC system depended, of course, on economic assessment and a collaborative deal with industry; yet research results were sufficiently advanced by 1973 to induce Brett to announce that the Department would want 'protection and recognition of its legitimate share of the industry property arising from the development'. It was not to be. Despite the 1974 commission's recommendation that the manufacture of limited quantities of telecommunications should be further examined, late in 1977 the Commission announced its decision to adopt L.M. Ericsson's SPC exchange system, AXE.

The Australian SPC system however, and its digital switching, had reached a successful operational stage. H.S. Wragge, a senior Research Laboratories member, presented a detailed account of the exchange model to an international symposium on switching in Kyoto, Japan, in 1976 and reported that the model had interconnected with all the different types of exchanges used in the Australian network, carried live traffic of some 1,000 calls a day for nearly a year, and was particularly 'effective in achieving a high degree of initial fault free operation'.[26] Without the industrial back–up needed for so major a switching system, however, Telecom's expertise was diverted to evaluating tenders for the imported electronic equipment and as a 'test bed' for further studies into remotely controlled switching stages and remotely operated exchanges. The event was illustrative. The size of the Australian market and general economies of scale were generally advanced as factors against indigenous 'development' work, and many ideas conceived in the Research Laboratories passed by way of staff movement to Australian subsidiaries and thence to the parent company overseas. L.M. Ericsson frankly acknowledged the contribution made by its Broadmeadows, Victoria, plant to its Stockholm operations in the automatic call distributor (ACD) system devised by staff drawn from working on the evolving system in the PMG Research Laboratories, Ericsson subsequently marketed ACD worldwide.[27] Surprisingly, in a period when high technology industry for Australia has been pressed by both coalition and Labor parties, the question of an Australian telecommunications industry based on a collaborative Telecom and industry, research and development effort, which is strongly supported by some Telecom research staff, has barely been examined.

One aspect of the PMG, and later Telecom, Research Laboratories' conduct appeared unique in Australia. They developed a co–ordinated and highly accountable system of research planning and performance. The system, institutionalised as research, development and innovation (RDI), was initiated by Eber Lane. As a new Director–General in 1972, Lane was struck by a certain *ad hoc* and overlapping organisation of research and development (R&D) which involved not only the

Research Laboratories but two headquarter's engineering divisions and resources in the State administrations as well. As the technology became more costly and sophisticated and its applications immense, Lane considered that it was essential that the selection and priority of innovative projects be carried out by a specialist group under scrutiny at the highest headquarter level. 'The fundamental intention, reason, purpose, etc, for the procedures', he minuted, 'is to ensure that research of any consequence will not take place other than on approved items; design work will be planned, priorities will be determined and no design work of consequence will be put in hand unless it is on an approved programme; and work will not be put into new technologies and innovations unless programmed and approved.'[28]

The outcome, in 1974, was the setting up of the three–year programme of research, development and innovation, launched at headquarters in June. While the first programme (1974/5–1976/7) was a headquarter's affair, subsequent programmes involved the States. The purpose of the programmes was to overview new systems, equipment and technical procedures proposed for telecommunications with justification, an estimate of resources required, and target 'in service' dates. The programmes were further designed to provide a vehicle for strategic decisions on projects to be pursued, the types of action required, and responsibilities for such action. Finally they were to provide an overview of resources engaged on various types of development activity within the total organisation and enable corporate priorities to be set.[29]

Lane would put his signature to this important piece of planning as the blueprint for Telecom took shape. It was, of necessity, tentative, the first year only was formally approved; yet its purpose was crystal clear — to streamline R&D programme planning and operation in the Laboratories, at headquarters and in the States, avoid duplication from lack of information (an acknowledged, and at times, fertile, phenomenon in the PMG) and to render a fully accountable overview of the organisation's undertakings in research, development and design. As such it was as orderly a piece of corporate policy making for resource allocation as could be found in any Australian research laboratory. When scholars began to probe the workings of the AAEC, and the CSIRO, its form of accounting and methods used by some of its major divisions in more recent years, the contrast between the PMG and the country's applied research colossus (even allowing for broad differences in mission, research activities and funding) were marked.[30] 'The emphasis in the preparation of this first programme', Lane set down in June 1974, 'should be on a close examination of work in hand to determine those items which should be continued, and perhaps accelerated, those where planned progress should be slowed, and those which should be substantially modified or eliminated. Out of this examination . . . will emerge a relationship between the different areas of activity and between short and long range projects that will provide a basis for the development of more specific guidelines for future programmes.'[31]

Only a month before, at a time when Ministerial pressures sought to discourage funding of projects which were self-perpetuating and low yielding in practical results, the chairman of the CSIRO wrote to one chief of division that 'the basic management concepts of CSIRO are such that the Executive is not, and has not sought to be, involved in programme details'.[32] The position had altered little by 1983.

Telecom Australia would adopt an even more pronouncedly 'top-down' research management approach in 1980 when the RDI select committee was finally set up, composed of the director business development, the general manager engineering, the general manager commercial services and the director research, to act as Lane's envisaged top level scrutinising group.[33]

Within this framework, diverse long term and short term research and development programmes were conducted. Telecom's research budget reached $20 million in 1980–1; the now extensive Research Laboratories at Clayton outside Melbourne employed some 540 staff, 200 of whom were 'professional' in June 1981 and almost the same total, technical staff. Engineers, many with higher degrees and with a strong concentration in electronic research, made up the largest sector (approximately 150 in 1981), while the range of some 50 scientists included chemists, physicists, metallurgists, together with three psychologists, and about ten computer science officers. Additionally, Telecom collaborated directly in some research areas with industry, contracted out annual sums rising to $500,000 and funded basic telecommunications research in centres of higher learning, through its membership of the Radio Research Board. In turn, Australian universities and colleges of advanced education provide graduate and post-graduate staff experienced in telecommunications research for employment in the Research Laboratories.[34]

Research ranged across broad fields. From Telecom's inception, digital coding and transmission techniques for voice, data and video signals held a central place. A pilot scheme on a digital data network using digital transmission and time division multiplexing was introduced on the Sydney–Canberra–Melbourne trunk route, and work was carried out on processes for the production of specialised and advanced semi-conductor devices. Solar energy applications moved ahead. Telecom took a significant lead in installing solar power based on solar photo voltaic modules in installations in isolated areas. First used at Wilkatana near Port Augusta in South Australia in 1974 for a subscribers radio telephone system and later in Western Australia in 1976 to power small telephone repeater stations at Roy Hill and Kumarina in the Pilbara, solar energy connected some 20 subscribers to a radio telephone system at Glen Valley, Victoria, in 1977 and, less than three years later, supplied the power for 13 repeater stations on the microwave route between Tennant Creek and Alice Springs. By 1980 this low power energy system also linked 13 islands in Torres Strait to the northern Australian mainland, figured on the Coen-Mossman microwave route to Cape York Peninsula, and served, at times in association with wind power, in distant areas of Tasmania. During 1979, with a background of innovative expertise, Telecom members joined a team and advised the Indian Government on the use of solar power.[35]

After much development work, solar power has been successfully introduced by Telecom at various sites and in differing climates throughout the continent, making Australia a world leader in the use of such technology. In 1977, Glen Valley, in the Victorian Alps, was the location for Australia's first solar-powered telephone exchange.

At Breona, in northern Tasmania, solar technology is adapted to power a single and remote public telephone.

Frank Henschke, senior technical officer, gives final inspection to the world's first major solar-powered link installed in 1979 on the 580km microwave telecommunications route between Alice Springs and Tennant Creek, NT.

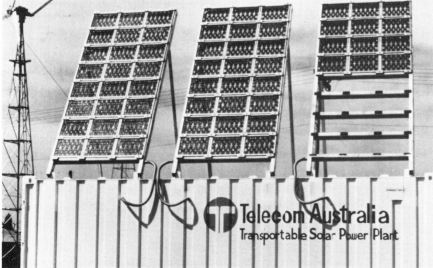

Telecom's Research Laboratories designed this fully transportable standard solar power plant for use wherever required.

In addition to the sun, the power of the wind had been harnessed as at the microwave repeater station on King Island, where three windmill generators are used to relay telephone conversations across the Bass Strait, between Tasmania and the mainland.

Ian McCahon Sinclair, Minister for Communications from 1980 to 1982. Sinclair was subsequently elected leader of the National Party in succession to Doug Anthony in 1984.

New customer facilities, backed by design and research, also streamed off Telecom's production line. A galaxy of acronyms heralded the Commission's thrust into important new commercial areas, the ADS (analogue datel services), DDS (digital data services) and AUSTPAC (packet switched data service) offered a new family of data communications products as the eighties began. Automatic mobile telephone services were introduced in Sydney and Melbourne late in 1981, and a telefinder radio paging service was in full swing nationally by February 1981. Multifeature telephones for the go-ahead consumer offering push-button dialling, internal paging, abbreviated dialling and automatic last-number re-dialling emerged in the small business 'Commander' system (Siemens and STC supplied) which was launched in 1981 and streamlined, many faceted 'Trimfones', 'Featurephones' were scheduled for 1982. Yet the solid traditionally spelt dial 'telephone' still satisfied most Australians and it had penetrated to 83 per cent of homes by early 1983.

Ian Sinclair was a heavyweight of a Minister. Elected to the House of Representatives as Country Party member for New England, New South Wales in 1963, his Ministerial experience included Shipping, Agriculture, Transport, Urban and Regional Development, and Primary Industry. He had been leader of the House of Representatives (with the exception of a nine-month absence from all office in 1979–80) and deputy leader of the coalition Country Party since 1975. Trained as a lawyer at Sydney University with experience in his father's accounting firm, Sinclair was also a part-time pastoralist, and a paradox. As spokesman for the Country Party before the Royal Commission of Inquiry into the APO in 1973, he had (it was difficult to believe in 1983) resisted the concept of partition of the PMG, arguing that the Department should be regarded 'as an essential service', 'an instrument of national development', and not as a statutory trading corporation. 'Its capital expenditure and recurrent losses', he gave evidence then, 'should be assisted by direct subvention from the Treasury and not by recourse to loan funds'.[36]

Several years later Sinclair had performed a *volte face*. As the fourth senior member of Fraser's free-enterprise cabinet, he had not only

The 1980s were to see the introduction of many new customer and business products. In September 1981 Telecom launched its automatic mobile telephone system in Melbourne and Sydney, giving full automatic access to customer vehicles using local, trunk and international networks.

Customers at home or in the office could now use the Digitel, Flip Phone, or Touch-a-matic range of telephones, the Commander small business system (SBS) series and a range of modern business aids, such as this Telex 2000, with many advanced features, including visual display and add-on floppy disk memory.

accepted and rationalised the statutory and trading form of Telecom Australia and Australia Post (now in his charge), but was determined both to decline to assist the Telecommunications Commission by 'subventions from the Treasury', and to buttress the Government's policy of imposing restriction on the size of Telecom's loan funds. The Minister was, as he agreed in an interview with the author, at least a 'semi–paradox'.[37]

The appointment of so senior a politician to the Communications portfolio was itself significant. If Staley had emerged as the first of the purposeful 'new men' in backing private sector diversification of telecommunications, Sinclair became the champion of an entre-preneurial bonanza in what he saw as 'the exciting new technologies of communications'. From the outset, the new Minister left the public and bureaucracy in no doubt of his support for private interests in communications through his early restructuring of the Broadcasting and Television Act.[38] In an address to Rotarians at Orange in March 1981 he stressed that the business world could look forward to participating in innovative devices that could be attached to the telephone and, in a reply to an opposition parliamentary question that same month requesting assurance that the domestic satellite would not effect Telecom's 'economic viability' or threaten the jobs of technicians, Sinclair roundly dismissed attempts at 'generating emotionalism about the impact of a technology designed to bring the benefits of improved facilities to the Australian people'.[39]

The Minister inherited a telecommunications authority whose borrowing levels had been severely cut. It was a policy Sinclair would extend. In the first days of his Ministry, acting chairman May noted publicly that Telecom's 'approved borrowing levels had been gener-ally $20 million to $30 million less than the Commission proposed'. But, buoyed up by his Government's commitment on the competing (though roughly costed) satellite, Sinclair was determined to keep a sharp eye on other telecommunications projects to ensure, he said, that they were 'within the ability of society to finance and to manage'.[40] Hence, while Telecom's overall profit continued to rise (from $211.5 million in 1979–80 to $232.5 million in 1980–1), it felt the severe bite of Government restraint. Moreover, as a result of a Treasury decision during 1981, the Commission also faced a daunting increase to 10 per cent in the rate of interest paid on the outstanding value of old capital advances negotiated with the Commonwealth since before 1975 — a burden that would add some $60 million to Telecom's expenditure from January 1982.

Yet even while the budget tightened, the network was pushing out. On major country axes, development forged ahead. The long coaxial cable project stretching from Ceduna, South Australia to Cobar, New South Wales, and on from Dubbo to Brisbane, started late in 1976, was completed in 1980 across 2,500 kilometres of the toughest, roughest country in Australia.[41] This cable, capable of carrying over 5,500 simultaneous telephone communications, STD, telex and television services linked Australia's two satellite earth stations at Ceduna and Moree and, stretching via Port Augusta, South Australia, Broken Hill,

Cobar and Moree, New South Wales, to Ipswich and Brisbane linked Western and South Australia and the eastern States and joined them by beamed INTELSAT satellite to the rest of the world.

The construction of the cable was a *tour de force*. Worked in sectors (like the overland telegraph line a century before), its route crossed the infamous 'hard–rock' of the Eyre Peninsula, tunnelled through the rugged Flinders Ranges, stretched into the flood plains of the Darling River and, close to Cobar, pierced the backbone of the Great Dividing Range. State teams drawn from South and Western Australia and Queenland soon lost count of the rock tonnage blasted and dug from the earth. At Wilcannia on the Darling River alone, over 100,000 tonnes of alluvial earth were removed to gouge out trenches at extra depth necessary to withstand the floods. Faced with widely differing climatic conditions and different 'bedding' for the cable across the route, the suppliers, Siemens Industries, Melbourne, adopted a method of regulating the cable amplifiers to suit ground temperatures.

Equally important and farreaching was the venture launched during 1980 to take modern communications to the sparsely settled

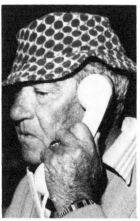

Vertical conquest of space. The Kimberley microwave project between Port Hedland and Kununurra, WA, completed in 1983 became the world's longest solar-powered communications link. The microwave repeater sites, such as this at Matterhorn (above), became the means by which wayside radio telephone services, connected to the nearest microwave repeater by individual solar powered radio telephones, could be set up (below). These gave telephone access to the outside world to 'the amazing people of the bush'.

regions of north–west Western Australia via the Kimberley microwave system. Planned in stages, the route between Port Hedland and Derby was completed in November 1982, while the second stage, following the Great Northern Highway, would reach Wyndham and Kununurra in September 1983. In a landscape of burning sunshine, 20 solar-powered repeater stations were installed along the 'super highway'. At the same time, across the continent, Queensland replaced its open wire lines along the Cape York Peninsula with a modern microwave extension of the Cairns–Mossman broadband system from Mossman to Coen.

While specific planning and execution of these major network extensions came from the States, managing director Curtis put his personal seal behind the remote area plans. 'Curtis was drawing the team all the time on this', said one senior Telecom official. 'It was his favourite baby.' It was also a strong commitment under the Telecommunications Act. Amid the rising tide of competition, there was, said Curtis, still the 'big question' of the nature of the national telecommunication system the Commission was trying to build. 'Are we going to provide', he reflected, 'the nation–wide services envisaged by the Act which require a strong cross–subsidy from the populated boomerang–shaped area from Adelaide to Brisbane [including Melbourne, Canberra and Sydney], or are we going to let other carriers into the main profit areas, have the Commission lose the more profitable traffic, and let the country look after itself?' Only Telecom, as Curtis rightly argued, would look after the outback, and the outback with its hostile country and hardship, and dogged and pioneering people made a powerful claim on his mind.

It was against this background of planning and progress that Telecom and its Commission confronted the uncompromising policy of the Government. By mid–1981 Prime Minister Fraser had publicly foreshadowed a major review of the activities of the Australian Telecommunications Commission. Telecom Australia was on notice. Curtis observed the growing schism between Telecom and the coalition free enterprise Government in plain terms. 'Telecom's success and its concept of meeting new business objectives', he said, 'has been an offence to Government. They feel it deeply in their souls . . . Just as technology was making it possible to succeed in the notion of a "universal service"', he said, 'the Government has taken decisions that make it impossible.'[42]

Ian Sinclair's role as Minister, and the National Country Party's deputy leader, was pivotal. Yet there was an evident dichotomy in his views. In private discussion, he justified a free enterprise approach to telecommunications in practical and ideological terms. The miner, the developer, the 'new breed of mechanised farmer' engaged in buying and selling were, he said, just as important in their communication needs as city businessmen, and the best way of getting them better service — including data service and the whole gamut of business terminals — was by opening up telecommunications to competition. While Telecom did a good job in expanding the system, Sinclair observed, 'technically it was still behind on phone installations and consumer-oriented services'. The Gold Coast and the outer Blue Mountain suburbs of Sydney, he stressed, were 'screaming for telephones'. While Sinclair had praise for his other communications Commission, the OTC, 'Telecom', he said, 'should be closer to running a business'. Importantly it should 'direct its funds to areas where they were most needed' and allow private enterprise to enter computerised data fields and the burgeoning business services.[43]

Like many Ministers who enter a technological portfolio with a layman's view, Sinclair was excited by the technology and the potential of privately-owned information systems. But there was some irrationality, a flaw in his financial reasoning. The 'directing' of Telecom funds to areas of remote subscriber needs, as he knew, made heavy financial claims: $27 million for the Ceduna-Brisbane cable; $19 million for the Port Hedland-Kununurra Microwave System for the Kimberleys; and $5 million for the microwave radio from Mossman to Coen. Cross-subsidies from the profitable basic telephone facility and local calls in metropolitan areas to 'lossy' country services, which Telecom revealed publicly for the first time in its annual report of 1979-80, were over $200 million a year, while Telecom's surplus for the same period, stood at $211.5 million.[44]

McKinsey's panacea for these problems had been simple but tough. Yet they had not recommended themselves to the Minister. The McKinsey Company's recommendation that Telecom tariffs should be restructured to minimise cross-subsidies while the Government provided direct capital grants for approved projects which were below the cost of capital, transcended the Minister's thinking. Searching for answers, he would appoint M.G. King, a former deputy general manager of CSR, early in 1981 to examine and report on the specific question of telecommunications terminal equipment.[45] Five months later, amid frustration and clear Government intimations that Telecom's monopoly 'could not be considered sacrosanct', managing director Curtis found himself in sudden and open clash with his Minister and cabinet.

Ironically the issue turned on the wage claims of technical staff. In May 1981 Telecom's major union, ATEA, harking back to the loose ends of their wages dispute of two years before and aware that the broad class of 'Telecom tradesmen' was not paid as well as their colleagues in State Government organisations or other Commonwealth Government service, entered a claim to management for an 8 per cent wage increase plus a $25 weekly industry allowance. Telecom management accepted the justice of the claim. 'We were a large employer making profits at the high end of the technology', said Curtis. 'We were gaining the highest profitability but paying less.'[46] A review of comparative wage and salary levels of Commonwealth and State employees undertaken by Telecom confirmed the point.

Tom May, as acting chairman, accordingly wrote to the Minister in April 1981 to seek approval for Telecom to negotiate with the ATEA on the claim. The Minister's reply to the Commission gave Telecom the right to negotiate within 'the wage indexation guidelines'. Sinclair was acting on cabinet instructions. His response to May followed a cabinet meeting which reviewed the detailed official report and endorsed Telecom's review of the salary disparity and gap that should be closed. But there was a rider: cabinet had told Sinclair that he was to 'oversight the situation' and that Telecom was to proceed in accordance with his instructions.[47]

Considerable uncertainty prevailed. Wage indexation guidelines had been introduced in Australia under the Whitlam Government in April 1975 as an attempt by the Conciliation and Arbitration Commission to adjust wages regularly for price movements and provide a fixed forum for the processing of other claims for improved wages and conditions. It was with the Arbitration Commission, Sinclair and most Ministers believed, that the Telecom matter should be finally tested. But, hung up on management's 'waiting' stance, first the APTU and subsequently the ATEA, indicated their determination to achieve their claim by placing limited work and telecommunications services bans.[48] The Government's position now turned on a negotiated settlement of the unions' claim ratified by the Arbitration Commission. The case was referred to the Arbitration Commission on 28 May. But, forced to public arbitration on what the Melbourne *Age* aptly called a 'Complex Pay Struggle Which Nobody Wants', the two unions increased their demands. Failure to find a means to settle the claim within the Arbitration Commission led to further bans and wider telecommunications breakdown and to an emergency meeting of the interdepartmental industry committee, the co-ordinating committee on pay and conditions in Australian government employment.

Once again Telecom found itself at the centre of a dislocating national dispute. While in private conference within the Arbitration Commission, Telecom and the unions sought a negotiated settlement which could be regarded as within the guidelines, Sinclair expressed a differing public view. In the present dispute, he told Parliament on 3 June, Telecom's comparative wage review did not take account of private industry and — the inference was clear — the matter could not be resolved by direct negotiations. It was within the Conciliation and Arbitration system that a capacity existed to 'refer to an anomalies procedure' in the interests both of Telecom employees and the public, and it was there that 'the Government believes wage negotiations should occur'.[49]

Sinclair, it would appear, had departed from the position conveyed by him in private to Telecom. As events progressed, his position also differed from cabinet's original decision not to oppose the negotiated settlement but to get the Conciliation and Arbitration Commission to agree immediately to part payment of the claim and settle the rest by a Full Bench.[50] His tenet, however, stood on slippery ground. Sir John Moore, President of the Conciliation and Arbitration Commission, saw the matter in another light. After several attempts to chair an 'anomalies conference' in the Telecom case and to give Full Bench sanction to the now consensually agreed wage conditions, Moore threw the responsibility back into the Government's lap. The Conciliation and Arbitration Commission, he gave judgment from the Full

Bench, could not 'recommend, endorse or ratify an agreement between Telecom Australia and its two major technical unions'. The matter of collective bargaining lay outside the wage indexation guidelines and was 'inconsistent with existing national wage case principles'.[51]

Moore's decision, startling to all parties, precipitated crisis. Telecom management clearly believed they were acting within the guidelines and, subject to Arbitration approval, could implement the agreement once the bans were removed. Curtis kept his Minister well informed. He knew, as he told Sinclair, that union officials had seen the agreed wage rises in 'cold hard print' and recognised that 'you can't take bones away from dogs'.[52] George Slater, the APTU's influential Federal secretary, also claimed publicly that the matter now rested in the Minister for Communications' hands. As Anne Summers of the *Australian Financial Review* critically surveyed the situation, the Minister had 'added to the confusion' by indicating during the week that the unions were entitled to wage increases of the size agreed to during the final phases of negotiation.[53] An emergency cabinet meeting called on the night of 10 June 1981, together with a late evening visit to Canberra by Curtis, his deputy chief general manager Smith and Telecom's industrial relations general manager O'Sullivan — Pollock was overseas — highlighted an advancing storm. On Friday 12 June Jack Curtis announced his resignation as Telecom's managing director.

Why? During that hectic week, Telecom management had sealed the agreement with their unions. Their action, taken as communications links strained and cracked around Australia, followed a consistent path. Curtis was clear he had not misled the Minister on the 'guidelines'. He had kept Sinclair informed both verbally and in writing. He had also communicated with Lansdown, secretary of the Department of Communications. Telecom, he said, 'had acted in good faith'.

By the week's end, both Fraser and Sinclair had made it plain that Telecom management had 'acted contrary to specific Cabinet instructions in dealing with the unions'. In measured language very different from the 'dressing down' administered in Ministerial rooms, the Prime Minister declared that he was 'not particularly enchanted' with the way Telecom conducted negotiations. It would, he asserted, be made clear to all statutory authorities that 'they can't run and cut loose the way Telecom appears to have on this particular occasion'.[54] Telecom top management had felt the lash. 'We expected a rough time and we got it', reflected one participant. 'It was a very harrowing experience . . . the nearest thing to a star chamber I can imagine.'

Curtis emerged with dignity from the political hullaballoo. 'Never resign, wait until you're sacked' rang the old adage. Curtis thought otherwise. He had steered Telecom through six constructive years. For the last two of these, his organisation had been consistently under fire. With one more year to go before retirement, he believed he had made his major contribution and that another managing director might be better able 'to bridge the gulf'. He offered his resignation, was given a chance to reconsider, but declined. Curtis had accepted the sacrificial role; but he did not wear the martyr's robe. 'We turned the whole system round', he said in an ABC interview next day. There was no body he could think of, that despite economic constraints and government restrictions, had 'progressed so fast and had refused to raise its prices over a period of five years'.

Amid the clamour of his going, it fell to one radical union leader to state employees' reaction in blunt terms. 'I am not in the business of defending Telecom', said the ATEA's New South Wales state secretary Cooper, 'but it seems to me that the Government is trying to use Telecom as a scapegoat for the failure of its own policies. It has always been in the Government's power to end the dispute by allowing Telecom to negotiate an agreement as it saw fit . . . It seemed to us throughout the dispute that Telecom kept the Government informed of progress in negotiations and that makes the Prime Minister's criticism of Telecom very unfair.'[55]

Curtis's departure cast a long shadow. Though he himself believed that no man's influence stretched beyond his time of service, he was modestly wide of the mark. He had shaped and led a telecommunications organisation that had performed a capital task, met capital targets and produced large capital returns. While he lacked the personality and 'nerve ends' for the manoeuvres of political power, he had substantially styled and motivated the enterprise of Telecom Australia. That he had done it for a year in 1980–1 without a Commission chairman, journalists were quick to note. 'Wanted', wrote the *Australian Financial Review*'s business and political columnist, 'Chanticleer', in a sardonic job description of the vacant managing directorship on 10 July 1981, the day Curtis quit office, 'Managing Director for Australia's largest business'.

> Unfortunately there may be changes in the organisation, but we are not quite sure what they will be or whether bits will be sold off. There will soon be an inquiry by somebody or other and successful applicants will learn of the terms of reference of the inquiry and who will conduct it, if they read the newspapers. Assuming the organisation remains intact, the appointee will report to the chairman, when one is found. He will also report to a Minister, a group of commissioners, numerous members of the Department of Communications, the Prime Minister, Treasury, Sir Phillip Lynch, interested backbenchers, Bill Mansfield, Kerry Packer and Doug Anthony. If he has the time, the managing director will administer 88,000 people, a cash flow of $12 million a day, and the most complex technological changes Australia has ever seen . . . Changes in operating policy of the organisation, as they affect the managing director, will be announced by the Minister in public speeches from time to time. Appointees should watch the newspapers for meetings of bodies such as the NSW Birdwatchers Association, Ballarat Grain and Feed Association and the Liberal Party's Mothers Guild — addressed by the Minister from time to time.

Curtis, it appeared, had helped 'Chanticleer' with his parody. It was a sharp swan song.

The man who inherited the managing directorship would have to steer Telecom through perhaps the most critical passage of its history. W.J.B. Pollock, acting MD for several months, was appointed to the top executive post in October 1981. At the same time, after an inexplicable hiatus of fifteen months, the Government announced the appointment of R.W. Brack as chairman of the Commission. Brack, vice–chairman of TAA and a former general manager of Australian Consolidated Industries was seen as an experienced and reliable administrator who would, in Minister Sinclair's words, 'bring a mix of business and government acumen and enterprise to what is one of Australia's most important statutory positions'!

Pollock, clear–sighted and pragmatic, a cool performer in the corridors of power, differed singularly from his predecessor in his administrative and political approach. He was less the planning zealot than Curtis, and he was not an engineer. Gordon Martin, former general manager engineering Telecom (and not the involved deputy chief general manager Smith) succeeded Pollock to the chief general manager's post.

Bill Pollock instantly took on the rough and tumble of the private sector–common carrier fight. In closer harmony with his Minister than Curtis had ever sought to be, he could not, however, influence the outcome of two bids made by Telecom to dominate a duo of major new telecommunications being discussed for introduction in Australia: cable television and videotex. With the appointment of the Australian Broadcasting Tribunal on cable television in mid–1981, Telecom had pressed its claim as the most efficient body to establish the cable TV network and to operate it 'in the national interest'. Telecom's proposal envisaged introducing the system (already in rather difficult operation in the USA) on present cost efficient coaxial cable technology, and leasing individual terminals to private organisations. But the tribunal's verdict was an unqualified 'No'. Scope, they concluded, should be given to private companies to provide communications services ranging from video pictures to electronic bank fund transfer and 'teleshopping'.[56]

Man at the top, W.J.B. Pollock, AM, who joined the PMG as a junior mechanic in 1938, and rose to head the Victorian administration from 1974 to 1975. He became managing director in November 1981 and was re-appointed for a second three-year term in February 1984.

The videotex outcome seemed equally glum. As early as 1980, after several years of study and investigation by Telecom of evolving videotex systems overseas, the Commission proposed to Government that Telecom should introduce a national public videotex system (based on the successful British 'Prestel') for the purpose of transmitting computer stored information over the switched telephone network and linking the telephone to television screens. Seen by many as the linchpin of a new information age, videotex could transmit data as diverse as weather, stock exchange information, news, hotel and transport bookings, entertainment, ordering, shopping, games, and even electronic newspapers and mail. Telecom, it was proposed, should again provide the basic network facilities and computer, and private enterprise the terminals and information.

Under pressure from Kerry Packer's Publishing and Broadcasting Ltd and Myers Ltd, owner of one of Australia's largest computer centres and leased–line networks for the transfer of details of its scattered sales and stores, Sinclair first declined Telecom's overture, returned later to 'think again', and finally told Parliament in October 1981 that Telecom could not compete in the videotex technology.

While Labor's shadow minister for science and technology, Barry Jones, attacked Sinclair for this 'savage but all too predictable attack on the country's intellectual capacity' and complained pithily that 'the Minister is taking more positions than the *Kama Sutra*', Telecom lost out tactically to the interests of private enterprise.[57]

Pollock, however, set his sails to catch the wind. He built good relations with his chairman and Minister and publicly acknowledged that not only were there long–term prospects for private enterprise sharing in major telecommunications areas, but that Telecom 'should welcome competition as a spur to efficiency'. To take a hard–line attitude now, he said as new managing director late in 1981, 'would destroy Telecom'. His strategy proved realistic. The foreshadowed public inquiry into telecommunications services in Australia was announced during his acting managing directorship on 23 September 1981.

Under the chairmanship of J.A. Davidson (chairman of Commonwealth Industrial Gases Ltd, whose name would stamp the review), the committee was to examine and report to the Minister for Communications on three fields:

(i)   the extent to which the private sector could be more widely involved in the provision of existing or proposed telecommunications services in Australia either alone or in conjunction with the Australian Telecommunications Commission;

(ii) the consequential change that might be necessary in statutory functions, duties, financial objectives and monopoly provisions of the Commission; and

(iii) the effectiveness of the Commission's operational policies and organisational arrangements.[58]

Unlike its major predecessor, the inquiry into the Australian Post Office of 1972–3, the Davidson inquiry was not a Royal Commission and the performance of its investigations proved considerably less probing and broad. Committee members, in addition to the chairman were one–time adviser to Government, Malcolm King, Professor of Communications, A.E. Karbowiak of the University of New South Wales (associated with the Telecom–ATEA exchange maintenance trials), and W.A. Dick, chartered accountant and chairman of Pacific Carpets International Pty Ltd.

In this battle for survival, Telecom would throw its defences into a major overview of its first six years.[59] Among the 143 public submissions to the inquiry which included media and industry, the Australian Telecommunications Employees Association (ATEA) gave Telecom fundamental support. It had hitched its wagon to Telecom's star during the anti–national carrier satellite skirmishes three years before. At its annual Federal Council meeting in Perth in October 1980, it moved further and (in the light of Staley's restrictive embargoes), announced its conviction that Telecom should be encouraged to maintain and extend its activities 'at the consumer interface of the telecommunications industry' to ensure genuine competition and an increase in choice to the consumer. In February ATEA consolidated its stand. Then, nine Telecom unions resolved to form a loose inter–union association to develop a joint strategy to meet the challenge of a Government bent on 'dismantling' Telecom. In one respect, it was self–defence. But ATEA clearly saw themselves as defenders of the 'ordinary Australian subscriber' and as bulwarks against domination of Australian communications from 'boardrooms overseas'. To fight the good fight, they hired publicists, consultants and research assistants, and allocated $200,000 to carry their educative, political and industrial campaign for the 'Australian connection' to the media, community and, finally, the hustings at the Federal election of March 1983. 'The record of Telecom Australia', read their submission to the Davidson inquiry, 'in overall terms in providing services to the Australian community has been commendable.' Since 1975 Telecom 'had become more efficient, it was offering a greater range of services, it was more responsive to customer needs, was achieving higher standards, and had achieved these objectives while lowering charges in real terms to the community'.[60]

Contrastingly, Telecom and its Commission seemed far less articulate in its public defence. While senior staff members participated in union and other seminars, Telecom's leaders waged a private fight. To make a song and dance in the hope of changing the situation, Roger Banks summed up top management's strategy, would be counter–productive. 'If you let the press get involved', he asserted, 'you lose control, and if you lose control, you can't win.' Yet this approach, while convincing to top floor executives of Telecom head-quarters, was alienating to many demoralised Telecom employees. It was also unenlightening and misleading to one important Telecom constituency, its own subscribers, a constituency Telecom was too often prone to overlook.

Pollock would justify his tactics pragmatically: it paid off. By his concerted lobbying, he would, throughout 1982 in association with Brack, wage a persistent assault on the bastions of relevant opinion — the Country party, the telecommunications industry, Government backbenchers, opposition supporters, the Country Women's Association and other concerned community groups. At the same time, he kept up a continuing dialogue with bureaucrats and his Minister. Hence, despite Telecom's public appearance as a latter-day Saint Sebastian heavily pierced with spears, Pollock's tactic brought returns. Financially Telecom was able to increase its expenditure on capital works spending by four per cent during 1982; its public loans rose, and new customer services gained range and penetration. Pollock was conspicuously confident. 'We have learned a lot in our first seven years', he told staff during 1982, 'Telecom 1982 is very different from Telecom 1975. We have developed a team of skilled and dedicated people who can rise to any heights when the chips are down. This is our greatest asset.'[61]

The Davidson report was tabled in Parliament by Sinclair's successor in the portfolio, N.A. Brown, on 28 October 1982. If all work ceased at Telecom that afternoon it was not surprising. Staff gathered in groups to hear internally broadcast reports. The recommendations hit Telecom at its core. With hindsight, many of them appear bizarre.

The Australian Telecommunications Commission, the report recommended, should be abolished and replaced by an incorporated company 'Telecom Australia Limited' owned 100 per cent by the Commonwealth Government. The company's relationship to the Commonwealth should be as a shareholder to company: it should set its own telecommunications prices (without the statutory powers of Ministerial direction) and manage its own staffing, contracting and purchasing policies. At the same time, terminal equipment, staff and assets associated with it should be transferred to an independent Telecommunications Equipment Company (the name was lively), 'TELEQUIP'.

Telecom Australia should be broken up. The private sector should be permitted to participate in all aspects of terminal equipment marketing and wiring; responsibility for technical standards was to be transferred from Telecom to an independent statutory authority; but Telecom Australia Ltd would be permitted to offer public leased network capacity and 'gateway' facilities to information and videotex service providers on a non–exclusive commercial basis. Telecom Australia Ltd was also named as the most logical organisation for control of cable television. On pricing, the news was no less brisk. The user paid. The new company's pricing policy should, said the report, reflect costs 'to a substantial degree'. It should minimise price discrimination, adopt timed local calls, but (a left–over from the discarded McKinsey report) 'direct subsidy funded from sources external to Telecom should be introduced for any class of subscriber which Government wishes to assist'.[62]

At the heart of the report lay the question of monopoly. Changing modes of telecommunications, growing public awareness of its great capabilities for improved information services, and the growing 'liberalisation' of current practices which Telecom endorsed, all pointed to an increase in, and healthy evidence of, the need for competition. 'The question', said the report, 'is not between competition or monopoly but how to allow competition to develop in a manner to gain the most benefit for the community.'[63]

Neil Brown, QC, the Melbourne barrister, who was to serve as Minister for Communications from 1982 until his defeat in the Federal election of 1983

In its fight against privatisation, Telecom management was to receive unsolicited support from within the ranks of its own staff, as this public meeting held by the ATEA at Bendigo, Victoria, in February 1983 shows.

While all staff were, in the report's recommendations, to be transferred with all existing rights and entitlements to either one of Telecom's suggested new parts, there were probably few who went home that evening who did not feel rather like the Melbourne *Age* cartoonist Tanner's Owl!

There were, however, ironies ahead. On 3 March 1983, Australia went to the polls and elected a Labor Government to office under Prime Minister Robert Hawke. Committed in its platform to the Australian Telecommunications Commission as the national carrier, the threat of a dismembered Telecom fell away. Unlike the United States and Britain, Australia would continue, at least for the foreseeable future, to preserve its established Governmental telecommunications authority.

'Hullo, mum!!!' 'BeepA' the owl, launched in 1979 to advertise Telecom's cheaper night time STD rates, portrayed on the morning after the tabling of the Davidson Report. From a cartoon by Tanner in the *Age* of Melbourne.

Lessons had been learnt on both political sides. Increasing competition in the 'add–on' market, as Senator John Button, Labor shadow minister for communications and subsequently leader of the Government in the Senate, had earlier indicated, would be contemplated provided it would give efficiency without inequitable effects and that the public sector would compete in such a way as to avoid fragmentation of the market and disturbance to an effective local manufacturing industry.[64]

Significantly the Liberal and coalition parties had also drawn back some distance from Davidson's revolutionising report. A major part of their conditioning was undoubtedly due to Pollock. He had concentrated on discussing with National Country Party Senators, members and other community leaders, the potential burden to rural dwellers and metropolitan subscribers of timed calls and Davidson's overriding principle of the 'user pays'. In an interview with the author in January 1983, Ian Sinclair, also gave warning that no history of telecommunications in Australia should end with the findings of the Davidson report. Sinclair, who had moved to the senior Defence portfolio in May 1982 while the inquiry was at work, had chosen not to give evidence to the Davidson committee but to make his judgments on the completed report. Clearly influenced by his managing director, he had given Pollock some clear encouragement to defend Telecom against the more extreme privations of the telecommunications review.[65]

Brown, as Minister for Communications, and his bureaucracy had also come to parley. Under persistent negotiation from Telecom, by January 1983 agreement had been forged with the Fraser Government that Davidson's turbulent recommendations would be implemented with careful liaison and only in measured stages. A letter from Lansdown, the secretary of the Department for Communications, to Pollock that month, confirmed that phase I, the 'Australian plan' containing Telecom's 46 positive responses to the Davidson report, should be implemented through 1983. Phase II, the AUSSAT satellite due for launch in 1985 and likely to bite into Telecom's communications areas, would, said Lansdown, 'require agreement and arrangements' and involve Telecom closely in all planning. Crucially, phase III, the 'breaking up' of Telecom had been projected far into the future.

'The Government', said Minister Brown, in a striking public policy reversal as the election campaign began, 'is committed to maintaining the essential common carrier role of Telecom . . . Telecom will remain, as it has been, the national terrestrial common carrier in telecommunications.' The Government had decided it would not implement timed calls; it did not propose to depart from the principle of cross–subsidies. 'It was essential', Brown now declared, 'that a national common carrier, particularly in a country as large as Australia, should be able to draw on its profitable services to subsidise other services that are costly to provide as a result of the great distances involved. We will not be implementing recommendations of the Davidson Report which would change the traditional methods of paying for telecommunications services in Australia.'[66]

Bill Pollock had triumphed. With chairman Brack, he had accomplished some wonders of political diplomacy on the old maxim, 'Never give way, and never give offence'.

The ATEA, campaigning explicitly in some electorates on the telecommunications issue, had contributed directly to the survival of Telecom.

The bureaucrats of the Department for Communications, had, bureaucratically, backed down.

The Right Hon. Ian Sinclair, who had come close to betraying fundamental National [Country] Party principles, was narrowly redeemed.

The BTS, the powerful lobby which had spearheaded the anti-telecommunications push and bolstered many of the recommendations of the Davidson inquiry, was disbanded in June 1983.

On 26 October 1983 Labor's Minister for Communications, Michael Duffy, spelt out the Hawke Government's official response to Davidson. Thanking the committee for their report, Duffy noted that Telecom was already taking a number of decisions and actions to make it more competitive, consistent with the many recommendations of the report. This, the Government recognised, was 'completely compatible with Telecom maintaining its traditional role as the national telecommunications common carrier'. The Government, however, rejected the inherent 'free market thrust' of the Davidson report. 'This Government's policy', Duffy summed up, 'is to ensure that the best possible services are available to the Australian public and that universal access is provided to the national telecommunications system at a price all can afford . . . Now that the Government has made its decision on the major recommendations . . . Telecom can get on with the job of providing, and continually developing, efficient and responsive telecommunications infrastructures and services in Australia.'[67]

'Signs are small measurable things', wrote George Eliot, 'but interpretations are illimitable . . . Starting a long way off the true point, and proceeding by loops and zigzags, we now and then arrive just where we ought to be.'[68]

17 Epilogue

This book has covered a wide canvas and much has been said of the developments and achievements of the past 130 years. Silence and isolation have been almost defeated. Economically and socially, the country of Deakin's 'magnificent distances' has advanced on the technology of communications. Telecommunication has played, and will continue to play, a central role in our national productivity and development. While smoke signals — the earliest telecommunications — greeted the first Englishmen who approached Australian shores, advanced electronic connections now link remote Aboriginals to a sophisticated information world.

By 1983 Australia had attained one of the highest rates of telephone penetration in the world.[1] It had also achieved (despite the popular tendency to complain at prices) a cheaper telephone service for residential and business customers than other major industrial countries with the exception of Canada, America and Japan.[2] In addition, as an outcome of its own distances and isolation from the developed centres of the northern hemisphere, Australia has become an important advocate for the needs and techniques of long-distance international telecommunications and a model for long-line internal communications that has earned it a leadership role among the developing countries of the Third World.

Accordingly Australia's influence at international telecommunications forums has tended to be greater than the size of its network might imply. Both the PMG and Telecom have played a major part in such developments as the planning of the worldwide automatic telephone systems in the 1960s, the present international system for frequency allocation through the International Frequency Registration Board, the preparation of manuals of advice and guidance for developing countries, and the provision of experts to give specialised aid to these countries. Many members of the PMG's Department and Telecom have held chairmanships of working parties and study groups of the CCITT (International Consultative Committee on Telephone and Telegraph) and the CCIR (International Consultative Committee on Radio Communications). The current Secretary General of the

International Telecommunications Union, a United Nations special agency, is an Australian, R.E. Butler, a one-time PMG telegraph messenger boy who rose to a senior position in external relations of the Department and held the post of Deputy Secretary General of the ITU before his election to the Secretary Generalship in October 1982.

Internationally, Telecom's reputation stands high. As the American managing director of AT&T International (Australia) lately summed up: 'Australia is a testing ground for any new system with Sydney and Melbourne representing markets as competitive as anywhere in the world.'[3]

With this behind it, and a recognised position as a frontier organisation in the field of computerised technology and industrial change, how does Telecom Australia envisage the future? And what, in the light of this historical study, are the institutional weaknesses and possible directions for reform?

With a record of outstanding progress in its first eight years, Telecom has entered a dynamic new telecommunications age. As its telephone service nears saturation and one telephone in virtually every household is anticipated by the end of this decade, Australian telecommunications have moved into an environment where high technology digital techniques, integrated circuits, optical fibres, 'intelligent terminals', videotex and satellite communication hold the key to far-reaching new services that will both aid national production and development and change the habits of the country. Technically Telecom's goals are well defined: to keep its services internationally up-to-date and competitive, with prices as low as possible, to attain maximum efficiency, reliability and security, and to foster the growth of a vigorous, viable modern communications and electronic industry with appropriate support industries.[4]

Telecom's ability to achieve its goals are well attested. The Telecom Research Laboratories, a report of an inquiry on Commonwealth laboratories commissioned by the Minister for Science and Technology, confirmed in 1983, 'permit complex investigations and advanced design and development programs to be undertaken' and 'indicate a capacity far beyond that of a network provider and closer to that of a design and development capability of a major supplier'.[5]

Under the Hawke Government new infrastructures have also been set in place. On the satellite front, Government announced its decision in November 1983 to have AUSSAT, originally intended to be a public company owned in part by both Government and the private sector, a company wholly owned by Government, with Telecom Australia having a quarter of the Government share. In addition, Telecom has recently received a ministerial go-ahead to introduce the first national, publicly accessible videotex communications service which, after consideration of tenders, is expected to be introduced towards the end of 1984.

If technically the scenario is comprehensive, what of the social goals of planning? Can Telecom Australia cope with the 'turbulent' social environment, foreshadowed in *Telecom 2000*, that is likely to accompany the spread of the revolutionary new technologies — the interactive telephone systems, the decentralisation of business and social activity through videoscreens, telephone and private data systems, the potential growth of 'wired cities', and the geographical concentrations and 'information ghettos' that satellite communication might promote?

Increasing public awareness of telecommunication futures invites some timely criticism here. Despite its broad successes as a provider of telecommunications services, Telecom Australia has failed conspicuously at times in its communication with the public. This failure appears to spring from an innate reluctance on the part of management to grasp the concept of the public's 'need to know' or to recognise the relevant interest of its 'constituency'. Thus, despite the presence of active public relations divisions at Headquarters and in each State, Telecom as an institution has not managed to convey important information about its plans and policies, its price structures, its basic cross-subsidisation between services, and its use of annual profits to expand its telecommunications grid, to the interested community. The participatory *Telecom 2000*, published in the first months of the Australian Telecommunications Commission, set a standard, but later reports and planning and objectives have not engaged the wider community. Instead, public interest issues involving Telecom — work related illnesses, the shortage of services in rapidly expanding areas of population, charges of links between some Telecom employees and SP bookmaking (a recurring refrain in the long history of the telephone) — are too often dealt with in the television media by bland bureaucrats who appear less than accountable to the public. 'Telecom has been paranoid about information,' says one long-term staff member reflectively. The issue runs deep. Open dialogue between the community and its telecommunications authority is crucial to decision making in an information society. Moreover, as this history shows, the organisation often failed to publicise its most innovative approaches, as for example the measures it adopted to ensure environmental protection at Bellenden Ker, and used closed strategies that sparked needlessly bitter controversies, as in the case of the now widely acclaimed Black Mountain Tower.

Other problems confront the telecommunications goliath. Telecom Australia has not to date been able to free itself from the influence of the Public Service Board as the 1972–3 Commission of Inquiry so positively intended, and hierarchical, bureaucratic procedures survive. While Telecom's top management has established a highly entrepreneurial role, this attitude has not percolated through the whole organisation and there are areas of protection and lack of competition, a whiff of the sheltered workshop, in middle management that subverts the blueprint for a creative and highly efficient instrumentality conceived by the founding Commission of Inquiry.

Nor has Telecom Australia, as the Commonwealth's largest employer, taken a leadership role in the field of women's career advancement despite the evidence given to the Commission of Inquiry and a timely prod delivered by Telecom's first woman commissioner,

Joan Hancock. 'Women's skills,' she noted in June 1975, 'are not being fully used' and the institutional structures of the new authority showed 'on a large scale, those characteristics of women within the low paid occupations and their limited advancement up the authority ladder'.[6] The position remains little altered today despite the succession of three women commissioners. While Telecom management has made some attempts to improve the situation, including the appointment of a handful of women as senior administrators, the presence of women managers in Telecom's business offices, the penetration of a few young women into the male technician and lineman grades, and a recent agreement between Telecom and the articulate Australian Telephone and Phonogram Officers' Association for the absorption of redundant telephone operators from obsolete manual services into other productive work, the organisation has far to go. Yet women will have an increasingly important part to play as Telecom confronts the implications of its expanding systems and new products.

Australia's history has been powerfully shaped by the spread of telecommunications. Distant, and tied formerly only by mail and a cable connection to the outside world, an Australian now heads the official international telecommunications community. We are all closely linked. Where we are going, and into what future, depends on every one of us.

1975 was to see one of the first PMG female intake into what had previously been a male preserve, such as the line staff. Here two Victorian women undertake training.

Appendixes

I

COMMONWEALTH POSTMASTERS–GENERAL, MINISTERS FOR POST AND TELECOMMUNICATIONS AND MINISTERS FOR COMMUNICATIONS 1901–83

	Term of office	State represented	Political affiliation[2]	Ministry
POSTMASTERS-GENERAL [1] (January 1901–December 1975)				
Sir John Forrest	1. 1.01–17. 1.01	WA	Lib/Prot.	Barton
Senator James Drake	5. 2.01– 7. 8.03	Qld	Lib/Prot.	Barton
Sir Philip Fysh	10. 8.03–24. 9.03	Tas.	FT	Barton
Sir Philip Fysh	24. 9.03–27. 4.04	Tas.	Prot.	Deakin
Hugh Mahon	27. 4.04–17. 8.04	WA	ALP	Watson
Sydney Smith	18. 8.04– 5. 7.05	NSW	FT	Reid–McLean
Sir Austin Chapman	5. 7.05–30. 7.07	NSW	Prot.	Deakin
Samuel Mauger	30. 7.07–13.11.08	Vic.	Prot.	Deakin
Sen. Josiah Thomas	13.11.08– 2. 6.09	NSW	ALP	Fisher
Sir John Quick	2. 6.09–29. 4.10	Vic.	Ind. Prot.	Deakin
Sen. Josiah Thomas	29. 4.10–14.10.11	NSW	ALP	Fisher
Charles E. Frazer	14.10.11–24. 6.13	WA	ALP	Fisher
Agar Wynne	24. 6.13–17. 9.14	Vic.	Lib/Prot.	Cook
William G. Spence	17. 9.14–27.10.15	NSW	ALP	Fisher
William Webster	27.10.15– 3. 2.20	NSW	ALP/Nat.	Hughes[3]
G.H. Wise	4. 2.20–21.12.21	Vic.	Nat.	Hughes
A. Poynton	21.12.21– 5. 2.23	SA	Nat.	Hughes
William G. Gibson	9. 2.23–22.10.29	Vic.	CP	Bruce–Page[4]
J.A. Lyons	22.10.29– 4. 2.31	Tas.	ALP	Scullin
A.E. Green	4. 2.31– 6. 1.32	WA	ALP	Scullin
J.E. Fenton	6. 1.32–13.10.32	Vic.	UAP	Lyons[5]
Sir Robert Parkhill	13.10.32–12.10.34	NSW	UAP	Lyons
Sen. A.J. McLachlan	12.10.34– 7.11.38	SA	Nat.	Lyons
A.G. Cameron	7.11.38– 7. 4.39	SA	CP	Lyons
A.G. Cameron	7. 4.39–26. 4.39	SA	CP	Page
Sir Eric Harrison	26. 4.39–14. 3.40	NSW	UAP	Menzies
H.V. Thorby	14. 3.40–28.10.40	NSW	CP	Menzies
Sen. George McLeay	28.10.40–26. 6.41	SA	Lib.	Menzies
T.J. Collins	26. 6.41–29. 8.41	NSW	CP	Menzies
T.J. Collins	29. 8.41– 7.10.41	NSW	CP	Fadden
Senator W.P. Ashley	7.10.41– 2. 2.45	NSW	ALP	Curtin
Sen. Donald Cameron	2. 2.45– 6. 7.45	Vic.	ALP	Curtin
Sen. Donald Cameron	13. 7.45–19.12.49	Vic.	ALP	Chifley
H.L. Anthony	19.12.49–11. 1.56	NSW	CP	Menzies
Sir Charles Davidson	11. 1.56–18.12.63	Qld	CP	Menzies
Sir Alan S. Hulme	18.12.63–26. 1.66	Qld	Lib.	Menzies
Sir Alan S. Hulme	26. 1.66–19.12.67	Qld	Lib.	Holt
Sir Alan S. Hulme	19.12.67–10. 1.68	Qld	Lib.	McEwen
Sir Alan S. Hulme	10. 1.68–10. 3.71	Qld	Lib.	Gorton
Sir Alan S. Hulme	10. 3.71– 5.12.72	Qld	Lib.	McMahon
L.H. Barnard	5.12.72–19.12.72	Tas.	ALP	Whitlam
L.F. Bowen	19.12.72–11. 6.74	NSW	ALP	Whitlam
Sen. Reginald Bishop	12. 6.74–11.11.75	SA	ALP	Whitlam
Peter J. Nixon	12.11.75–22.12.75	Vic.	NCP	Fraser

MINISTERS FOR POST AND TELECOMMUNICATIONS (December 1975–November 1980)

R.V. Garland	22.12.75– 6. 2.76	WA	Lib.	Fraser
E.L. Robinson	6. 2.76–20.12.77	Qld	Lib.	Fraser
A.A. Staley	20.12.77– 3.11.80	Vic.	Lib.	Fraser

MINISTERS FOR COMMUNICATIONS (November 1980)

I.M. Sinclair	3.11.80– 7. 5.82	NSW	NCP	Fraser
N.A. Brown	7. 5.82–11. 3.83	Vic.	Lib.	Fraser
M.J. Duffy	11. 3.83–current	Vic.	ALP	Hawke

1 The portfolio of Postmaster-General existed for threequarters of a century, from January 1901 to December 1975. It was held in the House of Representatives unless the holder's name is prefixed as a Senator, when it was held in the Upper House, the Senate.

2 Political affiliations are afflicted by the complexity of changes of title, political evolutions, and the later reappearance of party names. The Liberal Party of the first years of the century was essentially a protectionist party opposed to Conservative Free Trade and a different political grouping from the 'new' Liberal Party established as an offspring of the United Australia Party in 1945.

   The Country Party underwent a change of name to become the National Country Party of Australia in 1975 and the National Party of Australia in October 1982.

   Party abbreviations:
   ALP — Australian Labor Party
   CP — Country Party
   FT — Free Trade
   Lib. — Liberal
   Ind. Prot. — Independent Protectionist
   Nat. — Nationalist
   NCP — National Country Party
   Prot. — Protectionist
   UAP — United Australia Party

3 W.M. Hughes on three occasions requested the Governor-General for a commission to form a new ministry changing his official affiliation from ALP to Nationalist Party in 1915.

4 From 1923, outside the period of ALP governance, the Federal Government has been carried on by a coalition of the Nationalist or UAP or Liberal Party with the Country Party. The Bruce-Page Coalition of Nationalist and Country Party is the only government traditionally called by the two leaders' names. The Menzies, Holt, Gorton, McMahon and Fraser ministries, however, were all similar coalition governments which for long periods gave the Postmaster-General portfolio to their Country Party colleagues. The Page, Fadden and McEwen ministries were interim coalition governments founded in emergency periods and presided over briefly by Country Party prime ministers.

5 J.A. Lyons, who served as Labor Postmaster-General in the Scullin Ministry in 1929–31, left the ALP in February 1931 to lead the new United Australia Party taking with him a former ALP member, J.E. Fenton, who became his Postmaster-General in 1932.

PERMANENT HEADS OF THE POSTMASTER–GENERAL'S DEPARTMENT
AND MANAGING DIRECTORS OF TELECOM AUSTRALIA

SECRETARY OF THE PMG'S DEPARTMENT

Sir Robert Scott, Kt, ISO	1901–11
Justinian Oxenham, ISO	1911–23
H.P. (Sir Harry) Brown, Kt, CMG, MBE	December 1923–27: position retitled*

DIRECTOR–GENERAL OF POSTS AND TELEGRAPHS

H.P. (Sir Harry) Brown, Kt, CMG, MBE	1927–December 1939
Sir Daniel McVey, Kt, CME	1940–46
Lawrence B. Fanning, ISO	1946–49
G.T. (Sir Giles) Chippindall, Kt, CBE	1949–58
P.E. Vanthoff, OBE, MVO	1958
Charles Stradwick, OBE	1958–61
Frank P. O'Grady, CBE	1961–65
Trevor A. Housley, CBE	1964–68
Sir John Knott, Kt, CBE	1968–72
Eber F. Lane, CBE	1972–July 1975

MANAGING DIRECTOR, TELECOM AUSTRALIA

John H. Curtis, CB, FTS	1975–81
William J.B. Pollock, AM	1981–current

* The title of secretary of the Department, opposed by Brown as 'demeaning', was finally changed after persistent pressure in 1927.

UNIONS AND STAFF ASSOCIATIONS OF TELECOM AUSTRALIA

Union and staff association	Member-ship in Telecom	Type of work	Union overlap
ACOA Administrative & Clerical Officers Association	7,000	All types of clerical and administrative activities including personnel, accounting, industrial relations, and administrative/management	Some overlap with Heads of Departments, Divisions and Branches Association and Federated Clerks' Union
ADSTE Association of Draughting Supervisory and Technical Employees	1,500	Detail drafting and design drafting, and supervision of such work. Planning, programming, design and general technical assistance to professional engineers, and preparation of briefs on building layouts and services.	Major coverage. Some overlap with Professional Officers' Association. Some overlap with ATEA and Professional Officers' Association
APEA Association of Professional Engineers	600	Professional engineering work including engineering management	Approximately 1/5 of Telecom's engineers are members. The remainder are members of Professional Officers' Association (POA)
APSAA Australian Public Service Artisans' Association	850	Electrical and mechanical installation and maintenance, motor vehicle testing, repair; manufacture of cabinets; painting etc.	Shares membership (in some areas) with ATEA and with a number of other unions, e.g. ETU, AMWSU
APSA FDO Australian Public Service Association — Fourth Division Officers	3,500	Messenger and minor clerical duties, typing, data processing	Shares membership in Assistant area with APTU
APTU Australian Postal and Telecommunications Union	26,000	Installation and maintenance of conduits, cables, aerial lines, radio towers, etc. Operate plant (bulldozers, etc.) and drive motor vehicles. Carriage of stores, etc.	Supervisory positions are shared with EPOA
		Receipt storage and issue of stores	Coverage shared with FSPU
		Messenger and minor clerical duties	Coverage shared with Australian Public Service Association (Fourth Division Officers) and Federated Clerks Union
APTC HDDBA Australian Postal and Telecommunications Commissions Heads of Departments, Divisions and Branches Association	100	Controlling officers of the most significant functional areas in each State	Dominant coverage. Some overlap with Administrative and Clerical Officers' Association and Professional Officers' Association

Union and staff association	Member-ship in Telecom	Type of work	Union overlap
ATEA Australian Telecommunications Employees' Association	25,000	Installation and maintenance of telephone exchange equipment, radio and television broadcast transmitters and telephone subscribers equipment	Shares membership of Telecommunications Technical Officers with Telecommunications Technical Officers' Association (latter has roughly 25 per cent of total)
		Electrical, mechanical installation and maintenance and repair, renovation, etc. of equipment.	Membership shared with Australian Public Service Artisans' Association Electrical Trades Union Amalgamated Metal Workers' & Shipwrights Union, etc.
		Production planning, programming, design, equipment supply and laboratory work	Membership shared with Telecommunications Technical Officers' Association and ADSTE
ATPOA Australian Telephone & Phonogram Officers' Association	9,000	Assisting subscribers in arranging local, national and international telephone calls; receiving phonograms	
EPOA External Plant Officers' Association	600	Standards inspection or control of major line construction activities	
		Assisting engineers in planning, programming, etc. of lines work	Membership shared with APTU
POA Professional Officers' Association Australian Public Service	1,500	Professional engineering work including engineering management; professional scientific work in metallurgy, materials, etc.	Shares membership in professional engineering area with APEA — has bulk of staff in membership.
		Design drafting and supervision of drafting work	ADSTE has bulk of membership
TTOA Telecommunications Technical Officers' Association	1,200	Installation and maintenance of telephones exchange equipment, radio and television broadcast transmitters and telephone subscribers equipment	Shares membership with ATEA (which has roughly 75 per cent of total)
		Programming, design, equipment and supply laboratory work	Membership shared with ATEA and ADSTE
TTSOA Telecommunications Traffic & Supervisory Officers' Association	300	Supervision, management and administration of Chief Telegraph Office. Supervisors control telegraphists in a leading hand foreman situation. (Chief Telegraph Offices handle receipt and onward transmission of telegram traffic, as well as telex assistance)	Exclusive coverage

Union and staff association	Member-ship in Telecom	Type of work	Union overlap
UPCT Union of Postal Clerks and Telegraphists	500	Telegraphists — operation of teleprinters and other transmission equipment for despatch and receipt of telegrams	

The Australian Telecommunications Commission also deals with staff organisations which have a small minority of their membership in Telecom. Less than 50 would typically be employed from each organisation.

The organisations are —

AJA   Australian Journalists' Association
AMWSU   Amalgamated Metal Workers' and Shipwrights' Union
ASCJ   Australian Society of Carpenters and Joiners
ASE   Australian Society of Engineers
BWIU   Building Workers' Industrial Union
ETU   Electrical Trades Union
FCU   Federated Clerks' Union
FSPU   Federated Storemen and Packers' Union
NOPA   Non-Official Postmasters' Association
OPDU   Operative Painters' and Decorators' Union
PGEU   Plumbers and Gasfitters Employees' Union
PKIU   Printing and Kindred Industries Union
RANF   Royal Australian Nursing Federation
VBEFA   Vehicle Builders Employees' Federation of Australia

Source: Submission by Telecom Australia to the Public Inquiry into Telecommunications. Annexes, February 1982. Membership is for 1980.

IV
TELEGRAPHS AND TELEPHONES IN AUSTRALIA, 1899

Name of Colony	Telegraphs										Telephones & private wires		
	Miles open on 31st December (exclusive of telephones)*					Telegraph stations at end of year	Number of telegrams				Number of public exchanges	Miles of wire	Number of connections at end of year
	Postal department		Railway department		Cable		Inland (counted once)	Intercolonial received & despatched	Cablegrams received & despatched	Total			
	line	wire	line	wire									
Victoria	3,940	9,606	2,807	5,519	...	805	1,491,965	786,195	42,138	2,320,298	14	13,591[1]	4,407
New South Wales	13,663	88,718	2,691[7]	5,000[7]	...	945	1,922,640	972,261	54,806	2,949,707[2]	38[3]	...[4]	10,119
Queensland	10,202	18,968	...	...	45	456	1,203,864	198,107	8,080	1,410,051	11	3,108	2,036
South Australia	5,485	11,224	206	2,372	37	280	519,542	423,307	28,883	971,732[5]	10	3,305	1,320
Western Australia	5,941	8,749	...	...	...	155	803,507	298,943	34,063	1,136,513	10	2,869	2,115[6]
Total	39,231	87,265	5,704	12,891	82	2,641	5,941,518	2,678,813	167,970	8,788,301	83	22,873	19,997
Tasmania	2,000	3,252	404	692	428	275	250,958	128,190	1,518	380,666	5	815	1,010
New Zealand[0]	6,910	19,228	507[7]	977[7]	279	915	3,469,631	49,722	10,335	3,529,688	40	6,343	7,150
Grand total	48,141	109,745	6,615	14,560	789	3,831	9,662,107	2,856,725	179,823	12,698,655	128	30,031	28,157

NOTE — The telegrams refer to those transmitted and received (each telegram being counted only once).

* Telephone wire is included in the case of New South Wales.
0 Figures in this case are for the year ended 31st March 1900.
1 Excluding 1,389 miles of wire used solely for railway purposes.
2 Including messages in transitu, 162,356.
3 In addition there were 34 bureaux for the use of the public.
4 Included with telegraph wire.
5 Including messages in transitu, 146,910; but excluding about 100,000 international cablegrams transmitted on behalf of other colonies.
6 Including 318 connections at Government Departments.
7 Figures for 1898, later particulars not being to hand.

Source: Australian Statistics, compiled by the Government Statist of Victoria; South Australia, Parliamentary Papers, No.3A (Adelaide, Government Printer, 1901), Table XXIX, p.43.

V
POSTAL, TELEGRAPH AND TELEPHONE RETURNS OF THE DEPARTMENT,
1945–6 TO 1975

	Postal £	Telegraph £	Telephone £
1945–6	2,268,396	995,599	3,057,605
1946–7	2,840,582	148,009	2,534,266
1947–8	1,623,113	(1,325,949)	1,249,793
1948–9	(296,921)	(1,079,667)	(346,405)
1949–50	(1,153,559)	(721,872)	720,668
1951–2	(1,813,169)	(817,477)	(26,364)
1952–3	(544,662)	(899,829)	2,107,344
1953[1]	(2,146,818)	(1,452,750)	2,931,597
1954	(1,849,631)	(1,218,796)	3,221,100
1955	(2,253,588)	(800,036)	2,904,538
1956	(2,401,918)	(1,201,791)	3,178,431
1957	(1,526,168)	(637,580)	5,280,794
1958	(1,953,583)	(330,444)	6,294,207
1959	(850,577)	(41,503)	6,935,514
1960	728,218	(429,138)	129,173
1961	995,185	(171,295)	1,939,273
1962	(376,859)	(61,776)	(1,523,083)
1963	524,763	653,559	(1,941,303)
1964	478,145	892,016	(1,666,984)

		Telecommunications services[2]
1965	(1,309,095)	3,415,291
	$[3]	$
1966	(10,341,341)	10,217,224
1967	(23,580,078)	2,077,839
1968	(20,160,567)	10,512,461
1969–70	(19,868,129)	21,850,398
1971	(25,488,661)	23,845,906
1972	(11,253,385)	71,052,327
1973	(20,891,495)	62,114,674
1974	(54,518,000)	59,192,000
1975	(64,307,000)	95,126,000

1 Year ending June
2 Telegraph and telephone services were combined in 1965 when TRESS completed mechanisation of the public telegraph service
3 Decimal currency was introduced in Australia in 1966

Notes

Notes have been abbreviated in the interests of space. Where material is listed in the Select Bibliography in full, only author, abbreviated title and page references are given in the notes.

Telecom Australia denotes Headquarters, Melbourne (199 William Street, Melbourne, Vic. 3000); otherwise the State is given. Published or typescript material at Telecom Australia is located either in the library or in the information and publicity office. Telecom Australia files are held at central registry, Telecom Headquarters.

Telecom holds a selection of files covering the PMG period to 1975, in addition to Telecom files. Such historical PMG files which exist — as there has been extensive pruning — are held by Australian Archives, Brighton.

Abbreviations used in the Notes and Select Bibliography

ADB	*Australian Dictionary of Biography*
AFR	*Australian Financial Review*
AGPS	Australian Government Printing Service
ANU	Australian National University
ATR	*Australian Telecommunications Research*
CPD	*Commonwealth Parliamentary Debates*
H. of R.	House of Representatives
HUP	Harvard University Press
ITU	International Telecommunication Union
JIEA	*Journal of the Institution of Engineers*
JIR	*Journal of Industrial Relations*
JRAHS	*Journal of the Royal Australian Historical Society*
PA	*Public Administration* (Australia)
PP	Parliamentary Papers (In Colonial times these refer to the Votes and Proceedings of each Colony, viz.: *NSW PP, SA PP, Tas. PP, Qld PP, Vic. PP* and *WA PP*, and post-Federation to the Commonwealth Parliamentary Papers.)
OUP	Oxford University Press
RSSS	Research School of Social Sciences (ANU)
SUP	Sydney University Press
TJA	*Telecommunication Journal of Australia*
UQP	University of Queensland Press

1 NEWS FROM HOME

1 Banks's diary, quoted in Ann Mozley Moyal, *Scientists in nineteenth century Australia, A documentary history* (Cassell Australia, 1976) p.13.

2 K. Inglis, *The Australian colonists* (Melbourne, MUP, 1974), quoted p.33.

3 John Cobbold, *The history of Margaret Catchpole* (London, 1845).

4 *A history of the post office in Tasmania*, p.6.

5 Frank Crowley, *Colonial Australia 1788–1840, A documentary history of Australia*, Vol.1 (Nelson, 1980), p.548; and *The Australian Post Office, a brief history, 1809–1975* (APO, 1975).

6 *A history of the post office in Tasmania*, pp.7,13–14.

7 *Sydney Gazette*, 10 March 1828.

8 P.R. Heydon, *A History of the Postmasters' Association in Western Australia* (WA, 1979); J.K. Ewers, *The western gateway, A history of Fremantle* (City of Fremantle, 1971), p.21; information from WA Post and Telecom Museum.

9 *Report on the post office department, Victoria, to September 30 1862* (Vic. PP, Victoria, Govt Printer, 1862–3).

10 South Australia, *Report on the post office, telegraph and observatory departments of South Australia,* October 1884, *SA PP* 1884, No.191, Vol.IV, p.2.

11 Although the penal settlement was established at Moreton Bay in 1824, principal overseer, William Whyte, became the first designated, part-time postmaster from 1829. By 1839–40 most convicts had left the area. Rea, *Brisbane general post office*.

12 *ADB*, Vol.2, p.283.

13 *ADB*, Vol.1, pp.234–5.

14 A total of 170,000 convicts were imported into Australia from 1788 to 1868. Transportation ended in NSW in 1840; in Victoria in 1849; in Tasmania in 1853. Transportation to Western Australia begun in difficult labour and financial times in 1850, ended in 1868.

15 J. Bach, *A maritime history of Australia* (Nelson, Melbourne, 1976), p.105; and *Report on the post office dept . . . Victoria, 1862*, p.9.

16 Blainey, *Tyranny*, pp.143–4. The last Cobb & Co. 'Royal Mail' was discontinued in 1924.

17 *Report on the post office dept . . . 1862*, p.9.

18 *A history of Bourke post office* (1965); *A history of Yetman post office* (1973), National Library of Australia.

19 Robert Logan Jack, *Northmost Australia*, Vol.2 (Melbourne, George Robertson, 1922).

20 A.J. Boyd, *Old colonials* (SUP, facsimile edn, 1974), pp.79–81.

21 A History of the post office in Western Australia, 1829–1901 (Perth Post & Telecom Museum, typescript), p.4; and R. Buddrige, Detained in penal servitude.

22 Claire McCuskey, 'Women in the Victorian post office', in *Second women and labour conference papers*, 1980, Vol.1; Rea, *Brisbane General Post Office*, p.8; Buddrige, *op.cit.*; and Henry Handel Richardson, *Myself when young* (Heinemann, Melbourne, 1948), p.34.

23 See post office annual reports of the various Colonies. The recorded expenditure of the Colonies was generally double that of revenue received.

24 They hoped for a single vote each, compromised on two votes for the six Colonies, but eventually settled for one vote for Australia.

25 Anthony Trollope, *Australia and New Zealand* (1873). It was Trollope who designed the large red Victorian pillar box used well into the post–Second World War period.

2 'THE MOST PERFECT INVENTION'

1 Semaphores gained their greatest development in France where, used in conjunction with telescopes to extend the distance, they were widely deployed in the Napoleonic wars. By 1842 thousands of miles of these optical telegraphs were operated for government use by the French War Department. Brock, *Telecommunications industry*, 'The Telephone and Telegraph in Europe', ch.5. *See also* ITU, *From semaphore to satellite*.

2 Cf. Robert Thompson, *Wiring a continent, The history of the telegraph industry in the United States 1832–1866* (Princeton University Press, 1947).

3 *Argus*, June 1853.

4 The Victorian Surveyor-General, Lieutenant-General Sir Andrew Clarke, later claimed that, when early in 1853 he proposed the establishment of an electric telegraph, he was 'thought of as a visionary' and laughed at. R.H. Vetch, *Life of Lieutenant-General the Hon. Sir Andrew Clarke* (London, 1905), p.59.

5 *ADB*, Vol.5, pp.156–7; and *Argus*, 19 April 1887, McGowan's obituary notice, p.6.

6 Canada's first telegraph company, the Toronto, Hamilton, Niagara and St Catharine's Electro-Magnetic Telegraph Co. was formed by a group of businessmen in 1846.

7 Quoted G.W. Symes, Australia and world communications — A summary of develop-ments: 1830–70, *The centenary of the Adelaide–Darwin overland telegraph line*, p.3; and *ADB*, Vol.5, p.280.

8 SA, *Report on the post office, telegraph . . . 1884, op.cit.*, pp.4–5. This Report provides Todd's highly informative overview of the history of his Department.

9 The undergrounding technique had swallowed up two-thirds of Morse's $30,000 appropriation from Congress and, in desperation, the insulated wire was painfully unravelled by Morse's colleague, Cornell, and later erected on poles above ground. Cf. Thompson, *op.cit.*; Todd's comment, SA, *Report of the post office, telegraph . . . 1884, op.cit.*, p.5.

10 New South Wales, *Proceedings of the Legislative Council*, 1855 (Govt Printer, 1856) Vol.1, p.91, and Vol.3, p.608.

11 *Ibid.*, Vol.2, p.607. Costs cited varied greatly. McGowan quoted £85 per mile for the erection of posts, insulators and wire for the Melbourne–Sydney line excluding equipment, office furniture and station buildings.

12 *ADB*, Vol.3, pp.488–9.

13 Quoted Gribble, *What hath God wrought*, pp.3–4.

14 Cracknell succeeded J.J. Austin, first inspector of telegraphs in Queensland from October 1860. Rea, p.15.

15 Henry L. D'Emden, Early history of the post and telegraph offices, Tasmania, compiled from official records, 1901 (Telecom Australia, Hobart), typescript.

16 *Ibid.*, letter, 14 August 1857.

17 Letters and reports held by Telecom Australia, Hobart.

18 Letter to Colonial Secretary, Tasmania, 26 July 1861, *Report of superintendent of telegraphs, Tasmania*, (Tas. PP, Hobart Govt printer, 1862).

19 Victoria, *Report of the post office and telegraph department for the year 1870* (Vic. PP, Govt Printer, 1871).

20 SA, *Report on the post office, telegraph . . . 1884*, p.5; NSW, *Report of electric telegraph department*, 1859, 1860, 1861 and 1866, *NSW PP*; and *Report of superintendent of telegraphs*, Tas. PP, Tasmania, 16 June 1874.

21 Cf. *Report of the general superintendent of electric telegraph*, 31 December 1862 (Vic. PP, Victoria, 1862–3), pp.4–5.

22 John Moynihan, Some brief notes on owners and operators of early telegraph lines in Western Australia, 1869–73 (Perth, 1981) typescript; and Buddrige, Detained in penal servitude.

23 More accurately transcribed, 'mother failing fast'.

24 SA, *Report on the post office, telegraph . . . 1884*, p.6.

25 Margaret Kiddle, *Men of yesterday* (MUP, 1961), p.327.

26 *Report of the superintendent of telegraphs*, Tas. PP, Tasmania, August 1865.

27 Cf. Moyal, *Scientists in nineteenth century Australia*, *op.cit.*, Ch.7, p.160, and W.A. Gibbs, *The origins of Australian meteorology*, Dept of Science, Bureau of Meteorology (Canberra, AGPS, 1975).

28 SA, Boundary of New South Wales and South Australia printed by House of Assembly, 19 January 1869. *Report on the determination of the boundary line of the colonies of South Australia and New South Wales by Charles Todd . . .*, pp.1,2,5, *SA PP*.

29 *A statistical account of the seven colonies of Australasia, 1899-1900* (Sydney, Govt Printer, 8th issue, 1900), p.713.

3 WIRING A CONTINENT

1 Cameron, 'The story of the overland telegraph line'.

2 Charles Todd, public lecture notes, 1873, SA Archives.

3 Victoria, *Report of the department of electric telegraph*, 31 December, concluding report, 1 January 1859 (*Vic. PP*, Victoria Govt Printer, 1859), p.10.

4 Denison to McNaughtan, 14 June 1859 and 10 December 1858. Copies, Telecom Australia, Hobart.

5 Minutes, SA Executive Council, 20 January 1859.

6 W.L. Manser, The overland telegraph, Hons thesis, Adelaide University, 1961, pp.3,8-10. See also *SA PP*, 1870-1, No.24, p.2; Todd to Fergusson, 30 August 1869, SA, *Report on the post office, telegraph . . . 1884*, p.140; and report by C. Todd to Commissioner of Public Works on telegraph to King George's Sound, 10 July 1860, *SA PP*, 110 of 1860.

7 Letter from H.B.T. Strangways to H.W. Varley, 7 February 1908, SA Archives, and SA, *Report of the post office, telegraph . . . 1884*.

8 Quoted Taylor, *End to silence*, pp.30,32.

9 Todd's report of 8 October 1862, quoted Cameron, *op.cit.*, p.192.

10 Murphy, *Frederick Walker's expedition*.

11 BAT had cannibalised five cable companies: the Falmouth and Gilbraltar Cable Co.; the Anglo-American Cable Co.; the British India Cable Co.; the British India Extension Cable Co.; and the Eastern Asian Telegraph.

12 The Northern Territory was administered by the British government until 1863 when it passed to the government of South Australia. Its capital was the small town of Palmerston laid out in the early 1860s. Port Darwin was the strip of land along Palmerston's sea coast. In 1869, as plans for landing an overseas cable shaped, Port Darwin was surveyed as the Territory's port and capital, and the cable company's building and the post and telegraph offices were located there. In July 1907 Palmerston was incorporated in Port Darwin. Four years later, in April 1911, Port Darwin was named Darwin when the Northern Territory became a separate administrative entity.

13 Todd, public lecture notes, *op.cit.*

14 *Ibid.* Todd's later historical overview in SA, *Report on the post office, telegraph . . . 1884*, p.141, gives a slightly different version.

15 Todd, public lecture notes, *op.cit.*

16 *Ibid.*

17 SA, *Report on the post office, telegraph . . . 1884*, p.141.

18 Letter Todd to Ross, 7 July 1870, *ibid.*, p.142.

19 Taylor, *End to Silence*, pp.45,53,55.

20 SA, *Report on the post office, telegraph . . . 1884*, pp.143,148.

21 Taylor, *End to silence*, pp.50,57.

22 *ADB*, *(Vol.4)*, p.65; *Memoirs and Correspondence of Major General H.P. Babbage* (London, 1910).

23 Overland Telegraph — Port Augusta to Port Darwin, instructions to overseers in charge of works, copy, 21 pp. mimeo, Telecommunications Museum, Adelaide.

24 Diary of J. Beckwith, SA Archives and copy Telecommunications Museum, Adelaide.

25 Giles, 'Adelaide-Port Darwin telegraph line'. Extracts of Gile's journals are published in the issues of February, April, May, June, July, August and September 1888.

26 F.P. O'Grady, The overland telegraph line technology of the 1870s, in *The centenary of the Adelaide and Darwin telegraph line*, p.22.

27 M.J. Gooley, The Construction of the Overland Telegraph, Port Augusta to Darwin, *ibid.*, p.13.

28 SA, *Report on the post office, telegraph . . . 1884*, p.144.

29 Taylor, *End to silence*, pp.102-4.

30 R.C. Patterson, private diary, October 1871-November 1872, SA Archives.

31 *Report of Superintendent of Telegraphs*, Queensland, *Qld PP*, December 1870; *Report of Postmaster-General*, South Australia, *SA PP*, 19 May 1871.

32 Todd to his wife, 1 February 1872, Todd correspondence, SA Archives.

33 Woodrow, 'A century of telecommunications in the Northern Territory'.

34 SA, *Report on the post office, telegraph . . . 1884*, p.149.

35 Lieutenant Jekyll, 'The Telegraph and the Ashantee War', *Journal of Society Telegraph Engineers*, London, July 1875; and *SMH*, 21 September 1876.

36 Taylor, *End to silence*, p.167.

37 SA, *Report on the post office, telegraph . . . 1884*, p.149.

38 Blainey, *Tyranny*, p.304.

39 Governor Weld to Charles Todd, 3 December 1873, SA Archives; and Todd to F.P. Barlee, Colonial Secretary, Western Australia, quoted M.J. Gooley, The original telegraph line South Australia-Western Australia 1875-1877, its construction, people and localities, mimeo, Telecommunications Museum, Adelaide, p.4.

40 *Across the barrier.*

41 WA Legislative Council, Report from the

Superintendent of Telegraphs, Perth 19 August 1876, in *Reports Upon the Eucla Telegraph Line, WA PP* (Perth, 1876).

42 Richard Randall Knuckey diaries, SA Archives and quoted *The First East-West Link*, Telecom Australia pamphlet, April 1979.

43 Information from M.J. Gooley, Telecommunications Museum, Adelaide.

44 Report of the Postmaster-General, WA, 13 July 1876, in *Reports upon the Eucla line, op.cit.*

4 FROM TELEGRAPHY TO TELEPHONY

1 Geoffrey Blainey, *The rush that never ended* (MUP, 2nd edn, 1974), pp.91-2,208.

2 Tasmania, *Electric telegraph department report, Tas. PP*, 1 August 1875.

3 Blainey, *Tyranny*, pp.225-6.

4 N.G. Butlin, *Investment in Australian economic development 1886-1900* (Dept of Economic History, ANU), pp.292-3.

5 Australian Agricultural Co. Records, letters to General Superintendent Merewether, 5 September 1873, Archives of Business and Labour, RSSS, ANU, Canberra.

6 Cf. *Queensland votes and proceeding*, 1891, *Qld PP*, Vol.2, Electric Telegraph Regulations.

7 Goldsbrough Mort & Co. Papers, Series 2/92, cables received from London, January to November 1893, Archives of Business and Labour, RSSS, ANU.

8 Godfrey Linge, *Industrial awakening* (ANU Press, 1980), p.9.

9 Tasmania, Report of Superintendent of Telegraphs, *Tas. PP*, 11 September 1876.

10 SA, *Report on the post office, telegraph ... 1884, op.cit.*

11 10 July 1888, quoted R.B. Walker, *The newspaper press in New South Wales 1803-1920* (SUP, 1976), p.203.

12 Blainey, *Tyranny*, quoted p.224; and *Western Australian Times*, 25 February 1879, p.3.

13 Professor D. Kennedy, Durham College of Science, reported in 'A page from history', *Telecom Tasmania* (Telecom Australia).

14 Gerard E. Caiden *The ACTPA, A study of white collar public service unionism in the Commonwealth of Australia, 1885-1922* (occasional paper No.2, Dept of Political Science, RSSS, ANU, Canberra), pp.6-9. See Gribble, *op.cit.*

15 White, *A vital link*, p.4.

16 Memoirs of J.H. Lawrence, telegraphist at Eucla (Perth, Post and Telecom Museum), mimeo, p.11.

17 Quoted, J. Fitzpatrick, *The bicycle and the bush* (OUP, Melbourne, 1980), p.160.

18 Western Australia, *Report of postmaster-general and superintendent of telegraphs, 1896, WA PP.*

19 Lawrence, *op.cit.*, p.18, and cable/telegram 7 March 1885, Agent-General re European

Complications, Victorian State Archives p.85/783.

20 Western Australia, *Report of postmaster-general*, 1890, *WA PP.*

21 Tasmania, *Report of superintendent of telegraphs to Colonial Treasurer, Tas. PP*, 30 April 1877.

22 In the true PMG tradition, E.C.'s son Frank Kraegan made a third generation of communication men.

23 Baker, *Communicators and their first trade unions*, pp.65-7,93.

24 *ADB*, Vol.7, Baracchi, pp.166-7; and WA, *Report of the postmaster-general 1890, WA PP*, 1891-2, Vol.2, p.52.

25 Moyal, *Scientists in nineteenth century Australia*, p.75.

26 Baker, *op.cit.*, p.2.

27 Kernot's presidential address to the Victorian Institute of Engineers in March 1897.

28 *The palace of winged words* (Telecom Australia, Melbourne, 1980).

29 Three of Biggs's telephones are on display at the Queen Victoria Museum, Launceston.

30 *ADB*, Vol.6, pp.226-7.

31 *The cyclopedia of Victoria*, Vol.1 (Melbourne, 1903), pp.568-9.

32 Queensland *Superintendent of telegraphs report to Parliament, Qld PP*, 11 March 1878; and *Palace of winged words, op.cit.*

33 M. Cannon, *Life in the cities, Australia in the Victorian age* (Nelson, Melbourne, 1975), pp.118-20.

34 *Australian Sketcher*, 29 January 1881.

35 A.H. Freeman, A history of the telephone to 1887. The original subscribers held their rights in these 'purchase' lines until December 1911 when a special Act of Parliament provided for the acquisition of lines by the Commonwealth Postmaster-General.

36 Tasmania, *Report of superintendent of telegraphs*, 1881, *Tas. PP.*

37 C. Todd, Report of a visit to the inter-colonial conferences, *Journal of South Australian Electrical Society*, 1888, Vol.1, No.10, p.3.

38 Andrew Garran, *Picturesque atlas of Australia*, (facsimile edn, Lansdowne Press, 1980), p.82; and Victoria, *Postmaster-General annual report*, 1887, p.22. Brothels and 'houses of assignation' were declared illegal for telephone connection in 1904-5, PMG Circular Memorandum No.20, 8 January 1904, and PMG Statutory Rules 1905, No.67.

39 Karen Fitzsimmons Prior, A far too simple analysis, industrial work for women in the colonies of Australia 1857-1891, Preprint, February 1, and see Claire McCuskey, Women in the Victorian post office, *Second women and labour conference papers*, Vol.1, 1980.

40 Victoria, *Report upon the affairs of the post office and telegraph department for the year 1888* Employment of Females, (*Vic. PP*, Victoria Govt Printer, 1880-1), pp.21-2.

41 *New South Wales government gazette*, No.213, 30 May 1882.

42 *Telegraph* (Sydney), 6 July 1896; and the *Star* (Sydney), 4 July 1896.

43 Tasmania, *Report of superintendent of telegraphs*, 1877, *Tas. PP* (Hobart, 1878).

44 C. Kopsch, 'The electric exhibits at the Adelaide exhibition', *Journal South Australia Electric Society*, Vol.1, October 1877.

5 'BROTHERS IN ONE SERVICE'

1 Western Australia, *Report of the Postmaster-General for year 1900*, WA PP (Perth, 1901), p.16; Mr Batchelor, SA, *CPD*, H. of R., 1901-2, Vol.XI, p.1518, and Joseph Cook, quoted *Daily Telegraph*, 19 May 1899.

2 *The Transmitter*, 15 March 1901.

3 Address by Hon. J.D. Drake, Queensland Museum and Historical Society, GPO Brisbane, n.d. unpublished draft. 'History of the Post Office', ch. 'The federation of the Post Office' by Mrs Binns and Miss Ryan, Telecom Australia, Melbourne, discusses Barton's overtures to Philp in some detail.

4 F. Crowley (ed.), *A new history of Australia* (Heinemann, Melbourne, 1974), ch.7, p.266; W.K. Hancock, *Australia* (1961), p.66; and N.G. Butlin, 'Colonial Socialism in Australia' in H.A. Aitken (ed.), *The state and economic growth* (NY, 1956).

5 *CPD* Session 1901-2, *CPD*, Senate, Vol.1, 6 June 1901, pp.750.

6 *Ibid.*, pp.762-3; Gould, p.760.

7 *Ibid.*, pp.906,909,910,921.

8 *CPD*, H. of R. *ibid.*, pp.3608-9.

9 Commonwealth of Australia, Posts and Telegraph Department, *Report of the departmental committee of inquiry into the telegraph and telephone system of the states of the Commonwealth* (SA Govt Printer, Adelaide, 1901). The report sheds considerable light on the state of the telegraph and telephone art in Australia at the turn of the century. H.W. Jenvey, the Victorian representative, was the author of *Practical telegraphy* (George Robertson & Co., 4th edn, 1904).

10 Jonathan Pincus, 'Service at any cost', in Butlin, *Government and capitalism*, ch.5.

11 *Courier Mail* (Brisbane), 4 November 1902.

12 Commonwealth of Australia, *PP*, General Session 1905, Vol.11, Postmaster-General's Department, *Reports by Mr. John Hesketh, electrical engineer, on matters investigated by him during his recent tour in America and Europe* ... 8 September 1905, pp.1461-85; common battery exchange, p.1483. Hesketh's work for Queensland is commemorated in Hesketh House of Telecom Australia, Brisbane.

13 Commonwealth of Australia, *PP*, 1914-1917, Vol.IV, Report by J. Hesketh, May 1915, p.5611; and Commonwealth of Australia *PP*, 1906, Vol.2, *Telephone lines in country districts* by John Hesketh (read at the Sale Convention, Chamber of Agriculture, Victoria, 5 July 1906), p.1572.

14 The title of deputy Postmaster-General was given after Federation to PMG State heads. The title changed to deputy director, posts and telegraphs, in 1925 and to director, posts and telegraphs, in 1950.

15 Frank Kay, 'APEU-PTTA 1912-1962'.

16 Melbourne *Argus*, quoted in the *Courier Mail*, 10 July 1901.

17 L.F. Crisp, *Australia's national government* (Longman, Melbourne, 1967), p.325; and *CPD* H. of R. 1908, Vol.XLVI, p.10879. Deakin's biographer, Professor J. La Nauze, fails to mention this important event.

18 These included larger votes granted for telegraphs and telephones, the remodelling of telephone rates, estimates for extending the permanent staff, and the introduction in 1909 of Wheatstone instruments on inter-State telegraphs.

19 Bell's letter, 17 June 1910, Queensland Museum and Postal and Telecommunications Historical Society, Brisbane; *Courier Mail* (Brisbane), 8 July 1910; Parliament of the Commonwealth of Australia, *Report of the Royal Commission into postal services* (Victoria, Govt Printer, 1910), Appendix XXXIX. Evidence tendered by Dr. Bell of the United States of America, pp.2417-26.

20 *Report* 1910, p.9 (internal page numbering).

21 *Ibid.*, p.20.

22 Cf. Kewley and Rydon, 'Australian Commonwealth Government corporations'.

23 *Report*, 1910, *op.cit.*, pp.27,13.

24 Collins, *A voice from afar*.

25 PMG, *Third annual report*, 1912-1913, and PMG *Second annual report*, 1911-12, p.v.

26 Parliament of the Commonwealth of Australia, 1914-15, *Report on the business management of the postmaster-general's department of the Commonwealth of Australia*, Robert Murray Anderson, 25 August 1915 (*PP*, Govt Printer, Victoria, 1915).

27 Oxenham had been private secretary to Queensland's Postmaster-General and later charge clerk in the PMG's Department. He was appointed assistant secretary in 1907.

28 In the House of Representatives on 16 October 1913, 16 April 1914, 29 May 1914, and 13 and 29 May 1915, and in the estimates debates of July 1915.

29 D. Baker, 'From coo-ee to communications satellite', ch.7, p.182.

30 Sir Samuel Jones, The development of Australian telecommunications manufacturing industry, The centenary of the Adelaide-Darwin overland telegraph line, p.33; and *CPD*, H. of R. Deb. 1919, p.11724, Mr Fenton.

31 Ross, *History of radio in SA*, pp.16-22; M.J. Gooley, A report of early wireless telegraph in South Australia (PMG's Department, Adelaide, October 1964), mimeo; and *Adelaide Advertiser*, 14 September 1899.

32 Rottnest Island, WA, *Wireless telegraph experiments by the telegraph branch of the general post office to*

ascertain the practicability of establishing communication by that system between Rottnest Island and Perth (Perth, Govt Printer, 1899); and Premier of Tasmania to Prime Minister of Commonwealth, 4 October 1901, Commonwealth *PP*, 1901–2, Journals, Vol.1, p.883.

33 *Commonwealth of Australia Constitution Act* 63 and 64, Part V, para.51(v); and J.A. La Nauze, 'Other like services', Physics and the Australian Constitution, *Records of Australian Academy of Science*, November 1968, Vol.1, No.3, pp.36–44.

34 Ross, *History of radio in SA*, p.26.

35 Ross Curnow, 'The origins of Australian broadcasting', in Bedford and Curnow, *Initiative and organisation*, pp.50–1.

36 *Argus* (Melbourne), 13 July 1906, p.4; information J. Moynihan, Telecom Australia, Perth; and *CPD* H. of R. Vol.XXXIV, pp.4064–5.

37 Curnow, p.57; and E.T. Fisk, 'The application and development of wireless of Australia', *Proceedings of pan-Pacific science conference*, 1923, Vol.1 (Melbourne 1927), p.6210.

38 *ADB*, Vol.7, p.162; and PMG *First annual report*, 1910–11.

39 Blainey, *Tyranny*, pp.325–6.

40 PMG *Fifth annual report*, 1914–15, p.17; and *CPD*, H. of R. 20 August 1919, Vol.LXXXIX, p.11753.

41 F. Goss, 'Life in the never–never', ms, Telecom Museum, Adelaide; information from D. Grigg, Telecom Australia, Melbourne; V. Hopewell, The Story of Eucla Telegraph Repeating Station, Telecom Australia; and 'Early Days', Postal Telecommunications Historical Society, GPO Museum Brisbane.

42 *Commonwealth Gazette*, No.78, 8 November 1923, p.2152; and the *Argus* (Melbourne), 10 October 1922, p.6.

43 *Argus* (Melbourne), 13 October 1922, p.7. The rotary line switches were manufactured by American Telephones Ltd and supplied to the PMG by their subsidiary company in Sydney, Automatic Telephones (Australia) Ltd. In this case they supplanted the older type 'Keith' plunger telephone switches.

44 *Argus* (Melbourne) covered the inquiry on 10, 11, 12, 13, 16, 17, 21 and 23 October and 9 November 1922. And see *Commonwealth Gazette*, No. 40, 14 June 1923.

6 THE LONG REIGN OF 'POOH-BAH' BROWN

1 *ADB*, Vol.7, pp.437–9. On one point this entry is incorrect. Brown held no university degree. Information from Mr G. Brown, Melbourne. Telegram Australia House to Prime Minister's Department, ('most capable man in Britain') 9 August 1922, PMG Archives, PA 204/1/179, Australian Archives, Brighton, Victoria.

2 Hughes signed all telegrams in the protracted negotiations to obtain Brown's services in 1922. Minute paper of Executive Council, PMG's Department, 19 October 1922, approved Brown's appointment as adviser for one year. The third man of the Postal Advisory Committee was Mr Swanton.

3 *CPD*, H. of R., 28 March 1924. Brown's salary was £2,500 a year. The idea of a highly remunerated 'man at the top' had been first canvassed in Parliament by King O'Malley in the House of Representatives, 30 June 1915, p.448.

4 Kellock, 'Sir Harry Brown . . .'.

5 H.P. Brown, 'Telegraph and telephone development in Australia', address to the Victorian Postal Institute, 25 August 1927, *Telegraph and Telephone Journal*, August 1927, p.231.

6 *Ibid.*, and PMG *Annual reports* 1923–4, p.13; 1925–6, p.19.

7 Kellock, 'Sir Harry Brown . . .'.

8 PMG *Annual Report*, 1924–5, p.20; and Brown, *op.cit.*, p.13.

9 A.H. Kay, 'A short history of telecommunications', Faraday lecture, 1972 (APO, 1973), pp.16–17; and see Baker, *Communicators and their first trade unions*, for its impact on telegraphists, p.199.

10 APO Research laboratories, *Review of activities*, Golden Jubilee edn 1923–1973, pp.10,14–15.

11 Cf. A.F. Davies, 'Administrative style', *PA*, 1967, Vol.26, p.162.

12 Notes by H.P. Brown, 1957, in possession of his son G. Brown, together with six volumes of press cuttings.

13 *Punch*, 3 December 1925, p.29.

14 *Smith's Weekly*, 20 September 1930. The mail sorter with 71 conveyors, 114 electric motors and some two miles of belting was installed in Sydney in 1930 and later in Melbourne and Brisbane.

15 *ADB*, Vol.5, Kernot, pp.20–2; and Vol.6, Warren, pp.356–7.

16 PMG *First annual report*, 1910–11, p.13; and *Second annual report*, 1911–12, p.24. Strickland Gleed became supervising engineer, Sydney; Kilpatrick deputy–director, Perth; Reginald Partington, supervising engineer, Victoria; and Robert Lawson, chief engineer central office, in 1936. S.F. Kellock, unpublished ms in the possession of A. Kellock, Telecom Australia.

17 A campaign in the early 1950s to recruit engineers from Britain followed a notice in the 1948–9 annual report of a 'dearth of qualified men'. In 1971 a campaign in the Department anticipated adding 50 engineering graduates to the PMG. Recruitment of Engineers in USA, Report on exploratory visit to USA, May–June by E. Sawkins.

18 PMG *Eighth annual report*, 1917–18, p.34; *Ninth annual report*, 1918–19, p.23; interview J.R. Hutchinson 1982. The *Annual report* 1929–30 recorded that 'the educational and social facilities provided [by the Postal Institute] have been availed of to a great extent', p.19.

19 G.N. Smith, One man's career with the

Postmaster–General's Department, 1926–70. G.N. Smith left the service as State director of Posts and Telegraphs, Victoria.

20 *ADB*, Vol.8, pp.508–10; and L.P. Fitzhardinge, *A political biography, William Morris Hughes*, Vol.2 (Angus & Robertson, Sydney, 1979), p.476.

21 Brennan's dissenting opinion, Parliament of the Commonwealth of Australia, *Wireless communication*, Parliamentary Committee appointed to inquire into a proposed agreement in the Amalgamated Wireless (Australasia) Ltd, 12 July 1922, pp.13–15; and Fisk 'The application and development of wireless', *op.cit.*, p.626. One precedent was the 'mixed undertaking' which the Anglo-Persian Oil Company had negotiated with the Commonwealth Oil Refineries.

22 PMG *Thirteenth annual report*, 1922–3, p.20; R. Curnow, 'Communications and political power', in Bedford & Curnow, ch.4; and Fitzhardinge, *op.cit.*

23 *Wireless communication*, Parliamentary Committee . . ., *op.cit.*, p.14.

24 Fisk, 'The application and development of wireless', *op.cit.*, p.626.

25 Sir Earle Page, *Truant surgeon, The inside story of forty years of Australian political life*, ed. Ann Mozley (Angus & Robertson, Sydney, 1963), p.161.

26 Walker, *The Magic Spark*, p.17; and letter, *SMH*, 15 April 1924.

27 H.P. Brown, notes on broadcasting for address to Institution Electrical Engineers, Melbourne, 28 January 1931. *See also ADB* and Kellock, 'Sir Harry Brown'.

28 Judith Wright, 'To another housewife', *Collected poems 1942–1970* Angus & Robertson (Sydney, reprinted 1974), p.221.

29 Research Laboratories. Cf. APO Research laboratories, *Review of activities*, p.16; and *Telecom News*, April 1977, p.14, for Canberra broadcast.

30 Brown to secretary Prime Minister's Dept, Australian Archives, Brighton, MP 341, Box 248, Radio Miscellaneous.

31 Parliament of the Commonwealth of Australia, *Report of the Royal Commission on Wireless*, 5 October 1927, summary of recommendations, pp.viii, ix.

32 See Curnow, 'The national service', in Bedford & Curnow, ch.3.

33 H.P. Brown, 'The national network'. *The Listener-In*, 9 April 1932, p.28.

34 Letter H.P. Brown to departmental personnel, 28 June 1933. Copy made available by V.F. Kenna.

35 Brown, 'The national service', *op.cit.*, p.28.

36 '50 years of overseas phone calls', *Contact*, Journal of Overseas Telecommunication Australia, first issue, April 1980, pp.6–7,9–10; and PMG *Annual Report*, 1931–32, p.18.

37 Alistair Cooke, *Six men* (Penguin, 1978), p.70.

38 PMG *Annual reports*, 1929–30, p.19, and 1930–31, p.16.

39 Parliament of Commonwealth of Australia, 1929,

Parliamentary Standing Committee on Public Works, *Report . . . on the establishment of telephone communication between Perth and the eastern states* (Canberra, Govt Printer, 1919), p.iv.

40 'Tasmanian cable', *Advocate*, 29 November 1935; D.A. Grant and E. Rumpelt, 'The Bass Strait cable — 9 channel extension carrier system', *TJA*, February 1957, p.178; and 'Rottnest Island connection', *West Australian*, 2 April 1936. Rottnest was the last of Australia's pre-Federation exchanges taken over by the PMG's Department in 1936.

41 H.P. Brown letter to Reith, 17 November 1931; Brown press cuttings; and information received from George Brown, Melbourne. The propellor is now in the Museum of Science and Industry, Sydney. Australia's first internal airmail service was operated by Western Australian Airways. It ran from Geraldton via coastal ports to Broome from 1922 and was extended in 1924 to run from Perth to Derby.

42 Telecom Australia Archives Files 293/7/289 and 293/7/27.

43 'A song of the Telephone, 1910', reprinted *Teletechnician*, July 1983, Vol.64, p.125.

44 Page, *The flying doctor story*, pp.64–5,90 ff; and Ross, *op.cit*, pp.201–9. The Flying Doctor and other such stations were specifically exempt from Section 55 of the Wireless Telegraphy Act of 1924 which required licensed installations to be operated by a certified operator.

45 PMG *Annual report*, 1933–34, p.18; and *Broadcasting and the Australian post office, 1923–1973*, pamphlet (Melbourne, APO, 1973).

46 H.P. Brown address to the Postal Institute, 1927, *op.cit.*, and obituary, *TJA*, October 1967, p.211.

47 Quoted Kellock, *op.cit.*, pp.214–15.

48 *Commonwealth Government Gazette*, 9 November 1939, p.2367 and personal information.

49 Letter from Sir Harry Brown to A.B. Corbett, Director–General of Civil Aviation, 10 October 1939.

7 THE TELECOMMUNICATIONS WAR

1 ITU, *From semaphore to satellite*.

2 *CPD* Senate, 6 October 1949, Vol.204, p.1013, Postmaster–General Senator Cameron. Additionally some 760 PMG officers, said Cameron, were released for work in war organisations.

3 Claude Leonard, supervising engineer. Letter dated 28 November 1944 reporting on his period of PMG service in Darwin from November 1939–April 1942, Telecom Museum, Adelaide.

4 Interview with Claude Leonard, 1981; and G.O. Newton, 'Long distance telephone and telegraph installations in Australia during the war', *TJA*, February 1946, Vol.5, No.6, p.322.

5 Interview with J.L. Skerrett, 1982.

6 Letter, Operations Manager, Qantas, Sydney, to Director, Dept of Civil Aviation, 19 February 1942. Dept of Civil Aviation File 41/101/200, Australian Archives, MP 238/1.

404

7 George Tuthill (former senior technician, Adelaide), 'A Veteran Centre Tech Remembers', *Telecom*, No. 47, November 1979, p.17. This story is confirmed by Austin Jones in a letter to J. Lightfoot, secretary, Postal and Telecommunications Historical Society, Brisbane GPO Museum, January 1971.

8 *Advertiser* (Adelaide), 21 January 1942.

9 The two surviving PMG files, which unfortunately shed no light, are Postmaster-General's Department files relating to matters arising from the war, 1938-1950, W530, deposited at the Australian Archives, MP 721/1.

10 Letter, Austin Jones to Lightfoot, January 1971, *op.cit.*; and 'Key to memories. The day bombs fell on Darwin', Brisbane *Courier Mail*, 26 July 1982.

11 Skerrett interview; and Duke's account given in 'This was Australia's Pearl Harbour', *Sunday Mail* (Brisbane), 24 January 1971. Duke, who won a British Empire Medal for his wartime work, claimed he was the first to report the Darwin bombing and 'flash the message to the world'. The article provoked Austin Jones's correcting letter to Lightfoot. Other differing but only partially correct accounts are given by D. Lockwood, *Australia's Pearl Harbour* (Cassell, Melbourne, 1977); and Taylor, *End to silence*, pp.160-70.

12 Dept of Civil Aviation files, 1939-1945, file 4/101/200, Australian Archives, MP 238/1.

13 *Age* (Melbourne), 20 February 1942.

14 Douglas Gillison in his *Royal Australian Airforce 1939-1942*, Vol.1, in Series 3 (Air Series), *Australia in the war of 1939-1945* (Canberra, Australian War Museum, 1962), pp.430,431, gives the total dead from the bombing of 19 February as 238. The figure is qualified owing to the bombing of a hospital ship in harbour and some burials at sea. Skerrett sets the figure at 243. Interview, *op.cit.*, and *SMH*, 21 February 1942.

15 Newton, *op.cit.*, p.323; and R.M. Todd, 'Telecommunications development in Northern Territory', *TJA*, October 1972, pp.176-6; 'Developments in carrier telegraph transmissions', *TJA*, June 1944, Vol.5, No.1.

16 Skerrett interview, *op.cit.*

17 J.L. Skerrett, 'Developments in carrier telegraph transmission in Australia', Part 2, *TJA*, October 1944, pp.91-107.

18 Skerrett, 'Developments in . . .', Part 2, *op.cit.*; S.T. Webster, 'Developments in carrier telegraph transmission in Australia', *TJA*, Part 3, February 1945, Vol.5, pp.125-37, and N.J. McCay, *ibid.*, February 1961, Vol.12, No.6, p.390. The Defence Communications Committee was originally formed in 1924; its terms of reference were revised in 1938, and it took on a wider membership in 1941-2. Commonwealth Record Series, PMG's Dept correspondence 1938-1950, W2, Australian Archives.

19 Information received from G.N. Smith, 1982. *See*

also R.J. Kanaley, *Further recollections, 1929-1974*, NSW Telecommunication Society monograph; and W.C. Rhode, Defence Communication on the Cape York Peninsula, Queensland Postal-Telecommunications Historical Society, Brisbane, GPO Museum, typescript.

20 Information on the Torres Strait and New Guinea communications received from I.M. Gunn and N.J. McCay, 1982.

21 Skerrett, 'Developments in carrier telegraph transmissions', *op.cit.*, Part 2, p.107.

22 PMG *Annual report*, 1941-2; and Skerrett interview, *op.cit.*

23 W.F. Evans, *History of Radio Research Board 1926-1945* (Melbourne, 1973), pp.9-16. The board consisted of Madsen, Brown, Commander Cressell of the RAN, and Professor T.H. Laby, Dept of Physics, Melbourne University. The board also carried the support of the Department of Defence and the Wireless Institute of Australia.

24 Interview with L.M. Harris, 1982.

25 Cf. Australian Scientific Industry Association, *High and new technology: needs of Australian industry* (Australian Scientific Industry Association Position Paper, February 1983); and Stuart Macdonald, 'Faith, hope and disparity'.

26 The Radiophysics Advisory Board was set up with representatives from the CSIR, the PMG, the Departments of Defence and Munitions and the Service heads. Harris interview, *op.cit.*; and interview with Sir Frederick White, Canberra, 1983. White was later chairman of the CSIRO 1959-70. See also D.P. Mellor, *The role of science and industry*, Vol.5 in Series 4 (Civil) *Australia in the war of 1939-45* (Australian War Memorial, 1958), p.448.

27 Significantly, a CSIR wartime document entitled 'Council for Scientific and Industrial Research and Australian Telecommunications at War' makes the claim re radar: 'a band of scientists was hard at work in Australia. A new Division of CSIR was set up specially to undertake fundamental research connected with the new techniques, and to carry out the development, design and construction to the prototype stage of radar and associated equipment required by the Armed Forces.' In the lengthy description of equipment made, the document makes no mention of the problems encountered and of the vital developmental and engineering work of the PMG.

28 PMG Research Laboratories Monthly Report to the Director-General, September and October 1941, typescript, PMG Department minutes, Australian Telecommunications at War. Projects carried out for the Ministry of Munitions, 25 January 1946, Telecom Australia, Research Laboratories. See also A.S. Watson, 'Underwater inspection of the mainland-Tasmania telephone cable', *TJA* June 1940, p.17.

29 Development of the Australian telecommunications manufacturing industry since 1870, *The centenary of the Adelaide-Darwin overland telegraph*

line, *op.cit.*, p.34. Jones was himself a former PMG divisional engineer.

30 *TJA*, October 1939, Vol.2, No.5; *ibid.*, June 1946, Vol.6, No.1, and personal information.

31 *TJA*, February 1949, Vol.7, No.3, pp.128–9. Fanning was appointed deputy Director–General in February 1944.

32 *TJA*, 1940, Vol.3, No.1; and personal information.

33 Gavin Long, *The six years war* (Australian War Memorial and AGPS, 1973); information received from T. McNamara, former unit second-in-command of 3 Australia Corps Signals, 1982, and from J. Moynihan, Telecom WA.

34 MacArthur arrived in Australia on 17 March 1942 and assumed authority, agreed between the US and Australian governments, of supreme commander of the allied forces in the south-west Pacific area on 18 April 1942. He headquartered for five months in Melbourne at the Menzies Hotel and moved to Brisbane in July 1942. W. Manchester, *American Caesar: Douglas MacArthur 1880–1964* (Arrow, 1979), pp.24,261,270.

35 PMG *Annual report*, 1941–2, p.15; and *CPD*, Senate, July 1946, p.2686.

36 PMG *Annual report*, 1940–1, pp.15,16; 1941–2 p.16; and 1942–3 p.14.

8 'THE RINGING GROOVES OF CHANGE'

1 Alfred Lord Tennyson, *Locksley Hall*.

2 Interview with R. Turnbull, 1982, and *Report of the Commission of inquiry into the Australian post office*, Vol.1, April 1974 (AGPS, 1974), p.314.

3 *Report, ibid.*, p.319.

4 Quoted Blainey, *Tyranny*, p.333.

5 *CPD*, Senate, Vol.204, 6 October 1949, p.1016.

6 *CPD*, Senate, Vol.18, July 1946, Overseas Tele-communication Bill, Senator Donald Cameron, pp.2681–98; and H. of R., Vol.187, 20 June 1946, pp.1653–65.

7 PMG *Annual report*, 1949–50, pp.27,31; and PMG *Annual report*, 1950–1.

8 'A typical chart showing opportunities for advancement', 1934; and interview J.R. Hutchinson, 1982.

9 The PMG'S Department also became a member of the Board.

10 Chippindall's biography, *TJA*, February 1949, Vol.7, No.3, p.129.

11 Turnbull interview.

12 Commonwealth of Australia, *The Australian post office, ten years of progress*, 1 July 1947 to 30 June 1957. Report by the Director–General of Posts and Telegraphs, Sir Giles Chippindall.

13 Charles Ramond, *The art of using science in marketing*, quoted Martin Mayer, 'The telephone and uses of time', ch.10, in de Sola Pool, *The social impact of . . .*, p.225.

14 *Ten years of progress, op.cit.*, p.25.

15 PMG *Annual report 1956–7* pp.39–42.

16 Benchley quoted by John Brooks, 'The first and only century of telephone literature', in de Sola Pool, p.220.

17 Dorothy Parker, 'The telephone call', *The Penguin Dorothy Parker* (1977), p.120; and Shirley Hazzard, *The transit of Venus* (Penguin, 1981), p.143.

18 The radio revolution, Part 2: 1923–1973, in *OTC Information Broadsheet*, No.4.

19 Cf. John Langdale, 'Telex and data transmissions in the Australian economic system', *Proceedings of tenth New Zealand geography conference*, Auckland, 1979, p.98; PMG *Annual report*, 1965, Telex traffic 1955–1980, appendix; and R.W. McKinnon, 'Automatisation of the Australian telex network', Part 1, *TJA*, June 1965, Vol.15, pp.108–15.

20 *Moving the message, Telegraphs through the ages*, Telecom Australia, Public Relations Branch, January 1977; and private information from Peter Bethell, Telecom Australia, Melbourne. See also D. Richardson, 'Telegraph reperforator exchange switching system', *Teletechnician*, October 1956, pp.161–4.

21 *Australian Telegraphist*, August 1957, p.4.

22 *Report, op.cit.*, p.29.

23 *Australian Telegraphist*, August 1957, and see J. Baker, *op.cit.*, pp.262–74.

24 The full version of the ode is given in J. Baker, *op.cit.*, pp.59–60, and *Telecom News*, December 1981, No.70, p.17.

25 Information received from Dr Clive Coogan, Regional Administrative Officer, CSIRO, Melbourne; and see *ADB*, Vol.6, Sutton, pp.226–7.

26 *Courier–Mail* (Brisbane), 3 December 1955. Article by W. Brown based on interviews with Tom Elliott.

27 *Ibid.* The methods used by Elliott involved arc lamps to project the image onto the photo-electric cell of an electrically controlled scanning disc whose output was used to modulate a radio carrier. This reconverted into light images on the receiving sets.

28 Cf. APO Research laboratories, *Review of activities*, Golden Jubilee edn, pp.32–3; and *ATR*, May 1970, Vol.4, No.1, p.47, for Seyler's later contribution; also John Barth, '25 years of television', *Telecom News*, November 1981, p.23.

29 The Television Act of 1948 foreshadowed it.

30 *CPD*, H. of R., 12 October 1950, Vol.209, pp.715–16,721.

31 Falkinder, *CPD*, H. of R., 1949, Vol.204, p.822; Beale, 13 October 1949, Vol.205, p.1405; Casey, 12 October 1950, Vol.209, p.724; and Anthony, 1949, Vol.202, p.967.

32 *Report of the Royal Commission on television*, 29 September 1954, pp.2–3. Professor G.W. Paton, Vice–Chancellor of Melbourne University, was its chairman.

33 Hazlehurst, 'Advent of Commercial Television'.

34 *CPD*, H. of R., 12 October 1950, Vol.209, p.729.

35 *Ibid.*, March 1953, 2nd Reading of the National Television Bill.

36 *Broadcasting and the Australian Post Office 1923-1973*, and *Report of the Royal Commission on television*, pp.63,102.

37 Cecil Holmes, 'Television in Australia: A survey', *Meanjin*, April 1958, p.50.

38 Evidence by Chippindall to the Royal Commission on Television, quoted *Report, op.cit.*, p.54.

39 PMG *Annual report*, 1955-56. See also E.J. Wilkinson and J.D. Robertson, 'Expansion of transmitting station facilities for the national television service', *JIEA*, Oct.-Nov. 1964, p.263.

40 I.W. McLean, Telephone pricing and cross-subsidisation under the PMG, 1901-1975, Seminar delivered at Dept of Economic History, RSSS, ANU, 21 May 1982. I am indebted to this paper for its detailed information.

41 *Ibid.*, p.8.

42 *Ibid.*, p.11; and Telecom Australia.

43 *CPD*, H. of R., 25 November 1941, Vol.169, pp.1841-2; and information from Telecom Australia.

44 *CPD*, H. of R. 16 September 1959, Vol.24, pp.1094-7.

45 *Ten years of progress, op.cit.*, pp.59-61.

46 Parliament of Commonwealth of Australia, *Joint committee of public accounts, Nineteenth report* (Canberra, Govt Printing Office, 1955), Twelfth Report of the Committee, 13 April 1954, PMG's Department, p.373.

47 Alan Barnard, Cui bono: the post office at work, Seminar paper given to Dept of Economic History, RSSS, ANU, 25 August 1978, p.13.

48 *Ten years of progress, op.cit.*, pp.52-7.

49 See Cameron's long review of PMG post-war activities, *CPD*, Senate, 6 October 1949, Vol.204, pp.1013-20.

50 *SMH*, 15 September 1956; and *Who's who in Australia* 1965, p.229.

51 Parliament of the Commonwealth of Australia, *Report of the Hon. Mr. Justice R.L. Taylor, royal commissioner on alleged improper practices and improper refusal to co-operate with the Victoria police force on the part of persons employed in the Postmaster-General's Department in Victoria in relation to illegal gambling* (Canberra, 1963), and interview material.

52 Clement Semmler, *The ABC — Aunt Sally and sacred cow* (MUP 1981), p.27.

53 *CPD*, H. of R., 5 October 1955, Vol.8, p.1285.

9 DISTANCE AND DIVERSITY

1 *Progress - policy - plans* August 1959, published by authority of the Postmaster-General Hon. C.W. Davidson, OBE, MP (Commonwealth of Australia, 1959).

2 G.W. Larson, Development of telecommunications systems in Tasmania, Commonwealth of Australia, Postmaster-General's Department, paper presented to ANZAAS, Hobart, August 1965; interview with L.M. Harris, 1982; and W.E. Beard, 'Tasmania's radio telephone system', *TJA*, Feb. 1958, pp.72-82.

3 Quoted from 'A page from the past', Tasmanian *Telecom News*, February 1977.

4 Interview with K. Newham, Tasmania, 1981.

5 Interview with I. LeFevre, Hobart, 1981.

6 Bush fire disaster in Tasmania, Internal Telecommunications Division Report, PMG's Department, 1967.

7 Interview with M. Gooley, 1981. Gooley was supervising engineer at Murray Bridge, 1950-5.

8 Information from W.L. Caudle, State manager, Telecom WA, and from F. Gubbins, SA.

9 Cf. A. Gravell and R.J. Pontague, The development of telecommunication services to the north-west of Australia (Institution of Engineers, Australia, Annual Engineering Conference Papers, Perth, 1965), pp.187-98.

10 Information received from W. Harris, Brisbane.

11 Interviews with K. Petrie, State manager, D.M. Baker, chief engineer, A.B. Poulsen and N.G. Watson, Telecom Australia, Queensland.

12 *CPD* Senate, October 1949, Vol.202, p.1020.

13 *On the line*, September 1957, Vol.1, No.1.

14 PMG *Annual report*, 30 June 1960, p.18.

15 See J. Whybourne, 'Emergency telephone service civic exchange, Canberra', *TJA*, June 1964, pp.28-9; and P. Clark, 'Telecommunications' in *Canberra's Engineering Heritage* (Institution of Engineers, Australia, Canberra, 1982).

16 Interview with M. Power, deputy state manager, Telecom NSW, 1982.

17 Power, interview.

18 Interview with H.G. Shaw, Perth, 1981.

19 Interview with R. Turnbull, and R.W. Turnbull, B.F. Marrows, W.J.B. Pollock, 'Nation-wide dialling system for Australia', *TJA*, October 1958, p.134.

20 K. Beazley, WA *CPD*, H. of R., 15 September 1959, p.1017.

21 *Progress - policy - plans, op.cit.*, and *Community telephone plans for Australia, 1960*, PMG's Department, March 1960.

22 Turnbull, interview.

23 Britain began its all-numeral system in 1966.

24 Stradwick became general manager of the East Pacific-Australian International Telephone and Telegraph (IT&T) Corporation and vice-president of International Standard Electric Corporation.

25 *L.M. Ericsson 100 years*, Volume 11, *Rescue reconstruction worldwide enterprise, 1932-1976*, ch. by Arthur Attman, Three Key Markets, Mexico, Australia, Brazil 1977, p.244. During 1953 the enterprising Rowe presented a 60 line crossbar rural automatic exchange to the PMG for study and use in the Research Laboratories.

26 Interview with F.P. O'Grady, 1981; F.P. O'Grady, 'Australia Post adopts crossbar automatic switching systems', *TJA*, June 1959, Vol.12, No.2, p.6; and Braun and MacDonald, *Revolution in miniature*, pp.180–1.

27 *L.M. Ericsson 100 years*, Vol.2, Rowe to Aberg, 15 December 1958, and Aberg's reply, quoted pp.246–7.

28 *Ibid.*, p.247.

29 Ericsson is remembered by some PMG engineers for having 'forced' one particular type of PABX on the Australian scene.

10 THE TECHNOLOGISTS

1 John Crawford, 'The role of the permanent head', *PA*, Vol.13, 1954, p.154.

2 Letter to the author, 3 April 1981.

3 Arthur Attman, 'Three key markets . . .', *op.cit.*, p.246; *L.M. Ericsson 100 years*, Vol.2.

4 PMG *Annual report*, June 1967, p.8.

5 The Stewart-Brown Report 1960, PMG Files 156/3/229.

6 Harris-Brown-Dwyer Report, PMG Report on the organisation of professional and sub-professional staff, Research Laboratories, Engineering Division, 1962, mimeo, Telecom Australia.

7 APO Research laboratories, *Review of activities*, Golden Jubilee edn, p.12; interview with L.M. Harris; 'The research laboratories of the Postmaster-General's Department', *TJA*, October 1973, pp.60–3.

8 Interview with P.R. Brett; Brett, 'Aspects of future telecommunication services of particular relevance to Australia', *ATR*, special issue, symposium 'Whither communications?', 1973, Vol.7, No.3, pp.30–5; and APO Research laboratories, *Review of activities*, p.13.

9 F.P. O'Grady, 'Communications through satellites, horizons in science today', Golden Jubilee symposium, *POA Chronicle*, Nov. 1963, pp.3–4.

10 The distinction with television is worth noting. The PMG installed, maintained and operated the technical aspects of sound studios until the ABC took over this function in 1964; they also installed and maintained both sound and TV transmitters since the start of radio and TV. But the ABC have always installed, maintained and operated the technical aspects of TV studios without PMG–Telecom involvement.

11 Cf. L.D. Sebire & K.R. Collyer, 'The role of radio in the development of the remote areas', papers presented to the Institution of Engineers, Australia, Mildura, October 1969; and L.F. Pearson, 'The Australian outpost radio communication system'.

12 Cf. MacCullum, *Ten years of Television*, and Hall, *Supertoy*.

13 Information, Telecom WA; *Telecom News*, December 1981, No.90, p.19.

14 PMG *Annual report*, June 1964, p.8; H. White, 'Expanding overseas links: Seacom and Compac cables; space satellites', *Rydge's*, May 1967, Vol.40, pp.67–70. Two new major submarine coaxial cables were opened during 1976, the Tasman cable from Sydney to Auckland and the A–PNG cable from Cairns to Port Moresby, both capable of carrying up to 640 simultaneous telephone conversations.

15 Alan Hulme, Voices across Queensland, 1971, Queensland Postal and Telecommunications Historical Society, Brisbane.

16 *TJA*, February 1969, p.3; interview, W. Harris, Brisbane; and Max Wimmer, 'Days of penguins, humour and lasting friends', *Telecom News*, July 1981, No.65, p.22.

17 J. Moynihan, Developments in telecommunications in Western Australia, March 1981; and PMG *Annual report*, 1969–70, p.4.

18 *Telegen*, September 1969, p.1; Glenn's thanks, *West Australian*, 21 February 1962. A small earth station had been built c1960 at Muchea north of Perth in connection with Project Mercury.

19 Lloyd, *The education of the professional engineer*, p.227.

20 *Report of the Commission of Inquiry into the Australian Post Office*, April 1974, Vol.1, p.316.

21 *Research, development and innovation in Telecom Australia* (Telecom Australia, Melbourne, 1980). See also chapter 16.

22 C.P. Snow, *Science and government* (Mentor, 1962), p.71.

23 A.M. Wellington, *The economic theory of the location of railways* (Wiley, NY, 1888).

24 Newlands, 'APEA'. The Institution of Engineers, Australia, formed in 1920, was not eligible for registration as an organisation of employees under the Commonwealth Conciliation and Arbitration Act.

25 *The professional engineers' case* (Association of Professional Engineers, Australia, March 1961), Report to Members of the Association, p.1.

26 *Professional Engineer*, September 1970, p.2.

27 The Australian Postal Electricians Union was inaugurated as a Federal union under the new Arbitration (Public Service) Act of 1911. Kay, 'APEU-PTTA', p.50.

28 *Australian Postal Electrician*, 20 November 1931, p.23; and *Teletechnician*, 24 August 1942, p.1.

29 *Teletechnician*, June 1964, p.82.

30 Kay, 'APEU-PTTA', p.64.

31 *Teletechnician*, March 1958, pp.37–8, and Kay, p.62.

32 *Teletechnician*, June 1961, p.90.

33 Frank Waters, *Postal unions and politics, a history of the Amalgamated Postal Workers Union of Australia*, ed. D. Murphy (UQP, 1978), pp.19–20. The union was formed as the Amalgamated Postal Linemen's, Sorters and Letter Carriers' Association in July 1925 and changed its name to the Amalgamated Postal Workers' Union of Australia in February 1926.

34 Bertha Cleminson, Reminiscences of 44 years in the service of the Commonwealth of Australia, typescript, Queensland, Postal–Telecommunications Historical Society, Post Office Museum, Brisbane.

35 Minutes of the Royal Commission into the Postal Service, 1908–1910, Question 25214, quoted David Grigg, Female telephonists and nervous strain, typescript, Telecom Australia, Information and Publicity. Senator de Largie and David Storrer would, however, submit an important dissenting report to the Commission where they argued that females be given equal opportunity to rise to clerical posts in the PMG and that the just principles of equal pay to women for equal work with men be put into practice.

36 Brenda Maddox, 'Women and the switchboard' in de Sola Pool, op. cit.

37 Information from the Australian Telephone and Phonogram Officers' Association, The CTPOA — history of the association, 1975, typescript.

38 Report of the Committee of Inquiry into technological change, pp.31–2; and Kaye Hargreaves, Women at work (Penguin, 1982), pp.242–3.

11 THE END OF AN ERA

1 Adjustment of charges often reflected what was considered politically achievable rather than what was required. For example, on at least one occasion, a proposed tariff revision covering both postal and telecommunications charges was designed to yield a given revenue increase. Cabinet reduced the total increase, the minister reviewed the lower figure and, in the event, only the telecommunications charges were raised while posts went further into the red. Interview, Brian Jones, Melbourne.

2 PMG Annual report, 1958, p.6.

3 Jonathan Pincus, 'Service at any cost', in Butlin, Government and capitalism, ch.5; and see Appendixes.

4 A. Barnard, 'Cui bono? The post office at work', op.cit., Jonathan Pincus, op.cit., and I.W. McLean, 'Telephone pricing and cross–subsidisation under the PMG, 1901 to 1975', Working paper in Economic History, ANU, 1982, op.cit.

5 Pincus, op.cit.

6 J. Moynihan, 'Cost of a basic telephone service'; and see ch.8.

7 Cf. Pincus, op.cit.

8 AFR, 22 March 1965. The automation classification struggle is traced in Baker, Communicators and their first trade unions, pp.289–302.

9 Report of Commission of Inquiry into the Australian Post Office, Vol.2, Consultants Report, Cresap, McCormick & Paget.

10 ALP Constitution, Platform and Rules 1967; see Waters, Postal unions and politics, pp.239–40, for APWU's role.

11 Interviews with O'Grady, Jones. See also Baker, Communicators and their first trade unions, p.324.

12 Jones interview, and interview with Sir Alan Hulme, 1982.

13 Shaw interview.

14 Interview with Sir John Knott, 1982.

15 Evidence submitted by Eber Lane before the Commission of Inquiry into the Australian Post Office, 1973.

16 Hulme interview.

17 Interview Eber Lane, 1981, and other interview material. Lane's popularity in Queensland is commemorated in the 'Eber Lane Room' at the General Post Office Museum, Brisbane.

18 Report of the Commission of Inquiry . . ., Vol.1, pp.iv–v.

19 Interviews with Hon. Lionel Bowen MHR, 1981, and Sir James Vernon, 1981.

20 Courier Mail (Brisbane), 31 January 1973.

21 A.F. Spratt, 'Commissions of inquiry', Spratt, a first assistant Director–General, management services, from 1964–72, was deputy Director–General from 1973; and the Age, 1 February 1973.

22 Pollock was Senior Assistant Director–General, industrial relations; McQuitty, acting first Assistant Director–General, management services; Cullen and Brady were deputy assistant Directors–General, management services division, personnel branch.

23 Vernon interview.

24 Country Party submission to Commission of Inquiry into the Post Office, submission No. 264, Australian Archives, series No. CRS/A4067, exhibit No. 99.

25 ACOA submission, No. 351, p.24.

26 Interview with J. Baker, 1982, and oral testimony before commission of inquiry.

27 Bhattacharya, 'A productivity study of the Australian Post Office'.

28 Cullen, 'Productivity in the Australian Post Office'.

29 Amalgamated Postal Workers Union submission No. 298, summary of APWU Submission to the Commission of Inquiry into the Australian Post Office, pp.2–5. There were 45,000 members of the APWU at the time. Contract work is the letting out by tender of work to firms outside the Department.

30 Report of Commission of Inquiry, pp.151–2.

31 Association of Professional Engineers Australia submission No. 226, Australian Archives Series No. CRS/A4067, exhibit No. 39.

32 Submission by adviser on women's affairs, submission No. 382, exhibit no. 39, ibid.; comment on E. Reid's evidence, Hearings 23 July 1973 and Department's response to Ms Reid. Statement by the PMG's Department on submission No. 382, ibid.

33 Interview with J.J. Kennedy, 1982.

34 Report of Commission of Inquiry, Principal Conclusions and Recommendations, p.xiii.

35 *Report*, p.xvii, 321, and Paterson's evidence, pp.315–16.

36 *Report*, pp.189–92.

37 *Report*, quoted p.201.

38 *Report*, p.xxii.

39 *Report*, p.xxi, 189ff.

40 *Report*, p.xx–xxi, and ch.1, pp.155–96. The chapter 'Financial prospects' was written by Sir James Vernon.

41 *Report*, pp.xx–xxi, p.192.

42 *Report*, p.xxiii; ch.11. The chief engineer was subsequently designated general manager engineering.

43 *Report*, p.238.

44 *Report*, p.247.

45 *Report*, pp.249,251–2.

46 *Report*, pp.xxv–xxvi; 325ff.

47 There are two locations of Sydney's gateway exchange at Paddington and Broadway.

48 *Report*, Vol.1, pp.273–5.

49 *Report*, pp.281,295.

50 *Report*, pp.291,293–4.

51 *Report*, pp.295–6.

52 *Report*, pp.297–9, and Vernon interview.

53 *Ibid.*

54 *Report*, p.134.

55 Interview material, 1981.

56 *Age* (Melbourne), 26 April 1974.

12 'DOUBLE, DOUBLE, TOIL AND TROUBLE'

1 Shakespeare, *Macbeth* IV, i, 10.

2 Interview material.

3 Australian engineer George Julius had invented the totalisator in the early 1920s.

4 Minute, planning and research, letter, R.W. Turnbull, 16 October 1967, and letter, Turnbull, for Director-General, 9 May 1968, to Public Service Board, Telecom Australia, Central Registry File 330/15/125 CUDN.

5 Minute, *ibid.*

6 Note by L.M. Harris, 20 December 1968, *ibid.*

7 UNIVAC's 'turnkey' responsibility was 'to deliver a working system in accordance with the specifications at a fixed price subject to imposition of liquidated damages in certain circumstances'. Normally a 'turnkey' arrangement was one where the buyer purchased the entire technology, hardware and software, and simply 'turned the key' to activate the process.

8 Letter from Director-General, Dept of Health, to Director-General, APO, 7 May 1969, CUDN File, *op.cit.*

9 Minute Director-General to Deputy Director-General, E. Sawkins, 21 September 1970, and common data user network planning, letter no. 1, *ibid.*

10 Letters to unions, 12 December 1970; and Controller-General of Customs to Director-General Knott, 11 May 1971, *ibid.*

11 Minute from Postmaster-General to Director-General, Sir John Knott, 29 June 1971, *ibid.*

12 Quarterly progress report, 29 June 1971; letters exchanged between UNIVAC and APO, 15 September 1971 and 28 September 1971; letter 15 September 1971 from supply branch, APO, to managing director UNIVAC, Division of Sperry Rand (Australia) Ltd; and APO quarterly report on CUDN, January 1972, Telecom Australia, Central Registry File 330/15/125 CUDN.

13 Sperry Rand, 28 September 1971, to Director-General, *ibid.*

14 Letter SADG works programme, 27 March 1972, *ibid.*

15 Interview Lane, *op.cit.*

16 *Report of the Commission of Inquiry . . .*, Vol.1, pp.108–9, and cf. J.M. Bennett, Large computer project problems and their causes, Technical Report 188, Presidential address, Information Processing and Computer Science, 52nd ANZAAS Congress, Sydney, May 1982, for a general analysis of the problem.

17 Quoted *Age* (Melbourne), 8 April 1980; interview material. Technology improvement was claimed as a contributing cause in a Ministerial answer to a parliamentary question on CUDN on 24 September 1978. A.A. Staley indicated that 'progressive reductions in the price of leased lines as a result of improved technology in the trunk network and rapid development in mini-computers have been principal factors in the limited life of CUDN', *CPD*, H. of R., 24 October 1978, Vol.III, p.2243.

18 Interview material, and *Report of the Commission of Inquiry*, Vol.1, p.109.

19 TAA later fought and won concessions from the PMG on the original charges agreed.

20 W.K. Hancock, *The battle of Black Mountain, an episode of Canberra's environmental history*, p.3. Sir Keith Hancock was Emeritus Professor of the ANU.

21 Knott interview; and interview J. Anglin, Telecom Australia. W.F. Brigden, deputy assistant Director-General, buildings, was involved from the earliest conceptual stages through the development and construction of tower. Taylor, as SADG transmission and services, was the lead witness for the PMG in the tower controversy.

22 Postmaster-General Sir Alan Hulme favoured the tower. He believed that it 'would not influence the environment more adversely than existing structures' and that it would prove to be more pleasing than the separate installations that then existed. Telecom Australia File 439/2/318. The House of Representatives endorsed the report of the Parliamentary Standing Committee on Public Works on 11 October 1972.

23 Letter from Dr Bruce Kent, chairman of the Canberra Citizens to Save Black Mountain, to Postmaster-General Bowen, 9 April 1973, quoted *Canberra Times*, 10 April 1983; and Black

Mountain Tower Archives, Dr B. Kent, Dept of History, ANU. The protesters' case is fully developed in Hancock, *The Battle of . . .*, and W.K. Hancock, *Professing history* (SUP, 1976), ch.VI, 'Thinking and doing: Black Mountain'.

24 Discussion with Professor S. Kaneff, 1982; and Hancock, *The battle of . . .*, p.15.

25 The case for the PMG is given in F.L.C. Taylor and W.F. Brigden, 'The Black Mountain tower — an introduction', *TJA*, Vol.3, No. 2, 1981, Special issue, Telecommunications Tower, Canberra. See also L.J. Derrick, 'The tower radio functions and specification'; M.F. Cole, 'Design and construction'; and other contributed papers.

26 Taylor and Brigden, *ibid.*, p.92; discussion with F. Taylor; Hancock, *The battle of . . .*, p.12; Cass quoted, *Australian*, 1 March 1973, p.3.

27 Interview material, and *Australian*, 21 August 1973.

28 Hancock, *The battle of . . .*, pp.3–5; *Canberra Times*, 1 November 1973, p.3 (Smithers's verdict, and suspension ordered by the Minister for Works); cabinet decision, *Canberra Times*, 6 and 8 December 1973, p.3; and see Hancock, *Professing history*, Ch.VI, *op.cit.*; and Black Mountain Tower Archives, Dr B. Kent, ANU.

29 The NCDC's role and their archives lie outside the scope of this study. Their part is discussed by both Hancock, *The battle of . . .*; and Taylor and Brigden *op.cit.*

30 Quoted *Telecom*, No.53, June 1980.

31 *CPD*, H. of R., 25 February 1981. Answer to parliamentary question No. 81, and Telecom Australia, File 439/2/318.

32 Interview with A.B. Poulsen; and A.B. Poulsen, 'The Bellenden–Ker television project', Part 1, *TJA*, Vol.24, No.3, 1974, pp.276–87, and Part 2, A.B. Poulsen and P.J. Reed, *ibid.*, Vol.25, No.1, 1975, pp.48–52.

33 Alan Stretton, *The furious days, The relief of Darwin* (Collins, Sydney, 1976), p.201.

34 Darwin Disaster Cyclone Tracy, *Report by Director-General Natural Disasters Organisation on the Darwin Relief Operations*, 25 December 1974–3 January 1975 (Canberra 1975), pp.38–40.

35 Lane's letter to H. Kaye, Director of Posts and Telegraphs of South Australia–Northern Territory, quoted *ibid.*

36 Michael Foot, MP, quoted *New Scientist*, 21 January 1982, p.182.

37 *Canberra Times*, 25 April 1974.

38 He had succeeded L.H. Barnard who, as deputy Prime Minister, had held the portfolio for a fortnight. See Appendix I.

39 Interview with L. Bowen, *op.cit.*

40 Interview with D.M. Coleman, State manager, Telecom Australia, SA.

41 Other members were financial managers, D.M. Bright and R. Graham, Mrs G. Ettinger, executive secretary of the Australian Consumers Association, and E.H. Payne, first assistant secretary of the Department of the Special Minister of State.

42 *CPD*, Senate, Vol.63, Second Reading Speech, 23 April 1973, p.1257.

43 Interview with H. White, 1981. Minister Bowen claimed in the House that OTC had spent $900,000 on 'a large advertising campaign', *CPD*, H. of R. Vol.94, 3 June 1975, p.3259.

44 *Ibid.* (P. Nixon), p.3259; and McAuliffe, Senate, 11 June 1975, p.2536.

13 TELECOM RISING

1 Functions of Australian Telecommunications Commission, Telecommunications Act 1975, No.55 of 1975, Sections 5 and 6; 'special needs of people who reside in the country', Section 6, Clause b(iii).

2 *Ibid.*, Section 20.

3 Ministerial powers, *ibid.*, Sections 7 and 11.

4 *Ibid.*, Section Part VI, Sections 71–81, Financial provisions.

5 Sections 29, managing director, and 34–7, chief general manager, and decision-making in Telecom (Telecom Australia, typescript, n.d.).

6 Vernon and Bishop, quoted *Sun* (Melbourne), 30 June 1975.

7 R. Parker, *The government of New South Wales* (UQP, 1978), p.339.

8 Cf. J. Moynihan, 'Origins of our Telecom logo', *Telecom*, August 1977. Moynihan finds that the 'T' could derive from a script first used by Robert Hooke in the 17th century.

9 Telecom Australia, File 384/36/34 Central Registry, Minutes of meetings held between representatives of the PSB and the Department, 15 April 1975, concerning selection test procedures in the Commissions' recruitment and examination activities, and relationship with the Public Service Board.

10 9 July 1975, p.10.

11 The Australian Stores Supply and Tender Board purchased items common to all Commonwealth departments, e.g. stationery. As the largest department, the PMG had acted as the 'government agent'. Appropriately this group did not go to Telecom but to the 'new' small PMG.

12 Conciliation and Arbitration Commission, Case 2752 of 1976, The matter of the Australian Telecommunications Commission and the Professional Officers Association of Australia. Transcript of proceedings, 10 September 1976. Statement by Honorary General Secretary, R.A. Corin. For the APEA's early resistance, see ch.10, p.1. In 1976 the APEA submitted a dissenting statement.

13 *Telecom 2000*, pp.11–12.

14 *Outcomes from the Telecom 2000 report*, pp.33–4.

15 Corporate plan for Telecom Australia, 1977/78–1986/87 (Planning Directorate, December 1977), and *Highlights from our first*

corporate plan (Telecom Australia, pamphlet, n.d.).

16 Report on overseas visit May–June 1979, W.F. Cox, planning directorate, September 1979; and Australian Institute of Public Administration (SA Regional Group), Corporate planning a practical affair, Proceedings, 16 June 1982.

17 J.R. Smith, Giving service efficiently, address to five year engineering operations programme conference, 8 August 1978; and interview J. Smith 1981. Smith left Telecom in June 1983 with a high record of achievement to become chief general manager of the Victorian State Electricity Commission.

18 Interview, A. Kellock, Director of Finance, 1981; and chairman's statement, *Telecom* No. 1, August 1975.

19 Determination of rentals and charges, *Australian Government Gazette*, 29 August 1975.

20 Telecom Australia, *Annual report*, 1975–76, p.5.

21 Interview with J. Curtis, 1981; and Telecom Australia, *Annual report*, 1977–8.

22 Information from J. Curtis. The Act No. 94 of 1976, Clause 72(3A) authorised 'the issue of securities of such kinds as are prescribed' while Clause 72(4A) 'guaranteed' Commonwealth repayment of such loans.

23 Robinson, a Liberal, was briefly preceded in the new portfolio by WA Liberal, Victor Garland. See Appendix I.

24 Reark Research Pty Ltd, August 1976, quoted *Marketability makes sense*, Telecom Australia, pp.7,9.

25 Telecom Australia, *Annual report*, 1978, p.12.

26 Interview with R. Somervaille, 1981.

27 E.R. Banks, The marketing challenge of Telecom Australia, May 1978. Telecommunications Society of New South Wales monograph.

28 Cf. G. Brooks, *The telecommunications industry* (HUP, 1981), ch.11.

29 'Entering a brave new era of social electronics', *SMH*, 1 July 1975, p.6.

30 Banks, *op.cit.*

31 Public inquiry into telecommunications services in Australia (PITSA), C12, February 1982, submission by Telecom Australia (Davidson Inquiry).

32 W.J.B. Pollock, 'Telecom Australia and the telecommunications industry' in *The future of the electronic and telecommunications industries in Australia*, Institution of Engineers, Australian National Conference publication, 1978, No. 78/1, p.11. There were 4,800 datel installations in 1975–6 and some 10,400 in 1978–9.

33 George Patterson, *Status of the media*, Television (George Patterson Pty Ltd, 1979).

34 *Canberra Times*, 14 August 1982, letter.

35 Interview J. Curtis.

36 Tim Dare, 'The changing face of Telecom', part 1, *SMH* 24 January 1978.

14 THE 'NEW LUDDITIES'?

1 Information from C.J. Livingstone, Secretary Telecommunications Consultative Council, 1982.

2 Extract of minutes of PMG task directors and joint union group, 24 April 1975, Telecom Australia.

3 Interview K. Turbet, 1982.

4 *Staff Information Bulletin*, 27 April 1977, p.1.

5 Introduction of ARE and AXE switching systems by Telecom Australia, May 1979, Telecom Australia; Power, 'History of local telephone switching', and K. Blanch, 'The telephone revolution', *National Times*, 15–20 August 1977, and discussion with George Slater.

6 Interview with J. Curtis, 1981.

7 *Staff Information Bulletin*, No.1, 14 September 1976.

8 Quoted, Reinecke & Schultz, *Phone Book*, p.174.

9 Cooper quoted Blanch, *National Times*, *op.cit.*. For the union's position on the new machinery, see ATEA, *Telecommunications in Australia*, a submission to the Public Inquiry, February 1972, ATEA, Melbourne.

10 Quoted *Teletechnician*, May 1977, p.92.

11 Interview with R. Stradwick, 1982.

12 Letter from chief general manager, W. Pollock, to ATEA, 12 February 1976, quoted *Teletechnician*, April 1976, p.57.

13 Pollock, 'Dispute threatens Telecom Service', *AFR*, 1 August 1978; and Mansfield, quoted *ibid.*

14 *Age* (Melbourne), 10 August 1978; *AFR*, 7 August 1978.

15 Cf. Laurie J. Medway, 'Newspaper coverage of the Telecom dispute', *Australian Scan*, Dec. 1978–May 1979, No.5, pp.33–46.

16 *Age*, 10 August 1978.

17 *Age*, 11 August 1978.

18 *AFR*, 11 August 1978, p.1.

19 Letter from Minister Street to *Australian*, 18 August 1978, p.2.

20 *Australian*, 14 August 1978; and *AFR*, 16 August 1978.

21 Gaudron quoted, *AFR*, 16 August 1978; and *Australian*, 16 August 1978, p.2.

22 *Age*, 22 August 1978; and *Commonwealth Record*, Vol.3, No.33, 21–7 August 1978.

23 *Australian*, editorial, 23 August 1978; and *AFR*, 23 August 1978, p.10.

24 Cf. *SMH*, 25 August 1978. Telecom published their argument for deregistration in large print one-page advertisements in the major metropolitan newspapers over the signature of acting chairman, T.E. May, on 26 August 1978.

25 Quoted, Blanche d'Alpuget, *Robert J. Hawke, a biography* (Schwartz and Lansdowne Press, 1982), p.351.

26 Interview B. O'Sullivan, 1982. Hawke himself

agreed that Gaudron deserved much of the credit. D'Alpuget, *op.cit.*, p.352.

27 *Teletechnician*, September 1978, p.174.

28 *Staff Information Bulletin*, No.3, March 1977.

29 Interview with K. Turbet, 1982, and with Pollock, 1981.

30 Interview with P. Nolan, 1981.

31 *CPD*, H. of R., 24 August 1978.

32 Professor Karbowiak, professor of electrical engineering and head of the department of communications, was the author of *Trunk waveguide communication* and a former consultant to the British Post Office Research Laboratories on future communications. Trials of the two sets of exchanges (EMCs and ESCs) began on 1 July 1979 and were concluded in June 1980, and the reports of the assessors were submitted to the Conciliation and Arbitration Commission in June 1981. Robson found the ATEA–backed ESC mode of maintenance superior to the Telecom preferred EMCs. But Karbowiak judged there was little to choose between the two. In a wide-ranging analysis based on inspections overseas, he offered a third alternative, the 'EMA', a concept that grouped exchanges together on a district basis controlled from a central maintenance point. But resolution was far away. With Arbitration Commission hearings concluded in December 1981, Telecom and ATEA agreed to maintain the original EMC and ESC status quo while further negotiations went on. The matter was resolved ultimately in 1983.

33 D'Alpuget, *op.cit.*, p.72.

34 *Canberra Times*, 3 July 1979.

35 *SMH*, 3 July 1979, and *Australian*, 2 July 1979.

36 Quoted, *SMH*, 13 July 1979.

37 *Ibid.* Interviewer unnamed.

38 Cf. 'Chronology of a dispute', *Age* (Melbourne), 16 July 1979.

39 Telecom Australia, *Annual report*, 1979–80, p.73; editorial, *Australian*, 19 July 1979; Staples, 'Criticism of Telecom', *Age* (Melbourne), 22 November 1979, p.2; and Curtis, *ibid.*

40 Telecommunications Consultative Council document on new technology, 'Consideration of the introduction of technological change', 1979 (Telecom Australia).

41 'ATEA checks out the Myer report', *Teletechnician*, September 1980; interview with B. Mansfield, 1981; and Reinecke & Schultz, p.162.

15 THE POLITICS OF SATELLITES

1 APO Research laboratories, *Review of activities*, Golden Jubilee edn, p.34.

2 Telecommunications Planning Review 1974 (Planning and Programming Sub-Division PMG Department) was the outcome of this; and D. Snowden, *ATR*, 1970, Vol.4, No.1, pp.3–9. Snowden was a member of the Cooby Creek team.

3 P.R. Brett, 'Aspects of future telecommunications services . . .'.

4 *Telecom 2000*, p.69; *National satellite communication systems study*.

5 *Telecom 2000*, p.79.

6 *Ibid.*, p.80.

7 Bond was a consultant for RCA Alaska and PCA Global Communications. Letter K. Packer to Eric Robinson quoted Peter White, 'A DOMSAT for Australia'.

8 For IBM's participation, see Reinecke & Schultz, *Phone Book*, pp.100 ff. Robinson's statement, *CPD*, H. of R., Vol.106, p.1510.

9 *Ibid.*, p.1544.

10 Submission to the Commonwealth Government Task Force on National Communications Satellite Systems, January 1978, Telecom Australia, pp.8–9.

11 IBM submission, *ibid.*, quoted Reinecke & Schultz, p.107.

12 Transcript of hearings of the Commonwealth Government task force on the national communication satellite system, National Library of Australia and Department of Communications, Canberra.

13 *National communications satellite system report* (Canberra, AGPS, 1978) p.xiv, and p.125, para.10, 41–10.

14 The frequency range in which a satellite works is given by two numbers — e.g. 4/6. The first number is the 'DOWN' frequency band (4 gigahertz) used to transmit from the satellite to the many ground receiving stations, and the second number is the 'UP' frequency band (6 gigahertz) used to transmit the signal from the earth station to the satellite.

15 *Report*, *op.cit.*, annexe A, p.132, and interview material.

16 *Ibid.*, annexe A.

17 *CPD*, H. of R. 22 September 1978, Vol.111, p.1441.

18 Quoted *Video Age*, January 1983; and Reinecke & Schultz p.101.

19 Interview with Mrs J. Hancock, 1981.

20 Cf. Moyal, 'The Australian Atomic Energy Commission'.

21 Interview material; and Ian Reinecke, 'The Davidson inquiry, a personal view', paper delivered to the Telecommunications Society of Australia, NSW division, 1982.

22 White, *op.cit.*, p.243.

23 Interview with A.A. Staley.

24 *Ibid.*, and J. Penberthy, 'Tony Staley speaks out', *National Times*, 24 October 1982, p.40.

25 *CPD*, H. of R., 18 October 1979, p.2224.

26 National Communications Satellite System, *Working Group Report*, August 1978 (AGPS, 1979), p.ix.

27 Finance Department dissenting view, *ibid.*

28 Quoted *ibid.*, p.154.

29 Joint submission of the APTU and the ATEA to the working group, quoted *ibid.*, p.154; Peter Green quoted *Teletechnician*, May 1979, p.80.

30 Reinecke & Schultz, ch.6.

31 *CPD*, H. of R., 18 October 1979, pp.2237–8.

32 Staley interview, *op.cit.*

33 Interview with R.B. Lansdown, 1983.

34 Interview with J. Curtis, October 1981.

35 Telecom Australia, *Annual report*, 1979–80, p.88.

36 *A study of remote area telecommunications* . . ., National Report (Telecom Australia, August 1980), p.7, and a study of remote area telecommunications in the Northern Territory prepared by the Implementation and Management Group Pty Ltd, 4 vols (Telecom Australia, Melbourne, 1980). The consultant used the services of an anthropologist.

37 *A study of remote area telecommunications* . . ., p.17, and Reinecke, 'The Davidson inquiry'.

38 *AFR*, 14 July 1980.

39 Each satellite combined 4 high–powered and 11 low–powered transponders (a total of 15), the latter for national transmission purposes, and the four high–powered for 'spot beams' covering (a) Western Australia; (b) Northern Territory and South Australia; (c) Queensland; and (d) New South Wales, Victoria and Tasmania.

40 AUSSAT Pty Ltd, *Annual report*, 1982. Their satellite operated in the 11/16 gigahertz frequency.

41 Press statement by the Minister for Communications, 6 May 1982.

42 Reported 'Sayings of the week', *SMH*, 3 January 1983.

16 TIME OF CRISIS

1 Brock, *The telecommunications industry*, pp.239–41, and Brooks, *Telephone*, p.322, and *Business Week*, quoted Brooks, p.1.

2 Department of Industry, *Liberalisation of the use of British telecommunications network* by Michael E. Beesley.

3 *Telecom 2000*, pp.18,31. This it did. AWA's product 'Vocatex' was introduced in 1983.

4 *Ibid.*, pp.20–1.

5 *Ibid.*, pp.24–5.

6 *Outcomes from the Telecom 2000 report*, p.23.

7 *Ibid.*, pp.23–4.

8 TEI became a subsidiary of Plessey UK, in August 1963. The firm's name was changed to Plessey Telecommunications Pty Ltd in 1969 and to Plessey Australia Pty Ltd in 1974.

9 *Report of the Commission of inquiry* . . ., Vol.2, Consultants Report, Report by consultant on private contract work performed for the Australian Post Office, pp.25–6.

10 Inquiry into the Australian Post Office, submission by the APTU, Australian Archives Series No. CRS A4067, exhibit No. 86, attachment B.

11 *Report of Commission of Inquiry* . . ., Vol.1, p.313, and Committee of inquiry into technological change, *Report*, The communications industry, p.391.

12 ASTEC, *Science and technology in Australia 1977–78*, A Report to the Prime Minister by the ASTEC, Vol.2, p.506.

13 S. Cronstedt, The telecommunications industry, present and future problems on the telecommunications industry, paper given at seminar on the future of electronics and communication, March 1978. Institution of Engineers, Australia; and *Report of Commission of Inquiry*, Vol.1, pp.314, xxv.

14 The Australian Electronics Industry Association Submission to the Public Inquiry into Telecommunications Services in Australia 1982 (AEIA, Sydney), p.12.

15 Quoted I. Reinecke, *AFR*, 2 July 1980, p.5. France poured large sums into electronic switching and terminals from 1975 and planned to launch its government–owned domestic, Telecom 1, in the mid–1980s.

16 As a statutory body, Telecom paid neither taxes nor import duty, a situation seen as giving it a competitive advantage over industry. But Telecom's policy for industry decreed that, whenever a customer was liable to tax or duty, Telecom would load its prices to reflect that liability. Disgruntlement also existed over Telecom's exemption from pay rates or payroll tax. The point faded into insignificance, argued Telecom members, if private sector costs were compared with the total costs of employing staff in the public sector.

17 *APR*, 3 July 1980, pp.1,6.

18 Interview with R. Somervaille; and Staley, quoted Deborah Snow, 'Why Staley sacked Telecom boss', *National Times*, 6–12 July 1980.

19 *Capital and policy requirements for the 1980's* (McKinsey Report), June 1980, Telecom Australia, pp.i–viii.

20 Cf. Anne Summers, *AFR*, 24 June 1981.

21 The 'Goode Report', as it's known, was prepared by Robert Goode of the Mercer Company.

22 Reinecke & Schultz, p.53.

23 Quoted *Computer Weekly*, 9–15 November 1979, p.2.

24 *AFR*, 5 September 1980, and cf. Peter Holmes à Court, address to 51st ANZAAS Congress, 13 May 1981.

25 Brett, 'Aspects of future telecommunications services . . .'.

26 Interview with H. Wragge, 1983; and cf. I. Reinecke 'Telecom's research laboratories show a modest profile to the 1980s', *Communications Australia*, November 1982, pp.29–32.

27 *Ibid.*

28 PMG Department Minute paper 384/1/26, Programming of technical development and innovation, August 1972; and *ibid.*, Procedures for the introduction of a 3–year programme of

research, development and innovation in the APO, May 1974, Director-General's attached minute.

29 Australian Post Office, Director-General's Committee, Information Paper No.41, Three-year programme of research, development and innovation, June 1974.

30 See, e.g., Moyal, 'The Australian Atomic Energy Commission'; and Macdonald, 'Faith, hope and disparity'.

31 PMG's Department Minute Paper, 384/1/26. Guidelines for the preparation of the three year programme for research, development and innovation 1974/75–1976/77, signed 27 June 1974.

32 J. Price, 3 May 1974, to chief of the division of entomology, quoted Macdonald, 'Faith, hope and disparity'.

33 Telecom Australia, Headquarters, *RDI strategic guidelines*, December 1980.

34 Telecom Australia Research Laboratories, *Review of Activities 1980-1* (Australian Telecommunications Commission, 1981) and see ASTEC, *Science and technology in Australia, 1977-78, op.cit.*, ch.33.

35 Telecom Australia, *Annual reports*, 1976–77, 1977–78 and 1978–79, p.77, and *Review of activities 1980–81*.

36 Country Party submission to the Commission of Inquiry into the Australian Post Office, Australian Archives, series No. A 4067, exhibit No. 99.

37 Interview with the Right Hon. I. Sinclair, January 1983.

38 The amendments to the Act finalised in June 1981 assisted the proprietors Kerry Packer and Rupert Murdoch to enlarge their control of metropolitan television stations in Sydney and Melbourne.

39 Address to Rotarians, *Australian*, 18 March 1981, and *CPD*, H. of R., 24 March 1981, p.814.

40 Address to senior executives, Sydney, *Australian*, 31 March 1981.

41 A 300-kilometre radio system joined Cobar to Dubbo, NSW.

42 Interview with J. Curtis, October 1981.

43 Sinclair interview.

44 *Annual report*, 1979–80, p.25.

45 King was formally appointed by the Department for Communications late in January 1981. His report on terminal equipment was never released by the Department.

46 Curtis interview.

47 Cf. letter T.E. May to I. Sinclair, 16 April 1981, published *CPD*, H. of R., 3 June 1981; p.2983, in response to question from R. Hawke; and interview material from Telecom participants.

48 The APTU placed early bans on 18 May. The ATEA followed with bans and restrictions on 1 June 1981 after Arbitration negotiations began.

49 *CPD*, H. of R., 3 June 1981, pp.2983 ff.

50 Information from J. Smith, former deputy chief general manager.

51 *APR*, 11 June 1981; and cf. *CPD*, H. of R., 9 June 1981, p.334.

52 Curtis interview.

53 *AFR*, 11 June 1981.

54 Fraser, quoted *Sun* (Melbourne), 13 June 1981.

55 Cooper, quoted *AFR*, 16 June 1981.

56 Telecom submission to the Australian Broadcasting Tribunal on cable TV; and Australian Broadcasting Tribunal, *Cable and subscription television services*.

57 Videotex development, Telecom Australia, *Annual Reports* 1980–81, p.15, and 1981–82, p.14; Sinclair's statement, *CPD*, H. of R., 16 October 1981; Barry Jones, *ibid.*, 22 October 1981, grievance debate, pp.2379–80.

58 *Report of the Committee of Inquiry into telecommunications services in Australia*, Vol.1, p.1; and *CPD*, H. of R., 23 September 1981, p.1674.

59 Public Inquiry into Telecommunications Services in Australia. Submission by Telecom Australia, February 1982 and Annexes, 2 vols, Telecom Australia.

60 *The Professional*, February 1981, p.8; and ATEA, *Telecommunications services in Australia*, p.1.

61 Interview with W.J.B. Pollock; and 1981/82 Report to staff.

62 Telecom Australia, Special Staff Information Bulletin, 28 October 1982, No. 53, Davidson report.

63 *Report, op.cit.*, p.9.

64 John Button, speech to ATEA conference 12 October 1981, Sydney; and ALP response to the Davidson inquiry into Telecommunications, January 1983 (typescripts from the office of Senator Button).

65 Interview material.

66 Minister for Communications, media statement, February 1983; and see Minister for Communications Hon. N.A. Brown, press release, 27 January 1983, 'Minister welcomes Telecom response to Davidson inquiry'.

67 Press statement of the Minister for Communications, 20 October 1983.

68 George Eliot, *Middlemarch*.

EPILOGUE

1 85 per cent.

2 In the case of residential telephone services, Australia was third only to Canada and the USA. For business services, she held third position after the USA and Japan. Telecom Australia.

3 *SMH*, 23 May 1984, computer section, p.12.

4 *Telecom and Australia's Future Communications: Commitments and Objectives*. Telecom Australia, October 1983, 4 pp.

5 *Inquiry into Commonwealth Laboratories*, Vol.2, November 1983 (AGPS, Canberra, 1983), pp.32–4.

6 *Australian Post Office News*, June 1975.

Select Bibliography

Archival material for this study is located in the Postmaster-General's Department Archives at the Australian Archives, Brighton, Victoria and a small section of PMG Archives retained in Telecom Australia Archives, Headquarters, Melbourne.

Archival material relating to major commissions of inquiry is to be found in Submissions to the Commission of Inquiry into the Australian Post Office 1973-4, Australian Archives, Canberra, and in Transcripts of Hearings of the Commission of Inquiry into the Australian Post Office 1973-4, National Library of Australia, Canberra; in Submissions to the Committee of Inquiry into Telecommunications Services in Australia (Davidson Inquiry), Department of Communications Library, Canberra, and Submissions to the Commonwealth Task Force on National Satellite Communication System, 1978, Department of Communications Library, Canberra.

Valuable press cutting collections are held covering January 1973 to September 1975 and from 1975 to date on the APO and Telecom Australia at Telecom Australia, Engineering Library, Clayton, Victoria, and in the H.P. Brown newspaper collection (volumes in the possession of George Brown, Mitcham, Victoria).

The following journals relate to telecommunications and their history in Australia. *Australian Scan*, Journal of Human Communications; *Australian Post Office Magazine*, Official Journal of the Australian Postal Institute, 1954-1971; *The Australian Postal Electrician* (1915-1942); *Australian Telecommunications Research*; *Australian Telecommunications Review*; *Contact*, quarterly publication of Overseas Telecommunications Commission (Australia); *Journal of Electric Telegraph Society*, NSW, started 1891; *Journal of Institution of Engineers, Australia* (author and subject index of publications 1920-1968, pp. 175-80); *Journal of South Australia Electric Society*; *Media Information Australia*, quarterly journal of media research and media resources; *On the line*, PMG headquarters line staff engineering division, 1957-; *Telecom News*, published monthly, Telecom Australia headquarters, plus State editions, e.g. *Telecom News W.A.*; *Telecommunications Journal of Australia*, 1935-,

consolidated indexes 1935-70, Vols 1-20 & Vols 21-30 (Melbourne, 1972 & 1982); *Telegen*; *Telegraph Electrical Society Melbourne Journal*, 1874-1881; *Telephone Engineer and Management*, 1934-41, *Telephone Engineer*, 1941; *Teletechnician*, 1942-; *The Australian Telegraphist*; *The Professional Engineer*, journal of the Association of Professional Engineers, Australia; *The POA Chronicle*; *The Transmitter*, journal of NSW Electric Telegraph Society 1891-1908 and of the Australian Commonwealth Post and Telecommunication Association, 1908-1920.

OFFICIAL REPORTS

Reports relating to post, telegraph and telephone matters of the Australian colonies in the 19th century are to be found in the Parliamentary *Votes and Proceedings* of the respective colonial legislatures. Copies of some of the colonial reports are held in Telecom Australia Headquarters Library, Melbourne.

Australia. Commission of Inquiry into the Australian Post Office, *Report*, Canberra, 1974, 3 vols.

—— Committee of Inquiry into technological change in Australia, *Report* (AGPS, Canberra, 1980), (the CITCA or Myers committee), 4 vols.

—— Committee of Inquiry into telecommunications services in Australia, *Report* (AGPS, Canberra, 1982), 3 vols.

—— Commonwealth Government Task Force, *National communications satellite system report*, July 1978 (AGPS, Canberra, 1978).

—— —— *Working group report*, August 1979 (AGPS, Canberra, 1979).

—— Postmaster-General's Department, *Annual reports*, 1911-75.

—— Posts and Telegraph Department, *Report of the Departmental Committee of Inquiry into the telegraph and telephone systems, etc., of the States of the Commonwealth*, (Govt Printer, Adelaide, 1901).

—— *Progress-Policy-Plans* (published by authority of the Postmaster-General Hon. C.W. Davidson, 1959).

415

—— Report of Mr John Hesketh, Electrical Engineer on Matters investigated by him during his recent visit to Europe, *Report* (Govt Printer, 8 September 1905).

—— Ad Hoc Committee of Inquiry into the Commercial Accounts of the Post Office, *Report* (AGPS, Canberra, 1961).

—— Royal Commission on television. *Report.* (AGPS, Canberra, 1954).

—— Royal Commission on wireless. *Report*, together with appendices (Govt Printer, Melbourne, 1926-27).

—— Telecom Australia, *Annual reports*, 1975/6 to date.

Australian Science and Technology Council (ASTEC), *Science and Technology in Australia 1977-78.* A report to the Prime Minister by the Australian Science and Technology Council, December 1978. Vol.2, ch.33, Telecommunications (AGPS, Canberra, 1978), pp.505-20.

Cable and Subscription Television Services for Australia, Report. Australian Broadcasting Tribunal, August 1982 (The Jones Cable Television Report). (AGPS, Canberra, 1982.)

AUSTRALIAN MATERIAL: BOOKS, MONOGRAPHS AND TELECOM PUBLICATIONS

A history of the Post Office in Tasmania (PMG's Department, Hobart, n.d.).

A study of remote area telecommunications in the Northern Territory, 4 vols (Telecom Australia, Implementation and Management Group, Melbourne, 1980).

Across the barrier: communications across the Nullarbor (Telecom Australia, Melbourne, 1980).

Allen, Yolanda and Spencer, Susan, *The broadcasting chronology, 1809-1980* (Research and Survey Unit, Australian Film and Television School, Sydney, 1983).

Australian dictionary of biography, 1788-1939, Vols 1-9 (MUP, Melbourne, 1966-).

Australian Electronics Industry Association, *Communications and electronics 1982* (Sydney, 1982).

Australian Telecommunications Employees Association, *New telecommunications technology: social and economic issues* (Melbourne, 1978).

Australian Telecommunications Employees Association, *Telecommunications services in Australia: a submission to the public inquiry* (ATEA, Melbourne, 1982).

Baker, D., 'From coo-ee to communication satellite', ch.6 in *A century of scientific progress, the Royal Society of New South Wales* (Royal Society of New South Wales, Sydney, 1966).

Baker, John S., *Communicators and their first trade unions: a history of the telegraphist and postal clerk unions of Australia* (Unions of Postal Clerks and Telegraphists, Sydney, 1980).

Bateman, J., *History of the telephone in New South Wales* (J. Bateman, Croydon, NSW, 1980).

Bedford, Ian and Curnow, R., *Initiative and organisation* (Cheshire, Melbourne, 1963).

Blackwell, D. and Lockwood, D., *Alice on the line* (Rigby, Adelaide, 1965).

Blainey, G., *The tyranny of distance: how distance shaped Australia's history* (Sun Books, Melbourne, 1966).

Broadcasting and the Australian Post Office, 1923-73 (PMG's Dept, Melbourne, 1973).

Buddrige, R., *Detained in penal servitude, a biography of J.C. Fleming, WA's first superintendent of telegraphs*, mimeo (Post and Telecom Museum, Perth, 1981).

Butlin, N.G., Barnard, A. and Pincus, J.J., *Government and capitalism: public and private choice in twentieth century Australia* (George Allen & Unwin, Sydney, 1982).

Caiden, G.E., *Career service: an introduction to the history of personnel administration in the Commonwealth Public Service of Australia 1901-1961* (MUP, Melbourne, 1965).

Clune, Frank, *Overland telegraph: the story of great Australian achievement and the link between Adelaide and Darwin* (Angus & Robertson, Sydney, 1955).

Curnow, R., Collective bibliography of parliamentary debates on broadcasting in Australia (Dept of Government, University of Sydney).

Curtis, J.H., Communications in Australia, Academy of Technological Sciences Symposium on Manufacturing Resources, Canberra, October 1981.

Ford, B., Coffey, M. and Dunphy, D., *Technology and the workforce: an annotated bibliography* (Technology Research Unit, NSW Ministry of Technology for the Dept of Organizational Behaviour, University of New South Wales, Sydney, 1981).

Freeman, A.H., Automative telephony in the Australian Post Office (Australian Telecommunications Monograph No. 4, Telecommunication Society of Australia, Melbourne, 1973).

—— *History of the telephone to 1887* (Telecommunication Society of Australia, NSW Division, Historical Monograph No. 3, Sydney, n.d.).

Frenkel, S.J., (ed.), *Industrial action: patterns of labour conflict* (George Allen & Unwin, Sydney, 1980).

Gooley, M.J., The construction of the overland telegraph, Port Augusta to Darwin, in papers presented to a symposium on *The centenary of the Adelaide-Darwin overland telegraph line* (Institution of Engineers, Australia and APO, Adelaide, August 1972).

—— The original telegraph line South Australia-Western Australia 1875-1877, its construction, people and localities, mimeo (SA Telecom Museum, Adelaide).

Gribble, P.J., *What hath God wrought: a history of the Queensland telegraph service from 1861* (Telecom Australia, Brisbane, 1981).

Gosling, George W.H., *Telecommunications in*

education (Australian Council for Educational Research, Melbourne, 1972).

Hall, Sandra, *Supertoy: twenty years of Australian television* (Sun Books, South Melbourne, 1976).

Hancock, Sir Keith, *The battle of Black Mountain: an episode of Canberra's environmental history* (Dept of Economic History, RSSS, ANU, Canberra, 1974).

Hinckfuss, Harold, *Memories of a Signaller* (H. Hinckfuss, typeset by University of Queensland Press, 1982).

Holmes à Court, P., *Telecommunications in Australia in the '80's* (Telecommunication Society of Australia, NSW Division, Monograph No. 24, Sydney, 1981).

Information Technology Council, *Technological change: impact of information technology 1980* (AGPS, Canberra, 1980).

—— *Technological change: impact of information technology 1981* (AGPS, Canberra, 1981).

—— *Technological change: impact of information technology 1982* (AGPS, Canberra, 1982).

Inglis, K.S., *This is the A.B.C.: the Australian Broadcasting Commission, 1932–1983* (MUP, Melbourne, 1983).

Jones, Barry, *Sleepers, wake! technology and the future of work* (new edn, OUP, Melbourne, 1983).

Kanally, R.J., *An engineer's life with the PMG's Department, 1929–1974* (Telecommunication Society of Australia, NSW Division, Historical Monograph No. 10, Sydney, 1976).

Kanally, R.J., *Further recollections, 1929–1974* (Telecommunication Society of Australia, NSW Division, Monograph No. 9, Sydney, 1978).

Kolsen, H.M., *Public authority business undertakings (PABUs) in Australia* (Monash University, Dept of Economics and Politics, Seminar Paper No. 8/82).

Lamberton, D., MacDonald, S., and Manderville, T. (eds), *The trouble with technology* (Francis Pinter, London, 1983).

Lloyd, B.E., *The education of professional engineers in Australia* (3rd edn, Association of Professional Engineers, Melbourne, 1968).

MacCullum, Mungo, (ed.), *Ten years of television* (Sun Books, Melbourne, 1968).

Markey, Ray, *The trade union response to technological change in Australia* (Industrial Relations Research Centre Monograph, University of New South Wales, Sydney, 1983).

Moynihan, J.F., *All the news in a flash: the history of communications with Rottnest Island, 1829–1979* (Telecom Australia, Perth, in press, 1984).

—— Cost of a basic telephone service in Australian capital cities 1901–1983, mimeo (Telecom Australia, Perth).

—— *The first fifty years of telephone working between Western Australia and the eastern States 1930–80* (Telecommunication Society of Australia, WA Division, monograph, 1984).

National satellite communication systems studies (Telecom Australia, Planning Directorate, Melbourne, 1977).

Outcomes from the Telecom 2000 report (Telecom Australia, Planning Directorate, Melbourne, 1978).

Page, M., *The flying doctor story: 1928–1978* (Rigby, Adelaide, 1977).

Power, K.W., *National planning for local telephone exchanges* (Telecommunication Society of Australia, NSW Division, Monograph No. 6, Sydney 1977).

The future of the electronics and telecommunications industries in Australia (Melbourne, 1978), *Recommended guidelines for future policies: proceedings of conference* (Institution of Engineers, Australia, Barton, ACT, 1978).

Rea, Malcolm, *Brisbane General Post Office* (APO, Brisbane, 1972).

Reinecke, Ian, *The micro-invaders: how the new world of technology works* (Penguin, Ringwood, Vic., 1982).

Reinecke, Ian and Schultz, Julianne, *The phone book: the future of Australia's communications on the line* (Penguin, Ringwood, Vic., 1983).

Ross, J.F., *A history of radio in South Australia 1897–1977* (J.F. Ross, Plympton, SA, 1978).

Sinclair, James, *A History of the Postal and Telecommunication Services in Papua New Guinea* (OUP, Melbourne, 1984).

Soden, F.A., *et al.*, *100 years of the telephone*, (private limited edn, Burnley, Victoria, 1976).

Taylor, Peter, *An end to silence: the building of the overland telegraph line from Adelaide to Darwin* (Methuen, Sydney, 1980).

Telecom Australia — a brief portrait (Telecom Australia, Melbourne, 1979).

Telecom 2000: an exploration of the long-term development of telecommunications in Australia (Telecom Australia, Planning Directorate, Melbourne, 1976).

Telecommunication Society of Australia, SA Division, *Centenary souvenir 1874–1974: 100 years of service to telecommunications* (Adelaide, 1974).

Walker, R.R., *The magic spark: the story of the first fifty years of radio in Australia* (Hawthorn Press, Melbourne, 1973).

Ward, W.T. and Bryden, M.M (eds), *Public information: your right to know* (Royal Society of Queensland, Brisbane, 1981).

Waters, Frank, *Postal unions and politics: a history of the Amalgamated Postal Workers' Union of Australia* (UQP, St Lucia, 1978).

White, Jessie, *A vital link: Eucla and the Eyre highway* (Media Man, Perth, 1979).

Windschuttle, K., *The Media* (Penguin, 1984).

OVERSEAS MATERIAL: BOOKS AND REPORTS

American Telephone and Telegraph Company, *Long lines, the world's telephones* (Morris Plains, NJ, annual).

American Telephone and Telegraph Company, *Events in telecommunications history* (New York, NY, 1979).

Beesley, Michael E., *Liberalisation of the use of British telecommunications network* (HMSO, London, 1981).

Braun, E. and MacDonald, S., *Revolution in miniature: the history and impact of semiconductor electronics re-explored* (2nd edn, CUP, Cambridge, 1983).

British Telecom, *Further considerations relating to the British telecommunications network and proposals to permit competition* (London, 1981).

Brock, Gerald W., *The telecommunications industry: the dynamics of market structure* (MIT Press, Cambridge, Mass., 1981).

Brooks, John, *Telephone: the first hundred years* (Harper & Row, New York, NY, 1976).

Chapuis, R.J., *One hundred years of telephone switching 1878–1978. Part 1: 1878–1960's — manual and electrochemical switching* (North–Holland, Amsterdam, 1982).

Collins, Robert, *A voice from afar: the history of Canadian telecommunications* (McGraw, Toronto, 1977).

Corby, Michael, *The postal business, 1969–79: study in public sector management* (Nichols, London, 1979).

De Sola Pool, I., (ed.), *The social impact of the telephone* (MIT Press, Cambridge, Mass., 1977).

International Telecommunications Union, *From semaphore to satellite* (Geneva, 1965), written by Anthony R. Michaelis.

Lamberton, D., (ed.), *The economics of information and knowledge* (Penguin, Harmondsworth, 1971).

L.M. Ericsson 100 years Volume 1, Attman, Kuuse, Olsson, *The pioneering years, struggle for concessions crisis, 1876–1932.* Volume 2, Attman, Olsson, *The rescue reconstruction worldwide enterprise, 1932–1976.* Volume 3, Jacobaeus et al., *Evolution of the technology, 1876–1976.* (L.M. Ericsson, Orebro, Sweden, 1977).

Many voices, one world (UNESCO, Paris, 1980).

Meyer, John R., et al., *The economics of competition in the telecommunications industry* (Oelgeschlager, Gunn & Hain, Cambridge, Mass., 1980).

Pitt, D.C., *The telecommunications function in the British Post Office: a case study of bureaucratic adaptation* (Saxon House, Westmead, Hampshire, 1980).

Robertson, J.H., *The story of the telephone: a history of the telecommunications industry of Britain* (Pitman, London, 1947).

Schillar, Dan, *Telematics and government* (Ablex, Norwood, NJ, 1982).

Wilson, P.D., *The coming information age: an overview of its technology, economics and politics* (Longman, NY, 1982).

Young, Peter, *Power of speech: a history of Standard Telephones and Cables 1883–1983* (George Allen & Unwin, London, 1983).

JOURNAL ARTICLES

Banks, E.R., 'Crossbar switching equipment for the Australian telephone network', *Journal of the Institution of Engineers Australia* (*JIEA*), Vol.33, No. 4–5, pp.113–25.

Barnard, Alan, 'Broadcasting in the 1920's: government and private interests', *Prometheus*, Vol.1, No. 1, 1983, pp.98–126.

Bhattacharya, D., 'A productivity study of the Australian Post Office over the period 1961–62 to 1970–71', *Journal of Industrial Relations* (*JIR*), Vol.14, No. 4, pp.413–26.

Bradley, F.R., 'History of the electric telegraph in Australia', *Journal of the Royal Australian Historical Society* (*JRAHS*), Vol.20, 1934, pp.239–63.

Brain, P. and Donath, S., 'A corporate model of the Australian Telecommunications Commission: structure and applications', *Australian Journal of Management*, Vol.4, 1979, pp.27–54.

Brett, P.R., 'Aspects of future telecommunications services of particular relevance to Australia', *Australian Telecommunication Research* (*ATR*), Vol.7, No. 3, 1973, pp.30–5.

Buchanan, R.A., 'The British contribution to Australian engineering: the Australian dictionary of biography entries', *Historical studies of Australia and New Zealand*, Vol.20, No.8, 1983, pp.401–19.

Butler, R.E., 'Australian interests in the International Telecommunication Union', *Telecommunication Journal of Australia* (*TJA*), Vol.15, No. 3, 1965, pp.174–6.

Caiden, G.E., 'Some problems of white collar unionism in the commonwealth service', *Public Administration* (Australia) (*PA*), Vol.XXV, No.3, 1966, pp.233–51.

Cameron, A.R., 'The story of the overland telegraph line', Part I, *TJA*, Vol.5, No.4, 1945, pp.189–98, and Part II, *TJA*, Vol.5, No.5, 1945, pp.283–9.

'A cheap telephone system for farmers', *Journal of Agriculture of Western Australia*, Vol.1, 1900, pp.64–5, 73, 80.

Clement-Jones, T., 'Cable and satellite TV in the UK and Europe: the emerging legal issues', *Telecommunications Policy*, Vol.7, No.3, 1983, pp.204–14.

Cullen, R.B., 'Productivity in the Australian Post Office: a comment on the Bhattacharya analysis', *JIR*, Vol.15, No.4, 1973, pp.365–81.

Davis, E.B., 'The Woomera communications network', *Electrical and Mechanical Engineering Transactions*, Vol.EM 3, No.2, 1961, pp.53–68.

Encel, S., 'Communications and social change', *ATR*, Vol.7, No.3, 1973, pp.23–9.

Fisk, Sir Ernest, 'Radio engineering development in Australia', *JIEA*, Vol.10, No.4, 1938, pp.161–2.

Francis, C., 'Fault chasing: experiences of a telephone linesman in Northern Queensland', *Walkabout*, Vol.9, No.12, 1943, pp.23–5.

Freeman, A.H. and Gravell, A., 'Application of digital computers in telecommunication network planning', *Electrical and Mechanical Engineering Transactions*, Vol.EM 5, No.2, 1963, pp.27–40.

Giles, C., 'The Adelaide and Port Darwin telegraph line: some reminiscences of its construction', *Journal of the South Australian Electrical Society*, Vol.1, No.10-Vol.2, No.7, 1888.

Grant, N.E., 'Data transmission in the Australian Post Office', *Lasie*, Vol.2, No.5, 1972, pp.15-19.

Gravell, A. and Pontague, R.J., 'Development of telecommunication services to North West of Australia', *JIEA*, Vol.37, No.10-11, 1965, pp.367-79.

Hazlehurst, Cameron, 'The advent of commercial television', *Australian Cultural History*, No.2, 1982/3, pp.104-19.

Hayes, N.W.V., 'Carrier telephone and telegraph systems in Australia', *JIEA*, Vol.9, No.5, 1937, pp.195-202.

Hayes, N.W.V. and Atkins, R.J., 'Long line telephone and telegraph system of Australia', *JIEA*, Vol.2, No.9, 1930, pp.332-44.

Housley, T.A., 'Communications in modern society', *PA*, Vol.XXVI, No.2, 1967, pp.108-12.

Jones, B.F., 'The Post Office and the community', *PA*, Vol.XXVI, No.2, 1967, pp.113-32.

Kay, F., 'The story of the ... A.P.E.U.-P.T.T.A., 1912-1962', *Teletechnician*, Vol.XLV, No.3, 1962, pp.50-64.

Kaye, A.H., Morris, F.D., Sinnatt, J.F., Richards, P.H., Walklate, J.R. and Wilson, J.C., 'Broadband telecommunication systems', *JIEA*, Vol.33, No.6, 1961, pp.213-34.

Kellock, S.F., 'Sir Harry Brown in public administration, war work and commerce', *PA*, Vol.XXVI, No.3, 1967, pp.205-17.

Kerr, R.D., 'Some aspects of teleprinter switching', *TJA*, Vol.9, No.3, 1953, pp.129-39.

Kerr, R.M.J., 'The early history of the telephone in Victoria', *TJA*, Vol.13, No.5, 1962, pp.354-62.

Kewley, T.H. and Rydon, J., 'Australian commonwealth government corporations: a statutory analysis', *PA*, Vol.IX, No.1, 1950, pp.200-21.

Lamberton, D., (ed.), 'The information revolution', *Annals of the American Academy of Political and Social Science*, Vol.412, 1974.

Langdale, J., 'Competition in communications', *Telecommunications Policy*, Vol.6, No.4, 1982, pp.283-99.

────── 'Nodal regional structures of New South Wales', *Australian Geographical Studies*, Vol.13, 1975, pp.123-36.

Lawson, R., 'Sydney-Newcastle-Maitland telephone and telegraph cable', *JIEA*, Vol.11, No.9, 1939, pp.301-12.

Locksley, G., 'The political economy of satellite business', *Telecommunications Policy*, Vol.7, No.3, pp.195-203.

Macdonald, S., 'Faith, hope and disparity: an example of the public justification of public research', [CSIRO] *Search*, Vol.13, No.11-12, 1983, pp.290-9.

McMahon, J.F., 'Father Archibald Shaw: the wireless priest', *Journal of the Australian Catholic Historical Society*, 1983, pp.24-34.

McVey, D., 'The organisation of Empire telecommunication', *PA*, Vol.VI, No.2, 1946, pp.59-76.

Medway, Lauris J., 'Newspaper cover of the Telecom dispute 1978', *Australian Scan* (Journal of Human Communication), No.5, Dec. 1978-May 1979, pp.33-46.

Moyal, Ann, 'Telecommunications in Australia: an historical perspective, 1854-1930', *Prometheus*, Vol.1, No.1, 1983, pp.23-41.

Moyal, Ann Mozley, 'The Australian Atomic Energy Commission: a case study in Australian science and government', *Search*, Vol.6, No.9, 1975, pp.365-84.

Newlands, R.R., 'APEA (Association of Professional Engineers, Australia), early beginnings, formation and establishment', *The Professional Engineer*, Vol.25, 1971, pp.2-5.

Newstead, Anthony, 'Australia's Telecom 2000', *Telecommunications Policy*, Vol.1, No.2, 1977, pp.158-62.

O'Grady, F.P., 'Automation in the Post Office', *JIEA*, Vol.31, No.6, 1959, pp.125-42.

Pearson, L.F., 'The Australian outpost radio communication system', *TJA*, Vol.13, No.6, 1963, pp.456-8.

Pierce, W.B. and Jequier, N., 'The contribution of telecommunications to economic development', *Telecommunication Journal*, Vol.44, No.11, 1977, pp.532-4.

Power, J.M., 'The reticulist function in government: manipulating networks of communication and influence', *PA*, Vol.XXXII, No.1, 1973, pp.21-7.

Power, K.W., 'History of local telephone switching in Australia and background to the AXE decision', *TJA*, Vol.28, No.3, 1978, pp.207-16.

Ross, N.G., 'Developments in Post Office coordination with power authorities 1966-1969', *TJA*, Vol.20, No.2, 1970, pp.159-61.

Rydon, Joan, 'The Australian Broadcasting Commission, 1932-1942', *PA*, Vol.XI, No.1, 1952, pp.12-25, and 'The Australian Broadcasting Commission, 1942-1948', *PA*, Vol.XI, No.4, 1952, pp.190-205.

Schmidt, J.S. and Corbin, R.M., 'Telecommunications in Canada: the regulatory crisis', *Telecommunications Policy*, Vol.7, No.3, 1983, pp.204-15.

Shaw, H., 'Some aspects of management in the Post Office', *PA*, Vol.XIX, No.3, 1960, pp.248-56.

Spratt, A.F., 'Commissions of inquiry: The Post Office Inquiry', *PA*, Vol.XXXV, No.1, 1976, pp.69-75.

Standish, P.E.M., 'The Australian Post Office: a financial study', *PA*, Vol.XXIII, No.3, 1964, pp.212-34.

Taylor, F.L.C., Huston, J.A. and Sayer, G.E.,

420

'Telecommunication facilities between Western Australia and the eastern states', *JIEA*, Vol.37, No.9, 1965, pp.219–31.

Todd, L.W., 'Some aspects of staff training in the Postmaster–General's Department', *PA*, Vol.VIII, No.2–3, 1949, pp.80–6.

Turnbull, R.W., 'The Telecommunication Society of Australia, past, present and future', *TJA*, Vol.24, No.2, 1974, pp.99–105.

Turnbull, R.W. and Hams, G.E, 'Australian telephone and telegraph networks', *TJA*, Vol.14, No.2, 1963, pp.102–8.

Weal, S.E., '1876–1976: a century of telephony', *TJA*, Vol.26, No.2, 1976, pp.95–104.

White, Peter B., 'A DOMSAT for Australia: communications planning under strain', *Telecommunications Policy*, Vol.4, No.4, 1980, pp.240–8.

—— (ed.), *Satellite Telecommunications and Education, a resource guide for Australian educators* (Commonwealth–State advisory committee on the educational use of communications technology, November 1983).

Glossary of Terms and Abbreviations

AAC Australian Agricultural Company

AAEC Australian Atomic Energy Commission

ABC Australian Broadcasting Commission, 1932–1982; reconstituted as Australian Broadcasting Corporation 1983

ACD Automatic Call Distributor, a customer terminal device which holds and distributes calls to selected answering points

ACI Australian Consolidated Industries Ltd

ACOA Administrative and Clerical Officers Association

ACTU Australian Council of Trade Unions

add-on services *See* value–added services

ADP automatic data processing

ADR automatic disturbance recorder, a standard Australian installation used for supervising the working of the crossbar exchange

ADS analogue datel services

ALP Australian Labor Party

AM Amplitude modulation, in which the information to be transmitted modulates the amplitude of the carrier signal. This is the method used for MF broadcasting (2CH, 3LO, 4QR, 5AN, 6WF, 72R etc . . .)

ANA Australian National Airways

analogue signals electric analogues of sound or light signals produced by microphones, phonograph pickups, the playback heads for audio or video magnetic tapes, etc.

ANSO Automatic Network and Switching Objectives Committee

antenna arrangement of metallic rods and wires used to transmit or receive radio or television signals

ANU Australian National University

ANZAAS Australian and New Zealand Association for the Advancement of Science

ANZCAN cable linking Australia via Norfolk Island to New Zealand December 1983, and later to Canada

APEA Association of Professional Engineers, Australia

APEU Australian Postal Electricians' Union

APO Australian Post Office

APTU Australian Postal and Telecommunications Union

APWU Amalgamated Postal Workers Union of Australia

ARE automatic relay (crossbar) with stored programme control registers, a version of ARF (L.M. Ericsson)

ARF automatic relay (crossbar) main local exchange (L.M. Ericsson)

ARK automatic relay (crossbar) rural exchange (L.M. Ericsson)

ARM automatic relay (crossbar) 4–wire trunk exchange (L.M. Ericsson)

ASTEC Australian Science and Technology Council

ASV air to surface vessel

AT&T American Telephone and Telegraph Company

ATDA Australian Telecommunications Development Association

ATEA Australian Telecommunications Employees Association, formed April 1976 and superseding PTTA

ATPOA Australian Telephone and Phonogram Officers Association

ATS applications technology satellite

AUD Australian United Development Pty Ltd

AUSSAT AUSSAT Pty Ltd, incorporated as a company in November 1981 to operate a national telecommunications system in Australia

AUSTPAC name given to Telecom Australia's packet switched data transmission service

AWA Amalgamated Wireless (Australasia) Pty Ltd

AXE central stored programme control exchange, L.M. Ericsson exchange equipment available in both analogue and digital forms

bandwidth The difference between the highest and lowest frequency contained within a communication signal; or the range of frequencies which can be passed through a communications channel. *See* frequency.

BAT British Australian Telegraph Company

BBC British Broadcasting Corporation

beams As applied to satellite communications, refers to the area served/covered by a satellite antenna. There are receiver beams and transmit beams.
global: coverage of all of the earth which is 'visible' from the satellite
national: coverage of all of a nation's territory, e.g., all of Australia and the continental shelf

bearer medium for the transmission of communications, a term usually reserved for multi-channel communication

BGE British General Electric

BPO British Post Office

broadband The broadband system consists of both coaxial cable and microwave systems. The term broadband is used because these systems can carry signals of a wide range of frequencies.

BTM Bell Telephone Manufacturing Co. Antwerp, Belgium, a subsidiary of IT&T

BTS Business Telecommunications Services (Australia)

C band a frequency band at 6/4 gigahertz

cable An assembly of insulated conductors (usually copper) within either a lead, plastic or plastic-metal composite sheath. Cables include junction cables which connect telephone exchanges, exchange cables connecting subscriber to telephone exchanges, and other.

cable television (CTV) A television service transmitted by cable to specific receivers.

CAGEO Council of Australian Government Employees Organisations

CAMS computer augmented message systems

CANTAT I/II transatlantic cable

carrier system A system by which a number of telephone channels are multiplexed for transmission over open-wire lines or cables.

CATV community antenna television, a service where programmes received on a single antenna are amplified and distributed by cable to a given community

CAX country automatic exchanges, superseded the term RAX c. 1965

CCIR International Consultative Committee for Radio (Comité Consultatif International des Radio-communications)

CCITT International Consultative Committee for Telephony and Telegraphy (Comité Consultatif International Telephonique et Telegraphique)

CCTV closed circuit television

CEEP Commonwealth Employees (Employment Provisions) Act

CEPT Committee of European Posts and Telegraphs

circuit a two-way communication between two points comprising associated send and receive channels

CITCA Committee of Inquiry into Technological Change in Australia (the Myers Committee) 1978

coaxial cable A cable consisting of an insulated central conductor surrounded by a cylindrical conductor with additional insulation on the outside and covered with an outer sheath. As the two conductors are concentric the term 'coaxial' is used to describe the cable assembly.

common carrier a network which is owned and operated by an authority or organisation whose function is to provide common communication facilities to the public, e.g. in Australia, the PMG's Department and the Australian Telecommunications Commission — Telecom Australia

COMPAC Commonwealth submarine coaxial cable established to link Australia to New Zealand and Canada via Sydney, Auckland, Fiji, Hawaii and Vancouver, 1963

community plan the strategic plan launched in the late 1950s to introduce a telecommunications integrated STD dialling system in Australia and to mesh old and new community telephone plan embracing ELSA technologies into a comprehensive national plan

computer terminal a device which can connect to a computer, either at the site of the computer or remote from it and connected through a telecommunications link

COMSAT Comsat General Corporation (a communications satellite corporation) of the USA

conduit pipe into which cable is drawn for protection — generally laid underground

confravision conference whose participants are linked by television, also videoconference

COTC Canadian Overseas Telecommunications Corporation

CP Country Party

CRA Conzinc Riotinto of Australia Limited

crossbar a system for switching telephone calls which uses group relays rather than the uniselectors of the step-by-step (bimotional) switches. The term 'crossbar' comes from the crossing of horizontal and vertical bars that form part of the electromagnetic operation.

cross-subsidy a cross-subsidy occurs when profits made from one class of users of a given service are used to subsidise another class of users

CSIR Council for Scientific and Industrial Research (Australia) 1926–48

CSIRO Commonwealth Scientific and Industrial Research Organisation, successor of CSIR, 1948

CSR Colonial Sugar Refining Company

CTS communications technology satellite (Hermes)

CTV *See* cable television.

CUDN common user data network

DAS directory assistance service

DAS(C) directory assistance service (computer-based)

data a broad term used in telecommunications to denote basic elements of information which, after being translated into a suitable (digital) format, can be transmitted to and processed by a data terminal or computer

data base a structured set of data, a term principally used for data stored in a computer which may be 'accessed' using a computer terminal

data terminal a device capable of transmitting and-or receiving data over a telecommunication link

data transmission the sending of data from one part of a system to another over a tele-communication link

datel services transmission of data via the normal switched network: the converting equipment required for this purpose are called 'data modems'

DDS digital data service

demodulator a device used to recover the original signal from a modulated wave (see modulator)

DG Director-General

digital data network A network of data lines independent of the public switched network. This provided a dedicated (full-time) connection for the transmission of digital data between users of the network on a point to point basis.

digital signals signals in the form of a series of pulses, i.e., discrete states, for example, binary, two states, on/off or +/- or 0°/180°

DISPLAN The Victorian State Disaster Plan

DM delta modulation, a means of coding analogue signals into digital signals

DOMSAT domestic satellite

DRCS digital radio concentrator system

DTM district telecommunications manager

duplexing 'Duplex' means simultaneous two-way transmission

earth station radio station on earth used in conjunction with radio stations in space

EHF extremely high frequency, from 30 to 300 gigahertz

electromagnetic qualifies phenomena involving electromagnetic energy as distinct

electromagnetic wave wide range of vibrations travelling in vacuum at a speed of 3×10^{10} cm/sec. and ranging in order of increasing frequencies radio waves through infrared and visible and ultraviolet light, to X-rays and gamma rays

ELSA extended local service area (a geographical zone of service linked to one exchange within which certain tariff rates apply)

EMA exchange maintenance area

EMC exchange maintenance centre

ESA European Space Agency

ESC exchange service centres

exchange a centre of the network at which control of switching and transmission takes place

facsimile a system of information transfer which can transmit the content of documents

FACTS Federation of Australian Commercial TV Stations

FDM frequency division multiplexing, an analogue transmission system for simultaneous transmission of a number of voice and other signals

FM frequency modulation, in which the information to be transmitted modulates the frequency of the carrier

frequency The number of vibrations, waves or cycles per second of a periodic phenomenon. The unit of frequency is the Hertz (1 Hertz = 1 cycle per second) see Hz.

FYEOP Five Year Engineering Operations Plan (Telecom Australia)

FTS Fellow of Australian Academy of Techno-logical Sciences

gateway interconnection point between networks eg, between Telecom and OTC(A) networks

gigahertz or GHz *See* frequency *and* Hertz. GHz = 1,000,000,000 Hz. Frequencies in excess of about 1 GHz are generally described as microwave frequencies. Most of the world's high capacity trunk radio systems including satellite systems, operate in the microwave radio bands where carrier frequencies are specified and measured in GHz. Other prefixes are k, e.g, 3kHz = 3,000 Hz, and M, e.g., 3 MHz = 3,000,000 Hz.

GOC General Officer Commanding

GPO General Post Office

Hertz (Hz) A unit of frequency named after Heinrich Hertz (1857–1894) whose research provided the experimental confirmation of the electromagnetic waves predicted theoretically by James Clerk Maxwell (1831–1879). 1 Hertz = 1 cycle per second.

HF high frequency, 3MHz–30MHz

IBM International Business Machines

IDN Integrated digital network, a telecommunications transmission of a number of voice and other signals

IEE Institution of Electrical Engineers

INTELSAT International Satellite Organisation

ISD international subscriber dialling

ISO Imperial Service Order

IT&T International Telephone and Telegraph Corporation

ITU International Telecommunication Union, an organ of the United Nations

JUG Joint Union Group

K band a frequency of 14/12 Gigahertz

kHz kilohertz, *see* gigahertz

leased lines A transmission link or circuit leased by the common carrier for the exclusive use of one subscriber. It is not part of any public network.

LF low frequency, 30 to 300 kHz

line wire, cable, tube, conduit, fibreglass, waveguide or other physical medium used in connection with a telecommunications service

LME L.M. Ericsson

L of C Australian Line of Communication

MF medium frequency, 300 KHz to 3 MHz

MHz megahertz, *see* gigahertz

microwave A generic classification for radio waves about 1.5 Gigahertz frequency. Microwave systems are used in Australia as broadband radio carrier systems and require clear line of sight between antennae at each repeater station to pick up and transmit signals.

mobile services communication services, including telephony, facsimile, data which are not in a fixed place (e.g. car, vessel, aircraft). Radio is generally used as the transmission medium. Mobile services may operate in private networks owned by a single user, or can form a public network owned by the common carrier and shared by many users.

modem contraction of 'modulator and demodulator', used to connect equipment requiring its frequency band to be shifted from one place in the spectrum to another suitable for transmission in the analogue network. See modulator and demodulator

modulator a device to convert electrical signals from one form into another for sending purposes in a transmission system (see also demodulator)

MTS mobile telephone service (automatic).

multiplexing Multiplexing is the technique of transmitting more than one stream of information along a bearer such as a pair of wires, a coaxial cable or a trunk radio system. At present, each information stream (e.g., telephone channels) modulates a low powered carrier signal where carrier frequency is different from all others using that bearer. At the receiving end, each channel is demodulated in its own receiver. This multiplexing method is known as frequency division multiplexing.

Murray multiplex an electromechanical system for sending a number of telegraph signals over one telegraph circuit, named after its inventor Donald Murray

NASA National Aeronautics and Space Administration

NCDC National Capital Development Commission

network The infrastructure or complex of switching centres (exchanges) and connecting links to which customers' communication services, including telephone, telex, data, are connected. Segments of the network are described as the local network and the trunk network.

NLCC National Labour Consultative Council

NT Northern Territory

NTAMS Northern Territory Aerial Medical Service

NTP National Telecommunications Planning

open wires normally two wires (a pair) per circuit or line strung on insulators on poles

optical fibre a fine hair-like fibre of silicon along which coherent light waves can be transmitted as a carrier for many communications channels

OT overland telegraph

OTC Overseas Telecommunications Commission (Australia) established 1946

PABX private automatic branch exchange, a private branch exchange capable of automatic switching. See PBX

packet switching a data transmission service for smaller users where data is stored and forwarded in small packets as opposed to leasing data links

PANS peculiar and novel services

PBX private branch exchange, a switchboard and other apparatus which interconnects terminals (e.g. telephones) at the premises of a subscriber and connects them through the switchboard to an exchange. (PBX is the general term, see also PMBX and PABX)

PCM pulse code modulation. A means of coding an analogue signal into a digital signal, in which the original signal is defined by the patterns of the pulse groups. In much the same way as a movie film or TV picture consists of a series of slightly ·differing 'stills' or samples of the original action, an analogue sound signal can be sampled and reconstructed from the sample, provided the samples are taken often enough to preserve enough detail. In standard telephone PCM, the original analogue signal is sampled 8,000 times per second and each sample is then measured by a coding circuit which describes the sample amplitude as an eight bit digital word. At the receiving end, the samples are reconstructed by a decoder and the original signal (almost) reconstructed by passing the samples through a low pass filter.

phonophore a telephone adapted to allow speech over a telegraph circuit without interfering with telegraph signals

PMBX private manual branch exchange, a manually operated switchboard installed at the premises of a subscriber which is connected to a public exchange

PMG Postmaster–General's Department

POA Professional Officers' Association

POTS plain old telephone service

PREI Professional Radio and Electronics Institute of Australia

PSB Public Service Board

PTTA Postal and Telecommunications Technicians Association, *see* ATEA

PUG Postal Union Group

R&D research and development

RAX rural automatic exchange

RDI research, development and innovation

RF radio frequency

RFDS Royal Flying Doctor Service

RF spectrum The radio–frequency spectrum is that portion of the electromagnetic spectrum (see spectrum) which lies between 100 kHz and 100 GHz and is used for transmitting radio waves

RMS Royal Mail Steamer

satellite In the context of this book, a microwave repeater station in a circular equatorial orbit around the earth at a height of about 36,000 km above the earth's surface. In this configuration, the satellite appears stationary from points on the earth, hence the term 'geostationary satellite'.

SBS small business systems, a business telephone system marketed by Telecom under the name 'Commander'.

SBS Satellite Business Systems (USA) launched 1981

SEACOM South East Asia Commonwealth submarine cable system linking Australia (Cairns) Madang, Guam, Hong Kong, Jesselton and Singapore

semiconductor material whose conductivity lies approximately midway between that of a metal and of a good insulator. Semiconductors are the basic material in transistors and integrated circuit 'chips'.

SHF super high frequency from 3 to 30 GHz

slow scan video the transmission of images over a limited bandwidth necessitating the use of a low transmission rate and a slow scan rate

software a computer term describing computer programmes and operating systems

solid state in telecommunications technology parlance implies the exclusive use of semi-conductor devices

spectrum a range of electromagnetic wave frequencies, *see* electromagnetic waves

SPC stored programme control — solid state computer control for electronic telephone and telex exchanges

spot a limited area, usually a part of a country served by a satellite, e.g., Aussat's NE, SE, central and W. spot beams.

STC Standard Telephone and Cables Pty. Ltd, an IT&T subsidiary in UK and Australia

STD subscriber trunk dialling

step-by-step This switching system was invented by Almon B. Strowger of the USA towards the end of the 19th century. The heart of the system is the bimotional switch which enables a connection to be established between one pair of wires and any one of a hundred others, arranged in a square array of 10 × 10 pairs. The mechanism holding the 'originating' pair of conductors moves 'up and across' in direct response to the telephone dial. A series of bimotional switches, operating step–by–step in response to the dial on the originating telephone, provide the connection to the required telephone.

TAM telephone answering machines

TAT transatlantic telephone cable

TCN Television Corporation Network (channel 9)

TEI Telephone and Electrical Industries. The title of the company changed to Plessey in 1969.

Telco a telephone company, or the telephone company

teleprinter Otherwise known as a 'telex machine' or 'teletypewriter', it is the terminal device in telex networks.

TELESAT Canadian Satellite Corporation

telex An automatically switched network, separate from the normal switched telephone network, which is used for the transmission of printed messages. The terminal devices are called 'telex machines' or 'teleprinters'. They are very similar to ordinary typewriters from an operator's point of view.

10C an electronic (stored programme controlled) switching system used for switching trunk telephone calls

time division multiplexing the transmission of two or more signals over a common path by using successive time intervals for different signals.

traffic In telecommunications engineering terms, traffic refers to the volume of messages passing over the telecommunications system.

transponder The microwave receiver/transmitter (repeater) in a communications satellite. A satellite usually carries a number of transponders of a particular bandwidth and the number of transponders is often used as a measure of the capacity of the satellite.

TRESS Telegraph REperforator Switching System, an automatic teleprinter transmission system which stores telegraphic messages on perforated paper tape before automatically retransmitting them to their destination at capital city exchanges

Trunk a term used to describe long distance circuits, channels or networks used for linking widely spaced call switching centres, i.e. trunk traffic as distinct from local traffic.

TUG Telecommunications Union Group

UHF ultra high frequency, from 300 MHz to 3 GHz

value-added *or* **add-on services** a concept applied to services which are additional to those normally available on a network and for which the subscriber pays an additional charge

V vesting day

VF voice frequency, from about 200 Hz to 4 kHz.

VHF very high frequency, from 30 MHz to 300 MHz in the radio frequency spectrum

VLF very low frequency, from 3 to 30 kHz

videoconference *See* confravision.

WAAAF Women's Auxiliary Australian Air Force

CONVERSIONS

Imperial	Metric
one ounce (oz)	28.35 grams (g)
one pound (lb)	0.45 kilograms (kg)
one ton	1.02 tonnes (t)
one inch	2.54 centimetres (cm)
one foot	0.3 metre (m)
one yard	0.91 metre (m)
one mile	1.61 kilometres (km)

Index

427

434

436

U

UHF channels, 198
underground cable, 20, 105, 212; *see also* coaxial cable
unemployment, 141–2, 347
Union of Postal Clerks and Telegraphists, 189–90, 267, 268
unions and associations, 69, 96, 173, 261, 296, 315–35, *321*;
ACOA, 267, 268
APEA, 246–7, 268–9, 304
APEU, 231, 248, 249; subseq. PTTA, *q.v.*
APTU, 306, 330–1, 347, 352, 376, 377
APWU, 250, 251, 260, 268, 316
Association of Architects, Engineers, Surveyors & Draftsmen of Australia, 268
ATEA, 316, 320–9, *325*, 330, 331, 332, 333, 347, 352, 360, 375, 376, 378, 380–1, 384
ATPOA, 255, 388
Australian Commonwealth Post & Telegraph Officers' Assoc., 70; subseq. ATPOA, *q.v.*
Australian Postmasters Assoc., 268
Australian Public Service Assoc., 324
Australian Telegraph, Telephone Construction & Maintenance Union, 251; subseq. APWU, *q.v.*
Committee of Seven, 69
Electric Telegraph Society, 69
JUG, 315
NSW Operators Society, 69
POA, 248, 268, 304
Postal Linemen's Union, 251; subseq. APWU, *q.v.*
Postal Overseers Union, 268
PTTA, 185, 249, 268, 306, 316, 330–1; subseq. ATEA, *q.v.*
PUG, 315
Queensland Electric Telegraph Society, 69
South Australian Telegraph Officers' Assoc., 69
Telecommunication Technical Officers Assoc., 268
TUG, 315
Union of Postal Clerks & Telegraphists, 189–90, 267, 268
Universal Postal Union, 14
unions issues: ARE 11, 319–29; corporate planning, 305–6; Davidson report, 380–1; health & pay, 254; letter–sorter (mechanical), 250; PABX, 185; penal bans clause, 324–5, 326; PSB and arbitration, 259, 268, 272; Royal Commission, 267–9; satellite, 347, 352, 383–4; staff training, 249, 250; TRESS, 190–2; wage claim (1979), 330–3; (1981), 376–7, 378; word processor, 324
US Army, 160, 161
UNIVAC, 280–1, 282
universities, 129–30, 183, 244, 286, 368
Uren, T., 288

V

Vanthoff, P.E., 225, 232
Vernon, Sir James, 264, 269, 277, 295, 296, 299–300, 306
VHF channels, 198
Victoria, 6, 9, 12, 16–18, 72, 75, 79, 83, 103, 188, 219–21, 304, 317, 319, 363, 365, 366, 368

Videotex, 379–80
voice frequency repeater, 118, 125, 143, 155

437

W

Waagner–Biro, 290
wages, *see* salaries and wages
Walker, Frederick, 40
war, communication in, *see* Postmaster-General's Dept, wartime, and similar entries
Warren, W.H., 128
Waters, Frank, 268
Watling, Thomas, 2
weapons research, 213–14
weather reports, 32–3, 190
Webster, S.T., 159, 165, 166
Webster, William, 97, 106, 116
Weipa (Qld), 217
Weld, Sir Frederick, 56, 57
Wellington, A.W., 157
Wellstead, Mary, 59, 79
Westcott, John, 61
West Australian airways, 256
Western Australia, 5–6, 11, 13, 28–30, 56–60, 67–9, 78, 143, 147–8, 213–16, 218, 236, 242–3, 304, 333, 350, 368, 373–4
Western Electric Co., (US), 78
Western Union Corp. (US), 190, 351–2, 357
whalers (mail carriers), 2
Wheatstone system, 16, 25, 85, 95, 96, 122
Wheeler, Sir Frederick, 261
White, F., 167
White, Harold, 296, 339, 341; report, 341
White, Peter, 344
White, V., 251
Whitlam, E.G., 287, 288; govt, 264, 278, 294–5, 309
Wilks, William, 97
wind power, 212–13, 368, *370*
wire photo, 124, *124*
wireless communication, *see* radio broadcasting, telegraph, telephone, television broadcasting
Wise, Bernhard, 109
Witt, S.H., *123*, 125, 160, 166, *166*, 167, 168, 181, 195
women: and automation, 250, 252; A.G. Bell on, 98–9; careers in PMG, 79–83, 252–5, 262; discrimination against, 254; in early postal service, 6, 11–13; as line staff, *388*; in remote areas, 185; Royal Commission submission, 269; salaries, 252, 254; as telegraphists, 59, 79–80; union issues, 254, 255; in wartime, 172–3; wives of staff, 8, 55, 115, 126, 154, 157, 213; *see also* telephonists
Woods, S.T., 44
Woomera, 213, 214
Works, Dept of, 290
Wragge, H.S., 366
Wright, E.P., 232–3
Wright, Judith, 136

Y

Young, Emily, 157
Young, Sir John, 24